Lecture Notes in Computer Science   11635

Commenced Publication in 1973
Founding and Former Series Editors:
Gerhard Goos, Juris Hartmanis, and Jan van Leeuwen

More information about this series at http://www.springer.com/series/7410

Xingming Sun · Zhaoqing Pan ·
Elisa Bertino (Eds.)

Artificial Intelligence and Security

5th International Conference, ICAIS 2019
New York, NY, USA, July 26–28, 2019
Proceedings, Part IV

 Springer

Editors
Xingming Sun (iD)
Nanjing University of Information
Science and Technology
Nanjing, China

Zhaoqing Pan (iD)
Nanjing University of Information
Science and Technology
Nanjing, China

Elisa Bertino (iD)
Purdue University
West Lafayette, IN, USA

ISSN 0302-9743   ISSN 1611-3349   (electronic)
Lecture Notes in Computer Science
ISBN 978-3-030-24267-1   ISBN 978-3-030-24268-8   (eBook)
https://doi.org/10.1007/978-3-030-24268-8

LNCS Sublibrary: SL4 – Security and Cryptology

This Springer imprint is published by the registered company Springer Nature Switzerland AG
The registered company address is: Gewerbestrasse 11, 6330 Cham, Switzerland

Preface

The 5th International Conference on Artificial Intelligence and Security (ICAIS 2019), formerly called the International Conference on Cloud Computing and Security (ICCCS), was held during July 26–28, 2019, at New York University, New York, USA. Over the past four years, ICAIS has become a leading conference for researchers and engineers to share their latest results from research, development, and applications in the fields of artificial intelligence and information security.

We used the Microsoft Conference Management Toolkits (CMT) system to manage the submission and review processes of ICAIS 2019. We received 1529 submissions from 20 countries and regions, including USA, Canada, UK, Italy, Ireland, Japan, Russia, France, Australia, South Korea, South Africa, India, Iraq, Kazakhstan, Indonesia, Vietnam, Ghana, China, Taiwan, and Macao, etc. The submissions cover the areas of artificial intelligence, big data, cloud computing and security, information hiding, IoT security, multimedia forensics, encryption and cybersecurity, and so on. We thank our Technical Program Committee members and external reviewers for their efforts in reviewing papers and providing valuable comments to the authors. From the total of 1,529 submissions, and based on at least three reviews per submission, the Program Chairs decided to accept 230 papers, yielding an acceptance rate of 15%. The volume of the conference proceedings contains all the regular, poster, and workshop papers.

The conference program was enriched by a series of keynote presentations, and the keynote speakers included: Nasir Memon, New York University, USA; Edward Colbert, Virginia Tech Hume Center for National Security and Technology, USA; Quanyan Zhu, New York University, USA; Zhihua Xia, Nanjing University of Information Science and Technology, China; Tom Masino, TradeWeb, USA; etc. We thank them for their wonderful speeches.

There were 45 workshops organized at ICAIS 2019, covering all the hot topics in artificial intelligence and security. We would like to take this moment to express our sincere appreciation for the contribution of all the workshop chairs and their participants. We would like to extend our sincere thanks to all authors who submitted papers to ICAIS 2019 and to all Program Committee members. It was a truly great experience to work with such talented and hard-working researchers. We also appreciate the external reviewers for assisting the Program Committee members in their particular areas of expertise. Moreover, we want to thank our sponsors: Nanjing University of Information Science and Technology, Springer, New York University, IEEE Broadcast Technology Society (BTS) Nanjing Chapter, ACM China, Michigan State University, Taiwan Cheng Kung University, Taiwan Dong Hwa University, Taiwan Providence University, Nanjing University of Aeronautics and Astronautics, State Key Laboratory of Integrated Services Networks, and the National Nature Science Foundation of China.

May 2019

Xingming Sun
Zhaoqing Pan
Elisa Bertino

Organization

General Chairs

Yun Q. Shi	New Jersey Institute of Technology, USA
Mauro Barni	University of Siena, Italy
Xingang You	China Information Technology Security Evaluation Center, China
Elisa Bertino	Purdue University, USA
Quanyan Zhu	New York University, USA
Xingming Sun	Nanjing University of Information Science and Technology, China

Technical Program Chairs

Aniello Castiglione	University of Salerno, Italy
Yunbiao Guo	China Information Technology Security Evaluation Center, China
Suzanne K. McIntosh	New York University, USA
Zhihua Xia	Nanjing University of Information Science and Technology, China
Victor S. Sheng	University of Central Arkansas, USA

Publication Chair

Zhaoqing Pan	Nanjing University of Information Science and Technology, China

Workshop Chair

Baowei Wang	Nanjing University of Information Science and Technology, China

Organization Chairs

Edward Wong	New York University, USA
Zhangjie Fu	Nanjing University of Information Science and Technology, China

Technical Program Committee

Saeed Arif	University of Algeria, Algeria
Anthony Ayodele	University of Maryland University College, USA

Zhifeng Bao	Royal Melbourne Institute of Technology University, Australia
Zhiping Cai	National University of Defense Technology, China
Ning Cao	Qingdao Binhai University, China
Paolina Centonze	Iona College, USA
Chin-chen Chang	Feng Chia University, Taiwan, China
Han-Chieh Chao	Taiwan Dong Hwa University, Taiwan, China
Bing Chen	Nanjing University of Aeronautics and Astronautics, China
Hanhua Chen	Huazhong University of Science and Technology, China
Xiaofeng Chen	Xidian University, China
Jieren Cheng	Hainan University, China
Lianhua Chi	IBM Research Center, Australia
Kim-Kwang Raymond Choo	University of Texas at San Antonio, USA
Ilyong Chung	Chosun University, South Korea
Robert H. Deng	Singapore Management University, Singapore
Jintai Ding	University of Cincinnati, USA
Xinwen Fu	University of Central Florida, USA
Zhangjie Fu	Nanjing University of Information Science and Technology, China
Moncef Gabbouj	Tampere University of Technology, Finland
Ruili Geng	Spectral MD, USA
Song Guo	Hong Kong Polytechnic University, SAR China
Jinsong Han	Xi'an Jiaotong University, China
Mohammad Mehedi Hassan	King Saud University, Saudi Arabia
Debiao He	Wuhan University, China
Russell Higgs	University College Dublin, Ireland
Dinh Thai Hoang	University Technology Sydney, Australia
Wien Hong	Nanfang College of Sun Yat-Sen University, China
Chih-Hsien Hsia	National Ilan University, Taiwan, China
Robert Hsu	Chung Hua University, Taiwan, China
Yongjian Hu	South China University of Technology, China
Qiong Huang	South China Agricultural University, China
Xinyi Huang	Fujian Normal University, China
Yongfeng Huang	Tsinghua University, China
Zhiqiu Huang	Nanjing University of Aeronautics and Astronautics, China
Patrick C. K. Hung	University of Ontario Institute of Technology, Canada
Farookh Hussain	University of Technology Sydney, Australia
Hai Jin	Huazhong University of Science and Technology, China
Sam Tak Wu Kwong	City University of Hong Kong, SAR China
Chin-Feng Lai	Taiwan Cheng Kung University, Taiwan, China
Loukas Lazos	University of Arizona, USA

Sungyoung Lee	Kyung Hee University, South Korea
Bin Li	Shenzhen University, China
Chengcheng Li	University of Cincinnati, USA
Feifei Li	Utah State University, USA
Jiguo Li	Hohai University, China
Jin Li	Guangzhou University, China
Jing Li	Rutgers University, USA
Kuan-Ching Li	Providence University, Taiwan, China
Peng Li	University of Aizu, Japan
Xiaolong Li	Beijing Jiaotong University, China
Yangming Li	University of Washington, USA
Luming Liang	Uber Technology, USA
Haixiang Lin	Leiden University, The Netherlands
Xiaodong Lin	University of Ontario Institute of Technology, Canada
Zhenyi Lin	Verizon Wireless, USA
Alex Liu	Michigan State University, USA
Guangchi Liu	Stratifyd Inc., USA
Guohua Liu	Donghua University, China
Joseph Liu	Monash University, Australia
Mingzhe Liu	Chengdu University of Technology, China
Pingzeng Liu	Shandong Agricultural University, China
Quansheng Liu	University of South Brittany, France
Xiaodong Liu	Edinburgh Napier University, UK
Yuling Liu	Hunan University, China
Zhe Liu	University of Waterloo, Canada
Wei Lu	Sun Yat-sen University, China
Daniel Xiapu Luo	Hong Kong Polytechnic University, SAR China
Junzhou Luo	Southeast University, China
Xiangyang Luo	Zhengzhou Science and Technology Institute, China
Suzanne K. McIntosh	New York University, USA
Nasir Memon	New York University, USA
Sangman Moh	Chosun University, South Korea
Yi Mu	University of Wollongong, Australia
Jiangqun Ni	Sun Yat-sen University, China
Rongrong Ni	Beijing Jiao Tong University, China
Rafal Niemiec	University of Information Technology and Management, Poland
Zemin Ning	Wellcome Trust Sanger Institute, UK
Shaozhang Niu	Beijing University of Posts and Telecommunications, China
Srikant Ojha	Sharda University, India
Jeff Z. Pan	University of Aberdeen, UK
Wei Pang	University of Aberdeen, UK
Rong Peng	Wuhan University, China
Chen Qian	University of California Santa Cruz, USA
Zhenxing Qian	Fudan University, China

Chuan Qin	University of Shanghai for Science and Technology, China
Jiaohua Qin	Central South University of Forestry and Technology, China
Yanzhen Qu	Colorado Technical University, USA
Zhiguo Qu	Nanjing University of Information Science and Technology, China
Kui Ren	State University of New York, USA
Arun Kumar Sangaiah	VIT University, India
Zheng-guo Sheng	University of Sussex, UK
Robert Simon Sherratt	University of Reading, UK
Yun Q. Shi	New Jersey Institute of Technology, USA
Frank Y. Shih	New Jersey Institute of Technology, USA
Biao Song	King Saud University, Saudi Arabia
Guang Sun	Hunan University of Finance and Economics, China
Jiande Sun	Shandong Normal University, China
Jianguo Sun	Harbin University of Engineering, China
Jianyong Sun	Xi'an Jiaotong University, China
Krzysztof Szczypiorski	Warsaw University of Technology, Poland
Tsuyoshi Takagi	Kyushu University, Japan
Shanyu Tang	University of West London, UK
Xianping Tao	Nanjing University, China
Jing Tian	National University of Singapore, Singapore
Yoshito Tobe	Aoyang University, Japan
Cezhong Tong	Washington University in St. Louis, USA
Pengjun Wan	Illinois Institute of Technology, USA
Cai-Zhuang Wang	Ames Laboratory, USA
Ding Wang	Peking University, China
Guiling Wang	New Jersey Institute of Technology, USA
Honggang Wang	University of Massachusetts-Dartmouth, USA
Jian Wang	Nanjing University of Aeronautics and Astronautics, China
Jie Wang	University of Massachusetts Lowell, USA
Jing Wang	Changsha University of Science and Technology, China
Jinwei Wang	Nanjing University of Information Science and Technology, China
Liangmin Wang	Jiangsu University, China
Ruili Wang	Massey University, New Zealand
Xiaojun Wang	Dublin City University, Ireland
Xiaokang Wang	St. Francis Xavier University, Canada
Zhaoxia Wang	A-Star, Singapore
Sheng Wen	Swinburne University of Technology, Australia
Jian Weng	Jinan University, China
Edward Wong	New York University, USA
Eric Wong	University of Texas at Dallas, USA

Q. M. Jonathan Wu	University of Windsor, Canada
Shaoen Wu	Ball State University, USA
Shuangkui Xia	Beijing Institute of Electronics Technology and Application, China
Lingyun Xiang	Changsha University of Science and Technology, China
Shijun Xiang	Jinan University, China
Yang Xiang	Deakin University, Australia
Yang Xiao	The University of Alabama, USA
Haoran Xie	The Education University of Hong Kong, SAR China
Naixue Xiong	Northeastern State University, USA
Xin Xu	Wuhan University of Science and Technology, China
Wei Qi Yan	Auckland University of Technology, New Zealand
Aimin Yang	Guangdong University of Foreign Studies, China
Ching-Nung Yang	Taiwan Dong Hwa University, Taiwan, China
Chunfang Yang	Zhengzhou Science and Technology Institute, China
Fan Yang	University of Maryland, USA
Guomin Yang	University of Wollongong, Australia
Ming Yang	Southeast University, China
Qing Yang	University of North Texas, USA
Yuqiang Yang	Bohai University, USA
Ming Yin	Purdue University, USA
Xinchun Yin	Yangzhou University, China
Shaodi You	Australian National University, Australia
Kun-Ming Yu	Chung Hua University, Taiwan, China
Yong Yu	University of Electronic Science and Technology of China, China
Gonglin Yuan	Guangxi University, China
Mingwu Zhang	Hubei University of Technology, China
Wei Zhang	Nanjing University of Posts and Telecommunications, China
Weiming Zhang	University of Science and Technology of China, China
Xinpeng Zhang	Fudan University, China
Yan Zhang	Simula Research Laboratory, Norway
Yanchun Zhang	Victoria University, Australia
Yao Zhao	Beijing Jiaotong University, China
Linna Zhou	University of International Relations, China

Organizing Committee

Xianyi Chen	Nanjing University of Information Science and Technology, China
Yadang Chen	Nanjing University of Information Science and Technology, China
Beijing Chen	Nanjing University of Information Science and Technology, China

Huajun Huang	Central South University of Forestry and Technology, China
Jielin Jiang	Nanjing University of Information Science and Technology, China
Zilong Jin	Nanjing University of Information Science and Technology, China
Yan Kong	Nanjing University of Information Science and Technology, China
Yiwei Li	Columbia University, USA
Yuling Liu	Hunan University, China
Lirui Qiu	Nanjing University of Information Science and Technology, China
Zhiguo Qu	Nanjing University of Information Science and Technology, China
Guang Sun	Hunan University of Finance and Economics, China
Huiyu Sun	New York University, USA
Le Sun	Nanjing University of Information Science and Technology, China
Jian Su	Nanjing University of Information Science and Technology, China
Lina Tan	Hunan University of Commerce, China
Qing Tian	Nanjing University of Information Science and Technology, China
Yuan Tian	King Saud University, Saudi Arabia
Zuwei Tian	Hunan First Normal University, China
Xiaoliang Wang	Hunan University of Science and Technology, China
Lingyun Xiang	Changsha University of Science and Technology, China
Lizhi Xiong	Nanjing University of Information Science and Technology, China
Leiming Yan	Nanjing University of Information Science and Technology, China
Hengfu Yang	Hunan First Normal University, China
Li Yu	Nanjing University of Information Science and Technology, China
Zhili Zhou	Nanjing University of Information Science and Technology, China

Contents – Part IV

Encryption and Cybersecurity

A Gray-Box Vulnerability Discovery Model Based on Path Coverage

Chunlai Du[1(✉)], Xingbang Tan[1], and Yanhui Guo[2]

[1] School of Information Science and Technology,
North China University of Technology, Beijing 100144, China
duchunlai@ncut.edu.cn
[2] Department of Computer Science, University of Illinois Springfield,
Springfield, IL, USA

Abstract. With the increasing amount of codes and their complexity, the manual method of exploiting vulnerabilities is no longer able to meet the actual needs of vulnerability discovery. Therefore, more researchers are conducting automated vulnerability discovery models and related algorithms. In the real attack and defense scenario, the vulnerability discovery researchers rarely obtain the source code of the target software. Therefore, the non-white box mode of the target system or software is particularly urgent and necessary in the vulnerability discovery model and algorithm. Aiming to solve the above problems, this paper proposes a model for gray-box vulnerability discovery GVDM, which uses the tracking of path coverage to infer the internal structure of the application. The samples with low-frequency path are preferably selected during the sample selection phase using simulated annealing and genetic algorithms. The experimental results on the LAVA-M dataset justify the better performance of the proposed GVDM model, which finds more vulnerabilities than other fuzzers with high accuracy.

Keywords: Fuzzing · Gray-box fuzzer · Simulated annealing

1 Introduction

With the continuous upgrade of software functions, the software code size and the complexity of the architecture also increase, which inevitably leads to the existence of vulnerabilities in the software. According to CVE statistics shown in Table 1, the total number of vulnerabilities disclosed between 2017 and October 2018 is close to the total number of vulnerabilities in the past five years from 2012 to 2016. The growth of vulnerabilities in mobile devices [1] and IoT devices means that the security of all-platform devices is urgently needed.

Academia and industry focus on different attack surfaces, integrate different technologies, and actively explore various automatic vulnerability discovery solutions. For example, kAFL for kernel vulnerabilities, domato for browser DOM engine vulnerabilities, and guided gray-box Fuzzer AFLGo for patch testing and crash reproduction. Among the many methods of vulnerability discovery, fuzzing has achieved great success and has become the most effective and efficient vulnerability discovery solution

© Springer Nature Switzerland AG 2019
X. Sun et al. (Eds.): ICAIS 2019, LNCS 11635, pp. 3–12, 2019.
https://doi.org/10.1007/978-3-030-24268-8_1

Table 1. CVE disclosed the number of vulnerabilities.

Year	2012	2013	2014	2015	2016	2017	2018
Number of vulnerabilities	5297	5191	7946	6480	6447	14712	14327

[2]. OSS-Fuzz is a continuous fuzzing for open source software built by Google using libFuzzer and Sanitizers. In five months, the project generated 10 trillion input samples per day and continuously conducted fuzzing on 47 open source projects (such as Ffmpeg, Wireshark, SQLite3, etc.). Then the project found more than a thousand errors, in which 264 are potential security vulnerabilities.

This paper proposes a gray-box vulnerability discovery model GVDM based on path coverage in software. The validity of the model and algorithm is justified using a public dataset, LAVA-M dataset. The main contributions of this model are as follows:

- GVDM tracks the execution edges between two basic blocks to build a hierarchical relationship between basic blocks, helping fuzzer to infer the internal structure of the application.
- Through introduce genetic algorithm and simulated annealing, GVDM preferably selected input samples with the low-frequency path and achieve better performance.

2   Related Work

In recent years, many fuzzers have been constructed using various technologies, such as dynamic analysis, symbolic execution, and deep learning [3] have also become powerful support for the vulnerability discovery model. In the spirit of "the more covered code block, the more vulnerability to be found", many fuzzers use coverage as a path exploration guiding strategy [4, 5] and different ways were employed to obtain coverage, such as dynamic binary instrumentation using pin for binary instrumentation or intel-pt for hardware-level coverage tracking. Coverage information is useful for feedback-driven fuzzing, and there are many ways to improve coverage, such as symbolic execution.

In the sample selection procedure, fuzzer only selects those samples that may improve the efficiency of the fuzzing. Samples that perform low-frequency paths may help the fuzzing to explore more paths. Aflfast demonstrates that coverage-based fuzzing can be modeled as a Markov chain [6]. Sparks [7] et al. use Markov chains to model control flow graphs for programs to optimize those low-frequency exploration paths. Chen [8] used MCMC to utilize knowledge about the effectiveness of mutation, allowing those operators that were effective in the previous generation fuzzing to be selected with greater probability.

The internal structure inference in the application is closely related to the mutation strategy. TaintScope uses taint analysis to infer the checksum processing code and helps the fuzzer pass the checksum check [9]. Dowser [10] and BORG [11] used two techniques of taint analysis and symbol execution to assist the fuzzing. BORG aims buffer read errors and Dowser is against buffer overflow errors (including overflow and underflow). VUzzer [12] uses the control flow and data flow information extracted by static analysis and dynamic analysis to infer the internal structure and state of the program. Most of the current work only considers the number of executions of the edge, as the judgment of the execution frequency, however, they rarely record the execution order of the edges. To overcome this disadvantage, we dynamically track and record the execution order of the edges to better infer the internal space of the target program.

3 GVDM

Static analysis, genetic algorithm, simulated annealing, and dynamic binary instrumentation are employed to assist the fuzzing, and an improved scheme GVDM is proposed for the mutate-based, coverage-based gray-box fuzzer. The algorithm includes three modules: mutation strategy, runtime tracking, and sample selection. Based on the scheme mentioned above, the prototype system design of GVDM is shown in Fig. 1:

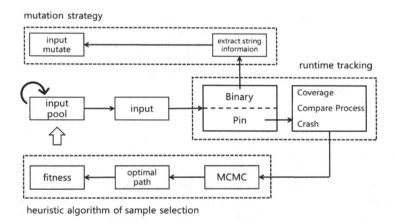

Fig. 1. Module diagram of GVDM prototype system

The prototype system GVDM uses static analysis to improve the value of mutation in the mutation strategy, and simulated annealing and genetic algorithm to evaluate sample in sample selection, dynamics binary instrumentation in runtime tracking to assist in coverage tracking, violation identification, and internal structure inference in the program.

The feedback-driven fuzzing method has proven to be an effective means of automating and comprehensively discovering vulnerabilities [13]. The genetic algorithm is precisely the connection hub of feedback and drive. In general, the feedback information collected by the runtime tracking is applied to the genetic algorithm to evaluate the fitness of each input sample in each generation. At the end of each generation, the genetic algorithm selects the samples with higher fitness values for the next generation.

3.1 Sample Mutation

GVDM uses four mutation strategies (bit flip, boundary value, simple arithmetic, random mutation) to mutate the input samples. In the boundary value strategy, in addition to the common values that are likely to cause boundary overflow, GVDM also extracts program-related information inside the application as a supplement to the boundary value (Table 2).

Table 2. Mutation strategy.

Mutation strategy	Mutation position	Mutation value	Mutation granularity
Bit flip	Sequential position	0/1 flip	Bit
Boundary value	Sequential position	Boundary value that easily trigger security vulnerability	Byte
Simple arithmetic	Sequential position	Fill the original position with simple arithmetic processing	Byte
Random mutation	Random position	Randomly generated value	Byte

In addition to the mutation process, the crossover between the two samples is also an effective complement for sample diversity. As a supplement to the sample diversity in addition to mutation, the over-proportion of the crossover will reduce the efficiency of the fuzzing, and the fuzzing will be trapped in the repetitive execution of path. GVDM controls the ratio of crossover and mutation to 1:9, which not only preserves the diversity of the sample but also prevents the fuzzing from falling into a repetitive path.

3.2 Runtime Tracking

The runtime tracking of GVDM mainly uses the Pintool from the dynamic binary instrumentation (DBI) framework pin to obtain edge coverage information and detect crash occurrences.

Edge Calculation. The pin defines a basic block as an instruction sequence set having only one entry and one exit, and the first address of each basic block serves as the address of the basic block. The execution path of the GVDM record is composed of the edges that the program executes, and the edge represents the transition from one basic block to another basic block.

GVDM get the basic block information executed by the program through the runtime tracking and calculates the sequential basic block transition as edges. Therefore, the edge is calculated from the previous basic block address and the current basic block address at the time of execution, such as:

$$edge_{(prev\_block,current\_block)} = (\text{prev\_block} \gg a) \oplus (\text{current\_block} \gg b), \qquad (1)$$

where a and b are set as 0 and 1.

Crash Classification. The Pintool collects the ten basic block addresses that are executed before the program crashes and uses the murmurhash3 hash algorithm to calculate the hash value for the address of the ten basic blocks, so as to judge the uniqueness of the program crash and remove the duplicate crash. The hash algorithm is as follows:

$$crash\_value = murmurhash3(bb_1 + bb_2 + \ldots + bb_{10}). \qquad (2)$$

$bb_1 \ldots bb_{10}$ is the address of the ten basic blocks before the crash.

3.3   Sample Selection

In the sample selection, different Fuzzers have a different propensity for sample selection, which is related to the original intention of the Fuzzer designer, and also reflects the direction that different Fuzzers pay more attention to when selecting samples. As shown in Table 3, this is the common sample selection tendency of Fuzzer.

Table 3. Common fuzzer sample selection tendency.

Fuzzer	Sample selection focus
AFL	Sample with small size and fast execution speed
AFLfast	Sample with explored low-frequency path
AFLGo	Sample closer to the target position
Vuzzer	Sample with explored deeper basic blocks
libFuzzer	Sample with hit more without-explored basic blocks
SlowFuzz	Sample with call more system resources

The simulated annealing algorithm is used in the sample selection to quickly find out the globally optimal path, which is a path with the lowest execution frequency in the program execution path space. Based the globally optimal path, calculating the correlation ratio between all input sample execution paths and the optimal path. The higher the correlation ratio, the lower the execution frequency of the sample execution path is, and the higher the fitness is. The path can be preserved to the next generation in the process of inheritance, thereby the frequency of execution of the low-frequency path will be increased.

Simulated Annealing. Simulated annealing algorithm is a kind of Markov Chain Monte Carlo method. The Markov chain state transition probability matrix is composed of the execution probability of each path in the program, the matrix $P_{n \times n} = (P_{ij}|i = 1, 2, \ldots, n; j = 1, 2, \ldots n)$.

P_{ij} is the execution probability of the path $path_{ij}$, which is probablity of the basic block i transits to basic block t and then transits to basic block j. The path $path_{ij}$ contains two edges, one is the edge of basic block i to basic block t $edge_{it}$, the other is the basic block t to the edge of the basic block j $edge_{tj}$. The execution probability of the path is P_{ij},

$$P_{ij} = \frac{C_{edge_{ij}}}{\sum_k^n C_{edge_{kt}}} (n = 1, 2, \ldots). \tag{3}$$

The execution frequency $C_{edge_{ij}}$ of edge $edge_{tj}$ is divided by the sum of the execution frequency of the $edge_{kt}$ with the basic block t as the endpoint. The algorithm for applying the simulated annealing algorithm to find the low-frequency execution path in application coverage is as follows:

There is an initial temperature T^0, and T^0 is a sufficiently large number. In the iterative process of the Anneal Arithmetic, the temperature T will decline gradually. So T^0 is the maximal temperature, that is $T_{max} = T^0$ in the end of the iterative process, we will get the minimum temperature T_{min} there is the Annealing factor,

$$Factor = -\log \frac{T_{max}}{T_{min}}. \tag{4}$$

The iterations $k = \{0, 1, 2, \ldots, n | n > 0\}$. For the temperature T, the probability of temperature drops with energy difference ΔE is $p(\Delta E)$, the solution is the path $Path$. Randomly choose a small number $\varepsilon \in (0, 1)$.

(1) Initialization: initialize the temperature T^0, and then select randomly a path $Path$ with the energy E;
(2) execute iteratively step 3 to step 6 n times:
(3) calculate the current temperature T:

$$T = T^0 \times e^{\frac{Factor \times k}{n}};$$

(4) For the rest paths set $Path = \{Path_1, Path_2, \ldots, Path_{n-1}\}$, select randomly one and calculate the energy difference ΔE.

$$\Delta E = E_k - E_{k-1},$$

$$p(\Delta E) = e^{\frac{\Delta E}{T}}.$$

(5) If $\Delta E > 0$ and $p(\Delta E) > \varepsilon$, select the current path $Path_k$ as the current solution of the path at present and replace the previous path with the selected path,

$$Path_{curr} = Path_k,$$

and choose the current energy E_k as the current solution of energy at present,

$$E_{curr} = E_k.$$

(6) if the current path is greater than the previous best energy, choose -the current energy as the best solution of energy:

$$E_{best} = E_{curr},$$

and the current path as the best path:

$$Path_{best} = Path_{curr}.$$

(7) T declines gradually and times of execution $k \leq n$, turn to step 2 to iteratively execute the algorithm. when the times $k > n$ or the rest paths set $Path = $ null, terminate the algorithm.

Fitness Calculation. Sample selection is mainly based on its fitness values. The samples with high fitness are considered to be good samples that may help the fuzzing to find more potential vulnerabilities. GVDM considers multiple characteristics of the input sample in the calculation of fitness, including sample size, execution time, execution path and comparison progress.

Fitness is the basis for the genetic algorithm to select samples. Genetic algorithms select better samples according to the design preferences and can ensure the diversity of samples to the greatest extent. The calculation of fitness cannot be biased towards a kind of characteristics of the input sample. Because that will cause the fuzzing to select those samples that are almost identical, which will damage the diversity of the sample and cause the fuzzing to stagnate.

The simulated annealing was used to efficiently find the optimal path, and the main feature of the fitness of the input sample in the genetic algorithm was calculated according to the correlation ratio between the sample execution path and the optimal path. The fitness calculation method used by GVDM is as follows:

$$\text{fitness}(input_t) = \alpha \frac{CompareProcess_t}{InputSize_t + ExecTime_t} + \beta \left(CorrelRatio \times \sum_{path_{begin} \text{ in } path_t}^{path_{end}} Weight_{path} \right)$$
$$(5)$$

Both α and β are constant and can be adjusted according to the actual operation of the fuzzer. $CompareProcess_t$ is the number of comparison values passed in the comparison operation on the sample execution path. $InputSize_t$ is the size of the input sample, and $ExecTime_t$ is the actual execution time of the input sample. $CorrelRatio$ is the correlation ratio of the sample execution path and the optimal path obtained by simulated annealing, $\sum_{path_{begin} \ in \ path_t}^{path_{end}} Weight_{path}$ is the sum of the weights of input sample execution path.

4 Experiments

The experimental environment is shown in Table 4:

Table 4. Experimental environment.

operating system	Ubuntu 16.04.1 64-bit
kernel version	4.10.0-42-generic
processor	Intel Core i7-6700
memory	20 GB
interpreter	pypy2-v6.0.0-linux64
pin	pin-3.6-97554

LAVA-M [14] is a vulnerability corpus generated by injecting many real errors into the source code of open source programs. It consists of four GNU Coreutils programs including uniq, base64, md5sum, and who. The data set is widely used in the evaluation of the effects of fuzzers.

As shown in Table 5 on the LAVA-M dataset, GVDM found most of the preset vulnerabilities in base64 (88.64%) and md5sum (70.18%), far exceeding the 38.64% and 1.75% that VUzzer found in the two programs (VUzzer does not work properly in md5sum). GVDM discovered vulnerabilities which were missed by VUzzer, such as 4144, 4145, and so on. In the uniq program, GVDM found 28.6% more than the FUZZERS, and a little less than VUzzer.

Table 5. Experiment comparison data.

Program	Total bugs	FUZZERS	SES	VUZZER	GVDM
uniq	28	7	0	27	9
base64	44	7	9	17	39
md5sum	57	2	0	0	40
who	2136	0	18	50	12

The experiment was evaluated on the LAVA-M dataset. The vulnerability number pairs found by GVDM and VUzzer are shown in Table 6. It can be found that there are many crossovers in the vulnerabilities discovered by GVDM and VUzzer.

Table 6. The number of vulnerabilities found on the LAVA-M dataset.

Program	Fuzzer	Vulnerability-ID
uniq	VUZZER	112, 130, 166, 169, 170, 171, 215, 222, 227, 293, 296, 297, 318, 321, 322, 368, 371, 372, 393, 396, 397, 443, 446, 447, 468, 471, 472
	GVDM	112, 130, 166, 169, 170, 171, 215, 222
base64	VUZZER	1, 222, 235, 276, 278, 284, 386, 576, 583, 584, 786, 788, 805, 806, 817, 841, 843
	GVDM	1, 222, 235, 276, 278, 284, 386, 556, 558, 560, 562, 566, 572, 573, 576, 582, 583, 584, 774, 778, 780, 782, 784, 786, 788, 790, 792, 798, 804, 805, 806, 815, 817, 831, 832, 835, 841, 842, 843
md5sum	VUZZER	1, 2, 3, 4, 5, 6, 7, 8, 9, 10, 14, 18, 20, 22, 26, 58, 59, 60, 63, 75, 79, 81, 83, 89, 137, 138, 159, 179, 255, 319, 341, 474, 475, 587, 672, 985, 1188, 1314, 1458, 1803, 1804, 1816, 1960, 2617, 3800, 4159, 4343, 4358, 4362, 4364
	GVDM	18, 60, 4144, 4145, 4158, 4159, 4193, 4160, 4342, 4343, 4356, 4358
who	VUZZER	*
	GVDM	1, 2, 6, 268, 269, 270, 271, 272, 273, 274, 279, 281, 284, 286, 289, 301, 302, 303, 307, 308, 314, 317, 320, 323, 326, 335, 341, 347, 353, 356, 359, 362, 365, 368, 371, 374, 380, 387, 547, 563

5 Conclusion

This paper presents a gray-box fuzzer for vulnerability discovery. By tracking the execution path, the internal structure of the program can be further inferred, and the samples performing the low-frequency path are selected by simulated annealing and genetic algorithm. Our experiments prove that this vulnerability discovery method is effective and can find more vulnerabilities.

Acknowledgment. This work was supported by Joint of Beijing Natural Science Foundation and Education Commission (KZ201810009011), Science and technology innovation project of North China University of Technology (18XN053).

References

1. Cui, J., Zhang, Y., Cai, Z., et al.: Securing display path for security-sensitive applications on mobile devices. Comput. Mater. Continua **55**(1), 17–35 (2018)
2. Gan, S., Zhang, C., Qin, X., et al.: CollAFL: path sensitive fuzzing. In: 2018 IEEE Symposium on Security and Privacy (SP), pp. 679–696. IEEE, San Francisco (2018)
3. Chen, L., Yang, C., Liu, F., et al.: Automatic mining of security-sensitive functions from source code. Comput. Mater. Continua **56**(2), 199–210 (2018)
4. Copos, B., Murthy, P.: Inputfinder: reverse engineering closed binaries using hardware performance counters. In: 5th Program Protection and Reverse Engineering Workshop. ACM, Los Angeles (2015)

5. Kargén, U., Shahmehri, N.: Turning programs against each other: high coverage fuzz-testing using binary-code mutation and dynamic slicing. In: 2015 10th Joint Meeting on Foundations of Software Engineering, pp. 782–792. ACM, Bergamo (2015)
6. Böhme, M., Pham, V.-T., Roychoudhury, A.: Coverage-based greybox fuzzing as markov chain. In: 2016 ACM SIGSAC Conference on Computer and Communications Security, pp. 1032–1043. ACM, Vienna (2016)
7. Sparks, S., Embleton, S., Cunningham, R., et al.: Automated vulnerability analysis: leveraging control flow for evolutionary input crafting. In: 23th Annual Computer Security Applications Conference (ACSAC), pp. 477–486, IEEE, Miami Beach (2007)
8. Chen, Y., Su, T., Sun, C., et al.: Coverage-directed differential testing of JVM implementations. In: 37th ACM SIGPLAN Conference on Programming Language Design and Implementation, pp. 85–99. ACM, Santa Barbara (2016)
9. Wang, T., Wei, T., Gu, G., et al.: TaintScope: a checksum-aware directed fuzzing tool for automatic software vulnerability detection. In: 2010 IEEE Symposium on Security and Privacy, pp. 497–512. IEEE, Berkeley (2010)
10. Haller, I., Slowinska, A., Neugschwandtner, M., et al.: Dowsing for overflows: a guided fuzzer to find buffer boundary violations. In: 22th USENIX Security Symposium, pp. 49–64. USENIX, Washington, D.C. (2013)
11. Neugschwandtner, M., Milani Comparetti, P., Haller, I., et al.: The BORG: nanoprobing binaries for buffer overreads. In: 5th ACM Conference on Data and Application Security and Privacy, pp. 87–97. ACM, San Antonio (2015)
12. Rawat, S., Jain, V., Kumar, A., et al.: Vuzzer: application-aware evolutionary fuzzing. In: The Network and Distributed System Security Symposium (NDSS), pp. 1–14. Internet Society, San Diego (2017)
13. Schumilo, S., Aschermann, C., Gawlik, R., et al.: kAFL: hardware-assisted feedback fuzzing for OS kernels. In: 26th USENIX Security Symposium, pp. 167–182. USENIX, Vancouver (2017)
14. Dolan-Gavitt, B., Hulin, P., et al.: Lava: large-scale automated vulnerability addition. In: 37th IEEE Symposium on Security and Privacy (SP), pp. 110–121. IEEE, San Jose (2016)

Quantum Network Coding Based on Entanglement Distribution

Tao Shang$^{(\boxtimes)}$, Ran Liu, Chengran Fang, and Jianwei Liu

School of Cyber Science and Technology, Beihang University,
Beijing 100083, China
shangtao@buaa.edu.cn

Abstract. Quantum network coding (QNC) is a new technology of quantum network communication. Since QNC can maximize the communication efficiency of quantum communication networks, it receives wide attention. As an important quantum communication resource, quantum entanglement plays a key role in the field of quantum communication and quantum computation, of course, including QNC. Several typical QNC schemes require quantum entanglement to achieve lossless quantum communication. However, none of these previous schemes mentioned the formation and distribution of quantum entanglement. Moreover, the entangled resources required by these schemes are more demanding and the required experimental environment is harsh, which is difficult to operate in practice. Therefore, with the help of entanglement distribution by separable states and probabilistic cloning, we propose a novel quantum network coding scheme based on entanglement distribution. This scheme can successfully achieve quantum entanglement distribution in the butterfly network. It is efficient in the use of quantum resources and has stronger resistance to environmental noise and other disturbances. We also point out that quantum discord, as a more general quantum communication resource, controls the realization of the whole communication process.

Keywords: Quantum network coding ·
Entanglement distribution by separable states ·
Quantum entanglement · Quantum discord

1 Introduction

In recent years, with the development of quantum communication technology [1, 2], quantum network coding (QNC) has attracted a lot of attention in quantum communication. It is also advantageous to improve the efficiency of transmission performance of a network. In 2006, Hayashi et al. [3] initiated the study of QNC for the butterfly network. The main problems of QNC lie in the exact copy of quantum states and the quantum operation of a qubit. The no-cloning theorem prevents the exact copy of an unknown qubit. So we can only use approximate cloning such as the universal cloning scheme [4].

© Springer Nature Switzerland AG 2019
X. Sun et al. (Eds.): ICAIS 2019, LNCS 11635, pp. 13–24, 2019.
https://doi.org/10.1007/978-3-030-24268-8_2

With the development of quantum technology, researchers began to introduce additional resources into quantum networks and aimed to achieve the perfect QNC scheme. Also, due to the no-cloning theorem, people believe that perfect quantum multicasting could not be achieved. Therefore, the vast majority of researchers focus on the problem of k-pairs (or multi-unicast problem). For example, Hayashi [5] proposed the perfect QNC scheme for the problem of k-pairs in the matrix of butterflies with a matted state between the sources. Kobayashi et al. [6] studied the role of classical communication in the quantum register network and proposed a QNC scheme capable of achieving a perfect quantum transmission for the k-pair problem in the general network. However, none of these previous schemes mentioned the formation and distribution of quantum entanglement. Therefore, it is necessary to consider the advantage of quantum entanglement and network coding and further study quantum network coding based on entanglement distribution.

Quantum entanglement is the fundamental and revolutionary application direction of quantum information theory. It cannot come from local operations and classical communication (LOCC) and represents a more complex relationship in the physical systems than in the classical world [7]. The common feature of all entanglements used so far is that entanglement is produced by a global operation in the systems that must be entangled, or result from a direct transmission of entanglement between the systems. Even the entanglements swapping, capable of establishing an entanglement between the systems that have no entanglements, is not an exception because the entanglement is transmitted directly among participants. Fortunately, quantum mechanics admits the different ways of establishing entanglement without the transmission of entanglements. In 2003, Cubitt et al. [8] proposed the entanglement distribution by separable states (EDSS) protocol, Kay [12] discussed and improved the protocol in 2012. Then the protocol was experimentally verified by Fedrizzi *et al.* [13]. EDSS synthesizes entanglement distillation and quantum information theory to realize entanglement distribution based on separable states. The creation of entanglements between two observers can be divided into local operations and the communication of a separable quantum system between the system.

Our QNC scheme aims to entangle two pairs of source nodes with two target nodes through local operations and the transmission of intermediate separable quantum systems from sources to targets. Once the state of the resource is established, no other classical communication is required to complete the transmission. Note that the preparation of resource states is only done through LOCC. No global quantum operation is executed in the initial stage and the entanglement is not present. In fact, Satoh et al. [14] designed the QNC scheme for quantum repeater networks which uses quantum entanglements between each adjacent node. The problem of Satoh's scheme is that they do not investigate the creation of entanglements between nodes. In addition, the consumption of quantum entanglements in their scheme is massive. In our scheme, we will use the distribution of entanglements by separable states. There is no need for the preparation of entanglements. As a result, we only need LOCC and the transmission of two separable quantum systems.

In this paper, we present two basic operations for QNC, namely EDSS and probabilistic cloning. The EDSS protocol can form the entanglement between two long-distance quantum systems with strong robustness. Probabilistic cloning can precisely clone quantum states that meet certain conditions with a certain probability. These two basic operations provide us with basic tools to implement a new QNC scheme.

2 Basic Operations

2.1 Entanglement Distribution by Separable States

In the EDSS protocol [8], the particles c, a and b are always in a separated state, i.e., they are not entangled. The quantum correlation therein is not easily affected by channel noise, and the protocol utilizes the quantum distillation technology to ensure strong robustness [9].

The EDSS protocol is described as follows:

(1) Alice and Bob start by preparing a (classically correlated) separable state, where Alice has particles a and c, Bob has particle b.
(2) Alice applies an operation on her two particles a and c, then sends particle c to Bob.
(3) Bob applies an operation on b and c, resulting in a state that contains (distillable) entanglement between a and b (tracing out c), even though c has remained separable from (ab) throughout.

Although the protocol above is abstract, one specific example is given:

(1) Alice and Bob prepare the qubits a, b, and c. The state of the entire system is:

$$\rho_{abc} = \frac{1}{6} \sum_{k=0}^{3} |\psi_k, \psi_{-k}, 0\rangle \langle \psi_k, \psi_{-k}, 0| + \sum_{i=0}^{1} \frac{1}{6} |i, i, 1\rangle \langle i, i, 1|$$

where $|\psi_k\rangle = \frac{1}{\sqrt{2}}(|0\rangle + e^{ik\pi/2} |1\rangle)$.

(2) Alice performs a CNOT operation on a and c, where a is the control bit. The state of the system is:

$$\sigma_{abc} = \frac{1}{3} |\psi_{GHZ}\rangle \langle \psi_{GHZ}| + \sum_{i,j,k=0}^{1} \beta_{ijk} \Pi_{ijk}$$

where $|\psi_{GHZ}\rangle_{abc} = \frac{1}{\sqrt{2}}(|000\rangle + |111\rangle)$, $\Pi_{ijk} = |ijk\rangle \langle ijk|$, and all β's are 0 apart from $\beta_{001} = \beta_{010} = \beta_{101} = \beta_{110} = \frac{1}{6}$.

(3) Alice sends c to Bob.
(4) Bob performs a CNOT operation on b and c, where b is the control bit. The final state of the system is:

$$\tau_{abc} = \frac{1}{3} |\phi^+\rangle_{ab} \langle \phi^+| \otimes |0\rangle_c \langle 0| + \frac{2}{3} I_{ab} \otimes |1\rangle_c \langle 1|$$

where $|\phi^+\rangle = \frac{1}{\sqrt{2}}(|00\rangle + |11\rangle)$.

(5) Bob measures the state of c. If the state of c is $|0\rangle$, the entanglement between a and b is established successfully. If the state of c is $|1\rangle$, then the entanglement between a and b failed to establish and the procedure is re-executed.

Note that there is no entanglement between c and ab in the whole process. There is only a classical correlation between initial states ρ_{abc}, so ρ_{abc} can be remotely prepared via LOCC.

2.2   Probabilistic Cloning

There are two types of quantum cloning techniques. One is definitive cloning, i.e., performing unitary transformations through the entire cloning process. The other is probabilistic cloning, which is unitary transformation and quantum measurement during cloning. Both of these types of quantum cloning are governed by the quantum no-cloning theorem. The quantum no-cloning theorem asserts that non-orthogonal states cannot be cloned, but it does not deny the possibility of inaccurate cloning. Thus, definitive cloning is dedicated to increasing the fidelity of inaccurate cloning, the realization and nature of definitive cloning were investigated in [11,16,17]. Gisin *et al.* [17] pointed out that the upper bound of the fidelity of a deterministic quantum copier with a single input and double output is 5/6. Furthermore, Duan *et al.* [18,19] put forward the technique of probabilistic cloning. In probabilistic cloning of a quantum system, quantum measurements are introduced to accurately clone a set of linearly independent quantum states with a certain probability.

The scheme of probabilistic cloning is described as follows:

(1) Preparation: Qubits a, b, and an additional qubit p. b and p are prepared to a certain initial state $|0\rangle$. The input bit of the original qubit a is $|\psi_s\rangle$.
(2) We choose the proper unitary evolution according to the input state of a, and apply a unitary operation to the whole system so that the final state is formed by the following two parts:

$$\sqrt{\eta}\,|\psi_s\rangle_a\,|\psi_s\rangle_b\,|0\rangle_p + \sqrt{1-\eta}\,|\psi_{ab}\rangle\,|1\rangle_p$$

(3) The state of p is measured. If the state of p is $|0\rangle$, the cloning is successful. a and b are two identical quantum states. If the state of p is $|1\rangle$, the clone fails.

From the above scheme, we can see that the probability of successful cloning is $\sqrt{\eta}$. The parameters η is defined as the cloning efficiency. It determines the performance of this clone. Further studies show that the upper bound of cloning efficiency depends on the set of input states [19]. For example, if the input state belongs to the set $\{|\psi_0\rangle, |\psi_1\rangle\}$, the maximum efficiency of the probabilistic quantum cloning machine is

$$\eta_{max} = \frac{1}{1 + \langle\psi_0|\psi_1\rangle}$$

3 Proposed QNC Scheme

Most of previous QNC schemes are based on the transmission of pure quantum states and do not consider noise during transmission. In reality, most quantum systems are in a mixed state. The reason is that the quantum system cannot be a perfect closed system, so the quantum system will certainly interact with the surrounding environment, and then evolve from a pure state into a mixed state. In the process of transmitting a quantum system, the noise in the channel can also interfere with the quantum. Although the ideal QNC schemes proposed in the past can achieve good results in theory, its communication efficiency will be greatly reduced due to the interference of various factors in the process of implementation [7].

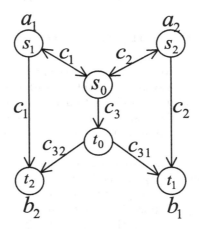

Fig. 1. Our QNC scheme

By virtue of the EDSS protocol, these factors can be taken into account to improve the robustness of QNC. Moreover, the entire network coding process does not involve the transmission of classical information, only through the transmission of an intermediate quantum state to build the maximal entanglement, and finally form a quantum teleportation channel between the sender and receiver of information. With this channel, the sender and receiver can securely transfer information.

The network setting is presented in Fig. 1. It is based on the butterfly network with all-quantum channels. Source nodes s_1 and s_2 simultaneously send quantum states to target nodes t_1 and t_2. s_0 and t_0 are two intermediate nodes. Quantum states are encoded at s_0 and decoded at t_1 and t_2.

Our QNC scheme is described as follows:

Step 1. The qubits a_1, b_1, c_1 are prepared at the nodes s_1, t_1. The qubits a_2, b_2, c_2 are prepared at the nodes s_2, t_2. Let the quantum be in a separable classically correlated state with each other. The density matrix of the system is expressed as:

$$\rho_{a_i b_i c_i} = \frac{1}{6} \sum_{k=0}^{3} |\psi_k, \psi_{-k}, 0\rangle \langle \psi_k, \psi_{-k}, 0| + \sum_{j=0}^{1} \frac{1}{6} |j, j, 1\rangle \langle j, j, 1| \quad i \in \{1, 2\} \qquad (1)$$

where $|\psi_k\rangle = \frac{1}{\sqrt{2}}(|0\rangle + e^{ik\pi/2} |1\rangle)$.

Step 2. At the node s_1, CNOT is operated on a_1, c_1 at the node s_1 where a_1 is the control bit. At the node s_2, CNOT is performed on a_2, c_2 where a_2 is the control bit. After the operation is completed, the state of the system is

$$\sigma_{a_i b_i c_i} = \frac{1}{3} |\psi_{GHZ}\rangle \langle \psi_{GHZ}| + \sum_{j,k,l=0}^{1} \beta_{jkl} \prod_{jkl} \quad i \in \{1, 2\}$$

where $|\psi_{GHZ}\rangle_{abc} = \frac{1}{\sqrt{2}}(|000\rangle + |111\rangle)$, $\prod_{jkl} = |jkl\rangle \langle jkl|$, and all β's are 0 apart from $\beta_{001} = \beta_{010} = \beta_{101} = \beta_{110} = \frac{1}{6}$.

Step 3. s_1, s_2 send c_1, c_2 to node s_0, respectively.

Step 4. The new quantum system c_3 is introduced at s_0, and the initial state of c_3 is $|0\rangle$. Quantum unitary transformation U_{CNOT} is performed on c_1, c_2, where c_2 is the control bit. The result of this operation is given to c_3.

Step 5. s_0 sends c_1 to t_2 via s_1 and s_0 sends c_2 to t_1 via s_1. c_3 is sent to the node t_0.

Step 6. At the node t_0, the probabilistic cloning of c_3 gives c_{31}, c_{32}. And c_{31}, c_{32} are sent to the node t_1, t_2, respectively.

Step 7. The CNOT operation is performed on c_2, c_{31} at the node t_1, where c_2 is the control bit. Then c_{31} is approximately equal to c_1. At the node t_2, CNOT is performed on c_1, c_{32}, where c_1 is the control bit. Then c_{32} is approximately equal to c_2.

Step 8. The CNOT operation is performed on c_{31}, b_1 at the node t_1, where b_1 is the control bit. At the node t_2, c_{32}, b_2 are CNOT, where b_2 is the control bit. After the operation is completed, the state of the system is

$$\tau_{a_i b_i c_{3i}} = \frac{1}{3} |\phi^+\rangle_{a_i b_i} \langle \phi^+| \otimes |0\rangle_{c_{3i}} \langle 0| + \frac{2}{3} I_{a_i b_i} \otimes |1\rangle_{c_{3i}} \langle 1| \quad i \in \{1, 2\} \qquad (2)$$

where $|\phi^+\rangle = \frac{1}{\sqrt{2}}(|00\rangle + |11\rangle)$.

At this moment, $|\phi^+\rangle_{a_i b_i} = \frac{1}{\sqrt{2}}(|00\rangle + |11\rangle)$ is maximally entangled. The ancilla c_{3i} clearly remains separable with respect the rest of the system, but the state now contains entanglement between a_i and b_i, i.e., the direct quantum teleportation channel of s_1, t_1, s_2, t_2 is established. Throwing away the ancilla leaves the state

$$\rho_{a_i b_i} = \frac{2}{3} |\phi^+\rangle \langle \phi^+| + \frac{1}{6} |01\rangle \langle 01| + \frac{1}{6} |10\rangle \langle 10|$$

4   Properties of the QNC Scheme

Firstly, we discuss the success probability of transmitting the qubit c to corresponding receivers. Then, by analyzing the final system state and extracting a maximally entangled state of a_i and b_i, we summarize another property. The properties of scheme are provided as follows.

Property 1. After the decoding processing in Step 7 of the QNC scheme, the probability of obtaining the correct corresponding c at the target nodes is $\frac{1}{1+\langle\psi_0|\psi_1\rangle}$.

Proof. If the qubit c_3 belongs to the set $\{|\psi_0\rangle, |\psi_1\rangle\}$, the maximum probability of cloning c_3 is $\sqrt{\frac{1}{1+\langle\psi_0|\psi_1\rangle}}$. So the maximum probability to make c_{31}, c_{32} equal to c_3 is $\frac{1}{1+\langle\psi_0|\psi_1\rangle}$. With quantum unitary transformation U_{CNOT} performed in Step 7, the maximum probability to make c_{31}, c_{32} equal to c_1, c_2 is $\frac{1}{1+\langle\psi_0|\psi_1\rangle}$.

Property 1 suggests that a larger overlap between the input states which leads to a larger $\langle\psi_0|\psi_1\rangle$, namely a smaller maximum cloning efficiency. So in order to make a large cloning efficiency, the input c needs to avoid overlapping.

Property 2: The maximal probability of obtaining maximally entangled states at the target nodes is 2/3.

Proof. We obtain the system state at Step 8 in Table 1. At the node t_1, t_2, we can get a maximally entangled state of a_i and b_i when c_{3i} is $|0\rangle$ with probability 1/3. Alternatively, if a deterministic effect is required, we can apply a local completely positive map (CPM) to b_i and c_{3i}, defined by $\varepsilon_{b_i c_{3i}} = \sum_i O_{b_i c_{3i}}^{(j)} \rho O_{b_i c_{3i}}^{(j)^+}$ with Kraus operators $O_{b_i c_{3i}}^{(1)} = I_{b_i} \otimes |0\rangle_{c_{3i}} \langle 0|, O_{b_i c_{3i}}^{(2)} = |0\rangle_{b_i} \langle 0| \otimes |1\rangle_{c_{3i}} \langle 1|, O_{b_i c_{3i}}^{(3)} = |0\rangle_{b_i} \langle 1| \otimes |1\rangle_{c_{3i}} \langle 1|$, satisfying $\sum_j O^{(j)^+} O^{(j)} = I$. Throwing away c_{3i} leaves the state $\rho_{a_i b_i} = tr_{c_{3i}}(\varepsilon_{b_i c_{3i}}(\tau_{a_i b_i c_{3i}})) = \frac{1}{3}|\phi^+\rangle\langle\phi^+| + \frac{1}{3}\prod 00 + \frac{1}{3}\prod 10$,

This state has non-positive partial transpose, so a_i and b_i must be (distilled) entangled. Thus the nodes s_1 and t_1 (s_2 and t_2) achieve the announced effect. The system state is shown in Table 2.

Table 1. System state at Step 8

a_i	b_i	c_{3i}	Probability
0	0	0	1/6
1	1	0	1/6
0	0	1	1/6
0	1	1	1/6
1	0	1	1/6
1	1	1	1/6

Table 2. Apply a CPM to b_i and c_{3i} and throw away c_{3i}

a_i	b_i	Probability
0	0	1/6
1	1	1/6
0	0	1/3
1	0	1/3

So we obtain the maximal probability of getting maximally entangled states $p_m = P_{\rho_{a_i b_i} = |\phi^+\rangle\langle\phi^+|} + P_{\rho_{a_i b_i} = |00\rangle\langle00|} = 1/3 + 1/3 = 2/3$.

According to the above properties, we can know that the efficiency of the QNC scheme depends on probabilistic cloning. Probabilistic cloning is different from definitive cloning, and it has a probability that cloning process comes to nothing. Once it succeeds, we will obtain the perfect copies of initial qubits. Wang and Cai [15] proposed a scheme to enhance the fidelity of quantum cloning machine using a weak measurement. They conducted a weak measurement on a qubit to make it easier to clone. If the result of a measurement is 'yes', the qubit will be fed to quantum cloning machine, otherwise, the qubit will be quitted. After the cloning process accomplishes, copies with high fidelity depend on the value of p will be obtained. Therefore, we can apply this idea to our scheme for a larger cloning efficiency. Before the probabilistic cloning of c_3, we conduct a weak measurement on it. If the result of a measurement is 'yes', we obtain the copies c_{31}, c_{32}. Otherwise, we quit c_3.

5   Performance Analysis

Since the distribution of entanglement by separable states is crucial in the QNC scheme, the EDSS properties deserve to be further discussed. We will discuss two important issues in this section. Firstly, what profit can the entanglement between the transmitter and the receiver gain under the exchange of a quantum carrier? Secondly, we try to find a relationship between the increase in entanglement and quantum discord, i.e., the non-classical correlations between senders and receivers.

To compare entanglement and discord at the same benchmark, we consider the entanglement measured by the relative entropy of the entanglement [20] and the discord is quantified by the relative entropy of the discord. The quantum relative entropy between two states ρ and σ is defined as:

$$S(\rho||\sigma) = -S(\rho) - tr(\rho \log \sigma)$$

where $S(\rho) = -tr(\rho \log \rho)$ is the von Neumann entropy of quantum state ρ. The relative entropy is monotonic under any completely positive trace-preserving map M [22], i.e.,

$$S(\rho||\sigma) \geq S(M(\rho)||M(\sigma))$$

The relative entropy of entanglement in the bipartition x versus y is defined as the minimum relative entropy

$$E_{x:y}(\rho) = \min_{\rho_{x:y}} S(\rho||\rho_{x:y})$$

between the joint state ρ of x and y and the set of separable states $\rho_{x:y} = \sum_i p_i \rho_x^i \otimes \rho_y^i$. Similarly, the relative entropy of discord is defined as the minimum relative entropy [23]

$$D_{x|y}(\rho) = \min_{\chi_{x|y}} S(\rho||\chi_{x|y})$$

between ρ and the set of quantum-classical states $\chi_{x|y} = \sum_j p_j \chi_x^j \otimes |j\rangle_y$. It can be shown that $D_{x|y}(\rho)$ corresponds to the minimal entropic increase resulting from the performance of a complete projective measurement $\prod_y$ over y: $D_{x|y}(\rho) = \min_{\prod_y} S[\prod_y(\rho)] - S(\rho)$ where $\prod_y(\rho)$ describes the state after the measurement $\prod_y$ [21]. Finally, mutual information between x and y is defined as $I_{x:y}(\rho) = S(\rho_{xy}||\rho_x \otimes \rho_y)$, with ρ_x and ρ_y, the reduced states of x and y. Mutual information quantifies the total amount of correlations present between x and y. It holds $I_{x:y}(\rho) \geq D_{x|y}(\rho) \geq E_{x:y}(\rho)$. Firstly, we discuss the properties of the general distribution of entanglements between Alice and Bob. The key step in the system is the transfer of a carrier from one place to another. The difference of entanglements through the bipartitions a: cb and ac: b, which corresponds to the situation after and before the transfer of the carrier, can be limited [24]. The lemma of the relative discord is provided as follows.

Lemma 1: For any tripartite state ρ_{abc}, we have difference of entanglement bounded by the relative discord:

$$|E_{a:bc}(\rho) - E_{ac:b}(\rho)| \leq D_{ab|c}(\rho) \tag{3}$$

Theorem 1: Assume u to be the initial state of a, b and c, and $g = M_{ac}(u)$ to be the state obtained from u by means of a local encoding operation M_{ac}, we have

$$E_{a:bc}(g) \leq E_{ac:b}(u) + D_{ab|c}(g)$$

Proof. Let us define u the initial state of a, b and c, and g the state obtained from u by means of a local encoding operation M_{ac}. A local operation on ac cannot increase entanglement in the ac:b, i.e., $E_{ac:b}(g) \leq E_{ac:b}(u)$. System c is then sent to b's site, where it interacts with b via a decoding operation meant to localize on b the entanglement between senders and receivers.

By combining the above description, we can have the theorem of local operation.

This theorem shows that the entanglement gain between distant locations is limited by the amount of quantum discord measured in the communication system [25].

Theorem 2: Assume u to be the initial state of a, b and c, and $g = M_{ac}(u)$ to be the state obtained from u by means of a local encoding operation M_{ac}, we have

$$E_{a:bc}(g) \leq E_{ab:c}(g) + D_{ac|b}(u)$$

Proof. In order to emphasize the importance of the appearance of discord rather than entanglement on the right-hand side of Eq. 3, we focus on the general conditions for the success of entanglement creation by means of a separable carrier. This corresponds to requiring

$$E_{b:ac}(g) = 0 \tag{4}$$

$$E_{ab:c}(g) = 0 \tag{5}$$

$$E_{a:bc}(g) > 0 \tag{6}$$

Equation 4 indicates that there is no initial entanglement between remote locations, i.e., ac and b. Equation 5 represents our description that the ancilla must be separable from a and b [23]. Equation 6 ensures that non-zero entanglement is established by the exchange of ancilla. Note that nonvanishing $a{:}bc$ entanglement does not necessarily imply the possibility of creating $a{:}b$ entanglement via the local decoding operation on bc.

In order to satisfy the conditions (3), besides the discord present in g, there must be discord on the receiver side already in the initial state u. It is seen by applying Eq. 3 again, but with the roles of b and c interchanged, and using the fact that discord does not increase under operations on the unmeasured systems, we can obtain the theorem of initial discord.

Finally, for a fixed dimension of the carrier, it is more efficient to use a separable carrier rather than an entangled one. On one hand, by sending a d-dimensional system that is maximally entangled with a similar one that remains with the sender, we can increase the shared entanglement by $\log_2 d$. On the other hand, [24] shows that by using separable states, the entanglement increase is strictly smaller than $\log_2 d$.

6   Security Analysis

The channels are tentatively useless after the evolution of the system, then attackers cannot get any message, so our scheme will achieve higher security during the communication. However, the channels may be under attack during the evolution of the system. We discuss two situations as follows.

Firstly, our scheme uses the EDSS protocol to successfully construct entanglement between two pairs of nodes. It can effectively defend against wiretap attack because the ancilla c_i is separable at all times during the evolution of the system [8]. So any attacker would fail to obtain the states a_i, b_i even if it can capture any ancilla c_i.

Secondly, the entanglement will fail to construct if any attacker replaced the ancilla c_i during the evolution. However, it is too difficult to replace the ancilla c_i accurately because of the quantum uncertainty principle. To avoid this situation, we can repeat the evolution and measure the system over and over again to check for the presence of attackers. Therefore, the success probability of constructing entanglement will increase.

From the above analysis, we can conclude that our scheme can be applied to the case of high security.

7   Discussion

First of all, we compare the previous QNC schemes with our scheme. The main comparison is whether the scheme involves the generation of quantum entanglement and the amount of entangled bits used. The specific comparison is listed

Table 3. Comparison of QNC schemes

Scheme	Generation of quantum entanglement	Amount of ebit
Prior Entanglement [3]	NOT involved	4
Quantum repeater [7]	NOT involved	7
Our scheme	Involved	2

in Table 3. We can see that none of the classical QNC schemes involve the generation of quantum entanglement and consume a large amount of entangled quantum resources.

Secondly, we find some differences from other QNC schemes which use a butterfly network. The channels of the other QNC schemes are one-way, while our scheme has two-way channels. At Step 3, c_1, c_2 are transmit to s_0 from s_1, s_2. Then at Step 5, they are retransmit to t_1, t_2 via s_1, s_2 after CNOT is performed on them. By means of two streams, we can decode at t_1, t_2 separately. Furthermore, if this network is generalized to the model of k-pair problem, we can specify some source-target pairs to complete decoding and construct entanglement arbitrarily by transmitting different c_i which could be of great benefit to realize access control between these target nodes.

8 Conclusion

In this paper, we proposed a new QNC scheme. The scheme successfully uses the EDSS protocol to achieve quantum entanglement distribution on the butterfly network. By comparing with the previous schemes, we found that this scheme was more efficient in the use of quantum resources and was more resistant to ambient noise and other disturbances. Probabilistic cloning is also a key step in the proposed QNC scheme. Finally, we analyzed the relationship between the entanglement distribution and the quantum discord existing in the system. Quantitative analysis of the scheme with quantum discord provides guidance for future research.

Acknowledgment. This project was supported by the National Natural Science Foundation of China (No. 61571024) for valuable helps.

References

1. Tan, X.Q., Li, X.C., Yang, P.: Perfect quantum teleportation via Bell states. Comput. Mater. Continua **57**(3), 495–503 (2018)
2. Zhong, J.F., Liu, Z.H., Xu, J.: Analysis and improvement of an efficient controlled quantum secure direct communication and authentication protocol. Comput. Mater. Continua **57**(3), 621–633 (2018)
3. Hayashi, M., Iwama, K., Nishimura, H., Raymond, R., Yamashita, S.: Quantum network coding. In: Thomas, W., Weil, P. (eds.) STACS 2007. LNCS, vol. 4393, pp. 610–621. Springer, Heidelberg (2007). https://doi.org/10.1007/978-3-540-70918-3_52

4. Buzek, V., Hillery, M.: Quantum copying: beyond the no-cloning theorem. Phys. Rev. A **54**, 1844 (1996)
5. Hayashi, M.: Prior entanglement between senders enables perfect quantum network coding with modification. Phys. Rev. A **76**(4), 538–538 (2012)
6. Kobayashi, H., Le Gall, F., Nishimura, H., Rötteler, M.: General scheme for perfect quantum network coding with free classical communication. In: Albers, S., Marchetti-Spaccamela, A., Matias, Y., Nikoletseas, S., Thomas, W. (eds.) ICALP 2009. LNCS, vol. 5555, pp. 622–633. Springer, Heidelberg (2009). https://doi.org/10.1007/978-3-642-02927-1_52
7. Bennett, C.H., Divincenzo, D.P.: Quantum information and computation. Nature **48**(10), 24–30 (1995)
8. Cubitt, T.S., Verstraete, F., Dr, W., Cirac, J.I.: Separable states can be used to distribute entanglement. Phys. Rev. Lett. **91**(3), 037902 (2003)
9. Bennett, C.H., Divincenzo, D.P., Smolin, J.A., Wootters, W.K.: Mixed-state entanglement and quantum error correction. Phys. Rev. A **54**(5), 3824 (1996)
10. Vidal, G., Tarrach, R.: Robustness of entanglement. Phys. Rev. A **59**(1), 141–155 (1999)
11. Braunstein, S.L., Caves, C.M., Jozsa, R., Linden, N., Popescu, S., Schack, R.: Separability of very noisy mixed states and implications for NMR quantum computing. Physics **83**(5), 1054–1057 (1998)
12. Kay, A.: Using separable bell-diagonal states to distribute entanglement. Phys. Rev. Lett. **109**(8), 080503 (2012)
13. Fedrizzi, A., Zuppardo, M., Gillett, G.G., Broome, M.A., Almeida, M.P., Paternostro, M., et al.: Experimental distribution of entanglement with separable carriers. Phys. Rev. Lett. **111**(23), 230504 (2013)
14. Satoh, T., Le Gall, F., Imai, H.: Quantum network coding for quantum repeaters. Phys. Rev. A **86**(3), 032331 (2012)
15. Wang, M.H., Cai, Q.Y.: High fidelity quantum cloning of two known nonorthogonal quantum states via weak measurement. arXiv:1806.08112v1 [quant-ph] (2018)
16. Mozyrsky, D., Privman, V., Hillery, M.: A Hamiltonian for quantum copying. Phys. Lett. A **226**(5), 253–256 (1997)
17. Gisin, N., Massar, S.: Optimal quantum cloning machines. Phys. Rev. Lett. **79**(11), 2153–2156 (1997)
18. Duan, L.M., Guo, G.C.: Probabilistic cloning and identification of linearly independent quantum states. Physics **80**(22), 4999–5002 (1998)
19. Duan, L.M., Guo, G.C.: A probabilistic cloning machine for replicating two nonorthogonal states. Phys. Lett. A **243**(5–6), 261–264 (1998)
20. Piani, M., Gharibian, S., Adesso, G., Calsamiglia, J., Horodecki, P., Winter, A.: All nonclassical correlations can be activated into distillable entanglement. Phys. Rev. Lett. **106**(22), 220403 (2011)
21. Nielsen, M.A., Isaac, C.: Quantum Computation and Quantum Information. Cambridge (2002)
22. Bennett, C.H., Shor, P.W.: Quantum information theory. Rep. Math. Phys. **10**(1), 43–72 (1998)
23. Abeyesinghe, A., Devetak, I., Hayden, P., Winter, A.: The mother of all protocols: restructuring quantum information's family tree. Proc. Math. Phys. Eng. Sci. **465**(2108), 2537–2563 (2009)
24. Madhok, V., Animesh, D.: Quantum discord as a resource in quantum communication. Int. J. Modern Phys. B **27**(01n03), 1345041 (2013)
25. Killoran, N., Steinhoff, F.E., Plenio, M.B.: Converting nonclassicality into entanglement. Phys. Rev. Lett. **116**(8), 080402 (2015)

Moving Target Defense in Preventing SQL Injection

Kaiyu Feng[1], Xiao Gu[1], Wei Peng[1], and Dequan Yang[2(✉)]

[1] School of Computer Science and Technology, Beijing Institute of Technology, Beijing, China
[2] Network Information Technology Center, Beijing Institute of Technology, Beijing, China
yangdequan@bit.edu.cn

Abstract. The database stores important information about the user, which make it a core part of the website. Therefore, database injection has become a serious cyber-attack. Traditional database injection defenses are passive defenses, which cannot detect new vulnerability before it is exposed. The Moving Target Defense (MTD) method that emerged in recent years has become a breakthrough to solve this problem. This paper mainly establishes the model to verify the possibility of dynamic defense application in database injection defense. This paper first introduces the related concepts SQLI and MTD, then we build models to compare the attack surface of the traditional static defense model and MTD one. It is concluded that with certain conditions, the dynamic defense model has a smaller attack surface, which indicate stronger defense ability.

Keywords: Moving target defense · SQL injection · Container

1 Introduction

Cybersecurity is a topic that has attracted more and more attention. It has penetrated into all aspects of computer science, such as web, IOT [1].

In the web system using databases to organize their data, SQL are used to storing, manipulating and retrieving data interacting with the databases. Almost every data record, such as bank account, password, personal information, are stored in databases and processed by SQL statement. Hence it makes SQL a popular target to be used by attacker to exploit the sensitive information. This approach is implemented by alter the valid SQL statement into malicious one, usually by using the feature of SQL grammar. The malicious statement, after executed by database server, can lead to some very serious consequences.

2 Summary on Attack Types

2.1 Union Query

This type of injection uses the UNION key word in SQL, which merge two queries to one. Technically, a union-based injection composes of both valid statement and invalid

© Springer Nature Switzerland AG 2019
X. Sun et al. (Eds.): ICAIS 2019, LNCS 11635, pp. 25–34, 2019.
https://doi.org/10.1007/978-3-030-24268-8_3

statement. As the example below: `SELECT * FROM table_name WHERE id=?;` The question mark represents the input. By construct -1 UNION SELECT * FROM other_table, an attacker can retrieve data from the certain table.

2.2 Tautologies

Tautologies is the most widely ways in SQLIA. It often be used in the subsection of WHERE statement. In this type of attack, the attacker construct a tautology to make the query always true. As the example below [2]:

```
USERNAME = 'Mohammad' and password = 'P@ssw0rd'
```

may become illegal reshaped query:

```
username = 'Mohammad' or 1 = 1 - and password =
'P@ssw0rd'
```

2.3 Alternate Encodings

This type of attack is hidden and dangerous as it can reshape the syntax of the attack into a normal one that intruder detection systems may not detect. The effectiveness of using alternate encodings in SQLIA is that the attacker reshapes the original SQLIA command to become a new normal syntax that contains embedded SQLIA [2].

2.4 Piggybacked Queries

By using "; ", this way of attack can attach an additional malicious query to the original query string. This type of attack can be especially harmful because attackers can use it tot to inject virtually any type of SQL command [3].

2.5 Malformed Queries

By taking advantage of error messages return from databases, attacker can figure out more detailed vulnerabilities of the databases. And even if the website does not echo back debug information, attacker can accomplish this by using a timing attack [3]. Such as
`legalUser0 AND ASCII SUBSRING select top 1 name from sysobjects; 1; 1>X WAITFOR 5.`

By measuring the time database response, attacker can determine whether the techniques mentioned above can be used.

3   Type of SQLIA and Related Work

3.1   Input Filtering Value Sanitization

It's a very common and direct way the web engineer would like to deploy to prevent SQLI as well as other type of precious code. The kind of method is implement usually by using a blacklist or even a whitelist to pre-process the input data in a way of filtering certain dangerous words. But it's not a safe way to prevent SQLI because it's always a gray area between safe input and gray input and the filter list is hard to be completed strong enough.

3.2   Parameterized Queries/Prepared Statements

This method is an effective and simple way to prevent attack by just adding a few lines of code into their program. The basic concept of this idea is to ensure that an attacker is not able to change the intent of a query. By prepared statements, even the input data is

$$1' \ or \ '1'='1'$$

the input will be considered as a whole.

3.3   Least Privilege Applied to Web Application and DBMS Accounts

Least privilege emphasize that a developer should always minimize the privileges that assigned to every database account. The detail to implement this including dividing one to multiple DB users and using views to minimize the access privilege.

3.4   Removal of Error Messages

Error message returned from the database could be gained by injecting syntactic incorrect SQL tokens to input field, which is commonly with useful debugging message including. These messages can facilitate injections.

This kind of vulnerability can be avoided by removing the error message from the web page or hide them.

3.5   Stored Procedure [4]

This approach is prompt by Ke Wei, M. Muthuprasanna and Suraj Kothari. By combining both static analysis and runtime validation. The basis technique includes control flow graph, retrieving a Finite State Automation from the EXEC procedure call and check the SQL statement of input.

Built-in stored procedure functions may be used by attackers by injecting malicious SQL queries. Normally, delimiter, such as " ; ", is used to append an attacking query followed by the legitimate query.

A stored procedure is a grope of programming statements which are prepared as a compiled form stored in the data dictionary. It can be used to improve productivity, preserve data integrity, control data access and get access to high level layer of the system. And it can be called by most of programs for its compiled form.

3.6   Using Server-Side Code Modification [5]

As per the proposed model when the two strings S1 and S2 are compared, they fail to match, and the attack will be detected.

- Actual Query:
  ```
  select * from student_details where roll_no= '';
  ```
- S1:
  ```
  roll_no= '';
  ```
- Attack Query:
  ```
  select * from student_details where roll_no='S123'
  +union+select+master.dbo.fn_varbintohexstr(password_has
  h)+from+sys.sql_logins+where+name+=+'sa' ;
  ```
- S2:
  ```
  roll_no=''+union+select+master.dbo.fn_varbintohexstr(
  password_hash)+from+sys.sql_logins+where +name+=+'sa';
  ```

Strings S1 and S2 are compared if they match then it is considered that there is no injection attack, and the query is sent to the database server for execution. Otherwise, the query would not be executed and the database send warning or error message to the web page.

3.7   Second-Order SQL Injection Detection Approach [6]

Second-order SQLI divide the injection to two stages: loading and constructing injection. They can be used in register and account management stage, for example. It is proposed by Chen Ping, Keywords randomization and proxy server are used when detect the second-order SQLI.

3.8   Length-Frequency-SQL Syntax Tree [7]

This method of SQL injection filtering mainly implemented by learning stage and filtering stage. We complete the learning process by constructing URL and SQL statement mapping tables which using crawler and database proxy technologies, and the filtering stage consists of three aspects. First, constraint the length of URL request. Second, monitor the connection frequency. Last, build a SQL syntax tree step by step to analysis the root nodes and features of subtrees. Simulation experiments and performance analysis results show that the proposed LFS filtering method can effectively prevent SQL injection attacks and is superior to keyword filtering methods and regular expression filtering methods in terms of interception rate and false alarm rate.

4 Moving Target Defence and Related Work in Preventing SQLI

4.1 Concept

Dynamic target defense aims at deploying and running uncertainty, random and dynamic networks and systems, making it difficult for attackers to discover the targets. By changing its various resources configurations and system attributes, the system presents attackers with constantly changing attack surfaces, making it more, it is the attacker conducts vulnerability analysis and penetration testing on a specific target and establishes an attack model, the system has undergone effective changes timely. These changes are enough to undermine the effectiveness of the attack model.

Dynamic target defense can also active deceive the attacker, disrupt the line of sight of the attacker, and bring it into a blind alley. It can also set up a bait to trick the attacker into attacking it and trigger an attack alert. In this way As a result, the cost and complexity of an attacker launching a successful attack will greatly increase. As a result, the probability of a successful attack will be reduced, and the Flexibility and security of the protected system will be effectively improved [8].

4.2 Common Realization Mechanism of Moving Target Defense

A large number of MTD strategies have been proposed in resent research. As put forward by Okhravi, Streilein [9], these MTD strategies can be classified into five different domains: Data layer, Software application layer, runtime environment layer, platform layer and network layer. The techniques include data randomization, N variant data diversification [10], fault-tolerant, random dynamic change or multi-state virtual system platform, randomize host/domain name mutation, intrusion tolerance system (ITS) [11], address space layout randomization (ASLR), Instruction Set Randomization (ISR), cost-effective disaster tolerance, self-protecting software system [12] and so on. In this paper we are focusing on the techniques that help to prevent SQLI. The approaches mentioned above are not specific to prevent SQLI but some of them, such as random host/domain name mutation or multi-state platform can protect a server from SQL injection to some extent.

5 Models Analysis

5.1 Proposed Model

One of the most basic models is the three-tier architecture model (Fig. 1). This model divides the entire business application into: User Interface layer, Business Logic Layer and Data Access Layer. In software architecture design, hierarchical structure is the most common and most important structure.

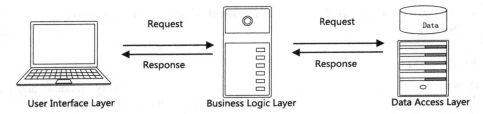

Fig. 1. Basic three-tier architecture model

The interface layer provides services to users. The business logic layer implements the logic of the entire system and interacts with the User Interface layer and the Data Access Layer. The Data Access Layer is responsible for a series of additions, deletions and changes the database, providing data services.

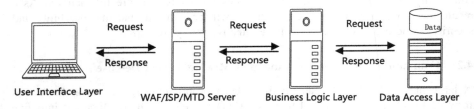

Fig. 2. Basic model with WAF/ISP or MTD Server

The user's input can be actually considered information flow, from the front end to the back end and to the database eventually. A WAF (web application firewall) or ISP (Intrusion Prevention System) is like a funnel that works between a browser and a web server to filter out threatening data (Fig. 2). The problem with the traditional model is that he can't do anything about a particular injection that is not identifiable, neither can it proactively discover new vulnerabilities.

In the SQLI dynamic defense model, we choose multiple implementations of different defense filtering systems, randomly changing the currently selected defense mode according to the time period and other conditions (such as the number of accesses and frequencies). Especially for SQLI, we can choose from the various methods mentioned above, or different current software combinations.

For traditional models, we describe its attack surface as a static, fixed-direction constant.

We can describe its attack surface as A variable, composed of multiple static fixed direction constants.

5.2 Modal Evaluation

For the traditional SQLI defense model, we assume that the attack surface has its S state space of $A = A0$. Relatively, For the MTD defense model, we assume that the state space of the attack surface S is

$$B = \{B_0, B_1, B_2, B_3, B_4, B_5\}$$

for a total of six state spaces. And we make

$$A_0 = \min\{B_n\}.$$

For both the attacker and the defender, we assume that neither of them has enough ability to grasp the specifics of the attack surface at every moment, for the reason it is the common cases in reality.

Furthermore, we can use the dynamic target defense effectiveness evaluation method to estimate the attack detection probability of the two models.

For the dynamic defense model, we assume that the transfer rules for these states are random, that is, each state has a probability transfer of 16.66%. Then we can calculate the final state expectation with the evaluation model from Yang's group [13]:

$$\bar{A} = \frac{1}{6}k_0 P_{d0} + \frac{1}{6}k_1 P_{d1} + \frac{1}{6}k_2 P_{d2} + \frac{1}{6}k_3 P_{d3} + \frac{1}{6}k_4 P_{d4} + \frac{1}{6}k_5 P_{d5}$$

We can assume that k (the initial value of the static system attack surface) also rises according to the angle, respectively

$$k_0 = 3, k_1 = 4, k_2 = 5, k_3 = 6, k_4 = 7, k_5 = 9$$

We also assume that the attack surface detection probability is

$$P_{d0} = 0.4, P_{d1} = 0.6, P_{d2} = 0.4, P_{d3} = 0.5, P_{d4} = 0.3, P_{d5} = 0.5$$

then the mathematical expectation of the dynamic attack surface is

$$\bar{A} = 2.533 < B$$

It can be seen that the attack surface of the dynamic attack surface at this time is expected to be smaller than any static attack surface.

6 Prospect of Combining Dynamic Defense with Containerization Technology

We need to note that in the past decade, in the industry, containerization technology is rapidly developing and is being applied to the production environment on a large scale [14]. Containerization technology led by Docker[1] helps companies develop, test, deploy, and operate faster.

Containerization technology is a widely recognized method of sharing server resources. The initial problem to be solved by these technologies is the isolation and

---

[1] The following uses the word "docker" to refer to the "containerization technology".

taking of resources such as servers, networks, memory, storage, etc. require by different software. Docker packages, integrates, and abstracts the underlying resources, breaking the independence between the physical structures, and allowing users to face more unified and isolated resources. In the development of containerization technology, people are not only attracted by the economic benefits brought by this technology, but also find that the underlying resources are hidden and isolated to some extent due to the abstraction witch is an effective defense method that cyber security is looking for.

Of course, even if the containerization technology of docker provides good isolation, its potential vulnerabilities still exist. The CVE official records that docker history version has more than 20 vulnerabilities. However, it is not difficult to notice that docker is what dynamic target defense looking for, which requires that the program itself may have a flaw, but can be dynamically transferred to switching its attack surface.

Containerization technology is an application technology that does not itself to provide new dynamic defense ideas of MTD. However, the automated container technology represented by kubernetes should be one of the good solutions to dynamics at the software engineering level and operating system level. Due to the quick start and small resource occupation, the creation, suspension, update and deletion of a container can be completed in a short time. Multi-application environments and dynamic target defenses for multiple operating systems just need such features. One of the functions of kubernetes is to automatically control the size and iteration of the container while ensuring that the container is always available. We believe this can provide a solution for the server to dynamically change multiple environments (Fig. 3).

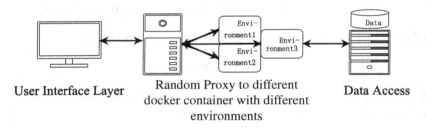

Fig. 3. MTD with docker container providing dynamic environment

In other aspects of cyber security, we can already see some approach that implements this idea, such as RELOCATE [15]. A container based moving target defense approach named RELOCATE is presented by Huang, Zhang and Liu. Under the premise of continuous service, RELOCATE switches the containers constantly. It ensures the safety of large scale multi-tenant service deployment by shorting the life cycle of containers. But in the aspect of SQLI protection, there still a long way to go and we can still expect more from it.

To the SQL injection, most of the cases require the attacker to perform a large number of test injections in a long time on the interface to obtain the final injection vulnerability. During this period, using the container technology of docker and kubernetes combined with the various dynamic defense techniques mentioned above, will effectively transfer the attack surface and block the hacker's injection process.

7 Conclusion

This paper introduces the concepts related to SQL and SQLI and verifies the rationality of the SQLI defense system based on Moving target defense system, providing its feasibility. As the increase of the number of states and the transfer frequency, the defense capability of the dynamic system will gradually exceed that of the traditional static system. Of course, in terms of specific implementation, dynamic defense has certain requirements for the confidentiality and reliability of the overall system.

The current work is only a preliminary analysis of the application of MTD in SQLI defense. In terms of implementation, we recommend using container wall orchestration techniques such as cabernets as a tool for implementation. And this is the subject to further research.

Acknowledgments. This work is partially supported by CERNET innovation Project (NGII20180407).

References

1. Zhang, H., Yi, Y., Wang, J., Cao, N., Duan, Q.: Network security situation awareness framework based on threat intelligence. CMC: Comput. Mater. Continua **56**(3), 381–399 (2018)
2. Qbea'h, M., Alshraideh, M., Sabri, K.E.: Detecting and preventing SQL injection attacks: a formal approach. In: 2016 Cybersecurity and Cyberforensics Conference (CCC) (2016)
3. Yeole, A.S., Meshram, B.B.: Analysis of different techniques for detection of SQL injection. Association for Computing Machinery, Mumbai, India (2011)
4. Wei, K., Muthuprasanna, M., Kothari, S.: Preventing SQL injection attacks in stored procedures. In: Australian Software Engineering Conference (ASWEC 2006) (2006)
5. Dalai, A.K., Jena, S.K.: Neutralizing SQL injection attack using server side code modification in web applications. Secur. Commun. Netw. **2017**, 12 (2017)
6. Ping, C.: A second-order SQL injection detection method. In: 2017 IEEE 2nd Information Technology, Networking, Electronic and Automation Control Conference (ITNEC) (2017)
7. Chen-Wang, H.A.N., Hui, L.I.N., et al.: SQL injection filtering method based on proxy mode. Comput. Syst. Appl. **27**(1), 98–105 (2018)
8. Cai, G.L., et al.: Moving target defense: state of the art and characteristics. Front. Inf. Technol. Electron. Eng. **17**(11), 1122–1153 (2016)
9. Okhravi, H., Streilein, W.W., Bauer, K.S.: Moving target techniques: leveraging uncertainty for cyber defense. Lincoln Lab. J. **22**, 1 (2016)
10. Cox, B., et al.: N-variant systems: a secretless framework for security through diversity. In: Proceedings of the 15th Conference on USENIX Security Symposium, vol. 15. USENIX Association, Vancouver (2006)
11. Nguyen, Q., Sood, A.: A comparison of intrusion-tolerant system architectures. IEEE Secur. Privacy **9**(4), 24–31 (2011)

12. Yuan, E., Malek, S.: A taxonomy and survey of self-protecting software systems. In: SEAMS 2012, Zürich, Switzerland (2012)
13. Yang, L., et al.: Performance assessment technique of moving target defense based on attack surface measurement. J. Command Control **1**(04), 453–457 (2015)
14. Xie, X., Yuan, T., Zhou, X., Cheng, X.: Research on trust model in container-based cloud service. CMC: Comput. Mater. Continua **56**(2), 273–283 (2018)
15. Huang, R., Zhang, H., Liu, Y., et al.: RELOCATE: a container based moving target defense approach. In: 7th International Conference on Computer Engineering and Networks (2017)

Design and Security Analysis of Certificateless Aggregate Signature Scheme

Li Cui$^{(\boxtimes)}$, Yang Heng, and Wu Gang

College of Information and Communication,
National University of Defense Technology, Xi'an, China
lcsy0304@126.com

Abstract. The existing certificateless aggregate signature schemes have problems in terms of security and efficiency: some schemes are not secure, which does not satisfy the claimed unforgeability, others are secure, but the calculation and communication cost are large. Based on the comprehensive consideration of security and efficiency, this paper designs a new certificateless aggregate signature scheme without bilinear pairing, proves the security of the scheme under the random oracle model and computational Diffie-Hellman problem. The new scheme not only overcomes the security problem of the existing scheme, but also has a fixed length of aggregate signature. The user does not need to exchange a large amount of information when performing single signature, so that users can dynamically join the aggregate signature.

Keywords: Bilinear pairing · Certificateless cryptosystem ·
Aggregate signature · Computational Diffie-Hellman problem

1 Introduction

Digital signature is one of the core technologies of information security which could provide security services such as authentication, integrity, non-repudiation and so on [1]. With the emergence of new network forms and network services, the study of digital signatures with special properties and their applications has become one of the research hotspots of cryptography. In 2003, Boneh et al. [2] first proposed the concept of aggregate signature. In an aggregate signature scheme, different users sign different messages separately, and these signatures can be combined into one signature, and the verifier can verify whether the signature is from the specified user by simply verifying the synthesized signature, thereby reducing the number of signature verification workload and signature storage space. In 2003, Al-Riyami and Paterson [3] proposed the concept of Certificateless Public Key Cryptography (CL-PKC). Because the certificateless cryptosystem avoids the certificate management problem in the traditional public key cryptosystem and solves the key escrow problem in the identity-based cryptosystem, it establishes a good balance between the traditional public key cryptography and the identity-based cryptography [4]. Therefore, the study of certificateless aggregate signature scheme has great theoretical significance and practical application value.

© Springer Nature Switzerland AG 2019
X. Sun et al. (Eds.): ICAIS 2019, LNCS 11635, pp. 35–45, 2019.
https://doi.org/10.1007/978-3-030-24268-8_4

Generally, there are two types of attackers against certificateless cryptography schemes: type I (The outsider) and type II (The malicious KGC). The outsider doesn't know the system's master key, but it has the ability to replace the legitimate user's public key. The malicious KGC knows the system's master key, but it does not have the ability to replace the legitimate user's public key. For type II attacker, there are two ways to attack: the passive attack and the active attack. The active attack is that the attacker not only knows the system's master key, but also construct other parameters to attack deliberately. The passive attack is that the attacker does nothing but know the master key. Through in-depth analysis of the existing certificateless aggregate signature schemes, it is found that the existing schemes mainly have two problems: security and efficiency.

On one hand, the scheme is not safe which cannot satisfy the claimed unforgeability. The aggregate signature scheme proposed by Zuo et al. [5] is not safe under the replace public attack of type I attacker, the attacker can arbitrarily forge the signature by replacing the user's public key. The scheme proposed in [6–12] is insecure under the passive attack of type II attacker, attacker can arbitrarily forge one user's signature on other messages after he got one legal signature of the user. The aggregate scheme designed in [13–15] is not safe under the active attack of type II attacker, the attacker can arbitrarily forge the user's signature.

On the other hand, although the scheme is secure, the length of the aggregate signature is not fixed, the calculation and communication overhead are large. For example, the certificateless aggregate signature scheme proposed in references [16–19] is secure, but the length of the aggregate signature increases linearly with the number of users. The length of the aggregate signature is long, and the communication and computation efficiency are low. The second improved scheme proposed by Zhou et al. [16] is secure and also with a fixed aggregate signature length. However, when generating aggregate signatures, the scheme requires a large amount of information exchange between users, which increases the communication overhead during the aggregate signature generation phase, while users cannot dynamically join the aggregate signature. In addition, most of the existing schemes [6–8, 10, 11, 13–15, 17–20] use bilinear pairing in the verification phase. From the theoretical analysis [21] and experimental results [22], it shows that under the condition of achieving the same safety strength, the calculation overhead of the bilinear pairing is about 20 times higher than that of the elliptic curve scalar multiplication. In summary, the existing schemes have problems of low computation and communication efficiency generally.

In summary, based on the advantages and disadvantages of the existing solutions, this paper designs a new certificateless aggregate signature scheme. This scheme is not only safe for the two types of attackers (The outsider and malicious KGC), but also has a fixed length of aggregate signature. This scheme's verification phase does not use the bilinear pairing operation, and the user can complete the individual signature independently without exchanging a large amount of information with each other. This solution not only has higher security, lower communication and computation overhead, but also allows users to dynamically join the aggregate signature.

2   New Certificateless Aggregate Signature Scheme

Because of the security and efficiency problems of the existing certificateless aggregate signature schemes, this paper summarizes the advantages and disadvantages of the existing schemes and designs a new certificateless aggregate signature scheme.

The new scheme consists of seven algorithms: system setup algorithm, user key generation algorithm, partial key generation algorithm, single signature algorithm, single signature verification algorithm, aggregate signature algorithm and aggregate signature verification algorithm.

(1) **System setup algorithm.** Set q as a large prime number, define an additive group G_1 of order q, and select P as the generator of the group G_1. The KGC randomly selects $s \in Z_q^*$ as the system's master key and calculates $P_{pub} = sP$, P_{pub} is the system's public key. Define three hash functions H_1, H_2, H_3: $\{0,1\}^* \rightarrow Z_q^*$, save the system's master key secretly, and expose the system's public parameters $\left(q, G_1, P, H_1, H_2, H_3, P_{pub}\right)$.

(2) **User key generation algorithm.** The user with identity ID_i selects $x_i \in Z_q^*$ as the secret value and calculates the corresponding public key $P_i = x_i P$.

(3) **Partial key generation algorithm.** KGC calculates $Q_i = H_1(ID_i, P_i)$, $d_i = sQ_i$, and sends d_i to the user ID_i, who generates the private key $S_i = (d_i, x_i)$.

(4) **Single-signature algorithm.** The user ID_i randomly selects $r_i \in Z_q^*$, calculates $R_i = r_i P$, $h_i = H_2(m_i, ID_i, P_i, R_i)$, $T = H_3(P_{pub})$, $V_i = d_i + h_i r_i + x_i T$, and outputs the signature of the message m_i as $\sigma_i = (R_i, V_i)$.

5. **Single-signature verification algorithm.** Verifier calculates $Q_i = H_1(ID_i, P_i)$, $h_i = H_2(m_i, ID_i, P_i, R_i)$ and $T = H_3(P_{pub})$, verifies whether the equation $V_i P = P_{pub} Q_i + h_i R_i + P_i T$ is true. If it is established, the user's signature $\sigma_i = (R_i, V_i)$ of message m_i is valid, otherwise, the signature must be rejected.

(6) **Aggregate signature algorithm.** Enter the identity-message-signature pair $(ID_i, m_i, \sigma_i = (R_i, V_i))(1 \leq i \leq n)$, the aggregator first calculates $h_i = H_2(m_i, ID_i, P_i, R_i)$ $(1 \leq i \leq n)$, then calculates $R = \sum_{i=1}^{n} h_i R_i$, $V = \sum_{i=1}^{n} V_i$, and outputs the aggregate signature $\sigma = (R, V)$.

(7) **Aggregate signature verification algorithm.** Enter the identity-message pair (ID_i, m_i) $(1 \leq i \leq n)$ and the aggregate signature $\sigma = (R, V)$. The verifier first calculates $Q_i = H_1(ID_i, P_i)$ and $T = H_3(P_{pub})$, then verifies whether the equation $VP = P_{pub} \sum_{i=1}^{n} Q_i + R + T \sum_{i=1}^{n} P_i$ is true. If it is established, it accepts the signature, otherwise the signature is invalid.

The new scheme adds the user's public key P_i to hash function H_1 and R_i to hash function H_2 to increase the correlation between the user's public key and the verification equation, so that to avoid attack from type I and type II attacker. At the same time, the new scheme carefully designs the equation of V_i and R so that the length of the aggregate signature does not increase with the number of aggregated users. Based on the above considerations, this paper has made the above scheme design.

3 Security Proof and Analysis of the New Scheme

3.1 Security Proof of the New Scheme

In the random oracle model, the security proof of the new scheme will be proved. The certificateless aggregate signature scheme faces two types of adversary A_1(Type I) and A_2(Type II). The literature [17] details the definition of the unforgeability and the corresponding games of the certificateless aggregate signature scheme under the adaptive chosen message and identity attacks of the two types of adversary, which will not be repeated here.

Theorem 1. In the random oracle model, if there is an adversary A_1, who can break the unforgeability of the new aggregate signature scheme with non-negligible advantages ξ after making adaptive chosen message and identity attack queries in polynomial times, then there is a distinguisher B who can take polynomial times to solve a CDH problem with non-negligible advantages $Adv[B] \geq \left(1 - \frac{1}{q_{H_1}}\right)^{q_{ppk} + q_s} \left(1 - (1 - \frac{1}{q_{H_1}})^n\right)\xi$ (wherein, q_{H_1}, q_{ppk} and q_s are the maximum number of H_1 query, partial key Generation query and single signature query A_1 could make. n is the user number of the aggregate signature scheme).

Proof: A_1 is an attacker while B is a challenger to the CDH problem. Given the triple (P, aP, bP), B's goal is to solve the CDH problem by using A_1, that is calculate abP.

B acts as a challenger and uses A_1 as a subroutine. B runs system parameter setup algorithm, generates the public parameter $(q, G_1, P, H_1, H_2, H_3, P_{pub})$(B set $P_{pub} = aP$, a is the system's master key) and sends it to A_1. B maintains lists $(L_1, L_2, L_3, L_{ppk}, L_{pk}, L_s)$ to track H_1 query, H_2 query, H_3 query, partial key generation query, public key generation query and signature query of A_1 respectively. At the beginning, each list is empty. B chooses identity ID_j as its challenging identity.

Query stage: The adversary A_1 makes the following query.

H_1 query: B keeps the list $L_1 = \{ID_i, P_i, a_i, Q_i\}$, initially empty. When B receives H_1 query from A_1, B does the following:

   ① If there is a corresponding tuple in the list L_1, then B returns Q_i to A_1;

   ② Otherwise, B performs public key generation query to obtain a value P_i. If $ID_i \neq ID_j$, B randomly selects $a_i \in Z_q^*$, sets $Q_i = a_iP$, adds $\{ID_i, P_i, a_i, Q_i\}$ to L_1 and returns Q_i; otherwise, B randomly selects $a_j \in Z_q^*$, calculates $Q_j = a_jbP$, adds the corresponding value to the list L_1 and returns Q_j.

H_3 query: B keeps the list $L_3 = \{P_{pub}, \beta, T\}$, initially empty. When B receives the H_3 query from A_1, if there is a corresponding tuple in the list, B returns T directly to A_1; otherwise, B randomly selects $\beta \in Z_q^*$, calculates $T = \beta$, adds $\{P_{pub}, \beta, T\}$ to list L_3 and returns T to A_1.

H_2 query: B keeps the list $L_2 = \{m_i, ID_i, P_i, R_i, h_i\}$, initially empty. When B receives the H_2 query from A_1, if there is a corresponding tuple in the list L_2, then value h_i is directly returned to A_1; otherwise, B randomly selects $h_i \in Z_q^*$, adds $\{m_i, ID_i, P_i, R_i, h_i\}$ to list L_2 and returns h_i to A_1.

Partial Key Generation query: B keeps the list $L_{ppk} = \{ID_i, d_i\}$, initially empty. When B receives a partial key generation query, if there is a corresponding tuple in the list L_{ppk}, B directly returns d_i to A_1; otherwise, A_1 performs H_1 query and gets $\{ID_i, P_i, a_i, Q_i\}$ from B. If $ID_i \neq ID_j$, $d_i = a_i P_{pub} = a_i a P$, returns d_i to A_1 and adds $\{ID_i, d_i\}$ to the list L_{ppk}; otherwise the simulation is terminated.

Public Key Generation query: B keeps the list $L_{pk} = \{ID_i, x_i, P_i\}$, initially empty. When B receives a public key generation query from A_1, if there is already a corresponding tuple in list L_{pk}, then P_i is directly returned to A_1; otherwise, B randomly selects $x_i \in Z_q^*$, calculates $P_i = x_i P$, returns P_i to A_1 and adds $\{ID_i, x_i, P_i\}$ to L_{pk}.

Secret value query: When A_1 asks for the secret value of ID_i, B searches the list L_{pk}. If the list contains the corresponding tuple of ID_i, then the corresponding secret value x_i is returned to A_1; otherwise, B performs the public key generation query, adds $\{ID_i, x_i, P_i\}$ to the list L_{pk} and returns the corresponding x_i to A_1.

Public key replacement query: When A_1 wants to replace the original public key P_i of ID_i with a new public key P_i', if the list L_{pk} contains the identity ID_i, B sets $P_i = P_i'$, $x_i = \bot$; if the list does not contain the corresponding tuple of ID_i, B sets $P_i = P_i'$, $x_i = \bot$, and adds it to L_{pk}.

Signature query: When B receives a signature query of identity-message-public key pair (ID_i, m_i, P_i) from A_1, B operates as follows:

① If $ID_i \neq ID_j$, B selects a random number $r_i \in Z_q^*$, calculates $R_i = r_i P$, $V_i = d_i + h_i r_i + x_i \beta$, generates a signature $\sigma_{ID_i} = (R_i, V_i)$ and returns it to the adversary A_1;

② Otherwise, B gives up and terminates the simulation.

Forgery phase: After polynomial times of the above queries, A_1 outputs a forged aggregate signature $\sigma = (R, V)$ of the identity-message-public key pair (ID_i, m_i, P_i) $(1 \leq i \leq n)$.

① If $ID_i \neq ID_j$ for all $ID_i (1 \leq i \leq n)$, B gives up and terminates the simulation;

② Otherwise (there is one $ID_i (1 \leq i \leq n)$ which is equal to ID_j), B can forge the signature.

If the signature is successfully forged, the forged signature must satisfy the verification equation:

$$VP = P_{pub} \sum_{i=1}^{n} Q_i + R + T \sum_{i=1}^{n} P_i$$

$$= P_{pub} \sum_{i=1, i \neq j}^{n} Q_i + P_{pub} Q_j + R + \beta \sum_{i=1}^{n} P_i$$

$$= P_{pub} \sum_{i=1, i \neq j}^{n} Q_i + aP \times a_j bP + R + \beta \sum_{i=1}^{n} P_i$$

$$= P_{pub} \sum_{i=1, i \neq j}^{n} Q_i + a_j P \times abP + R + \beta \sum_{i=1}^{n} P_i$$

Finally, B outputs $abP = (a_jP)^{-1}(VP - P_{pub} \sum_{i=1,i \neq j}^{n} Q_i - R - \beta \sum_{i=1}^{n} P_i)$. Therefore, B solves the CDH difficulty problem.

Then the probability of B's success is analyzed. First define the following events:

(1) E_1 is the event that B dose not exit during the partial key generation query and signature query.
(2) E_2 is the event that the attacker successfully forges an aggregate signature.
(3) E_3 is the event that the forgery phase has not been terminated.

In the partial key generation query, if the target identity ID_j is queried, it will exit and terminate the simulation. So the simulation will not exit if the target identity ID_j is not asked. For one query, the probability of not asking the target identity ID_j is $1 - \frac{1}{q_{H_1}}$. Since the adversary performs partial key generation query up to q_{ppk} times and the signature query up to q_s times, so the probability of not exiting in the partial key generation phase and the signature phase is $\Pr[E_1] \geq \left(1 - \frac{1}{q_{H_1}}\right)^{q_{ppk} + q_s}$. The probability of an attacker to forge a legitimate aggregate signature is $\Pr[E_2] \geq \xi$. If it is not terminated during the forgery phase, then the identity ID_j is included in the challenging aggregate signature, i.e. at least one identity is equal to ID_j. The probability that one identity is equal to ID_j is $\frac{1}{q_{H_1}}$, then the probability that at least one of the identities is equal to the target identity ID_j is $\Pr[E_3] \geq 1 - (1 - \frac{1}{q_{H_1}})^n$.

In summary, if an adversary can break down the new aggregate signature scheme in this article with non-negligible advantages ξ, then B can successfully solve the CDH difficult problem with the advantages $Adv[B] \geq \left(1 - \frac{1}{q_{H_1}}\right)^{q_{ppk} + q_s} \left(1 - (1 - \frac{1}{q_{H_1}})^n\right) \xi$.

Theorem 2. In the random oracle model, A_2 is the second type of attacker. If it can break down the unforgeability of the new aggregate signature scheme with non-negligible advantages ξ after making adaptive chosen message and identity attack queries in polynomial times, then there is a distinguisher B who can take a polynomial time to solve a CDH problem with non-negligible advantages $Adv[B] \geq \left(1 - \frac{1}{q_{pk}}\right)^{q_s} \left(1 - (1 - \frac{1}{q_{pk}})^n\right) \xi$ (q_{pk} and q_s are the maximum number of public key query and signature query A_2 could make, n is the user number of the aggregate signature scheme).

Proof: A_2 is an attacker while B is a challenger of the CDH problem. Given (P, aP, bP), B's goal is to solve the CDH problem through A_2, that is, calculates abP.

B uses A_2 as a subroutine and acts as a challenger. B runs the system setup algorithm, generates the public parameter $(q, G_1, P, H_1, H_2, H_3, P_{pub})$ (B sets $P_{pub} = \alpha P$, α is the system's master key. Because B is the second type of attacker, so B knows the master key α) and sends it to A_2. B maintains lists $L_1, L_2, L_3, L_{ppk}, L_{pk}$ and L_s

to track H_1 query, H_2 query, H_3 query, partial key generation query, public key generation query and signature query respectively. At the beginning, each list is empty. B chooses identity ID_j as its challenging identity.

Query stage: The adversary A_2 makes the following queries.

H_1 query: B keeps the list $L_1 = \{ID_i, P_i, Q_i\}$, initially empty. When B receives H_1 query from A_2, B does the following:

① If there is a corresponding tuple in the list L_1, then B returns Q_i to A_2;
② Otherwise, B performs public key generation query, gets P_i, randomly chooses $Q_i \in Z_q^*$, adds $\{ID_i, P_i, Q_i\}$ to list L_1 and returns Q_i to A_2.

H_3 query: B keeps the list $L_3 = \{P_{pub}, \beta, T\}$, initially empty. When B receives H_3 query from A_2, if there is a corresponding tuple in the list L_3, then B directly returns T to A_2; otherwise, B selects $\beta \in Z_q^*$ randomly, calculates $T = \beta bP$, adds $\{P_{pub}, \beta, T\}$ to list L_3 and returns T to A_2.

H_2 query: The process of making a H_2 query to B is the same as in Theorem 1.

Public key generation query: B keeps the list $L_{pk} = \{ID_i, x_i, P_i\}$, initially empty. When B receives a public key generation query from A_2, if there is a corresponding tuple in the list L_{pk}, then it directly returns P_i to A_2; otherwise, B performs the following operations:

① If $ID_i \neq ID_j$, B randomly selects $x_i \in Z_q^*$, let $P_i = x_iP$, adds $\{ID_i, x_i, P_i\}$ to L_{pk} and returns P_i to A_2;
② Otherwise, $ID_i = ID_j$, B randomly selects $x_j \in Z_q^*$, calculates $P_j = x_jaP$, adds the corresponding value to list L_{pk} and returns P_j to A_2.

Secret value query: The process of making a secret value query to B is the same as in Theorem 1.

Signature query: When B receives a signature query about identity-message-public key (ID_i, m_i, P_i), B operates as follows:

① If $ID_i \neq ID_j$, B selects a random number $r_i \in Z_q^*$, calculates $R_i = r_iP$, $V_i = \alpha Q_i + h_ir_i + x_i\beta bP$, generates the signature $\sigma_{ID_i} = (R_i, V_i)$ and returns it to the adversary A_2;
② Otherwise, B gives up and terminates the simulation.

Forgery phase: After the above query of polynomial times, A_2 outputs a forged aggregate signature $\sigma = (R, V)$ for the identity-message-public key pair $(ID_i, m_i, P_i)(1 \leq i \leq n)$.

① If $ID_i \neq ID_j$ is established for all identity $ID_i(1 \leq i \leq n)$, B gives up and terminates the simulation.
② Otherwise (there is one identity $ID_i(1 \leq i \leq n)$ which is equal to ID_j), B can forge the signature.

If the signature is successfully forged, then the forged signature must satisfy the verification equation:

$$VP = P_{pub} \sum_{i=1}^{n} Q_i + R + T \sum_{i=1}^{n} P_i$$

$$= \alpha P \sum_{i=1}^{n} Q_i + R + \beta b P \sum_{i=1}^{n} P_i$$

$$= \alpha P \sum_{i=1}^{n} Q_i + R + \beta b P \sum_{i=1,i\neq j}^{n} P_i + \beta b P P_j$$

$$= \alpha P \sum_{i=1}^{n} Q_i + R + \beta b P \sum_{i=1,i\neq j}^{n} P_i + \beta b P x_j a P$$

Finally, B outputs $abP = (x_j \beta P)^{-1} \left(VP - \alpha P \sum_{i=1}^{n} Q_i - R - \beta b P \sum_{i=1,i\neq j}^{n} P_i \right)$. Therefore, B finally solves the CDH problem.

Then the probability of B's success is analyzed. First define the following events:

(1) E_1 is the event that B dose not exit during the signature query.
(2) E_2 is the event that the adversary successfully forges an aggregate signature.
(3) E_3 is the event that the forgery phase has not been terminated.

In the signature query phase, if the target identity ID_j is queried, the simulation will quit, otherwise the simulation will not quit if the target identity will not be queried. For one query, the probability of not asking the target identity ID_j is $1 - \frac{1}{q_{pk}}$. Since the adversary makes signature query at most q_s times, therefore the probability of not exiting during the signature phase is $\Pr[E_1] \geq \left(1 - \frac{1}{q_{pk}} \right)^{q_s}$. The calculation of the probability of E_2 and E_3 is the same as in Theorem 1.

In summary, if an adversary can break down the new aggregate signature scheme in this article with non-negligible advantages ξ, then the challenger B can successfully solve the CDH problem with the advantages $Adv[B] \geq \left(1 - \frac{1}{q_{pk}} \right)^{q_s} \left(1 - (1 - \frac{1}{q_{pk}})^n \right) \xi$.

3.2   Analysis of the New Scheme

Compare the security of the existing certificateless aggregate signature scheme with the new scheme as follows, the results are shown in Table 1.

Table 1. Safety comparison of several schemes.

Scheme	Attack of the outsiders	Passive attack of the malicious KGC	Active attack of the malicious KGC
[5]	×	√	√
[10]	√	×	√
[15]	√	√	×
[16] -1	√	√	√
[16] -2	√	√	√
Our scheme	√	√	√

Note: √ resistible, × irresistible

Furthermore, the computation overhead of the proposed scheme is also compared, the results are shown in Table 2. In Table 2, the specific meanings of the relevant symbols are: SM represents the point multiplication on elliptic curve, BP represents bilinear pairing operation, H represents hash operation, and L represents the length of an element in the group.

Table 2. Computation cost of several schemes.

Scheme	Single sign	Aggregate signature verification	Length of the aggregate signature
[5]	2SM+2H	(2n+1)SM+3nH	(n+1)L
[10]	3SM+2H	2nSM+nH+2BP	2L
[15]	3SM+2H	4BP+1H	2L
[16] -1	2SM+1H	(2n+1)SM+2nH	(n+1)L
[16] -2	2SM+1H	(2n+1)SM+2nH	2L
Our scheme	3SM+2H	3SM+nH	2L

It can be seen from Table 1 that the scheme of [5, 10, 15] is not safe, attackers can forge a signature. Although the first improvement of [16] is safe, it can be seen from Table 2 that the aggregate signature has a long length and low communication efficiency. The second improvement of [16] is secure and has a fixed aggregate signature length. However, when generating single signatures, the scheme requires a large amount of information to be exchanged between users, which increases the communication cost of the aggregate signature generation phase. In summary, the certificateless aggregate signature scheme proposed in this paper is not only more secure than the previous schemes, but also has higher computation and communication efficiency.

4 Summary

Based on the analysis of the security risks of the existing certificateless aggregate signature schemes, this paper proposed a new certificateless aggregate signature scheme without bilinear pairing, proved the unforgeability of the scheme in the random oracle model and finally analyzed the efficiency of the scheme. The scheme has the characteristics of fixed length of aggregate signature, strong security, high computation and communication efficiency, which is applicable to network environments with limited bandwidth. In addition, users do not need to exchange a large amount of information when signing. It is convenient for users to dynamically join the aggregate signature.

References

1. Wang, M.J., Wang, J., Guo, L.H., et al.: Inverted XML access control model based on ontology semantic dependency. CMC: Comput. Mater. Continua **55**(3), 465–482 (2018)
2. Boneh, D., Gentry, C., Lynn, B., Shacham, H.: Aggregate and verifiably encrypted signatures from bilinear maps. In: Biham, E. (ed.) EUROCRYPT 2003. LNCS, vol. 2656, pp. 416–432. Springer, Heidelberg (2003). https://doi.org/10.1007/3-540-39200-9_26
3. Al-Riyami, S.S., Paterson, K.G.: Certificateless public key cryptography. In: Laih, Chi-Sung (ed.) ASIACRYPT 2003. LNCS, vol. 2894, pp. 452–473. Springer, Heidelberg (2003). https://doi.org/10.1007/978-3-540-40061-5_29
4. Cui, J.H., Zhang, Y.Y., Cai, Z.P., et al.: Securing display path for security-sensitive applications on mobile devices. CMC: Comput. Mater. Continua **55**(1), 017–035 (2018)
5. Zuo, L.M., Zhang, T.T., Guo, H.L., et al.: Certificateless aggregate signature scheme based on no pairing mapping. Comput. Eng. **43**(5), 313–316 (2017)
6. Wang, D.X., Teng, J.K.: Probably secure certificateless aggregate signature algorithm for vehicular ad hoc network. J. Electronica Inf. Technol. **40**(1), 11–17 (2018)
7. Du, H.Z., Huang, M.J., Wen, Q.Y.: Efficient and provably-secure certificateless aggregate signature scheme. Acta Electronica Sinica **40**(1), 72–76 (2013)
8. Zhang, Y.L., Li, C.Y., Wang, C.F., et al.: Security analysis and improvements of certificateless aggregate signature schemes. J. Electron. Inf. Technol. **37**(8), 1994–1999 (2015)
9. Pankaj, K., Saru, K., Vishnu, S., et al.: Secure CLS and CL-AS schemes designed for VANETs. J. Supercomput. (2018). https://doi.org/10.1007/s11227-018-2312-y
10. Xu, Y., Huang, L.S., Tian, M.M., et al.: A provably secure and compact certificateless aggregate signature scheme. Acta Electronica Sinica **44**(8), 1845–1850 (2016)
11. Du, H.Z., Wen, Q.Y.: Attack and improvement of a certificateless aggregate signature scheme. Acta Scientiarum Naturalium Univ. Sunyatseni **56**(1), 77–84 (2017)
12. Au, M.H., Mu, Y., Chen, J., et al.: Malicious KGC attack in certificateless cryptography. In: Proceedings of the ASIACCS 2007, New York, USA, pp. 302–311 (2007)
13. He, D.B., Tian, M.M., Chen, J.H.: Insecurity of an efficient certificateless aggregate signature with constant pairing computations. Inf. Sci. **268**, 458–462 (2014)
14. Fan, A.W., Xia, D.L., Yang, Z.F.: Security analysis and improvement of two certificateless aggregate signature schemes. J. Shandong Univ. (Nat. Sci.) **50**(9), 29–34 (2015)
15. Zhang, Y.L., Zhou, D.R., Li, C.Y., et al.: Certificateless-based efficient aggregate signature scheme with universal designated verifier. J. Commun. **36**(2), 331–338 (2015)

16. Zhou, Y.W., Yang, B., Zhang, W.Z.: Efficient and provide security certificateless aggregate signature scheme. J. Softw. **26**(12), 3204–3214 (2015)
17. Chen, H., Wei, S.M., Zhu, C.J., et al.: Secure certificateless aggregate signature scheme. J. Softw. **26**(5), 1173–1180 (2015)
18. Hu, J.H., Du, H.Z., Zhang, J.Z.: Analysis and improvement of certificateless aggregate signature scheme. Comput. Eng. Appl. **52**(10), 80–84 (2016)
19. Zhang, Y.J., Zhang, Y.L., Wang, C.F.: Security analysis and improvement of aggregate signature schemes. Comput. Appl. Softw. **34**(8), 307–311 (2017)
20. Liu, H., Wang, S.J., Liang, M.G., et al.: New construction of efficient certificateless aggregate signatures. J. Secur. Appl. **8**(1), 411–422 (2014)
21. Chen, L., Cheng, Z., Smart, N.P.: Identity-based key agreement protocols from pairings. Int. J. Inf. Secur. **6**(2), 213–241 (2007)
22. Cao, X., Kou, W.: A pairing-free identity-based authenticated key agreement scheme with minimal message exchanges. Inf. Sci. **180**(6), 2895–2903 (2010)

SuperEye: A Distributed Port Scanning System

Zibo Li[1(✉)], Xiangzhan Yu[1,2], Dawei Wang[3], Yiru Liu[3],
Huaidong Yin[3], and Shoushuai He[4]

[1] Harbin Institute of Technology, Harbin 150001, China
bonult@163.com, yxz@hit.edu.cn
[2] Institute of Electronic and Information Engineering of UESTC in Guangdong,
Dongguan, China
[3] National Computer Network Emergency Response Technical Team
Coordination Center of China, Beijing, China
stonetools@yeah.net, lyr030211@qq.com, 39006190@qq.com
[4] College of Communication Engineering,
Army Engineering University of PLA, Nanjing 210007, China
frldh@outlook.com

Abstract. With the rapid development of the Internet, more and more services are emerging on the Internet, but it also brings a lot of security risks. Scanning the services on the network by sending probe packets, user can know which host opens a specific service, and can also know statistical data related, which is very important for the network maintenance and discovering dangerous services. This paper focuses on SuperEye, a large-scale and interactive distributed port scanning system. In order to realize interactive port scanning, an enhanced version of TCP state transition automaton is defined to describe the interactive process of contracting and receiving packets. In order to improve the scanning efficiency and avoid triggering IDS, discusses the distribution of tasks, and the tasks are distributed with redundancy and then intermediate states of the task displayed in time, then process and store the returning results for analysis and statistics and at last show the visual results to users. The system interacts with users by friendly web pages. And heartbeat detection is also implemented to ensure the reliability of scanning tasks. Finally, a series of unit tests and integration tests are carried out, and it's sure that the completed system meets the expected development requirements.

Keywords: Port scanning · Finite automaton · Heartbeat detection · WebSocket

1 Introduction

Since the birth of the Internet, the network has gradually occupied an important position in people's lives. People access various services on the Internet and run a large number of applications or services on their own computers. As the size of the Internet has increased and the variety of services has increased, issues such as security have entered people's horizons. The services running on the network are uneven, and some services have loopholes due to their lack of design, and users are often unaware of this,

X. Sun et al. (Eds.): ICAIS 2019, LNCS 11635, pp. 46–56, 2019.
https://doi.org/10.1007/978-3-030-24268-8_5

giving attackers a chance. A port corresponds to a service, but even if there is a vulnerability in the service on one port, it will pose a potential danger to the entire operating system, and the so-called thousand-mile embankment collapses in the ant colony. On the other hand, some services are harmful, such as services designed to steal user privacy information, disseminate harmful information and attack other hosts, affecting social stability [1]. Most services have a fixed behavior pattern, and the characteristics for identifying these harmful services can be obtained through protocol analysis [2].

Using active port scanning technologies, combined with passive defense methods such as network monitoring systems and firewalls, can effectively avoid attacks and prevent problems before they occur [1]. A network service usually listens to the fixed port, and the open status of the port can roughly understand the open service of the target host [3]. Not just security related issues, it is also possible to use tools to count the number of specific services running on the network and then further analyze and count them, which is collecting information about these services. Unscrupulous hackers acquire vulnerabilities in a service, scan for services on the network, and exploit the related vulnerabilities to invade the system that provides the destination service. Therefore, service detection is essentially a double-edged sword. In the process of scanning a port, it may take several times to send and receive packets to identify the target service or protocol. While some software or services use their own application layer protocols, most scanning tools are difficult to detect such services, and the port scanning system SuperEye studied in this paper can solve these problems. And the system also has an excellent user interface, data statistics and analysis can also be displayed in an intuitive form.

The SuperEye system studied in this paper is a distributed port scanning system. We designed a simple script to write plugins for scanning in this paper. By modifying the source code of Masscan, it supports custom plugins for scanning. As the core of SuperEye, the control subsystem is responsible for managing distributed nodes, managing tasks, processing results, and visualizing results.

2 Related Work

Port scanning is the key content of network scanning. Network services usually listen to fixed ports, so through the openness of ports, you can get an idea of the open services of the target host. Based on the need of port scanning, the port scanner has gradually become a hot spot in the security field. The scanner can discover the distribution of various TCP ports of the remote host and the services provided. In terms of port scanning technologies, faster half-connection scanning is gradually evolved from full-connection scanning, and distributed scanning is more efficient and concealed [4]. Through distributed scanning, it is not easy to be detected by IDS (Intrusion detection system), and scanning traces are scattered on different hosts, which is less likely to be detected [5, 6].

In full-connection scanning, the first commercial scanner, the SATAN system, was introduced in 1995. SATAN is a security management, testing and reporting tool for analyzing networks and it can collect a lot of information from hosts on the network

[7]. In 1998, Renaud Derision launched a program called "Nessus", which was designed to provide the Internet community with a free, powerful, frequently updated and easy-to-use remote system security scanner [8]. There are also some open source free scanning tools such as Nmap. As the most well-known open source full-connection scanning tool, Nmap has a graphical interface Zenmap [9]. These full-connection scanning tools use the operating system's TCP/IP protocol stack for scanning. As for half-connection scanning, Zmap and Masscan are more famous. Since the system can maintain a limited number of connections, the efficiency is relatively low. Both Zmap and Masscan are stateless port scanners [10, 11]. "Stateless" means that the process of sending and receiving packets does not depend on the protocol stack of the operating system, and the packets are directly sent and received by the network card driver. However, Zmap only supports single-port scanning, and it requires loop scanning in multi-port situations, which is inefficient. Although there are many port scanning tools, most of their functions are relatively simple, or the efficiency is relatively low. Some integrated scanning tools have no statistical analysis of data, or less support for covert scanning.

3   Structure of the System

The system uses interactive scanning, so a large number of TCP connections need to be maintained. The number of TCP connections that the operating system can maintain is limited, which is much smaller than that required for detection. Therefore, the scanner uses a custom protocol stack to send and receive packets, which greatly improves system resource utilization. Even so, the port scanner is based on a single host, and the range of scanning in a short period of time is limited because the computing resources and network bandwidth of a single host are limited, which is still insufficient to support large-scale port scanning. So in order to improve the scanning speed, SuperEye adopts a distributed structure, and at the same time, it can avoid triggering the IDS [4].

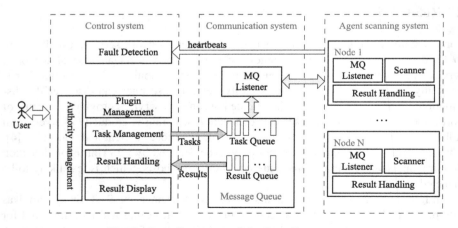

Fig. 1. Overall structure of the SuperEye system

When the amount of tasks is large, sending probe packets and receiving reply packets will generate a large amount of network traffic, which is likely to cause network congestion [8]. The distributed structure can reduce packet loss caused by network congestion. The overall structure of the SuperEye system is shown in Fig. 1. It is divided into three subsystems: the control subsystem, the communication subsystem and the scanning agent subsystem.

The control subsystem provides an external user interface, adopting the B/S architecture, and the user accesses various functions of the system through the browser, which is beneficial to the system's ease of use and future maintenance and upgrade. The control system is the core of SuperEye. The main functions include plugin management, task management, processing and visualization of scan results, and node fault detection. The system was built using Spring, using MySQL to store various data, and Redis as a cache.

The communication subsystem is built using RabbitMQ, which is the bridge between the control system and the proxy node. For each packet received, it is judged whether it is task fragmentation, heartbeat data or task result: if it is task fragmentation, it is moved from the task queue and then a proxy node receives the subtask, and if the collection fails, the task fragment is returned to the result queue; if it is heartbeat data, it is slightly processed and forwarded to the control system; if it is the task result, it is returned to the control system.

The scanning agent subsystem is built using Spring and a custom Masscan. And it's responsible for receiving tasks and returning results. The configuration items in the task include the parameters before the scanner scan and the plugin used for scanning. The core component of the agent subsystem is the scanner, which optimizes and expands the high-speed port scanner Masscan to load the plugin and control the TCP automaton. The plugin user written is used to describe the automaton. This paper designed the SuperEye script to write the plugin and so build a TCP state transfer automaton [12]. Each time the data sent is embedded in the state of the automaton, enabling interactive port scanning.

4   The SuperEye Script

For the versatility of port scanning, an interactive scan is used. The "plugin" mentioned in the paper can be regarded as a finite automaton based on TCP state, written in SuperEye script. The interaction process in Fig. 2 is similar to TCP protocol, in which the first two handshakes to establish a TCP connection and the four-way handshake to disconnect are ignored. Two adjacent reply states are considered to be a state of TCP, and some pattern matching work is performed in the reply state. The data of the sent packet is filled in the sending state, and the TCP interaction is implemented according to the state transfer automaton. If the state of a certain TCP interaction reaches the: "FIN" state, it can be determined that the destination port is enabled for the target service.

The automaton shown in Fig. 2 has a total of four states, namely "CONNECTED state", "Send state", "Reply state" and "FIN state". "CONNECTED" means that the first two handshakes are completed and TCP connection has established, and the next state is the "Send" state. The "Send" state defines the payload portion of the transmitted TCP packet, and waits for the arrival of the next response packet after the packet sent. After receiving the response packet, it enters the "Reply" state, and the "Reply" state can automatically output the matching result. After entering the reply state, pattern matching can be performed by using multiple reply states to perform multiple pattern matching, and then entering the next round of interaction, thereby forming an interactive port scan. The state transition to the "FIN" state indicates that the target service has been identified, and if the state cannot be transferred due to the mode mismatch, the current state is output and the automaton is exited.

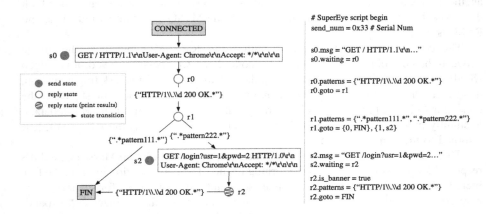

Fig. 2. State transfer automaton

Matching uses multi-pattern matching and byte number matching: the pattern matching substring can be a regular expression for regular matching; the number of bytes matches whether the number of bytes of TCP payload data is within the specified interval.

To describe the above automaton, we define a simple, interpretive script named SuperEye, which is similar to Nmap script. Masscan scans based on plugins written in this script. The syntax of the script can be used to define the operation of sending and receiving packets, the data of the packets sent, how to match after receiving the packets, and the jump of the state. The syntax specification is as follows:

- Use s_i to indicate "send state", attributes are "msg" and "waiting". Data filled into the payload of the transport layer is represented by "msg". And "waiting" is the state transferred to after sending the probe packet.
- Use r_j to indicate "reply state", attributes are "is_banner" (whether to output matching information), "patterns" (regular expression used to match), "len" (number of bytes in the data portion of the response packet) and "goto" (indicates a state jump).
- The send state node has an outdegree of 1, and the reply state node has an indegree and outdegree of no less than 1.

- The left and right symbols of all "=" symbols must be spaces.
- Note the escape characters in double quotes and regular expressions enclosed in curly braces.

When there are lots of states, the script is more complicated and it is easy to write wrong. In order to facilitate users to write their own plugins, the system provides a drag-and-drop graphical interface to maintain the plugins, similar to the form of online drawing flowcharts, and then the system converts the graphics into scripts. The graphical automaton is implemented using SVG (Scalable Vector Graphics). Each node or directed segment of the graphical automatic machine has some properties, including coordinates, width, height, and name on the artboard. And the graphical automaton can be translated into SuperEye script, which mainly uses the breadth-first traversal algorithm of the graph, and the user can edit the generated script to change some details.

5 Detailed Design and Implementation

In this section, the specific design and implementation of the modules of the control subsystem will be given.

5.1 Task Management

The main settings for a task are the IP address set, port set, and pattern set. Other settings for the task are packet sending rate, redundancy (for task redundancy allocation), IP address blacklist (some host addresses that do not actually exist), and whether non-target content should be output. Non-target content includes ports that are closed and ports of unreachable host. A task needs to be divided into several subtasks. After the user clicks to open the task, the task management module obtains the task configuration item from the database, and then fragments the IP address set and the port set according to the number of available working nodes, and then sends subtasks to the task queue one by one according to the redundancy. Each shard ID is unique and is used to integrate the results. The scanner uses a special randomization algorithm, and periodically return the scan status after starting the scan, and return the subtask result after the scan ends. The subtask status data in the heartbeat packet is continuously parsed and and processed during the scan, then transmitted to the result display module to be pushed to the browser. When all subtasks are completed, the results are merged, deduplicated, and persisted by user actions, and finally displayed.

5.2 Result Processing and Storage

When the subtask on the agent node is just completed, the result list in the form of "IP address, port status, reason (, banner)" is sent to the control system through the communication subsystem. Due to the redundancy setting during task partitioning, there are many redundant items in the task result. After receiving the result data sent by each node, the control system merges the data into the result set. The system uses the hash table of Redis to deduplicate, and the key is task ID, and Redis hash table has only three levels of structure, namely "KEY-HKEY-VALUE", so HKEY "IP port" which is the first two segments of the result item, and VALUE is the remaining part. Finally, the amount of various result items is counted during the merge process. After the results are merged, user chooses whether to persist them to MySQL.

5.3 Result Display

Task Status Display. In order to minimize the pressure on the server, the server uses the technology of actively pushing data to the browser to implement real-time update of the front-end page, instead of the traditional solution such as polling mode whose solutions have the disadvantages of large system resource consumption, low efficiency, and large server burden [13]. The browser communicates with the system through WebSocket to obtain real-time scanning progress, packet sending rate and hit number.

Visualization of Scan Results. After the task is completed, the different types of results are displayed in a pie chart after counted, and the result list is displayed in tabular form. The pie chart is a statistic for the results of one scan, and the ratio of several usages of the port is counted so as target service, other service, port opened, port closed, and host unreachable. These data are counted in the result processing module. Another result statistic is the comparison of the results of several tasks for the same set of configurations in time dimension, including the comparison of the number of results and the time spent for scanning, using histograms and line charts to display.

5.4 Fault Detection

Heartbeat detection techniques are commonly used for fault detection in distributed systems. The agent node periodically sends a heartbeat to the control system to report the status of the current node. If the heartbeat information is not received by the control system within a certain period, it can be determined that the proxy node is down or temporarily unavailable [14]. The agent system sends task progress messages and heartbeat messages using the same thread [15]. When the heartbeat is sent, some information of the current node such as the node ID and the heartbeat sending time are attached.

The control system maintains a list of cluster nodes and updates the list based on the node heartbeat. If the system does not receive the heartbeat of a node for a period of time, the node is removed from the job list. If the traditional fixed timeout mechanism is adopted, the system sets a timeout period T. If the heartbeat of a node is not received within the time T, the node is judged to be down or temporarily unavailable. When the value of T is too large, the system will not find the faulty node in time; if T is set too small, it may cause misjudgment, because the scanner on the agent node should send tens of thousands or even hundreds of thousands of packets per second. When the network is congested, the heartbeat time may time out and cause misjudgment. Therefore, in order to make the result of fault detection more accurate, the system adopts a dynamic timeout mechanism. The system performs correlation statistics based on $t_{i,1}, t_{i,2}, \ldots, t_{i,m}$ (time when heartbeats arrive) and $s_{i,1}, s_{i,2}, \ldots, s_{i,m}$ (the sending time of each heartbeat) in the last time T of the node N_i. And then dynamically adjusts the timeout period T_i of the node, and periodically checks whether it is alive. Assume that the minimum value of $t_{i,m} - s_{i,m}$ is M_i in one day and the minimum timeout threshold is T_0. The dynamic adjustment strategy is shown as follows:

$$T_i = \frac{\sum_{k=1}^{m-1} \left(t_{i,k} - s_{i,k} - M_i\right)}{m-1} * 0.3 + \left(t_{i,m} - s_{i,m} - M_i\right) * 0.7 + T_0, T_0 > T_s \quad (1)$$

Because the last heartbeat transmission time can better predict the next heartbeat transmission time, the weight of the last heartbeat transmission time is larger when calculating the timeout period. After detecting the fault of the node, the system notifies the task management module to check whether there is an ongoing task on the node, and if so, republish the corresponding subtask.

5.5   Access Control

User authentication and password encryption are the most basic access control functions. Permission resources include access to menus, clicks on a button on a page, and visibility of some page data. The system user authority control uses the RBAC (Role-Based Access Control) model. Each user can have multiple roles, and each role corresponds to multiple rights resources, forming a "user-role-privilege" mapping relationship. There is a "many-to-many" relationship between roles and permissions, and between users and roles. When the user logs in, all the roles of the user and the resources corresponding to each role are loaded from the database, and placed in the user session, and the permissions are verified every time the resources that need to be authorized are accessed. The initial role set by the system is the "super" role. This role has all the rights resources and cannot be modified. It also sets an initial user that is the super administrator and only it has the "super" role. The super administrator is responsible for managing roles and assigning roles to other users.

6   Experiments

In order to verify the correctness of the SuperEye system design, a series of experiments were conducted to test the system's functions and stability. The system uses four servers, one of which runs the control system and the remaining machines have scanners.

6.1   Webpage Test

Using Java to write 1000 threads to simulate http requests, while using the browser to access the page, the average response time is less than 2 s, and the system has no abnormal reaction. Test front-end pages on several major browsers including Chrome, Firefox, IE9+, Safari, etc. The page styles are basically the same, there is no obvious incompatibility.

6.2   Hit Ratio Compared with Nmap

Use the system to scan the global network to calculate the usage of protocols related to industrial control such as IEC-104. There are about 3.7 billion hosts in the world, so the scan uses 9 agent nodes, and the number of packets sent per second is 10 0000. Then scan different types of industrial control protocols, and at the same time, we also used Nmap to scan to compare the hit ratio. The hit number are shown in Fig. 3, indicating that the system runs smoothly and works normally.

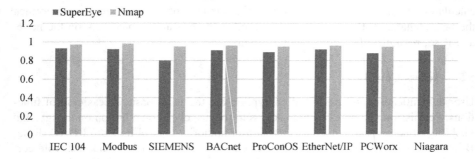

Fig. 3. Hit ratio compared with Nmap

According to SHODAN, there are 880 targets in the world, so we use 880 as the denominator, and other protocols also use this method. During the peak period of the network, there may be network congestion, resulting in a decrease in the hit rate. In general, the hit rate of our system is close to that of Nmap. The hit rate of the system is lower than that of Nmap, which is mainly caused by network packet loss. Under the same conditions, the time taken to scan using our system is about 69 min, which is much smaller than that of Nmap that is about a week.

7   Conclusion

The diversification of Internet services enriches people's lives, but also brings security risks. The discovery of specific services through the port scanning system is of great significance for network maintenance and regulation of illegal services. The research content of this paper is a large-scale customizable interactive port scanning system. According to the overall structure of the detection system. The innovative achievements are as follows:

- A kind of script for port scanning defined. A specific syntax is used to describe the transfer of TCP state during the port scanning process, the load of the packet to be sent, and the pattern matching of the packet payload.
- Distributed scanning. Designed and implemented a distributed architecture that facilitates faster scanning and concealed scanning.

- Visualization of the result data. The system realizes the real-time update of the scanning progress and the results of the analysis statistics in the form of pie charts and column charts.

Finally, through the test of each module and system integration test, the stability of the system and correctness of its design are verified.

Acknowledgement. This work was supported by National Key Research & Development Plan of China under Grant 2016QY05X1000, National Natural Science Foundation of China under Grant No. 61571144 and 61771166, and Dongguan Innovative Research Team Program under Grant No. 201636000100038.

References

1. Zhang, T., Hu, M., Yun, X., Zhang, Y.: Research and implementation of active detection technology for network information. Comput. Eng. Appl. (31), 17–20+43 (2004)
2. Du, Q., Kishi, K., Aiura, N., et al.: Transportation network vulnerability: vulnerability scanning methodology applied to multiple logistics transport networks. Transp. Res. Rec. J. Transp. Res. Board **2410**(2410), 96–104 (2014)
3. Du, Y.: Research on network service detection technology. J. Chin. People's Public Secur. Univ. (Nat. Sci. Edn.) **01**, 69–72 (2007)
4. Bou-Harb, E., Debbabi, M., Assi, C.: Cyber scanning: a comprehensive survey. IEEE Commun. Surv. Tutorials **16**(3), 1496–1519 (2014)
5. Anbar, M., Manasrah, A., Ramadass, S., Altaher, A., Aljmmal, A., Almomani, A.: Investigating study on network scanning techniques. Int. J. Digit. Content Technol. Appl. **9**, 312–320 (2013)
6. Modi, C., Patel, D., Borisaniya, B., et al.: Review: a survey of intrusion detection techniques in Cloud. J. Netw. Comput. Appl. **36**(1), 42–57 (2013)
7. Ran, S.: Research of Vulnerability Scanning Technology Based on Masscan. Nankai University, Nankai District (2016)
8. Anderson, H.: Introduction to nessus (2003)
9. Lyon, G.F.: Nmap Network Scanning: The Official Nmap Project Guide to Network Discovery and Security Scanning. Insecure, USA (2009)
10. Durumeric, Z., Wustrow, E., Halderman, J.A.: ZMap: fast internet-wide scanning and its security applications. In: Proceedings of Usenix Security Symposium, pp. 605–620 (2013)
11. Graham, R.D.: MASSCAN: Mass IP port scanner. https://github.com/robertdavidgraham/masscan. Accessed 03 July 2018
12. Garcia-Alfaro, J., Cuppens-Boulahia, N., Martinez, S., et al.: Management of stateful firewall misconfiguration. Comput. Secur. **39**(39), 64–85 (2013)
13. Skvorc, D., Horvat, M., Srbljic, S.: Performance evaluation of Websocket protocol for implementation of full-duplex web streams. In: International Convention on Information and Communication Technology, Electronics and Microelectronics, pp. 1003–1008. IEEE (2014)
14. Paalasmaa, J., Toivonen, H., Partinen, M.: Adaptive heartbeat modeling for beat-to-beat heart rate measurement in ballistocardiograms. IEEE J. Biomed. Health Inform. **19**(6), 1945 (2015)
15. Wang, S.: Design and Implementation of Communication and Heartbeat Module of Distributed Cluster Management System. Nanjing University (2014)

16. Wu, X., Zhang, C., Zhang, R., Wang, Y., Cui, J.: A distributed intrusion detection model via nondestructive partitioning and balanced allocation for big data. CMC: Comput. Mater. Continua **56**(1), 61–72 (2018)
17. Xie, X., Yuan, T., Zhou, X., Cheng, X.: Research on trust model in container-based cloud service. CMC: Comput. Mater. Continua **56**(2), 273–283 (2018)

An Improved Multi-classification Algorithm for Imbalanced Online Public Opinion Data

Xige Dang[1,2], Xu Wu[1,2,3(✉)], Xiaqing Xie[1,2], and Tianle Zhang[4]

[1] Key Laboratory of Trustworthy Distributed Computing and Service (BUPT),
Ministry of Education, Beijing, China
dangxige@sina.com, {wux,xiexiaqing}@bupt.edu.cn
[2] School of Cyberspace Security,
Beijing University of Posts and Telecommunications, Beijing, China
[3] Beijing University of Posts and Telecommunications Library, Beijing, China
[4] Cyberspace Institute of Advanced Technology,
Guangzhou University, Guangzhou, China
tlezhang@sohu.com

Abstract. When the datasets about online public opinion are imbalanced, the classifier is prone to sacrifice the accuracy of minority class to achieve the overall best performance. In order to solve this problem, an online public opinion text multi-classification algorithm based on random forest and cost-sensitive is proposed in this essay. The algorithm uses Naïve Bayes to construct cost matrix, chooses Gini index with misclassification cost to select the decision tree node. After the comparative experiment, the classifier has improved performance by 3% overall and 8% on minority classes, which can solve the problem of data imbalance to some extent.

Keywords: Online public opinion · Data imbalance · Multi-classification · Cost-sensitive · Random forest

1 Introduction

Social internet community, providing a communicating, discussing and information sharing platform for Internet users, has become an important carrier of internet information. As the Internet gradually permeates into people's daily life, the social internet community carries a great deal of useful information worth deeply digging. Text classification is an important foundation of data mining.

The social internet community has a wide range of users and a strong openness. There is a large amount of information being generated and disseminated everyday. The information which is sensitive to current events updates rapidly. This makes it extremely easy to appear the phenomena of information features centralizing. The large number of discussions about hot topics can easily lead to data imbalance. For the classifier that uses the text information in the social internet community as training sets and updates in real time, it is a long-standing problem that the data imbalance will have a great negative influence on the performance of the classifier.

© Springer Nature Switzerland AG 2019
X. Sun et al. (Eds.): ICAIS 2019, LNCS 11635, pp. 57–66, 2019.
https://doi.org/10.1007/978-3-030-24268-8_6

2 Background and Significance

Compared to the strict, standardized and accurate news information, the social internet community has a wider user foundation. Its openness makes the information obviously colloquialism and fragmented, and has relative superiority in real-time. The dissemination of information transcends the control of time and space. The information spreads rapidly and has short life cycle. However, its influence is very extensive and has become an important source of influence on online public opinion. The feature extraction and text classification of internet community information can effectively and accurately mine the discussion of hot topics, enabling Internet users to obtain relevant information systematically and centrally. It is also helpful for the supervision of the online public opinion.

Text classification is an important foundation of information retrieval and data mining. The original text classification is mainly based on the knowledge engineering method, and the logic rules are manually extracted according to the textual classification experience of domain experts as the basis for classification of computer texts. With the emergence of large-scale text processing needs, automatic text classification began to emerge. Text automatic classification is to use computer systems to automatically mark text according to a certain classification system or standard. Classification tool is based on the information of the document assigned to the existing classes. The idea of automatic text classification began from counting word frequency. After using factor analysis, it develops toward the machine-based learning and gradually mature. Compared with traditional text classification, machine learning pays more attention to the ability of automatic generation and dynamic optimization of models, and has achieved breakthrough in classification effect and flexibility. Up to now, the research of automatic text classification has entered the practical stage from the initial feasibility basic research and experimental research, and has been widely used.

Traditional classification algorithms usually assume that the training datasets are balanced. Most of them use the overall classification accuracy [1] as the learning objective and all the misclassified samples based on the same cost assumption. In the event of imbalanced datasets, the classifier will pay too much attention to the majority classes, tending to sacrifice the accuracy of minority classes to achieve the best overall performance. This makes the classifier although the overall performance is good, the minority class performance is poor. However, in practice, the cost of misclassifying minority class is often more than the cost of misclassifying majority class. The emergence of the above phenomenon is very unfavorable both for algorithm optimization and data mining.

At present, the improved algorithms for imbalanced datasets mainly start from two aspects: data level [2] and algorithm level [3]. Data level improvement is mainly taken in the data sampling process to make a certain strategy to get a balanced sample distribution, thereby improving classification performance. There are two main sampling strategies: oversampling [4] and undersampling. Improvements at the algorithm level include: changing the probability density, single-class learning classification, integrated algorithms, cost-sensitive learning, and using nuclear methods [5].

With the development of integrated learning, more and more researches introduce integrated learning [6] into the classification of imbalanced datasets. Integrated learning improves the final learning result by training multiple weak classifiers and integrating them. The integration of multiple weak classifiers can prevent over-fitting to a certain extent, thus reducing the deviation of single classifier on the imbalanced datasets. In addition, integrated learning takes multiple samples during training process and can be blended with imbalanced datasets to avoid additional learning costs.

Aiming at imbalanced training datasets, this essay proposes an improved text multi-classification algorithm based on the random forest with cost-sensitive introduced.

3 Related Algorithms Research

3.1 Cost-Sensitive

Cost-sensitive learning initially came from medical diagnostic issues [7]. In medical diagnostics, the cost of misdiagnosing a sick person as a disease-free person and misdiagnosing the patient as being diseased is far from equal. Cost-sensitive is to assign different costs to different mistakes. This idea is more practical in real life, and has wide application prospects in the field of intrusion detection, fraud detection and medical diagnosis.

In recent years, cost-sensitive algorithms have been proposed to solve the problem of imbalanced datasets. Adding the misclassification cost for each class, take the minimum misclassification cost as one of the learning objectives, so as to solve the low accuracy of minority classes due to the imbalanced datasets. The cost-sensitive learning algorithm that the cost-sensitive of each class is exactly the same is common machine learning algorithm. Therefore, the introduction of cost-sensitive is universal.

At present, there are quite a few cost-sensitive learning algorithms such as C4.5cs based on C4.5, meta-cost processing approach, using misclassification cost to adjust sample distribution, and some least-cost decision classification. Among these algorithms, the misclassification cost-sensitive algorithm based on Adaboost is widely regarded and concerned because of Adaboost's own remarkable performance.

However, the current cost-sensitive learning algorithm is mainly applicable to the binary-classification. For the multi-classification problem, only the sum of the misclassification costs can be calculated, and it is difficult to distinguish the differences in the costs of each class. The usual solution is to convert the multi-classification problem into a binary classification problem, and calculate the sum of the misclassification costs. However, this method obscures the differences in the misclassifications of different classes and it is difficult to obtain a classifier that is truly minimized the cost-sensitive.

3.2 Bayesian Algorithm

Bayesian school and classical frequency science are called as the two classical schools of modern statistics. Bayesian data analysis is based on a priori distribution, forming the empirical distribution according to the data features. The classifier based on

Bayesian method has strong model representing, learning and reasoning ability, and also shows high accuracy and fast speed in large-scale datasets.

Bayesian theory states that the probability of an event occurring can be estimated by calculating the frequency of past events. Probably, everything has uncertainties and different types of probabilities. In order to foresee the future, we must look at the past.

The probability that an event H occurs under the condition that event X has occurred is called the conditional probability of event H at a given event X, denoted P (H | X), also known as posterior probability, P (H) is priori probability. Posteriori probability is based on more information than prior probability. Bayes theorem is as Eq. 1.

$$P(H|X) = \frac{P(X|H)P(H)}{P(X)} \tag{1}$$

Bayesian provides a way to calculate the posterior probability. It observes the probability of different data for a given hypothesis based on the priori probabilities.

Bayesian classification model is based on statistical methods. Taking Bayesian theory as the basic theory, think the classification problem as an uncertain decision problem in accordance with the correct rate. Classifier classifies the uncategorized data by generalizing the training datasets. The representative Bayesian Classifiers include Naïve Bayesian Classifier, Bayesian Network Classifier, Tree-Extended Naïve Bayesian Classification Model, etc.

Bayesian classification has the following characteristics:

- Select the class with the highest probability as the sample classification.
- All attributes participate in the classification together.
- The attributes of the classification object can be discrete, continuous or mixed.

It is a basic and important task to mine the classifier according to a given training datasets. Bayesian classifier has a simple structure and good performance among many classifiers.

3.3 Random Forest

Random Forest is a tree-based integrated learning method based on Bagging algorithm and stochastic subspace technology [8]. The basic structure of random forest is the decision tree. Each decision tree corresponds to an independent identically distributed random variable. A decision tree is generated using a training set with random sampling and corresponding random variables. Improve the accuracy of classifier through the combination of multiple decision trees. The final output of the model is determined by the majority of the voting results for all the trees.

The selection of the best features of the decision tree node is generally based on the information gain, the information gain rate or the Gini index, and the corresponding decision tree types are ID3, C4.5 and CART. Information gain is the increment of information entropy before and after splitting the dataset according to the selected attribute. According to the definition of information entropy in information theory, the larger the information entropy, the higher the purity of data. Therefore, the greater the information gain, the better the attribute will be able to classify the samples. However, the information gain is more inclined to choose multi-valued attribute to split. To avoid the impact of meaningless multivalued attributes on the construction of decision tree, we can use the information gain rate for attribute selection. Similarly, the greater the rate of information gain, the better the classification performance.

In the process of random forest generation, there are two randomizations [9]. The first one is to select the training set for each tree using random sampling, and the second is to randomly select attributes from the overall characteristics and calculate to get the best split attribute. The decision tree in the random forest is free to grow without pruning in the process. This randomness allows random forest to solve the problem of over-fitting in single decision tree. Each tree in the random forest is a weak classifier with decision-making ability in one characteristic attribute, and finally becomes a powerful classifier [10].

4   Improved Algorithm Design

4.1   Algorithm Design Ideas

As a generation model, Bayesian classification is stable and insensitive to missing values. Meanwhile, Bayesian classifier is simple to calculate. It has no complicated iterative solving process and can be incremental training. However, naive Bayes based on independent assumptions is less effective when the attributes are relatively large. Because Bayesian judgment is based on the prior probability, the model effect is greatly influenced by the priori model of consumption. In addition, the model is also sensitive to the form of input data.

As a kind of integrated learning method, random forest has a great advantage over other algorithms and has better performance. Random forest can handle many high-dimensional features without feature selection. Relative to the decision tree, random forest has strong generalization ability. Due to the parallelization of the training process of random forest, its training speed is fast as well. For imbalanced datasets, random forest is able to balance errors to some extent [11]. The disadvantage of random forest is that over-fitting occurs on some classification problems with many noises. Moreover, random forest is not reliable for the training of weights for multivalued attributes.

Table 1. Algorithm comparison

	Advantage	Disadvantages
Naïve Bayes	Stable classification efficiency, insensitive to missing values	Based on independent assumptions and prior probabilities, the model is strongly influenced by assumptions
	Simple to calculate, can be training incrementally	Sensitive to input data representation
Random Forest	Be able to handle high-dimensional features without feature selection	Over-fitting when many noises exist
	Parallel training, fast training speed	Training of weights for multivalued attributes is not reliable

As can be seen from the comparison of Table 1, Bayesian has simple calculation, and its ability to describe the probability distribution of data is strong. Therefore, choosing Bayesian as the constructor of cost matrix can calculate the misclassification cost exactly and efficiently. However, the superiority to high-dimensional processing and strong generalization ability of random forest and its own error balance to the imbalanced data, introducing cost-sensitive, can solve the problem of imbalanced datasets on the premise of guaranteeing classification performance.

In summary, this essay chooses naive Bayes to construct cost matrix, and uses random forest algorithm introduced cost-sensitive to train classifier.

4.2   Construct the Cost Matrix

Adding cost-sensitive to random forest requires the identification of misclassification costs. For multi-classification problems, construct a cost-sensitive matrix. The element in the matrix represents the cost of predicting actual class j as class i. If i and j are not equal, the element value of the corresponding position is the cost of misclassification; if I and j are equal, then the classification is correct and the cost is 0.

Assuming that the classification features are independent with each other, use Naïve Bayes to construct the cost matrix.

Naive Bayes is based on the assumption that attributes are independent of each other on the basis of Bayesian algorithm. Supposing training dataset D includes samples of m classes, each sample can be represented by an n-dimensional feature vector, with class label C. For a sample in class k, suppose its feature vector values, and its class label is. Then under the independent assumption, we can get Eq. 2.

$$P(a_1, a_2, \ldots a_n | c_k) = \prod_{i=1}^{n} P(a_i | c_k) \tag{2}$$

Therefore, for training set D, calculate the prior probability of each class.

For a sample with known features, assume its feature vector x as. Calculate the conditional probability according to the Eq. 2. Calculate the posterior probability that sample belongs to each class combining class prior probability according to the Eq. 3.

$$P(c_i | x) = \frac{P(x|c_i)P(c_i)}{P(x)} = \frac{P(x|c_i)P(c_i)}{\sum_{i=1}^{m} P(x|c_i)P(c_i)} \tag{3}$$

This results in the probability that the sample belongs to each class. If the sample has a high probability of belonging to a class, the cost of misclassifying the sample into this class is small. Therefore, the naive Bayesian classifier is constructed by using the existing samples as the training set. Calculate the posterior probability that sample belongs to each class and associate with the sample's own class label. Take the reciprocal of the posterior probability as the misclassification cost corresponding to the position in the cost matrix and complete the construction of cost-sensitive matrix.

4.3   Train Random Forest

As a learning method based on feature subspace, random forest itself reduces the characteristic dimension of sample space during training and is suitable for processing high-dimensional data. Due to the randomness of its sampling, the sensitivity to imbalanced data is also relatively weak. Therefore, choosing random forest as the learning method of multi-classification on imbalanced datasets, and make further improvement.

The training process of random forest is as following

Input: training set D, the number of class m, the dimension of characteristic n, the number of decision tree k, node attribute selection algorithm, termination condition.

Output: random forest classifier, classification result.

- For i = 1: k;
- Using bootstrap, choose training set for each decision tree with putting back;
- Choose attributes randomly at the node, select the best attribute according to the node selection algorithm, split the dataset;
- Generate the decision tree according to the termination condition, do not do pruning;
- End;
- Determine the class for the sample to be classified by majority voting method;
- Output random forest classifier and classification result.

After getting the cost matrix through the naive Bayes model, we add cost-sensitive to the random forest and choose the CART decision tree to construct the random forest. CART uses the Gini index as the node selection algorithm. The smaller the Gini index, the better the classification effect. Calculate as Eq. 4.

$$Gini(T) = \sum 1 - P_i^2 \tag{4}$$

Introducing the cost into the Gini index, it can be written as Eq. 5.

$$GiniCost(T) = \sum A_{ij}P(i|t)P(j|t) \tag{5}$$

Among them, represents the cost of class j misclassifying as class i.

The classifier trained by node selection according to Eq. 5 which introduced cost-sensitive to random forest algorithm, can effectively solve the problem of data imbalance.

5   Experimental Verification

5.1   Experimental Design

This essay uses the university forum data and divides it into ten classes, including culture, economy, education, law, medicine, military, philosophy, politics, sports, science and technology, to test the algorithm. Among the ten classes, two of them have a larger sample size, four of them have an average samples and four of them have a smaller number of samples. Select science and technology, sports and medicine as representative classes from the three species above to observe the performance of classifier.

The performance evaluation of traditional classifier is mostly considering and calculating overall. The performance evaluation of imbalanced data classification should pay more attention to the minority classes [12]. Therefore, mainly evaluate from the following three aspects:

- Accuracy, including overall accuracy, minority class accuracy and majority class accuracy.
- Recall, pay attention to the recall rate of minority class.
- F-measure, the harmonic average value of the accuracy and recall rate of minority class. This performance is maximized with a balance of accuracy and recall.

5.2   Experimental Process and Result

Data in this essay comes from the university internet forum, 42617 corpus and ten classes in total. Using the improved classification algorithm in this essay to train the classifier, select the corresponding classes and index according to the experimental design to evaluate the classifier performance. The result is as Table 2.

Table 2. Performance of improved classifier

Class	Overall	Science and technology	Sports	Medicine
Total	42617	19413	4006	233
Correct	34619	17012	3240	183
Accuracy	81.2%	86.3%	80.9%	78.6%
Recall	43.0%	50.3%	43.9%	40.3%
F-measure	0.562	0.636	0.569	0.537

According to Table 2, the overall accuracy is 81.2%. Accuracy of minority class is 78.6%, below the 86.3% for majority class and 80.9% for average class. Similarly, recall rate and F-measure of the classifier in minority class are also slightly lower than the overall.

Because the improvement of algorithm to solve the problem of imbalanced data is usually make from data level and sample level, this essay chooses SVM algorithm based on SMOTE oversampling (referred to as SMOTE) on data level and continuous AdaBoost algorithm based on Bayes statistical inference (referred to as AdaBoost) on sample level to make comparisons with random forest algorithm based on cost-sensitive (referred to as GCRF) which is raised by this essay. The result is as Table 3.

Table 3. Performance of improved classifier

Class	Algorithm	Accuracy	Recall	F-measure
Overall	SMOTE	78.7%	38.3%	0.515
	AdaBoost	80.6%	41.5%	0.548
	GCRF	81.2%	43.0%	0.562
Majority class	SMOTE	84.2%	46.9%	0.602
	AdaBoost	85.6%	48.6%	0.620
	GCRF	86.3%	50.3%	0.636
Average class	SMOTE	79.3%	39.7%	0.529
	AdaBoost	80.9%	42.3%	0.556
	GCRF	80.9%	43.9%	0.569
Minority class	SMOTE	72.9%	28.5%	0.410
	AdaBoost	75.4%	36.1%	0.492
	GCRF	78.6%	40.3%	0.537

According to Table 3, the overall accuracy of GCRF classifier is 81.2%, which has a slight improvement over 78.7% of SMOTE and 80.6% of AdaBoost. There is also a slight improvement in recall and F-measure. However, for minority class, the accuracy of GCRF classifier is 78.6%, which is obviously higher than 72.9% of SMOTE and 75.4% of AdaBoost. There is also obvious improvement in recall rate and F-measure.

5.3 Experimental Analysis

In the overall performance of the classifier, the proposed algorithm improves the accuracy by 1%, the recall by 4% and the F-measure by 3%. It mainly relies on the randomness of random forest model itself and the relative insensitivity to imbalanced data, with not obviously superiority. Similarly, the accuracy of the algorithm is improved by 1%, the recall rate increased by 4% and the F-measure by 3% for majority class and average class.

However, for minority class, the proposed algorithm improves the accuracy rate by 4%, the recall rate by 12% and the F-measure by 9%. Compared to the two representative algorithms, the algorithm proposed by this essay has a certain increase in each evaluation index.

6 Conclusion

In the overall performance of the classifier, the proposed algorithm improves the accuracy by 1%, the recall by 4% and the F-measure by 3%. It mainly relies on the randomness of random forest model itself and the relative insensitivity to imbalanced data, with not obviously superiority. Similarly, the accuracy of the algorithm is improved by 1%, the recall rate increased by 4% and the F-measure by 3% for majority class and average class.

However, for minority class, the proposed algorithm improves the accuracy rate by 4%, the recall rate by 12% and the F-measure by 9%. Compared to the two representative algorithms, the algorithm proposed by this essay has a certain increase in each evaluation index.

Acknowledgements. This work is supported by the National Key Research and Development Plan (Grant No. 2017YFC0820603), BUPT's Graduate education reform project (2018Y003) and the Project of Chinese Society of Academic degrees and graduate education (2017Y0502).

References

1. Menardi, G., Torelli, N.: Training and assessing classification rules with imbalanced data. Data Mining Knowl. Discov. **28**(1), 92–122 (2014)
2. Estabrooks, A., Jo, T., Japkowicz, N.: A multiple resampling method for learning from imbalanced data sets. Comput. Intell. **20**(1), 18–36 (2010)
3. Lomax, S., Vadera, S.: A survey of cost-sensitive decision tree induction algorithms. ACM Comput. Surv. **45**(2), 16–35 (2013)
4. Fithian, W., Hastie, T.: Local case-control sampling: efficient subsampling in imbalanced data sets. PMC **42**(5), 1693–1724 (2014)
5. Maldonado, S., Weber, R., Famili, F.: Feature selection for high-dimensional class-imbalanced data sets using Support Vector Machines. Inf. Sci. **286**(1), 228–246 (2014)
6. Fernández, A., López, V., Galar, M., Jesus, M.J., Herrera, F.: Analysing the classification of imbalanced data-sets with multiple classes: binarization techniques and ad-hoc approaches. Knowl.-Based Syst. **42**, 97–110 (2013)
7. George, N.I., Lu, T.P., Chang, C.W.: Cost-sensitive performance metric for comparing multiple ordinal classifiers. Artif. Intell. Res. **5**(1), 135–143 (2016)
8. Kulkarni, V.Y., Sinha, P.K.: Random forest classifiers: a survey and future research directions. Int. J. Adv. Comput. **36**(1), 1144–1153 (2013)
9. Díez-Pastor, J.F., Rodríguez, J.J., García-Osorio, C., Kuncheva, L.I.: Random balance: ensembles of variable priors classifiers for imbalanced data. Knowl.-Based Syst. **85**, 96–111 (2015)
10. Wu, Q., Ye, Y., Zhang, H., Ng, M.K., Ho, S.-S.: Fores texter: an efficient random forest algorithm for imbalanced text categorization. Knowl.-Based Syst. **67**, 105–116 (2014)
11. Kim, A., Oh, K., Jung, J.-Y.: Imbalanced classification of manufacturing quality conditions using cost-sensitive decision tree ensembles. Comput. Integr. Manuf. **31**, 701–717 (2017)
12. Raeder, T., Forman, G., Chawla, N.V.: Learning from imbalanced data: evaluation matters. In: Holmes, D.E., Jain, L.C. (eds.) Data Mining: Foundations and Intelligent Paradigms. Intelligent Systems Reference Library, vol. 23, pp. 315–331. Springer, Heidelberg (2012). https://doi.org/10.1007/978-3-642-23166-7_12
13. Fang, S., et al.: Feature selection method based on class discriminative degree for intelligent medical diagnosis. CMC: Comput. Mater. Continua **55**(3), 419–433 (2018)
14. Xi, X., Sheng, V.S., Sun, B., Wang, L., Hu, F.: An empirical comparison on multi-target regression learning. CMC: Comput. Mater. Continua **56**(2), 185–198 (2018)

NCGs: Building a Trustworthy Environment to Identify Abnormal Events Based on Network Connection Behavior Analysis

Hangyu Hu[(✉)], Xuemeng Zhai, Mingda Wang, and Guangmin Hu

School of Information and Communication Engineering,
University of Electronic Science and Technology of China,
Chengdu 611731, China
huhangyuuestc@gmail.com

Abstract. With the continuous development and wide application of various network technologies, such as the mobile, wireless and sensors network, network services are becoming more and more high-speed, diversified and complex. Also, network attacks and infrequent events have emerged, making the promotion of network anomaly detection more and more significant. In order to control and manage the networks and establish a credible network environment, it is critical to facilitate an accurate behavioral characteristic analysis for networks, proactively identify abnormal events associated with network behavior, and improve the capacity of responding to abnormal events. In this paper, we use Network Connection Graphs (NCGs) to model flow activities during network operation. After we construct a NCG in a time-bin, then we can extract graph metric features for quantitative or semi-quantitative analysis of flow activities. And we also could build a series of NCGs to describe the evolution process of network operation. During these NCGs, we have conducted dynamic analysis to find out the outlier points of graph metric features by using Z-score analysis method so that we can detect the hidden abnormal events. The experiment results based on real network traces have demonstrated that the effectiveness of our method in network flow behavior analysis and abnormal event identification.

Keywords: Network Connection Graphs · Graph metrics · Dynamic analysis · Outlier detection · Event identification

1 Introduction

Recent years have witnessed the rapid improvement of various network technologies, such as the mobile, wireless and sensors network. These network technologies aim to connect everything in the cyber world and allow everything interacts with each other [1–3]. Since the advantages of these different network types, it is attracting tremendous attention from the academia, industry and government to carry on researches about network behavior analysis. However, with the increasing scale and complexity of the Internet and increasing frequency of network abnormal events, the volume, velocity and variety of data traffic travelling on network rises at an exponential rate; anomalous

© Springer Nature Switzerland AG 2019
X. Sun et al. (Eds.): ICAIS 2019, LNCS 11635, pp. 67–78, 2019.
https://doi.org/10.1007/978-3-030-24268-8_7

network events have the feature of erupting suddenly without known signatures, which could cause great catastrophe, thus network behavior analysis is still a problem which is important and urgently needed to be intensively explored.

The occurrence of network abnormal events originate by many reasons, such as bad operation of network devices, network operation errors, network intrusions (such as Denial of Service (DoS) attacks, flash crowds, port scanning and worm propagation), which will damage the normal functions of the network [4–7]. Therefore, the identification of network abnormal event is becoming an indispensable and essential part of network behavior analysis. In order to control and manage the network successfully and build a trustworthy network environment, it is necessary to analyze, extract and identify the connection relationship of the flow activities in real time and accurately, actively discover the type and abnormal behavior of the flow, and improve the ability of the network system to cope with the anomalous behavior of the network.

In our recent work, we have studied the problem of precisely identifying network flow behaviors and discovering the root cause of network events among a great deal of network flow data [8]. This paper is a continuation of recent work, by drawing on the concept of knowledge graph. And we propose Network Connection Graphs (NCGs), a new method used for network flow measurement, analysis and visualization over time. Firstly we collect network traffic and preprocess flow information in real time in order to construct data model for NCGs. Depending on the purpose of study, various rules can be used to determine nodes and edges in the graph. Then we extract graph metric features. It can intuitively reflect the different interaction between hosts in the network (for example, a certain number of packet exchanges), and avoid network encryption and other issues. After that, we analyze differences of NCGs in time series to detect the outlier-points and identify abnormal events by matching the connected patterns with corresponding graph metric features. The approach has been validated by using network traces from Abilene, Internet2 backbone communication network. The results have demonstrated that the effectiveness of our approach in capturing the connected patterns of network abnormal events, and scalability in both of static graph analysis and dynamic analysis, even for evolution graph analysis. In summary, NCGs provide an easy-to-understand, effective in mining and flexible on construction means to do contribution in network flow behavior analysis.

2   Related Work

There are commonly two kinds of methods in detecting and identifying network abnormal events which are divided into misuse based detection method and anomaly detection method. Both of them are particularly important in network management and monitoring, but nowadays are very difficult to achieve better results because of the impact of massive network data and other security and privacy factors.

From the perspective of fine and coarse level of analysis, traditional network behavior analysis methods can be divided into three levels under different granularity, as Fig. 1 shows: (a) packet level, such as signature-based application identification and well-known classification based on port number; (b) statistical technology of flow level; (c) network-wide level, which is the most coarse analysis method, often be considered as the complement for detailed and precise analysis method.

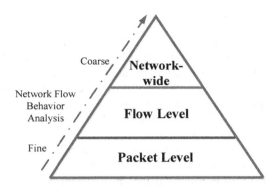

Fig. 1. Network behavior analysis granularity.

2.1 Packet Level Behavior Analysis

Packet level analysis method [9, 10] usually focus on the packet content including timestamp, IP addresses of source and destination hosts, port numbers opened for source and destination hosts, packet and byte counts, protocol, and TCP flags, etc. Table 1 shows the example of network packet data. The advantage of employing packet level analysis is to provide detail information about network interaction on the finest level of granularity.

The volume information of network traffic can be considered as a signal in the domain of signal processing. Figure 2 shows the volume of network traffic of one week trace with traffic every 5 min. Many researchers use time series analysis method, such as wavelet-analysis, PCA analysis, and ICA analysis.

Table 1. The example of network packet data

No.	Timestamp	SrcIP	DstIP	Sport	Dport	Proto.	#Bytes
1	0.00011	192.168.1.90	202.258.158.25	80	32548	6(TCP)	1540
2	0.00025	123.256.25.256	192.168.1.90	23548	80	6(TCP)	3340
3	0.000475	147.32.84.171	147.32.84.165	139	1040	6(TCP)	40
4	0.001953	147.32.84.171	147.32.84.165	139	1040	6(TCP)	44
...	......	......	......	......	......	......	......

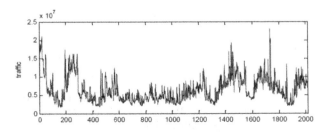

Fig. 2. Network traffic of one week traces (5 min for a time-bin).

2.2   Flow Level Behavior Analysis

Network operators lately have paid more attention on which new application or network event is flowing over the network that makes a wide range of network behavioral analyzing tasks focusing on the network flow data [11–13]. Network flows are active in host interactions so that we can make the most of connection relationship among various flows to analyze the behavioral characteristics of network flow, in particularly given a great number of IP-to-IP interaction flow data, how can we find interesting or suspicious behaviors, patterns and anomalies in real time through mining communication patterns, characterizing interaction structure, and modeling connection trends of new applications, users and other entities in the network. Thus this practical requirement has motivated a broad prospect for the development of a novel research field–network flow behavior analytics, being nowadays an interesting research domain.

2.3   Network-Wide Level Behavior Analysis

Network-wide behavior analysis [14, 15] which focuses on the global behavior information is including traffic, topology, and state information, globe level interaction information, link behavior information, etc. One of the network-wide level behavior analyses is shown in Fig. 3 by calculating different entropy of network-wide level properties.

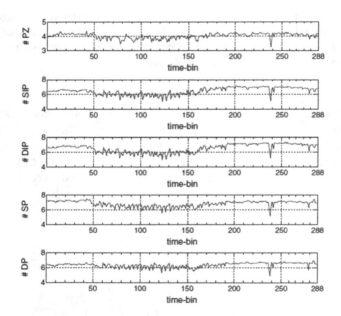

Fig. 3. Entropy values of network-wide level properties in one day time interval. Among them, PZ denotes packet size, SIP denotes Source IP addresses, DIP denotes Destination IP addresses, SP denotes Source Ports and DP denotes Destination Port [15].

3   Overview of Network Connection Graphs

In this section, we introduce knowledge graphs, Network Connection Graphs (NCGs), graph metric features and discuss how these features are used to quantify NCGs and identify network abnormal events.

3.1   Concepts of Network Connection Graphs

Definition 1: Knowledge graph is a structured semantic knowledge base to model connected relationships between various entities and reflect the knowledge information among them [16]. Its basic constituent unit is "entity-relationship-entity", as well as the related attribute values. This type of relational information could be used to construct various graph models to forming a network of knowledge structure.

Definition 2: A **Network Connection Graph (NCG)** is a graphical representation of interactions of various devices, which can be modeled as a directed connect graph $G = (V, E)$, where V is the set of vertices representing IP addresses in the interaction flows and E is the set of edges representing the relationships between numerous devices in networks. Let $n = |V|$ to represent the number of nodes and $m = |E|$ to represent the number of edges in a graph. The NCG is different from other graph models by setting weights to edges and attributed information to nodes, which is a special case of knowledge graph applied to network flow behavior analysis.

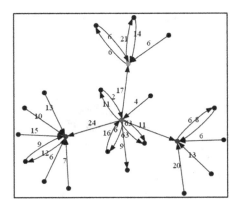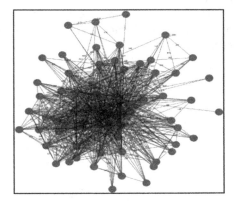

Fig. 4. A visualization example of NCG concept graph and actual NCG under real network trace.

3.2   Flow Knowledge Data Model Construction for NCGs

The data model for NCGs construction procedure is consists of two steps. The first step of it is to collect network flow data and pre-process these data into network flow. Since our approach does not require the detailed packet payload, we aggregate all information of network packet in transport layer header into flows based on an N-tuple flow— *<Time, SrcIP, DstIP, SrcPort, DstPort, Prot, Tcp_flag ...>* . Secondly, a graphical representation model of NCGs. Figure 4 is drawn with employing visualization software GraphViz [17] to show a visualization example of NCG concept graph and actual NCG under Abilene network traffic trace.

3.3 Quantifying NCG Graph Metric Features

NCG could be regarded as a type of weighted complex network structure. By drawing on the study of network science [18], we propose two kinds of graph metric features to describe behavioral of network flow connected relations and use these features to offer the quantitative or semi-quantitative analysis for network flow behaviors.

Basic metric features of NCG: describes the basic parameters of network topology, such as the number of nodes and edges, the average degree of nodes and so on. The occurrence of network events would cause a sudden change of these features by increasing or decreasing of nodes and edges, such as the suddenly shut down of FTP servers will result in the reduction of this feature.

Status metric features of NCG: this kind of feature represents the state and compactness of nodes and edges in the global structure of network, including the node strength, the density of graph, cluster coefficient of node, cluster coefficient of the global graph, etc. Note that some network events would not cause the change of network topology, but they would have an impact on the status of nodes and edges, such as NCG basic features may change little when DNS request failure happens, but the status features may change since the connection structure would develop into bi-mesh pattern from star pattern.

These above features could contribute a lot in summarizing various network connection patterns. Figure 5 shows a brief example of graph features of different connected structures.

Property	Formula				
Subgraph Type	$G=<V, E, A>$ V, Vertex set E, Edge set A, Adjacency matrix $A = (a_{ij})_{n*n}$	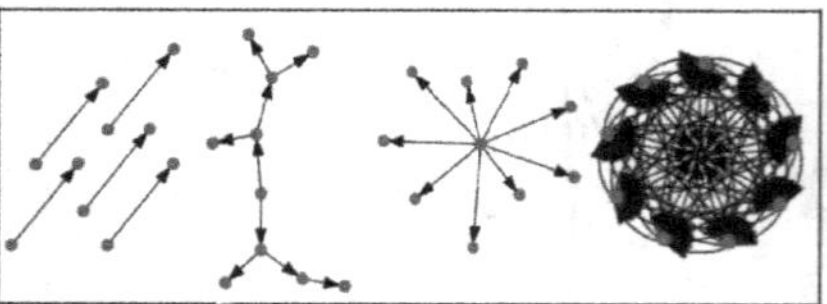			
#Nodes	m	10	10	10	10
#Edges	n	5	9	9	45
Avg. Deg	$K = \dfrac{1}{n} * \sum\limits_{i,j=1}^{n} a_{ij}$	1	1.8	1.8	9
Max. Connected Density	$MCD = \dfrac{Deg_{max}}{n-1} * 100\%$	0.11	0.33	1	1
In(%)	$In = \dfrac{m_{in}}{m} * 100\%$	50%	50%	90%	\
Out(%)	$Out = \dfrac{m_{out}}{m} * 100\%$	50%	10%	10%	\
In&Out(%)	$InO = \dfrac{m_{ino}}{m} * 100\%$	\	40%	\	100%
Max. Depth	$dep(v) = dep(u) + 1$	1	3	1	9

Fig. 5. A brief example of graph features of different connected structures.

3.4   Statistical Analysis for Graph Metric Features in NCGs

A NCG is corresponding to a vector space including the graph metric features, which means we could use some parameters to represent and distinguish NCG. Over the time, there are a lot of NCGs formed in each time-bin, thus as well as a series of graph metric features. However, when different network abnormal events occur, the structure changes of the NCG corresponding to the inherent characteristics are also different, which eventually result in the different changes of the graph metric features.

Therefore, we use the Z-score analysis method [19, 20] to find out the outlier-points of different graph metric features, and then identify the NCG of present moment as a suspicious state. There are several steps in this process, and also shown as in Fig. 6:

- Step1: Collecting network traffic and then aggregating packet data into network flow data;
- Step2: Constructing NCG over time to form a time series graph sequence;
- Step3: Extracting graph metric features for each a NCG of the graph sequence, and then build different sequence representations for various graph metric features; calculating the z-score for different feature sequences;
- Step4: Through deviation analysis to decide whether any graph metric features are under the anomalous state, and finally matching the features according to the inherent interactive characteristics of anomalies to identify the abnormal events.

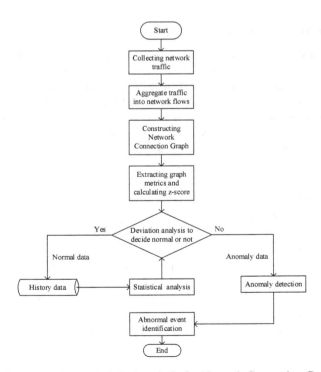

Fig. 6. Z-score based statistical analysis for Network Connection Graphs.

4   Experimental Results

To validate our approach in abnormal event identification, we used the sampled network flow dataset: Abilene [21], which belong to the Internet2 backbone network, connecting over 200 US universities and peering with research networks in Europe and Asia, and the topology structure [22] is shown in Fig. 7.

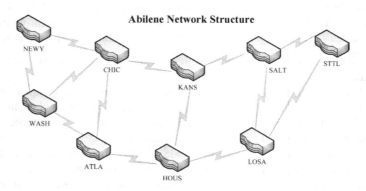

Fig. 7. Abilene network topology structure [22].

4.1   Static Graph Metric Feature Analysis

We have collected network flow data of Jan 11th in 2008. The trace is sampled with 5 min cycle and a NCG is generated every 5 min. We first calculate the graph metric features for different network applications in order to acquire connected characteristics of the normal flow data based on destination port number. Table 2 gives the graph metrics features for 6 kinds of well-known applications (including SMTP, DNS, HTTP, NetBIOS, eDonkey and WinMX). As shown in the table, we could draw a conclusion that the inherent interactive characteristics are different between each other.

Table 2. Graph metric features for different network applications.

App.	#Node	#Edges	Avg. Deg	MCD	Directionality		GCC	Max Dep
					Sink	Source		
SMTP	3146	4345	2.76	3.66%	47.97%	52.10%	75.43%	45
DNS	9155	20265	4.43	7.14%	36.70%	63.62%	92.61%	337
HTTP	12889	13185	2.05	6.39%	25.39%	74.61%	65.40%	4
NetBIOS	10969	10523	1.92	4.46%	95.54%	4.47%	4.54%	3
eDonkey	10161	14355	2.83	0.94%	36.55%	63.47%	85.86%	295
WinMX	5966	14015	4.70	5.52%	38.55%	61.46%	98.27%	523

4.2   Dynamic Graph Metric Feature Analysis

Figure 8 shows the dynamic changes of NCG graph metric features in 2008-01-11 network flow trace, including Avg.Deg, MCD, directionality (sink node ratio and source node ratio), GCC and Max depth. If the feature exceeds the threshold calculated by Z-score analysis method, we will label it out. Tables 3 and 4 respectively shows the outlier-point extraction of Avg. Degree feature and MCD in 2008-01-11 network flow trace. The No. 130 dataset and No. 90 dataset is detected as suspicious state by the Z-score analysis method. Then we compare the graph metric features of this dataset with any normal dataset, with results are shown in Figs. 9 and 10.

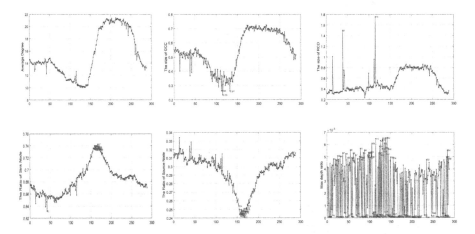

Fig. 8. Dynamic changes of NCG graph features in 2008-01-11 network flow trace.

Table 3. Outlier-point extraction of Avg. Degree in 2008-01-11 network flow trace.

	#Nodes	#Edges	Avg. Deg	MCD	Directionality			Size of GCC	Max. Depth
					Sink	Source	Ino		
No. 130 suspicious dataset	1902	3554	3.1	14.9%	61.5%	38%	0.5%	46.48%	4
No. 153 normal dataset	2447	5344	4.7	32.3%	66.8%	32.7%	0.5%	52.8%	4

Table 4. Outlier-point extraction of MCD in 2008-01-11 network flow trace.

	#Nodes	#Edges	Avg. Deg	MCD	Directionality			Size of GCC	Max. Depth
					Sink	Source	Ino		
No. 90 suspicious dataset	223	565	5.9	98.6%	59.6%	40.4%	0%	23.8%	1
No. 170 normal dataset	289	617	3.4	69.8%	64%	36%	0%	34.9%	1

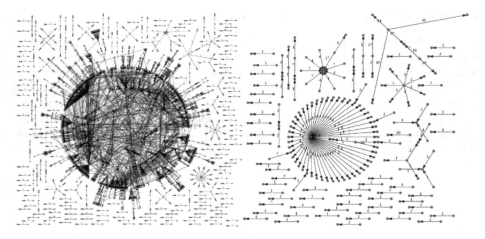

Fig. 9. NCG of No.130 suspicious dataset and NCG of No. 153 normal dataset.

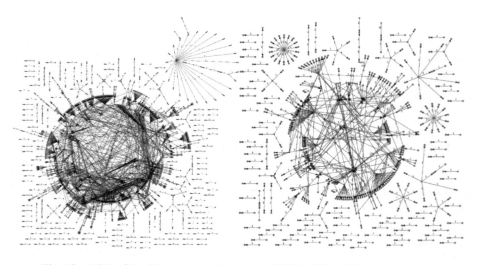

Fig. 10. NCG of No.90 suspicious dataset and NCG of No. 170 normal dataset.

4.3 Network Abnormal Events Visualization by Combining Manual Analysis and NCGs

We also validated our approach by manual label method in order to restore the complete connection relations of network abnormal events. Figure 11 shows the NCG visualization of DDoS attack and Worm propagation. From these two NCGs, we can conclude that their graph metric features are different from normal flows, especially compared with P2P structure based flow activities.

(a)   (b)

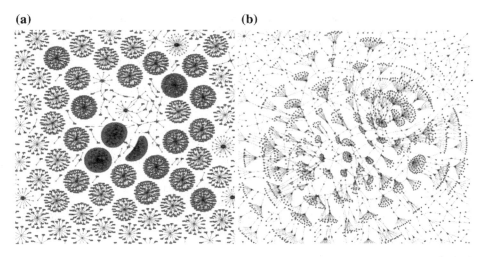

Fig. 11. NCG visualization of Abilene's trace: (a) DDoS attacks; (b) Worm propagation.

5 Conclusion and Prospection

In this paper, we propose the Network Connection Graphs (NCGs) as a novel tool to explore network flow activities by capturing the connected relationships of interaction flows. From the results of our experiments evaluated by real network traffic trace, combining with static analysis and dynamic analysis methods, we are effectively extract graph metric features for understanding network flow behaviors and identifying abnormal events. To our minds, our approach would contribute a lot to the foundation of next-generation communication network management and security service system development, and has implications for network security protection.

In the future work, aiming at increasing the robustness and effectiveness of our approach, we would start from sensitive analysis to improve the accuracy and performance in comparison with state of the art methods. Then we plan to investigate other dynamic analysis methods to thoroughly explore connected patterns for network events no matter normal or abnormal in order to completely characterize the network flow behaviors.

References

1. Whitmore, A., Agarwal, A., Da Xu, L.: The Internet of things—a survey of topics and trends. Inf. Syst. Front. **17**(2), 261–274 (2015)
2. Qi, Y.: Information potential fields navigation in wireless Ad-Hoc sensor networks. Sensors **11**(5), 4794–4807 (2011)
3. Yang, X.L., Shen, P.Y., Zhou, B.: Holes detection in anisotropic sensornets: topological methods. Int. J. Distrib. Sens. Netw. **8** (10), 135054 (2012)
4. Zarpelão, B.B., Miani, R.S., Kawakani, C.T., de Alvarenga, S.C.: A survey of intrusion detection in Internet of Things. J. Netw. Comput. Appl. **84**, 25–37 (2017)

5. Zhang, H., Yi, Y., Wang, J., Cao, N., Duan, Q.: Network security situation awareness framework based on threat intelligence. CMC: Comput. Mater. Continua **56**(3), 381–399 (2018)
6. Habeeb, R.A.A., et al.: Real-time big data processing for anomaly detection: a Survey. Int. J. Inf. Manag. (2018)
7. Cheng, J., Xu, R., Tang, X., Sheng, V.S., Cai, C.: An abnormal network flow feature sequence prediction approach for DDoS attacks detection in big data environment. CMC: Comput. Mater. Continua **55**(1), 095–119 (2018)
8. Hu, H., Zhai, X., Wang, M., Hu, G.: Linked-behaviors profiling in IoT networks using network connection graphs (NCGs). In: Sun, X., Pan, Z., Bertino, E. (eds.) ICCCS 2018. LNCS, vol. 11067, pp. 429–439. Springer, Cham (2018). https://doi.org/10.1007/978-3-030-00018-9_38
9. Barford, P., et al.: A signal analysis of network traffic anomalies. In: Proceedings of the 2nd ACM SIGCOMM Workshop on Internet Measurement. ACM (2002)
10. Zonglin, L., Hu, G., Yao, X.: Multi-dimensional traffic anomaly detection based on ICA. In: IEEE Symposium on Computers and Communications, ISCC 2009, pp. 333–336. IEEE (2009)
11. Karagiannis, T., Papagiannaki, K., Faloutsos, M.: BLINC: multilevel traffic classification in the dark. In: ACM SIGCOMM Computer Communication Review, vol. 35, no. 4, pp. 229–240. ACM (2005)
12. Iliofotou, M., Pappu, P., Faloutsos, M., Mitzenmacher, M., Singh, S., Varghese, G.: Network monitoring using traffic dispersion graphs (TDGs). In: Proceedings of the 7th ACM SIGCOMM Conference on Internet Measurement, pp. 315–320. ACM (2007)
13. Jin, Yu., Sharafuddin, E., Zhang, Z.-L.: Unveiling core network-wide communication patterns through application traffic activity graph decomposition. ACM SIGMETRICS Perform. Eval. Rev. **37**(1), 49–60 (2009)
14. Lakhina, A., Crovella, M., Diot, C.: Characterization of network-wide anomalies in traffic flows. In: Proceedings of the 4th ACM SIGCOMM Conference on Internet Measurement. ACM (2004)
15. Zhou, Y., Hu, G., Wu, D.: A data mining system for distributed abnormal event detection in backbone networks. Secur. Commun. Netw. **7**(5), 904–913 (2014)
16. Wang, Q., Mao, Z., Wang, B., Guo, L.: Knowledge graph embedding: a survey of approaches and applications. IEEE Trans. Knowl. Data Eng. **29**(12), 2724–2743 (2017)
17. GraphViz (2011). http://www.graphviz.org/
18. Lewis, T.G.: Network Science: Theory and Applications. Wiley, Hoboken (2011)
19. Cheadle, C., Vawter, M.P., Freed, W.J., Becker, K.G.: Analysis of microarray data using Z score transformation. J. Mol. Diagn. **5**(2), 73–81 (2003)
20. He, D., Chan, S., Ni, X., Guizani, M.: Software-defined-networking-enabled traffic anomaly detection and mitigation. IEEE Internet Things J. **4**(6), 1890–1898 (2017)
21. http://abilene.internet2.edu
22. https://en.wikipedia.org/wiki/Abilene_Network

Short Text Topic Recognition and Optimization Method for University Online Community

Xu Wu[1,2,3(✉)], Haitao Wu[1,2,3], Xiaqing Xie[1,2,3], Jin Xu[1,2,3], and Tianle Zhang[4]

[1] Key Laboratory of Trustworthy Distributed Computing and Service, Ministry of Education, Beijing, China
[2] School of Cyberspace Security, BUPT, Beijing, China
{wux,wht,xiexiaqing}@bupt.edu.cn
[3] Beijing University of Posts and Telecommunications Library, Beijing 100876, China
[4] Cyberspace Institute of Advanced Technology, Guangzhou University, Guangzhou 510006, China
tlezhang@sohu.com

Abstract. The university online community mainly records what happens in target areas and groups of people. It has the characteristics of timeliness, regional strong and clear target groups. Compared with Weibo and post-bar, university community's text topic recognition needs to solve the problems of large text noise, fast text update and short single text content. To this end, this paper proposes a method of building university topic model based on LDA topic model. Through the steps of original text's noise reduction, LDA (Latent Dirichlet Allocation (LDA), is a topic model commonly used in the field of machine learning and is often used for text categorization.) model recognition and weighted calculation of recognition results, etc., the event themes that characterize the common characteristics for university online community are obtained. Experiments based on real university online community's data show that the topic model of university popular events established by the topic recognition model of this paper can reflect some popular events in colleges and universities, so as to provide reasonable support for university management.

Keywords: University online community · University topic model · Popular events in colleges and universities

1 Introduction

The vigorous development of the Internet has made more and more netizens gather in the online community such as Weibo and post-bar and so on. In particular, college students express their views, discussed hot topics about their school in the university online community. As the active network community in Colleges and universities, the amount of information contained in the network community has increased geometrically. Correspondingly, the information related to all aspects of College Students' life

X. Sun et al. (Eds.): ICAIS 2019, LNCS 11635, pp. 79–90, 2019.
https://doi.org/10.1007/978-3-030-24268-8_8

has become a hot research contents. This paper focuses on the contents of university online community, proposes an improved LDA method for text topic recognition, and gives weight to the results. By calculating the weight, we can judge whether the output results can represent the corresponding topic model. The text of university network community has the problem of large text noise, fast text updating and short single text. To solve these problems, firstly, this paper extends the LDA model's stop word library and filters a large number of general useless replies to decrease the text noise. Then, uses the LDA topic model to generate a word vector group which can represent this topic, and each vector is given different weights. By calculating the weights, we can judge whether the topic model can truly represent the typical topic. Lastly, this paper establishes some topic models which can represent the typical events in universities. The experimental results show that the topic recognition model based on this paper can better reflect some of the hot events in universities than the traditional LDA topic model, so as to provide reasonable support for university management.

2   Related Research

2.1   Related Work

At present, some researches have used LDA topic model or improved LDA topic model to mine topic models in different fields. Zhu Maoran et al. use LDA model to identify the topic and its key words in the whole text set, and calculated the document-topic probability distribution in each time windows. Then the topic-lexical probability distribution is calculated by LDA model for each text set under each time window, and the similarity of different topics under different time windows is calculated, thus the evolution trend of topic strength is obtained. Finally, we get the change of thematic content through the probability distribution of words under similar themes. [1] Peng et al. embed a priori knowledge of word association, global feature words and subject emotion subordinate semantics in LDA model to improve LDA's ability to recognize feature words, affective words and their relationships. And it uses LDA model to extract the feature words and emotional words of product reviews, and take advantage of affective analysis technology [2]. To classify emotional polarity of product reviews Yi et al. introduce the strategic coordinates into the subject analysis of LDA patents, and fuses the time factors, using the internal and external correlation index to measure the relationship between the various parts of the subject. [3] Tan et al. apply the LDA model to the mining of hot topics, and constructs the identification process of Weibo hot topics. [4] Zheng et al. propose an improved LDA model ST-LDA to analyze Weibo topics. This model assigns a topic to each Weibo. In particular, when assigning a topic to each Weibo, not only the influence of posting time on the topic is considered, but also the influence of posting location on the topic is added. Thus, the model can assign a topic to each Weibo. The semantic similarity of Weibo published in adjacent time and space is classified into the same topic, which improves the comprehensibility of the topic. [5] Xu et al. use LDA topic model to analyze the topic relevance of blog content, redefine the link relationship between bloggers, and then classify the topics. [6] Shi et al. mainly explore the evolution of BBS as a topic in the network media in time, so as to find hot topics and no-hot topics, and better guide the netizens to understand what is happening. [7] He et al. proposes a simple and easy symmetric learning data augmentation model (SLDAM) for underwater target radiate-noise data expansion and generation. The SLDAM, taking the optimal classifier of an initial dataset as the discriminator, makes use of the structure of the classifier to construct a symmetric generator based on antagonistic generation. It generates data similar to the initial dataset that can be used to supplement training data sets. [8] Wang et al. proposes a natural language semantic construction method based on cloud database to improve natural language comprehension ability and analytical skills of the machine [9].

The research above has done a lot of work on the application level of LDA, and has also been extended based on this theory to optimize the topic recognition in specific areas. However, we can also see the shortcomings: on the one hand, LDA is an unsupervised learning model, the input content will greatly affect the accuracy of the output results, and these methods do not effectively de-noise the input data, which still has a lot of room for optimization; on the other hand, the output of the LDA model is considered the final result of the corresponding topic without considering the intrinsic correlation between the output of the LDA model. Although LDA model treats the segmentation results equally, the results of LDA model can be re-weighted to determine whether the results can represent the corresponding topic model.

2.2 LDA Model and Application

Latent Dirichlet Allocation (LDA), is a topic model commonly used in the field of machine learning and is often used for text categorization.

LDA was put forward in 2003 by Blei, David M., Ng, Andrew Y. and Jordan to predict the topic distribution of documents. It can give the topic of each document in the document set in the form of probability distribution. After analyzing some documents and extracting their topic distribution, it can cluster or classify the text according to the topic distribution.

Suppose there are M documents, corresponding to the d document, there are N_d words, that is, the input is as follows (Fig. 1):

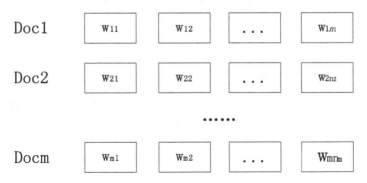

Fig. 1. The LDA Input schematic diagram.

In order to find the topic distribution of each document and the word distribution in each topic, this paper first assumes a topic number K, so that all distributions are based on K topics. Therefore, a specific LDA model can be obtained, as shown in the following Fig. 2:

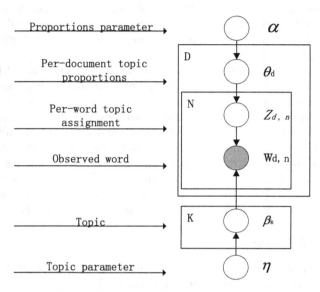

Fig. 2. The LDA model schematic diagram.

LDA assumes that the prior distribution of a document topic is a Dirichlet distribution, that is, for any document d, the topic distribution θ_d is:

$$\theta_d = Diriclet(\vec{\alpha}) \tag{1}$$

Among them, α is a distributed super parameter, which is a K dimensional vector.

LDA assumes that the prior distribution of words in a topic is Dirichlet distribution, that is, for any topic k, the word distribution β_k is:

$$\beta_k = Dirichlet(\vec{\eta}) \tag{2}$$

Among them, the parameter η is a V dimensional vector. V stands for the number of words in the word list.

For the nth word in any document d in the data, the distribution of the subject number z_{dn} is obtained from the topic distribution θ_d as follows:

$$z_{dn} = multi(\theta_d) \tag{3}$$

For this topic number, the probability distribution of word w_{dn} can be obtained as follows:

$$w_{dn} = multi\left(\beta_{z_{dn}}\right) \tag{4}$$

Thus, for M document topics, the corresponding data has multiple distributions of M topic numbers, so that $\alpha \to \theta_d \to \vec{z}_d$ constitutes a Dirichlet-multi conjugate. A posteriori distribution of document topics based on Dirichlet distribution can be obtained by Bayesian inference.

If the number of words for topic K in the dth document is $n_d^{(k)}$, the count of polynomial distributions can be expressed as:

$$\vec{n}_d = \left(n_d^{(1)}, n_d^{(2)}, \ldots n_d^{(K)}\right) \tag{5}$$

The posterior distribution of θ_d is obtained by using Dirichlet-multi conjugate is:

$$Dirichlet(\theta_d | \vec{\alpha} + \vec{n}_d) \tag{6}$$

For the distribution of subjects and words, if there is a Dirichlet distribution of K subjects and words, and the corresponding data has a polynomial distribution of K subject numbers, then $\eta \to \beta_k \to \vec{w}_{(k)}$ constitutes a Dirichlet-multiconjugate. Bayesian inference method can be used to obtain a posterior distribution of subject words based on the Dirichlet distribution.

If the number of words V in topic K is $n_k^{(v)}$, the number of polynomial distributions can be expressed as:

$$\vec{n}_k = \left(n_k^{(1)}, n_k^{(2)}, \ldots n_k^{(V)}\right) \tag{7}$$

By using Dirichlet-multi conjugation, the posterior distribution of β_k is obtained as:

$$Dirichlet(\beta_k | \vec{\eta} + \vec{n}_k) \tag{8}$$

Because the subject-generated words do not depend on a specific document, the topic distribution and the subject-word distribution of the document are independent.

3 Establishing the Theme Model of University Online Community

3.1 Text Topic Recognition Method in University Online Community

The concept of topic area is mostly adopted in the network community of colleges and universities. The topics discussed in the same topic area can be summed up as a kind of campus-related topics. Every post in the topic area revolves around a particular topic. If you ignore the useless responses in a single post, you can assume that all the responses are thematic responses. Considering these characteristics of college network community, this paper preprocesses the input text before generating topic distribution using LDA model, as shown in the following Fig. 3:

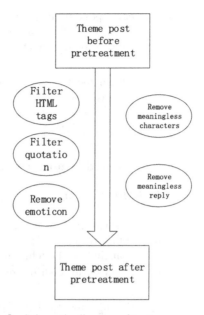

Fig. 3. Schematic diagram of text preprocessing

After pretreatment, the topic posts can be used as the input of LDA model to get the distribution of the topic words, because all the noises that affect the results are removed. And because each topic Posts contain only one topic, we can easily get the distribution of the topic words of a hot topic. As the LDA model is a bag of words model, the result can only show the frequency distribution of the subject words, and can not be divided in detail according to the weight of different words. According to the characteristics of the subject words in the topic model, this paper proposes a method of weight assignment according to the category of the subject words. By calculating the final weight results, we can get the result of weight assignment. Determine whether these topic phrases can correctly represent the corresponding topic models. Therefore, the whole process of text topic recognition in this paper is shown in the following Fig. 4:

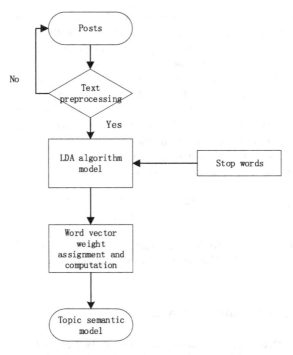

Fig. 4. Flow chart of text topic recognition

3.2 The Establishment of Popular Topic Model in University Online Community

The heat of the topic area in the network community reflects the students' attention to the corresponding events in universities. This paper investigates a large number of hot topics in the network community of colleges and universities, and obtains the topics closely related to colleges and universities shown in the following Fig. 5:

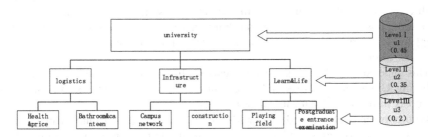

Fig. 5. Flow chart of text topic recognition

From the above chart shows, the hot topics related to the campus is divided into three categories, six small classes, which basically covers all aspects of campus life. This paper establishes the corresponding topic model bases on these six categories. The right-most side of the graph shows the weight of each level of the hot topic. For the model level, the letter u is used to represent the level, and $u_1u_2u_3...u_n$ is used to represent the corresponding level. For each level, this article uses the letter w to represent the corresponding weight, $w_1w_2w_3...w_n$ denotes the weight of the corresponding hierarchy, the letter $\lambda = \delta / \sum_0^n u$ denotes the compensation value, and the value of delta is related to the word frequency input by the LDA model. If the maximum word frequency is less than 0.1, then $\delta = 0.1$, and so on. The formula for calculating weight can be obtained as follows:

$$f(u, w) = \frac{u_1 * w_1 + u_2 * w_2 + u_3 * w_3 + ... + u_n * w_n}{u_1 + u_2 + u_3 + ...u_n} * \lambda \qquad (9)$$

The weighted result of the topic model can be obtained by using the above formula. If the result is greater than 0.5, the input text can be used to represent the corresponding topic model.

4   Experimental Results and Analysis

4.1   Text Topic Recognition Analysis of University Network Community

The University Forum of Beijing University of Posts and Telecommunications is one of the typical network communities in Colleges and universities. According to the different topics, the forum is divided into eight discussion areas, each of which includes the website, the campus of Beijing University of Posts and Telecommunications, academic science and technology, information society, humanities and arts, life style, leisure and entertainment, physical fitness, games and love of hometown. There are other discussion areas behind those areas. By analyzing the content of the discussion area, this paper draws a conclusion that posts posted on specific plates have obvious characteristics. For example, in the life fashion section, the discussion is mostly about life-related topics, such as canteen, bathroom, supermarket, and so on, while in the health care section, the discussion is mostly about hospitals, nursing and other topics. These topic posts also have a strong attribute: that is, the response below a topic post, except for some irrelevant replies, the rest of the replies are related to the topic of the topic post discussion.

This paper selects the posts related to campus life in the life style area of the forum of Beijing University of Posts and Telecommunications, and obtains the contents of each posts in the zone by means of web crawler.

Web crawler is also called web spider, or web robot. It is a kind of programs or scripts according to certain Rules that automatically grab information from the World Wide Web. In other words, it can automatically get the content of the web page according to the link address of the web page. If we compare the Internet to a big spider web, it has a lot of web pages, web spiders can get all of webpage's content. [10] In this paper, we can find the origin contents on the website like this (Fig. 6):

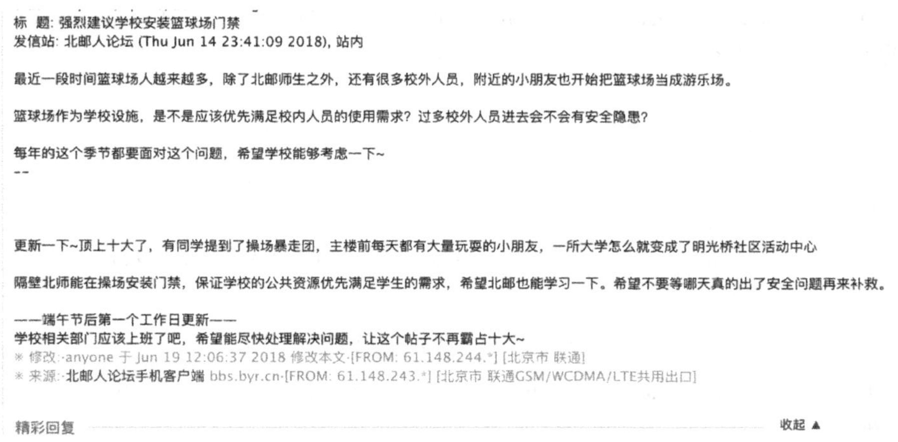

标 题: 强烈建议学校安装篮球场门禁
发信站: 北邮人论坛 (Thu Jun 14 23:41:09 2018), 站内

最近一段时间篮球场人越来越多，除了北邮师生之外，还有很多校外人员，附近的小朋友也开始把篮球场当成游乐场。

篮球场作为学校设施，是不是应该优先满足校内人员的使用需求？过多校外人员进去会不会有安全隐患？

每年的这个季节都要面对这个问题，希望学校能够考虑一下~
--

更新一下~顶上十大了，有同学提到了操场暴走团，主楼前每天都有大量玩耍的小朋友，一所大学怎么就变成了明光桥社区活动中心

隔壁北师能在操场安装门禁，保证学校的公共资源优先满足学生的需求，希望北邮也能学习一下。希望不要等哪天真的出了安全问题再来补救。

——端午节后第一个工作日更新——
学校相关部门应该上班了吧，希望能尽快处理解决问题，让这个帖子不再霸占十大~
※ 修改:·anyone 于 Jun 19 12:06:37 2018 修改本文·[FROM: 61.148.244.*] [北京市 联通]
※ 来源:·北邮人论坛手机客户端 bbs.byr.cn·[FROM: 61.148.243.*] [北京市 联通GSM/WCDMA/LTE共用出口]

精彩回复   收起 ▲

Fig. 6. The origin text on the website

The origin contents above can't use by LDA model before text preprocessing completed. We can see the whole text below (Fig. 7):

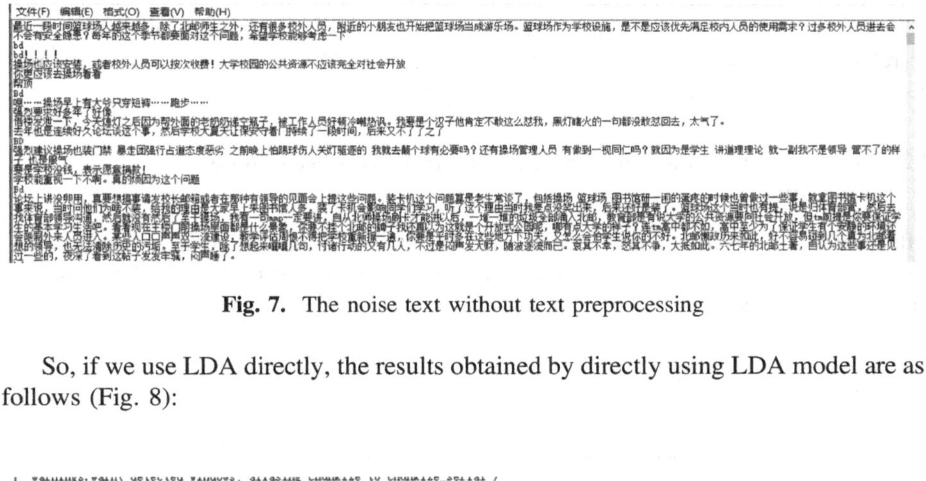

Fig. 7. The noise text without text preprocessing

So, if we use LDA directly, the results obtained by directly using LDA model are as follows (Fig. 8):

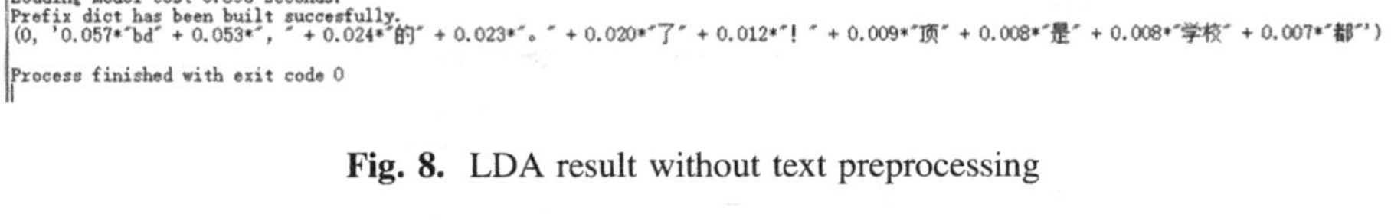

Fig. 8. LDA result without text preprocessing

As you can see, the phrases with the highest frequency are in turn "bd", "的", "了" and other characters that have nothing to do with the subject.

After the text preprocessing, the output of the LDA thematic model is shown in the following Fig. 9:

共计导入 1908 个停用词

Building prefix dict from the default dictionary ...

Loading model from cache C:\Users\wht\AppData\Local\Temp\jieba.cache

Loading model cost 0.912 seconds.

Prefix dict has been built succesfully.

(0, '0.017*"学校" + 0.015*"门禁" + 0.011*"北邮" + 0.011*"篮球场" + 0.010*"操场" + 0.008*"学生" + 0.007*"装" + 0.007*"领导" + 0.006*"每日" + 0.006*"真的"')

Fig. 9. LDA result using text preprocessing

Furthermore, a detailed comparison of the above results is shown in the following Table 1:

Table 1. A detailed comparison of the two results

Comparison item	Origin LDA	Improved LDA
Topic relevance	Weak	Strong
Accuracy rate	Low	High
Able to represent events	No	Yes

We can see that after the text preprocessing process proposed in this paper, the correlation between the topic distribution obtained by LDA model and the actual topic distribution involved has been effectively improved.

4.2 Verification of Popular Topic Model in University Online Community

After obtaining the frequency of the above-mentioned topic distribution words, different weights are assigned to them, and a topic model similar to the one shown in the Fig. 10 is obtained:

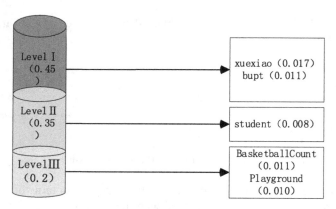

Fig. 10. An example model using the theory of this paper

So the weight of the vector frequency of the above words can be calculated like this:

$$f(u, w) = \frac{((0.017 + 0.011) * 0.45 + 0.008 * 0.35 + (0.011 + 0.010) * 0.2) * 0.1}{(0.017 + 0.011 + 0.08 + 0.011 + 0.010)^2}$$
$$= 0.6033$$

$$(10)$$

Because of $0.6033 > 0.5$, this paper can draw the conclusion that the above topic models can well represent the corresponding themes. That is: the content of the theme is related to the basketball court and playground closely related to the life of college students.

This conclusion also applies to other similar campus themes if we strictly fellow the steps above.

5 Summary and Prospect

The university online community is closely related to schools and students. How to dig up the information from it and serve the schools and students is the current concern of all colleges and universities. This paper focuses on the characteristics of university online community, proposes an improved LDA method for text topic recognition. Firstly, this paper extends the LDA model's stop word library and filters a large number of general useless replies to decrease the text noise. Then, uses the LDA topic model to generate a word vector group which can represent this topic, and each vector is given different weights. By calculating the weights, we can judge whether the topic model can truly represent the typical topic. Lastly, this paper establishes some topic models which can represent the typical events in universities. In the future, on the basis of this study, we can also establish other new thematic models according to the characteristics of universities, improve the calculation method of thematic model weight, and explore the development trend of thematic models of typical events in universities.

Acknowledgements. This work is supported by the National Key Research and Development Plan(Grant No. 2017YFC0820603), BUPT's Informatization Innovative Application Project, " privacy protection and data release on Campus big data" and the Open Project Fund of Key Laboratory of Trustworthy Distributed Computing and Service (BUPT), Ministry of Education.

References

1. Zhu, M., Wang, Y., Gao, S., Wang, H., Zhang, X.: Evolution of topic using LDA model: Evidence From Information Science Journals. J. Beijing Univ. Technol. **07**, 1047–1053 (2018)
2. Peng, Y., Wan, H., Zhong, L.: Fine-grained sentiment analysis algorithm of product reviews based on semantic weakly-supervised LDA. J. Mini-micro Syst. **05**, 978–985 (2018)

3. Yi, H., Wu, H., Ma, Y., Ji, F.: Technical topic analysis in patents based on LDA and strategic diagram by taking graphene technology as an example. J. Intell. **05**, 97–102 (2018)
4. Tan, C., Wang, C., Zhang, Y.: A hot topic identification based on LDA for Chinese microblog. J. Suzhou Univ. **04**, 71–77 (2014)
5. Zheng, Z., Jin, B., Cui, Y.: Study on recognition of spatial-temporal events based on microblogs. J. Comput. Sci. **10**, 214–219 (2016)
6. Xu, B., Zhao, C., Zhang, Y.: Topic community mining in blogosphere based on LDA. J. Comput. Digit. Eng. **11**, 40–43 (2012)
7. Shi, D., Zhang, H.: LDA model-based BBS topic evolution. J. Industr. Control Comput. **05**, 82–84 (2012)
8. He, M., Wang, H., Zhou, L., Wang, P., Ju, A.: Symmetric learning data augmentation model for underwater target noise data expansion. CMC: Comput. Mater. Continua **57**(3), 521–532 (2018)
9. Wang, S., et al.: Natural language semantic construction based on cloud database. CMC: Comput. Mater. Continua **57**(3), 603–619 (2018)
10. A simple web crawler for crawler learning. https://www.cnblogs.com/chenkun/p/5653459.html

A Survey on Network Traffic Identification

Qiuping Zhu[1(✉)], Dong Li[1,2], Yi Xin[1], Xiangzhan Yu[1],
and Guocai Mu[2]

[1] School of Computer Science and Technology,
Harbin Institute of Technology, Harbin, China
17s003115@stu.hit.edu.cn, {lee,xinyi,yxz}@hit.edu.cn
[2] Institute of Electronic and Information Engineering of UESTC in Guangdong,
Dongguan, China
240785491@qq.com

Abstract. With the rapid development of the Internet, the scale of Internet users has been expanding. At the same time, various mobile phone applications have emerged in an endless stream. While providing users with a variety of services, it also leads to the difficulty of user identification. All those things bring new challenges to traffic identification. Based on the importance of Internet traffic identification for Internet management and security, this paper describes the classification methods and problems faced by Internet traffic identification. Moreover, current work about user-related and application-related traffic identification methods is summarized and analyzed. At the end of this article, we will discuss the future research prospects of traffic identification and summarize the content of the article.

Keywords: Traffic identification · User-related identification ·
Application-related identification

1 Introduction

With rapid development of the network, the number of people using network is increasing. Moreover, the popularization of mobile intelligent terminal devices such as laptops, smartphones and tablets not only provide a convenient channel for people to use the network, but also closely integrate people's daily lives with the Internet. The Internet can be used for a variety of activities, like communication (such as Skype, WeChat), shopping (such as Amazon, Taobao), entertainment (such as Youtube, iTunes) and payment (such as Paypal, Alipay). The scale of network traffic continues to expand. As a result, the information contained in traffic is increasing. Up to October 2018, the size of Internet users exceeded about 4.0 billion [2]. More and more researchers are focusing on network traffic analysis and looking forward to getting useful information from it.

Some Internet service providers (ISPs) hope to better understand users and provide better services through traffic analysis, such as analyzing users' preferences from user behaviors and find users' potential interests. In addition, with the development of Internet application technologies, especially the development of technologies such as content search and hacking, the traffic generated by botnets in the Internet is gradually

X. Sun et al. (Eds.): ICAIS 2019, LNCS 11635, pp. 91–100, 2019.
https://doi.org/10.1007/978-3-030-24268-8_9

approaching or even surpassing the traffic generated by real users. Therefore, the ISPs are eager to solve difficult network management problems by network traffic analysis. For example, according to the traffic identification results, some strategies for blocking or adjusting the target traffic are implemented. What's more, part of criminals uses the Internet to implement cyber fraud. According to the FBI 2017 Internet Crime Report [1], cybercrime caused more than $5.52 billion losses up to 2017. Considering such circumstances, it is of practical significance to identify specific users (including criminals) through network traffic analysis.

Network traffic analysis can be traced back to the 1990s [3]. With the continuous development of the Internet, the methods of network traffic analysis are constantly changing. In the beginning, according to the information of the Internet assigned number authority (IANA) port number list [4], the protocol and function used by the packet can be analyzed in a superficial manner. However, some applications are based on self-defined protocols, which violates IANA's port allocation (without affecting their use). For example, some P2P applications used port 80 which used as the access port of web server generally to masquerade as their own function port, making port-based analysis increasingly unreliable. Hence, researchers started with the analysis of the packet payload. Sadly, with the widespread use of HTTPS, encrypted traffic created difficulties for payload-based method. There needs to be more ways to solve this problem. Husák [5, 6] generated a fingerprint by analyzing the SSL/TLS handshake to estimate the user-agent of the client in https communication. In order to better analyze network traffic, flow-based traffic identification technology is slowly entering researchers' field of vision. They use statistical analysis and machine learning methods to analyze as much information as possible from the flow. Masud [7] proposed a multiple log-file based temporal correlation technique to detect Command and Control traffic for identifying a botnet.

The rest of this paper is organized as followed: Sect. 2 will further introduce the classification of traffic identification and the challenges it faced. Section 3 is to analyze the related work about user-related and application-related traffic identification technologies. Section 4 looks forward to the future research prospects of traffic identification. Finally, the content of this article is summarized in Sect. 5.

2   Typical Traffic Identification Technology

This chapter will further elaborate on the classification of traffic identification technologies and introduce the difficulties of them.

2.1   Packet-Level Identification

The most primitive traffic identification technology is packet-level identification. Packet is a unit of data in a TCP/IP protocol communication transmission which consists of a header and a body. Typical examples include port-based methods and payload-based methods.

Port information is generally included in the packet header. Based on the ports registered on the IANA, traffic can be initially identified. For example, port 443 indicates a https packet. However, with the change of technology, some application services violate the IANA regulations and use self-defined protocols like some P2P applications use well-known port numbers, such as port 80, to disguise themselves as function ports. This reduces the accuracy of the port-based method. Nowadays, we generally no longer utilize the port-based method, but only use it as an auxiliary means for traffic identification. Ibrahim [8] represents signature statistical port classifier (SSPC) which combines port-based, payload-based and statistical methods to extract signature for identifying the www application traffic.

Unlike port-base method which only detects port numbers, payload-base method utilize deep packet inspection (DPI) technology. In addition to the transport layer, DPI adds application layer analysis to identify various applications and their content by maintaining existing rulesets that detect and match the payload of the packet. Bolzoni [9] proposed Payl Over Som for Intrusion DetectiON (POSEIDON) is a payload-base method that uses a self-organizing map (SOM) to classify payload data. However, considering the computational complexity brought by big data, the problem of data encryption brought by SSL/TLS, and the content identification problem brought by private protocols, the payload-base method has great limitations in its use. Researchers have also made many attempts in these areas. Under the premise of not reducing network throughput, Bloom filters are used by Clarke N to propose a hardware-based technology for detecting feature strings in the data stream [10]. Conti [11] proposed BlindBox, which implements DPI for encrypted traffic through the new protocol and the new encryption scheme, although it takes longer than using only SSL/TLS.

2.2   Flow-Level Identification

Since packet-based traffic identification technology does not perform well in the face of big data, encrypted data, and private protocols, most traffic identification technologies are now flow-based methods. Flow-based traffic identification technology is built on the concept of IP flows. A flow is the summary of a group of IP packets that share a set of common properties (e.g., source and destination IP addresses and port numbers) passing a network observation point during a certain timeframe [12]. Usually, a flow contains a five tuple (source ip, destination ip, source port, destination port, protocol type).

Flow-based traffic identification techniques typically use statistical methods and machine learning methods. The statistical method generally analyzes the characteristics of the flow through the number of packets, the flow rate, the flow interval and so on to achieve the purpose of identification. Liu [13] uses flow-based statistical network traffic classification to identify Thunder flow with high precision through feature extraction. Here, Thunder is a popular download software in China.

Machine learning methods are divided into supervised learning and unsupervised learning [14, 21, 22]. Supervised learning trains models based on pre-collected traffic data. Meidan [14] trained a multi-stage meta classifier to differentiate the traffic generated by IoT and non-IoT devices. Unsupervised learning uses clustering to achieve the purpose of identification. Zander [15] automatically classifies traffic according to statistical traffic characteristics for traffic classification and application identification. Although the accuracy of supervised learning is higher, its dependence on the training set is severe, which leads to high standards and requirements for the pre-collected traffic data. Moreover, it is impossible for supervised learning to identify the traffic of the application or user without the training data sets. Unsupervised learning has a natural advantage in identifying unknown traffic due to clustering. Relatively, its recognition accuracy is lower than that of supervised learning.

2.3   Challenges

Large-Scale Real-Time Data. With the implementation of 4G or even 5G technology, the network transmission rate is getting faster and faster so that the network throughput is gradually increasing which leads to the burst of the Internet real-time data. In such a scenario, how to analyze and manage network traffic in real time without affecting network throughput is one of the urgent problems to be solved in current research. This requires researchers to propose novel methods for identifying with low computational complexity and high availability.

Lack of Trusted Dataset. Currently, there are no publicly available trusted data sets for researchers to use in traffic analysis. Most of the researchers' experiment data comes from their own collection which resulted in incomplete data coverage for testing. As far as I'm concerned, a trusted data set, in addition to sufficient data, also has the following features. They should cover different phone models and different application versions due to their different performance on traffic. Covering different age groups also plays an important role because the usage habits of different age groups are quite different. Last but not least, covering different usage scenarios considering that everyone's usage habits in different scenarios may also different. Unfortunately, most of the current research data sets are unable to meet these standards. Therefore, a trusted public dataset is very necessary.

Encrypt Data. With the popularity of cybersecurity awareness, people are paying more and more attention to their privacy on the Internet. Most traffic on the network today uses encryption algorithms or private protocols so that traffic content becomes incomprehensible to eavesdroppers. Under such circumstances, how to analyze encrypted traffic without affecting user privacy through effective methods has become a problem that must be faced in research. Most of the existing methods are based on statistical methods and machine learning, and there is still much room for development.

The Impact of Third-Party Services. Due to the widespread use of content distribution networks (CDNs) and third-party advertising services, many application services directly call third-party interfaces to obtain advertisements or data content (such as images), resulting in many applications containing the same or similar traffic. Here the same or similar refers to the same ip address or ip address range for different applications. This creates a lot of interference with the identification of the application. Regrettably, research progress in this area has been slow.

User Identification. When the dynamic host configuration protocol (DHCP) is used in the LAN, the IP address assigned to each host changes dynamically which means the same IP may represent multiple users. At the same time, mobile users are also assigned multiple ips due to nature of mobile devices. Coupled with the large coverage of wifi today, it is no longer possible to locate a user by ip address. How to identify users in traffic in such a scenario is a problem.

3 Survey on Traffic Identification

Existing traffic identification can be roughly divided into two categories according to the purpose. One is user-related which dedicated to discovering the connection between traffic and users, identifying specific users or user behaviors, the identifying subject is a user [7, 16, 24]. The other is application-related focuses on the application information contained in the traffic, and the identification subject is the application [17–20]. This article will explain the current research situation from these two aspects.

3.1 User-Related Identification

With the development of social economy and the improvement of the level, the Internet is becoming more and more popular. The continuous development of mobile communication technology, while improving the comfort of people's network use, also subtly makes people's lives and network closely related. The gradual expansion of Wifi coverage, the introduction and use of IPv6, and so on, all of which may lead to the hiding of multiple users behind a single IP. At the same time, cyberattacks emerge in an endless stream. Attacks such as botnets allow attackers to hide themselves. Targeting users by IP only becomes impossible in the current network environment. Therefore, how to identify the users hidden behind this by traffic has its broad meaning and far-reaching influence.

Masud [7] assumes that the robot responds much faster than humans. This property can be detected by associating two log files, tcpdump and exedump, to detect the activity of the bot in the host where tcpdump is all network packets and exedump includes the start time of the application execution in the host. The experiment used five machine learning models to train and identify the data, all achieving high accuracy. Since the botmaster will automatically send all possible commands to the bot during the experiment, we have no way of knowing if the botmaster's transmission frequency is in line with the real application scenario and further research is needed.

Clarke [16] uses the meta-data of the traffic instead of the payload to identify the user. On the one hand, such analysis does not involve sensitive data related to user privacy in the traffic payload. On the one hand, the analysis of meta-data only greatly reduces the amount of data (probably saving 96.1% of the source data) which improves the efficiency of analysis and provides a new solution for real-time analysis. In this paper, a variety of training algorithms, number of neurons and number of inter nodes are chosen to compare different experimental effects and obtain optimal values. From the experimental results, the average recognition rate of users reached 87% by analyzing seven popular application services. However, it can be seen that the more the population using the application service, the lower the recognition rate. Consider a situation where the author's application is not only for these more popular applications, but also for some special applications like BaybyStory, an application for capturing lasting memories of your little one, is the recognition rate higher? Of course, this brings another problem. When using supervised learning, we can't collect all the app data and train the model according to it. Perhaps unsupervised learning is a possible solution, and the author also mentions this in their future work.

3.2   Application-Related Identification

Existing application-related identification methods are mostly based on feature extraction and supervised learning in machine learning [19, 20]. Yoon et al. signs the application by extracting the application behavior feature in [17]. Based on it, they use the sequence pattern algorithm for optimization in [18]. Jaiswal [20] and Conti [19] uses supervised learning to identify the application and application behavior. Their accuracy is shown in Table 1.

Table 1.   Accuracy of application-related identification.

Author	Method	Average precision	Average recall
Yoon et al. [17]	Behavior based signature using Candidate-Selection algorithm	1.0 in flow units	0.18 in flow units
		1.0 in byte units	0.57 in byte units
Shim et al. [18]	Behavior based signature using sequence pattern algorithm	1.0 in flow units	0.84 in flow units
		1.0 in byte units	0.68 in byte units
Conti et al. [19]	Supervised learning	0.93	0.92

Yoon et al. [17, 18] signs the business behavior patterns appearing in the first few request packets of multiple service flows when the application performs a specific function, and extracts behavior characteristics in their previous work. Since it uses the Candidate-Selection algorithm, the calculation is large, and the calculation result is more affected by the input flow. Therefore, the author used the sequence pattern algorithm to optimize performance and used seven popular apps covering all categories for experimental verification. The sequence pattern algorithm is a data mining technique that detects time series patterns from a database of values or sequences of events. By extracting a pattern with a specific order from different transactions, the author first extracts the sequence set, followed by extracting the sequence pattern from it. Finally, they identify the application according to the matching result of the sequence pattern and the traffic. The 7 application precisions used are up to 100%, and the memory consumption and execution speed are much better than the previous Candidate-Selection algorithm. However, the recall value of some applications is lower, such as Skype's recall value reached 53.49%. The guess is that during data preprocessing, neither the Candidate-Selection nor the Sequence-Pattern algorithm eliminated third-party traffic, such as advertising traffic and CDN servers (i.e. amazon), causing the impact of irrelevant traffic on the experimental results.

Jaiswal and Lokhande [20] use six machine learning algorithms, 10 statistical features and 25558 samples to train traffic classification models. The results show that AdaboostM1 is the fastest algorithm, but the tree-based algorithm (C4.5 and random forest) is the most efficient algorithm considering the maximum accuracy of random forests is as high as 99.7616%, and the accuracy of C4.5 classifier reaches 98.46%.

In addition to application identification, some researchers focus on the behavioral details of a single application. Conti [19] investigates the feasibility of identifying users' specific behavior on a mobile phone application by eavesdropping on encrypted network traffic. Similarly, the author uses supervised learning methods to classify user behaviors and conduct experimental analysis on three applications: Facebook, Gmail, and Twitter. The precision and recall of the three have reached more than 0.83. However, it still has all the common problems of supervised learning algorithms that it can only recognize the behaviors of the previous custom, but not the behaviors outside the definition. This has higher requirements for the researchers' ability to choose the train datasets.

Zhang et al. [23] explore how to identify application traffic when unknown applications exist. Their paper first uses a binary classification to extract sufficient negative training set. Then application signatures with flow correlation (ASFC) was proposed for training. ASFC uses a negative training set which presents unlabeled application and a positive training set from known application to train a binary classification as an application signature. Here, the subject of recognition is not a single flow, but correlated flows sharing the same 3-tuple {source ip, destination ip, Transport protocol}, which are modelled by "bag of flows" (BoF). The results show that this method performs better than other traffic identification methods when having unknown application flows.

4 Future Prospects

In the foreseeable future, due to the continuous development of Internet application requirements and models, we believe that traffic identification technology will develop in the following direction.

Automate the Generation of Datasets. Due to the lack of open and credible data sets, most researchers choose to collect data as needed, which results in a lot of tedious and repetitive work. Especially in application recognition, different applications perform differently on different versions of different devices, but researchers usually experiment in specific device and application version because of it. Therefore, it is necessary to develop an automated dataset collector/generator, which is the cornerstone of subsequent analysis.

Real-Time Identification. With the increase of network users and transmission rate, the network real-time traffic scale continues to increase. How to effectively identify and monitor real-time traffic has become one of the difficulties in research. It is a very effective method to reduce the amount of data analyzed while ensuring the recognition effect like Shim [18] only use the metadata in packets which reduce the size of data needed to be analyze. It takes only about 1 s to process the log provided by 30 hosts, provides real-time recognition. However, when the number of hosts increases, the efficiency of real-time recognition may be affected.

Remove the Impact of Third-Party Services. For a long time, most of the research has been devoted to the function of classification, that is, to find the difference between the traffic, which leads to deviations in the recognition results causing by the common services between some applications, such as the traffic of third-party advertising service providers and CDN service providers (i.e. amazon). Thinking in the opposite direction, if we start focusing on the commonality between traffic, can you eliminate the impact of third-party services? This is a subject to the experimental demonstration of the researchers.

User Identification. As mentioned above, identifying specific users from traffic has its practical significance. For example, to capture cybercriminals. However, due to the use of DHCP, the high coverage of wifi and the nature of mobile phones, we have been unable to locate a user simply by ip address because ip is dynamically allocated. New ways to identity user are urgently needed.

The Characteristics of the Flow. The commonality between flows can help us filter out invalid data, such as advertising traffic, and the characteristics between flows can help us better identify the data. For example, from some unique application traffic, users can be better understood. A user who uses the Baby Story application is likely to be a pregnant woman, which helps to distinguish her from other users. In addition, different user has different habits, which can also be reflected in the traffic, and helps us better identify users.

5   Conclusion

In this paper, we summarize the basic classification of traffic analysis methods and the challenges it faced. At the same time, the survey of user-related and application-related traffic identification research is briefly described and analyzed from the purpose of traffic analysis. Finally, we prospect the future research directions or research priorities of traffic identification technologies.

Acknowledgement. This work was supported by National Key Research & Development Plan of China under Grant 2016QY05X1000, National Natural Science Foundation of China under Grant No. 61771166, CERNET Innovation Project under Grant No. NGII20170101, and Dongguan Innovative Research Team Program under Grant No. 201636000100038.

References

1. FBI: 2017 Internet Crime Report. https://pdf.ic3.gov/2017_IC3Report.pdf. Accessed 10 Nov 2018
2. Internet Live Stats. http://www.internetlivestats.com/internet-users. Accessed 10 Nov 2018

3. Claffy, K.C., Braun, H.W., Polyzos, G.C.: A parameterizable methodology for Internet traffic flow profiling. IEEE J. Sel. Areas Commun. **13**(8), 1481–1494 (1995)
4. IANA Port Number List. https://www.iana.org/assignments/service-names-port-numbers/ service-names-port-numbers.xml. Accessed 10 Nov 2018
5. Husák, M., Čermák, M., Jirsík, T., et al.: HTTPS traffic analysis and client identification using passive SSL/TLS fingerprinting. EURASIP J. Inf. Secur. **2016**(1), 6 (2016)
6. Celeda, P.: Network-based HTTPS client identification using SSL/TLS fingerprinting. In: International Conference on Availability, Reliability and Security, pp. 389–396. IEEE Computer Society (2015)
7. Masud, M.M., Al-Khateeb, T., Khan, L., et al.: Flow-based identification of botnet traffic by mining multiple log files. In: International Conference on Distributed Framework and Applications, pp. 200–206. IEEE (2009)
8. Ibrahim, H.A.H., Nor, S.M., Jamil, H.A.: Online hybrid internet traffic classification algorithm based on signature statistical and port methods to identify internet applications. In: IEEE International Conference on Control System, Computing and Engineering, pp. 185–190. IEEE (2014)
9. Bolzoni, D., Etalle, S., Hartel, P., et al.: POSEIDON: a 2-tier anomaly-based network intrusion detection system. In: IEEE International Workshop on Information Assurance, 10 pp.-156
10. Dharmapurikar, S., Krishnamurthy, P., Sproull, T.S., et al.: Deep packet inspection using parallel bloom filters. IEEE Micro **24**(1), 52–61 (2004)
11. Sherry, J., Lan, C., Popa, R.A., et al.: BlindBox: deep packet inspection over encrypted traffic. ACM SIGCOMM Comput. Commun. Rev. **45**(5), 213–226 (2015)
12. Ise I.: Specification of the IP flow information export (IPFIX) protocol for the exchange of IP traffic flow information RFC 5101 (2008)
13. Liu, J., Liu, F., He, D.: The identification for P2P thunder traffic based on deep flow identification. In: International Conference on Cloud Computing and Intelligent Systems, pp. 504–507. IEEE (2013)
14. Meidan, Y., Bohadana, M., Shabtai, A., et al.: ProfilIoT: a machine learning approach for IoT device identification based on network traffic analysis. In: Symposium on Applied Computing, pp. 506–509. ACM (2017)
15. Zander, S., Nguyen, T., et al.: Automated traffic classification and application identification using machine learning. In: IEEE Conference on Local Computer Networks, Anniversary, pp. 250–257. IEEE (2005)
16. Clarke, N., Li, F., Furnell, S.: A novel privacy preserving user identification approach for network traffic. Comput. Secur. **70**, 335–350 (2017)
17. Yoon, S.H., Park, J.S., Kim, M.S., et al.: Behavior signature for big data traffic identification. In: International Conference on Big Data and Smart Computing, pp. 261–266. IEEE (2014)
18. Shim, K.S., Yoon, S.H., Sija, B.D., et al.: Effective behavior signature extraction method using sequence pattern algorithm for traffic identification. Int. J. Netw. Manag. **28**(5), e2011 (2017)
19. Conti, M., Mancini, L.V., Spolaor, R., et al.: Can't you hear me knocking: identification of user actions on android apps via traffic analysis. In: ACM Conference on Data and Application Security and Privacy, pp. 297–304. ACM (2015)
20. Jaiswal, R.C., Lokhande, S.D.: Machine learning based internet traffic recognition with statistical approach (2013)
21. Zander, S., Nguyen, T.T.T., Armitage, G.J.: Automated traffic classification and application identification using machine learning. In: IEEE Conference on Local Computer Networks. IEEE (2005)

22. Crotti, M., Dusi, M., Gringoli, F., et al.: Traffic classification through simple statistical fingerprinting. ACM SIGCOMM Comput. Commun. Rev. **37**(1), 5 (2007)
23. Zhang, J., Chen, C., Xiang, Y., et al.: Robust network traffic identification with unknown applications. In: ACM SIGSAC Symposium on Information. ACM (2013)
24. Gu, X., Yang, M., Fei, J., et al.: A novel behavior-based tracking attack for user identification. In: Third International Conference on Advanced Cloud & Big Data. IEEE (2016)
25. Shi, J., Zhang, Z., Li, Y., Wang, R., Shi, H., Li, X.: New method for computer identification through electromagnetic radiation. CMC: Comput. Mater. Continua **57**(1), 69–80 (2018)
26. Liu, Y., Peng, H., Wang, J.: Verifiable diversity ranking search over encrypted outsourced data. CMC: Comput. Mater. Continua **55**(1), 037–057 (2018)

A Survey of Network Security Situational Awareness Technology

Chen Chen[1(✉)], Lin Ye[1], Xiangzhan Yu[1,2], and Bailang Ding[2]

[1] School of Computer Science and Technology, Harbin Institute of Technology,
Harbin, China
chenchenhit@foxmail.com, {hityelin,yxz}@hit.edu.cn
[2] Institute of Electronic and Information Engineering of UESTC in Guangdong,
Dongguan, China
154024012@qq.com

Abstract. With the increasing importance of cyberspace security, the research and application of network situational awareness is getting more attention. The research on network security situational awareness is of great significance for improving the network monitoring ability, emergency response capability and predicting the development trend of network security. This paper describes the development and evolution of network situational awareness and analyzes the basic architecture of the current situational awareness system. Based on the situational awareness conceptual model, four main research contents of situational awareness are elaborated: network data collection, situational understanding, situational prediction and situational visualization. This paper focuses on the core issues, main algorithms, and the advantages and disadvantages of each method that need to be addressed at each research point. Finally, under the current development trend of big data processing technology and artificial intelligence technology, the application realization and development trend of network situational awareness are analyzed and forecasted.

Keywords: Situational awareness · Network security ·
Situational visualization

1 Introduction

In recent years, with the development of Internet technology, the attack methods have become more diversified, and the number of security vulnerabilities and security incidents has increased significantly. The research direction of network security has changed, from the research of single security issues to the overall situation of global networks. Network situational awareness is considered to be a new way to solve some current network security problems. It combines the detection of security events by all network sensors to provide real-time visibility into network security conditions and risks. It has become a hot research field at the forefront of the world.

There are two popular definitions of situational awareness. One was the concept of Situation awareness (SA) first proposed by Endsley in 1988 [1]. He defined the cognitive definition from artificial intelligence: situational awareness is the recognition of a

© Springer Nature Switzerland AG 2019
X. Sun et al. (Eds.): ICAIS 2019, LNCS 11635, pp. 101–109, 2019.
https://doi.org/10.1007/978-3-030-24268-8_10

large number of environmental elements in time and space, understanding their meanings, and predicting their status in the near future. Endsley's point of view is mainly on cognitive principles, mainly a top-down driven mental model, divided into three main parts: perception, understanding and projection. Another concept stems from the definition of the Joint Directors of Laboratories (JDL) data fusion model, which provides a more bottom-up, data-centric approach that defines situational awareness as an estimate and prediction of relationships between entities.

Although the network situation is used in different fields, the research on situational awareness in this paper is all about network security. After Endsley's groundbreaking work, research in this area has continued to deepen worldwide. In 1999, Bass believed [2] that in order to create network situational awareness, next-generation cyberspace intrusion detection systems would incorporate data from heterogeneous distributed network sensors. Since then, intrusion detection systems have been combined with situational awareness. And based on the JDL model of data fusion, he proposed a network situational awareness function model based on multi-sensor data fusion. The data fusion model has become a representative study at this stage. In 2000, McGuinness and Foy et al. [3] extended the fourth layer of the situational awareness model called Resolution. Resolution represents the countermeasures needed to deal with the interdependent risks in the network. In 2006, Tadda et al. [4] re-integrated a three-level model consisting of factor extraction, state perception and situational prediction, and proposed evaluation indicators and methods for situational awareness systems.

Therefore, this paper synthesizes the current research on the network security situation in the industry, and gives the following definition: Network security situational awareness refers to the analysis and visualization of various security elements in large-scale networks, and predicts the development trend, and finally assists the follow-up Decision making. The network security situational awareness system analyzes and predicts the current state and development trend of the network by collecting security data such as network traffic, security logs, security alarms, and threat intelligence, and using data analysis and machine learning techniques.

2   Network Security Situational Awareness

According to the different functions of the network situational awareness system, this paper summarizes the research content into four aspects:

- Network element collection
- Situational understanding
- Situation prediction
- Situation visualization.

The related technologies and research contents will be elaborated in four aspects.

2.1   Network Element Collection

Accurate and comprehensive extraction of security situation elements in the network is the basis of network security situational awareness research. Since the network has developed into a large nonlinear complex system with strong flexibility, it is very difficult to extract the network security situation elements. At present, the security posture elements of the network mainly include static configuration information, dynamic operation information, and network traffic information.

Franke et al. [5] believe that data acquired in network sensors (such as intrusion detection systems) can go directly into the data fusion process or be interpreted by decision makers. But it needs to be combined with other information, such as adding human understanding of security incidents. This combination helps improve overall network situational awareness. In addition, Jajodia et al. [6] assessed the vulnerability of the network by collecting vulnerability information from the network. Wang et al. [7] proposed an anti-attack concept by constructing an attack graph as a measure of security for different network configurations to give an indication of the current operation of the network.

On the other hand, data processing frameworks for large amounts of data are constantly evolving. Hadoop, based on MapReduce [8] technology, makes it possible to process terabytes of data. Spark [9], which focuses on memory computing, combines components such as streaming, machine learning, and graph computing to build a data calculation framework that provides a highly efficient and highly available data processing platform. In addition, the development of components such as Flink and Strom solves many of the difficulties in real-time processing, and people can better extract value from large amounts of data. At the same time, various data fusion algorithms can also be implemented in the big data framework. Security for large amounts of traffic is also evolving [27, 28].

Based on the current research situation, most methods only obtain data from a single aspect, cannot comprehensively consider information, and cannot dig into the internal relationship between data, which poses difficulties for later analysis. However, with the development of data mining technology, rapid processing of massive data becomes possible. Therefore, big data acquisition with intrinsic relevance is a trend of development in the future.

2.2 Situational Understanding

The understanding of network security situation refers to the integration of relevant data to obtain a macro network security situation. Data fusion is at the heart of the understanding of network security posture. According to Haines et al. [11]: Previous results have shown that no single control (such as IDS) can detect all network attacks. The network security situation assessment no longer studies a single event, but studies the overall security status of the network from a macro perspective. At present, data fusion algorithms are divided into the following categories: analytic hierarchy process, logical reasoning, probability analysis, and rule pattern matching.

Analytic Hierarchy Process. Bass first proposed a data fusion method for situational awareness [3]: Using the art and science of multi-sensor data fusion as a design framework, it can identify, track, classify and evaluate network-centric activities in complex infrastructure. The specific implementation method is to layer the data alarms according to the threat level from low to high, and the data at the same level is merged.

The analytic hierarchy process is to comprehensively consider various situational factors affecting the situation and establish several evaluation functions. The most representative rating function is the weighted average. The weighted average method is the most common and simple method of fusion based on mathematical models. Chen et al. [10] proposed a hierarchical cybersecurity threat situation quantitative assessment method. The implementation method is to weight the importance factor of the service and the host itself, calculate the threat index of the computing service, the host, and the entire network system, and then analyze the security posture of the network.

The analytic hierarchy process and the weighted averaging method can intuitively integrate various situational factors, and the implementation process is relatively simple. However, the main problem of this method is: There is no uniform standard for the choice of weights and the basis for stratification, most of which are based on domain knowledge or experience, and lack of objective basis.

Logical Reasoning. Logical reasoning mines the inherent logic between information and integrates information. The logical relationship between alarms is divided into: the similarity of alarm attributes, the relevance in the attack model, the correlation between the premise of the attack and the subsequent conditions. Ning et al. [11] analyzed the threatening situation of the network from the mass alarm information through alarm correlation. Morin et al. [12] used a representation language to normalize each network node based on a topology map of the network nodes, representing each event in a structured manner. This model provides the correlation logic between alerts to describe security events.

A typical algorithm for logical reasoning is fuzzy logic. Fuzzy logic is a mathematical method for people to reason about uncertain things, using fuzzy sets and fuzzy rules. In the network situation assessment, firstly, the single source data is locally evaluated, then the corresponding model parameters are selected, and the membership function is established for the local evaluation result, which is divided into corresponding fuzzy sets to realize the fuzzification of specific values, and the results are carried out. Quantify. After quantification, if a state attribute value exceeds a predetermined threshold, the local evaluation result is used as input for causal reasoning. Finally, the situational classification is identified by fuzzy rule reasoning, thus completing the assessment of the current situation.

The biggest advantage of logical reasoning is that it is easy to understand, and it can reflect the network security situation very intuitively. However, the limitation of this method is that it requires a detailed analysis of the type of attack, and this analysis is very difficult. And some unknown alarms can't make some judgments.

Probabilistic Analysis. The probability and statistics method makes full use of the statistical characteristics of prior knowledge and combines the uncertainty of information to establish a model of situation assessment. Bayesian networks and hidden Markov models are the most common methods of probability and statistics.

Bayesian network was defined by Pearl [1] in 1988 and became a research hotspot in the field of knowledge representation and reasoning for more than 20 years. In the network situation assessment, the Bayesian network uses a directed acyclic graph representation, nodes represent different situations and events, each node contains a conditional probability allocation table, and nodes use edges to connect, indicating the situation and events. Interdependence, after some nodes obtain evidence information, the Bayesian network spreads and fuses the information between nodes to obtain new situation information. Chen et al. [15] proposed a new method using Bayesian inference tools. The specific implementation is to use the layered model to re-define the decision fusion problem, and propose a Gibbs sampler to perform the fusion based on the posterior probability. Park et al. [16] added time factors to the original network. They propose a multi-instance Bayesian network that can be analyzed over time and incorporate high-level languages to handle complex situations and uncertainties.

The hidden Markov model is equivalent to a dynamic Bayesian network. Damarla et al. [17] proposed a situational awareness framework based on hidden Markov models. HMM is equivalent to a dynamic Bayesian network. In the network situation assessment, the transfer process of the network security state is defined as the implicit state, and the security events at different time points are defined as the sequence of observation values, and the HMM model is trained using the sequence of observation values and the implicit state. Finally, the model is used to evaluate the situation.

Probabilistic analysis based methods can fuse all data and prior knowledge, and the reasoning process is clear and easy to understand. However, this model requires a large amount of data and takes a long time in the training process. This method has some difficulties in feature extraction and model construction.

Rule Pattern Matching. The rule pattern method is to build an evaluation model based on expert knowledge and experience, and analyze the security posture of the entire network through pattern matching. At present, the D-S evidence combination method and the gray correlation algorithm are the research hotspots.

The D-S evidence fusion method was first proposed by DEMPSTER [18] and then refined by SHAFER [19]. The D-S evidence fusion method is a measure of the support for each possible decision of the single source data, that is, the degree of support for the decision using the data information as evidence. Then look for a synthetic rule of evidence. By repeatedly applying the synthesis rules, the algorithm finally achieves the degree of support for a certain decision and completes the process of data fusion. Sabata et al. [20] proposed a multi-source evidence fusion method to complete the fusion of distributed real-time attack events and realize the perception of network situation. Zhang et al. [21] improved the D-S theory by introducing Bhattacharyya distance, evidence confidence and modified combination rules, and effectively solved the conflict of evidence in DS evidence theory. The grey system theory was first proposed by Deng [22] and is a theoretical method for dealing with uncertain information. The basic idea of gray correlation analysis is to judge whether the connection is tight according to the similarity of the geometry of the sequence curve. The closer the curve is, the greater the degree of association between the corresponding sequences, and vice versa. Hu et al. [23] proposed an improved adaptive grayscale model to analyze the situation that the network security situation is "S" curve.

Algorithms based on rule patterns generally need to mine the intrinsic patterns between data, which can be adapted to uncertain situations without prior information. However, this method may have problems with the explosion of the number of associated patterns and the conflict of evidence, so it will have a great impact on the results.

2.3 Situation Prediction

The prediction of the network security situation refers to predicting the development trend of the network in the future according to the historical information and current state of the network security situation. Due to the randomness and uncertainty of cyber-attacks, predicting the change of security situation is a complex nonlinear process, thus limiting the use of traditional prediction models. At present, network security situation prediction generally adopts methods such as neural network and time series prediction.

Neural network is a commonly used network situation prediction method. The algorithm uses multiple associated neurons as the structure of the model, linking the inputs to the output. The algorithm adjusts the parameters by means of gradient descent and other methods to construct a prediction model. Ying et al. [24] improved the BP neural network by using wavelet neural network (WNN) to predict the network situation. The neural network model has many parameters, strong adaptability, and good nonlinearity fitting, so it has strong robustness. However, since the effect of the model depends on the quality of the feature engineering, and the model requires a large amount of computational power for training, it cannot be used in some environments.

Time series prediction method reveals the law of network situation change with time through time series, and predicts the future situation according to this law. The prediction process uses the top N values of the sequence to predict the next M values. Commonly used for time series are HMM algorithm, autoregressive moving average method and so on.

The current situation prediction method mainly uses machine learning, which has good convergence and fault tolerance, and can handle large-scale data. However, in the real network environment, there is often a mutual game between the attacker and the defender. Therefore, the hybrid model based on game theory is the future development direction.

2.4 Situation Visualization

Visualization is an important part of situational awareness. The data collected from various network sensors is abstract and fragmentary, and people cannot understand the analysis very quickly. Therefore, we need to perform aggregate analysis on multi-source data to extract high-level situational results and display them using some visualization techniques. Many visualization systems are data driven. Host and server monitoring is one of the manifestations for a single data source. Users can get information about system load, network link status, abnormal traffic, and so on. These are all visual methods for basic information. When multiple servers are interconnected to form a large-scale cluster, it is necessary to display the host connection diagram, monitor the traffic status between the hosts, and monitor the traffic between the internal cluster and the external network. However, these methods simply count the basic data, and the invisible threat situation and attack mode cannot form an intuitive display.

Current research focuses on hierarchical visualization, attack visualization, and interactive visualization. Chen et al. [10] conducted hierarchical analysis of multiple data sources and presented them according to different categories. Beaver et al. [25] visualize the attack by screening the information generated by the IDS and collecting the results of multi-source cleaning. Phan et al. [26] proposed a time-centric visualization system that classifies events by interacting with humans and iteratively produces visual charts.

With the advancement of computer graphics and visual technology, many modeling methods continue to evolve. Visualization methods are fully applied at every stage of network situational awareness. Future interactive situational visualization technology will become a trend.

3 Outlook

Through the narrative of the four aspects of the network situational awareness field, we discuss the advantages and disadvantages of various algorithms. At present, the research on network situational awareness is still in the development stage, so many problems need to be further solved. This paper believes that there are several aspects to the future research direction.

Fusion of Massive Data. At present, the data sources on which situational awareness depends are increasing, making the integration method more and more difficult. At the same time, the network situation understanding requires high-quality data alarm as a data source. Due to the detection level of IDS and various firewall systems, the alarm quality is not very high. How to extract high-quality data sources and carry out efficient and rapid integration is the future development trend. At present, deep learning has received extensive attention, and its performance and accuracy have reached a very good level. Therefore, data fusion technology based on deep learning will develop rapidly.

Situational Understanding of Incomplete Warning. The robustness of the network situational awareness system will be tested when there is an error, omission, or new type of alarm in the device that generated the data. Therefore, how to face the unknown missing data is also a problem that needs to be solved. At present, some methods based on logical reasoning, probability and so on require prior knowledge, which requires experts to analyze the entire network and summarize the relevant laws. Methods that do not require prior knowledge are often severely affected by data quality issues, and therefore require more efficient algorithms.

Visualization of Situation. Situational visualization is the most intuitive way to understand the situation, and the results of data fusion and situational understanding need to be represented using appropriate representations. At present, many papers tend to study the content of fusion and prediction, ignoring the importance of visualization in situational awareness. Therefore, with the development of visualization technology, situational awareness will become more direct and concise.

Situation Prediction in a Complex Environment. The randomness and uncertainty of network attacks determine that the change of security situation is a complex non-linear process. At present, the methods of situation prediction are mainly probabilistic models and machine learning models, which have good effects on regular time series. But it does not reflect the complex trend changes very well. Therefore, the mathematical model based on causality needs further research.

4   Conclusion

As the scale of the Internet continues to expand, the number of cyber threats continues to increase. How to comprehensively and accurately detect network situation is a problem that needs to be solved. This paper introduces the definition and development status of current network situational awareness, and describes four aspects of situational awareness: network security situation factor collection, situation understanding, situation prediction and situation visualization. The current algorithms and related advantages and disadvantages of these four aspects are analyzed. With the development of deep learning and big data technology, people have made significant progress in dealing with multi-source data, and there are still some problems to be solved. Finally, this paper gives the problems that the situational awareness needs to solve in the future and the direction of development. I hope that through the development of related algorithms, it will bring more benefits to human beings.

Acknowledgement. This work was supported by National Key Research & Development Plan of China under Grant 2016QY05X1000, National Natural Science Foundation of China under Grant No. 61872111, and Dongguan Innovative Research Team Program under Grant No. 201636000100038.

References

1. Endsley, M.R.: Design and evaluation for situation awareness enhancement. In: Proceedings of the Human Factors Society Annual Meeting, vol. 32, no. 2, pp. 97–101. SAGE Publications, Los Angeles (1988)
2. Bass, T.: Multisensor data fusion for next generation distributed intrusion detection systems (1999)
3. McGuinness, B., Foy, L.: A subjective measure of SA: the crew awareness rating scale (CARS). In: Proceedings of the First Human Performance, Situation Awareness, and Automation Conference, Savannah, Georgia, vol. 16 (2000)
4. Tadda, G., Salerno, J.J., Boulware, D., et al.: Realizing situation awareness within a cyber environment. In: Multisensor, Multisource Information Fusion: Architectures, Algorithms, and Applications 2006, vol. 6242, p. 624204. International Society for Optics and Photonics (2006)
5. Franke, U., Brynielsson, J.: Cyber situational awareness – a systematic review of the literature. Comput. Secur. **46**, 18–31 (2014)
6. Jajodia, S., Noel, S., O'Berry, B.: Topological analysis of network attack vulnerability. In: Kumar, V., Srivastava, J., Lazarevic, A. (eds.) Managing Cyber Threats, pp. 247–266. Springer, Boston (2005). https://doi.org/10.1007/0-387-24230-9_9
7. Wang, L., Singhal, A., Jajodia, S.: Measuring the overall security of network configurations using attack graphs. In: Barker, S., Ahn, G.-J. (eds.) DBSec 2007. LNCS, vol. 4602, pp. 98–112. Springer, Heidelberg (2007). https://doi.org/10.1007/978-3-540-73538-0_9
8. Bu, Y., Howe, B., Balazinska, M., et al.: HaLoop: efficient iterative data processing on large clusters. Proc. VLDB Endowment **3**(1–2), 285–296 (2010)
9. Zaharia, M., Xin, R.S., Wendell, P., et al.: Apache spark: a unified engine for big data processing. Commun. ACM **59**(11), 56–65 (2016)

10. Chen, X.Z., Zheng, Q.H., Guan, X.H., et al.: Quantitative hierarchical threat evaluation model for network security. J. Softw. **17**(4), 885–897 (2006)
11. Ning, P., Cui, Y., Reeves, D.S., et al.: Techniques and tools for analyzing intrusion alerts. ACM Trans. Inf. Syst. Secur. (TISSEC) **7**(2), 274–318 (2004)
12. Morin, B., Mé, L., Debar, H., et al.: A logic-based model to support alert correlation in intrusion detection. Inf. Fusion **10**(4), 285–299 (2009)
13. Pearl, J.: Probabilistic Reasoning in Intelligent Systems: Networks of Plausible Inference. Elsevier, Amsterdam (2014)
14. Mahoney, S.M., Laskey, K.B.: Constructing situation specific belief networks. In: Proceedings of the Fourteenth Conference on Uncertainty in Artificial Intelligence, pp. 370–378. Morgan Kaufmann Publishers Inc., (1998)
15. Chen, B., Varshney, P.K.: A Bayesian sampling approach to decision fusion using hierarchical models. IEEE Trans. Sig. Process. **50**(8), 1809–1818 (2002)
16. Park, C.Y., Laskey, K.B., Costa, P.C.G., et al.: Predictive situation awareness reference model using multi-entity bayesian networks. In: 2014 17th International Conference on Information Fusion (FUSION), pp. 1–8. IEEE (2014)
17. Damarla, T.: Hidden markov model as a framework for situational awareness. In: 2008 11th International Conference on Information Fusion, pp. 1–7. IEEE (2008)
18. Dempster, A.P.: Upper and lower probabilities induced by a multivalued mapping. In: Yager, R.R., Liu, L. (eds.) Classic Works of the Dempster-Shafer Theory of Belief Functions, vol. 219, pp. 57–72. Springer, Heidelberg (2008). https://doi.org/10.1007/978-3-540-44792-4_3
19. Shafer, G.: A Mathematical Theory of Evidence. Princeton University Press, Princeton (1976)
20. Sabata, B., Ornes, C.: Multisource evidence fusion for cyber-situation assessment. In: Multisensor, Multisource Information Fusion: Architectures, Algorithms, and Applications 2006, vol. 6242, p. 624201. International Society for Optics and Photonics (2006)
21. Zhang, W., Ji, X., Yang, Y., et al.: Data fusion method based on improved DS evidence theory. In: 2018 IEEE International Conference on Big Data and Smart Computing (BigComp), pp. 760–766. IEEE (2018)
22. Deng, J.L.: Properties of relational space for grey system. Grey Syst. (1988)
23. Hu, W., Li, J., Chen, X., et al.: Network security situation prediction based on improved adaptive grey Verhulst model. J. Shanghai Jiaotong Univ. (Sci.) **15**(4), 408–413 (2010)
24. Jibao, L., Huiqiang, W., Xiaowu, L., et al.: A quantitative prediction method of network security situation based on wavelet neural network. In: ISDPE, pp. 197–202. IEEE (2007)
25. Beaver, J.M., Steed, C.A., Patton, R.M., et al.: Visualization techniques for computer network defense. In: Sensors, and Command, Control, Communications, and Intelligence (C3I) Technologies for Homeland Security and Homeland Defense X, vol. 8019, p. 801906. International Society for Optics and Photonics (2011)
26. Phan, D., Gerth, J., Lee, M., Paepcke, A., Winograd, T.: Visual analysis of network flow data with timelines and event plots. In: Goodall, J.R., Conti, G., Ma, K.L. (eds.) VizSEC 2007, pp. 85–99. Springer, Heidelberg (2008)
27. Cheng, J., Ruomeng, X., Tang, X., Sheng, V.S., Cai, C.: An Abnormal Network Flow Feature Sequence Prediction Approach for DDoS Attacks Detection in Big Data Environment, CMC: Computers. Materials & Continua **55**(1), 095–119 (2018)
28. Xiaonian, W., Zhang, C., Zhang, R., Wang, Y., Cui, J.: A distributed intrusion detection model via nondestructive partitioning and balanced allocation for big data, CMC: computers. Mater. Continua **56**(1), 61–72 (2018)

Multi-function Quantum Cryptography Protocol Based on Bell State

Zheng Tao[1] (ID), Xiang Gao[1], Shibin Zhang[1(✉)], Yan Chang[1],
and Jinyue Xia[2]

[1] Chengdu University of Information Technology,
Chengdu 610225, Sichuan, China
cuitzsb@cuit.edu.cn
[2] International Business Machines Corporation (IBM), New York, USA

Abstract. Most of the current quantum cryptographic protocols can only perform a single function, and quantum resources are not fully utilized. In this paper, we propose a multi-function quantum cryptographic protocol based on the Bell state. This protocol can perform quantum private query (QPQ), quantum identity authentication (QIA), and quantum key distribution (QKD) functions. In the QPQ function part, this protocol can effectively improve database security and user privacy. In the QIA function part, this protocol can complete a two-way identity authentication function, which can effectively improve the reliability of identity authentication. In the QKD function part, this protocol can complete the key distribution function efficiently and reliably, and can maximize the utilization efficiency of quantum resources. With a rigorous security analysis, we proves that this protocol can defend against JM attacks, entanglement measurement attacks and external attacks.

Keywords: Bell state · Multi-function · Quantum private query ·
Quantum identity authentication · Quantum key distribution

1 Introduction

Cryptosystem is the backbone of information security. With the rapid development of quantum technology, especially the advent of quantum computation, the classical cryptosystem was unable to meet the security needs of informationization. Therefore, quantum cryptosystem which is based on quantum mechanics and aims to exchange information absolutely safe in theory has attracted more and more attention in the last thirty decades. In 1984, Bennett and Brassard proposed the first quantum key distribution protocol (QKD), as known as BB84 [1]. After that, a number of quantum private communication schemes has been proposed, including quantum key distribution (QKD) [2–5], quantum secure direct communication(QSDC) [6–11], quantum secret sharing(QSS) [12–16], quantum private comparison (QPC) [17, 18], quantum dialogue (QD) [19, 20], quantum private query (QPQ) [21–28], quantum identity authentication (QIA) [29–32] and many other achievements[33, 34].

Quantum key distribution (QKD) is one of the most successful applications of quantum information technology [2, 3]. It can provide unconditionally secure key

X. Sun et al. (Eds.): ICAIS 2019, LNCS 11635, pp. 110–119, 2019.
https://doi.org/10.1007/978-3-030-24268-8_11

distribution between two remote participants, Alice and Bob. The security of QKD is guaranteed by the fundamental laws of quantum mechanics. In order to make it more robust, Lo et al. proposed the measurement-device-independent QKD (MDI-QKD) protocol, which can remove all detector side-channel attacks that are the major security loopholes in QKD systems. These protocols rigorously prove the security of the key distribution process, but few people consider how to improve the efficiency of particle utilization in the QKD process, that is, how to use all particles for eavesdrop detection and quantum key distribution, minimizing Waste of particle resources in the QKD process.

In another area of application of quantum resources, symmetrically private information retrieval (SPIR) problem also has solutions in the quantum scenarios, like the quantum symmetrically private information retrieval (QSPIR), namely the quantum private queries (QPQ). Giovannetti et al. proposed a novel cheat-sensitive QPQ protocol (GLM-protocol) [26], where the database is represented by an oracle operation which is performed on the coming query states. Although most attempts have aimed at reducing the communication complexity of the protocols, it is shown that the reduction in communication and computational complexity is less valuable than achieving a practical protocol. Because of the use of the oracle operation, the above protocols are difficult to implement for large database and high-dimensional oracle operation. To solve this problem, Jakobi et al. for the first time proposed a novel and practical QPQ protocol (J-protocol) based on SARG04 [3] QKD protocol [27]. Using SARG04 QKD protocol, an asymmetric key can be distributed between Alice and Bob, which is used to encrypt the whole database. Alice only knows few bits of the key, which ensures the database privacy. J-protocol can be easily generalized to large database. In 2012, Gao et al. proposed a flexible QPQ scheme (G-protocol) [28] which shows better performance in flexibility, security and communication complexity. However, these papers do not solve the user privacy problem very well, and the process of the protocol is complicated.

Since Bennett and Brassard published the first QKD protocol [1], many quantum communication protocols, including quantum identity authentication (QIA) protocols, have been suggested in the research [32]. Although the QKDs provide unconditional security, they still require an authentication prior to the communication. In most of QIA protocols, quantum entangled states are used [30, 31]. The maintenance of entangled states is a major obstacle to realization. To compensate for this limit, some protocols use classical cryptography with QKD. For instance, DuŜek [29] suggested a quantum identification protocol where the BB84 QKD is used to share an identification sequence as common secret information. After Alice and Bob share these secret sequences, they use a classical channel for identity authentication. In order to improve the security and flexibility of identity authentication, we have proposed a two-way identity authentication protocol in this agreement, which can guarantee the privacy of both parties.

In this paper, a multi-function quantum cryptography protocol has been proposed. Through the quantum cryptographic protocol proposed in this paper, we can complete the quantum private query, quantum identity authentication, and quantum key distribution function at one time, which means that quantum resources can be utilized most efficiently through this protocol.

The organization of this paper is demonstrated as follows. In Sect. 2, we propose our protocol. In Sect. 3, the security of this protocol is discussed. At last, the conclusion is given.

2 The Protocol

Step 1: Alice prepares 2N qubits which are randomly in one of the states $\{|00\rangle, |11\rangle, |\phi^+\rangle, |\phi^-\rangle\}$. Here

$$|\phi^+\rangle = \frac{1}{\sqrt{2}}(|00\rangle + |11\rangle)$$

$$|\phi^-\rangle = \frac{1}{\sqrt{2}}(|00\rangle - |11\rangle)$$

The first and second qubits compose the pair 1(denotes as P_1), the third and fourth qubits composes pair 2 (denotes as P_2)... the 2n−1th and 2nth qubits composes pair n (denotes as P_n). All of these qubit pairs composes sequence $S = \{P_1, P_2...P_{n-1}, P_n\}$. Then Alice sends sequence S to Bob.

Step 2: When Bob receives the sequence S, he first chooses some qubit pairs as checking pairs to detect Alice's malicious behavior. For each checking pair, Bob measures each qubit in the Z basis or Bell basis randomly. Then Bob announces the position of these checking pairs and asks Alice to announce the prepared state. If the prepared basis and measurement basis are different, Bob cannot check Alice's behavior, which the probability is 1/2; if the prepared basis and the measurement basis are same, Bob's measurement result should be same as Alice's prepared state. If the error rate is higher than the predetermined error rate, they abort the protocol. Otherwise, they discard the decoy pairs, then continue to the next step. This step can prevent Alice sending the fake states or the external eavesdropper using the intercept-resent attack.

Step 3: After confirming that Alice is not cheating, and there is no eavesdropper, Bob measures each qubit in the Z basis or Bell basis randomly, and Bob records the measurement base used for each pair of particles. When Bob uses the Z-based measurement for the particles at the ith position, he records the key value corresponding to the i position as 0. When he uses the Bell base to measure the ith position, he records the key value corresponding to the ith position as 1. Then he generates a binary string $key_b = \{0, 1\}^N$. For each pair, Bob announce "0" or "1", where "0" represents his measurement result is in one of the states $\{|00\rangle, |\phi^+\rangle\}$; "1" represents his measurement result is in one of the state $\{|11\rangle, |\phi^-\rangle\}$. It should be noted that, if Bob's measurement result is in one of the state $\{|\psi^+\rangle, |\psi^-\rangle\}$, he will deduce that Alice is cheating, therefore he aborts the protocol.

Step 4: Similar to the SARG04 QKD protocol, Alice can deduce the oblivious key according to her prepared state and Bob's announcement. For example, if Alice prepares the state $|00\rangle$, and Bob announces "0", Alice cannot deduce the key, which the probability is 1/2; however if Bob announces "1", Alice will know that Bob must use the "wrong basis", and then she can deduce the raw key is "1". After the above Steps, Alice and Bob can get the raw key which Bob knows the whole key and Alice only knows the 1/4 key. Table 1 shows the relationship between Alice's prepared state and Bob's measurement result.

Next we discuss the completion of Quantum private query (QPQ), Quantum identity authentication (QIA), and Quantum key distribution (QKD) with this protocol.

Table 1. The relationship between Alice's prepared state and Bob's measurement result

Alice's prepared state	Bob's measurement basis (raw key)	Bob's measurement result (announcement)	Alice's deduction
$|00\rangle$	Z basis (0)	$|00\rangle$ (0)	Cannot deduce
	Bell basis (1)	$|\phi^+\rangle$, (0)	Cannot deduce
		$|\phi^-\rangle$ (1)	1
$|11\rangle$	Z basis (0)	$|11\rangle$ (1)	Cannot deduce
	Bell basis (1)	$|\phi^+\rangle$, (0)	1
		$|\phi^-\rangle$ (1)	Cannot deduce
$|\phi^+\rangle$	Z basis (0)	$|00\rangle$ (0)	Cannot deduce
		$|11\rangle$ (1)	0
	Bell basis (1)	$|\phi^+\rangle$ (0)	Cannot deduce
$|\phi^-\rangle$	Z basis (0)	$|00\rangle$ (0)	0
		$|11\rangle$ (1)	Cannot deduce
	Bell basis (1)	$|\phi^-\rangle$ (1)	Cannot deduce

2.1   Quantum Private Query

Step 5: After step 4 is completed, Alice and Bob can get the raw key which Bob knows the whole key and Alice only knows the 1/4 key. Just as Jakobi et al. provided the practical QPQ protocol (J-protocol), and to reduce the bits Alice known in the raw key the shared in the above steps, Alice and Bob execute classical post-processing to the final key. We suppose the length of raw key is kN, where k is a natural number, Alice and Bob break raw key up into k parts, thus length of each parts is N. By adding the k parts bitwise, the raw key becomes a final key with length N. Bob knows the whole key, while Alice only knows several bits. The process is similar to that in J-protocol, G-protocol and Y-protocol. If Alice knows nothing of the final key after this post-processing, the protocol should be restarted.

Step 6: At last, Bob can encrypt the database using One-Time-Pad(OTP). Suppose Alice knows the jth bit in the final key, and she wants to know the jth item in the database, she will announce a shift value s = j − i. So Bob can shift his final key by s. Finally Bob encrypted the whole database and sent it to Alice. According to i and j, Alice can correctly get the item which she paid for it. At this point, this protocol has completed the quantum private query (QPQ) function.

2.2 Two-Way Quantum Identity Authentication

Step 7: After step 4 is completed, Alice and Bob can get the raw key which Bob knows the whole key (denoted as key_{Bob}) and Alice only knows the 1/4 key (denoted as key_{Alice1}). Alice announces the particle position and key value corresponding to the known key in key_{Alice1}. Bob queries the key value key_{Bob1} of the corresponding particle position in the key_{Bob} according to the content published by Alice. If $key_{Alice1} = key_{Bob1}$, Bob passes Alice's identity authentication, the agreement goes to the next step, otherwise, the agreement is cancelled.

Step 8: Bob sends the measured particle sequence (denoted as S_1) to Alice. Alice randomly selects some particles for sequence S_1 to detect eavesdropping. She randomly selects the Z basis or the Bell basis to measure the selected particles. Alice informs Bob of the particle position information she selected and asks Bob to publish the status information of these particles in S_1 (Similar to step 3, Alice can detect if Bob is cheating, therefore he aborts the protocol). After completing the bit error rate detection, Alice discards the eavesdropping particles and notifies bob to announce all the particle position information in the Z-base state in sequence S_1. Alice performs Z-based measurements on these particles. According to the coding rules published by Bob in step 3, Alice encodes the measured particles to obtain key_{Alice2}. At this time, Bob announces the key value key_{Bob2} of the corresponding position. If $key_{Alice2} = key_{Bob2}$, Alice passes the authentication of Bob. At this point, this protocol has completed the two-way identity authentication (two-way QIA) function.

2.3 Quantum Key Distribution

Step 9: After completing step 8, Alice performs a Bell-based measurement on the remaining particles (theoretically all of the Bell state particles), and also obtains the key string key_{Alice3} according to the encoding rule published by Bob in step 3. Alice combines the key string $key_{Alice} = key_{Alice1} + key_{Alice2} + key_{Alice3}$ according to the order of receiving sequence S_1. At this time, $key_{Alice} = key_{Bob}$ holds, and Alice shares a string of identical binary key strings with Bob. At this point, this protocol has completed the quantum key distribution (QKD) function.

3 Examples of the Protocol

We give an example of the protocol in this section, explaining in detail how this protocol accomplishes QIA and QKD functions. Note that: in our example, Alice and Bob's encoding rules follow the rules that Bob published in step 3. To be more clearly, for each pair, Bob announce "0" or "1", where "0" represents his measurement result is in one of the states $\{|00\rangle, |\phi^+\rangle\}$; "1" represents his measurement result is in one of the state $\{|11\rangle, |\phi^-\rangle\}$.

3.1   Examples of Two-Way QIA

Examples of Step 7

We assume that the particle sequence obtained after bob measurement is $S_1 = \{|00\rangle, |\phi^-\rangle, |\phi^+\rangle, |11\rangle, |\phi^+\rangle, |11\rangle, |00\rangle, |\phi^-\rangle, |\phi^+\rangle, |11\rangle, |\phi^+\rangle, |11\rangle\}$, thus $Key_{Bob} = \{010101010101\}$.

Alice can correctly release the 2nd, 4th, and 6th bits of the key, and Alice's key is $Key_{Alice1} = \{?1?1?1??????\}$. Alice announces Key_{Alice1}, and Bob checks the value of the corresponding position in Key_{Bob}. Since $Key_{Bob1} = Key_{Bob(2,4,6)} = \{111\} = Key_{Alice1}$ is established, Bob authenticates the identity of Alice.

Examples of Step 8

Bob sends the sequence S_1 to Alice, Alice selects the first, third, and eighth bits, randomly selects the measurement base for eavesdropping detection, and informs Bob to announce the particle state information of the corresponding position in S_1. After the eavesdropping test passes, Alice informs Bob to announce all the particle positions and key values in the Z-base state in sequence S_1 (removing the particles used for eavesdrop detection). That is, bob publishes $Key_{Bob2} = Key_{Bob(4,6,7,10,12)} = \{11011\}$, and Alice performs Z-based measurement on the particles in her hands according to the position announced by Bob, and obtains $Key_{Alice2} = \{11011\}$. Because $Key_{Alice2} = Key_{Bob2}$ is established, Alice passes the identity authentication of bob.

3.2   Examples of QKD

Examples of Step 9

Alice performs a Bell-based measurement on the remaining particles (the 2nd, 5th, 9th, and 11th bits remain) to obtain the key sequence $Key_{Alice3} = \{1000\}$. Alice combines the key sequences Key_{Alice1}, Key_{Alice2} and Key_{Alice3} in the subscript order when receiving the sequence s1 to obtain a Key_{Alice}. At this point, $Key_{Alice} = Key_{Bob} = \{110100101\}$ is established, they finish the quantum key distribution (QKD).

4   Security Analysis

According to the protocol description, the security analysis of this protocol mainly focuses on QPQ and two-way QIA. Note that: the JM attack analysis and the Entangled-Measurement attack analysis for QIA is similar to QPQ (The main safety hazard appears in step 8), so we will not repeat the security analysis.

4.1   The Outsider Attack

4.1.1   The Outsider Attack of QPQ

Compared with QPQ based on B92 protocol, our protocol can stand against an external eavesdropper. Suppose Eve is a malicious eavesdropper who wants to know Alice's secret item in the database. Because one-time-pad (OTP) is proved to be unconditionally secure, as long as Eve does not know the oblivious key, he cannot get the confidential information. In order to get the oblivious key, he needs to know Bob's operation (whether measure the qubit pair in the Z basis or in the Bell basis). In step 3, Bob will announce some information, only if Eve knows Alice's initial state, he can deduce the secret key. Therefore Eve may take an Intercept-resend attack, however without Alice prepared basis, his malicious behavior will be caught easily. For example, in step 1, suppose Alice prepares state $|00\rangle$ and send them to Bob. Eve may intercept the sequence S, and measures them in Z basis or Bell basis randomly. If he uses right basis (in this case is Z basis), his malicious behavior will not be caught; however if he uses the wrong basis (in this case is Bell basis), he will get the measurement result $|\phi^+\rangle$ or $|\phi^-\rangle$ with equal probability. In step 2, when Bob uses the Z basis to measure the checking sequence, Eve's malicious behavior will be caught with the probability of 1/4. As the checking photons are large enough, he will be caught easily.

4.1.2   The User Privacy of QPQ

Most of the current protocol are cheat-sensitive QPQ protocol. "Cheat-sensitive" means that dishonest database holder Bob will run the risk of being detected if he tries to obtain Alice's query address. In our protocol, Bob only announce in the public channel in step 4, that gives him no chance to send a fake quantum state. Because Alice does not announce anything, so Bob cannot deduce Alice's prepared states. For example, if Bob's measurement result is $|00\rangle$, he cannot judge whether Alice is sending $|00\rangle$, $|\phi^+\rangle$ or $|\phi^-\rangle$. Therefore our protocol has a perfect user privacy.

4.1.3   The Outsider Attack of QIA

As the analysis of QPQ, Eve may intercept the sequence S_1, and measures them in Z basis or Bell basis randomly. If he uses right basis (in this case is Z basis), his malicious behavior will not be caught; however if he uses the wrong basis (in this case is Bell basis), he will get the measurement result $|\phi^+\rangle$ or $|\phi^-\rangle$ with equal probability. In step 8, when Alice uses the Z basis to measure the checking sequence, Eve's malicious behavior will be caught with the probability of 1/4. As the checking photons are large enough, he will be caught easily too. More importantly, this protocol is a two-way QIA protocol. Anyone who has a dishonest behavior on either Alice or Bob will be detected. Therefore, this quantum protocol is safe and reliable for QIA purposes.

4.2   The JM Attack

In QPQ protocol, we assume Alice is dishonest, i.e. she will try every means to get more oblivious key illegally (more than 1/4 of the raw key) in our protocol. In this section, we will analyze two kind of attack from Alice, i.e. the joint-measurement (JM) attack and entangled-measurement attack.

In 2016, Wei et al. pointed out that the JM attack poses a noticeable threat to the database security in the QPQ protocol. By taking such attack strategy, the malicious user Alice can deduce more item from the database without being caught. To conduct a JM attack, the malicious Alice must hold the states and knows which states contribute the final key simultaneously. However our protocol can resist such kind of attack.

Because in step 1, Alice holds the carrier state, however she doesn't know which states contributes the final key in step 4, she cannot take the joint-measurement attack, because the carrier states are not in her hand anymore after she sending the sequence S to Bob in step 1. Therefore, because the two essential elements for JM attack is isolate, Alice cannot perform the JM attack. More generally, Alice can prepare an entangled states, instead of $\{|00\rangle, |11\rangle, |\phi^+\rangle, |\phi^-\rangle\}$. If Alice can pass the eavesdropping check, Alice will know which qubits will generate a final key and performs joint-measurement to those qubits in her hand. However this malicious behavior will be caught easily. For example, Alice will prepares this quantum state in step 1

$$|\Psi\rangle = \frac{1}{\sqrt{2}}[|000\rangle + |111\rangle]_{123}$$

$$= \frac{1}{\sqrt{2}}[(0+1)(00+11) + (0-1)(00-11)]_{123}$$

Alice keep the first qubit in her hand, and sends particle 2 and 3 to Bob. After Bob receive the particle 2 and 3, he will measure them in Z basis or Bell basis, here we suppose Bob measure them in the Bell basis. Bob will get the measurement result $|\phi^+\rangle$ or $|\phi^-\rangle$ with equal probability. We suppose Bob's measurement result is $|\phi^-\rangle$. Then in step 2, Bob will ask Alice publish her prepared basis and result. Because Alice doesn't know which basis Bob chooses, Alice can only publish the answer randomly. For example, if she announces "Bell basis and $|\phi^+\rangle$", Bob will know Alice must sending the fake states, Therefore Alice cannot send the entangled states in order to perform the JM attack.

5 The Entangled-Measurement Attack

The malicious user Alice may take an entangled-measurement attack. Without loss of generality, the malicious Alice may prepare some auxiliary particles $|e\rangle$, and perform unitary operation U to entangle them with the particles in sequence S. After the operation U, state $|0\rangle, |1\rangle$ will change to:

$$U \otimes |0e\rangle = a|0e_{00}\rangle + b|1e_{01}\rangle,$$
$$U \otimes |1e\rangle = b'|0e_{10}\rangle + a'|1e_{11}\rangle,$$

The entangled state $|\phi^+\rangle$ will change to:

$$|\phi\rangle_{Eve} = U \otimes |\phi^+\rangle$$
$$= \frac{1}{\sqrt{2}}[(a|0e_{00}\rangle + b|1e_{01}\rangle) \otimes |0\rangle + (b'|0e_{10}\rangle + a'|1e_{11}\rangle) \otimes |1\rangle]$$
$$= \frac{1}{\sqrt{2}}(a|0e_{00}0\rangle + b|1e_{01}0\rangle + b'|0e_{10}1\rangle + a'|1e_{11}1\rangle)$$

When Bob perform the Bell measurement on the checking pairs, only if $|a'| = |a|$, he can escape from the detecting which the probability is $P_{Eve} = \frac{|a|^2 + |a'|^2}{2} = |a|^2$. As the checking photons are large enough, she will be caught easily.

6 Conclusion and Discussion

In this paper, we proposed a novel Quantum cryptography protocol based on Bell state. Our protocol is a multi-function quantum protocol, which can be used to perform QPQ, QIA, and QKD functions. This protocol can improve the utilization efficiency of entangled particles, and can complete a variety of practical functions by preparing only one primary particle. Therefore, our protocol doesn't need the wave-length filter and PNS technique, and our protocol only need 4 kinds of quantum states and realize almost perfect user privacy. By using Bell entangled state, our protocol show better performance in the collective-noise channels.

Acknowledgments. The authors would like to thank the reviewers and editors who have helped to improve the paper.

This work is supported by the National Key Research and Development Project of China (No. 2017YFB0802302), the National Natural Science Foundation of China (No. 61572086, No. 61402058), the Innovation Team of Quantum Security Communication of Sichuan Province (No. 17TD0009), the Academic and Technical Leaders Training Funding Support Projects of Sichuan Province (No. 2016120080102643), the Application Foundation Project of Sichuan Province(No. 2017JY0168), the Key Research and Development Project of Sichuan Province (No. 2018TJPT0012), the Science and Technology Support Project of Sichuan Province (No. 2016FZ0112, No. 2018GZ0204).

References

1. Bennett, C.H., Brassard, G.: Quantum cryptography: public key distribution and coin tossing. In: Proceedings of IEEE International Conference on Computers, Systems and Signal Processing, pp 175–179. IEEE, Bangalore (1984)
2. Bennett, C.H., Brassard, G., Mermin, N.D.: Quantum cryptography without Bell theorem. Phys. Rev. Lett. **68**, 557–559 (1992)
3. Scarani, V., Acin, A., Ribordy, G., Gisin, N.: Quantum cryptography protocols robust against Photon number splitting attacks for. Phys. Rev. Lett. **92**, 057901 (2004)
4. Deng, F.G., Long, G.L.: Controlled order rearrangement encryption for quantum key distribution. Phys. Rev. A **68**, 042315 (2003)
5. Li, X.H., Deng, F.G., Zhou, H.Y.: Efficient quantum key distribution over a collective noise channel. Phys. Rev. A **78**, 022321 (2008)
6. Long, G.L., Liu, X.S.: Theoretically efficient high-capacity quantum-key-distribution scheme. Phys. Rev. A **65**, 032302 (2002)
7. Deng, F.G., Long, G.L., Liu, X.S.: Two-step quantum direct communication protocol using the Einstein-Podolsky-Rosen pair block. Phys. Rev. A **68**, 042317 (2003)
8. Deng, F.G., Long, G.L.: Secure direct communication with a quantum one-time pad. Phys. Rev. A **69**, 052319 (2004)

9. Wang, C.: Quantum secure direct communication with high-dimension quantum superdense coding. Phys. Rev. A **71**, 044305 (2005)
10. Ye, T.Y., Jiang, L.Z.: Improvement of controlled bidirectional quantum direct communication using a GHZ state. Chin. Phys. Lett. **30**(4), 040305 (2013)
11. Chen, Y., Man, Z.X., Xia, Y.J.: Quantum bidirectional secure direct communication via entanglement swapping. Chin. Phys. Lett. **24**(1), 19 (2007)
12. Hillery, M., Buzek, V., Berthiaume, A.: Quantum secret sharing. Phys. Rev. A **59**, 1829–1834 (1999)
13. Karlsson, A., Koashi, M., Imoto, N.: Quantum entanglement for secret sharing and secret splitting. Phys. Rev. A **59**, 162–168 (1999)
14. Xiao, L., Long, G.L., Deng, F.G., Pan, J.W.: Efficient multiparty quantum-secret-sharing schemes. Phys. Rev. A **69**, 052307 (2004)
15. Deng, F.G., Zhou, H.Y., Long, G.L.: Circular quantum secret sharing. J. Phys. A **39**, 14089–14099 (2006)
16. Cleve, R., Gottesman, D., Lo, H.K.: How to share a quantum secret. Phys. Rev. Lett. **83**, 648 (1999)
17. Yang, Y.G., Wen, Q.Y.: J. Phys. A - Math. Theor. **42**, 055305 (2009)
18. Tseng, H.Y., Lin, J., Hwang, T.: Quantum Inf. Process. **11**, 373 (2012)
19. Zhang, Z.J., Man, Z.X.: Secure direct bidirectional communication protocol using the Einstein- Podolsky-Rosen pair block. arXiv:0403215 pdf (2004)
20. Zheng, C., Long, G.F.: Quantum secure direct dialogue using Einstein-Podolsky-Rosen pairs. Sci. China-Phys. Mech. Astron. **57**(7), 1238–1243 (2014)
21. Chor, B., Goldreich, O., Kushilevitz, E., Sudan, M.: Private information retrieval. In: Proceedings 36th IEEE Symposium on Foundations of Computer Science. IEEE Press (1995)
22. Gertner, Y., Ishai, Y., Kushilevitz, E., Malkin, T.: Protecting data privacy in private information retrieval schemes. J. Comput. Syst. Sci. **60**(3), 592–629 (2000)
23. Shor, P.: Polynomial-time algorithms for prime factorization and discrete logarithms on a quantum computer. SIAM J. Comput. **26**(5), 1484–1509 (1997)
24. Liu, B., Gao, F., Huang, W., Wen, Q.Y.: QKD-Based quantum private query without a failure probability. Sci. China-Phys. Mech. Astron. **58**(10), 100301 (2015)
25. Yang, Y.G., Sun, S.J., Xue, P., Tian, J.: Flexible protocol for quantum private query based on b92 protocol. Quant. Inf. Process **13**(3), 805–813 (2014)
26. Giovannetti, V., Lloyd, S., Maccone, L.: Quantum private queries. Phys. Rev. Lett. **100**(23), 230502 (2008)
27. Jakobi, M., et al.: Practical private database queries based on a quantum-key-distribution protocol. Phys. Rev. A **83**(2), 022301 (2011)
28. Gao, F., Liu, B., Wen, Q.Y.: Flexible quantum private queries based on quantum key distribution. Opt. Exp. **20**(16), 17411–17420 (2012)
29. DuŜek, M., Haderka, O., Hendrych, M., Mayska, R.: Quantum identification system. Phys. Rev. A **60**, 149 (1999)
30. Stinson, D.R.: Cryptography: Theory and Practice, 3rd edn. CRC Press, Boca Raton (2005)
31. Kang, M.S., Hong, C.H., Heo, J., Lim, J.I., Yang, H.J.: Controlled mutual quantum entity authentication using entanglement swapping. Chin. Phys. B **24**, 090306 (2015)
32. Mihara, T.: Quantum identification schemes with entanglements. Phys. Rev. A **65**, 052326 (2002)
33. Tang, X., Juan, X., Duan, B.: A memory-efficient simulation method of Grover's search algorithm. CMC: Comput. Mater. Continua **56**(2), 307–319 (2018)
34. Tan, X., Li, X., Yang, P.: perfect quantum teleportation via Bell states. CMC: Comput. Mater. Continua **57**(3), 495–503 (2018)

The Attack Case of ECDSA on Blockchain Based on Improved Simple Power Analysis

Wan Wunan[1(✉)], Chen Hao[1], and Chen Jun[2]

[1] School of Cybersecurity, Chengdu University of Information Technology,
Chengdu 610225, China
nan_wwn@cuit.edu.cn
[2] School of Computer, Chengdu University of Information Technology,
Chengdu 610225, China

Abstract. Blockchain is an emerging distributed computing technology of decentralization. The cryptography is used to ensure integrity, anonymity, privacy and immutability. Security of blockchain rely on cryptographic algorithms. However, cryptographic primitives typically get broken or weakened due to increase computational power and advanced cryptanalysis of the side channel methods. The cryptographic algorithms of blockchain will face side channel attacks. In this paper, we present the systematic analysis of threats on broken digital signature of the transaction data. And an improved SPA against ECDSA is presented with the power feature model in this paper. An attack case is given, and the private key of ECDSA can be recovered by using the proposed attack method with a power trace. Then the countermeasure of equivalent power consumption at atomic level is given by adding empty operations in point doubling and addition operations for hardware devices of blockchain.

Keywords: Cluster · Correlation power analysis (CPA) ·
Module exponentiation · K-means · Side channel attack

1 Introduction

The blockchain idea originates from the foundational article entitled "Bitcoin: a peer-to-peer electronic cash system" [1], authored by Satoshi Nakamoto in 2008. At present, blockchain can be viewed as a novel decentralized architecture and distributed computing paradigm, and has be used widely in many areas. Technically speaking, blockchain technology consists of many different aspects of technology including cryptography, Peer-to-Peer (P2P) technology and consensus mechanisms over distributed network [2]. Among these techniques, cryptography is the key component to ensure the integrity, anonymity, privacy and immutability in the blockchain. However, cryptography techniques were usually broken with increasing computational power of the attacker. For example, side channel attack methods have been proposed against many cryptographic algorithms.

Impact analysis of blockchain protocol when the underlying cryptographic algorithms are broken was proposed by Giechaskiel et al. [3]. Massashi Sato et al. had analyzed the needs of transition of cryptographic algorithm and shown the way to extend the validity of blockchain applying the long-term signature scheme which was standardized in ETSI [4]. To enforce the security and to improve performance in blockchain, Bitcoin mining machines are implemented based on hardware chips, and cryptographic algorithms such as hash functions, ECDSA digital signature can be applied at the hardware level by using FPGA or ASIC. However, An adversary has a wide range of choices in attack strategies for hard devices of blockchain, including timing analysis [5], simple power analysis (SPA) [6, 7], differential power analysis (DPA) [8], correlation power analysis (CPA) [9], template analysis [10, 11]. Template Attacks on ECDSA was proposed by Medwed et al. in 2008 [10]. Hence, Fan et al. were able to perform an attack on the scalar multiplication [12–14]. At SAC2013, Bauer et al. gave a Big Mac attack on ECC [8]. The implementation uses a side-channel countermeasure called Side-Channel Atomicity. Jean-Luc Danger introduced the improved Big Mac attack on ECC [9]. LUO Peng proposed chosen-message SPA against ECC in 2016 [6]. And so ECC implementations are vulnerable to side channel attacks.

Even if such side channel attacks are away from being practical in blockchain system at present, it is crucial to anticipate the impact of these attacks so that the countermeasures can be put in place [15, 16]. In this paper, we provide a broken case study of the private key on ECDSA by the practical SPA method with a power trace. The countermeasure of equivalent power consumption at atomic level is given by adding empty operations in point doubling and addition operations. This is given to secure cryptography technology against side channel attacks for hardware devices of blockchain. Finally, the research results are summarized and a perspective of the future work in this research area is discussed in this paper.

The rest of this paper is organized as follows: Sect. 2 introduces signature of blockchain and elliptic curve scalar multiplication algorithm; Sect. 3 introduces elliptic curve scalar multiplication algorithm. Power characteristic model of double point and double atomic operation are given. And an effective SPA attack based on atomic operation are presented, and we gives an atomic level of equal power defense measures. Section 4 concludes the full text and makes a preliminary discussion on future research directions worthy of attention.

2 Preliminary

In this section, we will provide brief background information about digital signature in blcokchain.

2.1 Digital Signatures in Bitcoin

Figure 1 shows the basic data structure of blockchain [17, 18]. In Bitcoin, The blockchain is a public log of all Bitcoin transaction that have occurred, combined together in components called blocks. Transactions use a scripting language that determines the owners of coins.

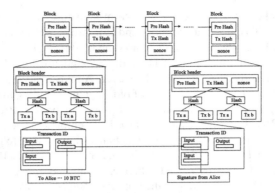

Fig. 1. The blockchain data structure

A digital signature is given to each transaction and stored in the block with the transaction. Digital signature scheme in the blockchain protocol is to verify the transaction data is produced by the key owner, and integrity of the transaction data. The digital signature scheme in Bitcoin is the Elliptic Curve Digital Signature Algorithm (ECDSA) with the secp256kl parameters, as shown Fig. 2.

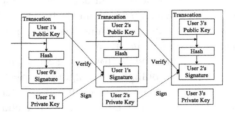

Fig. 2. Transaction signature procedure

2.2   Threats on the Digital Signature of the Transaction Data

The security of ECDSA relies on the difficulty of the elliptic curve discrete logarithm problem (ECDLP). That is, ECDSA is theoretically security. But with putting forward advanced cryptanalysis, such as the side channel methods, the cryptographic algorithms are broken and weaken, there arise following two kinds of threats [4].

Threat 1: If the private key can be broken, the adversary can make impersonate the user and move coin to other account. That is, the future transactions are impersonated.

Threat 2: If hash value on the transaction data can be calculated, the adversary can obtain the 2nd pre-image or a value which produce the same hash value (collision). This causes, the permutation of the transaction data to be signed by producing same hash value from other transaction data.

2.3   Security of ECDSA

ECDSA is the elliptic curve version of the digital signature algorithm. Algorithm 1 shows how to computer a signature [10].

Algorithm 1 ECDSA Algorithm

Input $D=(q,P,n,\text{Curve})$, private key d, message m

Output: Signature (r,s)

---

1. Select the random k, $1 \leqslant k \leqslant n$
2. Computer $[k]P=(x_1,y_1)$, where $0 \leqslant x_1 \leqslant q\text{-}1$
3. Computer $r= x_1 \bmod n$. if $r=0$, then go to step 1
4. Compute $e=\text{H}(m)$
5. Compute $s=k^{-1}(e+dr) \bmod n$. if $s=0$ then go to Step1.
6. Return (r,s)

If we can get the secret key d, ECDSA is referred to as a full break. According to Algorithm 1, if the ephemeral key k is known for a signature(r, s), then we can calculate the secret key d from formula (1) and (2).

$$r = x_1 \ \bmod \ n. \ ([k]P = (x_1 y_1)) \tag{1}$$

$$S = k^{-1} \ (\text{H}(m) + dr) \ \bmod \ n \tag{2}$$

For ECDSA, If an attacker is able to reveal the ephemeral key k, ECDSA implementation can be broken in practices. Step 2 in Algorithm 1 is the scalar multiplication $[k]$ P, given a point P on $E(F_q)$ and an integer k, is the most important and costly operation for ECC. We will briefly describe the implementation of the scalar multiplication on ECC.

2.4 Implementations of Scalar Multiplication

The scalar multiplication can be implemented with the well-known double and add algorithm based on the Left-to-Right binary *NAF*(Non Adjacent Form) mixed

---

Algorithm 2 Left-to-Right binary NAF scalar multiplication

Input:k, $P \in E(F_q)$

Output: $[k]P$

---

1. $Q \leftarrow \infty, i=i+1$;
2.   while $k \geq 1$ do
    2.1 if （$k \bmod 2$）$=1$ then
        $u_i = 2 - k \ (mod \ 4); \ k = k - u_i$
    else
        $u_i = 0$
    end if
    2.2 $k=k/2$
    2.3 $i=i+1$
3. for $j=i\text{-}1$ to 0
    3.1 $Q = 2Q$
    3.2 if $u_j = 1$then
        $Q = Q + P$
        else if $u_j = -1$then $Q = Q - P$ end if
    end if
4. return Q

coordinates multiplication. Algorithm 2 gives the details of the NAF scalar multiplication used in our work.

To avoid costly divisions when using the formulae affine coordinate, Jacobian or Jacobian-affine mixed coordinate are used. The Jacobian point (X, Y, Z) corresponds to the affine point $(X/Z^2, Y/Z^2)$. And the point at infinity as $O = (1, 1, 0)$ in Jacobian coordinate. We give doubling formulas in the Jacobian projective coordinate system. Let $P = (x_1, y_1, z_1)$, $Q = 2P = (x_2, y_2, z_2)$ is computed as:

$$\lambda_1 = 3x_1^2 + az_1^4, \quad \lambda_2 = 4x_1y_1^2, \quad \lambda_3 = 8y_1^4, \quad x_2 = \lambda_1^2 - 2\lambda_2, \quad y_2 = \lambda_1(\lambda_2 - x_3) - \lambda_3,$$
$$z_2 = 2y_1z_1$$

Algorithm 3: Doubling using Jacobian coordinate.

Input: $P(x, y, z)$, $T=a$

Output: $Q(x_1, y_1, z_1) = 2P$, T

1. $T_1 = y_1^2$ $\{T_1 \leftarrow y_1^2\}$
2. $T_2 = 2x_1$ $\{T_2 \leftarrow 2x_1\}$
3. $T_2 = T_1T_2$ $\{T_2 \leftarrow 2x_1y_1^2\}$
4. $T_2 = 2T_2$ $\{T_2 \leftarrow 4x_1y_1^2\}$, computed as λ_2
5. $T_1 = T_1^2$ $\{T_1 \leftarrow y_1^4\}$
6. $T_1 = 8T_1$ $\{T_1 \leftarrow 8y_1^4\}$, computed as λ_3
7. $T_3 = x_1^2$ $\{T_3 \leftarrow x_1^2\}$
8. $T_3 = 3x_1^2$ $\{T_3 \leftarrow 3x_1^2\}$
9. $T_3 = T_3 + T$ $\{T_3 \leftarrow 3x_1^2 + az^4\}$, computed as λ_1, $z = 1$
10. $T_4 = T_3^2$ $\{T_4 \leftarrow (3x_1^2 + az_1^4)^2\}$
11. $x_1 = T_4 - 2T_2$
12. $T_4 = T_2 - x_1$ $\{T_4 \leftarrow (\lambda_2 - x_3)\}$
13. $T_4 = T_3T_4$ $\{T_4 \leftarrow \lambda_1(\lambda_2 - x_3)\}$
14. $y_1 = T_4 - T_1$
15. $T_4 = y_1z_1$
16. $z_1 = 2T_4$
17. $T_1 = 2T_1$ $\{T_1 \leftarrow 16y_1^4\}$
18. $T = TT_1$ $\{T \leftarrow az_1^4\}$ $az_1^4 = a(2yz)^4 = az^4 \times 16y^4$
19. return $Q(x_1, y_1, z_1)$, T

For speeding up the addition, the modified Jacobian coordinates is introduced by Cohen et al. Let $P = (x_1, y_1, z_1)$ is represented by the Jacobian coordinates, and $Q = (x_2, y_2, z_2)$ is represented by the affine coordinates. The sum $R = Q + P = (x_3, y_3, z_3)$ is computed as:

$$\lambda_1 = x_2 z_1^2, \ \lambda_2 = y_2 z_1^3, \ \lambda_3 = \lambda_1 - x_1, \ \lambda_4 = \lambda_2 - y_1, \ x_3 = \lambda_4^2 - (\lambda_3^3 + 2x_1 \lambda_3^2),$$
$$y_3 = \lambda_4 (x_1 \lambda_3^2 - x_3) - y_1 \lambda_3^3, \ z_3 = z_1 \lambda_3$$

Algorithm 4: Addition using affine-Jacobian mixed coordinates.

Input: $P=(x_1,y_1,z_1)$ in the Jacobian coordinates , $Q=(x_2,y_2)$ in the affine coordinates, $T=az_1^4$, $z_1=1$

Output: $R=Q+P=(x_3,y_3,z_3)$, T

1. $T_1 = z_1^2$ $\{T_1 \leftarrow z_1^2\}$
2. $T_2 = z_1 T_1$ $\{T_2 \leftarrow z_1^3\}$
3. $T_1 = x_2 T_1$ $\{T_1 \leftarrow x_2 z_1^2\}$,   computed as λ_1
4. $T_2 = y_2 T_2$ $\{T_2 \leftarrow y_2 z_1^3\}$,   computed as λ_2
5. $T_3 = T_1 - x_1$ $\{T_3 \leftarrow x_2 z_1^2 - x_1\}$,   computed as λ_3
6. $T_4 = T_2 - y_1$ $\{T_4 \leftarrow y_2 z_1^2 - y_1\}$,   computed as λ_4
7. $T_1 = T_3^2$ $\{T_1 \leftarrow \lambda_3^2\}$
8. $T_2 = T_1 T_3$ $\{T_2 \leftarrow \lambda_3^3\}$
9. $T_5 = T_4^2$ $\{T_5 \leftarrow \lambda_4^2\}$
10. $x_3 = 2x_1 T_1$ $x_3 \leftarrow 2x_1 \lambda_3^2$
11. $x_3 = T_2 + x_3$ $x_3 \leftarrow \lambda_3^3 + 2x_1 \lambda_3^2$
12. $x_3 = T_5 - x_3$ $x_3 \leftarrow \lambda_4^2 - (\lambda_3^3 + 2x_1 \lambda_3^2)$
13. $T_5 = T_1^2$ $\{T_5 \leftarrow \lambda_3^4\}$
14. $T_1 = x_1 T_1$ $\{T_1 \leftarrow x_1 \lambda_3^2\}$
15. $T_1 = T_1 - x_3$ $\{T_1 \leftarrow x_1 \lambda_3^2 - x_3\}$
16. $T_2 = y_1 T_2$ $\{T_2 \leftarrow y_1 \lambda_3^3\}$
17. $y_3 = T_4 T_1$ $\{y_3 \leftarrow \lambda_4 (x_1 \lambda_3^2 - x_3)\}$
18. $y_3 = y_3 - T_2$ $\{y_3 \leftarrow \lambda_4 (x_1 \lambda_3^2 - x_3) - y_1 \lambda_3^3\}$
19. $z_3 = z_1 T_3$ $\{z_3 \leftarrow z_1 \lambda_3\}$
20. $T = TT_5$ $\{T \leftarrow az_3^4\} \ az_3^4 = a(z_1 \lambda_3)^4 = az_1^4 \lambda_3^4$
21. Return $R(x_3,y_3,z_3)$, T

The scalar multiplication is subject to side channel attack technique since Kocher first introduced a power analysis attack based on execution time measurements in 1996 [5], such as simple power analysis (SPA) [6, 7]. Implementations of the scalar multiplication may allow revealing the secret key d if they leak information the ephemeral key k.

In following section, we explain why the scalar multiplication is very well studied as target from at atomic level, and give a case attack based on improved SPA. The countermeasure will be presented.

3 Improved SPA Method and Countermeasure of Scalar Multiplication

3.1 Power Model of Scalar Multiplication

In real attack environment, the existence of noise in the power traces is inevitable. The total power consumption of the cryptosystem may then be determined as follows:

$$P_{total} = P_{op} + P_{data} + P_{el.noise} + P_{const} \tag{3}$$

Where P_{total} is the total power, P_{op} is the operation dependent power consumption, P_{data} is the data dependent power consumption, $P_{el.noise}$ denotes power resulting from the electronic noise in the hardware, P_{const} is some constant power consumption, depending on the technical implementation.

According to the implementation of scalar multiplication, point doubling and addition operations mainly include modular multiplication, modular addition, modular subtraction, shift and load date of the large integers at atomic level. Theoretically, the power characteristics of each operation are not the same in according to the Hamming weight power model. When bit jumps of the operation is more, and power consumption is greater.

Atomic operations according to double and add algorithm can be subdivided, including modular multiplication, modular addition, modular subtraction, shift and load date, where modular multiplication is denoted as $P_{op\_mod\_mul}(a, b)$, modular addition $P_{op\_mod\_add}(a, b)$, modular subtraction $P_{op\_mod\_sub}(a, b)$, shift $P_{op\_shift}(a)$ and load date $P_{op\_load}(a)$. According to their power characteristics, they can be divided into three categories, as illustrated in Table 1.

Table 1. Power characteristics of different arithmetic operations

Power characteristics	Operation
P_{High}	$P_{op\_mod\_mul}(a, b)$
P_{Medium}	$P_{op\_mod\_add}(a, b)$, $P_{op\_mod\_sub}(a, b)$, $P_{op\_shift}(a)$
P_{Low}	$P_{op\_load}(a)$

In Algorithm 3, there are mainly 19 atomic operations for point doubling, including 8 modulus multiplication, 2 modulus addition, 3 modulus subtraction, 9 shift. And point addition has 21 atomic operations in algorithm 4, including 13 modulus multiplication, 5 modulus addition, 5 modulus subtraction, 5 shift. The operation power P_{op} of doubling and addition can be represented as follow:

$$P_{op\_double} = 8P_{op\_mod\_mul} + 9P_{op\_shift} + 2P_{op\_mod\_add} + 3P_{op\_mod\_sub} \qquad (4)$$

$$P_{op\_add} = P_{op\_sub} = 13P_{op\_mod\_mul} + P_{op\_shift} + P_{op\_mod\_add} + 5P_{op\_mod\_sub} \qquad (5)$$

According to power characteristics of different atomic level operations, The power consumption P_{op} has the big difference between point addition and point doubling, so the power consumption P_{total} is difference. We are able to distinguish between point addition and point doubling by P_{High} number of each point operation.

3.2 Feature Analysis and Extraction of Power Traces for Scalar Multiplication

According to Subsect. 3.1, it is known that three types power characteristics of scalar multiplication with P_{High}, P_{Medium}, P_{Low}, as shown Fig. 3. Because load data occurs between two operations, power characteristics of load data is obviously lower than other operations.

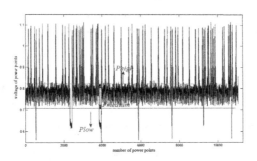

Fig. 3. Three types of power characteristics of scalar multiplication

Point addition and doubling can be divided by number of P_{High} of each segment. If there is 8 P_{High} in a segment, the operation is point doubling, and if there is 13 P_{High}, is point addition or subtraction. As is shown Fig. 4. Another, point subtraction has the same operation process as point addition, but the operand is different. The one operand of point subtraction is $-P$, the operand of point addition is P. Load data needs increase negative operation in point subtraction, so low power characteristics P_{Low} is wider. We can judge the segment is addition or subtraction by power characteristics P_{Low} of the front and back of the segment.

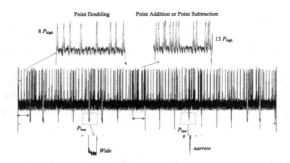

Fig. 4. Power characteristics of point doubling, addition and subduction operations

3.3 An Attack Case Based on SPA Against Scalar Multiplication

In according to the Algorithm 2 in Sect. 2.4, the 4th step can be classified into three types: doubling-addition, doubling-subtraction, doubling, as shown Fig. 5.

When $u_j = 0$, the operation is doubling.
When $u_j = 1$, the operation is doubling-addition.
When $u_j = -1$, the operation is doubling-subtraction.

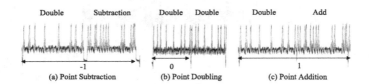

Fig. 5. Power characteristic of three types of point operations

The key NAF (k) value can be estimated by analyzing the doubling, doubling and subtracting of scalar power curve, as shown Fig. 6.

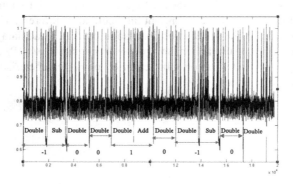

Fig. 6. Simple power attack of the private key k

And we can extract each segment of power trace by the characteristics P_{Low}. Each segment is denoted Seg_i, the steps of SPA against scalar multiplication as follows:

Step 1: Firstly, The power trace is segmented according to the power characteristic P_{Low}, as is denoted $Seg = \{Seg_0, Seg_1, \ldots\ldots, Seg_n\}$.

Step 2: Classify three cluster sets of the data set Seg, $C = \{c_0, c_1, c_3\}$, where the cluster c_0 is point doubling, and c_1 is point addition, and c_2 is point subtraction.

The principle of classification: For each segment Seg_i, if it has 8 P_{High}, then Seg_i is divided into the cluster c_0. If it has 13 P_{High}, then Seg_i is divided into the cluster c_1 when P_{low} of the segment is narrow, and Seg_i is divided into the cluster c_2 when P_{low} of the segment is wide.

Step 3: Set initial value $i = 0, j = 0$. We can obtain the key value of NAF (k) as fellows:

When $Seg_{i+1} \in c_0$, then $u_j = 0$, $i = i + 1$, $j = j + 1$
When $Seg_{i+1} \in c_1$, then $u_j = 1$, $i = i + 2$, $j = j + 1$
When $Seg_{i+1} \in c_2$, then $u_j = -1$, $i = i + 2$, $j = j + 1$

Step 4: According to the value of NAF (k), the ephemeral key k can be broken finally.

3.4 Countermeasure of SPA on ECC

The key of successful simple power analysis on scalar multiplication is that power trace can leak information of differential point operations. According to the algorithm 2, there is the dependency between three point operations and the ephemeral key k. Therefore, the defense must start from atomic level of scalar multiplication implementation process. Power consumption of each operation must be equal. So, empty operations are increased in point addition or point doubling, as shown in formulas (6) and (7) and in Table 2.

$$(Rand(R_1) * Rand(R_2)) \bmod q \tag{6}$$

$$(Rand(R_1) + Rand(R_2)) \bmod q \tag{7}$$

Where $Rand$ is random function.

Where $\blacktriangle$ represents null modulus multiplication, $\bigstar$ represents null modulus addition.

Table 2 shows that, addition and doubling respectively increase null operations, including modular multiplication and modular addition in order to achieve equal power consumption. Moreover, random delay can be obtained. Side channel attack based on chosen message is invalid for the countermeasure in this paper.

Table 2. Countermeasure of equivalent power consumption at atomic level

	Doubling		Addition
1.	$T_1 = y_1^2$	1.	$T_1 = z_1^2$
2.	$T_2 = 2x_1$	2.	★
3.	$T_2 = T_1T_2$	3.	$T_2 = z_1T_1$
4.	▲	4.	$T_1 = x_2T_1$
5.	▲	5.	$T_2 = y_2T_2$
6.	$T_2 = 2T_2$	6.	$T_3 = T_1 - x_1$
7.	★	7.	$T_4 = T_2 - y_1$
8.	$T_1 = T_1^2$	8.	$T_1 = T_3^2$
9.	$T_1 = 8T_1$	9.	★ ★ ★
10.	$T_3 = x_1^2$	10.	$T_2 = T_1T_3$
11.	$T_3 = 3x_1^2$	11.	★ ★
12.	$T_3 = T_3 + T$	12.	★
13.	$T_4 = T_3^2$	13.	$T_5 = T_4^2$
14.	▲ ★	14.	$x_3 = 2x_1T_1$
15.	$x_1 = T_4 - 2T_2$	15.	$x_3 = T_2 + x_3$ ★
16.	$T_4 = T_2 - x_1$	16.	$x_3 = T_5 - x_3$
17.	$T_4 = T_3T_4$	17.	$T_5 = T_1^2$
18.	▲	18.	$T_1 = x_1T_1$
19.	$y_1 = T_4 - T_1$	19.	$T_1 = T_1 - x_3$
20.	$T_4 = y_1z_1$	20.	$T_2 = y_1T_2$
21.	▲	21.	$y_3 = T_4T_1$
22.	$z_1 = 2T_4$	22.	$y_3 = y_3 - T_2$
23.	$T_1 = 2T_1$	23.	$z_3 = z_1T_3$
24.	$T = TT_1$	24.	$T = TT_5$

4 Conclusions

This paper proposed an attack case of ECDSA in blockchain. The paper analyzes the major cause of power difference between point doubling and addition operations from atomic operations for ECDSA, and the countermeasure of equivalent power consumption at atomic level is given by adding empty operations in point doubling and addition operations. This is given to secure cryptography technology against side channel attacks for hardware devices of blockchain. Finally, the research results are summarized and a perspective of the future work in this research area is discussed in this paper.

Acknowledgments. The authors would like to thank the reviewers for their detailed reviews and constructive comments, which have helped improve the quality of this paper. This work was supported in part by the National Key Research and Development Project of China (No. 2017YFB0802302), the Science and Technology Support Project of Sichuan Province (No. 2016FZ0112, No. 2017GZ0314, No. 2018GZ0204), the Academic and Technical Leaders

Training Funding Support Projects of Sichuan Province (No. 2016120080102643), the Application Foundation Project of Sichuan Province (No. 2017JY0168), the Science and Technology Project of Chengdu (No. 2017-RK00-00103-ZF, No. 2016-HM01-00217-SF).

References

1. Nakamoto, S.: Bitcoin: A Peer-to-Peer Electronic Cash System. Bitcoin Consulted (2008)
2. Jiang, X., Liu, M.Z., Yang, C., Liu, Y.H., Wang, R.L.: A blockchain-based authentication protocol for WLAN mesh security access. Comput. Mater. Continua 58(1), 45–59 (2019)
3. Giechaskiel, I., Cremers, C., Rasmussen, K.: On bitcoin security in the presence of broken crypto primitives. IACR ePrint Archive, 2016/167 (2016)
4. Sato, M., Matsuo, S.: Long-term public blockchain: resilience against compromise of underlying cryptography. In: IEEE European Symposium on Security & Privacy Workshops, pp. 1–8 (2017)
5. Kocher, P., Jaffe, J., Jun, B.: Differential power analysis. In: Wiener, M. (ed.) CRYPTO 1999. LNCS, vol. 1666, pp. 388–397. Springer, Heidelberg (1999). https://doi.org/10.1007/3-540-48405-1_25
6. Peng, L.U.O., Huiyun, L.I., Kunpeng, W.A.N.G., Yawei, W.A.N.G.: Chosen message attacks method against ECC implementations. J. Commun. 35(5), 79–86 (2014)
7. Goubin, L.: A refined power-analysis attack on elliptic curve cryptosystems. In: Desmedt, Y. G. (ed.) PKC 2003. LNCS, vol. 2567, pp. 199–211. Springer, Heidelberg (2003). https://doi.org/10.1007/3-540-36288-6_15
8. Bauer, A., Jaulmes, E., Prouff, E., Reinhard, J.R., Wild, J.: Horizontal collision correlation attack on elliptic curves. Cryptogr. Commun. 7(1), 91–119 (2015)
9. Coron, J.-S.: Resistance against differential power analysis for elliptic curve cryptosystems. In: Koç, Ç.K., Paar, C. (eds.) CHES 1999. LNCS, vol. 1717, pp. 292–302. Springer, Heidelberg (1999). https://doi.org/10.1007/3-540-48059-5_25
10. Medwed, M., Oswald, E.: Template attacks on ECDSA. In: Chung, K.-I., Sohn, K., Yung, M. (eds.) WISA 2008. LNCS, vol. 5379, pp. 14–27. Springer, Heidelberg (2009). https://doi.org/10.1007/978-3-642-00306-6_2
11. Zhang, Z., Wu, L., Mu, Z., Zhang, X.: A novel template attack on wNAF algorithm of ECC. In: 2014 Tenth International Conference on Computational Intelligence and Security (CIS), pp. 671–675. IEEE (2014)
12. Pang, S.C., Tong, S.Y., Cong, F.Z., et al.: A efficient elliptic curve scalar multiplication algorithm against side channel attacks. In: Proceedings of the 2010 International Conference on Computer, Mechatronics, Control and Electronic Engineering (CMCE 2010), pp. 361–364. Springer, Berlin (2010)
13. Fan, J.F., Guo, X., De Mulder, E., et al.: State-of-the-art of secure ECC implementations: a survey on known side-channel attacks and countermeasures. In: 2010 IEEE International Symposium on Hardware-Oriented Security and Trust (HOST), pp. 76–87. IEEE (2010)
14. Fan, J., Gierlichs, B., Vercauteren, F.: To infinity and beyond: combined attack on ECC using points of low order. In: Preneel, B., Takagi, T. (eds.) CHES 2011. LNCS, vol. 6917, pp. 143–159. Springer, Heidelberg (2011). https://doi.org/10.1007/978-3-642-23951-9_10
15. Chen, T., Li, H., Wu, K., Yu, F.: Countermeasure of ECC against side channel attacks: balanced point addition and point doubling operation procedure. In: Asia Pacific Conference on Information Processing, pp. 465–469 (2009)

16. Nascimento, E., Chmielewski, Ł., Oswald, D., Schwabe, P.: Attacking embedded ECC implementations through CMOV side channels. https://eprint.iacr.org/2016/923.pdf
17. Liu, A.D., Du, X.H., Wang, N., Li, S.Z.: Research progress of blockchain technology and its application in information security. Ruan Jian Xue Bao/J. Softw. **29**(7), 2092–2115 (2018). (in Chinese). http://www.jos.org.cn/1000-9825/5589
18. Deng, Z.L., Ren, Y.J., Liu, Y.P., Yin, X., Shen, Z.X., Kim, H.J.: Blockchain-based trusted electronic records preservation in cloud storage. Comput. Mater. Continua **58**(1), 135–151 (2019)

A Weight-Based Channel Estimation Implementation Algorithm

Jian Liu$^{(\boxtimes)}$ and Yalin Yuan

University of Science and Technology Beijing, Beijing, China
liujian@ustb.edu.cn, yuanyalin81@163.com

Abstract. In vehicular communication, due to the variable channel environment, higher requirements are placed on the performance of channel estimation. In this paper, a baseband communication system based on IEEE802.11p is established, and several channel estimation algorithms are evaluated in the simulation environment. Based on the training sequence and data pilot in the IEEE802.11p frame structure, the two are combined and a weight-based channel estimation algorithm is proposed. The simulation results show that the algorithm improves by 1–2 dB under 10^{-4} conditions.

Keywords: Channel estimation · IEEE 802.11p · Least square · Weights

1 Introduction

In general, when the OFDM signal is transmitted in a wireless environment, the amplitude and phase of the signal are severely distorted due to the selective fading of the time and frequency of the channel [1]. In order to recover the transmitted signal at the receiver, we usually use the channel estimation technique to obtain the channel information and then compensate the received signal [2]. If the channel estimation performance is improved, not only the complexity of the subsequent processing process can be reduced, but also the performance of the entire wireless communication system can be improved.

The IEEE 802.11p standard is based on the IEEE 802.11a protocol and evolved from a series of adaptations to the automotive application environment. After years of development, it has become one of the mainstream standards in the field of vehicular wireless communication systems [3–6]. The main content of the IEEE802.11p protocol is to specify the baseband physical layer design standard for the vehicle wireless communication system [7]. Based on the research of IEEE802.11p protocol, we establish the physical layer model of the OFDM communication system and realize the FPGA design for this model.

In the actual vehicle driving, the Doppler effect caused by the propagation of Doppler, the long distance scattering caused by the delay expansion and the

This work is supported by National Major Project (No. 2017ZX03001021-005).

X. Sun et al. (Eds.): ICAIS 2019, LNCS 11635, pp. 133–142, 2019.
https://doi.org/10.1007/978-3-030-24268-8_13

non-stationary channel statistical characteristics caused by the scattering point all make the vehicle channel show a very strong time variability [8–11], so it is necessary to design a channel estimation algorithm suitable for changeable channels. In this paper, several common channel estimation algorithms are introduced and by comparing and analyzing these algorithms, a weight-based channel estimation algorithm is proposed. In this algorithm, we use the training sequence and data pilot contained in the frame structure inherent in IEEE802.11p, and combine the channel estimation values obtained by the two according to different weight ratios, and perform simulation verification.

2   System Model

Firstly, the general framework of OFDM baseband system based on IEEE802.11p is built. As shown in Fig. 1, the design of the transmitter is a process of forming an OFDM frame, including Signal, Data, and Preamble. The processing of Signal and Data is basically the same, including convolution, interleaving, modulation, insertion of pilot, IFFT, cyclic prefix addition and other processing modules. However, there are certain differences between the two, such as the convolution rate, the depth of interleaving, the modulation method, and so on. The Preamble is located at the forefront of the frame structure and is used for receiver synchronization, channel estimation, and the like.

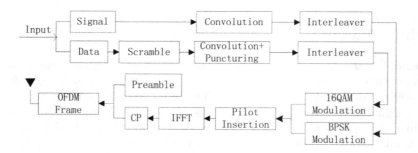

Fig. 1. Transmitter

As shown in Fig. 2, the receiver design is the process of OFDM frame parsing. Synchronization is performed by Preamble in the frame structure, followed by FFT transformation, and data compensation is completed by channel estimation and phase tracking. Then, according to the corresponding module of the transmitter, the Signal and Data are demodulated, deinterleaved, decoded, etc., and the received signal is restored to the original information.

The pilots in the data are distributed in two ways, a block pilot distribution and a comb pilot distribution [12,13]. As shown in Fig. 3, In an OFDM system with bulk pilot distribution, the continuous multiple OFDM symbols constitute a frame, and all the subcarriers in a frame are all inserted into the pilot signal

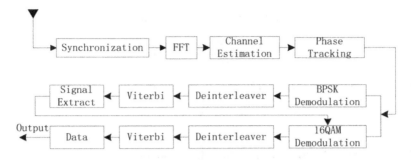

Fig. 2. Receiver

at a fixed time interval, so the pilot signal of the block pilot distribution is continuous in the frequency domain, it appears as a training sequence in IEEE 802.11p. The pilot symbols are spaced apart between subcarriers at any time. This distribution is called a comb pilot distribution, which is continuous in the time domain, so it has better adaptability to channel variations, it appears as a data pilot in IEEE 802.11p.

Fig. 3. Frame Structure of PPDU

3   Channel Estimation Implementation Algorithm

3.1   Common Channel Estimation Algorithm

There are many commonly used channel estimation algorithms. Here we focus on LS channel estimation, MMSE channel estimation, and LMMSE channel estimation.

LS Channel Estimation. LS channel estimation is the most common channel estimation method. The frequency domain received signal of the OFDM pilot is modeled as

$$Y = XH + N \tag{1}$$

where Y is the received signal, X is the transmitted signal, H is the frequency domain response of the channel, and N is the channel noise.

The LS estimation algorithm is to minimize the following squared errors:

$$H_{LS} = arg\{min\{(Y - XH_{LS})^H(Y - XH_{LS})\}\} \tag{2}$$

Find the partial derivative of the H_{LS} in (2), and make the equation zero:

$$\frac{\partial (Y - XH_{LS})^H (Y - XH_{LS})}{\partial H_{LS}} = 0 \tag{3}$$

The frequency response to get the channel estimate is:

$$\hat{H}_{LS} = X^{-1} Y \tag{4}$$

MMSE Channel Estimation. Since the LS algorithm is not highly accurate due to noise interference, the minimum mean square error (MMSE) channel estimation is proposed. It uses the second-order statistical properties of the channel to reduce the mean square error and greatly improves the accuracy of the channel estimation [14–16]. The channel estimation is modeled as

$$\hat{H}_{MMSE} = R_{HY} R_{YY}^{-1} Y \tag{5}$$

where R_{HY} is the cross-covariance matrix of channel transfer function and received signal, and R_{YY} is the auto-covariance matrix of the received signal.

$$R_{HY} = E\{HY^H\} = E\{H(HX + N)^H\} = R_{HH} X^H \tag{6}$$

$$R_{YY} = E\{YY^H\} = E\{(HX + N)(HX + N)^H\} = X R_{HH} X^H + \sigma_n^2 I_N \tag{7}$$

Substituting (6) and (7) into (5), the estimated value of the MMSE channel is modeled as

$$\hat{H}_{MMSE} = R_{HH}(R_{HH} + \sigma_n^2 (X^H X)^{-1})^{-1} \hat{H}_{LS} \tag{8}$$

where R_{HH} is the auto-covariance of the channel frequency response H, which is related to the channel characteristics, and σ_n^2 is the variance of the noise.

LMMSE Channel Estimation. It can be seen from (8) that the MMSE channel estimation method involves the inverse operation of the matrix, which is more complicated, and the calculation amount increases exponentially as the number of operation points increases. In order to reduce the complexity, by using $E\{(X^H X)^{-1}\}$ instead of $(X^H X)^{-1}$, the linear minimum mean square error (LMMSE) channel estimate can be obtained as

$$\hat{H}_{LMMSE} = R_{HH}(R_{HH} + \frac{\beta}{SNR})^{-1} \hat{H}_{LS} \tag{9}$$

where β is related to the constellation modulation method, such as 1 in QPSK modulation and 17/9 in 16QAM modulation, SNR represents the average signal to noise ratio [17, 18].

3.2   New Weight-Based Channel Estimation Algorithm

The training sequence designed in this paper or the data pilot can use the above LS, MMSE, and LMMSE methods to obtain the channel estimation value. MMSE and LMMSE involve matrix operations, which have high complexity and are not suitable for hardware requirements in FPGA design. Therefore, this paper uses LS channel estimation algorithm. From the frame structure in the second section, the training sequence is continuous in the frequency domain and discontinuous in the time domain, which is suitable for a static channel environment. In contrast, data pilots are continuous in the time domain and discontinuous in the frequency domain, which is more suitable for dynamic channel environments. However, since the data pilots are not continuous in the frequency domain, an interpolation algorithm is needed to make them continuous. In this paper, the simplest one-dimensional linear interpolation is used, which is to calculate the channel frequency response of the intermediate data subcarrier by using the channel frequency response estimates of two adjacent pilot subcarriers [19, 20].

$$\hat{H}_{m+1} = (1 - \frac{l}{L})\hat{H}_p(m) + \frac{l}{L}\hat{H}_p(m+1) \tag{10}$$

In the equation (10), $\hat{H}_p(m)$ and $\hat{H}_p(m+1)$ are estimated pilot channel responses, and $\hat{H}_{m+1}$ is the channel response at the data symbol.

Although the channel frequency response based on the data pilot is more suitable for a variable channel environment, the data pilot is too small, the frequency response value obtained by simply using the data pilot has a large error. Therefore, the channel estimation values obtained by the training sequence and the data pilot are combined according to a certain weight ratio, a better channel frequency response value is obtained [21, 22].

In the frame structure of IEEE802.11p, we can obtain four known pilot data. Since the channel estimates obtained by the data pilots are closer to the true values, we assume that the four channel estimates [23] are true values, and the channel estimates obtained from the four pilots [24] corresponding to the training sequence are subjected to error calculation. It can be concluded from the analysis that the channel estimation algorithm based on data pilot performs better under low SNR conditions, and the channel estimation algorithm based on training sequence performs better under high SNR conditions. Therefore, at a low SNR (0dB), we can obtain the maximum value of error A_{max}. By changing the SNR, different absolute error values E_{abs} are obtained, which are divided by the maximum value A_{max} to obtain the weight value α.

$$\alpha = \frac{E_{abs}}{A_{max}} \tag{11}$$

Then the new channel estimate is:

$$\hat{H}_{new} = \alpha\hat{H}_{pilot} + (1 - \alpha)\hat{H}_{preamble} \tag{12}$$

where $\hat{H}_{pilot}$ is the channel estimation value obtained after the data pilot is interpolated, and $\hat{H}_{preamble}$ is the channel estimation value obtained by the training sequence.

4 Performance Evaluation

In this paper, the performance of the IEE802.11p baseband system is evaluated by the Matlab simulation platform.

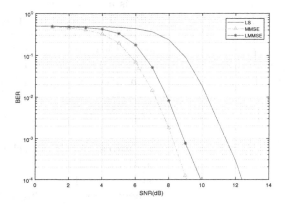

Fig. 4. LS, MMSE, LMMSE comparison

As shown in Fig. 4, the simulation obtains bit error rate curve of three channel estimations based on the training sequence LS, MMSE, and LMMSE, the MMSE algorithm has the best performance and the LS algorithm has the worst performance. The LMMSE algorithm is a simplification of the MMSE algorithm, both in terms of computational complexity and performance between MMSE and LS.

As shown in Fig. 5, the simulation obtains bit error rate curve of the channel estimation algorithm based on the training sequence and the data pilot under different signal to noise ratio conditions. The channel estimation algorithm based on data pilot performs better under low SNR conditions, and the channel estimation algorithm based on training sequence performs better under high SNR conditions.

As shown in Fig. 6, the simulation results show that the error values of the data pilot and training sequence channel estimation change with the signal to noise ratio.

As shown in Fig. 7, the simulation obtains comparison of new weight-based channel estimation algorithms with other algorithms.

When we implement the above algorithm in FPGA, we need to use Matlab's algorithm and result as a reference. However, the data of the two are not the

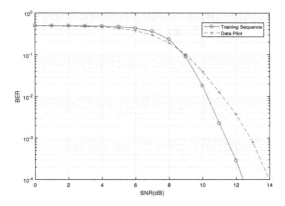

Fig. 5. Channel estimation comparison based on training sequence and data pilot

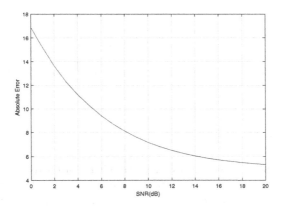

Fig. 6. Error value based on data pilot and training sequence channel estimation

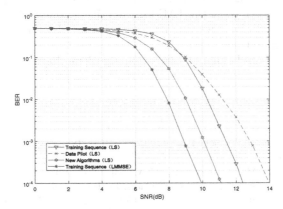

Fig. 7. Comparison of new weight-based channel estimation algorithms with other algorithms

same, which requires fixed-point design. As shown in Fig. 8, although the performance of the system after the fixed point is slightly reduced, it is basically the same as before the fixed point.

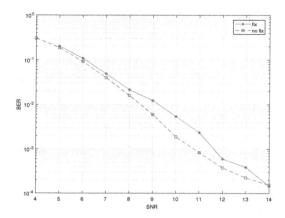

Fig. 8. Performance comparison between fixed-point system and unpointed system

5   Conclusion

In this paper, the channel estimation algorithm is researched and implemented by establishing a baseband communication system based on IEEE802.11p. Based on the two channel estimation schemes of training sequence and data pilot, we propose a new weight-based channel estimation algorithm. The simulation results show that the algorithm significantly improves the system performance, although slightly lower than the LMMSE algorithm, but in terms of complexity, the weight-based channel estimation algorithm is better than the LMMSE algorithm. Therefore, the complexity and performance of the integrated system design, the weight-based channel estimation algorithm better achieves this goal.

References

1. Ku, M.L., Huang, C.C.: A refined channel estimation method for STBC/OFDM systems in high-mobility wireless channels. IEEE Trans. Wirel. Commun. **7**(11), 4312–4320 (2008)
2. Shirmohammadi, M., Damavandi, M.A.: Blind channel estimation of MIMO-OFDM systems in satellite communication. In: International Conference on Information and Communication Technology Convergence, pp. 704–709. IEEE (2015)
3. Han, S., Zhao, K., Yang, L.Q., et al.: Performance evaluation for multi-antenna vehicular communication based on IEEE 802.11p standard. In: International Conference on Computing, Networking and Communications, pp. 1–5. IEEE (2016)

4. Wang, B., Gu, X., Yan, S.: STCS: a practical solar radiation based temperature correction scheme in meteorological WSN. Int. J. Sens. Netw. **28**(1), 22–33 (2018)
5. Choi, J.Y., Mun, C., Yook, J.G.: Adaptive channel estimation based on a decision method using a long preamble for the IEEE 802.11p. In: Vehicular Technology Conference: VTC 2017-Spring, pp. 1–5. IEEE (2017)
6. Bazzi, A., Masini, B.M., Zanella, A., et al.: On the performance of IEEE 802.11p and LTE-V2V for the cooperative awareness of connected vehicles. IEEE Trans. Veh. Technol. **66**, 10419–10432 (2017)
7. Yang, Y.: Inter-vehicle cooperative channel estimation for IEEE802.11p systems. In: Vehicular Technology Conference. IEEE (2016)
8. Walter, M., Shutin, D., Dammann, A.: Time-variant Doppler PDFs and characteristic functions for the vehicle-to-vehicle channel. IEEE Trans. Veh. Technol. **66**, 10748–10763 (2017)
9. Mecklenbrauker, C.F., Molisch, A.F., Karedal, J., et al.: Vehicular channel characterization and its implications for wireless system design and performance. Proc. IEEE **99**(7), 1189–1212 (2011)
10. Wang, B., Gu, X., Zhou, A.: E2S2: a code dissemination approach to energy efficiency and status surveillance for wireless sensor networks. J. Internet Technol. **8**(4), 877–885 (2017). https://doi.org/10.6138/JIT.2017.18.4.20160815
11. Wang, B., Gu, X., Ma, L., et al.: Temperature error correction based on BP neural network in meteorological wireless sensor network. Int. J. Sens. Netw. **23**(4), 265–278 (2017)
12. Liu, P., Wang, X., Chaudhry, S.R., et al.: Secure video streaming with lightweight cipher PRESENT in an SDN Testbed (2018)
13. Zhang, K., Xue, L.: Iterative weight LS channel estimation in time domain for OQAM/OFDM systems. In: IEEE International Conference on Computer and Communications, pp. 158–161. IEEE (2017)
14. Liu, K., Ke, X.: Research of MMSE and LS channel estimation in OFDM systems. In: International Conference on Information Science and Engineering, pp. 2308–2311. IEEE (2010)
15. Khan, M.N.I., Alam, M.J.: Noise reduction algorithm for LS channel estimation in OFDM system. In: International Conference on Computer and Information Technology, pp. 310–315. IEEE (2013)
16. Sutar, M.B., Patil, V.S.: LS and MMSE estimation with different fading channels for OFDM system. In: International Conference of Electronics, Communication and Aerospace Technology, pp. 740–745 (2017)
17. Desai, M.V., Gupta, S., Dalal, U.D.: DCT-SVD based channel estimation technique in IEEE 802.16e DL-PUSC system. In: International Conference on Emerging Technology Trends in Electronics, Communication and Networking, pp. 1–6. IEEE (2015)
18. Tong, Z.R., Guo, M.J., Yang, X.F., et al.: Performance comparison of LS and LMMSE channel estimation algorithm for CO-OFDM system. Appl. Mech. Mater. **130–134**, 2965–2968 (2012)
19. Hung, K.C., Lin, D.W.: Pilot-aided multicarrier channel estimation via MMSE linear phase-shifted polynomial interpolation. IEEE Trans. Wirel. Commun. **9**(8), 2539–2549 (2010)
20. Dong, X., Lu, W.S., Soong, A.C.K.: Linear interpolation in pilot symbol assisted channel estimation for OFDM. IEEE Trans. Wirel. Commun. **6**(5), 1910–1920 (2007)
21. Fertl, P., Matz, G.: Channel estimation in wireless OFDM systems with irregular pilot distribution. IEEE Trans. Sig. Process. **58**(6), 3180–3194 (2010)

22. Zhang, C., Zhao, H., Li, J., et al.: Experimental study of weighted inter-frame averaging based channel estimation for CO-OFDM system. In: Optical Fiber Communications Conference and Exhibition, pp. 1–3. IEEE (2014)
23. Li, Y.Y., Huang, Z., Ma, Y.G., Wen, G.J.: acSB: anti-collision selective-based broad-cast protocol in CR-AdHocs. CMC: Comput. Mater. Contin. **56**(1), 35–46 (2018)
24. Jiang, Y., Zhong, X.L., Guo, Y., Duan, M.X.: Communication mechanism and algorithm of composite location analysis of emergency communication based on rail. CMC: Comput. Mater. Contin. **57**(2), 321–340 (2018)

Multi-party Quantum Communication Complexity on Composite Boolean-Valued Function

Wenbin Yu[1,3]([✉]), Zangqiang Dong[2], Wenjie Liu[1], Zhiguo Qu[1], Xiaolong Xu[1], and Alex Xiangyang Liu[1,3]

[1] Jiangsu Collaborative Innovation Center of Atmospheric Environment and Equipment Technology (CICAEET), Jiangsu Engineering Center of Network Monitoring, School of Computer and Software,
Nanjing University of Information Science and Technology,
Nanjing 210044, Jiangsu Province, People's Republic of China
yuwenbil@msu.edu
[2] The Department of Computer Science and Application,
Zhengzhou Institute of Aeronautical Industry Management, Zhengzhou 450015,
Henan Province, People's Republic of China
[3] Department of Computer Science and Engineering, Michigan State University,
East Lansing, MI 48824-1226, USA

Abstract. The performance of communication complexity depends on the selected computation model. Even on the specific model the quantum communication complexity is not always better than the classical one. This paper investigates the quantum communication complexity based on a multi-party computation model of the composite Boolean-valued function. On this model we design a quantum distributed algorithm to obtain the upper bound of quantum communication complexity. The result shows that the performance gap between quantum and classical communication complexity depends on the infinity order of function domain's square root and users' number. In the best situation the performance of the quantum communication complexity wins the quadratic level of advantage than the classical one. And sometimes the classical way is more efficient than the quantum one.

Keywords: Quantum algorithm · Quantum communication · Quantum complexity

1 Introduction

This model was first introduced by Yao [1] with classical communication complexity (CCC for short). Thereafter, some investigations show that if the quantum computation and communication are allowed, some two-party and three-party quantum communication complexity (QCC for short) will be degraded, which has been proven impossible in the classical case.

© Springer Nature Switzerland AG 2019
X. Sun et al. (Eds.): ICAIS 2019, LNCS 11635, pp. 143–154, 2019.
https://doi.org/10.1007/978-3-030-24268-8_14

With more attention given on the research of QCC, there have been many studies on various computation models. Paper [2] investigates the Hamming Distance problem with the prior shared entanglement. Paper [3] studies the communication complexity in the model of the remote quantum state preparation. Papers [4, 5] concern the single channel communication complexity with the two-party Boolean function, pointing out that there is an exponential level reduction in the communication complexity of the quantum method compared with the classical one. Papers [6–10] present the lower bound of the QCC based on the various models of two-party computation. Papers [11] study the applying of the Kolmogorov complexity and combination methods in the QCC area. Paper [12] presents the QCC of the symmetric function on the condition of none error upper bound. Paper [13] studies the QCC with prior shared entanglement based on the two-party computation model with the binary inner product function. Recent research shows that quantum Zeno-Effect could be used in QCC [14] and quantum private information retrieval has linear QCC [15].

By now, the investigation on QCC is heading for the Multi-Party Computation (MPC for short) model [16–20]. Paper [16] develops a multi-party quantum communication complexity under the k-ary Boolean function model. Paper [17] presents the QCC based on the NOF (Number-On-Forehead) model. Paper [18] involves with the QCC based on the random k-party NOF model. Paper [19] investigates on the strong non-determinative multi-party QCC under the NOF and the NIH (Number-In-Hand) model. Paper [20] discusses a special simplified multi-party communication experiment, and shows that the quantum communication gains an exponential level of performance improvement over the classical case. Paper [23] provides a quantum query complexity for triangle finding problem. Paper [24] proves a special case of QCC when the Alice and Bob are restricted to using classical communication. Paper [25, 26] present two novel quantum algorithms related to QCC, which are applied to the quantum secure communication and quantum signature scheme respectively.

In general, it is an important method to reduce the communication complexity adopting the model of the prior shared quantum entanglement. But the prior assignment of the shared entanglement resource will cause communication overhead, which is not taken into consideration usually. Meanwhile, although the quantum method can gain a high performance advantage, such as exponential decrease in communication complexity, in more multi-party computation model, the classical way may reveal its advantage more efficiently than the quantum one. For this problem, it's necessary to signify the performance bound between the quantum way and the classical one. In this paper, we investigate the multi-party QCC without prior shared entanglement based on an MPC model with a composite Boolean-valued function, design a special distributed algorithm and presents the performance bound of communication complexity for the quantum communication and the classical one.

2 The Multi-party QCC Based on the Composite Boolean-Valued Function

2.1 The MPC Model Based on the Composite Boolean-Valued Function

In this section we introduce the MPC model based on the composite Boolean-valued function. Supposing that there are K users, marked as user 1 to user K, provided with the function

$$
\begin{cases}
user1: & y_1 = g_1(x) \\
user2: & y_2 = g_2(x) \\
\quad\vdots & \quad\vdots \\
userK: & y_K = g_K(x)
\end{cases}
$$

in turn. The kth user wants to compute the function $g_k(x)$, $1 \leq k \leq K$. The function $\{g_k(x)|1 \leq k \leq K\}$ could be arbitrary function in the application, but only satisfying that they share the same function domain and codomain. Besides, denote the function $F(y_1, y_2, \cdots, y_K)$ as an arbitrary K-ary Boolean-valued function, only to satisfy that $F(y_1, y_2, \cdots, y_K) \in \{0, 1\}$ and $y_k = g_k(x)$, $1 \leq k \leq K$.

Without loss of generality, denote the domain of function $g_k(x)$ as $X = \{x|0 \leq x \leq N - 1, x \in \mathbb{Z}\}$, the length of $\mathbf{X}$ is N. For the convenience let N be an integer that satisfies $N = 2^n$ (As for the case of $2^n < N < 2^{n+1}$, simply have $N = 2^{n+1}$, the expanded part of $\mathbf{X}$ does not influence on the solving of the problem), therefore it's feasible to use the length of $n = \log N$ bits information to describe the function domain. And similarly, supposing that the codomain of $g_k(x)$ is $Y = \{y|0 \leq y \leq H - 1, y \in \mathbb{Z}\}$, and the length to store the codomain information is $h = \log H$ bits. So we have

$$
g_k(x) : X \rightarrow Y
$$
$$
F(y_1, y_2, \cdots, y_K) : Y^K \rightarrow \{0, 1\}
$$
$$
F(g_1(x), g_2(x), \cdots, g_K(x)) : X \rightarrow \{0, 1\}
$$

In summary, the goal of our research on the multiparty computation task is to find a solution x to equation $F(g_1(x), g_2(x), \cdots, g_K(x)) = 1$ by comparing the results of K arbitrary functions $\{g_k(x)|1 \leq k \leq K\}$ calculation held by the multi-users.

2.2 The MPC Model Based on the Composite Boolean-Valued Function

With the traditional classical methods, the users need communication for sharing their function value in MPC model. It's easy to see that users should send as few messages as possible among them to compare their computation results and achieve the task. Here we present the description of the Classical Optimal (CO for short) algorithm for the MPC model on the condition that the sharing of the random number is forbidden.

The algorithm is described as follows: first, every user prepares one vector W_k with length of N, and save the computation result of the corresponding function $g_k(x)$ in W_k, that is

$$W_k = [g_k(0), g_k(1), \cdots, g_k(N-1)], \quad 1 \leq k \leq K$$

Obviously, W_k stores $N \times h$ bits of information. Second, to gather all the calculation results of the users' functions and converge to one user, it takes at $K-1$ times of communications in the classical methods. At last, applying the collected message the function $F(y_1, y_2, \cdots, y_K)$ at the last user and obtaining the final result, the solution x is found.

Without loss of generality, denote user 1 as the message gathering center for the rest. Then we present the steps of the CO algorithm for the MPC model, the following algorithm begins with user 2.

CO algorithm:

Step 1 User k calculate his function $g_k(x)$, save the result into the prepared vector W_k and send it to user 1.

Step 2 Check whether user k is the final one. If not, let user $k+1$ executes Step 1; else, user K executes Step 3.

Step 3 User 1 calculates his own function $g_1(x)$, then calculates function $F(y_1, y_2, \cdots, y_K)$ based on all the received vectors W_k from other users, and outcomes the solution to the model.

Algorithm ends.

For a specific MPC model, according to a certain form of the function $g_k(x)$ and $F(y_1, y_2, \cdots, y_K)$, the CO algorithm can be optimized correspondingly, which will considerably lower the average communication cost. But in the worst case, this kind of MPC model shows the same level of communication cost.

Theorem 1. With the CO algorithm, the upper bound of communication complexity is $O(KN\log H)$.

Proof. According to the above statements on the algorithm, it can be inferred that the communication cost of the algorithm at least is

$$Nh(K-1) + CK = N(K-1)\log H + CK \tag{1}$$

Where C is a constant, CK is the affiliate communication amount used to specify the concrete algorithm and show the feedback of the final results. By Eq. (1), we can find that the upper bound is

$$O(KN\log H)$$

2.3   Method: Distributed Oracle Operation and Quantum Distributed Algorithm

Based on the foregoing MPC model, we construct the quantum distributed (QD for short) algorithm with DOO and Grover iteration [21].

The Function and Operator Definition Related to the QD Algorithm

The initialization of the algorithm starts with user 1. First, user 1 needs to prepare an n qubits state $|0\rangle^{\otimes n}$, then apply the Hadamard transformation $H^{\otimes n}$ on it, which will make the n qubits at an uniform superposition state $|\Psi\rangle = \frac{1}{\sqrt{N}}\sum_{x=0}^{N-1}|x\rangle$. Quantum state $|\Psi\rangle$ is used to save the N values of the user function domain, where $|x\rangle = |0\rangle, |1\rangle, \cdots, |N-1\rangle$ are the N eigenstates corresponding to the indices of the N values in the function domain. The quantum state $|\Psi\rangle$ is the initial input of user 1, the h qubits $|g_k(x)\rangle$ is used to save the calculated message about x for the kth user.

Second, define the quantum state sequence $\{|\varphi_k\rangle|1 \leq k \leq K\}$ and $\{|\psi_k\rangle|1 \leq k \leq K\}$, where

$$|\varphi_k\rangle = |x\rangle|g_1(x)\rangle|g_2(x)\rangle \cdots |g_{k-1}(x)\rangle$$
$$|\psi_k\rangle = |x\rangle|g_1(x)\rangle|g_2(x)\rangle \cdots |g_{K-k}(x)\rangle$$

It can be seen that $|\varphi_k\rangle$ and $|\psi_k\rangle$ are $n+(k-1)h$ and $n+(K-k)h$ qubits respectively. Especially we have $|\varphi_1\rangle = |x\rangle$ when $k = 1$ and $|\psi_K\rangle = |x\rangle$ when $k = K$, both of which are of n qubits length.

Moreover, define the unitary operator sequence $\{U_k|1 \leq k \leq K - 1\}$, where U_k is a $n + kh$ dimensional operator. It is used to operate on the last qubit of the input states, add it to $g_k(x)$ with the mod H. Especially when $k = 1$, U_1 is an n dimensional unitary operator. The quantum circuit is described in Fig. 1.

Fig. 1. The quantum circuit of operator U_k.

It can be verified that the operator U_k is a reversible unitary transformation, and the reversible operator of U_k satisfies the condition $U_k^{-1} = U_k^{H-1}$. The same type of operators with U_k is applied in the Deutsch–Jozsa [22] algorithm once. In the quantum computation, the quantum calculation circuits which satisfy the reversible transformation condition are proved to be physically realizable.

Still, define the $n + (k-1)h$ dimensional unitary operator Oracle, which is an expansion of the Oracle operator in the Grover's quantum search algorithm [21], that is

$$|x\rangle|g_1(x)\rangle|g_2(x)\rangle \cdots |g_{K-1}(x)\rangle$$
$$\xrightarrow{Oracle} (-1)^{F(g_1(x),g_2(x),\cdots,g_K(x))}|x\rangle|g_1(x)\rangle|g_2(x)\rangle \cdots |g_{K-1}(x)\rangle$$

Obviously, the Oracle operator is unitary as well as reversible, therefore is physically realizable.

Finally, apply the operator sequence $\{U_k|1 \leq k \leq K-1\}$ and operator Oracle we defined to the quantum state sequence $\{|\varphi_k\rangle|1 \leq k \leq K\}$ and $\{|\psi_k\rangle|1 \leq k \leq K\}$, then there are

$$|\varphi_k\rangle|0\rangle^{\otimes h} \xrightarrow{U_k} |\varphi_{k+1}\rangle$$
$$|\psi_k\rangle \xrightarrow{U_{K-k}^{H-1}} |\psi_{k+1}\rangle|0\rangle^{\otimes h}$$
$$|\varphi_K\rangle \xrightarrow{Oracle} |\psi_1\rangle$$

Distributed Oracle Operation

As is shown in Fig. 2, we separate the DOO algorithm into three phases. Phase 1 is a forward communication process from user 1 to user K. During this phase, every user applies the unitary operator in the sequence $\{U_k|1 \leq k \leq K-1\}$ to the quantum states in the sequence $\{|\varphi_k\rangle|1 \leq k \leq K\}$ in order, and transfers the result to the next user one by one. Therefore, the result of each user's calculation will finally be transferred to user K.

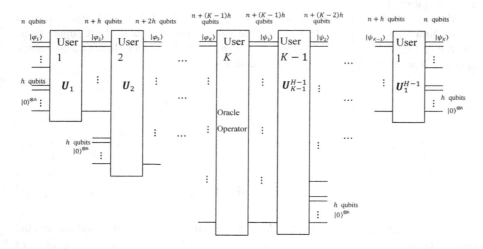

Fig. 2. The quantum circuit of DOO.

In the second phase, user K applies the Oracle operator to quantum state $|\varphi_K\rangle$ and gets the quantum state $|\psi_1\rangle$. Meanwhile, all the quantum states corresponding to the solution of the MPC model will get a phase reverse, so that the solution can be marked.

The third phase is the reverse communication process from user K to user 1. Every user applies the unitary operator in the sequence $\{U_k^{-1}|1 \leq k \leq K-1\}$ to the quantum states in the sequence $\{|\psi_k\rangle|1 \leq k \leq K\}$ in turn, and transfers the result to the next user, then the quantum states carrying the solution mark will be delivered to user 1. So the entire process of DOO algorithm is as follows.

DOO algorithm:

(1) The forward communication phase from user 1 to user K.

Step 1: The initial input is that user 1 receives the quantum state $|\varphi_1\rangle$.

Step 2: The current user receives quantum state $|\varphi_K\rangle$, then adds h qubits $|0\rangle^{\otimes h}$ to its last qubit as the auxiliary quantum state.

Step 3: The current user applies operator U_k to the outcome of step 2 to get quantum state $|\varphi_{k+1}\rangle$.

Step 4: The current user transfers quantum state $|\varphi_{k+1}\rangle$ to the next user.

Step 5: The next user goes to Step 2 to start. Repeating this process till the quantum state $|\varphi_K$ is transferred to the last user K.

(2) User K executes the Oracle operator on the received quantum state $|\varphi_K\rangle$, gets state $|\psi_1\rangle$. Sends $|\psi_1\rangle$ to user $K-1$.

(3) The backward communication phase from user $K-1$ to user 1

Step 1: The initial input is that user $K-1$ receives the quantum state $|\psi_1\rangle$.

Step 2: The current user receives the quantum state $|\psi_k\rangle$, applies the operator U_{K-k}^{-1} to it and gets state $|\psi_{k+1}\rangle|0\rangle^{\otimes h}$.

Step 3: The current user removes the last h qubits $|0\rangle^{\otimes h}$ from the quantum state $|\psi_{k+1}\rangle|0\rangle^{\otimes h}$ and gets the state $|\psi_{k+1}\rangle$.

Step 4: The current user sends $|\psi_{k+1}\rangle$ to the previous user.

Step 5: The previous user goes to Step 2 and start operating. Repeating this process till the quantum state $|\psi_{k-1}\rangle$ is transferred to user 1.

Step 6: User 1 gets the quantum state $|\psi_{k-1}\rangle$, applies the operator U_1^{-1} to it and gets the state $|\psi_K\rangle|0\rangle^{\otimes h}$; Then removes the last h qubits $|0\rangle^{\otimes h}$ and gets $|\psi_K\rangle$.

Algorithm ends.

The QD Algorithm:

In the DOO algorithm, we take the quantum state as the information carrier. Through the process of delivering and sharing quantum states within multi users, each user executes the corresponding operation on the quantum state signal to cooperate with a joint distributed computation task. As for the MPC model, the operation the DOO algorithm performs on the input quantum state $|\varphi_1$ can be written as:

$$\text{DOO: } |x\rangle \rightarrow (-1)^{F(g_1(x),g_2(x),\cdots,g_K(x))}|x\rangle.$$

This means when every turn of DOO algorithm is carried out, the quantum eigenstates corresponding to the solutions will get a phase reverse.

In order to implement QD algorithm, we need to apply the aforementioned DOO algorithm to the Grover iteration. Here we present one time of the Grover iteration steps:

Step 1: Applying the DOO algorithm. Check whether each value index is the solution of MPC model or not.

Step 2: Apply Hadamard transform $H^{\otimes n}$ to the result of step

Step 3: Carry on conditional phase shift to the outcome of Step 2, so as to make every base state other than $|0\rangle$ gets -1 phase shift, i.e. $|x\rangle \rightarrow -(-1)^{\delta_{x,0}}|x\rangle$.

Step 4: Apply the Hadamard transform $H^{\otimes n}$ to the result of Step 3.

According to the features of the Grover algorithm, we notice that as the iteration times approach $O(\sqrt{N})$ the weights of some eigenstates of the n qubits representing the function domain will grow big enough, where these eigenstates are all solutions to the MPC model. If we measure the eigenstates on the n qubits after iteration, we'll obtain the solution to the problem with an ultimately large probability.

2.4 The Multi-party QCC

The QD algorithm means that the quantum computation and communication method can be taken to solve the MPC model. However, how many communications the QD algorithm takes in solving the MPC model remains a request for the survey and deduction on the communication complexity. Section 2.4 gives the presentation of the QCC on MPC model.

Theorem 2. With QD algorithm, the upper bound of communication complexity is $O\left((K\log N + K^2\log H)\sqrt{N}\right)$.

Proof. As Fig. 3 shows, each iteration of DOO consists of two processes: the forward and backward communication process. In the forward process, every user delivers quantum state to the next one by one, which at least needs the communicating cost

$$(K-1)\log N + K(K-1)h/2.$$

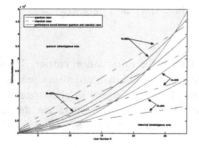
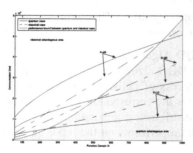

Fig. 3. The communication cost comparison of QD and CO algorithm for N = 100 and K = 10 respectively. (Color figure online)

The backward process from user K to user 1 in delivering the quantum state bears the same communication cost with the forward stage. Hence, in one total iteration, the communication cost at least is

$$2(K-1)\log N + K(K-1)h = 2(K-1)\log N + K(K-1)\log H.$$

Since the algorithm needs $O(\sqrt{N})$ iterations in all, thus with the QD algorithm the upper bound is

$$O\left((2(K-1)\log N + K(K-1)\log H)\sqrt{N}\right) \tag{2}$$

For abbreviation, we have

$$O\left((K\log N + K^2\log H)\sqrt{N}\right) \tag{3}$$

By observing Eqs. (2) and (3), we notice that the first term in Eq. (3) satisfies the condition $O\left(K\sqrt{N}\log N\right) \ll O(KN\log H)$, therefore the second term in Eq. (3) decides the order of magnitude of the QCC. Concerning the relative correlation of each variable in the second term, we can theoretically make the comparison of communication complexity between the classical and the quantum way.

In the first place, if $O(K) = O(\sqrt{N})$, we have $O\left(K^2\sqrt{N}\log H\right) = O(KN\log H)$, that means when the users' number K is of the same infinity order with the square root of the domain $\sqrt{N}$, the quantum method have the same communication complexity with the classical method. In this case, the QCC is $O(KN\log H)$.

To the next, when $O(K) > O(\sqrt{N})$, that means the order of the infinity of user K is higher than $\sqrt{N}$, so we have $O\left(K^2\sqrt{N}\log H\right) > O(KN\log H)$. This means the QCC will exceed the classical case. In this case, the QCC goes over $O(KN\log H)$.

Finally, when $O(K) < O(\sqrt{N})$, that means the order of infinity of user K is lower than $\sqrt{N}$, then $O\left(K^2\sqrt{N}\log H\right) < O(KN\log H)$. This means the QCC is less than $O(KN\log H)$. For the extreme case, when $O(K) \leq O(\log_H N)$, the QCC will be decided by the first term of Eq. (3), $O\left(K\sqrt{N}\log N\right)$, consequently the QCC will be reduced at nearly a quadratic level compared with the classical case. Hence, when $O(\log_H N) < O(K) < O(\sqrt{N})$, the QCC is between $O\left(K\sqrt{N}\log N\right)$ and $O(KN\log H)$.

In a word, from the comparison on the communication complexity of the QD and CO algorithm, it can be seen that, the performance gap of the QCC and CCC relies on the relation of the infinity order between the users' number K and the square root of the function domain $\sqrt{N}$. Considering this situation, we list the communication complexity relations in Table 1.

Table 1. Communication complexity comparison between quantum and classical ways.

The relation of K, N and H	QCC	Performance comparison	CCC
$O(K) \leq O(\log_H N)$	$O\left(K\sqrt{N}\log N\right)$	Nearly quadratic level less than	$O(KN\log H)$
$O(\log_H N) < O(K) < O(\sqrt{N})$	$O\left(K^2\sqrt{N}\log H\right)$	Less than	
$O(K) = O(\sqrt{N})$	$O\left(K^2\sqrt{N}\log H\right)$	Equal to	
$O(K) > O(\sqrt{N})$	$O\left(K^2\sqrt{N}\log H\right)$	More than	

2.5   Performance Comparison Between CO and QD Algorithm

In Sect. 2.4, we present the comparison results on communication complexity of the QD and CO algorithm, which shows the performance difference counts on the relation of users' number K and function domain N. The result proves that QD algorithm's complexity gains a nearly quadratic level reduction compared to the CO algorithm in the best case; however, under a bad case, the QD algorithm has a higher communication complexity than that of the CO algorithm.

According to Theorem 1, the communication overhead of CO algorithm can be calculated; and similarly, the communication overhead of QD algorithm can be calculated based on Theorem 2. The iteration times of the QD algorithm can be estimated with the upper bound of the Eq. (4)

$$R \leq \frac{\pi}{4} \sqrt{\frac{N}{M}}. \tag{4}$$

Assuming the solution's number M to be 1, the information length of the function codomain h to be 2 bits. In the calculation process, all the auxiliary communication overhead is neglected (It doesn't influence the performance analysis of the algorithm).

The left part of Fig. 3 shows the communication cost of QD and CO algorithm increases with the increasing of the users' number K. Here the function domain parameter N is set to 200, 400, 600, 800 respectively,and let user number parameter K varies from 2 to 30. We can see that, when N is fixed to 200 and the users' number K is under 10, the communication cost of the QD algorithm is lower than that of the CO algorithm; when K is over 10 users, the communication cost of QD algorithm begins to increase. As Fig. 3 describes, the red line marks the performance bound of quantum and classical algorithm. In the right-down area of this line, the communication cost of the classical algorithm is lower than that of the quantum one with the same parameter; while in the left-upper area, the quantum case predominates over the classical one in the same condition, it has a comparatively lower communication cost.

The right part of Fig. 3 shows the communication cost of QD and CO algorithm increases with the increasing of the function domain N. Set users' number K to be 12, 20, 28, and function domain parameter N to increase from 60 to 1000. It's illustrative that when K is set to 12 and N is around 250, the QD algorithm begins to manifest its dominance over the CO algorithm. This trend gradually becomes more significant, especially when N is a very large number, the communication cost of QD algorithm gets a nearly quadratic level of reduction compared to the CO algorithm. This situation is also exhibited by the red line in Fig. 3 that marks the performance bound on the quantum and classical case.

3   Conclusion

In this paper, we investigate the QCC based on the MPC model of composite Boolean-valued function, presenting the CCC upper bound of this issue as O(KNlog$H$). Furthermore, a QD algorithm of the MPC model is presented and proves the QCC upper bound to be $O\big((K\log N + K^2\log H)\sqrt{N}\big)$. From the theory analysis and numerical experiment result, we establish that, when the square root of function domain and the user number are of the same order of infinity, there is no distinct performance difference between QD algorithm and CO algorithm; when the users' number is of higher infinity order than the square root of domain, QD has a higher communication cost. On this occasion, QD algorithm does not take predominance over the CO algorithm which is a proper choice for this model. When the square root of the domain is of higher infinity order than the user number, the QD algorithm reveals its privilege in performance: on one side, with the increase of function domain, the communication cost of the QD algorithm will approach quadratic level lower than the CO algorithm; On the other side, when the function domain grows big enough, the QD algorithm will get to a 100% average correct ratio very soon.

In conclusion, which way is more efficient is determined by the parameters of this model. It means that we need to make choice between the quantum way and the classical one according to the parameters' relations in order to get the optimal performance in practice. Finding the more general models and obtaining the performance gap between QCC and CCC will be the future work.

Acknowledgement. Supported by the National Natural Science Foundation of China under Grant Nos. 61501247, 61373131 and 61702277, the Six Talent Peaks Project of Jiangsu Province (Grant No. 2015-XXRJ-013), Natural Science Foundation of Jiangsu Province (Grant No. BK20171458), the Natural Science Foundation of the Higher Education Institutions of Jiangsu Province (China under Grant No. 16KJB520030), the NUIST Research Foundation for Talented Scholars under Grant Nos. 2015r014. Partially supported by the China-USA Computer Science Research Center.

References

1. Yao, A.C.-C.: Some complexity questions related to distributed computing. In: Proceedings of the 11th Annual ACM Symposium on Theory of Computing, New York, NY, USA, pp. 209–213 (1979)
2. Huang, W., Shi, Y., Zhang, S., et al.: The communication complexity of the Hamming distance problem. Inf. Process. Lett. **99**(4), 149–153 (2006)
3. Jain, R.: Communication complexity of remote state preparation with entanglement. Quantum Inf. Comput. **6**(4–5), 461–464 (2006)
4. Gavinsky, D., Kempe J., Kerenidis, I., et al.: Exponential separations for one-way quantum communication complexity with applications to cryptography. In: STOC 2007: Proceedings of the 39th Annual ACM Symposium on Theory of Computing: 11–13 June 2007, San Diego, California, USA, pp. 516–525 (2007)
5. Montanaro, A.: A new exponential separation between quantum and classical one-way communication complexity. Quantum Inf. Comput. **11**(7–8), 574–591 (2011)
6. Klauck, H.: One-way communication complexity and the Nečiporuk lower bound on formula size. SIAM J. Comput. **37**(2), 552–583 (2007)
7. Montanaro, A., Winter, A.: A lower bound on entanglement-assisted quantum communication complexity. In: Arge, L., Cachin, C., Jurdziński, T., Tarlecki, A. (eds.) ICALP 2007. LNCS, vol. 4596, pp. 122–133. Springer, Heidelberg (2007). https://doi.org/10.1007/978-3-540-73420-8_13

8. Klauck, H.: Lower bounds for quantum communication complexity. SIAM J. Comput. **37** (1), 20–46 (2007)
9. Jain, R., Zhang, S.: New bounds on classical and quantum one-way communication complexity. Theor. Comput. Sci. **410**(26), 2463–2477 (2009)
10. Jain, R., Klauck, H.: The partition bound for classical communication complexity and query complexity. 25th Annual IEEE Conference on Computational Complexity – CCC, Boston, Massachusetts, USA, 9–12 June 2010, pp. 247–258 (2010)
11. Kaplan, M., Laplante, S.: Kolmogorov complexity and combinatorial methods in communication complexity. Theor. Comput. Sci. **412**(23), 2524–2535 (2011)
12. Sherstov, A.A.: The unbounded-error communication complexity of symmetric functions. Combinatorica **31**(5), 583–614 (2011)
13. Cleve, R., Van Dam, W., Nielsen, M., et al.: Quantum entanglement and the communication complexity of the inner product function. Theor. Comput. Sci. **486**, 11–19 (2013)
14. Tavakoli, A., Anwer, H., Hameedi, A., et al.: Quantum communication complexity using the quantum Zeno effect. Phys. Rev. A **92**, 012303 (2015)
15. Baumeler, A., Broadbent, A.: Quantum private information retrieval has linear communication complexity. J. Cryptol. **28**(1), 161–175 (2015)
16. Kerenidis, I.: Quantum multiparty communication complexity and circuit lower bounds. Math. Struct. Comput. Sci. **19**(1), 119–132 (2009)
17. Lee, T., Schechtmsn, G., Shraibman, A.: Lower bounds on quantum multiparty communication complexity. In: Proceedings of the 24th Annual IEEE Conference on Computational Complexity, Paris, France, 15–18 July 2009, pp. 254–262 (2009)
18. Beame, P., Huynh, T.: Multiparty communication complexity and threshold circuit size of AC (0). SIAM J. Comput. **41**(3), 484–518 (2012)
19. Villagra, M., Nakanishi, M., Yamashita, S., et al.: Tensor rank and strong quantum nondeterminism in multiparty communication. IEICE Trans. Inf. Syst. **E96d**(1), 1–8 (2013)
20. Trojek, P., Schmid, C., Bourennane, M., et al.: Experimental multipartner quantum communication complexity employing just one qubit. Nat. Comput. **12**(1), 19–26 (2013)
21. Grover, L.K.: Quantum mechanism helps in searching for a needle in a haystack. Phys. Rev. Lett. **79**, 325–328 (1997)
22. Nielsen, M., Chuang, I.L.: Quantum Computation and Quantum Information, 7th edn, pp. 171–271. Cambridge University Press, Cambridge (2010)
23. Francois, L.G., Shogo, N.: Multiparty quantum communication complexity of triangle finding. In: 12th Conference on the Theory of Quantum Computation, Communication and Cryptography (2017). https://doi.org/10.4230/lipics.tqc.2017.6
24. Shima, B.H., Ashwin, N., Renato, R.: Communication complexity of one-shot remote state preparation. IEEE Trans. Inf. Theory **64**(7), 4709–4728 (2018)
25. Mingming, W., Chen, Y., Reza, M.: Controlled cyclic remote state preparation of arbitrary qubit states. CMC: Comput. Mater. Continua **55**(2), 321–329 (2018)
26. Faguo, W., Xiao, Z., Wang, Y., Zhiming, Z., Lipeng, X., Wanpeng, L.: An advanced quantum-resistant signature scheme for cloud based on Eisenstein ring. CMC: Comput. Mater. Continua **56**(1), 19–34 (2018)

BlockZone: A Blockchain-Based DNS Storage and Retrieval Scheme

Wentong Wang[1], Ning Hu[2(✉)], and Xin Liu[3(✉)]

[1] National University of Defense Technology, Changsha 410073, China
[2] Cyberspace Institute of Advanced Technology, Guangzhou 510006, China
huning@gzhu.edu.cn
[3] Changsha University, Changsha 410022, China
xin.liu@ccsu.edu.cn

Abstract. DNS is an important infrastructure of the Internet, providing domain name resolution services. However, there is a serious centralization problem in terms of DNS architecture and management. To solve the problem of DNS centralization, we propose a blockchain-based decentralized DNS storage and parsing scheme BlockZone. Without changing the existing DNS protocol, BlockZone takes DNS name server as the node in the blockchain network and each node stores all the record information of the whole network. The record in the node ensures consistency by consensus algorithm. We propose an improved PBFT consensus algorithm for DNS, which has the advantages of fast consensus and low traffic. Experiments show that the parsing and authentication efficiency of BlockZone is 37.8% higher than that of DNSSEC, and the improved consensus algorithm is improved by 4 orders of magnitude in efficiency than PoW-based consensus algorithm.

Keywords: DNS · Blockchain · DNS decentralization

1 Introduction

Domain Name System (DNS) is the key component of Internet. Its main function is to create domain name and IP address mapping and provide domain name resolution service. With the development of Internet, DNS has been endowed with other application functions, such as DKMI standard [1] (Domain Keys Identified Mail, DKIM), load balancing [2], domain name blockade [3]. In order to work properly, most applications of the Internet need DNS to provide services.

Although DNS system plays an important role in the Internet, there are serious centralization problems in DNS, including the centralization of DNS architecture, storage mode and management. Although DNS adopts hierarchical structure design, the overall structure is centralized, and the root server serves as the control center of the whole system. The validity of the signature is determined by the structure of trust chain

Supported by Project of National Defense Science and Technology Innovation Zone (Grant No. 18-H863-01-ZT-005-027-02), National Natural Science Foundation of China (U1636215) and Project of Hunan Provincial Department of Education (Grant No. 14C0095).

X. Sun et al. (Eds.): ICAIS 2019, LNCS 11635, pp. 155–166, 2019.
https://doi.org/10.1007/978-3-030-24268-8_15

[4]. The root server acts as the anchor node of the whole trust chain. DNSSEC, as a centralized authentication method, results in low verification efficiency, high computational overhead and complex key management [5]. As a center of trust, the root server also has security risks [6, 14].

To solve the problem of DNS centralization, we innovate a decentralized blockchain-based DNS storage and retrieval scheme BlockZone. BlockZone exchanges the DNS zone file with the blockchain through smart contracts to facilitate DNS zone file management. Using a combination of blockchain and external storage, the complete data is stored in the external storage, and the file hash value of the resource record, the external link address, and the public key information for verifying the external data are stored in the blockchain. The blockchain ensures the authenticity and integrity of the DNS data, and the external storage expands the storage space of the blockchain to improve system scalability. In this paper, we make the following contributions:

- We use blockchain technology to design a decentralized DNS architecture, and design and implement a distributed storage and retrieval scheme BlockZone.
- We propose a blockchain-based DNS resource record verification scheme based on BlockZone, which improves the verification efficiency by 37.8% compared with DNSSEC.
- We propose an improved PBFT consensus algorithm. Compared with the PoW consensus algorithm, the throughput of the improved PBFT algorithm is improved by four orders of magnitude. Compared with the PBFT algorithm, the improved PBFT algorithm reduces the bandwidth consumption in the transaction process.

2   Motivation

In this section, we describe the motivation for building decentralized naming systems that have no central point of trust and provide the relevant background on blockchain.

2.1   Problems in Current DNS

Single Point Failure. As the first layer server in domain name resolution, DNS root server plays an important role. Only through the root server can the address information of top-level domain name server be obtained. As the control center of DNS parsing process, DNS root server has a single point failure. There have been many attacks on the root server [7, 8, 15], which has caused serious impact on the stable operation of the entire Internet.

Inequality in the Control of the Internet. The centralized structure of DNS leads to security threats to the sovereignty of cyberspace, including two aspects: one is the domain name loss risk [9], which can be achieved by deleting the top-level domain name records of a specific country from the root server and refusing to provide the registration of the domain name of that country. The other is the denial of access risk [9], which rejects requests for resolutions from a country's top-level domain in the root server and its mirror server.

Deployment Problem of Security Solutions Based on PKI Facilities. Although there are many DNS enhancements or alternatives proposed at present, these research solutions are difficult to deploy on a large scale due to changing the DNS protocol or incompatibility with the DNS system. For example, although 89% of top-level domain servers deploy DNSSEC, the deployment rate of second-level domain names is only 3% [10], which makes it difficult to play DNSSEC role in practical applications.

2.2   Research Motivation

The basic idea of this paper is to construct a decentralized DNS system based on blockchain, and synchronize the information in different domains of DNS into the blockchain through smart contracts. Due to the limited storage space of the blockchain, the files in the domain are stored in the external database, and the index and hash value of the data are stored in the blockchain. With the feature that blockchains are tamper-resistent, the indexes and hashes stored in the blockchain ensure the authenticity and integrity of the records stored in the external database.

3   BlockZone Overview

To ensure the authenticity and integrity of the DNS resource record, we propose a DNS resource record storage and retrieval scheme BlockZone based blockchain without changing the DNS protocol. The BlockZone system model is shown in Fig. 1. BlockZone is divided into three layers, including user layer, storage layer, and blockchain layer. The detailed definition of each layer is as follows.

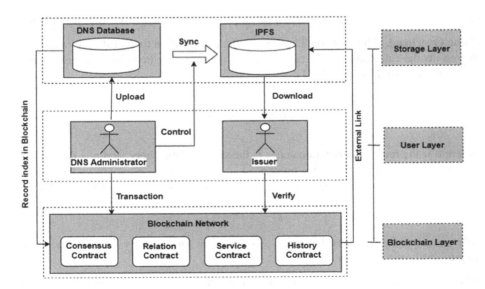

Fig. 1. Overview of Blockstack's architecture.

3.1   BlockZone Layers

BlockZone Layers. Blockchain layer mainly provides three functions: storing DNS resource records, indexing key DNS resource records in external storage, and tracing DNS resource records.

User Layer. The user layer mainly contains two kinds of users: DNS administrator and search user.

- **DNS administrator.** The DNS administrator is responsible for DNS database information registration and update, and synchronizes DNS key data to external storage. The smart registration is used to write DNS registration information, update information and recorded hash value, signature information, and external storage link address into the block.
- **DNS user.** The DNS uses the DNS client to query the resource record corresponding to the domain name. For the retrieved IP address, query the blockchain and the records in the external storage to verify the authenticity and integrity of the record.

Storage Layer. The storage layer is responsible for storing critical DNS resource records. IPFS stores the record information submitted by each DNS administrator. Each IPFS corresponds to a hash address that identifies the identity, and stores the hash address of the identity and the hash value of the record information in the blockchain to ensure the resource record authenticity and integrity.

3.2   Formal Description

The following is a formal description of the BlockZone storage and parsing process.

Time Overhead. The function T represents the computation time cost. The function T represents the calculation of the time cost, and the time that the DNS server executes a query is expressed as formula (1).

$$T_D = \sum_{i=0}^{n} t_d(d, s_i) \tag{1}$$

where d is the retrieved domain name, s is the server of the query, and n is the number of servers required for the query process.

The query time of DNS system based on blockchain is shown as formula (2).

$$T_B = t_B(d, s, K) \tag{2}$$

where d is the domain name to search, s is the server for the query, and K is the secret key to verify the signature.

Storage Overhead. The additional storage overhead required for DNS centralized authentication is V_D. The storage overhead per server is $v(r, s)$ shown as formula (3).

$$V_D = \sum_{i=0}^{n} v(r, s_i) \tag{3}$$

$$v(r, s_i) = RRSIG + DNSKEY + DS + NSEC$$

where RRSIG, DNSKEY, DS and NSEC are additional records needed for DNS to add validation process.

Let the additional storage overhead for blockchain-based verification be V_B and the storage overhead T of each server is $\mu(r, s)$ shown as formula (4).

$$V_B = \sum_{i=0}^{n} \mu(r, s_i) \tag{4}$$

$$\mu(r, s_i) = HASH + LINKADDR + K$$

Where *HASH, LINKADDR, K* are records hash, external link address and verification secret key in the blockchain respectively.

4 System Implementation

4.1 Data Storage

In order to facilitate the writing of DNS resource records into the blockchain, Blcok-Zone constructs four kinds of smart contracts, including: Consensus Contract (CC), Relationship Contract (RC), Ownership Contract (OC), History Record Contract (HC). Through these four kinds of contracts, DNS hierarchical relationships, resource records, and historical update information are written into the blockchain. In order to make the contracts between nodes independent of each other, the contract can only be created by the generated contract. The details of each contract are shown in Fig. 2.

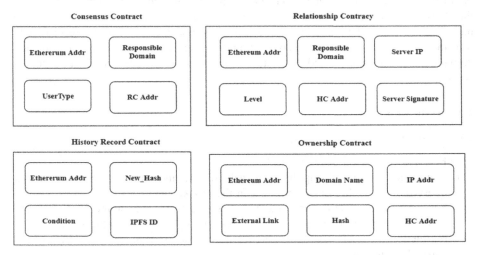

Fig. 2. BlockZone smart contracts

4.2   Node Addition

Assume that the server node joining the system has installed the Ethereum client and created the Ethereum address. The specific adding process is as follows:

(1) The registration node submits a registration application to the blockchain network, including the Ethereum address, the domain name information, the server level, and the identity information.
(2) Consensus contract pushes the message to the voting pool node for confirmation.
(3) The voting pool node checks whether the domain name information is legal and not registered. If the domain name is legal and not registered, the registration is successful, otherwise the registration fails.
(4) The consensus contract processes the voting result, and if the voting result is legal, the relationship contract is created, otherwise the registration information is discarded.
(5) Consensus contract forwards the registration message to the relationship contract.
(6) The relationship contract transfers the registration message to the corresponding server node.
(7) The superior server node agrees to authorize the node and sends the application information and its own signature to the relationship contract.
(8) The relationship contract compiles the registration information and the authorization server signature and creates a service contract.
(9) Relationship contract writes the registered information into the service contract.
(10) The address of the service contract is returned to the application node, and the node uses the service contract to perform domain name information operation.

4.3   Data Update

Assuming that the server node to update the zone file has been registered in the system, the database management component of the server node synchronizes the resource record in the external IPFS system, and links the zone file in IPFS, the record hash. Information is sent to the service contract, and the service contract stores the updated domain name information and generates a historical contract to record the updated content.

4.4   Data Retrieval

The specific process is as follows:

(1) End user initiates a query request.
(2) The trusted server looks up the local cache record, and if there is no hit, initiates a query request to the service contract in the blockchain.
(3) Service contract queries the storage record. If the record is stored in the domain name and the query content is the corresponding IP address, the IP address is returned. If the query content is another record, the external storage address of the zone file is returned.

(4) The trusted server receives the return result of the service contract. If the user queries the IP address corresponding to the domain name, the IP address will be returned. If other records are recorded, the server looks for external storage.

(5) Trusted server lookups external storage.

(6) The trusted server computes the hash of the external zone file and compares it with the hash returned by the service contract. If the two are the same, the external file is not tampered with and the corresponding resource record is retrieved.

(7) Return the query result.

4.5   Consensus Algorithm

Considering the limitations of PBFT algorithm in terms of network bandwidth and node communication mode, combined with the characteristics of blockchain, the improved PBFT algorithm does not require each message to be sequenced first. Each node only needs to complete the verification and confirmation of the message, which reduces the three broadcasting processes of PBFT to two times and reduces the communication overhead of the network.

Symbol Description. Let the number of nodes participating in the consensus be N, and the maximum number of malicious nodes that can be tolerated is f, then N must satisfy the formula $N \geq 3f + 1$. The nodes participating in the consensus are divided into two types: the master node m and the slave node s. To ensure the authenticity and integrity of the message, in the process of sending the message, the signature value sig is expressed as $sig_{msg} = \sigma(hash(msg))$ where σ is the signature function, msg is the message to be sent and $hash$ is the hash function.

In each round of consensus process, the data set needed is recorded as view v, which is numbered from 0. If the current set does not reach consensus, it needs to go to the next set until consensus is reached. The nodes involved in the consensus process are also numbered. Each round, one node is chosen as the master node and the other nodes are chosen as the slave nodes.

Algorithm Flow. Assume that the nodes participating in the consensus initially have the same initial state, that is, the initial block height h, the previous block hash, and the version number are consistent. The relationship between the initial view number and the primary node number is shown in formula (5).

$$v = 0$$
$$m = (h + v) \bmod N \tag{5}$$

If the non-consensus node receives the transaction information, the message is forwarded. The consensus node has a master node to initiate a consensus request, and the child consensus node receives the transaction message, and then verifies the correctness of the message. If the message is verified, the information is saved, and the slave nodes broadcast consensus confirmation message, otherwise broadcast view update message. When the consensus process is over, delete the transaction information, update the view and block height, and prepare to enter the new consensus stage.

The flow chart of the algorithm is the operation process of formula (1) as shown in Algorithm 1.

View Update. When the master node fails and does not broadcast the consensus request message within the specified time t or the child node broadcast view update message does not get *2f* node confirmation or the number of consensus confirmation nodes is less than *2f*, the view update operation is performed.

View Update Workflow. The process of view updating is shown below.

a. First increase the view v = v + 1.
b. The child node sends a view update message.
   $< ViewChange, h, v, s, v', Sig_{msg} >$, where *ViewChange* represents the message type as view update, h is the current block height, v current view number, s is child node number, v' is new view number, Sig_{msg} is the message signature.
c. If the consensus node accepts the number of view update broadcast messages, the view is updated to v', the master node is updated to $m + 1$, and a new consensus process begins.
d. If the number of received view update messages does not reach *2f*, return to step *a* to continue.

Algorithm 1. Improved Consensus Algorithm

Input: v, s, h
Output: $newBlock$
1: **if** $(CurrentNode == SlaveNode)$ **then**
2:     $recv\_msg(msg :< ConsensusRequest >)$;
3:     **if** (check msg is right) **then**
4:         $broadcast(msg :< ConsensusConfirm >)$;
5:     **else**
6:         $ViewChange(v, m, h)$;
7:         goto step 1;
8:     **end if**
9: **else**
10:     $wait$;
11:     $broadcast(msg :< ConsensusRequest >)$;
12: **end if**
13: **if** $(ConfirmNum > 2f)$ **then**
14:     $broadcast(newBlock)$;
15:     $ViewChange(v, m, h)$;
16:     goto step1;
17: **end if**

---

5 Performance Evaluation

In order to test the validation efficiency of this scheme, we compare and analyze the validation method based on DNSSEC, including query efficiency: query throughput, network traffic, transmission delay and space occupancy. To reduce transmission delay and real response verification efficiency, the *queryperf* tool of BIND9 is used to test. In order to simulate real DNS messages, different RRs are included in the test process, including A, MX and NS resource records.

5.1 Experimental Setup

The blockchain construction environment is set up as follows: 6 Linux 16.04 virtual machines, each of which is Intel(R) Core(TM) i5.7200 and the memory is 2G. The blockchain network uses Ethereum, the test network chooses Kovan, and the external storage uses IPFS.

The DNS setup environment is as follows: BIND-9.10.4 DNS server, 5 Linux16.04 virtual machines, each of which is Intel(R) Core(TM) i5.7200, 2G memory, and 4 as zone servers. 1 set as a parser. The throughput test is performed using the queryperf tool that comes with the BIND server. The network structure is shown in Fig. 3.

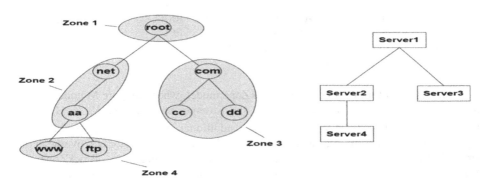

Fig. 3. DNS network topology diagram

5.2 Experimental Results

The throughput in this scenario is defined as the number of queries that the server can process per second. To simulate the real DNS server, verify the DNSSEC verification efficiency. In each server responsible for zone 1–4, it contains 1 SOA record, 1 NS record, 10 MX records, and 1000 A records respectively. We use the *queryperf* tool to build different resource record query requests. The initial query is 10^4 times, each time increasing 10^4 times respectively, to test the throughput of the parser.

Table 1 shows the throughput of 10^4 queries between different servers. There is no central server in BlockZone and no hierarchical structure is used, so the throughput takes the average of server nodes.

Table 1. DNS, DNSSEC, BlockZone server query throughput comparison

Scheme	Root server	Top level server	Second level server
DNS	16860	14720	12640
DNSSEC	13790	11940	8920
BDRNS	2850		

The storage overhead of DNSSEC is shown in Table 2. Calculation of formula (3). The encryption algorithm uses RSA, and the key length is 1024 bits. The storage overhead is $=379 + |zone| + |name| + |label|$, where $|zone|$ is the size of the zone file, and $|name|$ is the name of the next record in NSEC. $|label|$ is the identified resource record type, such as A, RRSIG, NSEC. When $|name|$ takes 4octets, $|label|$ takes 1 byte, then $V = 384 + |zone|$. When a server stores N zone files, then $V_D = N * V$, V_D is a linear function about V.

Table 2. DNSSEC storage overhead.

Record types	Storage overhead (octets)	Description
DNSSKEY	18 + key size	RSA or ECC
DS	36	SHA-1
RRSIG	46 + key size + |zone|	RSA
	70 + |zone|	ECC
NSEC	23 + |name| + |label|	

Calculation of formula (4). In the BlockZone model, when there are M nodes in the network, N zone files are stored, and the storage overhead is $V_B = M * N * (V' + V_{Block})$, where $V' = V - 384$ and the additional storage cost in the block is V_{Block}. For comparison, we assume $V_{Block} \approx 384$ (the actual storage overhead is smaller than 384octets). Therefore, the storage overhead in BlockZone is $V_B = M * N * V = M * V_C$, then, V_B is the linear function about V_D. The storage overhead on each server is $V' = V - 384$.

Consensus Algorithm Test. Throughput is an important indicator of the consensus algorithm. The definition of throughput is the number of transactions completed per unit time as shown in formula (6).

$$TPS_{\Delta t} = \frac{TotalTrans\ actions}{\Delta t} \tag{6}$$

Compared with other consensus algorithms, the result is shown in Fig. 4. Compared with the PoW consensus algorithm, the throughput is improved by 4 orders of magnitude. Compared with the PBFT algorithm, the improved PBFT algorithm supports node dynamic join, and the bandwidth consumption is also reduced.

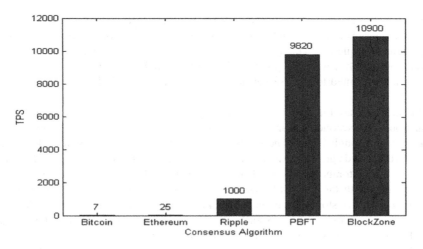

Fig. 4. Improved PBFT algorithm compared with other consensus algorithms

6 Related Work

Namecoin [11] is the first blockchain-based DNS system. As a fork of Bitcoin, Namecoin modified the storage content of Bitcoin, allowing the blockchain to store name-value data in addition to transactions. Other functions and mechanisms are the same as Bitcoin, and Bitcoin miners use the combined mining method to provide proof of Bitcoin and Namecoing workload. Namecoin uses a virtual.bit top-level domain that is not officially registered with the current DNS system. This means that Namecoin is isolated from the traditional DNS system, and users cannot resolve.bit domain names without installing other parsing software.

OneName [12] provides an online identity service that runs on top of Namecoin. OneName's idea is to create a name-value pair in the blockchain that associates the name with different online identities such as email, GitHub, Twitter, and Bitcoin addresses. OneName users can confirm ownership of these accounts by referencing their OneName name through a specific message channel in different systems.

Blockstack [13] is the first domain name system to run directly on the Bitcoin block. Its predecessor is the OneName built on top of Namecoin. Due to the security issue of Namecoin, Blockstack proposed to construct a virtual chain layer on top of Bitcoin to separate the data plane from the control plane. Similar to Namecoin, Blockstack also uses .app, .id virtual domain names to identify different namespaces, and requires security-specific parsing software to resolve such domain names.

7 Summary and Conclusion

In the parser throughput test, BlockZone increased by 37.8% compared to DNSSEC. Since BlockZone adopts a non-central structure, the parser forwards the authentication requests to different service nodes separately, which improves the verification efficiency of the entire system. In the server throughput test, if the cache misses in the parser, the query is directly sent to the root server, causing the root server to process the query request frequently. This is one of the limitations of the centralized structure, and the central node has a single point of failure risk. In BlockZone, the query request pressure is distributed to each server node, which is more stable for the entire network system.

BlockZone uses the PBFT consensus algorithm to process nearly thousands of transactions per second, ensuring that resource records are quickly stored in the blockchain. Although BlockZone saves all node information records in each node, as the resource records are frequently updated, the length of the blockchain will increase rapidly, and the storage overhead of the blockchain will gradually increase.

Compared with the DNSSEC, BlockZone improves the authentication efficiency. Compared with the storage overhead, BlockZone is M times of DNSSEC (M is the number of server nodes), but on each server, since the signatures, secret keys, and DNSSEC new records are not stored, Storage overhead is 384octets lower than DNSSEC.

References

1. Hansen, T., et al.: Domain keys identified mail (DKIM) service overview. RFC 5585 (2009)
2. Leighton, T.: Improving performance on the internet. Commun. ACM **52**(2), 44–51 (2009)
3. Levine, J.: DNS blacklists and whitelists. IETF RFC 5782 (2010)
4. Ateniese, G., Mangard, S.: A new approach to DNS security (DNSSEC). In: The 8th ACM Conference on Computer and Communications Security, pp. 86–95 (2001)
5. Lian, W., Rescorla, E., Shacham, H., et al.: Measuring the practical impact of DNSSEC deployment. In: USENIX Security, pp. 573–588 (2013)
6. Herzberg, A., Shulman, H.: DNSSEC: security and availability challenges. In: Communications and Network Security, pp. 365–366 (2013)
7. Events of 2015-11-30, 04 December 2015. Retrieved 18 Dec 2015
8. Moura, G.C.M., Schmidt, O., Ricardo, H., et al.: Anycast vs. DDoS: evaluating the November 2015 root DNS event (PDF). In: Proceedings of the ACM Internet Measurement Conference (IMC 2016). ACM, Santa Monica, November 2016
9. Binxing, F.: Discussion on autonomous root domain name system based on national union from "Network Sovereignty". Inf. Secur. Commun. Priv. **12**, 35–38 (2014)
10. Chung, T., Rijswijk-Deij, R.V., Choffnes, D., et al.: Understanding the role of registrars in DNSSEC deployment. In: Internet Measurement Conference, pp. 369–383 (2017)
11. Namecoin [EB/OL]. https://Namecoin.info
12. OneName [EB/OL]. https://onename.com/
13. Ali, M., Nelson, J., Shea, R., et al.: Blockstack: a global naming and storage system secured by blockchains. IN: 2016 USENIX Annual Technical Conference, pp. 181–194 (2016)
14. Meng, R., Rice, S.G., Wang, J., Sun, X.: A fusion steganographic algorithm based on faster R-CNN. CMC: Comput. Mater. Continua **55**(1), 001–016 (2018)
15. Cui, J., Zhang, Y., Cai, Z., Liu, A., Li, Y.: Securing display path for security-sensitive applications on mobile devices. CMC: Comput. Mater. Continua **55**(1), 017–035 (2018)

Robust Analysis of Grid System Based on Complex Network Attack Mode

Jun Xiang[1](✉), Jiao Zhu[1], Shuyang Guo[1], Yue Chen[2], and Zhizhong Qiao[3]

[1] Hainan Power Grid Co., Ltd., Hainan 570203, China
`xiangj@hn.csg.cn`
[2] Nari Technology Development Co., Ltd., Nanjing 210033, China
[3] NARI Information and Communication Technology Co., Ltd.,
Nanjing 210033, China

Abstract. With the continuous construction of the grid, its scale is getting larger and larger and the degree of connection is becoming more and more complicated, which means the structure of the grid gradually meets the characteristics of complex networks. Through the modeling of the structure of the grid system and the analysis of complex network theory, different attack modes (i.e., attack strategy of degree node, immediate node, and random node) in the complex network are proposed which are utilized to do the robust analysis of grid system. The IEEE-57 and IEEE-300 node systems are chosen for simulation verification. Based on the results, the connectivity of the system presents different results in different attack modes. Among them, the random attack has the least impact on the system, while the median attack is the most serious. This also corresponds to the definition of the mediator.

Keywords: Robust analysis · Complex network attack mode · Grid system · Simulation verification

1 Introduction

At the end of the 20th century, Watts and Strogatz of Cornell University in the United States published "Collective Dynamics of Small-World' Networks" [1], and the small world network model was first presented to people. There has been a wave of research on complex networks around the world. In 2013, Pagani and Aiello published "The power grid as a complex network: A survey" in "Physica A" [2], which explained that generators and transmission lines can be abstracted into nodes and edges in the network in the power grid. To model, you can use the theory of complex networks to study power networks. So far, researchers in the field of power systems have begun to analyze power systems from the perspective of complex networks [3–6]. Applying the complex network theory, combined with the actuality of the power system, the initial load of the node is defined by the electrical interface, and the cascading failure model is established. The normalized fault scale, average connectivity level and weighted network

© Springer Nature Switzerland AG 2019
X. Sun et al. (Eds.): ICAIS 2019, LNCS 11635, pp. 167–177, 2019.
https://doi.org/10.1007/978-3-030-24268-8_16

efficiency are used to evaluate the evolution of the small world power grid. The change in robustness. The analysis results show that with the increase of network capacity, the robustness of the small world power grid is enhanced, but when the network capacity reaches a certain value, the increased capacity has little impact on the robustness of the small world power grid [7]; with the development of the small world power grid Evolution, the connection between nodes is enhanced, and its overall robustness is also enhanced. Therefore, when planning and designing the power system, the capacity of the power grid should be scientifically and reasonably determined according to the actual situation. It is also possible to refer to the development and evolution mode of the small world power grid to obtain a power grid with strong robustness and low cost. Network robustness refers to the ability of a network to maintain its operation after a node or edge in the network fails due to external interference.

Complex networks are an important method for studying complex systems. The network view of complex systems research has become a new perspective accepted by researchers [8,9]. Compared with other research methods, complex network theory emphasizes the topological characteristics of the system, can properly reflect the dynamic formation process of the network, and reveal some macroscopic properties of the system. These have the robustness and anti-risk ability for analyzing complex networks. Important reference value. Robustness is generally considered to be the robustness of complex systems, and is the key to the survival, maintenance, and continuous service of complex networks in abnormal and dangerous situations. Albert and Barabasi compared the connectivity of ER random graphs and BA scale-free networks to the robustness of node removal in [10].

Two kinds of node removal strategies are studied. One is the random failure strategy, which completely removes some nodes in the network randomly. The second is the deliberate attack strategy, that is, from the removal of the most moderate node in the network, the consciously removes the highest degree in the network. Node. It is the non-uniformity that makes the scale-free network highly vulnerable to deliberate attacks: as long as the consciously removing the nodes with the largest number of values in the network will have a great impact on the connectivity of the entire network [11]. Scientists in different fields have explored this problem and found that robust but fragile is one of the most important and basic features of complex systems [12]. Broder et al. studied the robustness of large-scale WWW sub-networks. Sexual discovery only removes all nodes with degrees greater than 5 to completely destroy the connectivity of the WWW [13]. These studies are qualitative in terms of robustness, and the study of the impact of complex network structures on robustness is not sufficient. Based on the classical node admittance matrix model, this paper classifies nodes, simplifies calculations, and proposes three different attack strategies from the perspective of complex networks. Using static analysis methods, the structural structure is robust from the perspective of grid system. The influence of sex is finally verified by using IEEE-57 system and IEEE-300 system as examples.

The remaining parts of the paper are organized as follows: In Sect. 2, some preliminaries (i.e., the complex network and robustness index of grid system) are introduced. And in Sect. 3, Robust analysis of grid system based on different attack modes (i.e., attack strategy of degree node, immediate node and random node) in complex network is detailedly introduced, which consists of there parts: attack mode, attack simulation process and experiment results. Finally, Sect. 4 is dedicated for conclusion and discussion.

2   Preliminary

2.1   Complex Network and Its Spread and Influence

With the continuous construction of the power grid, the scale of the power grid is getting larger and larger, and the degree of connection is more and more complicated [14]. In recent years, more and more scholars have applied complex network theory to power systems, so that the structure of the power grid gradually meets the characteristics of complex networks and solves a variety of problems. The characteristics of complex networks are often hidden in their statistical properties, and many concepts have been proposed for their statistical properties [15–18]. Because of its many concepts, only three basic concepts used in this article are introduced.

(1) Shortest path length
    In the network, the shortest path length $l_{i,j}$ is defined as the number of edges on the shortest path between any two points i and j.
(2) Degrees
    In the network, the degree k_i of node i is defined as the number of edges connected to the node. So intuitively, if the degree of a node is greater, then the node is more important in a sense.
(3) Intermediation
    In the network, some nodes are not very large, but this node may play a role as a bridge between the two parts of the network, indicating that this node is also very important, so it is defined in all nodes of the network, The number B_i of the shortest path through all the nodes i is the mediator of node i.

Based on the propagation process of the d-dimensional small world network described by the NW network model, Moukarzel studied the propagation equation of the d-dimensional small world network more specifically [19]. The idea is to start from the initial infected node of the network, (1) the virus starts to propagate at constant speed 1; (2) the density of the long-range connection endpoint in the network is ρ; (3) the propagation process is continuous; The probability of encountering a long-range endpoint at the source endpoint is ρ. Then, the average total infection amount $V(t)$ is obtained by the following form and integral equation [20]:

$$V(t) = \Gamma_d \int_0^1 \tau^{d-1}[1 + 2pV(t - \tau)]d\tau \tag{1}$$

After scaling and differentiation, a linear propagation equation of the following form can be obtained [20].

$$\frac{\partial^d V(t)}{\partial t^d} = 1 + V(t) \tag{2}$$

Considering the influence of various nonlinear obstacles in the process of propagation, then, the average total infection amount $V(t)$ is obtained by the following form and integral equation [21]:

$$V(t) = \Gamma_d \int_0^1 \tau^{d-1} \left[1 + \xi^{-d} V(t - \tau) - \mu V^2(t - \tau) \right] d\tau \tag{3}$$

After the above formula is scaled and differentiated, the following nonlinear equation can be obtained [21]:

$$\frac{\partial^d V(t)}{\partial t^d} = \xi^d + V(t) - \mu \xi^d V^2(t) \tag{4}$$

Where ξ is the NW length scale and μ is the interaction coefficient. When considering a one-dimensional case, it is inversely proportional to the degree of complexity in a complex network [22], i.e., $\xi \sim 1/k$. The above formula is the expression of the total amount of network propagation $V(t)$ in the small world. In the case of the unbalanced system, the parameters will fluctuate. The physical meaning of such fluctuations is the errors, faults, etc. of complex network nodes and connected edges.

2.2   Robustness Index of Grid System

Robustness refers to the ability of the system to maintain its original performance when the structure or size changes occur in the system [23]. The structural robustness of the grid can be considered as the ability of the grid system to maintain its original power supply function after the structure of the grid changes.

The robustness of complex networks is the key to the survival, maintenance, and continuous service of complex networks in the event of node parameter failure (fluctuations) [24]. A more rigorous definition refers to the characteristics of the control system that maintains relevant performance under certain parameters (such as system structure, size, etc.) [25]. In a complex network, if most nodes in the network are still connected after removing a small number of nodes, then the connectivity of the network is said to be robust to node failures [26].

Artificial giant systems such as power networks and communication networks are increasingly dependent on the daily production and life of human beings. A serious problem is faced: How reliable are these networks? In fact, although hundreds of routers fail on the network every moment, the Internet is rarely affected. The performance of the life system is more robust: although there are thousands of errors in the cells, such as mutations and protein errors, there are very few serious consequences in life, and the source of this toughness mainly comes from within the system. In the network parameters with random fluctuations, there are factors in the system that cause the network structure to abruptly change, and there are also factors (damping) that make the system gradually stabilize before the network disaster.

For real networks, whether it is artificial giant systems such as Internet, telecommunication networks, power networks, large-scale circuits, or natural networks such as various metabolic networks, food chain networks, etc., are open, unbalanced, nonlinear and complex. The system is a typical object of non-balanced statistical physics research. It is in this case that a non-equilibrium network is proposed in correspondence with an equilibrium network. The number of nodes in the system described by the unbalanced network and the connected edges of the nodes are not fixed, but grow with time. The unbalanced complex network model can be constructed in the following ways: (1) the number of network nodes and the connected edges of nodes grow continuously with time; (2) the growth of network nodes and connected edges is in a fixed way: such as connection Preference, etc. [27]; (3) The internal and external network systems have the exchange of basic physical quantities and information; (4) There are fluctuations between nodes and even edges. Compared with the actual network system, the resulting unbalanced complex network model is a better model for describing the real network.

The nonlinear open system described by this unbalanced complex network model differs from traditional statistical methods in that it: (1) treat events occurring in the system as random events; (2) treat the processes occurring as random processes (3) Add some uncertainty directly into the dynamic equations describing the system. This method of studying the statistical properties of a large number of events, directly from the probability characteristics of random events and stochastic processes, is commonly referred to as Stochastic approaches [28].

Therefore, according to the particularity of the grid system, the following two indicators of the robustness of the grid system are defined.

(1) Grid node removal ratio

The grid node removal ratio is defined as: in the grid, the ratio of the number of nodes removed by the grid system to the number of nodes in the grid is:

$$PN = \frac{n_b}{N}, \tag{5}$$

here, N is the total number of nodes in the grid; n_b is the number of grid structures removed due to failure.

(2) Maximum connectivity of the grid system

Maximum connectivity of a power grid system After a fault occurs in a grid, due to the withdrawal of certain components, a connected network may be split into several isolated networks that are connected by itself. Then the maximum connectivity of the grid system is defined as the maximum connectivity after the fault. The ratio of the number of nodes in the subset to the total number of nodes in the grid:

$$S = \frac{n_r}{N}, \tag{6}$$

here, N is all nodes of the entire network; n_r is the number of nodes in the largest connected subset after the failure.

3   Robust Analysis of Grid System Based on Attack Modes in Complex Network

In the actual power grid, the topology of the original power grid will be changed more or less due to faults and the like. This includes the initial point of failure and the exit of the cascading failure node due to the initial point of failure. This paper focuses on the number of components removed and the impact of the strategy on the robustness of the grid system, i.e., static analysis, without considering the cascading failure response caused by grid nodes or tidal current distribution after removal.

3.1   Attack Mode

In a complex network, the component removal method of the network can be divided into deliberate removal and random removal according to the way it is removed. Removing these nodes does not have a major impact on the connectivity of the entire network. However, it is this non-uniformity that makes scale-free networks highly vulnerable to deliberate attacks: consciously removing the nodes with the fewest values in the network can have a significant impact on the connectivity of the entire network. In the power network studied in this paper, the attack objects of the deliberate and random attacks that simulate the fault are nodes or edges. According to the particularity of the power grid system, the following three attack modes are formulated:

(1) Attack strategy of degree node (degree attack): firstly remove the maximum degree node in the network, then calculate the degree of each node in the new network, and then remove the node, and repeat until the set grid node removal ratio is satisfied.

(2) Attack strategy of intermediate node (median attack): first remove the maximum number of network mediation nodes, then calculate the number of nodes in the new network, and then remove the node, and repeat until the set grid node is removed ratio.

(3) Attack strategy of random node (random attack): randomly remove the number of nodes whose number of grid node removal ratios are set. Due to the contingency of random attacks, repeat the test for 20 times.

3.2   Attack Simulation Process

The robustness analysis of grid system based on static analysis method only considers the influence of grid topology on its own robustness, and does not consider the redistribution of power flow and its chain reaction caused by the removal of components in the grid. So we are studying the impact of different attack modes on the robustness of the grid system in the case of setting different grid node removal ratios. The specific process is as follows:

(1) Initialization: The network topology is generated based on the initial data, and the parameters such as the number and degree of each node of the network are calculated, and the grid node removal ratio of this test is determined.
(2) Node removal is performed according to the selected attack mode until the set value is satisfied.
(3) Generate the final network topology model, calculate the maximum connectivity of the grid system of the model and record the data.
(4) Repeat multiple times, record the maximum connectivity of the final topology under different set values and different attack modes, and plot the curve with the grid removal ratio setting. The flow chart is shown in Fig. 1.

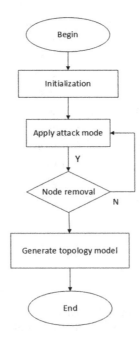

Fig. 1. Process about robust analysis of grid system based on complex network attack mode.

3.3   Experiment

According to the algorithm described above, the IEEE-57 node system and the IEEE-300 node system are selected for simulation verification.

(1) IEEE-300 node system

According to the attack method set in the previous method, the attack is performed in the maximum degree, the maximum number of media, and the random mode. The relationship between the maximum connectivity (S) of the grid system and the grid node removal ratio (PN) is shown in Table 1.

According to the above simulation results, it can be seen that in different attack modes, the connectivity of the system presents different results, in which the random attack has the least impact on the system, while the median attack presents the most serious, which is also the definition of the mediator. Compatible. After the degree attack is 15% set value, the drastic drop of connectivity indicates that when the system node is missing to a certain extent, the quantity changes to the qualitative change.

Table 1. IEEE-300 node system S results in different set PN values and different attack modes.

PN setting value (%)	S (degree attack)	S (median attack)	S (random attack)
0	1.0000	1.0000	1.0000
1	0.8983	0.9831	0.9831
3	0.8559	0.5678	0.9746
5	0.7966	0.3983	0.9407
7	0.6610	0.3051	0.9237
9	0.6356	0.2542	0.9237
11	0.5510	0.1520	0.9019
13	0.5018	0.1500	0.8937
15	0.5000	0.1451	0.8812
17	0.2819	0.1391	0.8647
19	0.2819	0.0951	0.8430

(2) IEEE-57 node system

According to the attack method set in the previous method, the attack is performed in the maximum degree, the maximum number of media, and the random mode. The relationship between the maximum connectivity (S) of the grid system and the grid node removal ratio (PN) is shown in Table 2.

It can be seen that the simulation results are similar to those of the IEEE-300 node system. In different attack modes, the random attack has the least impact

Table 2. IEEE-57 node system S results in different set PN values and different attack modes.

PN setting value (%)	S (degree attack)	S (median attack)	S (random attack)
0	1.0000	1.0000	1.0000
1	0.9845	0.9845	0.9845
3	0.8959	0.9678	0.9546
5	0.8866	0.9583	0.9307
7	0.8410	0.9451	0.9237
9	0.6356	0.9042	0.9137
11	0.5510	0.1520	0.9019
13	0.5018	0.1105	0.8967
15	0.5000	0.0999	0.8895
17	0.2819	0.0971	0.8548
19	0.2819	0.0953	0.8436

and the median attack has the greatest impact. In terms of system collapse, the IEEE-57 node has begun to cause serious system stagnation at the smaller PN setting than the IEEE-300 node, which indicates that the robustness of the system is also related to its own scale.

4 Conclusion

This paper classifies the nodes in the system through power network modeling, and uses the complex network related theory to analyze it statistically and obtain its statistical description index. Different attack models (i.e., attack strategy of degree node, immediate node and random node) based on complex network theory are developed for their networks, and the descriptive indicators of the robustness of the system structure are also defined. Finally, the IEEE-300 and IEEE-57 node systems are attacked according to different modes under different set values, and the conclusion that the system mediation number is larger is more important. At the same time, the conclusion that the system robustness is related to its scale is obtained. Because its complex network characteristics can be considered in future grid design to improve its robustness.

In the next work, we will study the influence parameters of complex network robustness based on complex network propagation and response and derive the interaction coefficients of complex networks, which can be used as a basic parameter to measure the robustness of complex networks.

References

1. Watts, D.J., Strogatz, S.H.: Collective dynamics of small-world networks. Nature **393**, 440–442 (1998)
2. Pagani, G.A., Aiello, M.: The power gridas a complex network: a survey. Phys. A Stat. Mech. Appl. **392**(11), 2688–2700 (2013)
3. Zhang, X., Tse, C.K.: Assessment of robustness of power systems from the perspective of complex networks. In: IEEE International Symposium on Circuits and Systems, pp. 2684–2687 (2015)
4. Zeng, A., Shen, Z., Zhou, J., et al.: The science of science: from the perspective of complex systems. Phys. Rep. **714**, 714–715 (2017)
5. Chen, Z., Wu, J., Xia, Y., et al.: Robustness of interdependent power grids and communication networks: a complex network perspective. IEEE Trans. Circ. Syst. II Express Briefs **65**, 115–119 (2017)
6. Liang, M., Liu, F., Gao, C., et al.: Robustness analysis of the complex network. In: Data Driven Control and Learning Systems, pp. 638–643 (2017)
7. Bhatu, B., Shah, H.Y.: Customized approach to increase capacity and robustness in image steganography. In: International Conference on Inventive Computation Technologies, pp. 1–6 (2017)
8. Nardelli, P.H.J., Cardieri Jr., P., Kretzschmar, W.A., Latva-Aho, K., et al.: Interference networks: a complex system view. Eprint arxiv (2013)
9. Ivanov, I.V.: Epistemology of computational biology and modeling of complex heterogeneous systems (2015)
10. Albert, R., Jeong, H., Barabasi, A.L.: The diameter of the world wide web. Nature **401**(6), 130–131 (1999)
11. Joo, W., Kwak, S., Youm, Y., et al.: Brain functional connectivity difference in the complete network of an entire village: the role of social network size and embeddedness. Sci. Rep. **7**(1), 4465 (2017)
12. Grindrod, P., Stoyanov, Z.V., Smith, G.M., et al.: Primary evolving networks and the comparative analysis of robust and fragile structures. J. Complex Netw. **2**(1), 60–73 (2018)
13. Wang, H., Ding, X., Huang, C., et al.: Adaptive connectivity restoration from node failure(s) in wireless sensor networks. Sensors **16**(10), 1487 (2016)
14. Xia, L.L., Song, B., Jing, Z.J., Song, Y.R., Zhang, L.: Dynamical interaction between information and disease spreading in populations of moving agents. CMC: Comput. Mater. Continua **57**(1), 123–144 (2018)
15. Yao, J., Xiao, P., Zhang, Y., et al.: A mathematical model of algal blooms based on the characteristics of complex networks theory. Ecol. Model. **222**(20), 3727–3733 (2011)
16. Redelico, F.O., Proto, A.N.: Complex networks topology: the statistical self-similarity characteristics of the average overlapping index. In: Proto, A., Squillante, M., Kacprzyk, J. (eds.) Advanced Dynamic Modeling of Economic and Social Systems. SCI, vol. 448, pp. 163–174. Springer, Heidelberg (2013). https://doi.org/10.1007/978-3-642-32903-6_12
17. Lei, M., Xie, B.: Research on the characteristics of complex networks in area joint air defense command information system. In: WIT Transactions on Modelling & Simulation, pp. 593–600 (2014)
18. Jiang, Y.W.: Study on the characteristics of complex networks in network user behavior. J. China Acad. Electron. Inf. Technol. (2017)

19. Moukarzel, C.F.: Spreading and shortest paths in systems with sparse long-range connections. Phys. Rev. E Stat. Phys. Plasmas Fluids Related Interdisc. Top. **60**(6), R6263-6 (1999)
20. Yang, X.S.: Chaos in small-world networks. Phys. Rev. E Stat. Nonlinear Soft Matter Phys. **63**(2), 046206 (2001)
21. Yang, S.K., Chen, C.L., Yau, H.T.: Control of chaos in Lorenz system. Chaos Solitons Fractals **13**(4), 767–780 (2002)
22. Newman, M.E.J., Watts, D.J.: Scaling and percolation in the small-world network model. Phys. Rev. E **60**(6), 7332–7342 (1999)
23. Tanaka, G., Kai, M., Aihara, K.: Dynamical robustness in complex networks: the crucial role of low-degree nodes. Sci. Rep. **2**(1), 232 (2012)
24. Wang, Z.F., Yan, D.Q., Wang, R.D., Xiang, L., Wu, T.T.: Speech resampling detection based on inconsistency of band energy. CMC: Comput. Mater. Continua **56**(2), 247–259 (2018)
25. Abdi, N., Kitous, O., Grib, H., et al.: Evaluation of the robustness of the enzymatic hydrolysis in batch and continuous mode by a central composite design. J. Food Process. Preserv. **42**(1), e13330 (2017)
26. NetAnswer: Robustness of self-consolidating concrete. Materials & Structures
27. Newman, M.E.J.: The structure and function of complex networks. SIAM Rev. **45**(2), 167–256 (2003)
28. Guo, B.H., Cai, S.H., Zhu, J.Q.: Small world network bifurcation driven by non-equilibrium fluctuation. J. Sichuan Normal Univ. (Nat. Sci.) **31**(5), 631–634 (2008)

A Secure Data Aggregation Protocol in VANETs Based on Multi-key FHE

Bo Mi[1], Hongyang Pan[1], Darong Huang[1(✉)], Tiancheng Wei[1], and Xingfeng Wang[2]

[1] Institute of Information Science and Engineering,
Chongqing Jiaotong University, Chongqing 400074, China
drhuang@cqjtu.edu.cn
[2] College of Cybersecurity, Sichuan University, Chengdu, China

Abstract. For sake of data aggregation in VANETs, a protocol is devised based on multi-key fully homomorphic encryption (MFHE). In order to introduce practical properties, such as scalability, into the proposed protocol, a dynamic topology is utilized to structure the very-basic framework. To address the problem of dynamic changes with respect to floating nodes, linear secret sharing scheme is applied to multi-key fully homomorphic encryption with threshold decryption, and then the partial sharing decryption is proposed. Performance analysis illustrated that the proposed scheme is feasible and the complexity expands. Under the universal composability frame, the proposed protocol is also proved to be semantically secure.

Keywords: VANETs · Data aggregation · MFHE · GSW ·
Linear secret sharing · Threshold decryption

1 Introduction

With the expansion of the data and the increase in the accounting overhead, it is natural to store the clients' data and perform the expensive computation on the remote powerful "cloud" servers. Although the "cloud" can provide considerably many advantages in costs and functionality, how to protect the data privacy has become one of the most serious problems in the process.

Fully homomorphic encryption (FHE), which was first proposed by Gentry in 2009 [1], can perform arbitrary circuits on encrypted data as the plaintext. FHE was initially designed to only involve one user and one cloud. However, there are many scenarios including multiparty communication, such as multiuser to one core, which could carry out the FHE operation under different keys. Multi-key FHE (MFHE) [7, 8] is an interesting result derived from it.

Further, we can consider a more complex situation in VANETs. Considering a basic VANETs data aggregation protocol with clusters abstractly, VANETs can be divided into many clusters which consist of vehicle members. In the process of data aggregation, the vehicle members will broadcast their traffic data to complete aggregations. In traffic transportation, we need to achieve the safety aggregation of vehicle

© Springer Nature Switzerland AG 2019
X. Sun et al. (Eds.): ICAIS 2019, LNCS 11635, pp. 178–190, 2019.
https://doi.org/10.1007/978-3-030-24268-8_17

data [9, 13, 14] within a certain range to complete various functions, such as early warning, congestion control and so on (Fig. 1).

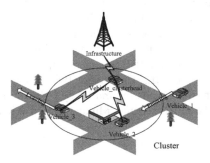

Fig. 1. VANETs

In order to achieve data aggregation privately, FHE could be used in the communication in VANETs with a set of natural and stringent requirements. First, we should protect the privacy information. Second, with the dynamic change of VANETs topology, we need to ensure the correctness of data aggregation. And some MFHE schemes make these requirements true partially. But the dynamic change also put up some new requirements for MFHE. For example, with the increase or decrease of the node number, an MFHE scheme should achieve a multi-hop homomorphic encryption.

Based on MFHE and threshold decryption, we present a secure 3-round protocol of data aggregation in VANETs. We applied an MFHE scheme based on GSW [8] and a Two-Round MPC protocol [16] to complete the data aggregation. And then in the dynamic situation, the linear secret sharing scheme has been used to cut apart the secret key and store the sharing separately on the other nodes. With the reduction of vehicle nodes, the sharing of the node left from the cluster will be reconstructed from the other nodes which are still in it to finish the decryption of the final ciphertext.

1.1 Our Results and Techniques

In order to achieve the data aggregation in VANETs, we make some changes:

Based on the threshold encryption, the linear secret sharing has been applied to realize the variant partial decryption. By the linear secret sharing, a secret key will be split into the other nodes. Then we can reconstruct the variant partial decryption of the secret key using one-round communication. And then we can complete the threshold decryption.

To construct the 3-round data aggregation protocol in VANETs, we applied the Two-Round MPC protocol based on MFHE to complete the basis communication, and the variant partial decryption to ensure the reliability in the dynamic situation. In the dynamic situation of VANETs, each secret key will be split into some sharing for the other nodes. If one vehicle leaves the cluster, the variant partial decryption will be executed for this node to complete the final decryption.

1.2 Other Related Work

The basic idea of performing the evaluation between the ciphertexts encrypted by different keys using the homomorphic encryption schemes was first proposed by López-Alt, Tromer and Vaikuntanathan [7]. Their protocol, however, was built on the NTRU scheme which relied on a non-standard assumption, referred to as the Decisional Small Polynomial Ratio assumption. Clear and McGoldrick [8], on the basis of GSW IBFHE schemes [6] and GPV IBE schemes [10], constructed a new approach to achieve the multi-identity IBFHE. Coincidentally, based on the standard LWE assumption, the approach implements the multi-key FHE of [11]. Based on the Clear and McGoldrick's multi-key FHE scheme, Mukherjee and Wichs [16] proposed a two-round MPC protocol.

1.3 Organization

In Sect. 2, we introduce the notation used in this paper and the related definition of the MFHE with threshold decryption. In Sect. 3, we show the threshold decryption and the variant partial decryption. In Sect. 4, we show how to construct the data aggregation and analyze the security and performance.

2 Preliminary

Notations. Throughout, we let λ denote the security parameter and $\mathrm{negl}(\lambda)$ denote a negligible function. We represent elements in $\mathbb{Z}_q$ as integers in the range $(-q/2, q/2]$. Let $\mathbf{x} = (x_1, \ldots, x_n) \in \mathbb{Z}_q^n$ be a vector. We use the notation $\mathbf{x}[i]$ to denote the i-th component scalar. Similarly, for a matrix $\mathbf{M} \in \mathbb{Z}_q^{n \times m}$, we use $\mathbf{M}[i, j]$ to denote the scalar element located in the i-th row and the j-th column. And, for an integer $x \in \mathbb{Z}_q$, we use $x[i]$ to denote the i-th bit. The infinity norm of a vector $\mathbf{x}$ is defined as $\|\mathbf{x}\|_\infty = \max_i(|\mathbf{x}[i]|)$. The norm of matrices is defined similarly.

2.1 Multi-key FHE with Threshold Decryption

We start with the definition of Threshold multi-key FHE which has been proposed in [16].

Definition 2.1. Threshold multi-key FHE scheme (TMFHE) *is a multi-key FHE scheme with two additional algorithms* PartDec, FinDec *described as follow:*

- $p_i \leftarrow \mathrm{PartDec}(\hat{c}, (pk_1, \ldots, pk_N), i, sk_i)$: *On input an expanded ciphertext under a sequence of N keys and the i-th secret key output a partial decryption p_i.*
- $\mu \leftarrow \mathrm{FinDec}(p_1, \ldots, p_N)$: *On input N partial decryption output the plaintext μ.*

Now we propose our definition for the variant partial decryption. 3 algorithms have been inserted into the new definition as follow:

Definition 2.3. Threshold multi-key FHE scheme* (TMFHE*) *is a threshold multi-key FHE scheme with three additional algorithms* SecSplit, SharPartDec, SharFinDec *described as follow:*

- $\{s_j\}_{j \in [N] \setminus \{i\}} \leftarrow$ SecSplit(N, i, sk_i): *On input a secret key sk_i and the number of parties N output $N - 1$ sharing.*
- $sp_j \leftarrow$ SharPartDec$(\hat{c}, (pk_1, \ldots, pk_N), j, s_j)$: *On input an expanded ciphertext under a sequence of N keys and the j-th sharing s_j output a partial sharing decryption sp_j.*
- $p_i' \leftarrow$ SharFinDec$(sp_1, \ldots, sp_N)$: *On input N partial sharing decryptions output the partial decryption p_i'.*

This definition requires correctness and security as follow:

Simulator Security. *There exists a PPT simulator S^{vthr} which, on input the index $j \in [N]$ and all but the i-th sharing $\{s_j\}_{j \in [N] \setminus \{i\}}$, the evaluated ciphertext $\hat{c}$ and the k-th secret key sk_k produces a simulated partial sharing decryption $sp_i' \leftarrow S^{vthr}(sk_k, \hat{c}, i, \{s_j\}_{j \in [N] \setminus \{i,k\}})$ such that:*

$$sp_i' \stackrel{comp}{\approx} sp_i$$

where $sp_i \leftarrow$ SharPartDec$(\hat{c}, (pk_1, \ldots, pk_N), i, s_i)$.

Correctness. *The following holds with probability 1:*

$$\text{FinDec}(p_1, \ldots, p_i', \ldots, p_N) = \mu$$

where $p_i' \leftarrow$ SharFinDec$(sp_1, \ldots, sp_N)$.

2.2 Other Related Definitions

Now we give some related definitions which would be used in the rest of this paper.

Definition 2.4 (B-Bounded Distribution). *A distribution ensemble χ, supported over the integers, is called B-bounded if*

$$\Pr_{e \leftarrow \chi}[|e| > B] \leq \text{negl}(\lambda).$$

Definition 2.5 (Statistical Indistinguishability). *For two distribution ensembles X, Y, over a finite domain Ω. X, Y is statistical indistinguishable, denoted by $X \stackrel{stat}{\approx} Y$, if*

$$\Delta(X, Y) \leq \text{negl}(n).$$

where $\Delta(X, Y) \stackrel{def}{=} \frac{1}{2} \sum_{\omega \in \Omega} |X(\omega) - Y(\omega)|$.

3 Threshold Decryption via Linear Secret Sharing

We now show how to construct the variant threshold decryption from MFHE by linear secret sharing. It proceeds in 3 parts, which is shown as follow:

1. We show how to perform the threshold decryption and the variant based on linear secret sharing for this scheme.
2. We show the correctness and security of the variant threshold decryption.

3.1 Variant of Threshold Decryption Based on Linear Secret Sharing

This part is to implement the variant threshold decryption for the MFHE construction and its reconstruction on the sharing of one's secret key.

The threshold decryption is implemented by the following 2 functions **PartDec**($\ldots$) and **FinDec**($\ldots$):

- **PartDec**($\hat{c}, i, sk_i$): On input an expanded ciphertext $\hat{c} = \hat{\mathbf{C}} \in \mathbb{Z}_q^{nN \times mN}$ in [8] and the i-th secret key $sk_i = \mathbf{t}_i \in \mathbb{Z}_q^n$ do the following:

  1. Parse $\hat{\mathbf{C}}$ as consisting of N sub-matrices $\hat{\mathbf{C}}^{(i)} \in \mathbb{Z}_q^{n \times mN}$ such that $\hat{\mathbf{C}} = \begin{bmatrix} \hat{\mathbf{C}}^{(1)} \\ \vdots \\ \hat{\mathbf{C}}^{(N)} \end{bmatrix}$.

  2. Define $\hat{\mathbf{w}} \in \mathbb{Z}_q^{nN}$ as $\hat{\mathbf{w}} = [0, \ldots, 0, \lceil q/2 \rceil]$.

  3. Then compute $\gamma_i = \mathbf{t}_i \hat{\mathbf{C}}^{(i)} \hat{\mathbf{G}}^{-1}(\hat{\mathbf{w}}) \in \mathbb{Z}_q$ and output $p_i = \gamma_i + e_i^{sm} \in \mathbb{Z}_q$ where $e_i^{sm} \xleftarrow{\$} \left[-B_{smdg}^{dec}, B_{smdg}^{dec} \right]$ is a random noise where $B_{smdg}^{dec} = B_\chi 2^{d\lambda \log \lambda}$.

- **FinDec**($p_1, \ldots, p_N$): Given $p_1, \ldots, p_N$, compute the sum $p = \sum_{i=1}^N p_i$. Output $\mu := \left| Round \left(\frac{p}{q/2} \right) \right|$.

As mentioned in the Sect. 1, the increase and decrease of the node number will affect the encryption and decryption of the MFHE scheme in the multi-hop environment. When it increases, we can make evaluation ciphertexts expanded in the next hop. And if a node leaves, we make use of linear secret sharing scheme to solve it. A new parameter r will be set as $r = r(\lambda, d)$. The variant based on the linear secret sharing consists of the following 3 algorithms:

- **SecSplit**(N, i, sk_i): On input a secret key sk_i, parse $sk_i = \mathbf{t}_i = [t_{i,1}, t_{i,2}, \ldots, t_{i,n}] \in \mathbb{Z}_q^n$. For $j \in [n]$ compute the sharing of $t_{i,j}$ as follow:

  1. Sample 2 vectors $\mathbf{x}_j = [x_{j,1}, \ldots, x_{j,i-1}, x_{j,i+1}, \ldots, x_{j,N}] \xleftarrow{\$} \mathbb{Z}_q^{N-1}$ and $\mathbf{k}_j = [k_{j,1}, \ldots, k_{j,N-2}] \xleftarrow{\$} \mathbb{Z}_q^{N-2}$ for $\forall k_1 \neq k_2 \in [N] \setminus \{i\}$, $\left| x_{j,k_1} - x_{j,k_2} \right| \geq r$.
  2. Compute the vector $\mathbf{y}_j \in \mathbb{Z}_q^{N-1}$ as follow:

$$\mathbf{y}_j = [(1^{N-1})^T, \mathbf{x}_j^T, (\mathbf{x}_j^2)^T, \ldots, (\mathbf{x}_j^{N-2})^T] \cdot \begin{bmatrix} t_{i,j} \\ \mathbf{k}_j^T \end{bmatrix}$$

$$= [y_{j,1}, \ldots, y_{j,N-1}] \in \mathbb{Z}_q^{N-1}$$

and the sharing is output as follow:

$$\begin{bmatrix} (x_{1,1}, y_{1,1}) & \cdots & \cdots & (x_{n,1}, y_{n,1}) \\ \vdots & \ddots & & \vdots \\ \vdots & & \ddots & \vdots \\ (x_{1,N}, y_{1,N}) & \cdots & \cdots & (x_{n,N}, y_{n,N}) \end{bmatrix}$$

These tuples in the same row are the sharing received by the same party, and the tuples in the same column are the sharing split by the same value.

- **SharPartDec**$((x_{i,j}, y_{i,j}), \hat{c}, i, k, N)$: On input a sharing tuple $(x_{i,j}, y_{i,j})$, the expanded ciphertext $\hat{c} = \hat{\mathbf{C}} \in \mathbb{Z}_q^{nN \times mN}$, the index k of the secret key $\mathbf{t}_k$ and the index i of the i-th component scalar $t_{k,i}$, execute the following steps:

1. Parse $\hat{\mathbf{C}}$ as consisting of $n \times N$ vectors $\hat{\mathbf{c}}^{(i)} \in \mathbb{Z}_q^{mN}$ such that $\hat{\mathbf{C}} = \begin{bmatrix} \hat{\mathbf{c}}^{(1)} \\ \vdots \\ \hat{\mathbf{c}}^{(nN)} \end{bmatrix}$

2. Difine $\hat{\mathbf{w}} \in \mathbb{Z}_q^{nN}$ as $\hat{\mathbf{w}} = [0, \ldots, 0, \lceil q/2 \rceil]$.

3. Then compute the partial sharing decryption $(v_{i,j}, \tau_{i,j})$ as follow:

$$v_{i,j} = x_{i,j} \hat{\mathbf{c}}^{(kn+i)} \hat{\mathbf{G}}^{-1}(\hat{\mathbf{w}}) + e_i^{smx} \in \mathbb{Z}_q$$

$$\tau_{i,j} = y_{i,j} \hat{\mathbf{c}}^{(kn+i)} \hat{\mathbf{G}}^{-1}(\hat{\mathbf{w}}) + e_i^{smy} \in \mathbb{Z}_q$$

where $e_i^{smx}, e_i^{smy} \xleftarrow{\$} \left[-B_{smdg}^{vdec}, B_{smdg}^{vdec} \right]$ is a random noise where $B_{smdg}^{vdec} = 2^{d\lambda \log \lambda}$.

- **SharFinDec**$((v_{i,j}, \tau_{i,j})_{i \in [n], j \in [N] \setminus \{k\}})$: Given all the partial sharing decryptions $(v_{i,j}, \tau_{i,j})_{i \in [n], k \in [N] \setminus \{k\}}$, compute the variant partial decryption as follow:

$$p'_j = \sum_{i=1}^{n} \sum_{\substack{j=1 \\ j \neq k}}^{N} \tau_{i,j} \prod_{\substack{h=1 \\ h \neq j \\ h \neq k}}^{N} v_{i,h} / (v_{i,h} - v_{i,j})$$

and then output p'_j.

3.2 Correctness and Simulation Security

Now, we testify the correctness along with security of our partial sharing decryption

Theorem 3.1. *The above variant procedures of threshold decryption for* MFHE *satisfy correctness and simulation security.*

Correctness. Here the entire scheme is same as MFHE except the variant of threshold decryption based on linear secret sharing. If $(v_{i,h}, \tau_{i,h})$ and $(v_{i,j}, \tau_{i,j})$ are the partial sharing decryption of a secret key t_k, then we have

$$
\frac{v_{i,h}}{v_{i,h} - v_{i,j}} = \frac{x_{i,h}\hat{\mathbf{c}}^{(kn+i)}\hat{\mathbf{G}}^{-1}(\hat{\mathbf{w}}) + e_h}{(x_{i,h} - x_{i,j})\hat{\mathbf{c}}^{(kn+i)}\hat{\mathbf{G}}^{-1}(\hat{\mathbf{w}}) + (e_h - e_j)}
$$

$$
= \frac{x_{i,h}}{x_{i,h} - x_{i,j}} \cdot \frac{\hat{\mathbf{c}}^{(kn+i)}\hat{\mathbf{G}}^{-1}(\hat{\mathbf{w}}) + e'}{\hat{\mathbf{c}}^{(kn+i)}\hat{\mathbf{G}}^{-1}(\hat{\mathbf{w}}) + e''}
$$

where $e' = e_h/x_{i,h}(x_{i,h} - x_{i,j})$, $e'' = (e_h - e_j)/(x_{i,h} - x_{i,j})$. The equation can be generalized into the following form:

$$
\sum_{i=1}^{n}\sum_{j=1}^{N} \tau_{i,j} \prod_{\substack{h=1 \\ h \neq j \\ h \neq k}}^{N} v_{i,h}/(v_{i,h} - v_{i,j})
$$

$$
= \sum_{i=1}^{n} \frac{(\hat{\mathbf{c}}\hat{\mathbf{G}}^{-1}(\hat{\mathbf{w}}) + e')^{N-1}}{(\hat{\mathbf{c}}\hat{\mathbf{G}}^{-1}(\hat{\mathbf{w}}) + e'')^{N-2}} \cdot t_{k,i}
$$

$$
= (\frac{\hat{\mathbf{c}}\hat{\mathbf{G}}^{-1}(\hat{\mathbf{w}}) + e'}{\hat{\mathbf{c}}\hat{\mathbf{G}}^{-1}(\hat{\mathbf{w}}) + e''})^{N-2}(t_k\hat{\mathbf{C}}^{(k)}\hat{\mathbf{G}}^{-1}(\hat{\mathbf{w}}) + t_k e')
$$

where $\hat{\mathbf{c}}$ is a row vector of $\hat{\mathbf{C}}$. It is easy to see that $\hat{\mathbf{c}}\hat{\mathbf{G}}^{-1}(\hat{\mathbf{w}})$ is much larger than e' and e'', and the value of $(\frac{\hat{\mathbf{c}}\hat{\mathbf{G}}^{-1}(\hat{\mathbf{w}}) + e'}{\hat{\mathbf{c}}\hat{\mathbf{G}}^{-1}(\hat{\mathbf{w}}) + e''})^{N-2}$ is very close to 1. So the correctness is primarily determined by $t_k\hat{\mathbf{C}}^{(k)}\hat{\mathbf{G}}^{-1}(\hat{\mathbf{w}}) + t_k e'$.

If $\hat{\mathbf{C}}$ is an evaluated ciphertext encrypting a bit μ and the secret key is $\hat{\mathbf{t}} = [\mathbf{t}_1, \ldots, \mathbf{t}_N]$, then we have $\hat{\mathbf{t}}\hat{\mathbf{C}}\hat{\mathbf{G}}^{-1}(\hat{\mathbf{w}}^T) = \mu(q/2) + e$. Now, one can observe that decryption without threshold decryption works correctly as long as $\|e\|_\infty \leq q/4$.

If the threshold decryption with partial sharing decryption is executed, the final result must be correctly decrypted by the function **FinDec**(…). So we take t_k's variant partial decryption and the other partial decryption as input. And we have

$$
\sum_i (\mathbf{t}_i\hat{\mathbf{C}}^{(i)}\hat{\mathbf{G}}^{-1}(\hat{\mathbf{w}})) + t_k e' + e^{sm} = \mu(q/2) + e + t_k e' + e^{sm}
$$

Lemma 3.2. *Let $\hat{\mathbf{C}}$ be the evaluated ciphertext of the above* **MFHE** *scheme and e be the decryption noisy after a homomorphic evaluation of a d-level circuit $\mathcal{C}$. The noisy e has norm upper bound $B_\chi 2^{O(d \log \lambda)}$.*

Proof. We refer the reader to [8] for details.

Lemma 3.3. *Let p be the final decryption of the above* **Threshold Decryption** *scheme generated by function* **FinDec(...),** *and e^{sm} be the "smudging noisy" of p. The noisy e^{sm} has norm upper bound $B_\chi 2^{O(d\lambda \log \lambda)}$.*

Proof. We refer the reader to [16] for details.

Lemma 3.4. *Let p'_k be the final result of the above* **Variant Partial Decryption** *scheme and $\mathbf{t}_i e'$ be the "variant smudging" noisy. The noisy $\mathbf{t}_k e'$ has norm upper bound $B_\chi 2^{O(d\lambda \log \lambda)}$.*

Proof. Let $\mathbf{t}_i e'$ be the "variant smudging" noisy. Recall that, $\mathbf{t}_i = [-\mathbf{s}_i, 1]$ with $\mathbf{s}_i \leftarrow \chi^{n-1}$, and $\mathbf{e}' = [e'_1, \ldots, e'_N]$. And for any $i \in [n]$, $e'_i \leq \frac{2^{d\lambda \log \lambda}}{r}$. Therefore, we have $\mathbf{t}_i e' \leq \frac{nB_\chi 2^{d\lambda \log \lambda}}{r} = B_\chi 2^{O(d\lambda \log \lambda)}$.

So e has norm $|e| \leq B_\chi 2^{O(d\log \lambda)}$, $\mathbf{t}_i e'$ has norm $|\mathbf{t}_i e'| \leq B_\chi 2^{O(d\lambda \log \lambda)}$ and e^{sm} has norm $|e^{sm}| \leq B_\chi 2^{O(d\lambda \log \lambda)}$. Since $q = B_\chi 2^{\omega(d\lambda \log \lambda)}$, we have $|e + \mathbf{t}_i e' + e^{sm}| \leq q/4$ and correctness holds.

Security. We construct the simulator $\mathcal{S}^{vthr}$ as below:

On input sharing $(x_{u,j}, y_{u,j})_{u \in [n], j \in [N] \setminus \{i,k\}}$, an evaluated ciphertext $\hat{c}$ and the secret key $\mathbf{t}_k$ generating secret sharing $(x_{u,j}, y_{u,j})$, outputs the *simulated partial sharing decryption* as the below steps:

1. Construct n matrices $\{\mathbf{MX}_u = [\mathbf{x}_u, \mathbf{x}_u^2, \ldots, \mathbf{x}_u^{N-2}] \in \mathbb{Z}_q^{N-2 \times N-2}\}_{u \in [n]}$ and n vectors $\{\mathbf{Vy}_u = [\mathbf{y}_u - \mathbf{t}_{k,u}] \in \mathbb{Z}_q^{N-2}\}_{u \in [n]}$ where $\mathbf{x}_u = [\ldots, x_{u,j}, \ldots]_{j \in [N] \setminus \{i,k\}}^T \in \mathbb{Z}_q^{N-2}$, $\mathbf{y}_u = [\ldots, y_{u,j}, \ldots]_{j \in [N] \setminus \{i,k\}}^T \in \mathbb{Z}_q^{N-2}$ and $\mathbf{t}_{k,u} = [t_{k,u}, \ldots, t_{k,u}]^T \in \mathbb{Z}_q^{N-2}$. And then compute n vectors $\{\mathbf{k}_u = (\mathbf{MX}_u)^{-1} \cdot \mathbf{Vy}_u \in \mathbb{Z}_q^{N-2}\}_{u \in [n]}$.

2. Sample a vector $\mathbf{Sx}_i = [x'_{1,i}, \ldots, x'_{n,i}]^T \overset{\$}{\leftarrow} \mathbb{Z}_q^n$ and for each $u \in [n]$ compute $y'_{u,i} = [1^n, x'_{u,i}, (x'_{u,i})^2, \ldots, (x'_{u,i})^{N-2}] \cdot \begin{bmatrix} t_{k,u} \\ \mathbf{k}_u \end{bmatrix}$. And we have $\mathbf{Sy}_i = [y'_{1,i}, \ldots, y'_{n,i}]^T$.

3. For each $u \in [n]$ compute the u-th simulated partial sharing decryption:

$$v'_{u,i} = x'_{u,i} \hat{c}^{(kn+u)} \hat{\mathbf{G}}^{-1}(\hat{\mathbf{w}}) + e_u^{smx} \in \mathbb{Z}_q, \tau'_{u,i} = y'_{u,i} \hat{c}^{(kn+u)} \hat{\mathbf{G}}^{-1}(\hat{\mathbf{w}}) + e_u^{smy} \in \mathbb{Z}_q$$

where $e_u^{smx}, e_u^{smy} \overset{\$}{\leftarrow} \left[-B_{smdg}^{vdec}, B_{smdg}^{vdec}\right]$. Then output the simulated partial sharing decryption $sp'_i = \{(v'_{u,i}, \tau'_{u,i})_{u \in [n]}\}$.

The real value sp_i and the simulated sp'_i are almost statistically indistinguishable.

4 Data Aggregation Protocol in VANETs

In this section, we now describe our secure aggregation protocol in VANETs within the cluster through 3 rounds of communication. The following two procedures are supplemented in [16].

Increase. When a new vehicle participants in the cluster, the next hop computation should be executed within $N + 1$ nodes after the final decryption of the last hop.

Decrease. When a vehicle in the cluster leaves, the original protocol will have some changes in the 3rd round which supplements the variant partial decryption of the vehicle's secret key.

4.1 Data Aggregation Protocol Against $N-1$ Corruptions

We have some similar processes with the two-round MPC protocol in [16], so we will not dwell on these. We remind readers to consult [16] for details. And now we describe the additional process. Let $f : (\{0, 1\}^{\ell_{in}})^N \to \{0, 1\}^{\ell_{out}}$ be the function to compute.

Round 1. Each party P_k executes the key generation function of the MFHE scheme in [16], and then broadcast the public key pk_k

Round 2. Each party P_k on receiving values $\{pk_i\}_{i\in[N]\setminus\{k\}}$ executes the following steps:

- Split the secret key $\{\{s_j\}_{j\in[N]\setminus\{k\}}\} \leftarrow \text{SecSplit}(N, k, sk_k)$.
- Execute the MFHE encryption function for the secret key sharing $\{cs_{i,g} \leftarrow \text{Encrypt}(pk_i, s_i[g])\}_{i\in[N]\setminus\{k\},g\in[2n\lceil\log q\rceil]}$ bit-by-bit and then broadcast these ciphertexts.

Round 3. On receiving these values $\{cs_{k,g}\}_{g\in[2n\lceil\log q\rceil]}$, if all vehicles are still in the cluster, the final decryption will be executed as [16]. And if the vehicle P_s leaves the cluster, the following steps will be executed:

1. Each P_k decrypts these sharing ciphertexts $\{cs_{k,g}\}_{g\in[2n\lceil\log q\rceil]}$ encrypted by pk_k of the secret key sk_s and reconstructs s_k.
2. Each P_k computes the partial decryption $p_k^{(j)} \leftarrow \text{PartDec}(\hat{c}_j, k, sk_k)$ and the variant partial decryption $(\tau_k^{(j)}, \upsilon_k^{(j)}) \leftarrow \text{SharPartDec}(s_k, \hat{c}_j, k, N)$ of P_s for all $j \in [\ell_{out}]$.
3. Then P_k will broadcast all the above values $\{p_k^{(j)}, \upsilon_k^{(j)}, \tau_k^{(j)}\}_{j\in[\ell_{out}]}$.

Output

1. On receiving the values $\{p_k^{(j)}\}_{j\in[\ell_{out}]}$ run the final decryption to obtain the j-th bit $\{y_j \leftarrow \text{FinDec}(p_1^{(j)}, \ldots, p_N^{(j)})\}_{j\in[\ell_{out}]}$ and then Output $y = y_1 \cdots y_{\ell_{out}}$.
2. On receiving the values $\{p_i^{(j)}, \upsilon_i^{(j)}, \tau_i^{(j)}\}_{j\in[\ell_{out}],i\in[N]\setminus\{s\}}$, run the partial sharing decryption to obtain $\{p_s^{(j)\prime} \leftarrow \text{SharFinDec}(\{\upsilon_i^{(j)}\tau_i^{(j)}\}_{i\in[N]\setminus\{s\}})\}_{j\in[\ell_{out}]}$ and then run the final decryption to obtain $\{y_i \leftarrow \text{FinDec}(p_1^{(j)}, \ldots, p_i^{(j)\prime}, \ldots, p_N^{(j)})\}_{j\in[\ell_{out}]}$.

Then Output $y = y_1 \cdots y_{\ell_{out}}$.

4.2 Correctness and Security Analysis

Formally we prove the following theorem.

Theorem 4.1. *Let f be a poly-time computable deterministic function with N inputs and 1 output. Let the scheme* MFHE = (Setup, Kengen, Encrypt, Expand, Eval, PartDec, FinDec, SecSplit, SharPartDec, SharFinDec) *be a multi-key FHE scheme with variant threshold decryption. Then the protocol described in Sect. 4.1 UC-realize the function f against any semi-honest adversary corrupting exactly N-1 vehicles in a cluster.*

Proof. The correctness of the protocol follows in a straightforward way from the correctness of the underlying variant threshold MFHE scheme.

To prove the security we construct an efficient (PPT) simulator $\mathcal{S}$ for any adversary corrupting exactly *N-1*. Let A be a semi-honest adversary, P_h be the only honest party and P_s be the vehicle left the cluster.

The Simulator. In round 2, the simulator encrypt 0s as the simulated sharing encryption $\{cs'_{k,g}\}_{g\in[2n\lceil\log q\rceil]}$ instead of the real ones. In round 3, it computes the simulated variant partial decryption $sp_i' \leftarrow \mathcal{S}^{vthr}(sk_s, \hat{c}, i, (s_j)_{j\in[N]\setminus\{s,h\}})$ instead of the correctly computed values generated via SharPartDec(...).

Hybrid Games. We now define a series of *hybrid games* that will be used to prove the indistinguishability of the real and ideal worlds:

$$\text{IDEAL}_{\mathcal{F},\mathcal{S},\mathcal{Z}} \overset{comp}{\approx} \text{REAL}_{\pi,\mathcal{A},\mathcal{Z}}$$

The output of each game is always just the out of the environment.

The game $\text{REAL}_{\pi,\mathcal{A},\mathcal{Z}}$**:** This is exactly an execution of the protocol π in the real world with environment $\mathcal{Z}$ and semi-honest adversary $\mathcal{A}$.

The game $\text{HYB}^1_{\pi,\mathcal{A},\mathcal{Z}}$**:** In this game, we modify the real world experiment as follows. Assume that P_h is given the simulated sharing encryption $\{cs'_{k,g}\}_{g\in[2n\lceil\log q\rceil]}$ after round 2. In the 3rd round, instead of broadcasting a correctly generated sharing encryption $\{cs_{k,g}\}_{g\in[2n\lceil\log q\rceil]}$, it broadcasts simulated ones.

The game $\text{IDEAL}_{\mathcal{F},\mathcal{S},\mathcal{Z}}$**:** In this game, we modify the game $\text{HYB}^1_{\pi,\mathcal{A},\mathcal{Z}}$ as follows. Assume that P_h is given all the sharing $\{s_j\}_{j\in[N]\setminus\{s,h\}}$ of the secret keys $\mathbf{t}_s$ after round 2. In the 3rd round, instead of broadcasting a correctly generated variant partial decryption sp_i generated via SharPartDec(...), it broadcasts simulated ones $sp_i' \leftarrow \mathcal{S}^{vthr}(sk_s, \hat{c}, i, \{s_j\}_{j\in[N]\setminus\{s,h\}})$.

Claim 4.2. $\text{REAL}_{\pi,\mathcal{A},\mathcal{Z}} \overset{stat}{\approx} \text{HYB}^1_{\pi,\mathcal{A},\mathcal{Z}}$

Proof. The only changes between those experiments are in generating encryption of party P_h. We have the following lemma:

Lemma 4.3. *The* MFHE *scheme described in Sect. 3.1 satisfies semantic security.*

The semantic security of the above MFHE scheme has been proved in detail in reference [8]. We refer the reader to [8] for details. So the encryptions are also computationally indistinguishable.

Claim 4.4. $\mathrm{HYB}^1_{\pi,\mathcal{A},\mathcal{Z}} \overset{comp}{\approx} \mathrm{IDEAL}_{\mathcal{F},\mathcal{S},\mathcal{Z}}$

Proof. The only changes between those experiments are that the variant partial decryption of party P_h is generated through simulator $\mathcal{S}^{vthr}$ instead of correctly using SharPartDec(…). By simulation security the variant partial decryptions are statistically indistinguishable hence so are the experiments.

This concludes the proof of the theorem.

4.3   Complexity Analysis

In this section, we analyze the communication complexity and computational complexity of our protocols. And for simplicity, we will take the vehicle P_h as the example to carry out the analysis.

In round 1, the public keys are generated and broadcasted in the cluster. So for fixed parameters, the communication complexity is $\omega(d^2 \lambda^2 (\log \lambda)^2)$. In round 2, it is $\omega(\ell_{in}d^2 \lambda^2 (\log \lambda)^2) + \omega(d^3 \lambda^3 (\log \lambda)^3)$. In round 3, it is $\omega(\ell_{out}d\lambda(\log \lambda))$. As described above, the total communication complexity is

$$\omega(\ell_{in}d^4 \lambda^4 (\log \lambda)^4) + \omega(d^5 \lambda^5 (\log \lambda)^5).$$

In the execution of the entire protocol, the function Encrypt(…) has been invoked for $\ell_{in} + 2n(N-1)\log q$ times. And the function performs nm^4 multiplication operations every time. So the computation complexity is

$$\omega(\ell_{in}d^4 \lambda^4 (\log \lambda)^4) + \omega(d^5 \lambda^5 (\log \lambda)^5).$$

We list the differences in complexity between our scheme and some other related scheme in Table 1. Compared with the previous scheme.

Table 1. Complexity comparison.

	Communication complexity	Computation complexity
Clear and Mcgoldrick [8]		$\omega(\ell_{in}d^4 \lambda^4 (\log \lambda)^4)$
Mukherjee and Wichs [16]	$\omega(\ell_{in}d^4 \lambda^4 (\log \lambda)^4)$	$\omega(\ell_{in}d^4 \lambda^4 (\log \lambda)^4)$
Our scheme	$\omega(\ell_{in}d^4 \lambda^4 (\log \lambda)^4) + \omega(d^5 \lambda^5 (\log \lambda)^5)$	$\omega(\ell_{in}d^4 \lambda^4 (\log \lambda)^4) + \omega(d^5 \lambda^5 (\log \lambda)^5)$

5   Conclusion

This paper main contributes to the data aggregation protocol based on MFHE in VANETs. To adapt the existed schemes to the new situation, a novel protocol based on MFHE is proposed. The main conclusion as follow:

Considering the dynamic structure of the vehicle cluster, after the variant partial decryption, we can realize the data aggregation in the more complex situation. And the multi-hop evaluation can be performed in this environment. On the other hand, because too many cryptographic suites and matrix operations are invoked, the performance of the proposed scheme is much lower than that of the previous one. The above will be the focus of our future research.

Acknowledgement. This work is supported by National Science Foundation of China P.R. (NSFC) under Grants 61573076, 61703063, 61663008; the Scientific Research Foundation for the Returned Overseas Chinese Scholars under Grant 2015-49; the Program for Excellent Talents of Chongqing Higher School under Grant 2014-18; Science and Technology Research Project of Chongqing Municipal Education Commission of China P.R. under Grants KJ1705121, KJ1600518, KJ1705139, KJ1605002, KJZD-K201800701; Chongqing Research Program of Basic Research and Frontier Technology under Grant CSTC2017jcyjAX0411; Chongqing Municipal Social Livelihood Science and Technology Innovation Project under Grant CSTC2016shmszx30026; Program of Chongqing Innovation and Entrepreneurship for Returned Overseas Scholars of China P.R under Grant cx2018110; Graduate Education and Innovation Foundation Project of Chongqing Jiaotong University under Grant 2018S0145.

References

1. Gentry, C.: Fully homomorphic encryption using ideal lattices. In: STOC 2009, vol. 9, no. 4, pp. 169–178 (2009)
2. Brakerski, Z., Vaikuntanathan, V.: Efficient fully homomorphic encryption from (standard) LWE. In: Foundations of Computer Science, pp. 97–106. IEEE (2011)
3. Plantard, T., Susilo, W., Zhang, Z.: Fully homomorphic encryption using hidden ideal lattice. IEEE Trans. Inf. Forensics Secur. **8**(12), 2127–2137 (2013)
4. Gentry, C., Halevi, S.: Fully homomorphic encryption without squashing using depth-3 arithmetic circuits. In: Annual Symposium on Foundations of Computer Science, vol. 47, no. 10, pp. 107–109 (2011)
5. Brakerski, Z., Gentry, C., Vaikuntanathan, V.: (Leveled) fully homomorphic encryption without bootstrapping. ACM Trans. Comput. Theory **6**(3), 1–36 (2014)
6. Gentry, C., Sahai, A., Waters, B.: Homomorphic encryption from learning with errors: conceptually-simpler, asymptotically-faster, attribute-based. In: Canetti, R., Garay, J.A. (eds.) CRYPTO 2013. LNCS, vol. 8042, pp. 75–92. Springer, Heidelberg (2013). https://doi.org/10.1007/978-3-642-40041-4_5
7. Lópezalt, A., Tromer, E., Vaikuntanathan, V.: On-the-fly multiparty computation on the cloud via multikey fully homomorphic encryption. In: Proceedings of the Annual ACM Symposium on Theory of Computing, pp. 1219–1234 (2012)
8. Clear, M., McGoldrick, C.: Multi-identity and multi-key leveled FHE from learning with errors. In: Gennaro, R., Robshaw, M. (eds.) CRYPTO 2015. LNCS, vol. 9216, pp. 630–656. Springer, Heidelberg (2015). https://doi.org/10.1007/978-3-662-48000-7_31

9. Wan, S., Zhang, Y., Chen, J.: On the construction of data aggregation tree with maximizing lifetime in large-scale wireless sensor networks. IEEE Sens. J. **16**(20), 7433–7440 (2016)

10. Gentry, C., Peikert, C., Vaikuntanathan, V.: Trapdoors for hard lattices and new cryptographic constructions. In: DBLP, pp. 197–206 (2008)

11. Lyubashevsky, V., Peikert, C., Regev, O.: On Ideal Lattices and Learning with Errors over Rings. ACM (2013)

12. Regev, O.: On lattices, learning with errors, random linear codes, and cryptography. ACM (2009)

13. Wan, S.: Energy-efficient adaptive routing and context-aware lifetime maximization in wireless sensor networks. Int. J. Distrib. Sens. Netw. **2014**(2), 112–116 (2014)

14. Wan, S., Zhang, Y.: Coverage hole bypassing in wireless sensor networks. Comput. J. **60** (10), 1536–1544 (2017)

15. Peikert, C., Shiehian, S.: Multi-key FHE from LWE, revisited. In: Hirt, M., Smith, A. (eds.) TCC 2016. LNCS, vol. 9986, pp. 217–238. Springer, Heidelberg (2016). https://doi.org/10.1007/978-3-662-53644-5_9

16. Mukherjee, P., Wichs, D.: Two round multiparty computation via multi-key FHE. In: Fischlin, M., Coron, J.-S. (eds.) EUROCRYPT 2016. LNCS, vol. 9666, pp. 735–763. Springer, Heidelberg (2016). https://doi.org/10.1007/978-3-662-49896-5_26

17. Regev, O.: On Lattices, Learning with Errors, Random Linear Codes, and Cryptography, pp. 84–89. ACM (2005)

18. Gopinath, V., Bhuvaneswaran, R.S.: Design of ECC based secured cloud storage mechanism for transaction rich applications. CMC: Comput. Mater. Continua **57**(2), 341–352 (2018)

19. Zhong, J., Liu, Z., Xu, J.: Analysis and improvement of an efficient controlled quantum secure direct communication and authentication protocol. CMC: Comput. Mater. Continua **57**(3), 621–633 (2018)

Research on SQL Injection and Defense Technology

Zongshi Chen, Mohan Li, Xiang Cui, and Yanbin Sun[✉]

Cyberspace Institute of Advanced Technology, Guangzhou University,
Guangzhou, China
sunyanbin@gzhu.edu.cn

Abstract. With the rapid development of Internet technology, more and more dynamic web sites based on the B/S three-tier architecture have been established. At the same time, the security issues exposed by the websites are increasing, and the situation is not optimistic. Today, a large number of Web systems use a database to store various data of a website, which may be the user's personal information, or may be a company's trade secret information. If this information is leaked, it is a huge loss and risk to the individual or the company. SQL injection attacks can achieve the purpose of obtaining illegal data, so it is conceivable that the harm of SQL injection is huge. From the point of view of SQL injection, SQL injection attacks are still one of the most common and most dangerous attacks. This paper introduces the concept and technical principle of SQL injection attack, introduces the type of SQL injection, analyzes the basic implementation process of SQL injection attack, and finally gives the defense method of preventing SQL injection and summarizes some researches on SQL injection.

Keywords: SQL injection · Web security · Database security

1 Introduction

The security risk of injecting vulnerabilities is always in the OWASP top 10 [1] most serious security risks from 2004 to 2017. An injection vulnerability occurs when untrusted data is sent to the interpreter as part of a command or query. Injection vulnerabilities include SQL, NoSQL, OS, and LDAP injection. The focus of this article is on SQL vulnerabilities. SQL vulnerabilities are actually what we call SQL injection attacks. In 2000, Rain Forest Puppy released a report on SQL injection called "How I hacked PacketStorm" [2]. Since then, researchers have never stopped researching SQL injection. So far, research on SQL injection has done a lot of work.

SQL injection attacks have three characteristics. The first feature is that there are many variants, and different attackers have different SQL injection methods. The second feature is that the attack is simple. There are many SQL injection attack tools on the Internet. Those who know nothing about SQL injection only need to use these tools to easily attack or destroy the target website. The third feature is that the attack is extremely harmful. Due to the defects of the web language itself and the lack of

X. Sun et al. (Eds.): ICAIS 2019, LNCS 11635, pp. 191–201, 2019.
https://doi.org/10.1007/978-3-030-24268-8_18

developers with secure programming, most web application systems have the possibility of being attacked by SQL injection, and once the attacker succeeds, the attacker can Control the entire web application system to make any modifications or steals of the data, and the destructive power is reached to the extreme. The harm caused by SQL injection is even more serious than Distributed Denial of Service (DDOS) [3]. DDOS only makes the network paralyzed, but SQL injection will lead to more serious information leakage, network control and so on. Therefore, it is necessary to learn SQL injection.

The second section of this article will describe the concepts and principles of SQL injection. The third section describes the type of SQL injection. The fourth section briefly describes the general process of SQL injection attacks. The fifth section focuses on the defense methods of SQL injection and the methods of learning SQL injection against others.

2   The Concept and Principle of SQL Injection

2.1   The Concept of SQL Injection Attack

The definition of SQL injection attack is that the attacker uses the SQL security vulnerability existing in the website, inserts malicious SQL statements into the user input parameters, and finally spoofs the database server to execute malicious SQL commands to illegally obtain sensitive information such as user passwords.

The user input parameter is data input by the user in the webpage, for example, the user name and password entered in the login page belong to the user input parameter. Attacker can directly access the database and obtain data through a SQL injection attack, which poses a great security risk to the system.

2.2   The Technical Principle of SQL Injection

The principle of SQL injection is as follows. First, construct special inputs based on the SQL syntax, and then pass those inputs as parameters to the web application. After that, the maliciously constructed SQL command is injected into the website database through the WEB server for execution. Eventually perform various unauthorized operations on the database, such as query, update, delete, access, and so on.

The essence of SQL injection is the append command. The default SQL command of the website daemon is a normal command called "constant" in the program, and the user-controlled input such as user name, password, etc. is called "variable". SQL injection is implemented by spelling together constants and variables as SQL instructions. For the convenience of understanding, the SQL injection flow is shown in Fig. 1.

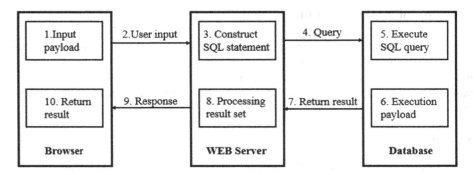

Fig. 1. SQL injection

The login verification module is taken as an example to illustrate the implementation principle of the SQL injection attack.

In the web application login verification program, there are two parameters "username" and "password". The program performs the authorization operation by the user's input username and password. The principle is to authorize access by looking up the results of the username and password in the user table.

Assume that the procedure for background login verification is as follows, taking the PHP code as an example [4]:

```php
<?php
$username = $_POST['username'];
$password = $_POST['password'];
$sql = "Select * from users where username='$username' and password='$password'";
$result = mysql_query($sql);
if (!result) {
    die('<pre>' . mysql_error() .'</pre>' );
}
```

After the user enters the correct username and password (for example, the correct username: admin, password: password), the SQL query executed by the database is: select * from users where username = 'admin' and password = 'password'. As a result, there is a piece of data in which the user name is "admin" and the password is "password" in the query data, and finally enters the background successfully. However, when the user enters the username and password as Alice' or '1' = '1, the database query statement is: select * from users where username = 'Alice' or '1' = '1' and password = 'Alice' or '1' = '1'. Since the content input by the user is not detected, the database server is equivalent to executing the statement: select * from users, regardless of whether there is Alice' or '1' = '1 user in the database, the data will be returned and the login will be successful. Thus, the harm of SQL injection can be imagined.

3   Type of SQL Injection

The type of SQL injection can be divided into 5 types of SQL injection attacks according to the SQL syntax used in SQL injection, which are error injection, joint query injection, multi-state query injection, boolean-based blind injection and time-based blind injection [5]. Below I will describe these five SQL injection types one by one.

3.1   Error Injection

The main reason which causes the error injection is that the server does not close the error echo. When the attacker sends some maliciously constructed input query parameters to the website, some error information of website server can be obtained. According to the error information, some key information of the server is leaked.

The error message is the error reported by the database server executing the wrong SQL statement, not the error message designed by the web developer. For example, if we enter "select * from stu—+" at the SQL injection point, and "stu" is a non-existent database table that is randomly entered, it will return an error like this: Table 'dvwa.stu' doesn't exist. From this error message we got the name of the database.

3.2   Joint Query Injection

The joint query injection is to obtain the data of the database by connecting two different SQL statements through "UNION".

Specifically, the first SQL statement is generally provided to the user's normal query sql statement, and the second SQL statement is generally constructed by the attacker, they are connected through UNION. However, it should be noted that the number of fields in the query of two SQL statements in the UNION query must be the same, otherwise the SQL statement will not be successfully executed. For example, "select Firstname, Surname from users union select 1, 2 from users", the "Firstname" and "Surname" fields are provided in the SQL query provided by the website, and two fields must be constructed after constructing the SQL statement. We generally use "order by" to guess the number of fields in the original SQL statement.

3.3   Multi-statement Query Injection

Multi-statement query injection is also known as stacked query injection. In SQL statements, the semicolon ";" is used to indicate the end of a statement, and the next statement can be constructed after the end of an SQL statement. Compared with federated query injection, multi-statement query injection can construct any type of statement, and can perform database operations such as deletion, update, and addition.

For example, if you construct "1'; drop table user#" in the user input parameter, the database will actually execute: select * from users where id = '1'; drop table test#, the drop table operation will be directly executed after the query ends.

3.4   Boolean-Based Blind and Time-Based Blinds

Blind injection based on Boolean and blind injection based on time are theoretically blind injection. Blind injection means that the WEB server shields the error message generated by the SQL server returned to the user, and the attacker cannot directly obtain useful information through the error information of the database.

The difference between a Boolean blind and a time-based blind is that Boolean injection can be easily judged by using the customized page information returned by the web page. Whether the malicious input we construct is feasible, whether it can be injected, and time-based blindness. Note that when the page does not return any error information or does not output the data information detected by the joint query injection, the information acquisition can only be performed by using a function in the database that can extend the response time.

For example, when the time-based blind injection target is Mysql database, we can use the sleep() function in the if() function to perform SQL injection attacks. The following code is a SQL statement constructed for time blind injection, the function is to get the length of the current database name:

```
Select FirstName, Surname form users where id=1' and if (asci (substr (database( ), 1, 1 ) )
= 115, sleep(10), 1 ) --+
```

These kinds of SQL injection types are mainly aimed at constructing malicious SQL statements to obtain database data by using different SQL syntax used in SQL injection, and there is no difference in essence.

4   The General Process of SQL Injection Attacks

SQL injection attacks can be done manually, or through tool software such as Ming Xiaozi, D, sqlmap, etc. But no matter which kind of attack method is used, basically it is first to construct a special statement to detect the SQL vulnerabilities existing in the Web program, and then perform illegal operations according to the corresponding vulnerabilities, and finally obtain the database data and obtain the highest authority of the server.

We all know that the simplest and most basic SQL query statement is "select field name from table name". It is not difficult to conclude that if we want to get the data information in the database, we must first know the table name and field name. At the same time, there may be slight differences in database functions for different databases, so in order to construct SQL statements effectively, we must first know which database the website uses.

The above knowledge is not difficult to get, SQL injection attacks generally go through the process:

1. Determine whether there is an injection point and whether it can be injected;
2. Guess which database, get the basic information of the database, such as version;
3. Guess the name of the table, get the name of the table;
4. Guess the field name and get the field name;
5. Guess the field value and get the field value.

5   Defense of SQL Injection Attacks

The harm caused by SQL injection attacks is terrible. The harm is not serious, it may only tamper with the information of the web page. If the harm is serious, the sensitive information of the database user or the private information will be leaked. Even the entire web server will be controlled by the hacker. This is very dangerous.

In order to minimize the loss caused by SQL injection attacks and increase the difficulty of SQL injection attacks, we can implement some preventive strategies and measures. We can generally prevent SQL injection attacks at the code and platform layers.

5.1   Defense at the Code Level

Verify User Input
User input verification is the process of testing the input received by the application to ensure it meets the criteria defined in the application. It can be as simple as limiting a parameter to a type, or as complex as using regular expressions or business logic to validate input [6]. The method of verifying user input can be simply divided into blacklist filtering and whitelist filtering.

Blacklist verification means rejecting all input that appears in the list. Usually, it is determined whether the input is accepted by determining whether there is a sensitive character. The sensitive characters are usually single quotes('), double quotes("), semicolons(;), and so on.

Whitelist verification means that only the specified conforming input is accepted. For example, the input data type, data content, data size [7], etc. are accepted by the user in the trusted list, otherwise it is not accepted.

Blacklist-based verification methods are much weaker than whitelist-based verification. It is unrealistic to rely on artificially adding all the sensitive characters to the blacklist. It is also possible that whitelisting may affect the use of normal users due to incomplete consideration. However, whether it is based on blacklist or whitelist defense methods, it has a great effect on preventing SQL injection.

Java, C#, HTML5, PHP, etc. all have their own format code to verify user input. Take PHP as an example, use the preg_math function to verify the parameters of the form.

```php
<?php
$AdminName = $_POST['AdminName'];
If ( preg_math("/^[A-Za-z] {12-16}$/D", $ AdminName) ) {
   // Verification success!
}
?>
```

Use Parameterized Query Statements

One of the most fundamental reasons for the SQL injection attack is the ability to dynamically construct the generated SQL statement and then send it to the database for execution [8]. In order to prevent the characters entered by the user from being executed as SQL instructions, we can use parameterized query statements.

Parametric queries are currently the most effective defense against SQL injection attacks. The main idea of a parameterized query statement is as follows. First send the default SQL statement of the website to the database server for pre-compilation to generate a template, and then send the template back to the web server. After that, the user's input can only represent one parameter string, and can't be constructed as a new SQL statement. This eliminates the user-entered characters being executed as SQL statements, eliminating SQL injection.

Take PHP as an example to implement parameterized queries:

```
<?php
$AdminName = $_POST['AdminName'];
$AdminPw = $_POST['AdminPw'];
Result = Db.Execute("select admin where AdminName='"+ AdminName +"' and AdminPw='"+ AdminPw +"'")
If(Result){
    // Verification success!
}
?>
```

Use Hexadecimal Encoding

Parametric queries can protect against all first-order SQL injection attacks, but they are powerless for second-order SQL injection attacks.

As mentioned above, SQL injection belongs to the first-order SQL injection, which means that the user input containing the attack payload is directly spliced into the dynamic SQL statement of the web application structure through the web input, so that the dynamic SQL statement is submitted to the database for execution and finally obtained unauthorized. Access technology [9], in which the attack load refers to the SQL statement that causes the original query logic of the SQL statement to be tampered with after being spliced by the SQL query, so as to implement the SQL statement that performs the illegal function [10].

Second-order SQL injection [11] is different from first-order SQL injection. The attack payload is injected into the WEB application and is not executed immediately to trigger the vulnerability. Instead, it is stored in the database and stored in the database when other operations are requested. The malicious code in the database will be retrieved and dynamically combined with the SQL statement of the WEB application into a new SQL statement to implement SQL injection attacks.

There are also many defense methods for second-order SQL injection, but they are not completely defense. In order to be able to almost completely prevent or even solve the second-order SQL injection attack, we can use ASCII hexadecimal encoding (that is, use a 2-digit hexadecimal number to represent one character). The hexadecimal ASCII encoding of the string entered by the user prevents any executable SQL code from being inserted into the data, thus completely preventing the SQL injection attack [12].

All of the above mentioned are basic defense methods. There are also many people studying for more efficient defense methods or systems, and there are many achievements.

Muthuprasanna, et al. [13] propose a SQL detection and prevention technique, which is a fully automated technique that combines static analysis with runtime verification. In the static analysis phase, the author uses the Java String Analysis library for static analysis, representing SQL queries as finite state automata (SQL-FSM) and treating them as SQL graphs. In the runtime verification phase, it is illegal to use the static data structure to audit the SQL statement, so that it is safe to mark the currently detected statement. In addition to defending against SQL injection, the detection defense technology proposed by the author has two advantages. The first advantage is that there is no need to modify the code. The second advantage is that it speeds up web access.

Min and Kun proposed an idea of using regular expressions to detect and defend against SQL injection, and they also developed a simple system using Snort's regular expressions [14]. This system only needs two steps to detect and defend SQL injection. The first step is to design the rules of regular expressions. The second step is to execute regular expressions with snort. Regular Expressions Compared to SQL-FSM, regular expressions are more mature and easier to program and implement. However, this method also has disadvantages. The design of regular expression rules has a certain degree of limitation, which depends mainly on the performer's technology.

Encryption technology can not only do simple data encryption to ensure confidentiality, but also apply to SQL injection defense. An article mentions the use of Advanced Encryption Standard (AES) and RSA encryption for two-stage encryption to prevent SQL injection [15]. The author proposes to encrypt the user name and user password with AES, while the SQL statement is encrypted with the RSA algorithm. This defense method is feasible, but it also has shortcomings. The downside is the management and maintenance of the key, and this defense method is not useful for URL-based SQL injection. Mittal and Jena also use encryption to prevent and detect SQL injection. They proposed a technique based on Bitslice AES encryption to prevent and detect SQL injection [16]. Using this technique, you can prevent second-order SQL injection.

Naresh Duhan and Bharti Saneja proposed an efficient way to detect and prevent the notorious SQL injection problem [17]. Combine client-side validation with identity-based cryptography (IBC) to implement two layers of defense to solve SQL injection. The first layer of defense is client-side validation, which is implemented by applying static validation constraints to user input. The constraints can be the type of the data, the length of the string, or some special characters. The second layer of defense is IBC, which is the second line of defense against SQL injection. The key used for encryption is generated based on the combination of email addresses, and each user's key is unique. The advantage of this defense method is that it is efficient and easy to implement. More importantly, it not only detects and prevents known types of SQL injection attacks, but also detects and prevents new types of SQL injection attacks.

Voitovych, et al. [18] made a defense system for SQL injection attacks. The main functional modules of this system are verification checkers, filters and error handlers. This system is very simple to implement, and it is not a new technology. It is essentially a method of checking and filtering to implement SQL injection defense.

Input validation is used to verify user input to ensure that the data entered is trustworthy and secure. Therefore, the way to input verification is to detect and defend against SQL injection, but it may have a problem of low detection accuracy. Lin, et al. [19] concluded that the input validation error occurred because only one filter rule was used. In order to solve the shortcomings of input verification, they proposed an automatic mechanism to improve the selection of filtering rules. They also made a defense system consisting of a test framework and a security gateway. The system they designed can achieve high detection rates.

5.2   Defense on the Platform Level

Defense against SQL injection attacks not only set protection mechanisms at the code level, but also protect against SQL injection attacks at the platform level. Insecure database configurations or vulnerabilities in the database platform can lead to the risk of SQL injection. So for SQL injection at the platform level, we can use the methods described below to defend against SQL injection.

Correct Configuration of the Web Server

The WEB server structure is large and complex, which makes the WEB server inevitably flawed in terms of security. Properly configuring the web server can reduce the risk of SQL injection. We can implement the security configuration of the WEB server from the following three aspects:

- Modify the server initial configuration: Once the server's brand is known by the hacker, the server's default configuration will be revealed, such as username and password. So we have to modify the initial configuration of the server.
- Install server security patches in a timely manner: By installing security patches, you can continuously improve your server to avoid vulnerabilities.
- Turn off the server's error message: According to the error information of the database, it is easier for the hacker to perform SQL injection, so we must configure the web server to block the error message.

The Correct Configuration Database

For the correct security configuration of the database, it is also one of the ways to reduce the risk of SQL injection. For example, database security configuration should follow the principle of least privilege [20]. Only grant the user the necessary permissions without over-authorization. The principle of least privilege can effectively reduce SQL injection and prevent important data leakage in the database. In addition to configuring the database, we mainly configure the database from the following two aspects:

- Modify the database initial configuration
- Upgrade the database in time

Use Web Application Firewall (WAF)

By configuring security parameters or rules such as WAF access control list, it can effectively prevent SQL injection attacks to a certain extent.

Security Settings for Script Parsing

For scripting languages such as ASP and PHP, some security settings are involved in their configuration files. We can increase the difficulty of SQL injection by properly configuring these security settings and reduce the risk of SQL injection.

In the case of PHP, we can set "magic_quotes_gpc" to "on" and "safe_mode" to "on".

6 Conclusion

With the advent of the information age, the number of Internet users has increased, and the number of websites has soared, and the web security situation has become increasingly severe. SQL injection attacks have become one of the most common attacks in web attacks. Therefore, learning and studying the principles of SQL injection attacks, the implementation process of attacks, and the knowledge of SQL injection defense have far-reaching significance for securing web security. In recent years, big data, cloud security [21], AI have also been rapidly developed, all of them are very useful researches for SQL injection.

Acknowledgments. This work is funded by the National Key Research and Development Plan (Grant No. 2018YFB0803504) and the National Natural Science Foundation of China (No. U1636215).

References

1. Tan, J.: OWASP releases top ten web application security risks. Comput. Netw. (23), 52–53 (2017)
2. Puppy, F.R.: How I hacked PacketStorm: a look at hacking WWW threads by means of SQL —part 2. EDPACS **28**(3), 1–6 (2000)
3. Cheng, J., Xu, R., Tang, X., Sheng, V.S., Cai, C., et al.: An abnormal network flow feature sequence prediction approach for DDoS attacks detection in big data environment. Comput. Mater. Continua **55**(1), 095–119 (2018)
4. Ou, X., Yang, S.: Study on the principle and prevention technology of SQL injection attack. Digital Technol. Appl. (04), 216 (2016)
5. Halfond, W.G., Viegas, J., Orso, A.: A classification of SQL-injection attacks and countermeasures. In: IEEE International Symposium on Secure Software Engineering, vol. 1, pp. 13–15, March 2006
6. Shi, H., Ye, W.: SQL Injection Attack and Defense, 2nd edn. Tsinghua University Press, Beijing (2013)

7. Xu, J.: SQL injection attack principle and application in database security. Comput. Program. Skills Maint. (18), 104–106(2009)
8. Bo, Z.: Research on SQL injection attack and detection technology. Inf. Secur. Commun. Secur. (5), 90–92 (2010)
9. Herrero, Á., Corchado, E., Bajo, J., Pinzón, C.I., De Paz, J.F., Corchado, J.M.: idMAS-SQL: intrusion detection based on MAS to detect and block SQL injection through data mining. Inf. Sci. **231**, 15–31 (2013)
10. Kieyzuna, A., Guo, P.J., Jayaraman, K, et al.: Automatic creation of SQL injection and cross-site scripting attacks. In: Proceedings of the 31st International Conference on Software Engineering (ICSE), pp. 199–209. IEEE Computer Society, Washington, DC (2009)
11. Ollmann, G.: Second-order code injection attacks. Technical report. NGSSoftware Insight Security Research (2004)
12. Fu, X., Gong, X.: A general encoding method for solving SQL injection vulnerabilities. J. Yancheng Inst. Technol.: Nat. Sci. Ed. (1), 5–8(2015)
13. Muthuprasanna, M., Wei, K., Kothari, S.: Eliminating SQL injection attacks - a transparent defense mechanism. In: Eighth IEEE International Symposium on Web Site Evolution. IEEE Computer Society (2006)
14. Min, W., Kun, L.: An improved eliminating SQL injection attacks based regular expressions matching. In: International Conference on Control Engineering & Communication Technology. IEEE Computer Society (2012)
15. Balasundram, I., Ramaraj, E.: An Authentication scheme for Preventing SQL Injection Attack Using Hybrid Encryption (PSQL1-HBE) **53**(3), 359–368 (2011). ISSN 1450-216 X
16. Mittal, P., Jena, S.K.: A fast and secure way to prevent SQL injection attacks. In: Information & Communication Technologies. IEEE (2013)
17. Duhan, N., Saneja, B.: A two tier defense against SQL injection. In: International Conference on Signal Propagation & Computer Technology. IEEE (2014)
18. Voitovych, O.P., Yuvkovetskyi, O.S., Kupershtein, L.M.: SQL injection prevention system. In: Radio Electronics & Info Communications. IEEE (2016)
19. Lin, J.C., Chen, J.M., Liu, C.H.: An automatic mechanism for sanitizing malicious injection. In: International Conference for Young Computer Scientists. IEEE (2008)
20. Qi, C.: Web security development: SQL injection attacks and web page hanging horses. Programmer (7), 102–104 (2008)
21. Zhang, H., Yi, Y., Wang, J., Cao, N., Duan, Q., et al.: Network security situation awareness framework based on threat intelligence. Comput. Mater. Continua **56**(3), 381–399 (2018)

A Review of the Factorization Problem
of Large Integers

Xinguo Zhang, Mohan Li, Yu Jiang, and Yanbin Sun[(✉)]

Cyberspace Institute of Advanced Technology, Guangzhou University,
Guangzhou, China
sunyanbin@gzhu.edu.cn

Abstract. Large integer decomposition is the most direct attack method of
RSA public key encryption algorithm, and it is closely related to the security of
RSA. Therefore, the problem of large integer decomposition has become a
problem for cryptographers and mathematicians. The main purpose of this paper
is to discuss the current research situation of large integer decomposition
problem, analyze the basic principle and implementation method of the current
mainstream large integer decomposition algorithm, and forecast the future
research trend of large integer decomposition.

Keywords: Large integer decomposition · RSA · Security

1 Introduction

As a public key encryption algorithm that is still relatively safe, RSA is widely used in
encryption and signature authentication, such as signature authentication in Android
[1]. The flow of the RSA encryption and decryption algorithm is to find two large
prime integer p, q, obtain $n = p * q$, $\varphi(n) = (p - 1) * (q - 1)$, generate a random
integer $e < n$, find $e * d(mod\ n) = 1$, throw p, q, then we get the public key (n, e), the
private key (n, d), the public key will be published on the network. Let m be plaintext
and c be ciphertext. The sender then encrypts with the public key advertised by the
recipient and the recipient decrypts it with his private key. The formula is as follows:

$$c = m^e\ mod\ n \tag{1}$$

$$m = c^d\ mod\ n \tag{2}$$

From the above RSA encryption and decryption process, we can see that when we
can get p, q through n, then we can decrypt the ciphertext arbitrarily. The process of
obtaining p, q from n is the process of decomposition of large integer. At present, it is
generally believed that the difficulty of cracking RSA is equivalent to the difficulty of
decomposition of large integer. Whether it can solve that the decomposition of large
integer will directly determine whether RSA is safe. Therefore, the problem of large
integer decomposition has important application value.

This paper first discusses the current status of the study of the large integer
decomposition problem, and then analyzes the basic principles of the classical large

© Springer Nature Switzerland AG 2019
X. Sun et al. (Eds.): ICAIS 2019, LNCS 11635, pp. 202–213, 2019.
https://doi.org/10.1007/978-3-030-24268-8_19

integer decomposition algorithm. Finally, the future research trend of the large integer decomposition problem is prospected.

2 Research Status

A natural integer greater than 1 can be written as the product of its prime factor. The problem of large integer decomposition is to find out what the specific values of these prime factors are. When the prime factor of the composite integer is very large, it will be very difficult to violent cracking it. At present, the large integer decomposition problem cannot be proved as a non-solvable problem in polynomial time, nor can it be proved as a solvable problem in polynomial time. Before 1970, it was very difficult to decompose 20 decimal integer. In the 1970s and 1980s, large integer decomposition has a relatively large development, by 1991 can successfully decompose the 110-digit decimal large integer [2]. In order to encourage more people to study the problem of large integer decomposition, RSA Laboratories proposed the RSA Decomposition Challenge in 1991. In the Challenge, RSA Laboratories provides some decimal integers from 100 to 617, and said that no matter what organization and individual complete the decomposition of these integers in any way, you can get the cash reward of the corresponding integer of successful decomposition. But until now only 232 decimal digits were successfully decomposed. The following table shows large integer decomposition situation so far (Table 1):

Table 1. RSA modulus decomposition

RSA integer	Decimal digits	Binary digits	Factored on	Factored by
RSA-576	174	576	December 3, 2003	Jens Franke [3]
RSA-180	180	596	May 8, 2010	S.A.Danilov [4]
RSA-190	190	629	November 8, 2010	A.Timofeev [5]
RSA-640	193	640	November 2, 2005	Jens Franke [6]
RSA-210	210	696	September 26, 2013	Ryan Propper [7]
RSA-704	212	704	July 2, 2012	Bai Shi [8]
RSA-220	220	729	May 13, 2016	S.Bai, P.Gaudry [9]
RSA-768	232	768	December 12, 2009	Thorsten Kleinjung [10]

At present, representative large integer decomposition algorithms can be divided into three categories: large integer decomposition algorithms with special attributes, such as trial division, Pollard's rho algorithm, Pollard's p-1 algorithm, Lenstra elliptic curve decomposition, Fermat factorization method, Euler factorization method; general large integer decomposition algorithms, such as Dixon algorithm, Quadratic sieve, Rational sieve, General integer field sieve; other categories of algorithms, such as Shor algorithm. Below, we will review and analyze the algorithms of the classic large integer decomposition in the past.

3 Decomposition Algorithm for Large Integer with Special Properties

3.1 Trial Division

Trial division is a relatively old method used to decompose large integer. Its essence is an Exhaustive method. The idea of this algorithm is very simple: use the large integer n to sequentially remove the integer between 2 and $\lceil \sqrt{N} \rceil$ until the remainder is 0. Then the integer is a prime factor of the large integer n. If until $\lceil \sqrt{N} \rceil$ still does not find a integer with a remainder of 0, then the large integer n is a prime. This algorithm is usually used when the large integer n itself is relatively small or there are relatively small factors. When n is large and its factor is large, it is no longer suitable for this method.

3.2 Pollard's Rho Algorithm

Pollard's rho algorithm is a large integer decomposition algorithm invented by John Pollard in 1975 [11]. It was improved by Brent in 1980. Pollard's rho algorithm is mainly based on the cyclicity of modular arithmetic and Floyd's circular search algorithm [12]. The basic idea is as follows: We assume that the large integer N has a prime factor p. We first select an initial function, usually selected as $g(x) = (x^2 + 1) \bmod n$ or $g(x) = (x^2 - 1) \bmod n$, and select an initial value $x_0 = 2$, So we can get a bunch of random integer $\{x_0, x_1 \ldots \ldots x_n\}$ less than n and satisfies Eq. 3. Since the modulo operation is cyclic, there will be $x_i \equiv x_j \bmod p$. Since we don't know what p is, we need to calculate $d = gcd(|x_i - x_j|, N)$, when d is not 1 and n, d is a factor of N. At this time, we have to find the right x_i, x_j. At this point we want to use Floyd's loop lookup algorithm. Floyd's loop-finding algorithm, also known as Floyd's Tortoise-Rabbit algorithm, uses the speed of the turtle and the rabbit to move the two pointers. The sequence pointer obtained above knows to find $x_i \equiv x_j \bmod p$.

$$x_{i+1} = (x_i^2 + 1) \bmod n (x_{i+1}, x_i \in [0, n-1]) \tag{3}$$

According to the above description, the algorithm flow of the method is as follows:

1. $x = 1$, $y = 1$, $d = 1$, select $g(x) = (x^2 + 1) \bmod n$
2. $x = g(x)$, $y = g(g(y))$
3. Calculate $d = gcd(|x_i - x_j|, N)$
4. When $d = 1$ or $x = n$, return 2. Otherwise d is a factor of n

In order to get the same integer of two modulo p in one sequence, how long should our sequence length be? This issue is similar to a birthday attack. Let us assume that the sequence length we obtained is k, then the probability that there is no duplicate integer in this sequence is Eq. 4, the probability of having a repeated integer in this sequence is $1 - p$. When k = $\sqrt{p}$, the probability of having a repeating integer in this sequence is 50%. We find that when the factor of the large integer n is relatively large, we need a longer sequence, that is, a large enough difference is needed to obtain the same integer of two modulo p.

$$p = \frac{365}{365} \frac{364}{365} \cdots \cdots \frac{365 - k + 1}{365} = \frac{\prod_{i=0}^{k-1} 365 - i}{365^k} \tag{4}$$

3.3 Pollard's p-1 Algorithm

Pollard's p-1 algorithm is also a large integer decomposition algorithm invented by John Pollard in 1974 [13]. The algorithm is based on Fermat's theorem. The theorem is described as follows: p is a prime integer, and the integer of random selections is $1 < a < p$, then $a^{p-1} modp \equiv 1$. The idea of the algorithm is as follows: We assume that the large integer N has a prime factor p, according to the Fermat's theorem, $a^{p-1} modp \equiv 1$ then $a^{k(p-1)} modp \equiv 1$, $(a^{k(p-1)}) - 1) modp = 0$, $a^{k(p-1)} - 1 = kp$. At this time $gcd(a^{k(p-1)} - 1, N) = p$, then we need to construct $k (p - 1)$, we know that p is a prime integer, then $p - 1$ must be a composite integer. Here we assume that $p - 1$ can be composed of some small prime integer smaller than b. Then we can continue to use these small prime integer to try to construct M, which constitutes a multiple of $(p - 1)$, and then solves a prime factor p of n. The algorithm flow is as follows:

1. Select a random integer B
2. Construct $M = \prod_{prime q \leq B} q^{k_q}$, (where q is less than all primes of B, k_q is a random value)
3. Select a random integer of a and N to be prime, usually choose a to be 2, calculate $g = gcd(a^M, N)$
4. When $g = 1$ or $g = n$, return to the second step
5. When $1 < g < n$, return g

The time complexity of the algorithm is $O(B \log B(\log n)^2)$ it can be seen that when the $p - 1$ of the prime factor p of large integer can be written as a product of several small prime integer, use the algorithm is more efficient for large integer decomposition.

3.4 Elliptic Curve Decomposition Method

In 1985, Hendrik Lenstra invented the elliptic curve decomposition method [14]. The algorithm is an integer decomposition algorithm with sub exponential runtime, which is commonly used to decompose 50–60 digit decimal integer. The best result of using this algorithm today is to decompose a large 83-bit integer. The basic idea of the elliptic curve decomposition method is as follows: The basic idea of the algorithm is similar to Pollard's p-1 algorithm, except that the multiplicative group in Pollard's p-1 algorithm is replaced by the additive group in the elliptic curve. The addition on the elliptic curve is different from the addition of our normal coordinate points. The formula for the addition on the elliptic curve is defined as follows: the known elliptic equation $y^2 = (x^3 + ax + b)modn, p(x_1, y_1), q(x_2, y_2)$ Then

$$p + q = (((\frac{y_1 - y_2}{x_1 - x_2})^2 - x_1 - x_2)modn, ((\frac{y_1 - y_2}{x_1 - x_2})(x_1 - x_3) - y_3)modn) \qquad (5)$$

$$2p = (((\frac{3x_1^2 + a}{2y_1})^2 - 2x_1)modn, ((\frac{3x_1^2 + a}{2y_1})(x_1 - x_4) - y_4)modn) \qquad (6)$$

The basic flow of the algorithm is as follows:

1. Select three random integer x_0, y_0, a_0 and let $b = (y_0^2 - x_0^3 - ax_0)modn$. Thus we get an initial elliptic equation $y^2 = (x^3 + ax + b)modn$ and the initial point $A(x_0, y_0)$ on the elliptic equation
2. Calculate KA using the ellipse addition formula. In the addition formula, you need to calculate the inverse of $(x_1 - x_2)modn$ or $2y_1$ modn. If the inverse does not exist, you can find $gcd((x_1 - x_2), n)$ or $gcd(2y_1, n)$, if the inverse exists, treat KA as A, repeat step 2
3. Return when $gcd((x_1 - x_2), n)$ or $gcd(2y_1, n)$ is not d, otherwise go to step 1.

The elliptic curve decomposition method is the fastest in the large integer decomposition algorithm with special properties, and its time complexity is $O(e^{(\sqrt{2}+O(1))\sqrt{\ln p \ln \ln p}})$. It can be seen that like the Pollard's p-1 algorithm, the smaller the factor that makes up n, the smoother the n is in the ellipse addition group, the faster the algorithm is.

3.5   Fermat Factorization Method

The Fermat factorization method is an integer decomposition method that Fermat found more than 300 years ago. The basic idea of the Fermat decomposition method is as follows: When the large integer n has a decomposition form of $n = ab$, then let $t = \frac{a+b}{2}$, $s = \frac{a-b}{2}$. N can be written as $n = (\frac{a+b}{2})^2 - (\frac{a-b}{2})^2$, $n = t^2 - s^2$ when we don't know what a and b are, we can turn the problem into finding t, s in $n = t^2 - s^2$. At this time, $n = t^2 - s^2 = (t - s)(t + s)$. When neither $t + s$ nor $t - s$ is 1, $t + s$ and $t - s$ are factors of n. The algorithm flow is as follows:

1. Initialize $t = \lfloor \sqrt{N} \rfloor$
2. $t = t + 1$
3. $s = t^2 - N$
4. When s is not a square integer jump to 2, otherwise continue
5. Return $t + \sqrt{s}$, or $t - \sqrt{s}$

It can be seen from the basic idea and flow of the algorithm $(\frac{a-b}{2})^2 = s = t^2 - N$, $t = \sqrt{N + (\frac{a-b}{2})^2}$, so When the difference between a and b in $n = ab$ is small, that is, a and b are close to $\sqrt{N}$, we only need to cycle through a few rounds to get the result, using this algorithm, we can get the result quickly, but when the difference between a and b is large, it will need to loop a lot of rounds. When n is large, the algorithm will have a hard time getting results.

3.6 Euler Factorization Method

The Euler factorization method was first discovered by Marin Mersenne, but the algorithm was widely used until Euler's promotion a hundred years later. Therefore, the algorithm is also called Euler factor decomposition method. The basic idea of the algorithm is as follows: We first find the sum of two different squares of the big integer n, i.e. $n = a^2 + b^2 = c^2 + d^2$, then $a^2 - c^2 = b^2 - d^2$, then $(a - c)(a + c) = (d - b)(d + b)$, we let $k = gcd(a - c, d - b)$, $h = gcd(a + c, d + b)$. Then we can get $a - c = kl$, $a + c = hm$, $d - b = km$, $d + b = hl$. Then according to Brahmagupta Fibonacci theorem, $(k^2 + h^2)(l^2 + m^2) = 4n$, then $n = (l^2 + m^2)\left(\left(\frac{k}{2}\right)^2 + \left(\frac{h}{2}\right)^2\right)$. Then we succeed in breaking down the large integer n. The algorithm flow is as follows:

1. Select $a = 0$, $sign = 0$;
2. $a = a + 1$, $b = n - a^2$
3. When b is the square integer, $sign = sign + 1$ and save (a_{sign}, b_{sign}), $a_{sign} = a$, $b_{sign} = \sqrt{b}$
4. Returns 2 when sign is not 2 and $a < \sqrt{n}$
5. Calculate $A = a_1 - a_2$, $B = a_1 + a_2$, $C = b_1 - b_2$, $D = b_1 - b_2$
6. Calculate $k = gcd(A, C)$, $h = gcd(B, D)$, $l = \frac{A-C}{k}$, $m = \frac{A+C}{k}$
7. Return $(l^2 + m^2)$ or $\left(\left(\frac{k}{2}\right)^2 + \left(\frac{h}{2}\right)^2\right)$

There is a problem with this algorithm. Not all composite integer have this form of large integer decomposition. It can be easily proved that when a integer can be written in the form of $4k + 3$, it can't be expressed as the sum of two squares. Then when n has a prime factor of $4k + 3$, the integer will not be decomposed using this method.

4 Decomposition Algorithm for General Large Integer

4.1 Dixon Algorithm

The Dixon algorithm was designed by Carleton mathematician Dixon in 1981 [15]. The basic idea of the algorithm is as follows: For a large integer n we find $x^2 \equiv y^2 modn((x \pm y)modn \neq 0)$, then we will easily find $gcd(x + y, n)$ or $gcd(x - y, n)$ as a factor of n, the Fermat decomposition method mentioned above is to use the traversal method to directly find $x^2 \equiv y^2 modn$ is x, y. However, as x increases, the square integer becomes very sparse, which makes the x, y of $x^2 \equiv y^2 modn$ difficult to find, resulting in the Fermat decomposition method when the factor difference of n is relatively large. It will be more complicated. It is difficult to find the square integer directly, then we can find some weaker conditions, that is, we can indirectly look for a few integer so that the product is a square integer. We can find some k_i composed of small prime integer, so that $k_i = \prod_{primep_j < b} p_j^{i_j}$ satisfies $x_i^2 \equiv k_i modn$. The k_i inside is called the b-smooth integer. Then look for two or more expressions that satisfy $x_i^2 \equiv k_i modn$, and these formulas satisfy formula (7), then we find that the left and right are flat, we indirectly get $x^2 \equiv y^2 modn$, so that the factor $gcd(x + y, n)$ or $gcd(x - y, n)$ of n can be obtained.

$$x_1^2 x_2^2 \ldots \ldots x_n^2 \equiv \prod_{primtp_j < b} p_j^{1_j + 2_j + \ldots n_j}(modn)((1_j + 2_j + \ldots n_j)mod2 \equiv 0) \quad (7)$$

The algorithm flow is as follows:

1. Select a B such that $list1 = [p_1, p_2, \ldots \ldots, p_n]$, where the elements are all primes less than B
2. $a = \lfloor \sqrt{n} \rfloor$
3. $a = a + 1$
4. Calculate $k \equiv a^2 modn$
5. If k can be composed of elements in list1, k is represented as $\prod_{primep_j < b} p_j^{i_j}$, and the coefficients of p_i are stored in a list in order.
6. Combine the list with the previous list as a new list. If you can get all the elements in the list to be even, continue, otherwise return 3
7. Calculate $x = (a_1 a_2 \ldots \ldots a_n)modn$, $y = \prod_{primtp_j < b} p_j^{(1_j + 2_j + \ldots n_j)/2}(modn)$
8. Returns 3 when $x \equiv \pm ymodn$, otherwise returns $gcd(x + y, N)$

We find that there are only 10,000 squares within 100000000, and the integer that can be decomposed by prime integer less than 30 within 100000000 has 88413. The integer of squares is much lower than the smoothing integer. We find $\prod_{primep_j < b} p_j^{i_j} \equiv a^2 modn$ established formula will be easier. But the algorithm looks for $\prod_{primep_j < b} p_j^{i_j} \equiv a^2 modn$ The formula that is established is still using the traversal method, which means that when n is large, n decomposition is still very difficult.

4.2 Quadratic Sieve

The Quadratic sieve was developed by Carl Pomerance in 1980s on the basis of the Schroeppel's linear sieve [16]. The algorithm is similar to the Dixon algorithm and is currently used to process integers of 50–100 decimal digits. The basic idea of the algorithm is as follows: First we choose a function $y(x) = (x + \lceil \sqrt{n} \rceil)^2 - n$. Then we sequentially calculate $y(0)$, $y(1)$, $y(2)$... corresponding to $x = 0, 1, 2.....$ Decompose $y(0)$, $y(1)$, $y(2)$, and combine some of the smaller factors to form a factor library $F = \{ p_1, p_2, p_3 \ldots \ldots p_k \}$. Construct the equation $y(x) \equiv (x + \lceil \sqrt{n} \rceil)^2 - n \equiv 0(mod\, p_i)$, substituting each factor in the factor library, solving $x \equiv (\sqrt{n} - \sqrt{n})(mod\, p_i)$, using We can solve a series of function values that contain this factor. Then the function value is decomposed. If all factors can fall in our factor library after decomposition, the coefficients decomposed into each factor are stored in a vector $v_i = [i_1, i_2 \ldots \ldots i_k]$.

Combine the vectors into a matrix $V = \begin{bmatrix} v_1 \\ v_2 \\ \vdots \\ v_m \end{bmatrix}$, let $S = [s_1, s_2 \ldots \ldots s_m]$ (s_i take 0 or 1),

and solve the equation $S \cdot V \equiv [0, 0, \ldots \ldots 0] mod 2$ S vector, s_i is 1 corresponding function value decomposition type multiplication, we can get $a^2 \equiv b^2 mod n$, then gcd $(a + b, n)$ or $gcd(a - b, n)$ is a factor of n. The algorithm flow is as follows:

1. Construct the equation $y(x) = (x + \lceil \sqrt{n} \rceil)^2 - n$, and substitute $x = 0,1,2\ldots$ into the equation to obtain $y(0), y(1),\ldots$, the integer of values depends on The size of n
2. Decompose $y(0), y(1), \ldots$, and save the smaller prime integer into the factor library $F = \{p_1, p_2, p_3 \ldots \ldots p_n\}$. The size of the factor library depends on the size of n.
3. Solving $y(x) \equiv (x + \lceil \sqrt{n} \rceil)^2 - n \equiv 0(mod p_i)$, $x \equiv (\sqrt{n} - \lceil \sqrt{n} \rceil)(mod p_i)$, we can get a series of solutions $x_i mod p_i$ save
4. Factoring each solution into the equation, if it can be written as $(x_i + \lceil \sqrt{n} \rceil)^2 - n = \prod_{p_j \in F} p_j^{i_j}$, then $(x_i + \lceil \sqrt{n} \rceil, (i_1, i_2 \ldots \ldots, i_k))$ Stored
5. Form $v_i = [i_1, i_2 \ldots \ldots i_k]$ into a matrix $V = \begin{bmatrix} v_1 \\ v_2 \\ \vdots \\ v_m \end{bmatrix}$ and solve the S vector in the equation $S \cdot V \equiv [0, 0, \ldots \ldots 0] mod 2$
6. Corresponding to the formula of $s_i = 1$, multiply the left and right sides respectively to obtain $a = \prod_{s_i = 1} (x_i + \lceil \sqrt{n} \rceil)$, $b = \prod_{s_i = 1} \prod_{p_j \in F} p_j^{i_j}$.
7. Return $gcd(|a + b|, n)$ or $gcd(|a - b|, n)$

The equation selected in the algorithm is not unique, as long as it has an equation of the form $y(x) = x^2 - n$. A better improvement is to choose the equation $y(x) = (ax + b)^2 - n$. Where $a | b^2 - n$. Then the original is equal to $a^2 x^2 + 2abx + b^2 - n = a^2 x^2 + 2abx + ka = a(ax^2 + 2bx + k)$, if a is set to square, we just need to make the function $(ax^2 + 2bx + k)$ a square number. The time complexity of the algorithm is $O(e^{(1 + o(1))\sqrt{\ln n \ln \ln n}})$. Compared with the Dixon algorithm, it is no longer searched according to the traversal method, but reduces our search range according to our factor library, and the secondary screening factor decomposition method can search each type of solution in parallel, it is easier to put the algorithm is transformed into a parallel algorithm to accelerated operation. But the matrix V in our algorithm is a sparse matrix. When n is large, the matrix V will be too large to be stored.

4.3   General Integer Field Sieve

The General integer field sieve was proposed by Pollard around 1990 [17]. The basic idea of the algorithm is still to find that $x^2 \equiv y^2 mod n((x \pm y)mod n \neq 0)$ holds x, y. So the question is still how to quickly find x, y. Here we first search a d-degree polynomial f and an integer m, so that $f(m) \equiv 0 mod n$, let α be a solution of f, but α is not in the modulo n congruence ring, then we can put α Enter a new ring in the integer ring. At the same time, we can also get a ring homomorphism function g(x) from integer ring to new ring. We need to filter the k-group pairs (a_0, b_0), (a_1, b_1),......, (a_k, b_k) so that $\prod_{i=0}^{k} (a_0 + b_0 m) mod n$ On the integer ring is a square integer x^2 and $\prod_{i=0}^{k} (a_0 + b_0 \alpha) mod n$ is a square integer β^2 on the new ring, according to the homomorphic function We can find that β^2 corresponds to y^2 in the rational integer field. At this point we find x, y satisfies $x^2 \equiv y^2 mod n$. The time complexity of the integer field screening method is formula 8, is the fastest algorithm for the decomposition of large integer. The current breakthrough in the decomposition of large integer is to use the algorithm or some variant based on the algorithm. When the algorithm is implemented, a relatively large matrix is generated, and the matrix operation needs to be solved to screen out the pairs we need. Therefore, the algorithm and the secondary screening method also have memory issues. Although the algorithm can use a high-degree polynomial than the second sieve method, the algorithm has a more complicated process than the secondary sieve method.

$$O(\exp((\frac{64}{9} + O(1))^{\frac{1}{3}}(\ln n)^{\frac{1}{3}}(\ln \ln n)^{\frac{2}{3}})) \tag{8}$$

5   Other Algorithms

5.1   Shor Algorithm

The Shor algorithm is a quantum algorithm proposed by Peter Shor in 1994 [18]. Quantum algorithms are algorithms that run on quantum computers. The basic idea of the algorithm is as follows: First we choose a random integer $a < N$, and $gcd(a, N) = 1$, and set the function $f(x) = a^x mod n$, find the smallest r so that $f(x) = f(x + r)$ holds, when r is even or $a^{\frac{r}{2}} mod n = -1$, re-select a, otherwise return $gcd(a^{\frac{r}{2}} + 1, N)$ and $gcd(a^{\frac{r}{2}} - 1, N)$, then the problem translates into how to find r quickly. Here we use the QFET algorithm and then use the properties of the continuous fraction to calculate r. The minimum time complexity of the Shor algorithm is formula 9, indicating that the algorithm is likely to be completed in polynomial time. The time complexity is much smaller than that of the integer domain screening method. This algorithm is more effective than the traditional algorithm. In 2001, IBM successfully used the Shor algorithm to decompose 15 into 3 and 5 using NMR quantum computers [19]. By 2014, quantum computers can be used to decompose 56153 into 233 and 241, but here is the use of adiabatic sub-calculation (AQS) to decompose 56153.

$$O((\log n)^2 (\log \log n)(\log \log \log n)) \tag{9}$$

6 Summary and Outlook

6.1 Algorithm Summary

The essence of the above algorithm is to use n some mathematical methods to convert some smooth integer, which can be combined by some relatively small integer. The general idea can be divided into n or n factors are smooth, such as trial and error. Pollard's rho algorithm is that when n is smooth, the algorithm can get the result very quickly. Pollard's p-1 algorithm establishes the p-1 of the factor p of n to be smooth, and the algorithm can get the result very quickly. Large integers are smooth in the other of the group, and the elliptic curve decomposition is based on the fact that large integer is smooth in the elliptic curve addition group. The polynomial generates a smooth value to construct a factor of a large integer. For example, Dixon algorithm, quadratic screening method, common number field filtering method, are all using a polynomial constructing factor library to generate a smooth value and construct a factor of a large integer (Fig. 1).

6.2 Outlook

From the above picture, although the decomposition of large numbers has developed rapidly in recent decades, no new algorithms and ideas for large number decomposition have been proposed since the 1990s. Most of the work is based on correction and optimizing general integer field sieve. Moreover, general integer field sieve has various problems such as large memory and complicated algorithm flow, which makes it difficult to perform decomposition of large numbers of 1024-bit binary even on a large computer. The development of large number decomposition in the last decade or so has mostly relied on the development of computer computing power and hardware. So in the future we should look for new algorithms for decomposing large numbers and find some algorithms that are more suitable for hardware. At the same time, we find that

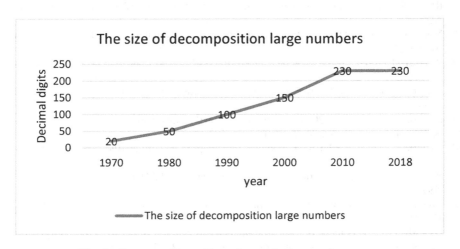

Fig. 1. Decomposition of large integer in the past forty years

using quantum algorithms to decompose large numbers is theoretically superior to using traditional methods to decompose large numbers. So how to optimize quantum computer [20] is also a hot topic of large number decomposition.

7 Conclusion

The study of the large integer decomposition problem has developed rapidly in recent decades. It is also difficult to solve the 20-digit decimal number in the past. But now we can use a large computer to decompose 232-bit decimal numbers. In addition to the rapid development of computer computing power in recent decades. The study of the large number decomposition algorithm has also played a crucial role in the continuous breakthrough in recent decades. Although it has not been possible to prove whether the large number decomposition has a polynomial solution, we have been raising the lower limit of the time complexity of the large number decomposition algorithm. I believe that the problem of large integer decomposition in the future will be well resolved.

Acknowledgments. This work is funded by the National Key Research and Development Plan (Grant No. 2018YFB0803504) and the National Natural Science Foundation of China (No. U1636215).

References

1. Li, D., Luo, M., Zhao, B.: Provably secure APK redevelopment authorization scheme in the standard model. Comput. Mater. Cortinua **56**(3), 447–465 (2018)
2. Pomerance, C.: A tale of two sieves. Not. AMS **43**(12), 1473–1485 (1996)
3. MathWorld Headline news. http://mathworld.wolfram.com/news/2003-12-05/rsa/. Accessed 24 Oct 2018
4. Factorization of RSA-180. https://eprint.iacr.org/2010/270.pdf,last. Accessed 24 Oct 2018
5. RSA-190 factored. https://mersenneforum.org/showpost.php?p=236114&postcount=1,last. Accessed 24 Oct 2018
6. MathWorld Headline news. http://mathworld.wolfram.com/news/2005-11-08/rsa-640/,last. Accessed 24 Oct 2018
7. RSA-210 factored. https://www.mersenneforum.org/showpost.php?p=354259,last. Accessed 24 Oct 2018
8. Factorization of RSA-704 with cado-nfs. https://eprint.iacr.org/2012/369.pdf,last. Accessed 24 Oct 2018
9. Factorization of RSA-220 with cado-nfs. https://members.loria.fr/PZimmermann/papers/rsa220.pdf,last. Accessed 24 Oct 2018
10. Factorization of a 768-bit RSA modules. https://eprint.iacr.org/2010/006.pdf,last. Accessed 24 Oct 2018
11. Pollard, J.M.: A Monte Carlo method for factorization. BIT Numer. Math. **15**(3), 331–334 (1975)
12. Brent, R.P.: An improved Monte Carlo factorization algorithm. BIT Numer. Math. **20**(2), 176–184 (1980)
13. Pollard, J.M.: Theorems of factorization and primality testing. In: Proceedings of the Cambridge Philosophical Society, vol. 76, no. 3, pp. 521–528 (1974)

14. Lenstra, H.W.: Factoring integers with elliptic curves. Ann. Math. **126**(3), 64–73 (1987)
15. Dixon, J.D.: Asymptotically fast factorization of integers. Math. Comput. **36**(153), 255–260 (1981)
16. Pomerance, C.: The quadratic sieve factoring algorithm. In: Beth, T., Cot, N., Ingemarsson, I. (eds.) EUROCRYPT 1984. LNCS, vol. 209, pp. 169–182. Springer, Heidelberg (1985). https://doi.org/10.1007/3-540-39757-4_17
17. Lenstra, A.K., Lenstra, H.W. (eds.): The Development of the Number Field Sieve. LNM, vol. 1554. Springer, Heidelberg (1993). https://doi.org/10.1007/BFb0091534
18. Shor, P.W.: Polynomial-time algorithms for prime factorization and discrete logarithms on a quantum computer. In: 35th Annual Symposium on Foundations of Computer Science, pp. 124–134. IEEE Computer Society Press, Los Alamitos (1994)
19. Vandersypen, L.M.K., Steffen, M.: Experimental realization of Shor's quantum factoring algorithm using nuclear magnetic resonance. Nature **414**(6866), 883–887 (2001)
20. Tang, X., Xu, J., Duan, B.: A memory-efficient simulation method of Grover's search algorithm. Comput. Mater. Continua **57**(2), 307–319 (2018)

A Comparison of Machine Learning Algorithms for Detecting XSS Attacks

XiaoLong Chen, Mohan Li, Yu Jiang, and Yanbin Sun[✉]

Cyberspace Institute of Advanced Technology, Guangzhou University,
Guangzhou, China
sunyanbin@gzhu.edu.cn

Abstract. With the rapid increase of web applications, the problem of XSS (cross-site scripting) attacks in Web applications is becoming more and more serious. In the face of more and more complex and changeable XSS attacks, the traditional XSS defense method cannot solve the problem of XSS security, inefficient and accurate recognition effect is poor. Therefore, this paper summarizes the method of XSS recognition based on the machine learning algorithm, classifies different machine learning algorithms according to the recognition strategy, analyzes their advantages and disadvantages, and finally looks forward to the development trend of XSS defense research, hoping to play a reference role for the following researchers.

Keywords: Web applications · XSS recognition · XSS defense ·
Machine learning

1 Introduction

In the era of explosive growth of Web applications, people get great convenience from Web sites and web apps, but they are also surrounded by web cross-site scripting attacks. In the 2017 Global cybersecurity report released by Trustwave, the most common types of cyberattacks in 2016 were disclosed, with XSS attacks accounting for 20.1% of the top ten total attacks, accounting for 13% of all attacks, and in all high-risk vulnerability statistics, the number of XSS vulnerabilities ranked first with 29.6%, which is enough to show that the current XSS attack situation is very serious. And once a user or website is attacked by XSS, the harm is considerable. For example, hackers can steal users' cookie through XSS malicious scripts and steal user accounts, make illegal transfers, etc. Or they can control enterprise data through XSS malicious scripts, such as reading, deleting, tampering, adding enterprise-sensitive data, and even using XSS malicious scripts combined with other vulnerabilities to implement DDoS attacks on websites. The consequences of these hazards are serious, so researchers have taken a series of methods to defend against XSS attacks.

© Springer Nature Switzerland AG 2019
X. Sun et al. (Eds.): ICAIS 2019, LNCS 11635, pp. 214–224, 2019.
https://doi.org/10.1007/978-3-030-24268-8_20

2   Traditional XSS Defense

Traditional XSS defense is mainly based on two ideas, one is to filter the user's input, the other is to escape the content that is output to the website. Input filtering for users is mainly based on pattern matching. Pattern matching is the most commonly used way to detect web malicious code, according to the filtering idea can be divided into blacklist filtering and whitelist filtering. As the name suggests, blacklist filtering is the filtering of input that can be a threat to websites and users, such as XSS malicious code that typically implements its malicious functionality through JavaScript scripts, so we can match the keywords such as <script>, alert, prompt, document, cookie and other characters in the input, then delete or replace the keywords, so malicious XSS code cannot launch attacks.

The whitelist filtering method is the same, but the different idea is to keep only the keywords and characters required by the site, for example, the input requirements of the site can only be 0 to 9 digits and A to Z lowercase letters, the rest of the characters cannot be entered, then even the normal input containing other characters will be filtered out. Of course, this filtering method can largely avoid XSS attacks, but it also affects the function and scope of application of the website to a certain extent.

The idea of output escaping and input filtering is similar. The difference is that output escaping is character escaping the content of the user input that will be displayed on the page or executed on the browser, and the sensitive characters that may trigger XSS are transferred or encoded into normal characters, so that XSS malicious code cannot be executed. And keyword filtering is to perform feature matching before user input enters the website, so output escaping can be used as a supplementary measure for keyword filtering, for unfiltered XSS attack statement escaping can avoid XSS attacks to a greater extent.

3   Defects of Traditional XSS Defense

Although the traditional defense measures based on filtering rules and output escape can avoid XSS attacks to some extent, the disadvantages are also obvious: The XSS attack statement is flexible, the speed of filtering rule library update is difficult to keep up with the change speed of XSS attack statement combination rules, It is extremely time-consuming and error-prone to manually discover the keyword combination rules for new XSS attack statements. And when the output is escaped, the way to escape is determined based on the context information of the current location, and it is a tedious task to decide how each location should be escaped in the face of so many and complex pages. And it is not the site security maintenance personnel who decide how to escape, but the specific business personnel (because the business personnel decides how the current location should be displayed), so it is difficult for all business personnel to understand the XSS statement rules. If not handled properly, it will generate more XSS vulnerabilities, so it is not an easy task to determine the escaping rules completely manually.

Just as Qiu, et al. [1] faced heterogeneous data in city big data, XSS data is also becoming more and more heterogeneous, for example, XSS statements are hidden in

URL links, pictures and even script files, which are difficult to be recognized by traditional methods. Traditional XSS defenses are also less effective against XSS attacks combined with other means, such as ransomware and RDF protocols [2].

In order to automatically identify XSS attacks and perform XSS defenses, web security researchers have proposed XSS recognition technology based on machine learning.

4   Overview and Suggestions on the Application of Machine Learning in XSS Detection

Machine learning algorithms applied to XSS recognition have been researched since long ago, but early research is more focused on the detection of malicious web pages. For example, Cohen [3] applied the decision tree algorithm to the detection of Web pages in 1996. Kan and Thi [4] was also one of the first researchers to apply machine learning algorithms to malicious Web page detection, and their work in 2005 focused on keywords in URLs and their location in URLs. Ma, Saul, Savage, and Voelker [5] focus on using online learning to detect malicious Web pages from URLs features. In the research work of Kazemian, Ahmed [6], for the first time, they applied unsupervised machine learning algorithms k-means and affinity propagation to the detection of malicious Web pages. In the study of Krishnaveni and Sathiyakumari [7], they used naive Bayesian [8], decision trees, and multi-layer perceptron (MLP) to classify attacks containing XSS Web pages. Wu and Lin [9] use hidden markov models to detect cross-site scripting attacks, and compared with logistic regression and naive bayesian algorithm, achieved better accuracy and recall rate. Vishnu and Jevitha [10] used support vector machine, J48 decision tree and bayesian algorithm to predict the cross-site scripting attack. Zhang [11] explored a new method for finding frequent itemsets of eigenvectors of XSS attacks using apriori and FP-growth algorithms. Liu, Fang and Liu [12] and others use deep learning to detect cross-site scripting attacks, and use the Word2vec word vector model to deal with XSS features, compared with the traditional machine learning algorithm ADtree and AdaBoost algorithms used by Wang [13], better accuracy and recall rates have been achieved. Next, this paper will briefly analyze the processing flow of each machine learning algorithm in XSS detection and its advantages and disadvantages.

In addition, the work done by the above researchers is more reflected in the passive defense of XSS. For active defense of XSS, just like the method proposed by Chen, et al. [14], which automatically mines security-sensitive functions from source code, we can also consider automatically mining security-sensitive functions of Web programs and correcting them before attackers attack. For the XSS adversarial examples attacks on the trained model, as Zeng, et al. [15] used adversarial learning for distant supervised relation extraction, we can also conduct adversarial learning on the machine learning model based on the generative adversarial networks before the attacker attacks, so as to improve the robustness of XSS detection model.

5   Application Process of Different Machine Learning Algorithms in XSS Detection

This section will briefly analyze how each machine learning algorithm is applied to the detection and recognition of cross-site scripting attacks, and the advantages and disadvantages of each machine learning algorithm in cross-site scripting attack recognition processing.

5.1   Naive Bayes

The naive bayesian algorithm is based on Bayesian theorem, and the naive bayesian classification is the simplest and common classification method in Bayesian classification. Bayesian theorem is as follows:

$$P(B|A) = \frac{P(A|B)P(B)}{P(A)} \tag{1}$$

As a Bayesian rule based on statistical method, the naive bayesian hypothesis has an important assumption that each feature is independent of each other, and it classifies by calculating the probability and cost associated with each decision. Specifically, for a data to be classified, the posterior probability of each class is calculated, and the data to be classified belongs to the class with the highest posterior probability. In the training process, each observation sample in the training set can incrementally increase or decrease the probability of hypothesis occurrence [16]. The naive bayesian algorithm can usually achieve high classification accuracy and its calculation cost is relatively small, but as mentioned earlier, the naive bayesian algorithm is based on the premise that each feature is independent of each other, and the characteristics of cross-site scripting attack statement are usually closely related. Therefore, this will affect the recognition accuracy of Naive Bayes algorithm for cross-site scripting attacks to a certain extent, and in the research of Nunan, et al. [17], the overall performance of SVM in cross-site scripting attack recognition is better than that of the Naive Bayesian algorithm.

Moreover, when the naive bayesian classifier trains according to XSS samples, it may have unbalanced XSS data, which is also the problem faced by all XSS classifiers in training. Some effective sampling algorithms, such as bidirectional self-adaptive resampling algorithm [18], can be adopted to mitigate the impact on the model detection effect to a certain extent.

5.2   K-means

K-means Algorithm is an unsupervised clustering algorithm, which is a typical representative of the target function clustering method based on prototype. Prototype-based clustering algorithm assumes that the clustering structure can be characterized by a set of prototypes, which is very common in real clustering tasks. K-means need to determine a parameter K, which indicates the number of clusters generated by K-means, and in calculating the similarity between the cluster and the cluster, K-means takes the European distance as the similarity measure, which is to find the optimal classification corresponding to an initial clustering center vector V, so that the evaluation index J is the smallest. The algorithm uses the sum of squares of errors as the clustering criterion function. Specifically, given the sample set $D = \{x_1, x_2, \ldots x_m\}$, k-means algorithm divides clusters of $C = \{c_1, c_2, \ldots c_k\}$ to minimize squared error [19]:

$$E = \sum_{i=1}^{k} \sum_{x \in C_i} \|x - \mu_i\|_2^2 \qquad (2)$$

In order to minimize the square error, the K-means algorithm uses greedy strategy to approximate the squared error by iterative optimization.

Shar, Tan [20] proposed a cross-site script attack prediction model based on classification and clustering. They used the research content of cluster-based intrusion detection of Portnoy [21], that is, the optimal parameter N (the percentage of maximum clustering) containing a large number of vulnerable clusters is 15%. In such a K-means clustering model, their predictors average 76% recall rate and 39% accuracy, indicating that they are effective without labeled training data. Although it is not as accurate as supervised learning, it is much easier to construct an unsupervised model such as k-means clustering than to construct a supervised model for attack detection.

5.3 Decision Tree

Decision tree is a kind of supervised learning algorithm, which is widely used as a classification method. According to the structure of the decision tree, the decision tree can be divided into a binary decision tree and a multi-fork tree. For example, some decision tree algorithms only generate a binary tree (where each internal node just branches out two branches), while other decision trees may generate a non-binary tree, where each node represents an attribute, the branch path is selected according to the value of the attribute, and the leaf node represents the result of the classification.

The training of decision tree algorithms for identifying cross-site scripting attack statements consists of two main processes: construction and pruning. First of all, according to the various feature attributes in the attack statement to construct the decision tree, such as branch determination based on the value of some sensitive keywords (including Script, document, alert, etc.); then pruning (specifically divided into pre-pruning and post-pruning) gives "subtraction" to branches that have little effect on the classification results, which can reduce the amount of calculation or increase the accuracy of classification.

Krishnaveni and Sathiyakumari [7] use decision tree algorithm to identify cross-site scripting attacks, and achieve the same good recognition effect as multi-layer perceptron (MLP). In Vishnu and Jevitha's [10] experiments, the decision tree algorithm has the same performance as Bayesian and SVM in correctly identifying cross-site scripting attacks, and it is less easy to identify attack statements as benign ones, and the time taken for model generation is less than SVM but more than Bayesian algorithm.

5.4   Association Rules

Association rule analysis is an algorithm that discovers interesting associations and related relationships between itemsets from large amounts of data, and a classic application of association rules is the placement of supermarket shelves (such as the famous story of beer and diaper). There are two important concepts in the association rule algorithm, one is the support, the other is the confidence, the support indicates that the dataset contains the proportion of an item set record, the specific formula is as follows:

$$\text{Support}(X \Rightarrow Y) = \frac{Number\ of\ records\ containing\ both\ X\ and\ Y}{Total\ number\ of\ data\ sets\ recorded} \tag{3}$$

Confidence indicates the probability that Y is pushed out by x in the case where the precondition x occurs. A simple understanding is a conditional probability. The specific formula is as follows:

$$\text{Confidence}(X \Rightarrow Y) = \frac{Number\ of\ records\ containing\ both\ X\ and\ Y}{The\ data\ set\ contains\ the\ number\ of\ records\ of\ X} \tag{4}$$

The common association rule algorithm are Apriori algorithm and FP-Growth algorithm. Apriori algorithm is a traditional association rule algorithm, and when using Apriori algorithm to mine the association rules of cross-site script attack statement, it is usually necessary to split the statement according to some special characters, and then the association of these separated parts is calculated, the following steps are mainly used when calculating the association:

1. According to the minimum support, the words satisfying the support degree are selected from the segmented word set to form a frequent set;
2. Combine the results from the first step to form a candidate set, and add only one word that is not in the original item set for each combination;
3. Scan the word set again, select the two-two combination that satisfies the support, and get a new frequent set;
4. Frequent sets are combined again. Each combination only adds a word that is not found in the original item set to form a new candidate set;
5. Scan the initial set of words, select the item sets that satisfy the support from the candidate set, and form a new frequent set;
6. Repeat the above steps to finally obtain a frequent set with strong correlation, select the item sets with strong associations according to the confidence in frequent set, and obtain the strong correlation between the words in the statement.

And the part with strong correlation constitutes the feature rule of the statement together. But the Apriori algorithm scans the whole dataset every round, and the efficiency is very low, so the FP-Growth improves the algorithm and only scans two times in the process of operation, which greatly improves the efficiency. The strong association relationship of each part of the statement obtained by association rule can be used as an important content of feature extraction in other algorithm operation.

5.5   Support Vector Machine

Support Vector Machine (SVM) is a two-class model, which divides the dataset by looking for a hyperplane, and in order to make the classification result better, the principle is to maximize the separation of the data set. Specifically in the classification of cross-site scripting attack statements, their intuitive representation is as follows (Fig. 1):

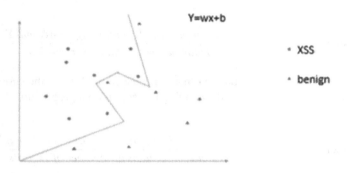

Fig. 1. SVM model diagram

For Web access datasets, if the normal statement and the cross-site scripting attack statement can be clearly distinguished after feature vectorization, the training process of the SVM is very simple, and the attack statement can be separated from the normal statement by a simple plane. But in reality normal statements and attack statements are usually nested with each other, there is no obvious distinction, so the normal statement and attack statement cannot be separated by a simple linear plane, and it is necessary to map the statement data which cannot be separated by linear plane into the high dimensional space through the very important kernel function in SVM, and then divide it through the hyperplane. The choice of kernel function will directly affect our final classification results. In the experiment of Choi, Choi, Ko [22], the data set and code dictionary obtained by using n-Gram generated malicious code and pattern matching are applied to the SVM classifier, and the cross-site scripting attack code was effectively detected, which achieved better performance than the naive bayesian and keyword mode methods.

5.6   Hidden Markov Models

The Hidden Markov model (HMM) is a statistical model used to describe a Markov process with implicit unknown parameters, the difficulty of which is to determine the implicit parameters of the process from observable parameters, and then use these parameters for further analysis, such as pattern recognition. Further understanding is actually the simplest dynamic Bayesian network, which is used for modeling time series data. The graph model structure is as follows (Fig. 2):

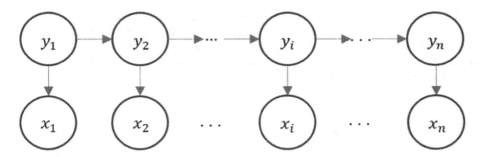

Fig. 2. Markoff model diagram

The value of the observed variable of the hidden Markov model depends only on the state variable, that is, the x_t is determined by y_t, and the state y_t at time t only depends on the state y_{t-1} at time t − 1, that is, the state of the next moment of the system is determined only by the current state and does not depend on any previous state. Based on this dependency, the combined probability distribution of all variables is [19]:

$$P(x_1, y_1, \ldots, x_n, y_n) = P(x_1|y_1) \prod_{i=2}^{n} P(y_i|y_{i-1})P(x_i|y_i) \tag{5}$$

When Wu Jr [9] use the above hidden Markov model to detect cross-site script attack statements, the HTTP request of the statement is first converted into a token sequence, and then the time relationship in the token sequence is modeled by HMM model to determine the XSS attack. Specifically, the token sequence extractor converts HTTP requests into token sequences. The HMM-based token correlator uses HMM to extract the token correlation of adjacent tokens in the token sequence, and the XSS attack detector is responsible for determining whether the input token sequence contains any XSS attacks and where the attacks are. The experimental results show that 100% of all cross-site script attacks can be identified, and the rate of misidentification (recognizing benign statements as attack statements) is only 0.3%, which has a very good recognition effect.

5.7 Deep Learning

The concept of deep learning originates from the research of artificial neural network, and the multi-layer perceptron (MLP) with multi-hidden layer is a kind of deep learning structure, and the typical deep learning model is a deep neural network. Hinton [23] in the Deep Belief network (DBN) proposed the non-supervised greedy layer-by-layer training algorithm, which helps to solve the optimization problems related to deep structure, and this is the core algorithm of deep learning training. Specifically, every time a layer of hidden nodes is trained, the output of the previous layer of hidden nodes is used as input, while the output of the current layer of hidden nodes is used as input of the next layer of hidden nodes. Finally, the whole network is trained with BP algorithm [24] (Fig. 3).

Using deep learning to detect cross-site scripting attacks, it is necessary to vectorize the sample statements and then train the deep learning algorithm model. When using the trained model to predict the newly entered statements, it is also necessary to carry out the same vectorization, through the calculation of the model, to determine whether it is an attack statement. The figure is as follows:

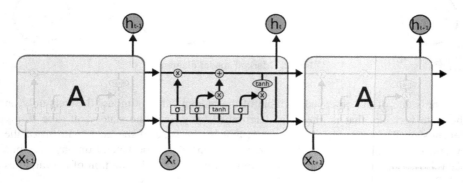

Fig. 3. LSTM model diagram

In the experiment of Liu, Fang and Liu [12], they used word2vec [25] to generate word vectors, Word2vec was a software tool developed by Google to train word vectors, and the word vectors generated by Word2vec were able to preserve the semantic information of words. Therefore, the semantic relations of each part of attack statements are also preserved, and the traditional machine learning algorithm cannot achieve this. And finally use the long-length memory (LSTM) recurrent neural network to establish the classification model, the final accuracy of the model is 99.5%, and the recall rate is 97.9%, which is a very good detection effect.

6   Conclusion

This paper mainly introduces the application of different machine learning algorithms in the detection and recognition of cross-site scripting attacks, including the classical unsupervised machine learning algorithms, such as Association rule algorithm(Apriori) and K-means clustering algorithm, as well as support vector machine, decision tree, naive bayesian and other supervised learning algorithms, and the most popular deep learning algorithms at the moment, such as lstm (long time memory model). Each machine learning algorithm has different application scenarios when detecting attacks, in different cases to choose the appropriate algorithm can achieve the best results. I hope this paper can bring some help to the following researchers.

Because this paper mainly introduces the application of each algorithm in cross-site scripting attacks detection and recognition, and does not introduce the situation of their combination use, such as the combination of Apriori algorithm and other algorithms, so the next important research direction is the machine learning algorithm combined to detect cross-site scripting attacks. Moreover, the machine learning algorithm introduced in this paper is mainly used in the recognition of cross-site scripting attacks, and does not explore how to extract the characteristics of attack statements more intelligently and efficiently, so it is also an important research direction to study how to extract the feature rule of XSS attack statements accurately and efficiently by machine learning algorithm.

Acknowledgments. This work is funded by the National Key Research and Development Plan (Grant No. 2018YFB0803504) and the National Natural Science Foundation of China (No. U1636215).

References

1. Qiu, J., Chai, Y., Liu, Y., et al.: Automatic non-taxonomic relation extraction from big data in smart city. IEEE Access **6**, 74854–74864 (2018)
2. Wang, Z., Liu, C., Qiu, J., et al.: Automatically traceback RDP-based targeted ransomware attacks. Wirel. Commun. Mobile Comput. (2018)
3. Cohen, W.W.: Learning trees and rules with set-valued features. In: AAAI/IAAI, vol. 1, pp. 709–716 (1996)
4. Kan, M., Thi, H.: Fast webpage classification using URL features. In: Proceedings of the 14th ACM International Conference on Information and Knowledge Management, pp. 325–326. ACM (2005)
5. Ma, J., Saul, L.K., Savage, S., Voelker, G.M.: Identifying suspicious URLs: an application of large-scale online learning. In: Proceedings of the 26th Annual International Conference on Machine Learning, ICML, pp. 681–688 (2009)
6. Kazemian, H.B., Ahmed, S.: Comparisons of machine learning techniques for detecting malicious webpages. Expert Syst. Appl. **42**(3), 1166–1177 (2015)
7. Krishnaveni, S., Sathiyakumari, K.: Multiclass classification of XSS web page attack using machine learning techniques. Int. J. Comput. Appl. **74**(12), 36–40 (2013)
8. Bayes, T., Bayes, T.: An essay towards solving a problem in the doctrine of chances. Resonance **8**(4), 80–88 (2003)
9. Wu Jr, Y.T., Lin Jr, S.J., Liu Jr, E.S., et al.: Cross-site scripting attack detection based on hidden Markov model (2009)
10. Vishnu, B.A., Jevitha, K.P.: Prediction of cross-site scripting attack using machine learning algorithms. In: Proceedings of the 2014 International Conference on Interdisciplinary Advances in Applied Computing. ACM (2014)
11. Zhang, W.: Research on XSS vulnerability detection model based on feature injection. Lanzhou University of Technology (2016)
12. Fang, Y., Li, Y., Liu, L., et al.: DeepXSS: cross site scripting detection based on deep learning. In: Proceedings of the 2018 International Conference on Computing and Artificial Intelligence, pp. 47–51. ACM (2018)
13. Wang, R., Jia, X., Li, Q., et al.: Machine learning based cross-site scripting detection in online social network. In: 2014 IEEE International Conference on High Performance Computing and Communications, 2014 IEEE 6th International Symposium on Cyberspace Safety and Security, 2014 IEEE 11th International Conference on Embedded Software and System (HPCC, CSS, ICESS), pp. 823–828. IEEE (2014)
14. Chen, L., Yang, C., Liu, F., et al.: Automatic mining of security-sensitive functions from source code. Comput. Mater. Continua **56**(2), 199–210 (2018)

15. Zeng, D., Dai, Y., Li, F., et al.: Adversarial learning for distant supervised relation extraction. Comput. Mater. Continua **55**(1), 121–136 (2018)
16. Alpaydın, E.: Introduction to Machine Learning, 2nd edn. The MIT Press, Cambridge (2010)
17. Nunan, A.E., Souto, E., Dos Santos, E.M., et al.: Automatic classification of cross-site scripting in web pages using document-based and URL-based features. In: 2012 IEEE Symposium on Computers and Communications (ISCC), pp. 000702–000707. IEEE (2012)
18. Han, W., Tian, Z., Huang, Z., et al.: Bidirectional self-adaptive resampling in internet of things big data learning. Multimedia Tools Appl. 1–16 (2018)
19. Zhou, Z.: Machine Learning, 1st edn. Tsinghua University Press, Beijing (2016)
20. Shar, L.K., Tan, H.B.K., Briand, L.C.: Mining SQL injection and cross site scripting vulnerabilities using hybrid program analysis. In: Proceedings of the 2013 International Conference on Software Engineering, pp. 642–651. IEEE Press (2013)
21. Portnoy, L., Eskin, E., Stolfo, S.: Intrusion detection with unlabeled data using clustering. In: ACM CSS Workshop on Data Mining Applied to Security (2001)
22. Choi, J.H., Choi, C., Ko, B.K., et al.: Detection of cross site scripting attack in wireless networks using n-Gram and SVM. Mobile Inf. Syst. **8**(3), 275–286 (2012)
23. Hinton, G.E., Osindero, S., Teh, Y.W.: A fast learning algorithm for deep belief nets. Neural Comput. **18**(7), 1527–1554 (2006)
24. McClelland, J.L., Rumelhart, D.E., PDP Research Group.: Parallel distributed processing. Explor. Microstruct. Cogn. **2**, 216–271 (1986)
25. Mikolov, T., Chen, K., Corrado, G., et al.: Efficient estimation of word representations in vector space. arXiv preprint arXiv:1301.3781 (2013)

A Survey of Privacy-Preserving Techniques for Blockchain

Yuchong Cui[1], Bing Pan[1], and Yanbin Sun[2(✉)]

[1] School of Electronics and Information Engineering, Jinan University,
Zhuhai, China
[2] Cyberspace Institute of Advanced Technology, Guangzhou University,
Guangzhou, China
sunyanbin@gzhu.edu.cn

Abstract. Blockchain technology is an important innovation of fintech area. It mainly consists of distributed data storage, P2P propagation, consensus mechanism and encryption algorithm. From the cryptocurrency to IoT (Internet of things), the blockchain technology has been applied to many areas. However, it faces some challenges, especially for personal privacy preservation. Though there exist some studies on the privacy issue of blockchain, it still lacks a systematic review of the privacy preserving techniques for blockchain technology. This paper focuses on some methods to protect personal private data in blockchain and newly developing areas combined with blockchain. Further, we discuss the limitation of existing techniques and future development direction.

Keywords: Blockchain · Privacy-preserving · Cryptocurrency · IoT

1 Introduction

Bitcoin is the first widely used application of blockchain. Since the debut of bitcoin in 2008, it attracted the world's attention. As long as internet exists, P2P transaction can be done without the third-party platform. That is the reason why investors are not afraid that bitcoin will face inflation and think highly of it. Few years later, people began to find out why bitcoin can be used stably and they finally focus on its underlying technique, blockchain.

Blockchain is an open decentralized ledger technology and smart contract infrastructure platform, which can make everything programmable, store and share data. The data includes payment history [1], bitcoin [2], smart contract, etc. Because the ledger can only be written on the base and shared by other nodes in the network, even the nodes with mutual distrust can easily verify the data and rely on a consensus mechanism to achieve consistency. Its appearance has driven a new revolution. For example, blockchain technology can be used to trace the record of equipment and coordinate transactions between equipment automatically, which means the blockchain technology can be perfectly utilized in IoT.

While blockchain can improve the efficiency, decrease the cost and protect the data, it still encounters serious privacy issues. Because different nodes require the same data to be calculated and verified, the data on the blockchain is required to be public. This

X. Sun et al. (Eds.): ICAIS 2019, LNCS 11635, pp. 225–234, 2019.
https://doi.org/10.1007/978-3-030-24268-8_21

increases the transparency and credibility of the data as well as the risk of privacy disclosure. There is no doubt that some nodes are not willing to make the details public, with which adversary can infer personal information and extort clients. However, conventional techniques are not suitable for blockchain because the way of storage of data has changed.

In this paper, we first introduce the background of blockchain including its core techniques and privacy issues. Then, we show existing privacy-preserving techniques for cryptocurrency. Further, the applications in IoT with new privacy problems and solutions will be focused. In the end, we will envision future directions on the topic.

2   Background

This section introduces four major techniques employed in blockchain, which are distributed ledger, asymmetric encryption techniques, consensus mechanism and smart contract. Then, we point out the risks and analyse the causes and possible consequences.

2.1   Core Techniques for Blockchain

Distributed ledger is a decentralized ledger without central node. All nodes are responsible for updating data and monitoring each transaction. When a new transaction occurs, all nodes confirm and verify the facticity with asymmetric encryption techniques. After that, all nodes synchronize the new ledger. The block propagation mechanisms can be divided into the following categories [3]: advertisement-based propagation, sendheaders propagation, unsolicited push propagation, relay network propagation and push/advertisement hybrid propagation. In Ethereum, that node A requests block synchronization from node B includes four processes. Blockchain can be regarded as a byzantine fault system, the consensus mechanism of which can prevent any nodes from being tampered. It mainly includes PoW (Proof of Work), PoS (Proof of Stake), PBFT (Practical Byzantine Fault Tolerance), and DPoS (Delegated Proof of Stake) [4]. The two most popular blockchain systems (i.e., Bitcoin and Ethereum) use the PoW mechanism. PoW mechanism uses the solution of puzzles to prove the credibility of the data. The puzzle is usually a computationally hard but easily verifiable problem, which is often relative to hash. When a node creates a block, it must resolve a PoW puzzle. For example, in bitcoin system, the hash rate entitles nodes to keep accounts. Only one node can win the competition in a round. This leads only a winner can complete a round of bookkeeping and others can only update information, resulting in new blocks. Smart contract refers to automatically executing some early defined principles. The appearance of smart contract enlarges the applied range of blockchain, the simplest example of which is vendor.

2.2   Privacy Issue

The privacy issue can be divided into two parts. One is that the route of information in network layer can be used to infer identity of client. At first, attackers collect nodes' IP address, analyzing their locations and online rules. Based on the associated topology, attackers can find out the cluster-head node. Koshy et al. [5] proposed that utilizing special transaction helped to look for head node. Kaminsky et al. [6] put forward a theory that the first node to send information is the head node. Biryukov et al. [7] optimized the theory. They think it is possible to locate the head node by using the order of time in which neighbor nodes forward information. Based on the above information, it is possible for attackers to associate the transaction information captured in the network layer with the IP address of the head node, thereby threatening the user's identity privacy. The other is that the details of transactions can tell much information. Using these details, attackers can summarize relationships among nodes, trace special transaction and discover transaction principle. There is no doubt that in financial area companies are not willing to tell their competitors modes of business operation.

3 Typical Strategies of Privacy Preserving

This section mainly introduces typical strategies of privacy preserving in cryptocurrency and IoT area.

3.1 CoinJoin

CoinJoin is a method of bitcoin transaction compression which aims to improve privacy by discarding unnecessary information. A coinjoin transaction is where multiple people have agreed to form a single transaction, while some of the outputs have the same value. A casual observer of the blockchain cannot tell who an output belongs to. Each user provides an IO address and sends it to the primary node for mixing. A key privacy protection role in CoinJoin is the primary node, which still may be controlled by attackers. Chaining technology and blinding technology are utilized to solve this problem. The so-called chaining technology means that the users will randomly select and mix multiple primary nodes, and eventually output them. The so-called blinding technology means that the users do not directly send the IO address to the transaction pool, but select a primary node randomly, and pass the input and output to the specified primary node. Unless attackers know about adequate primary nodes, with one single node they can't infer the real identity. Dash is the representative of CoinJoin.

However, CoinJoin still have its defects. For one thing, the communication between nodes will reveal some private information. For another, if some nodes break the rule, the process will stop, and attackers can use this theory to launch the Denial-of-Service attack. Ruffing et al. proposed a protocol named Coinshuffle [8] based on CoinJoin to solve the first problem. Bissias et al. designed Xim [9] to increase the cost of launching Denial-of-Service attack.

3.2 Stealth Address and Ring Signature

These two technologies are aimed to be independent of primary nodes. Stealth address technology can solve the problem that IO address has some kinds of relationship. We assume that A is a sender and B is a receiver. Firstly, A uses the address of B to make a disposable public key with ECC (Elliptic curve cryptography), accompanied by overhead information. B can use its private key to test the existence of public key and generate another private key with the information of specific transaction to sign up the transaction.

Although stealth address can keep receivers' address variable and therefore attackers cannot judge the relationship between address, it still cannot make senders and receivers anonymous. Hence, ring signature technique is raised, as shown in Fig. 1.

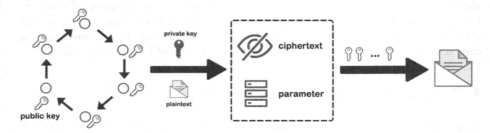

Fig. 1. Ring signature

A ring signature scheme is defined by two procedures [10]:

- ring-sign (m, P1, P2..., Pr, s, Ss) which produces a ring signature σ for the message m, given the public keys P1, P2, ..., Pr of the r ring members, together with the secret key Ss of the s-th member (who is the actual signer).
- ring-verify (m, σ) which accepts a message m and a signature σ (which includes the public keys of all the possible signers), and outputs either true or false.

In fact, a signer uses the public key of other possible signers to produce a ring with a break, and then uses the private key to connect the break into a complete ring. Any verifier can verify whether a ring signature is generated by a possible signer using the public key of a ring member. Monero is the representative.

3.3 Zcash

What if adversaries use their public keys to hide in the ring? Zcash use Zero-Knowledge Proof to avoid this problem, enabling users to hide information with cryptocurrency itself. Zero-Knowledge Proof refers to the ability of the certifier to convince the verifier that a claim is correct without providing any useful information to the verifier. Zcash utilizes a kind of zero knowledge proof named zkSNARK [11], building a chaff-coin pool. This method uses Quadratic Arithmetic Program (QAP) to check that the two polynomials match at one randomly chosen point. If the certifier knew in advance which point the verifier would choose to check, they might be able to craft polynomials that are invalid, but still satisfy the identity at that point [12]. The chaff-coin pool uses mint process and pour process to achieve anonymity, as shown in Fig. 2.

At first, the so-called mint process is that the clients use a certain amount of change exchange commitment and add it to a list. The commitment must be calculated by a disposable serial number and the private key. When users want to use the Zcash, they are supposed to provide the serial number and utilize zkANARK to prove that he knows the private key of a specific commitment without revealing identity. However, there are two new problems [13]. One is that the sender can judge the recipient is spending money through the serial number. The other is that the receiver must spend the money immediately, otherwise it may be withdrawn by the sender.

In order to solve these two problems, an operation called pouring is employed. The operation is to turn a coin into more coins that owning their own key, number, serial number with a series of zero knowledge. Except the sender nobody knows who the recipient is, and the sender cannot get the serial number of the new coin. Therefore, sender cannot use the coin and know when the receiver spent the new coin.

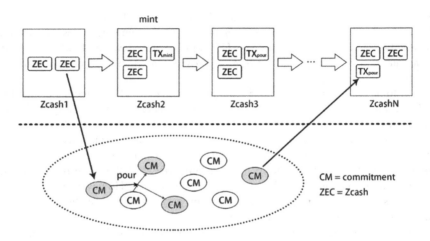

Fig. 2. Chaff-coin pool

Besides senders and receivers, miners will confirm the transaction without knowing the identities of senders and receivers. Miner only need to verify the Zero-Knowledge Proof of the transaction's initiator, confirming that the transaction initiator can use one of the commitments in the list and placing the corresponding serial numbers of the commitments in the list. Miners do not know who uses the specific commitment, but simply know that a commitment has been used.

3.4 Hawk

Not only transactions are public but also contract-related information is. Kosba et al. [14] propose Hawk, a novel framework for developing privacy-preserving smart contracts. Imitating Zcash, clients can use mint and pour technology to hide their identities and then set the target of pour to the address of smart contract. The miners, after receiving the transaction, will calculate the correct result with secure multiparty computation. Secure multiparty computation is a classical algorithm in cryptology for using secrets to cooperate between entities.

The contract can be divided into two parts: private portion and public portion. The private data and financial function related codes can be written into the private portion, and codes that do not involve private information can be written into the public portion to make it fair. The Hawk contract is compiled into three pieces. (1). The program that will be executed in all virtual machines of nodes, just like smart contracts in Ethereum. (2). The program that will only be executed by the users of smart contracts. (3). The program that will be executed by the manager, which is a special trustworthy party in Hawk [3]. But it is worth an attention that Hawk keeps the input of the contract's code private rather than the code.

3.5 Coco Framework

JP Morgan designed a mechanism for financial system called Quorum, which is based on Ethereum. It keeps most of the protocol and the way to generate nodes. But Quorum innovatively uses Raft-Based Consensus [15] and imitates Hawk to divide transactions into private portion and public portion. It provides a function for privatization of transaction and contract.

For a long time, performance, privacy and organizational management have been the big problems for enterprise-level users. That is because in the design of public blockchain, the first to considerate is how to get different nodes to reach a consensus. And the environment of different nodes is usually anonymous, untrustworthy, potentially hostile. Therefore, in order to prevent malicious behavior, transactions are not generally encrypted for everyone to monitor and verify. At the same time, it applies Byzantine fault tolerant algorithm to reach a consensus. However, that leads the technologies for protection, performance and privacy protection in the public blockchain to form a contradictory relationship [16].

In order to solve the problem above, Microsoft Azure raised the Coco framework. Coco can integrate with existing protocols such as Ethereum, Quorum and Corda [17] and dispose of their problems. Coco fully utilizes TEE (Trusted Execution Environment), such as Intel SGX [18] and VSM, building authentic network. Not only can TEE prove code is right, but also ensure that the internal data are invisible and cannot be tampered with at runtime, which means it can ensure the confidentiality and integrity of the key code and data. Therefore, the application of blockchain can be run efficiently in fully trusted member nodes. Besides, Coco separates the consistency protocol out, selects leader nodes to deal with external transactions. After leader is elected, the traditional consensus process of blockchain can be avoided according to the guarantee of TEE [19].

3.6 LSB

The ubiquitous Internet of Things (IoT) through RFIDs, GPS, NFC and other wireless devices is capable of sensing the activities being carried around Industrial environment so as to automate industrial processes [20]. Since it's recognized that blockchain can be perfectly used in blockchain, this section introduces a lightweight scalable blockchain for IoT proposed by Ali Dorri et al. The LSB consists of overlay and smart home, as shown in Fig. 3.

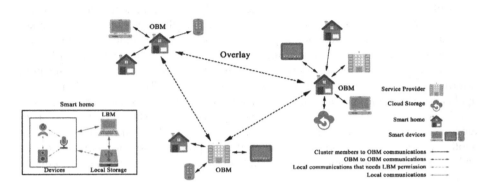

Fig. 3. LSB

The overlay is comprised of various entities, known as overlay nodes, including the smart home, represented by the Local BlockManager, mobile devices, Service Provider (SP) servers, and cloud storage (used by smart home devices for storing data) [21]. The overlay network can consist of many nodes. Thus, to ensure scalability, we assume that the public BC is managed by a subset of the overlay nodes with each cluster selecting a Cluster Head (CH). CHs are responsible for managing the BC and are thus referred to as Overlay Block Mangers (OBMs). An OBM is supposed to verify new block which is generated by other OBMs prior and aimed to be combined with its blockchain. Transactions in overlay nodes have four keys: genesis, store, access and monitor. Each overlay nodes must create a genesis transaction as the starting point for its ledger in the blockchain. Then, each node has its own data base and access to get the data. Besides, each node generates a monitor for SP to get real-time data from a device.

The overlay transactions are stored in the blockchain. Each block consists of transactions and block header. The block header contains the following: hash of the previous block, blockgeneratorID, and signatures of the verifiers. The hash of the previous block in the public BC ensures immutability. If an attacker tries to change the previous transaction, the hash previously stored in the next block will not be consistent and expose the attack. LSB uses changeable public keys as the identity of overlay nodes to protect the privacy of users in the overlay. Sometimes two end points that are communicating may need to know the real identity of each other. To solve this problem, a unique public key will be used to encrypt the transaction against the attackers who want to sniff the information. The cloud storage can be the adversary for it is able to use the data to find real identity. To protect against this de-anonymization of devices, the overlay node uses different credits to store the data of each of its devices, which prevents the cloud from identifying different devices of the same overlay node.

Smart home contains its own devices, block manager and storage. Local private BC that keeps track of transactions and has a policy header to enforce users' policy for incoming and outgoing transactions [22]. Transactions between entities that belong to the same smart home are referred to as local transactions. Local transactions are encrypted by a shared key between the two entities involved in the transaction. The LBM generates shared keys for devices, using the generalized Diffie-Hellman protocol [23]. When a permission is denied, the LBM will mark the previously distributed key as invalid by sending a control message to those entities that use the key for transaction. In the smart home, the local block manager enforces home owner policies to ensure his control over exchanged data, thus protects his privacy [22].

Eckhoff et al. proposed a privacy-friendly smart city which strive to integrate information technology into every aspect of city life [24]. They classified smart city applications and the technologies that enable them, such as smart mobility, smart buildings and so on. In the smart cities, five types of privacy should be focused. They are location, state of body & mind, behavior & action, social life and media. Big data is another study point in smart cities. Qiu et al. [25] proposed how to extract automatically Non-Taxonomic relations from big data in smart city to improve the performance of the system.

Shi proposed a novel ensemble learning algorithm for IoT security [26]. It could be used in the coalition. Given the limited space available, we won't explore it in this article.

4   Future Directions

Although there exist many privacy-preserving techniques for blockchain, they respectively have their limitations and need to be further researched.

First, though some algorithms of cryptology are safe, they should be future studied. We can maximum the efficiency, thereby we can put more privacy-preserving techniques into mobile platform. Take Zcash as an example. Although the verification of the proof of zkSNARK takes little time, the emergence of proof takes much with obtaining large memory, which means it is hard to be employed on the phone. Second, the most popular consensus mechanism is PoW. However, PoW wastes lots of computing resources. To solve this problem, a hybrid consensus mechanism of PoW and PoS is being developing in Ethereum [27]. Third, some protocols for communication is too complicated, resulting in being more likely attacked by malicious software.

Besides, with the application of blockchain in many areas, specific demands determine specific methods to meet the requirements of clients. Finally, privacy protection should not be used as a sheltering technique for criminals against the law. Appropriate regulatory mechanisms should be set in the blockchain to prevent the criminals from using the platform.

5   Conclusion

In this paper, we focus on the privacy-preserving techniques for blockchain. At first, we introduce some background of blockchain. By listing core techniques for blockchain and privacy issue, we raise five existing privacy-preserving techniques for blockchain.

Each technique has its own advantages, differently used in various areas. Furthermore, we discuss newly developing areas combined with blockchain. Finally, we summarize efficiency enhancements and suggest a few future directions in this area.

Acknowledgments. This work is funded by the National Key Research and Development Plan (Grant No. 2018YFB0803504) and the National Natural Science Foundation of China (No. U1636215).

References

1. Nakamoto, S.: Bitcoin: a peer-to-peer electronic cash system (2008)
2. Wood, G.: Ethereum: a secure decentralized generalized transaction ledger. Ethereum Project Yellow Paper, vol. 151 (2014)
3. Li, X.: A survey on the security of blockchain systems (2018)
4. Zheng, Z., Xie, S., Dai, H.-N., Wang, H.: Blockchain challenges and opportunities: a survey. Int. J. Web Grid Serv. **14**(4), 352–377 (2016)
5. Koshy, P., Koshy, D., McDaniel, P.: An analysis of anonymity in bitcoin using P2P network traffic. In: Christin, N., Safavi-Naini, R. (eds.) FC 2014. LNCS, vol. 8437, pp. 469–485. Springer, Heidelberg (2014). https://doi.org/10.1007/978-3-662-45472-5_30
6. Kaminsky, D.: Black Ops of TCP/IP (2011). https://dankaminsky.com/2011/08/05/bo2l11/
7. Biryukov, A., Khovratovich, D., Pustogarov, I..: Deanonymisation of clients in Bitcoin P2P network. In: Proceedings of the 21st ACM Conference on Computer and Communications Security, pp. 15–29. ACM, New York (2014)
8. Ruffing, T., Moreno-Sanchez, P., Kate, A.: CoinShuffle: practical decentralized coin mixing for bitcoin. In: Kutyłowski, M., Vaidya, J. (eds.) ESORICS 2014. LNCS, vol. 8713, pp. 345–364. Springer, Cham (2014). https://doi.org/10.1007/978-3-319-11212-1_20
9. Bissias, G., Ozisik, A.P., Levine, B.N., et al.: Sybil-resistant mixing for bitcoin. In: Proceedings of the 2015 ACM Workshop on Privacy in the Electronic Society, pp. 149–158. ACM, New York (2014)
10. Rivest, R.L., Shamir, A., Tauman, Y.: How to leak a secret. In: Boyd, C. (ed.) ASIACRYPT 2001. LNCS, vol. 2248, pp. 552–565. Springer, Heidelberg (2001). https://doi.org/10.1007/3-540-45682-1_32
11. Ben-Sasson, E., Chiesa, A., Tromer, E.: Succinct non—interactive zero knowledge for a von Neumann architecture. In: Proceedings of NSENIX Security Symposium, pp. 781–796. USENIX Association, Berkeley (2014)
12. Sodamnsure. https://blog.csdn.net/zhaiguowei/article/details/809355252. Accessed 06 July 2018
13. Zhang, X., Jiang, Y., Yan, Y.: A glimpse at blockchain: from the perspective of privacy (2017)
14. Kosba, A., Miller, A., Shi, E., Wen, Z., Papamanthou, C.: Hawk: the blockchain model of cryptography and privacy-preserving smart contracts. In: IEEE Symposium on Security and Privacy, pp. 839–858 (2016)
15. Fixanoid. https://github.com/jpmorganchase/quorum/blob/master/docs/raft.md. Accessed 04 Dec 2018
16. Microsoft Research Asia. https://zhuanlan.zhihu.com/p/28597205. Accessed 18 Aug 2017
17. Shamsasari. https://github.com/corda/corda. Accessed 15 Dec 2018
18. lzha101. https://github.com/intel/linux-sgx. Accessed 13 Nov 2018
19. Bing. https://zhuanlan.zhihu.com/p/37099018. Accessed 21 May 2018

20. Kaur, J., Kaur, K.: A fuzzy approach for an IoT-based automated employee performance appraisal. Comput. Mater. Continua **53**(1), 23–36 (2017)
21. Dorri, A., Kanhere, S.S., Jurdak, R., Gauravaram, P.: LSB: a lightweight scalable blockchain for IoT security and privacy (2017)
22. Dorri, A., Kanhere, S.S.: Blockchain for IoT security and privacy: the case study of a smart home (2017)
23. Delfs, H., Knebl, H.: Introduction to Cryptography, vol. 2. Springer, Heidelberg (2002)
24. Eckhoff, D., Wagner, I.: Privacy in the smart city – applications, technologies, challenges and solutions (2017)
25. Qiu, J., Chai, Y., Liu, Y., Gu, Z., Li, S., Tian, Z.: Automatic non-taxonomic relation extraction from big data in smart city. IEEE Access **6**, 74854–74864 (2018). https://doi.org/10.1109/access.2018.2881422
26. Shi, C.: A novel ensemble learning algorithm based on D-S evidence theory for IoT security. Comput. Mater. Continua **57**(3), 635–652 (2018)
27. Xiao xi. https://blog.csdn.net/fidelhl/article/details/50520572. Accessed 14 Jan 2016

A Survey of Software Reverse Engineering Applications

Zhuangyou Chen[1], Bing Pan[1], and Yanbin Sun[2(✉)]

[1] School of Electronics and Information Engineering,
Jinan University, Zhuhai, China
[2] Cyberspace Institute of Advanced Technology,
Guangzhou University, Guangzhou, China
sunyanbin@gzhu.edu.cn

Abstract. With the development of software, software maintenance and software security become an important research of software engineering. Software reverse engineering plays an irreplaceable role in software maintenance and software security. In this paper, the applications of software reverse engineering in software maintenance and malware analysis, as well as the legitimacy of software reverse engineering research are briefly discussed, and then software reverse engineering, disassembly, decompilation and so on are introduced. Related technique such as software protection technology, static analysis technology, dynamic analysis technology are described. Then, we discuss the application of software reverse engineering, such as software maintenance, software vulnerability mining, malware analysis and so on. In addition, we also describe how to use software reverse engineering to learn the method of software cracking, so as to resist reverse attack and improve the ability of anti-piracy of software itself.

Keywords: Software reverse engineering · Software maintenance · Software vulnerability mining · Malware analysis · Anti-piracy

1 Introduction

The scale and complexity of software system have increased considerably over the past few years, the life cycle of software is becoming longer and longer, and the traditional software development method can not meet the needs of today's development. Practical research shows that the cost of software maintenance has been increasing. In the 1970s, the maintenance cost of software was 35%–40% of the total budget of the software, and it increased to about 60% in the 1980s. In recent years, this value has risen to about 80%. Software maintenance in software engineering takes up a lot of time and cost of the whole software engineering, and the time of software maintenance is much spent in program understanding. In addition, many software manufacturers need to transplant software systems to web to meet the needs of many users, which further increases the need for software maintenance. Software maintenance has become one of the most important issues in software engineering. As a new research field in software engineering, software reverse engineering can help developers understand programs and

© Springer Nature Switzerland AG 2019
X. Sun et al. (Eds.): ICAIS 2019, LNCS 11635, pp. 235–245, 2019.
https://doi.org/10.1007/978-3-030-24268-8_22

improve the efficiency of software maintenance. At the same time, after the release of software, the security problems of software emerge endlessly-the security vulnerabilities exist in the software itself, which makes the software vulnerabilities once they exist and will be discovered in the current network environment of rampant virus. In a very short period of time, the lawless elements will make a new Trojan horse maliciously exploit the vulnerability, and the software will become the target of the hacker attack, which will bring the users serious security risks. Therefore, it is necessary to mine and repair the vulnerabilities in time. Software reverse engineering can help technicians mine software vulnerabilities and eliminate hidden dangers. Software piracy has caused direct economic losses to software enterprises and has posed a serious threat to the development of software technology. However, it is very difficult to prevent software piracy completely, the best way is to increase the difficulty of software itself being pirated, so as to improve the ability of software itself to prevent piracy. It is necessary to learn software reverse engineering [1] so as to understand and familiarize with software cracking methods, so that we can know ourselves and know our enemies and do a good job in such technologies as software cracking and protection. In addition, in the current Internet, malware is everywhere, which is a serious threat to network security. From the 1988 CERT due to the Morris worm Since the establishment of the incident, the Internet security threat incidents have been rising year by year, and the growth trend has become more rapid in recent years. The statistical results [2] show that the "cloud security" system of Ruixing has intercepted a total of 31.32 million virus samples in the period from January to June 2017. The number of virus infections is 2.34 billion, which tells us the importance of antivirus technology, and viruses often exist in the form of binary files, so it is often necessary to reverse analyze. To understand the structure and behavior of the virus, to analyze how it exists in the network, and to measure and eliminate the harm it brings. Therefore, software reverse engineering is a way for the software programmers to study and exchange the programs, benefit the users, and help us to create a good environment for the computer software.

Nowadays, more and more attention has been paid to the technical research related to reverse engineering in academic circles. Since 2000, the number of related papers on software reverse engineering has increased dramatically. WCRE (the Working Conference on Reverse Engineering) has been held yearly to explore and expand the techniques of reverse engineering [3], Computer-aided software engineering (CASE) and automated code generation have contributed greatly in the field of reverse engineering [4]. In addition, other international conferences on reverse engineering for IWPC (the International Workshop on Program Comprehension) and PASTE (the Workshop on Program Analysis for Software Tools and Engineering) be held once a year. Many software companies in China have carried out software reverse engineering research one after another. The development of software reverse engineering is best witnessed by the growing external industry of online games.

On the legitimacy of software reverse engineering, in the United States and many other countries, products or manufacturing laws are protected by trade secrets, so long as they are reasonably obtained, products or laws can be reverse engineered, and software reverse engineering is considered legal for the sake of interactivity. In order to obtain the thought and function elements implied in a copyrighted computer program and to obtain them for lawful reasons, when only the method of dismantling is used, according to the law, dismantling is the fair use of copyrighted works. In addition, although China has formulated the "Regulations on the protection of the computer software", "Registration ordinance of the copyright of the computer software" and other laws and regulations, they are not involved in the reverse engineering of the software. Instead, in early 2007, law [5] was enacted to recognize the legitimacy of reverse engineering for learning research. This removes the last obstacle for developers engaged in software reverse engineering and promotes the development of software reverse engineering technology.

2 Basic Concept

Software reverse engineering is the process of identifying software components, their interrelationships, and representing these entities at a higher level of abstraction that can be used in program understanding and system renovation [6]. Generally, the whole process of software reverse analysis is referred to software reverse engineering, and the technology used in this process is called software reverse engineering technology.

Reverse engineering of software can be accomplished by various methods. The three main groups of software reverse engineering are analysis through observation of information exchange, disassembly using a disassembler and decompilation using a decompiler.

Three concepts are closely related to software engineering: forward engineering, reverse engineering and reengineering, which were proposed by Cross and Chikofsky in 1990. Among them, forward engineering is a traditional process from the high-level abstract and logically independent design to the physical design of the system. Reverse engineering is the analysis of the system to determine the interaction between the components of the system, to represent the system in other forms, or to represent the process of the system at a higher level of abstraction (this process does not change the system). Reengineering is not the scope of this paper.

The concepts associated with software reverse engineering are as follows:

Disassembly: the process of converting from machine language to assembly language;

Decompilation: the process of converting from machine language to high-level language;

Although decompilation technology exists, the relative immaturity of machine code decompilation, it is presently the case that for large, commercial reverse engineering projects, a good disassembler, such as IDA Pro, is probably a better option than a decompiler.

Function relation call graph: refers to the form of a graph to represent the function between the call relationship;

Control flow diagram: the possible flow direction through which all basic blocks are executed in a process in the form of a graph, and also reflects the real-time execution process of a process. Nowadays, there are several types of control flow diagrams, such as change control flow diagram and process control flow diagram.

Data dependency graph: a graph that represents the dependencies between data in a program.

3   Basic Process

The first step: research the software protection method, bypass the protection verification mechanism. At present, many software to maintain the software is not cracked, usually using a series of software protection technology, such as common serial number protection, shell protection, anti-debugging, anti-reverse and so on. Therefore, these software protection verification mechanisms need to be bypassed before analysis, so that the program code can be further analyzed.

The second step: disassembles the target program, carring on the analysis to the program code. After the first step, we can get the executable file without software protection. Then, we can use IDA Pro to analyze the target program statically, and use OllyDbg to dynamically debug the program, so as to obtain the key information and understand the design ideas of the program. This is the most critical step.

The third step: according to the second step of the key information to generate software design ideas, architecture, algorithms and other related documents.

The forth step: if it is malware, it can develop a program to deal with the malware. If the program of reverse analysis is software, the target software can be reengineered to develop a more perfect or more suitable application software.

4   Correlation Technique of Software Reverse

4.1   Software Protection Technology

Software protection technology [7] is that software developers seek all kinds of effective methods and technologies to protect software copyright, increase the difficulties of piracy, or extend the time of software cracking, so as to prevent software from being used illegally as much as possible. Today, the technology is also used by some users to protect malware from reverse analysis.

According to whether special hardware equipment is used, software protection technology can be divided into hardware based protection and software based protection. The hardware-based protection means that the protection needs to be bound to a special hardware device. At present, the main way of hardware protection is to use a cryptographic lock, commonly known as an encrypted dog. The protection mode based on software refers to the protection mode that does not need the special hardware equipment. It generally adopts the digital license which binds with the terminal hardware and software information, also known as the electronic authorization form.

Only by deeply understanding the software protection mechanism can we remove the software protection mechanism and get the target program without the software protection mechanism, so as to carry on the subsequent analysis. In many cases, removing software protection mechanisms is the first step in software reverse analysis.

4.2   Static Analysis Technology

The static analysis technology [8] is to analyze the program flow from the program code which is disassembled, and to start with the prompt information, to understand the function of each module in the software and the relationship between the modules and the programming ideas, so as to obtain the useful information of the software. In most cases the analysis is performed on some version of the source code, and in the other cases, some form of the object code. Facilitate further understanding of the program, analysis of software functions or detection and elimination of defects in the software.

Static analysis can fully analyze the program, ensure that all execution paths of the program are detected, and not be limited to specific execution paths, so as to obtain as much information as possible from the program code. This information can be used as a supplement to dynamic analysis to verify the security of the program before dynamic debugging and to understand the code function of the program.

4.3   Dynamic Analysis Technology

Dynamic analysis technology [9] is to understand the function of the program or discover the program problem by dynamically debugging the program, controlling the execution process of the program to be debugged. For dynamic program analysis to be effective, the target program must be executed with sufficient test inputs to produce interesting behavior. There are many types of dynamic analysis, one of them is fault localization, which has been shown that one can refactor the test cases in order to get better results [10]. The main steps of the dynamic analysis are as follows:

(1) load the target program with the debugging tools such as OllyDbg [11], then run the program, track the execution flow of the program briefly, analyze the function of the program and find the key module or program segment.
(2) by setting breakpoints and other ways, the key module or program segment is tracked and debugged in detail, and then the module is tracked and analyzed in detail. Understand the function of the key code, so as to understand the design ideas and functions of the program.

5   Applications of Software Reverse Engineering

5.1   Software Maintenance

Software maintenance [12] is defined in the IEEE Standard for Software Maintenance, IEEE 1219 [IEEE 1219], as the modification of a software product after delivery to correct faults, to improve performance or other attributes, or to adapt the product to a modified environment. In the actual work of maintaining a software, there are often problems such as no source code, the turnover of company personnel, the lack of all kinds of documents during the development, and the difficult situation of software maintenance. The main reason is that part of the code in the program can not be understood. At this time, the software reverse engineering technology can be used to analyze the code of the target system, to model the target system to provide useful information to help the understanding, so that the software design can be derived, and the complete development document can be obtained. In order to help maintainers understand the original system, better to maintain and update the system, software reverse engineering is primarily designed help maintainers solve programs understand the problem. The main process of software reverse engineering to help maintainers carry out software maintenance are as follows:

(1) The test cases are designed according to the performance and function of the software, and then the program is understood according to the execution process and the results of the test cases, and the test cases are constantly revised and updated, so as to deepen the understanding of the software programs.

(2) By decomposing binary code into functions, analyzing the whole software flow statically, understanding the structure of the program, describing the function calling diagram and the control flow diagram of the program, the execution path of the program is described intuitively. Helps to understand the execution process and functions of the program.

(3) The key module or program segment in the program is deeply analyzed, and dynamic analysis technology is used to track and debug the key code repeatedly, which helps the analyst to understand the execution mode and the structure of the program. Combined with the results of static analysis in the second step, the control flow and data flow information of the whole program are analyzed step by step, the design is deduced and the complete document is established.

In recent years, new reverse engineering methods for extracting information from source code and version logs have also attracted academic attention. For example, Wu [13] is a visualization tool for analyzing and browsing software artifacts, related versioning information, and data in CVS databases. The application of visual technology in version control has great potential. It can assist the development process and improve the efficiency of program understanding in software maintenance and development.

5.2 Software Vulnerability Mining

In computer security, software vulnerability is a weakness in design, implementation, operation or internal control, which can be exploited by a Threat Actor, such as an attacker, to perform unauthorized actions within a computer system. Today, many automatic hole mining technology emerge in endlessly, based on the source code for automatic leak problems of mining technology, also has the research to solve, such as large programs based on the security of sensitive function decomposition method [14] can help to solve in dealing with large-scale programs, many automatic hole mining technology in the path of the explosion, state explosion, low efficiency and so on. This way, you can find vulnerabilities in the source code. However, in real work, when evaluating non-open source and professional applications, the evaluators get executable programs. In this case, software reverse analysis is needed to help understand the program and exploit software vulnerabilities. Software vulnerability mining methods based on software reverse engineering are as follows:

(1) Input tracing method: through static analysis tools such as IDA Pro, all possible input points in the program are determined, and the relationship between modules is analyzed to generate data dependency diagram and control flow diagram. Then we use dynamic debugging tools such as OllyDbg to set breakpoints on input points and track debugging step by step, further verify the vulnerabilities found by static analysis and obtain dynamic execution information, and detect the specific vulnerability patterns according to the obtained information.

(2) Through static analysis tools provided by the script language, such as IDA pro provided by IDC scripts, automatic analysis mining software vulnerabilities.

(3) Through static analysis, detect the unsafe functions used in the program, such as strcpy, printf, so as to find the software vulnerabilities.

(4) Combining static and dynamic analysis: static analysis is able to achieve high code coverage with low accuracy, and the dynamic analysis is just the opposite. Therefore, many researches attempt to integrate these two techniques in order to neutralize their drawbacks and maximize their advantages. There are two main methods: Integrating static and dynamic analysis and static analysis to guide the dynamic analysis to generate test cases.

The first method, which is proposed by Aggarwal [15] in his paper, is an Integrate dynamic and dynamic analysis for software vulnerability. In this paper, the static and dynamic vulnerability mining engines are implemented, the code is analyzed independently and juxtaposed, and the analysis results are synthesized as the output. The main process is that the source code is checked to obtain the data from all the unsafe function calls, and then the obtained data is analyzed dynamically and statically. This method is relatively simple, but difficult to achieve the purpose of vulnerability mining.

The second method: static analysis guides the dynamic analysis of generating test cases [16], which is mainly software reverse engineering combined with fuzz technology for vulnerability mining.

Fuzz, also known as fuzzy testing, is a testing technique used to discover software vulnerabilities. It sends random, heuristic, protocol based composite data and code to the external interface of the software, causing exceptions to the target software. To find a loophole.

The combination of software reverse engineering and fuzz technology can make both advantages and disadvantages complement each other, and combine automation with purpose to a certain extent, and automatically mine software vulnerabilities.

Taking buffer overflow vulnerability as an example, the process of vulnerability mining is analyzed. The main process is to disassemble the key functions of buffer overflow such as strcpy strcat by disassembly tools such as IDA pro, so as to analyze and extract characteristic codes from them. According to the characteristic code, these key functions are located, and then the proxy server software is dynamically loaded with OllyDbg, and the program is broken to analyze which data filtering is not strict enough, so as to find the location of the vulnerability.

5.3 Malware Analysis

Nowadays, malware [17] has become the main threat to the information security at present. The malware is popular in variety, and the attack techniques and forms of malware are becoming more and more covert and complicated, and the harm caused by malware is becoming more and more serious. For example, some attackers use information hiding technology [18] to embed malicious programs into ordinary picture files. As long as people open and take a look at this seemingly ordinary picture, their computers will be hacked. Therefore, thorough analysis and understanding of malware, so as to better prevent and study malware is necessary. However, malware is usually in the form of executable program, so it is necessary to use software reverse analysis technology to analyze malware.

Malware refers to all malicious programs, including worms, computer viruses, backdoors, which are designed to destroy the reliability, availability, security and data integrity of computers or network systems, or consume system resources. The method by which malware analysis is performed typically falls under one of two types:

(1) static malware analysis: the process of analyzing program instructions and structure to determine the function of a program without executing the program [19].
(2) dynamic malware analysis: the second step of malicious code analysis, which is typically done when static malware analysis enters a dead end, such as when malicious code is confused. It is through the malicious code runtime monitoring, as well as the running system condition check, to understand the real function of malicious code. Dynamic analysis is an effective method to identify the function of malicious code. However, before dynamic analysis of malicious code, you must establish a security environment, such as virtual machine or sandbox dynamic analysis, so that you can avoid the business host or other hosts exposed to the threat of malicious code, so as to avoid these unexpected and unnecessary risks [19].

The main processes of software reverse engineering analysis of malware are as follows:

The first step is static analysis: using IDA pro and other analysis tools to analyze the static features and function modules of malware, extract malware feature string, feature code segment, data flow feature and control flow feature [20], etc. The function module of malware and the flow chart of each function module are analyzed to understand the behavior characteristics of malware and the function of malware is preliminarily analyzed.

The second step is dynamic observation: system monitoring tools are used to observe the changes of system environment in the course of malicious code running, and the functions of malware are judged by these changes.

The third step is dynamic debugging: using dynamic debugging tools such as OllyDbg to track the system functions and command characteristics used in the execution of malware, so as to further analyze the functions of it.

5.4   Piracy Prevention Technology

With the development of computer technology, the function of computer software is becoming more and more powerful, the development cost is higher and higher, and the cost of software replication is almost zero, which causes the software developed by developers to be illegally acquired by others. As a result, software developers and investors caused huge losses. Therefore, it is necessary to study software reverse engineering, understand and familiar with software cracking methods, so as to research and apply the technology of resisting software reverse attack, and improve the security of software itself. The applications of software reverse engineering in software protection are as follows:

(1) By learning software reverse engineering technology and learning the ways and techniques of bypassing software protection, such as de-shell technology, the software protection technology, such as shell, hardware protection and so on, can be improved to improve the difficulties of software cracking.

(2) Learning the process of disassembly and static analysis in software reverse, so as to understand which symbol information can make the program easy to read close to the source code, and then eliminate the symbol information and increase the difficulty of reverse analysis.

(3) In the process of static analysis, flower instructions, confusing program flow and other methods will make the analysis more difficult. Learning static analysis technology can add flower instructions to the program more pertinently, confuse the program flow, etc. Thus, the purpose of resisting the static analysis of the program by the attacker is achieved.

(4) Learn the techniques of dynamic analysis in reverse engineering, understand the process and signs of dynamic debugging of programs, and some commonly used dynamic debugging tools, and then defend them from an attacker's point of view: by detecting the flags of the program being debugged, Parent process detection, virtual machine protection and some special code are used to prevent the reverse analyzer from debugging and tracking the program step by step and setting breakpoints, so as to resist the dynamic debugging of the program by the attacker.

6   Conclusion

Through the above analysis, with the development of computer technology, the software field is facing more and more competition and challenge, and the problem of software security is becoming more and more serious and paid more and more attention to. Software reverse engineering plays an irreplaceable role in software maintenance, software vulnerability mining, malware analysis, anti-piracy and so on. It can not only help us cope with a series of challenges in software maintenance, better deal with security problems such as software vulnerabilities and malicious code, but also improve the ability of software piracy prevention. In addition, it can also be used in unfamiliar software fields that lack the appropriate information. In this case, learn the advanced design ideas and techniques of others by using software reverse engineering technology. It can be seen that software reverse engineering promotes the progress of software engineering technology and makes software better serve people.

Acknowledgments. This work is funded by the National Key Research and Development Plan (Grant No. 2018YFB0803504) and the National Natural Science Foundation of China (No. 61702220, 61702223).

References

1. Ge, X., Prywes, N.: Reverse software engineering of concurrent programs. In: 1990 Proceedings of the 5th Jerusalem Conference on Information Technology, Next Decade in Information Technology, 22–25 October 1990. IEEE (1990)
2. Beijing Ruixing Information Technology Co., Ltd., National Information Center Information and Network Security Department, China Network complete report for the first half of 2017. http://www.sic.gov.cn/archiver/SIC/UpFile/Files/Default/20170807115920801889.pdf
3. WCRE. Computer Science bibliography. Archived from the original on 14 March 2017. http://dblp.uni-trier.de. Accessed 22 Feb 2018
4. Eilam, E.: Reversing: Secrets of Reverse Engineering. Wiley, Hoboken (2005). ISBN 978-0-7645-7481-8
5. Supreme People's Court (SPC). Interpretation of the Supreme People's Court on Some Issues Concerning the Application of Law in the Trial of Civil Cases Involving Unfair Competition Article 12 (2007)
6. Yang, S.: Research on recovering early aspects in aspect-oriented software reserve engineering. In: ICCASM 2010, Taiyuan, China. IEEE (2010)
7. Nazarlou, M.M.: Deliberate software protection technologies. In: ICIS. IEEE (2011)
8. Wagner, D.: Static analysis and computer security: new technique for software assurance. Ph.D. dissertation, pp. 29–52, Fall (2000)
9. Masri, W., Podgurski, A.: Algorithms and tool support for dynamic information flow analysis, 385–404 (2009). https://doi.org/10.1016/j.infsof.2008.05.008
10. Xuan, J., Monperrus, M.: Test case purification for improving fault localization. In: 22nd ACM SIGSOFT International Symposium on the Foundations of Software Engineering, FSE 2014, November 2014
11. Yunschuk, O.: OllyDbg: 32-bit assembler level analysing debugger for Microsoft® Windows® (version 2.01) [EB/OL], 05 Feb 2014. http://ollydbg.de/
12. Pigoski, T.: Software maintenance (PDF), Chapter 6. In: SWEBOK. IEEE. Accessed 05 Nov 2012
13. Wu, X., Murray, A., Storey, M., Lintern, R.: A reverse engineering approach to support software maintenance: version control knowledge extraction. In: 11th Working Conference on Reverse Engineering, 8–12 November 2004. IEEE (2004)
14. Chen, L., Yang, C., Liu, F., Gong, D., Ding, S.: Automatic mining of security-sensitive functions from source code. CMC: Comput. Mater. Continua **56**(2), 199–210 (2018)
15. Aggarwal, A., Jalote, P.: Integrating static and dynamic analysis for detecting vulnerabilities. In: COMPSAC (2006)
16. Leek, L.R., Baker, G.Z., Brown, R.E., Zhivich, M.A., Lippmann. R.P.: Coverage maximization using dynamic taint tracing. Technique report (2006)

17. Burji, S., Liszka, K.J., Chan, C.: Malware analysis using reverse engineering and data mining tools. In: Proceedings of 2010 International Conference on System Science and Engineering (ICSSE), pp. 619–624. IEEE Computer Society, Washington DC (2010)
18. Meng, R., Rice, S.G., Wang, J., Sun, X.: A fusion steganographic algorithm based on faster R-CNN. CMC: Comput. Mater. Continua **55**(1), 001–016 (2018)
19. Honig, A., Sikorski, M.: Practical Malware Analysis. No Starch Press, San Francisco (2012). ISBN 9781593272906
20. Yu, B., Fang, Y., Yang, Q., Tang, Y., Liu, L.: A survey of malware behavior description and analysis, 584–590 (2018). https://doi.org/10.1631/FITEE.1601745

A Fast IP Matching Algorithm Under Large Traffic

Guanjun Guo[1]([⊠]), Yi Xin[1], Xiangzhan Yu[1,2], Likun Liu[1], and Houhua Cao[2]

[1] School of Computer Science and Technology, Harbin Institute of Technology, Harbin 150001, China
{17S103185,liulikun}@stu.hit.edu.cn,
{xinyi,yxz}@hit.edu.cn
[2] Institute of Electronic and Information Engineering, UESTC, Dongguan, Guangdong, China
tershou@163.com

Abstract. By introducing the idea of data compression storage and not distinguishing between intermediate node and termination node, we propose a new matching algorithm for the IP with mask. The worst-case space complexity of the algorithm is fixed. The comparison of the experiments' result shows that the new algorithm has superior performance. In the case of a large set of patterns, its matching performance is better, which is very suitable for application in IDS systems with large traffic and very strong real-time requirements.

Keywords: Matching algorithm · IP address · Data compression

1 Introduction

With the increasing amount of data on the Internet, which is useful or useless, we need to find useful ones. In the field of information security, the principle of the IDS system is to identify and detect the abnormal behavior of the traffic after the protocol is restored. Therefore, the process of identifying and detecting becomes the core part of the whole system. Reducing the detection response time and reducing the required computing resources are two ways to improve system performance [1]. At the same time, in order to improve system performance, ISP upgrades from hardware and software [2]. On the hardware, it can improve performance through multi-core parallel and improved scheduling methods. However, one of the disadvantages is that the scalability of the hardware and the flexibility of the scheduling method are limited, so the improvement of the matching module becomes more and more important. In the existing IDS system, maintaining system load balancing and protecting data integrity are key issues [3]. At the same time, identifying and detecting malicious traffic through IP and port is an important way of traffic detection, which has become an important breakthrough point for improving system performance. In this article, our main contributions are as follows:

We designed an automaton storage structure storage node for the mode set compression storage with masked IP and port. The storage node borrows from the AC automaton but the idea is completely different. One important difference is the state node of the new automaton. The intermediate state node and the terminating state node are not distinguished, but the structure of all the state nodes is equivalent. The other point is that the state transition is not performed by a character string, but the state transition of the state is performed by the state of 0 and 1. The specific design architecture will be covered in Sect. 3.1.

We design a status bit to be stored in each automaton state node. This status bit is used to speed up the fast insertion speed of the newly added pattern string during the process of building the automaton and to realize the fast jump lookup when the automaton matches the search. At the same time, we have ensured the dynamic insertion of the pattern string into the existing structure of the automaton in the existing automaton storage structure and the accuracy of the new automaton through the improvement and experiment in detail.

The structure of this paper is as follows: Sect. 2 we introduced the related work. Section 3 describes our new algorithm, and we show our experimental results in Sect. 4. Finally, we summarize the results of the experiments with the AC automaton algorithm and our new algorithm and discuss the next work.

2 Related Work

In order to meet the real-time requirements under large traffic, researchers have been improving the performance of existing IDS systems. Some researchers are focusing on multi-core related research [4], while others are more focused on core pattern matching algorithms. The difference between the two research points is that the former focuses on the improved architecture of the system. In many cases, it is associated with the scheduling problem, and the latter belongs to the classic string matching algorithm field. Since the content we are studying in this article belongs to the latter, we here mainly explain the research results of pattern matching. Previous matching algorithms include three categories: prefix searching, suffix searching and factor searching. Prefix-based AC [5] algorithm and suffix-based WM [6] algorithm and string-based SBOM [7]. The AC algorithm is the most efficient and typical algorithm based on prefix search. It receives all pattern strings by using a finite automaton and then processes each input character through an automaton. Although the performance of the AC algorithm is very stable during the matching phase, it is not sensitive to the size of the mode set size. This can effectively resist the algorithm attack in time, but the memory usage is extremely sensitive to the number of the pattern set. However, with the size of the pattern set increasing, the storage space of the automaton grows exponentially. According to actual statistics, when the mode combination reaches 350,000 levels, the memory usage is 7G. If you reach a million-level memory footprint will reach dozens or even more than 100G, which is unbearable for any security system. Therefore, the application of the AC algorithm is that the mode set size is not particularly large. When the mode set size is large, the general practice is to optimize the algorithm for compressing the memory. Currently, there is an improved algorithm based on the structure of Bitmap to compress the state table of the AC automaton [8]. The LDM [9] algorithm divides the text into overlapping windows and then performs an accurate scan based on

the idea of time complexity. There is also an algorithm for improving scanning efficiency by recording a plurality of characters in one state [3]. The WM algorithm is a
representative algorithm based on suffix search. It firstly constructs a jump table, a
prefix table and a hash table in the beginning, and then it sets a scan window whose
size is the length of the shortest mode in the pattern set. Then taking the k-grams into
the whole block hash, and the hash value is transferred to the jump table to determine
jump distance. The WM algorithm is suitable for situations where the text string size is
much larger than the pattern string and the pattern set hit probability is lower. This is
because the jump can be directly performed because it is possible to determine that
there is no match according to the jump table, which greatly reduces the number of
comparisons. The initialization time and memory usage of the WM algorithm are
smaller than the construction and initialization time of the AC algorithm, and the
scanning time is best in the best case, but the disadvantage is that the scanning speed
depends on the length of the shortest mode string and the scanning time is not Stability.
When the rate of hitting is high, the performance of the algorithm comes down
immediately. Some people have improved the special case where the jump distance is 0
but not matched [10]. The pretty representative matching algorithm based on sub-string
scanning is SBOM algorithm and the SBDM algorithm. Since the algorithm is not
dominant in time or space, it is used less in general. In addition, we can usually uses
some special hardware [11–13], such as FPGA [14]. These schemes are generally
difficult to reprogram and update the patterns set under the large size patterns set.

In this paper, we use the uniformity of IP address to compress the storage of the
pattern set, which solves the original automaton's shortcoming of storage space
growing linearly as the set of patterns increases. In addition, for the storage structure of
the automaton, we set the flag bit to enable the new pattern to be accurately inserted
into the automaton and realize the state jump when matching. In particular, when the
automaton is built, the pattern to be inserted is transferred by the first node of the
automaton according to checking the bit until the closest parent node with the pattern
(IP) is found. Last, it is determined to insert this pattern into the existing automaton
storage structure by comparison.

3   IP Address Multi-mode Matching Algorithm

3.1   Design of Automaton

After designing the algorithm based on the idea of bitwise matching of the PAT tree,
how to construct the automaton based on the set of IP address pattern strings with
masks. The patterns to be stored by the automaton are as follows, where the mode
number Pi is equivalent to the rule number, the IP address mask in the pattern string is
between 24 and 32, and the port is 0 for any port (see Table 1). Therefore, each state
node of the automaton is designed, including the IP address, the number of mask bits,
the port number and the check bit, and the left and right child pointers. We also leave
an extended pointer for other attribute extensions (see Table 2).

Table 1. Typical pattern rule

Pattern string pi	ip_key	Mask	Port	Others
1	0x ff ff ff ff 255.255.255.255	30	0	NULL
2	0xff ff ff fd 255.255.255.253	30	0	NULL
3	0xff ff ff fd 255.255.255.253	31	0	NULL
4	0x ff fe ff fc 255.254.255.252	32	65536	NULL

Table 2. The state node

Name	Description
ip_key	*IP*
bit_index	*Recording check position*
node [9]	*Link header pointers for different masks under the same IP*
Left	*Left child*
Right	*Right child*

3.2 Initialization

In the new algorithm our proposed, the main attribute of the automaton node is an IP address. The storage structure of the automaton is a binary tree, and the character that causes the state transition to occur is 0 or 1. When the traversal path goes to the check bit. When it is greater than 24, all the nodes on the node's sub-tree are pushed into the queue and then all the stored nodes are matched, so the failure pointer is no longer needed in this case. The new automaton only has a goto table, which is the construction process of the search structure. In this algorithm, since the mode combination is the same format, the IP address plus mask and port are unified formats and characters, so there is no case where one mode is a subset and prefix of another mode, so it also avoids the processing of additional termination states and reduce the construction time of the automaton in this algorithm. The idea of the algorithm is to insert all the pattern rules into the automaton one by one until all the modes are read. First, the binary sequence of the pattern string is read from left to right, and the state transition of the automaton is performed according to the mark bit on each state node of the automaton until the automaton node whose current automaton node is closest to the pattern to be inserted is found. The specific implementation process is that when the automaton is an empty data structure, there is only one head pointer at this time, and the head node pointed to by the head pointer assigns its check bit to −1, and the first mode is inserted at the right of the head node. At this point, the automaton structure is no longer empty. The following pattern insertion process is as follows: first, bitwise matching is started from the automatic head node, and the automaton performs state transition until reaching the deepest node of the automaton, which is the automaton state node that is closest to the pattern to be inserted. We record the node as t, and record the father of t as p, and then compare the node t with the mode to be inserted. If the IP addresses are equal, the IP already exists. In order to insert the new pattern into the existing node, we create an array and its length is 9 to store the list pointers, which are corresponding to 9 digits from 24 to 32 according to hash function respectively. Therefore, the patterns with the same IP and different mask will be stored in this automaton node. On the contrary, it means that the IP address in the mode to be inserted does not exist in the automaton structure at this time. We first find the location to be inserted into the mode to be inserted, and then determine the checkpoint of the new automaton state node, and finally create a new automaton node, loop the above process until all pattern strings are inserted (Fig. 1).

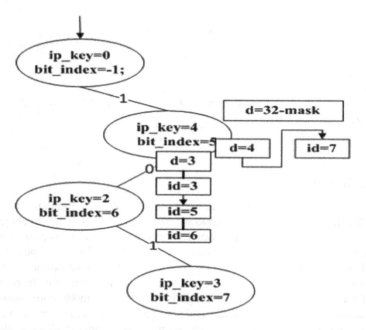

Fig. 1. Schema rule storage structure with the same IP and different masks.

3.3   Matching Algorithm

The core goal of our proposed algorithm is to hit the rules efficiently and completely. The IP to be matched is transferred according to the character of the check bit of the automaton state node. When the check bit is greater than or equal to 24, the state nodes on the matching path before the node are not the node where the pattern of the hit is located, and the next check bit is greater than or equal to 24. However, the check bit of all nodes of its sub-branch are greater than 24. Then we need to match these nodes. Based on this idea, I designed a queue in this paper, putting the node and its sub-branches into it and traversing these nodes. Even if this sub-tree is a full binary tree, the number of nodes is at most 256. When searching, we also prune many nodes and sub-branches, so it performs pretty well.

Pseudo code is shown as follows:

Matching algorithm

INPUT: Pair <a, b>

1. Scan down from the automatic head node

2. WHILE the node is exits and a has not end DO

3.   The bit_index of the current automaton status node is x.

4.   The position x of binary sequence is y

5:     IF y is equal to 1 THEN

6:         Enter the right child node

7:     IF y is equal to 0 THEN

8:         Enter the left child node

9:     IF x>=24 THEN

10:        Enter all nodes of the node sub-tree into the scan queue

11:    Scan queue for scanning processing

12:    IF node hit

13:        Record its rule number

4   Experiment Results

4.1   Experimental Environment

We use a system with Intel Core (TM) i7-6700HQ CPU 2.60 GHz, quad-core, where each core has two hardware threads, 32 KB L1 data cache (per core), 256 KB L2 cache (per core), and 8 MB L3 cache (shared among cores), 16G Memory. The system runs Linux Cent-OS 7, DPDK is installed to capture packets. Our program runs with 8 threads in parallel, one thread is used to capture packet and preprocess, three threads are used to parse in parallel the application protocol, the remaining four threads work for parallel matching.

4.2   Algorithm Correctness Test

Since this topic is to support a million-level mode set, it is necessary to test the correctness of the algorithm, and match the 1.5G size test text ip.txt with the 100K, 500K, 1000K, 5000K, and 10000K mode sets. Then analyze the records in the output array after the algorithm is executed, and compare it with the actual correct number of hits to verify the correctness of the algorithm (Table 3).

Table 3. The results of matching for different numbers rules

The number of rules	The number of hits	The number of correct hits	Accuracy
100K	4158	4158	100%
500K	8097	8097	100%
1000K	20373	20365	99.96%
5000K	70671	70661	99.98%
10000K	210045	210045	100%

4.3   Construction Performance

To evaluate the potential performance gains of our algorithm, we first analyzed the three components of the algorithm. The first part is a performance comparison of the build process for the automaton, in which the time measurement unit is milliseconds. The construction process of the automaton essentially inserts the individual pattern strings into the constructed automaton storage structure. Our proposed new algorithm spends less time each time than the AC algorithm when the pattern string is inserted into the automaton storage structure. Especially when the mode set size is relatively large, the time performance is more obvious (Fig. 2).

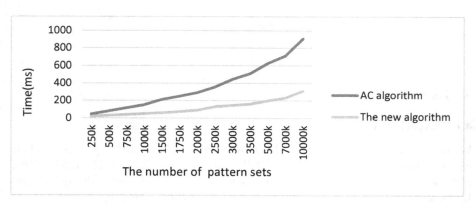

Fig. 2. Comparison of construction performance for two algorithms.

4.4   Memory Occupancy

The memory growth of the original AC algorithm is also exponential, which is consistent with the traditional classical AC algorithm, but the growth rate of both algorithms is reduced after optimization, and the automatic algorithm memory occupancy of the new algorithm is better than AC. The results show that the algorithm is significantly reduced (Fig. 3).

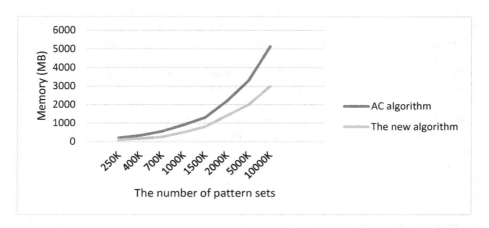

Fig. 3. Comparison of memory usage for two algorithms.

4.5 Matching Performance

First, we constructed some patterns sets for different sizes, and then we used the same environment to experiment with the new algorithm proposed in this paper and the original AC algorithm. The results show that the performance of the new algorithm proposed in this paper is about 6 times than the AC optimization algorithm when matching IP addresses (Fig. 4).

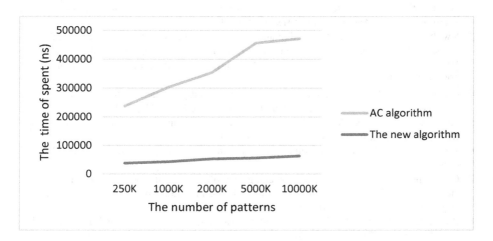

Fig. 4. Average matching time for different sizes of patterns

5 Conclusion

In the original intrusion detection system, the matching method of the IP address under the large mode set (more than one million) is not efficient, and it is difficult to deal with the system's more and more matching requests. This paper mainly completed the following work: We first analyze and summarize the principles, advantages and disadvantages of the classic matching algorithm. At the same time, the problem of the IP address is analyzed, and the state of the automaton is determined by using the bit-matching idea of the PAT tree. The structure of the node is designed for the storage structure, and the fastest state jump is achieved by setting the check mark bit, and the idea of hashing, binary search, and classification storage greatly improves the performance of the new algorithm. Finally, we propose a new algorithm for IP address matching.

In the future, we plan to optimize the matching part of the system from two aspects: firstly, we improve the performance of universal algorithm. Secondly, we also focus on the improvement of algorithm performance for related scenarios.

Acknowledgement. This work was supported by National Key Research & Development Plan of China under Grant 2016QY05X1000, National Natural Science Foundation of China under Grant No. 61771166, CERNET Innovation Project under Grant No. NGII20170101, and Dongguan Innovative Research Team Program under Grant No. 201636000100038.

References

1. Cheng, J., Ruomeng, X., Tang, X., Sheng, V.S., Cai, C.: An abnormal network flow feature sequence prediction approach for DDoS attacks detection in big data environment. CMC: Comput. Mater. Continua **55**(1), 095–119 (2018)
2. Liu, L., Zhang, H., Yu, X., et al.: An efficient security system for mobile data monitoring. Wirel. Commun. Mob. Comput. **2018**, 1–10 (2018)
3. Kwok, T.T.-O., Kwok, Y.-K.: Design and evaluation of parallel string matching algorithms for network intrusion detection systems. In: Li, K., Jesshope, C., Jin, H., Gaudiot, J.-L. (eds.) NPC 2007. LNCS, vol. 4672, pp. 344–353. Springer, Heidelberg (2007). https://doi.org/10.1007/978-3-540-74784-0_35
4. Guangming, T., Ping, L., Dongbo, B.Y.: Revisiting multiple pattern matching algorithms for multi-core architecture. J. Comput. Sci. Technol. **26**(5), 866–874 (2011)
5. Aho, A.V., Corasick, M.J.: Efficient string matching: an aid to bibliographic search. IEEE/ACM Trans. Commun. **18**(6), 333–340 (1975)
6. Wu, S., Manber, U.: A fast algorithm for multi-pattern searching. Technical report TR-94-17 (1994)
7. Commentz-Walter, B.: A string matching algorithm fast on the average. In: Maurer, Hermann A. (ed.) ICALP 1979. LNCS, vol. 71, pp. 118–132. Springer, Heidelberg (1979). https://doi.org/10.1007/3-540-09510-1_10
8. Zhang, Y.J., Zhang, W.Z.: A multiple-pattern matching algorithm based on bitmap. J. Harbin Inst. Technol. **42**(2), 277–280 (2010)
9. He, L.T., Fang, B.X., Yu, X.Z.: A time optimal exact string matching algorithm. J. Softw. **92**(16), 676–683 (2005)

10. Zhang W. An improved Wu-Manber multiple patterns matching algorithm[C]// IEEE International Conference on Electronic Information and Communication Technology. IEEE, 2017:91
11. Baker, Z.K., Prasanna, V.K.: Time and area efficient pattern matching on FPGAs. In: FPGA, pp. 223–232 (2004)
12. Clark, C., Lee, W., Schimmel, D., Contis, D., Kon, M., Thomas, A.: A hardware platform for network intrusion detection and prevention. In: NP (2004)
13. Lee, J., Hwang, S.H., Park, N., Lee, S.-W., Jun, S., Kim, Y.S.: A high performance NIDS using FPGA-based regular expression matching. In: SAC 2007, pp. 1187–1191 (2007)
14. Bremler-Barr, A., David, S.T., Harchol, Y., et al.: Leveraging traffic repetitions for high-speed deep packet inspection. In: Computer Communications, pp. 2578–2586. IEEE (2015)

An Effective Load Balance Using Link Bandwidth for SDN-Based Data Centers

Xiaosen Zeng[1,4], Dongbin Wang[2,3(✉)], Shuwen Han[5], Wenbin Yao[1], Zhao Wang[2], and Rui Chen[2]

[1] School of Computer Science, Beijing University of Posts and Telecommunications, Beijing, China
{zengxiaosen, yaowenbin}@bupt.edu.cn
[2] School of Cyberspace Security, Beijing University of Posts and Telecommunications, Beijing, China
{dbwang, wangzhao, chen_rui}@bupt.edu.cn
[3] National Engineering Laboratory for Mobile Network Security (BUPT), Beijing, China
[4] Key Laboratory of Trustworthy Distributed Computing and Service (BUPT), Ministry of Education, Beijing, China
[5] Article Numbering Center of China, Beijing, China
hanshw@ancc.org.cn

Abstract. The burst traffic will be likely to cause congestion, packet loss and degrading network service quality. If the traffic load in the data center is unbalanced, the packet lost will occur in the bottleneck link. In this paper, we propose a load-balancing algorithm using the remaining bandwidth of the bottleneck link and the average link remaining bandwidth in the path for SDN-based data centers. A score is ranking for each path according to the link load in the path and the path with the largest score is selected to transfer the traffic. The traffic is redistributed periodically to different paths that can avoid the occurring of heavy load link. The experiment results show that the proposed algorithm can reduce the load of the congested link, the packet loss and achieve better performance in load balance.

Keywords: Data center network · Software definition network · Load balance · Congestion

1 Introduction

In data center networks, the traditional network architecture fails to provide a global perspective, so its limitations in management difficulty, scalability are gradually highlighted [1]. The control plane is separated from the data plane using the OpenFlow protocol in software defined network, and the centralized controller can get a global perspective [2, 3]. Many applications based on the SDN technology have appeared. For example, Wan [4] proposed a security software appliance in SDN-based control systems, and Cheng [5] proposed a DDOS attack detector based on SDN.

The central controller has the global perspective in the network and can load balance in different paths by distributing flow rules to the switches. The traffic in SDN can be distributed to each path as evenly as possible. So we can avoid traffic congestion

© Springer Nature Switzerland AG 2019
X. Sun et al. (Eds.): ICAIS 2019, LNCS 11635, pp. 256–265, 2019.
https://doi.org/10.1007/978-3-030-24268-8_24

on the over-loading links and reduce the packet loss rate which can improve network service quality. Due to the programmability of the control layer, SDN technology can make load balance more effective and more flexible.

With the development of SDN technology, several typical routing algorithms for load balancing have emerged, such as ECMP algorithm [6], DLB algorithm [8], HEDERA algorithm [9], and FSEM algorithm [10]. ECMP used as default routing algorithm in data centers do not consider the load of alternative paths, and flows associated to user tasks are easily routed over congested paths that affects the user experience. DLB is used to forward flows with a greedy approach and the imbalance of the overall network is prone to happen. Simulated Annealing scheduler is proposed in HEDERA, and the slow convergence is an obvious shortcoming. The FSEM algorithm is a global load balancing algorithm that considers packet count, byte count and the port forwarding rate of the critical link. But the average link load in FSEM is not taken into account, and the reschedule on congested link is not fully valued. So the balance between alternative paths is not ideal, and packets will be lost due to burst traffic.

An effective load balance using link bandwidth called LBLB is proposed. LBLB algorithm considers the remaining bandwidth of the critical link and the remaining average link bandwidth of the path. Compared with FSEM, LBLB can effectively reduce the load of congested links and the packet loss rate when burst traffic happens.

The remainder of this paper is organized as follows. Section 2 presents related work. Section 3 presents the design of LBLB algorithm. Section 4 presents the performance evaluation. Section 5 presents the conclusions. Section 6 presents the acknowledgment.

2 Related Work

Nowadays, load balancing technology for SDN-Based data centers has been extensively studied.

Hopps proposed ECMP algorithm [6], which statically stripe flows across available paths using flow hashing. Some paths are overloaded and some paths are lightly loaded, because the bandwidth of alternative paths and the flow size are not taken into account. Packets on those congested links are prone to loss due to burst traffic.

Dijkstra algorithm [7] calculates the hop counts of all alternative paths and selects the shortest path to install forwarding rule. However, this method does not consider network status information.

Li et al. [8] proposed the DLB algorithm, which uses the single-hop greedy method to select the least congested link for each hop. The greedy algorithm is the local optimum, resulting in unbalanced load.

AI-Fares et al. [9] proposed the HEDERA algorithm, which estimates the natural demand of flows and use placement algorithms to calculate good paths for them, such as Global First Fit. The advantage of Global First Fit is that the speed is fast. However, flow size and link bandwidth are not fully evaluated. The optimal solution with Simulated Annealing can be achieved, but the astringent is too slow.

Li et al. [10] proposed FSEM algorithm, which considers hops of alternative path, bytes received by the critical switch, and the forwarding rate. However, the average load of the reachable path is not considered, and the flow re-routing on congested link has not been considered seriously. Some links of alternative paths cannot reserve sufficient volume for bust traffic and packet loss may occur due to burst traffic.

Long et al. [13] proposed a rescheduling mechanism named Single-Hop LABERIO. First, this mechanism sorts links by their occupied bandwidth and selects the busiest link for alarm. Secondly, this mechanism sorts flows on this link and set the object flow to be the biggest flow. Then LABERIO calculates all alternative paths for the object flow according to the source address and the destination address. At last LABERIO scores for each alternative path, and the lightest one with the highest score is selected.

3   Algorithm Formulation

In order to provide sufficient bidirectional bandwidth, data center network usually adopts hierarchical multi-network topology, such as fat tree [11], as shown in Fig. 1. Fat-tree topology contains multiple paths among hosts so it can provide higher avail-

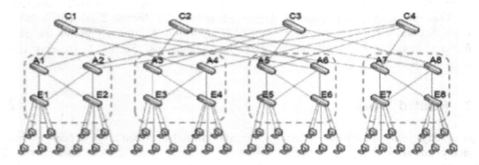

Fig. 1. Fat tree topology of data center network.

able bandwidth than a single-path tree with the same number of nodes. In recent years, it has been adopted in many data center [12].

The occupied bandwidth of the link can be obtained by the central controller. Some definitions using by LBLB are presented in the following. The serial number of path and the serial number of the link in this path are represented by i and j respectively. $Trans_{ij}$ suggests the traffic in link j on the path i during the monitoring time interval T. Bw represent the link bandwidth. Bw_{ij} and $BwRest_{ij}$ represents the occupied bandwidth and the remaining bandwidth respectively. $MinBwRest_i$ means the minimum remaining bandwidth of the path i.

$$Bw_{ij} = Trans_{ij}/T \tag{1}$$

$$BwRest_{ij} = Bw - Bw_{ij} \tag{2}$$

$$MinBwRest_i = min\{BwRest_{i1}, BwRest_{i2}, \ldots, BwRest_{in}\} \tag{3}$$

The min remaining bandwidth of all links in one path can reflect the congestion of this path. So $BwRest_i$ is considered as the bottleneck remaining bandwidth of path in this paper. When the bottleneck remaining bandwidth is small, the load of this path is heavy. If we select this path to reschedule, congestion and packet loss will be likely to occur. Therefore, the bottleneck remaining bandwidth of the path is considered as one of the most critical factor for routing.

BwMeanRest means the average remaining bandwidth of one path. According to formula (2), average remaining bandwidth of path i is as follows:

$$BwMeanRest_i = (BwRest_{i1} + BwRest_{i2} + \ldots + BwRest_{in})/n \tag{4}$$

The two critical routing factors mentioned above can affect the load balancing. According to formula (3) and formula (4), $score_i$ represent the score of the path i and the path with the max score will be selected as the forwarding path.

$$score_i = \alpha * \log_{10}(MinBwRest_i + 1) + \beta * \log_{10}(BwMeanRest_i + 1) \tag{5}$$

After a series of experiments, we found that when the ratio of α and β is 1:1, the load balancing effect is good. So the value of α and β will be set to fifty percent below.

LBLB algorithm is used in Packge-in and Reschedule stage. In these stage, we use LBLB algorithm to choose path among all alternative paths.

The LBLB algorithm of this paper is as follows:

Algorithm 1 LBLB Algorithm

1: init $score_i$ of each path with 0
2: set bestPath as the first path in acceptPaths
3: set bestScore to 0
4: For $path_i$ in acceptPaths
5:    init α, β
6:    compute the rest bandwith of the most congested link, $BwRest_i$
7:    compute the mean rest bandwith of all links, $BwMeanRest_i$
8:    set x to $\log_{10}$ ($BwRest_i + 1$)
9:    set y to $\log_{10}$ ($BwMeanRest_i + 1$)
10:   assign $score_i$ equal to the value of $\alpha* x + \beta * y$
11:   If the value of $score_i$ is larger than the value of bestScore
12:      set bestScore to $score_i$
13:      set bestPath to $path_i$
14:   EndIf
15: EndFor
16: At last, reschedule this flow with the bastPath.

The mechanism for rerouting in this paper is as follows:

Algorithm 2 Reschedule Algorithm

1: linkAferSorted represent links collection sorted by bandwidth in network
2: set rescheduledFlag to false
3: For link in linkAfterSorted
4:    If rescheduledFlag is true
5:       break
6   EndIF
7:    For flow in link
8:       If rescheduledFlag is true
9:          break
10:      EndIF
11:      compute all path between flow.src and flow.dst as paths
12:      compute acceptPaths that can hold this flow in paths as acceptPaths
13:      If acceptPaths.size is 0
14:         continue
15:      EndIF
16:      set objectPath as the best path in acceptPaths using LBLB
17:      set rescheduledFlag to true
18:   EndFor
19: EndFor

---

4 Performance Evaluation

In order to evaluate the load-balancing effect of LBLB, we use Mininet to simulate the network topology in Fig. 1. We connect eight hosts to each edge layer switch of the fat-tree topology. The source host and the destination host are selected respectively in Fig. 1 and random traffic are generated from 1 Mbps to 27 Mbps between the source host and the destination host.

The reason for generating traffic in random mode is to verify the universality of the load balancing algorithm. Because the traffic mode is not fixed in the data center, the communication between each source host server and the destination host server is not fixed. So in this paper, each host randomly selects any host other than itself as the destination host, and then generates random traffic in the host pair.

As shown in the formula (5), we calculate each path score of each available path and then select the path with the highest score to install flow rules. When the traffic passes through the switches, it will be forwarded according to the rules in the flow table. Finally, we implement load-balancing in data centers.

In order to verify the effectiveness of load balancing, the ability to avoid congestion, and the ability to reduce packet loss due to burst traffic, we compare LBLB with FSEM algorithm and ECMP algorithm.

4.1 Load Balancing Evaluation

Standard Deviation of Bandwidth Utilization Rate of all Links. Standard deviation of bandwidth utilization rate of all links in the network topology is used as one of the evaluation standard for load balancing. The smaller the value is, the more balanced the network is, that also means the stronger the ability to avoid congestion.

Average Packet Loss Rate. Average packet loss rate is used to evaluate the performance for load balancing. If the load is unbalanced, those congested links will be easily congested that means packets will be lost when those congested links encounter burst traffic.

Average Bandwidth Usage Rate of all Links. Average bandwidth usage rate of all links is also an important load balancing evaluation. If the network load is unbalanced, some link load is high and some link load is light. The link with light load is not fully utilized due to bandwidth, resulting in the average bandwidth utilization rate of links low.

4.2 Comparative Analysis of Load Balancing Effect

$\delta 1$ is the standard deviation of bandwidth utilization rate of all links included in the fat-tree topology as shown in (6).

$$\delta 1 = \sqrt{\frac{\left[\sum_{i=1}^{n}(linkBwUsedRate - meanBwUsedRate)^2\right]}{n}} \qquad (6)$$

linkBwUsedRate represents the bandwidth utilization rate of the link and mean-BwUsedRate represents the average bandwidth utilization rate of all links.

In random mode, when each source host in the fat-tree structure randomly selects the destination host to generate random traffic from 1 Mbps to 27 Mbps, we compare $\delta 1$ of the LBLB algorithm, FSEM and ECMP algorithm.

As show in Fig. 2, the load balancing effect achieved by LBLB is better than the FSEM and ECMP. Due to not considering the average remaining bandwidth of all links in alternative paths, the load balancing effect of FSEM and ECMP is worse than LBLB.

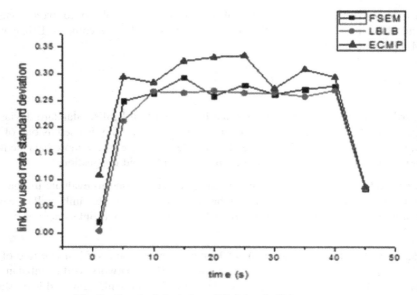

Fig. 2. Standard deviation of link bandwidth usage rate

δ2 is the average ratio of the lost packets to the total packets numbers in the fat-tree topology. The calculation formula of δ2 is as shown in (7), where psi represents the number of packets sent by the source node of flow i, and pri represents the number of packets received by the receiver node of flow i:

$$\delta2 = \frac{\sum_{i=1}^{n} \frac{psi}{pri}}{n} \tag{7}$$

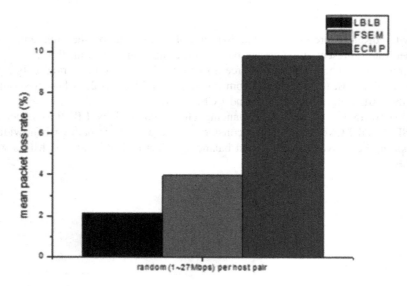

Fig. 3. Mean packet loss rate.

As shown in Fig. 3, the packet loss rate of LBLB algorithm and FSEM algorithm is lower than that of ECMP. This is because the routing strategy of ECMP algorithm does not consider the real time bandwidth which are closely related to load balancing. If we don't take account of them, bandwidth will not be used well. Therefore, load balancing cannot be performed well, and condition about congestion and packet loss is serious.

At the same time, the load balancing algorithm LBLB of this paper is lower than the FSEM algorithm. It is because our solution can distribute the traffic more reasonably to alternative path than the FSEM algorithm, so that the load of each alternative path is more average. In summary, for the evaluation of packet loss rate, our solution performs better than the other two algorithms.

Average bandwidth usage rate of link $\delta 3$ is shown in Fig. 4. We generate random traffic varying from 1 Mbps–27 Mbps for the host pair, and periodically calculate the average link bandwidth usage rate every 5 s in this experiment.

$$\delta 3 = \frac{\sum_{i=1}^{n} bwUsageRateOfLink}{n} \tag{8}$$

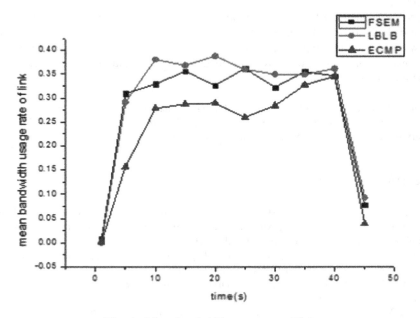

Fig. 4. Mean bandwidth usage rate of link

If the load on the links is not balanced, the packet on the congested link will be lost due to burst traffic, and the bandwidth on the link with light load will not be fully utilized. So the overall network bandwidth will be relatively low.

As show in Fig. 4, the LBLB algorithm in this paper can make the network more balanced, avoiding some link congested and some link load light.

5 Conclusion

In data centers, when network is unbalanced, burst traffic will cause congestion and packet loss on the bottle link and network service quality will be degraded. In this paper, we present an effective load-balancing mechanism, LBLB, which is used in the two phases of Package-in and rescheduling.

In rescheduling phase, LBLB periodically monitors the bandwidth utilization rate of the link, and then selects the most congested link for traffic rescheduling to avoid network congestion.

LBLB algorithm analyzes the remaining bandwidth of the bottleneck link and the average remaining bandwidth of the alternative path. The remaining bandwidth of the bottleneck link directly determines whether packets on the path will be lost. The average link remaining bandwidth reflects the average load of the path. According to fat-tree topology, those latter links in one path are likely to have traffic imported by other paths. So in order to provide sufficient bandwidth to transfer the traffic, we consider the average remaining bandwidth in LBLB. After a series of analysis and experiments, we verify that these two factors play a very important role in load balancing.

The performance of LBLB is compared with that of FSEM and ECMP on the standard deviation of link bandwidth usage rate, packet loss rate, and link average bandwidth usage rate. Experiments show that LBLB performs better in load balancing with lower packet loss rate, lower link load standard deviation, higher average link bandwidth usage rate.

Acknowledgment. This work was supported in part by national key research and development program (No. 2016YFB0800302) and national science and technology major project of the ministry of science and technology of China (No. 2012BAH45B01).

References

1. Zhang, C.K., Cui, Y., Tang, H.Y., Wu, J.P.: State-of-the-art survey on software-defined networking (SDN). Ruan Jian Xue Bao/J. Softw. **26**(1), 62–81 (2015). http://www.jos.org.cn/1000-9825/4701.htm. (in Chinese with English abstract)
2. McKeown, N., et al.: OpenFlow: enabling innovation in campus networks. In: ACM SIGCOMM Computer Communication (2008)
3. Nunes, B., Mendonça, M., Ng, X.: A survey of software-defined network programmable networks. To app Tutorials (2014)
4. Wan, M., Yao, J., Jing, Y., Jin, X.: Event-based anomaly detection for non-public industrial communication protocols in SDN-based control systems. CMC: Comput. Mater. Continua **55**(3), 447–463 (2018)
5. Cheng, J., Xu, R., Tang, X., et al.: An abnormal network flow feature sequence prediction approach for DDoS attacks detection in big data environment. CMC: Comput. Mater. Continua **55**(1), 95–463 (2018)
6. Hopps, C.E.: Analysis of an equal-cost multi-path algorithm. J. Allergy Clin. Immunol. 281–196 (2010)

7. Dijkstra, E.: A note on two problems in connexion with graphs. Numerische mathematic **1** (1), 261–271 (1959)
8. Li, Y., Pan, D.: OpenFlow based load balancing for Fat-Tree networks with multipath support. In: Proceedings of 12th IEEE International Conference on Communications (ICC 2013), Budapest, Hungary, pp. 1–5 (2013). Patrice Godefroid. Automated Whitebox Fuzz Testing. Microsoft (Research)
9. AI-Fares, M., Radhakrishnan, S., Raghavan, B., et al.: Hedera: dynamic flow scheduling for data center networks. In: Proceedings of the 7th USENIX Conference on Networked Systems Design and Implementation, San Jose, USA, pp. 281–296 (2010)
10. Li, J., Chang, X., Ren, Y., Zhang, Z., Wang, G.: An effective path load balancing mechanism based on SDN. In: Proceedings of the 13th International Conference on Trust, Security and Privacy in Computing and Communications (TrustCom), pp. 527–533. IEEE Computer Society Press, Washington (2014). http://doi.org/10.1109/TrustCom.2014.67
11. Qiao, L., Yin, X.H., Zhuo, D.I., et al.: Research on SDN network architecture for electric power big data platform. Electr. Power Inf. Comrnun. Technol. **12**(6), 1–6 (2015)
12. Sun, Y., Cherg, J., Shi, K.: Data center network architecture. ZTE Commun. **11**(5), 5–9 (2013)
13. Long, H., Shen, Y., Guo, M., Tang, F.: LABERIO: dynamic load-balanced Routing in OpenFlow-enabled networks. In: 2013 IEEE 27th International Conference on Advanced Information Networking and Applications, pp. 290–297 (2013)

Zero-Day Vulnerability Risk Assessment and Attack Path Analysis Using Security Metric

Ziwei Ye$^{(\boxtimes)}$, Yuanbo Guo, and Ankang Ju

Zhengzhou Information Science and Technology Institute,
Zhengzhou 450001, China
yezw2014@163.com

Abstract. Zero-day vulnerability has been considered one of the most serious threats to network security at present. Current researches on zero-day vulnerability risk assessment are mainly focused on the number of necessary zero-day vulnerabilities for attack to exploit to reach the target. However, in practice, it is difficult to realize risk assessment of single zero-day vulnerability by existing methods. In this paper, a zero-day vulnerability and attack path risk assessment method is proposed for internal network. Four kinds of security metrics and a zero-day vulnerability discovery and zero-day attack graph generation algorithm are designed. By contrasting the preconditions with postconditions of known vulnerabilities, attack complexity and impact of zero-day vulnerabilities in various contexts are analyzed. Experimental results show that the proposed method can quantitatively assess risk of single zero-day vulnerability and attack path from multiple dimensionalities.

Keywords: Zero-day vulnerability · Security metric · Attack graph ·
Attack path · Risk assessment

1 Introduction

Among the threats to network security, attack exploiting zero-day vulnerabilities (hereinafter referred to as "zero-day attack") is one of the hardest measures to defend against. It is in much difficulty predicting location, type and exploiting way of zero-day vulnerability. And with the development of attack technology, existence form and exploiting way of zero-day vulnerabilities are more and more complex and diverse. Due to the inherent agnosticism of zero-day vulnerabilities, zero-day attacks have become one of the best breakthroughs attackers can take when facing a network difficult to compromise. Software or hardware vendors and security companies cannot repair or provide mitigation solutions before discovering zero-day vulnerabilities. Evaluating the location and risk of zero-day vulnerability could effectively guide security hardening of target network when zero-day attack has not occurred, increase attack cost, and reduce the probability of attack success, so as to strive more time for defender to take suitable countermeasures. How to assess risk of zero-day vulnerabilities has become an issue widely studied by scholars in recent years.

© Springer Nature Switzerland AG 2019
X. Sun et al. (Eds.): ICAIS 2019, LNCS 11635, pp. 266–278, 2019.
https://doi.org/10.1007/978-3-030-24268-8_25

At present, studies for risk assessment of zero-day vulnerabilities are mainly divided into two categories. The first category is to assess the number and location of potential zero-day vulnerabilities in network. Wang et al. [1, 2] propose a security metric called k-zero day security based on attack graph. It is assumed that all remote services in network may have zero-day vulnerabilities, and network security is evaluated according to the minimum number of zero-day vulnerabilities that attacker needs to exploit to compromise the target host. Futhermore, methods for assessing the diversity of equipment and services and the impact of known vulnerabilities on network security are presented in [3, 4]. Multiple algorithms are proposed to evaluate the k-zero day security of large-scale networks without generating a complete attack graph [5]. The above literatures focus on how to assess network security given a pre-generating zero-day attack graph, but don't delve into how to generate zero-day attack graph. Yang et al. [6] propose a zero-day attack graph generation method. Vulnerabilities are divided into remote privilege promotion vulnerabilities, DDoS vulnerabilities, remote information leakage vulnerabilities and other vulnerabilities. Each type of vulnerabilities is modeled respectively to predict zero-day vulnerabilities and extend general attack graph. This study mainly shows a zero-day attack graph generation algorithm, and do not elaborate how to assess risk of zero-day vulnerabilities and attack paths.

The second category of research is to analyze the location of zero-day vulnerability and decide efficient defense during attack occurring. Sun et al. [7, 8] design and implement a graph-based method for discovering zero-day attack paths. Through the integration of system call, log, intrusion detection alarm and other security information, zero-day attacks which are occurring would be detected. On the basis of [7, 8], Bayesian Network is further used to infer the probability that the target host has been compromised by zero-day attacks [9], which leads to higher accuracy and universality. The above studies identify zero-day attack path of a single host at operation system level, and are more fine-grained compared with other researches related to zero-day vulnerabilities based on the attack graph. Joshi et al. [10] propose a zero-day vulnerability identification and risk assessment framework to analyze abnormal traffic in network, in order to detect possible zero-day attacks and generate a zero-day attack graph for guiding forecasting of zero-day attacks.

By summarizing the existing researches, it is concluded that in practices, due to the lack of information of zero-day vulnerabilities characteristics, the first type of research would predict a large number of zero-day vulnerabilities that may not exist or whose risk is uncertain. It results that these methods cannot distinguish the importance of different zero-day vulnerabilities. Defender could only treat all zero-day vulnerabilities equally, and cost a lot but obtain an unsatisfactory effect. Meanwhile because of the real-time detection of zero-day attacks, the second kind of research not only have higher requirements for network traffic monitoring and analysis capabilities, but also are likely to occur that the monitoring and analysis system has not yet reached an accurate conclusion while the attack has been already completed.

Attack graph is such a technology used to show the way and process of attacking the target network, so as to find vulnerable hosts and paths in network and guide defender to harden the network [11]. In network penetration, specific continuous attack behaviors can be called an attack path from the origin host to the target host, and attack graph graphically shows all attack paths that can be found by defender. On one hand, we can compare the risk of possible attack paths from boundary hosts to potential targeted hosts. On the other hand, we can analyze the attacker's ability and infer the subsequent attacks in real time when attack occurs, so as to take countermeasures. Risk assessment is one of the most important applications of attack graph. By constructing attack graph of the whole network, the possibility of important hosts being attacked, risk of each host, and the programs or services that are most vulnerable can be calculated and analyze. According to these information, defender can increase protection mechanism and select safer software to reduce security risk of network and harden network. Traditional attack graph technology mainly relies on network vulnerability, topology, security configuration and other information to generate and analyze attack graph. Since the characteristics and scores of each known vulnerability can be queried in vulnerability databases such as NVD [12, 13], it is feasible to evaluate security risk based on the attack graph which is composed of known vulnerabilities. At present, there are a lot of related achievements in academic circles [11, 14].

In order to realize the risk assessment of single zero-day vulnerability and attack path, avoiding handling all zero-day vulnerabilities equally and selecting unreasonable protective measures, in this paper we propose a zero-day vulnerability risk assessment and attack path analysis method using security metrics. Firstly, security metrics are proposed to comprehensively judge attack path and network security. Then, a zero-day vulnerability discovery and zero-day attack graph generation algorithm is proposed by matching preconditions and postconditions of known vulnerabilities in network. The necessity, exploiting difficulty and risk of zero-day vulnerabilities under various contexts are studied. Formulas are given to illustrate how to calculate the proposed security metrics given zero-day attack graph and single zero-day vulnerability risk. The main contributions of this paper are as follows:

(1) Zero-day vulnerability security metrics and calculation formulas are proposed to quantify the network security, which provides a basis for analyzing network security in different network contexts.
(2) An algorithm for zero-day vulnerability discovering and zero-day attack graph generation is proposed to provide a basis for zero-day vulnerability risk assessment and network security analysis.
(3) The necessity, attack complexity and impact of single zero-day vulnerability in various contexts are analyzed. It is used to determine the risk score of zero-day vulnerabilities in specific network contexts and apply it to the calculation of security metrics.

2 Proposed Method

2.1 Security Metrics

As described in Chapter 1, existing researches indicate that it is feasible to use attack graph for zero-day vulnerability risk assessment. However, since the various features of zero-day vulnerability are unknown, new security metrics need to be defined [15, 16]. k-zero day safety metric is proposed in literature [1]:

- k-zero day safety

This metric represents the minimum number of zero-day vulnerabilities that an attacker needs to exploit to reach the target. And the minimum number is the value of k. The more zero-day vulnerabilities an attack path contains, the less likely it is to be chosen by attacker. When the number of zero-day vulnerabilities on a path is less than the preset k-value, the path and network are considered unsecure.

k-zero day safety metric has been proven to be effective for network security assessment and network hardening. Several researches discuss how to apply this security metric under different network conditions. But k-zero day safety "simply count show many distinct zero day vulnerabilities a network can resist, regardless of what vulnerabilities those are [1] ". Defender can only decide which hosts in network to harden based on the security metric, but cannot determine to what extent each host should be hardened. Therefore, more security metrics are needed to provide more fine-grained guidance for network hardening.

To achieve an accurate risk assessment of single zero-day vulnerability and zero-day attack path, we propose the following security metrics:

- Minimum zero-day vulnerabilities attack path length

Attack paths in zero-day attack graph consist of known vulnerabilities and zero-day vulnerabilities. When the minimum number of zero-day vulnerabilities an attacker needs to exploit is known, the attack path containing the minimum number of zero-day vulnerabilities is called minimum zero-day vulnerabilities attack path. The length of this path is determined by the number of known vulnerabilities. The longer the path is, the greater the attacker costs. When there are multiple such paths, the probability of shorter path selected by the attacker is higher. If there is a path whose total length is less than the preset value, the path is considered unsecure.

- Exploitability of zero-day attack path

Exploitability of an attack path reflects the overall probability that an attacker will follow the path from the original host to the target host successfully. It is clear that exploitability of all vulnerabilities in an attack path together determine the exploitability of the attack path. The shorter the attack path and the higher exploitability of vulnerabilities, the higher exploitability of the attack path and the easier it is for the attacker to realize the goal. If the exploitability of a zero-day attack path is higher than the preset value, the path is considered unsecure.

- Risk of zero-day attack path

To reach the target, an attacker usually needs to compromise multiple hosts in network along an attack path. Even if the attacker's target is only the final host, other compromised hosts on the path may bring additional benefits. Therefore, the overall risk of zero-day attack path is determined by all hosts and vulnerabilities on the path. If the risk of a zero-day attack path is higher than the preset value, the path is considered unsecure.

2.2 Zero-Day Attack Graph

In this paper we expand the initial attack graph by discovering potential zero-day vulnerabilities to generate a zero-day attack graph. The various security metrics proposed in Sect. 2.1 need to be calculated on the basis of zero-day attack graph.

It is noteworthy that in practice, there may be a large number of zero-day vulnerabilities in network. Conditions and results of part of zero-day vulnerabilities are the same as some known vulnerabilities. Attacker can directly exploit known vulnerabilities without spending extra effort on discovering and exploiting these zero-day vulnerabilities. This kind of vulnerabilities is not considered in this article.

We define attack graph and zero-day attack graph as follows:

Definition 1: Attack graph AG

Attack graph AG is a directed graph $AG = (C, V, E)$, where C is a set of conditions (include initial conditions, preconditions, and postconditions), V a set of vulnerabilities, and E a set of edges. AG satisfies the following conditions: For $\forall v \in V$, $pre(v)$ is precondition, while $post(v)$ is postcondition. $(\land pre(v)) \rightarrow (\land post(v))$ indicates that vulnerability v can be exploited when preconditions are met, and attacker would obtain postcondition of vulnerability v by successful exploitation.

Definition 2: Zero-day attack graph $ZDAG$

$ZDAG = (C', V', E')$, where $C' = C \cup C^0$, $V' = V \cup V^0$, and $E' = E \cup E^0$. C^0, V^0, and E^0 respectively represent the condition set of zero-day vulnerability, the set of zero-day vulnerability, and the set of new edges brought by zero-day vulnerabilities.

In order to minimize the size of zero-day attack graph and facilitate subsequent risk assessment, we make the following assumptions:

(1) There is only one zero-day vulnerability per host on the same attack path.
(2) Zero-day vulnerabilities that can be exploited by lower privilege, are more difficult to exploit than zero-day vulnerabilities that require higher privilege.
(3) Zero-day vulnerability that helps attacker to obtain a higher privilege, is riskier than zero-day vulnerability that helps attacker to obtain a lower privilege.
(4) Zero-day vulnerability is assumed to allow attacker to directly obtain the minimum privilege required to exploit follow-up vulnerabilities. For example, suppose that host 1 and host 2 can communicate with each other, and attacker's target is to obtain the local privilege on host 2. There is a zero-day vulnerability on host 2 that could allow attacker to gain local privilege or root privilege. By statistical analysis of vulnerabilities recorded in NVD, it is obviously that in most cases vulnerabilities that can lead to root privilege is more difficult to exploit than vulnerabilities that can lead to local privileges under the same precondition. For attacker, obtaining local privilege can achieve the goal, without the need of spending extra cost to discover and exploit more complex vulnerabilities to gain root privilege. In this case, only zero-day vulnerabilities that enable an attacker to obtain the minimum privilege to meet the target are considered.
(5) Ignore zero-day vulnerabilities that may cause cyclic attack and denial of service attack.

Based on the above assumptions, we propose the following algorithm to discover zero-day vulnerabilities and generate zero-day attack graph.

Algorithm 1: zero-day vulnerability discovery and zero-day attack graph generation algorithm
Input: initial attack graph $AG=(C,V,E)$, set of hosts $H=\{h_1,h_2,......,h_n\}$
Output: zero-day attack graph $ZDAG=(C',V',E')$
1: int $j=1$;
2: for $(k=1; k\leq m; k++)$
3:    for$(i=1; i\leq m$ && $i\neq k; i++)$
4:      if$(pre(v_i)\rightarrow host_a$ && $post(v_k)\rightarrow host_a$ && $pre(v_i)\leq post(v_k))$
5:        create v^0_j;
6:        $pre(v^0_j)=post(v_k)$;
7:        $post(v^0_j)=pre(v_i)$;
8:        create $e^0(pre(v^0_j)\rightarrow v^0_j)$;
9:        create $e^0(v^0_j\rightarrow post(v^0_j))$;
10:       $j++$;
11:     else end
12:   end
13: end
14: print ZDAG;

Algorithm 1 takes the initial attack graph and host set as input. n is the number of hosts in network, and m the number of known vulnerabilities. The preconditions and postconditions of vulnerabilities existing on two devices that can access each other are identified according to network topology. When the following conditions are met:

(1) The postcondition of vulnerability a and the precondition of vulnerability b are all certain privilege of a specific host x;
(2) The postcondition of vulnerability a cannot satisfy the precondition of vulnerability b. That is, the privilege obtained by exploiting a is insufficient to successfully exploit b;
(3) There is no vulnerability on host x that can enable attacker to obtain the precondition of vulnerability b after successfully exploiting vulnerability a.

It can be supposed that there is a zero-day vulnerability i on host x, and the precondition and postcondition of zero-day vulnerability i are respectively the postcondition of vulnerability a and the precondition of vulnerability b. In zero-day attack graph, the zero-day vulnerability i locates between vulnerability a and vulnerability b.

In mainstream operating systems such as Windows, Linux, and Mac OS, privileges on a host can be divided into three categories:

(1) No privilege. Attacker can only perform operations that the target host allows remotely, or exploit vulnerability to promote privilege;
(2) Local privilege. Attacker is able to perform operations allowed by the administrator as legal user locally, but cannot achieve complete control;
(3) Root privilege. Attacker can completely control target host.

Table 1. Possible combinations of *post(v_a)* & *pre(v_b)*

	post(v_a)	pre(v_b)
1	None	None
2	None	Local
3	None	Root
4	Local	None
5	Local	Local
6	Local	Root
7	Root	None
8	Root	Local
9	Root	Root

At this point, there are nine possible combinations for the postcondition of vulnerability a and the precondition of vulnerability b, as shown in Table 1.

In cases (1) (4) (5) (7) (8) (9), the postcondition of vulnerability a could satisfy the privilege required to exploit vulnerability b. Hence no additional zero-day vulnerability is required for higher privilege. For (2) (3) (6), vulnerability a usually exists on the host which is mutually accessible to x in case (2) and (3), and on host x in case (6). Vulnerability b, in case (2) and case (6), usually exists on a host that has mutual access to x, while case (3) on host x.

NVD is one of the most commonly used vulnerability databases. It follows the CVSS standard [17] and provides characteristics such as attack vectors, attack complexity, and impact of each vulnerability. Attack complexity indicates the difficulty of successfully exploiting the vulnerability. Its value range is (0, 10]. The higher score, the lower difficulty. Impact signifies damage to confidentiality, integrity, and availability of target host, with the range of (0,10]. The higher score, the more serious consequences. The statistical analysis of vulnerabilities recorded in NVD shows that in (2) (3) (6) the attack complexity and impact of vulnerabilities are all satisfied (3) > (6) > (2). Referencing CVSS standard, we set attack complexity and impact of zero-day vulnerabilities the maximum value of each level. In case (3), the attack complexity level of zero-day vulnerabilities is low, while the attack complexity score 10, and impact score 10. In case (6), the attack complexity level is medium, while the attack complexity score 8, and impact score 7. In case (2), the attack complexity level is high, while the attack complexity score 6, and the impact score 4 (Table 2).

Table 2. Attack complexity and impact score of zero-day vulnerability

	Attack complexity level	Attack complexity score	Impact score
(2)	High	6	4
(3)	Low	10	10
(6)	Medium	8	7

2.3   Security Metric Calculation

The security metrics proposed in Sect. 2.1 can be calculated based on the information of attack complexity and impact of vulnerabilities. In this section we give a detailed calculation of each security metric.

In the four security metrics used in this article, the k-zero day safety and minimum zero-day vulnerabilities attack path length can be derived directly from the number of vulnerabilities in the path. Exploitability of zero-day attack path is calculated using the following formula:

$$ex(p) = \prod_{i=1}^{l-a} \frac{ac(v_i)}{10} * \prod_{j=1}^{a} \frac{ac(v_j^0)}{10} \tag{1}$$

$ex(p)$ indicates exploitability of attack path, while l length of attack path, and a number of zero-day vulnerabilities. $ac(v_i)$ indicates attack complexity of known vulnerability, and $ac(v_j^0)$ of zero-day vulnerability. Attack complexity of known vulnerabilities is obtained from NVD.

Risk of zero-day attack path is calculated by the following formula:

$$rd(p) = \sum_{i=1}^{n-a} k_i * rd(v_i) + \sum_{j=1}^{a} k_j * rd(v_j^0) \tag{2}$$

$rd(p)$ indica v_j^0 s risk of attack path. $im(v_i)$ indicates impact of known vulnerability, and $im(v_j^0)$ of zero-day vulnerability. k_i and k_j indicate weight of hosts where vulnerabilities are located. The specific values of k_i and k_j can be set according to actual context of target network. For example, the weight of server should be higher than that of PC, and the weight of hosts storing important files should be higher than hosts storing general files.

3   Experiment and Analysis

The experimental network is set up referenced literatures [4–6, 11], as shown in Fig. 1:

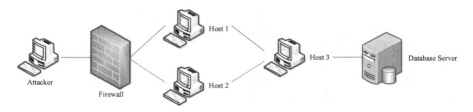

Fig. 1. Experiment network settings

One hardware firewall, three internal hosts and one database server are deployed in target network. The firewall is used to filter network traffic, prevent various attacks from outside and information leakage from inside. Host 1 and host 2 receive and process all kinds of requests from external network to converge the requests to host 3. Host 3 issues data query requests to database server and receives query results. The results are transferred to host 1 and host 2 from host 3. Attacker can only initially attack the firewall from external network. After the firewall compromised, hosts and database server in target network could be further penetrated. The access control matrix is shown in Table 3. 1 indicates that host A can access host B, and 0 on the contrary.

Table 3. Access control matrix

Host A \ Host B	Attacker	Firewall	DB Server	Host 1	Host 2	Host 3
Attacker		1	0	0	0	0
Firewall	1		0	1	1	0
DB Server	0	0		0	0	1
Host 1	0	1	0		0	1
Host 2	0	1	0	0		1
Host 3	0	0	1	1	1	

Information of known vulnerabilities in this network is shown in Table 4.

Figure 2 shows the initial attack graph generated based on the above information. Squares boxes indicate attacker's privilege on controlled host, while oval boxes the vulnerabilities which could be exploited. Edges pointed to oval box from squares box means that the privilege is a precondition of the vulnerability, and the opposite edges means that the privilege is a postcondition of the vulnerability. Initially, attacker is in network location. After the firewall compromised, if attacker attacks host 2, only local privilege of host 2 can be obtained, and no other attacks can be further launched. If firstly attacks host 1, attacker can successively obtain root privilege of host 1, host 3, and database server, and finally get sensitive information from database server.

Table 4. Information of known vulnerabilities

Location	CVE ID	CVSS Score	Attack Complexity	Impact
Firewall	CVE-2018-0101	10.0	10.0	10.0
Host 1	CVE-2017-0290	9.3	8.6	10.0
Host 2	CVE-2014-3566	4.3	8.6	2.9
Host 3	CVE-2013-4782	10.0	10.0	10.0
DB server	CVE-2017-8464	9.3	8.6	10.0

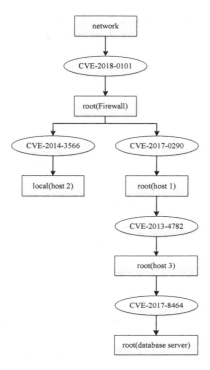

Fig. 2. Initial attack graph

By the proposed algorithm in Sect. 2.2 with the initial attack graph as input, the zero-day attack graph is generated and shown in Fig. 3.

Comparing the zero-day attack graph with the initial attack graph, there are two potential zero-day vulnerabilities v_1^0 and v_2^0 on host 2. *Root (host 2)* is root privilege of host 2 that attacker can't obtain by exploiting known vulnerability but only by v_1^0 or v_2^0. Without exploiting v_1^0 or v_2^0, attacker can only obtain local privilege of host 2, and could not exploit CVE-2013-4782 to attack host 3. With the help of v_1^0 or v_2^0, attacker can obtain root privilege of host 2, and further exploit CVE-2013-4782 to attack host 3. Assume that attacker's target is root privilege of database server. In the initial attack graph, attacker has only one attack path, namely CVE-2018-0101 → CVE-2017-0290 → CVE-2013-4782 → CVE-2017-8464. Set this path as path 1. After introducing zero-day vulnerabilities, attacker has two new attack paths to choose. Set attack path CVE-2018-0101 → CVE-2014-3566 → v01 → CVE-2013-4782 → CVE-2017-8464 as path 2, and another path CVE-2018-0101 → v02 → CVE-2013-4782 → CVE-2017-8464 as path 3. In the zero-day attack graph, *pre(v_1^0)* is *local (host 2)*, and *post(v_1^0)* is *root (host 2)*. *pre(v_2^0)* is *root(firewall)* (the same as *non (host 2)*), and *post (v_2^0)* is *root (host 2)*. According to Sect. 2.2, v_1^0 conforms to case (6). Its attack complexity level is medium, while attack complexity score 8, and impact score 7. v_2^0 conforms to (3), whose attack complexity level low, while attack complexity score 10, and impact score

10. Set the firewall weight to 1, hosts weight to 1, and database server weight to 2. The calculating results of security metrics for three paths are provided in Table 5.

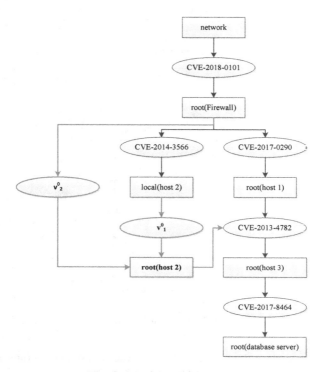

Fig. 3. Zero-day attack graph

Table 5. Zero-day attack graph security metric

Security metric	Path 1	Path 2	Path 3
k-Zero Day Safety	x	1	1
Minimum Zero-day vulnerabilities attack path length	4	5	4
Exploitability of Zero-day Attack Path	0.7396	0.5917	0.8600
Risk of Zero-day Attack Path	50.0	49.9	50.0

In Table 5, by the introduction of zero-day vulnerability v_1^0, length of path 2 is greater than path 1, and exploitability and risk are smaller. It is concluded that the introduction of v_1^0 does not significantly improve security risk of the network, and there is no need for targeted defense against v_1^0.

By the introduction of zero-day vulnerability v_2^0, length of path 3 is the same as that of path 1, while exploitability greater and risk the same as path 1. It is concluded that the introduction of v_2^0 improves exploitability of the attack path under the premise of changeless length and risk. Targeted defense against v_2^0 is required.

According to the security metrics proposed in Sect. 2.1, when the preset values of security metrics meet the following four requirements simultaneously, the network is secure, otherwise it is unsafe:

(1) Minimum number of zero-day vulnerabilities required to reach the target is less than 1;
(2) Minimum zero-day vulnerabilities attack path length is less than 4;
(3) Exploitability of zero-day attack path is greater than 0.8600;
(4) Risk of zero-day attack path is greater than 50.0.

4 Conclusion

Zero-day vulnerability is one of the most concerned security threats for both attacker and defender. Even if reliable defense mechanisms are adopted in network, it is difficult for defender to completely prevent zero-day attacks or minimize the damage when zero-day attack actually occurs due to the lack of sufficient information. Therefore, designing novel security metrics and assessing risk of potential zero-day vulnerability has become one of the key issues in recent years in network security field.

In this paper we design security metrics based on attack graph for risk assessment of zero-day vulnerability and zero-day attack path analysis. A zero-day vulnerability discovery and zero-day attack graph generation algorithm is proposed. Attack complexity and impact of zero-day vulnerability in various contexts are analyzed, to quantize risk of zero-day vulnerability.

Compared with two kinds of previous zero-day vulnerability risk assessment methods introduced in Sect. 1, our method implements risk assessment of single zero-day vulnerability and attack path analysis. Since it is a pre-assessment before attack occurs, the analytical efficiency issue faced by real-time analysis methods could be ignored. Experimental results demonstrate the feasibility and effectiveness of our method in practice.

Preset values should be set for all presented security metrics. Zero-day vulnerability risk assessment results reflect the security of target network under the preset conditions. Therefore, network security is determined by preset metric values and risk assessment result. For the same assessment result, if the preset values are changed, network security may be changed together with the modification of preset metric values. For networks with higher security level, lower preset values should be set, otherwise higher.

In future work, we will introduce more variables beneficial to zero-day vulnerability risk assessment to further improve accuracy.

References

1. Wang, L., Jajodla, S., Singhal, A., et al.: k-zero day safety: measuring the security risk of networks against unknown attacks. Lect. Notes Comput. Sci. **11**(1), 573–587 (2010)
2. Wang, L., Jajodla, S., Singhal, A., et al.: K-zero day safety: a network security metric for measuring the risk of unknown vulnerabilities. IEEE Trans. Depend. Secur. Comput. **11**(1), 30–44 (2014)
3. Wang, L., Zhang, M., Jajodia, S., Singhal, A., Albanese, M.: Modeling network diversity for evaluating the robustness of networks against zero-day attacks. In: Kutyłowski, M., Vaidya, J. (eds.) ESORICS 2014. LNCS, vol. 8713, pp. 494–511. Springer, Cham (2014). https://doi.org/10.1007/978-3-319-11212-1_28
4. Zhang, M., Wang, L., Jajodia, S., et al.: Network diversity: a security metric for evaluating the resilience of networks against zero-day attacks. IEEE Trans. Inf. Forensics Secur. **11**(5), 1071–1086 (2016)
5. Albanese, M., Jajodia, S., et al.: An efficient approach to assessing the risk of zero-day vulnerabilities. In: International Conference on Security and Cryptography, pp. 1–12. IEEE, Iceland (2013)
6. Yang, Y., et al.: An augmented 0-day attack graph generation method. DEStech Trans. Comput. Sci. Eng. (aice-ncs) (2016)
7. Dai, J., Sun, X., Liu, P.: Patrol: revealing zero-day attack paths through network-wide system object dependencies. In: Crampton, J., Jajodia, S., Mayes, K. (eds) ESORICS 2013. LNCS, vol. 8134, pp. 536–555. Springer, Heidelberg (2013). https://doi.org/10.1007/978-3-642-40203-6_30
8. Sun, X., Dai, J., Liu, P., Singhal, A., Yen, J.: Towards probabilistic identification of zero-day attack paths. In: Communications and Network Security, pp. 64–72. IEEE (2016)
9. Sun, X., Dai, J., Liu, P., Singhal, A.: Using Bayesian networks for probabilistic identification of zero-day attack paths. IEEE Trans. Inf. Forensics Secur. **13**(10), 2506–2521 (2018)
10. Joshi, C., et al.: An enhanced framework for identification and risks assessment of zero-day vulnerabilities. Int. J. Appl. Eng. Res. **13**(12), 10861–10870 (2018)
11. Ye, Z., Guo, Y., et al.: Survey on application of attack graph technology. J. Commun. **38**(11), 121–132 (2017)
12. National Vulnerability Database. https://web.nvd.nist.gov. Accessed 10 Nov 2018
13. Chen, L., Yang, C., Liu, F., Gong, D., Ding, S.: Automatic mining of security-sensitive functions from source code. CMC: Comput. Mater. Continua **56**(2), 199–210 (2018)
14. Hong, J., Kim, D., Chung, C.: A survey on the usability and practical applications of graphical security models. Comput. Sci. Rev. **26**, 1–16 (2017)
15. Zhang, H., Yi, Y., Wang, J., et al.: Network security situation awareness framework based on threat intelligence. CMC: Comput. Mater. Continua **56**(3), 381–399 (2018)
16. Wang, L., Sushil, J., Anoop, S.: Network Security Metric. Springer, Switzerland (2017)
17. Common vulnerability scoring system. http://www.First.org/cvss. Accessed 10 Nov 2018

Research on Content Extraction of Rich Text Web Pages

Hangfeng Yang, Hui Lu$^{(\boxtimes)}$, Shudong Li, Mohan Li, and Yanbin Sun

Cyberspace Institute of Advance Technology, Guangzhou University,
Guangzhou 510006, China
luhui@gzhu.edu.cn

Abstract. Obtaining effective information from Web pages has become a hot topic in the Internet data processing industry. Based on this, this paper studies the extraction of rich text Web pages. First, this paper designs a method to extract rich text page titles and release times. After a large number of data sets statistics, it is found that almost all the body titles are in the title tag, so a tag-based regular matching algorithm is designed. By writing the code to test the algorithm, the average extraction accuracy is more than 80%. For the extraction of release time, a common regular expression is used to match the full text of a web page and filter according to the position difference of each timestamp in the web page. Set the rule to filter the first occurrence of the timestamp is the release time. Test the algorithm, and the average extraction accuracy of the local data set is over 75%. Secondly, this paper designs a method to extract the text of rich text web pages. On the basis of the training data set, the logical regression model, random forest model and support vector machine model were respectively trained through the cross validation of ten folds. Model fusion was performed on the three models to identify the class tag of the body. Again tested on the test data set, the experimental results show that the average accuracy is 95.6%, the recall rate index was 0.948, 0.923, f1 to further determine the web page text in class labels can be 100% extraction. Finally, this paper evaluates the proposed algorithm and proposes corresponding improvements.

Keywords: Row block distribution function · Tag path feature system · Model fusion

1 Research Background

Getting effective information from Web pages has become one of the key issues in the Internet data processing industry. With the continuous development of science and technology, computer network has become popular, its scale is getting larger and larger, the behavior of network users is becoming more and more complex, and the network data is also growing exponentially. The network information is more and more abundant, and the text information of the network is also growing. Obtaining text information from the Web has become the main channel for people to obtain information. However, in the massive information contained in Web pages, the frequently used means such as search engines can not quickly and massively extract text information, nor can they find effective content through the original text information.

© Springer Nature Switzerland AG 2019
X. Sun et al. (Eds.): ICAIS 2019, LNCS 11635, pp. 279–287, 2019.
https://doi.org/10.1007/978-3-030-24268-8_26

Therefore, we need to study the extraction and mining methods of Web text information. In order to carry out this research, we need to understand some web page extraction technologies, and promote the use of rich-text web content extraction technology to promote its development.

2 Research Purpose and Significance

The main purpose of this paper is to obtain the text content contained in HTML of any web page type, and design an intelligent algorithm to extract the title, publishing time and text information of the page, and store the extracted data.

Massive data generated by Internet contains a lot of information, which has become an important source of data for governments and enterprises. Through the Internet, we can quickly obtain a large amount of public web page data, and analyze and mine these data, from which we can extract valuable information. Help and guide us in business decision making, public opinion analysis, social investigation and policy formulation. However, most web data is presented in semi-structured data format, and the information we need is often overwhelmed by a large number of "noise" data, such as advertisements, icons and links. How to extract information from web pages effectively is always a thorny problem in the Internet data extraction industry.

3 Research Status at Home and Abroad

As an important form of information transmission, the Internet is mainly transmitted in the form of text. In essence, the classification of Internet web pages belongs to the category of text classification. To sum up, in recent years, the development of automatic text classification can be roughly divided into three processes: feasibility study of automatic text classification method, automatic classification based on expert system and automatic classification using relevant machine learning algorithm. The original text classification relies on manual processing, which requires the staff involved in text classification to have a good understanding and grasp of knowledge in various fields. In addition, the manual classification method has low feasibility, high early investment, and is not suitable for text classification scenarios of big data attributes.

Compared with foreign countries, domestic research on text classification methods started relatively late. Professor hou hanqing started at the beginning of the 21st century. In recent years, with the development of computer and Internet technologies, more and more high requirements have been placed on the automatic text classification technology. The automatic text classification technology has attracted more and more attention from people and attracted the attention of ARS and relevant researchers.

Nowadays, researchers usually use vector space in mathematical concepts to describe text vectors. However, if the word frequency statistics method and word segmentation algorithm are directly used to obtain the various dimensions of text feature vectors to represent the text, then the vector dimension will be very large. Text vectors without pre-processing will not only bring huge computational cost to the subsequent analysis and extraction work, but also the efficiency of the whole process is usually very low. In most cases, it will damage the accuracy of text classification and relevant clustering algorithm, so it is difficult to get satisfactory results. To sum up, on the basis of ensuring the significance of the original article, it is necessary to further screen the text vectors to find the most representative text features within the range of text features. In order to solve this series of possible problems, the most effective and direct method is to reduce the dimension of text vector by feature selection algorithm.

4 Design and Implementation of Algorithm

For the extraction of rich text web pages, the algorithm is designed from the aspects of title, publishing time and text. The following three modules are used to design the algorithm respectively. By comparing the form of local data set and online source code of web pages, it is found that the title is basically fixed in the content labeled with title, so only regular matching pattern needs to be constructed to extract the title content (Fig. 1).

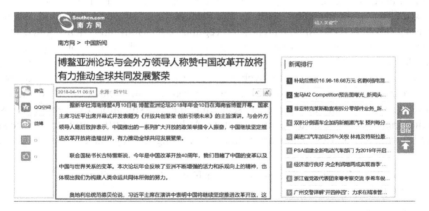

Fig. 1. A screenshot of a web page of the southern network (Color figure online)

The algorithm designed in this paper needs to extract the title in the red box, the release time in the green box, the text in the purple box and other information, and eliminate the noise number in the yellow box.

4.1 Data Preprocessing

The original data of nearly 1600 webpages from 12 websites such as Beiqing, China and Tencent are captured by web crawler technology as shown in Table 1.

Table 1. List of sample data collected by websites

Site	Pagenum	Site	Pagenum	Site	Pagenum
Beiqing	100	Tencent	136	Renming	104
China	115	Xinhua	184	Qianlong	107
Dazhong	150	Yaowen	143	Wangxin	101
Guangming	160	Zhengyi	120	Shijie	111

In a way the text information extraction system in order to ensure the quality of text information extraction and extraction efficiency, should be depending on the type of web page when collecting information using different extraction methods, using machine learning method of dynamic extraction contains pictures of web page for the most part, common web page, the use of the line judge block distribution function method. In conclusion, it can be found that before extracting relevant text information, the original rich text web pages should be classified according to the purpose of text extraction, and the data processing of rich text web pages should be completed by using the pre-processing algorithm system designed previously. Algorithm of web page code due to block the distribution function of the description of the structure itself is not sensitive, because the line algorithm for rich text page title block distribution function, the extraction of information such as the release time effect is not good, so it is necessary through the design matches the regular expression, and then applied to the extraction after pretreatment module of web page text, so the corresponding page text title, release time and other information can be extracted easily. After the extraction, the information such as the title of the web page, the time of publication, and the record of the corresponding web page row block are stored and then transmitted to the next algorithm module. So far, it can be seen that the classification of web pages is a function included in the data cleaning module. At last, the text title, publishing time and other information of web pages are extracted by using the regular expression model.

4.2 Algorithm Implementation Based on Row Block Distribution Function

Define 1 [5] **(Block text vector).** Based on the line number in the preprocessed text vector, we take the K lines around it, which together are called a block text vector;

Define 2 [5] **(Row length).** The source code of rich text web pages and the total number of text characters after deleting all irrelevant modifiers contained in each line of code text are called line block length;

Define 3 [5] **(Row block distribution function).** The row number of block text vector is x axis, and its row block length is Y axis distribution function;

According to the above definition of the line block distribution function, we can see that the correct text area should all be a region with the maximum value and continuous existence in the distribution function Fig. 2, which often contains a line number as a fast rising point and a line number as a fast descending point.

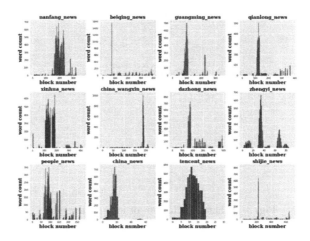

Fig. 2. Row block distribution function diagram

Therefore, the problem of text extraction from rich text web pages is transformed into the line numbers of two boundary points: the fast ascending point and the fast descending point on the line block distribution function. The line block vector range of these two boundary points contains the text area of the current rich text web pages.

4.3 Extracting Web Page Text Based on Machine Learning Algorithm

The label path scoring algorithm can be used to screen out all nodes that contain body content. Because of the objective existence of noise data, the extraction of the text problem is transformed into the classification of the text and noise data from the set containing the text data and noise data, and this is a typical dichotomous problem.

So we extract the characteristics of three kinds of strong classAttrCount amount (class label attribute), wordCount (Chinese characters) under the class label, punctuationCount punctuation (number) to construct the local data sets, through this training, build three supervised machine learning model logic regression model, support vector machine (SVM) model and random forest model, the last of the three model fusion model and use the final fusion model to predict the tag data is the data under the posts or noise.

Logical regression model, random forest model and support vector machine model are trained in local data sets, and then an integration model is trained by model fusion technology. The schematic diagram of the integration model is shown in Fig. 3.

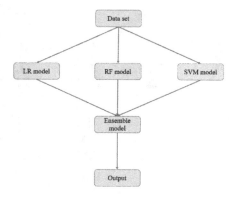

Fig. 3. Schematic diagram of integrated model

The final tag value is predicted through the integrated model, and the prediction results are shown in Table 2.

Table 2. Integrated model prediction results

Count	Accuracy	Recall score	f1 score
1	0.956	0.923	0.941
2	0.955	0.923	0940
3	0.954	0.922	0.939
4	0.955	0.923	0.941
5	0.957	0.924	0.943

5 Result Analysis of Algorithm

The row block distribution function algorithm extracts the text contents of the rich text web page as shown in Fig. 4.

The experimental results of Fig. 4 show that the extraction accuracy of static web pages, such as Beiqing, Qianlong and Yaowen, is higher than 90%, and the content extraction of rich text web pages is more complete, but the dynamic web pages such as Xinhua, Mass Net and Justice Web are more complete. The accuracy of web page extraction is over 80%. The reason for the failure of extracting text is that different website design styles are different, and different front-end designers have different design artists for web pages.

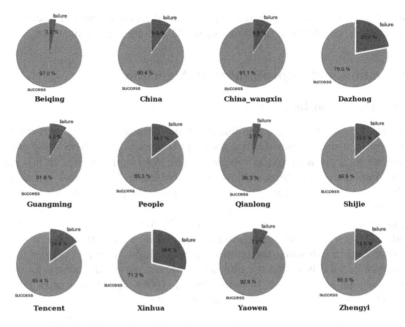

Fig. 4. The results of the relevant website page text extraction

6   Result Analysis Based on Machine Learning Algorithm

Logical regression model, support vector machine model, random forest model and integration model are trained in the training set. The prediction results of the label values of the text are shown in Table 3.

Table 3. Comparison between machine learning algorithms

Model	Accuracy	Recall score	f1 score
LR model	0.823	0.522	0.638
SVM model	0.904	0.914	0.877
RF model	0.941	0.912	0.909
Ensemble model	0.956	0.923	0.948

The results of Table 3 show that the predictive effect of logistic regression model is the worst among the single models, with the average accuracy of 82.3%, recall rate of 0.522 and F1 index of 0.638; the predictive effect of support vector machine model is the second, with the average accuracy of 90.4%, recall rate of 0.914 and F1 index of 0.877; and random forest model is the second. The prediction accuracy is the best, the average accuracy rate is 94.1%, the recall rate is 0.923, and the F1 index is 0.948. Through the fusion of logistic regression model, support vector machine model and

Stochastic Forest model, the integrated model has the best prediction effect, with an average accuracy of 95.6%, a recall rate of 0.923 and a F1 index of 0.948.

7   Evaluation and Improvement of Algorithm

7.1   Advantages and Disadvantages of the Algorithm

The series of algorithms designed in this paper not only have a good extraction effect on news web content, but also have a good extraction effect on BBS, blog and other communication media with text as the media. The algorithm designed in this paper is simple to implement, the time complexity is polynomial time, and it has natural portability for enterprise integration. It can be used for government departments to supervise online public opinion, and it can also be used for business. For example, text mining is carried out in BBS of a certain commodity to analyze the sales volume, word of mouth and other valuable information for improving corporate profits.

However, when extracting the content of webpage body title, a regular matching algorithm can be used based on the title tag. However, part of the content of webpage body title does not necessarily exist in the title tag. If this algorithm is used, the correct title content cannot be extracted. When the content of the body of the web page is small enough, or even when there is no noise data, the body extracted by the row and column distribution function algorithm will be replaced by noise data, so the body cannot be recognized, leading to the failure of the body content extraction.

7.2   Algorithm Improvement

Since this algorithm depends on the size of training data samples, the larger the sample size of training data, the better the extraction effect. Due to time reasons, this algorithm does not have enough time for training in sufficient quantity of data, therefore, in the later time and the amount of data under the condition of enough, can train every site corresponding to the high accuracy of the model, for each site one-to-one model is set up, with the increasing of the amount of data and time, can extract the sites and ideally should be increasing accuracy. Ideally, all sites would be 95% or more accurate.

Acknowledgment. The authors would like to thank the anonymous reviewers for their helpful comments for improving this paper. This work is supported by the National Natural Science Foundation of China under grant (No. 61572153, 61672020, U1803263, 61871140, 61872100) and the National key research and development plan under Grant No. 2018YFB0803504.

References

1. Hang, L.: Statistical Learning Method. Tsinghua University Press, Beijing (2012)
2. Jiazhen, C., Yan, G., Qiang, L., et al.: An automatic text extraction method for short text web pages. Chin. J. Inf. Sci. **30**(1), 8–15 (2016)
3. Qi, W., Shiwei, T., Dongqing, Y., et al.: Automatic extraction of Web topic information based on DOM. Comput. Res. Dev. **41**(10), 1786–1791 (2004)

4. Wenli, L., Lechao, W., Chunlei, S.: Research on document information extraction method based on HTML tree and template. Comput. Appl. Res. **27**(12), 4615–4617 (2010)
5. Xin, C.: General Web Page Text Extraction Based on Line Block Distribution Function. Information Retrieval Research Center of Harbin University of Technology. http://code.google.com/p/cx-extractor/
6. Ronglum, L.: Text Classification and Related Research. Fudan University, Shanghai (2005)
7. Zhao, C., Dongmei, Z.: Web information extraction technology overview. Comput. Appl. Res. **27**(12), 4401–4405 (2010)
8. Wenbei, H., Jing, Y., Junzhong, G.: Research on the algorithm of extracting body information of web pages based on block. Comput. Appl. **27**(s1), 24–26 (2007)
9. Xin, H., Zhipeng, X.: Similarity measurement of web page structure based on simple tree matching algorithms. Comput. Res. Dev. **44**(z3), 1–6 (2007)
10. Gongqing, W., Jun, H., Li, L.L., et al.: Online web news content extraction based on label path feature fusion. J. Softw. **27**(3), 714–735 (2016)
11. Wu, G.Q., Hu, J., Li, L., Xu, Z.H., Liu, P.C., Hu, X.G., Wu, X.D.: Online Web news extraction via tag path feature fusion. Ruan Jian Xue Bao/J. Softw. **27**(3), 714–735 (2016)
12. Cowie, J., Lehnert, W.: Information extraction. Commun. ACM **39**(1), 80–91 (1996)
13. Han, W., Tian, Z., Huang, Z., Li, S., Jia, Y.: Bidirectional self-adaptive resampling in imbalanced big data learning. Multimed. Tools Appl. (2018). https://doi.org/10.1007/s11042-018-6938-9
14. Qiu, J., Chai, Y., Liu, Y., ZhaoQuan, G., Li, S., Tian, Z.: Automatic non-taxonomic relation extraction from big data in smart city. IEEE Access **6**, 74854–74864 (2018). https://doi.org/10.1109/ACCESS.2018.2881422
15. Wu, C., Zapevalova, E., Chen, Y., Zeng, D., Liu, F.: Optimal model of continuous knowledge transfer in the big data environment. CMES: Comput. Model. Eng. Sci. **116**(1), 89–107 (2018)
16. Meng, R., Cui, Q., Yuan, C.: A survey of image information hiding algorithms based on deep learning. CMES: Comput. Model. Eng. Sci. **117**(3), 425–454 (2018)

Network Protocol Analysis Base on WeChat PC Version

Weixiang Chen, Hui Lu$^{(\boxtimes)}$, Mohan Li, and Yanbin Sun

Cyberspace Institute of Advance Technology, Guangzhou University,
Guangzhou 510006, China
luhui@gzhu.edu.cn

Abstract. IM (Instant Messaging), also known as real-time communication, is a real-time communication system that allows people to use the network to communicate text messages, files, voice and video in real time. With the sustainable development of informatization construction at home and abroad, IM has also become a theme in the development of Internet informatization. In China, Tencent QQ, WeChat, Fetion, Aliwangwang and other IMs are used more and more widely, which occupy a large number of markets. The share of WeChat stands out in the highly competitive IM market and is gradually becoming the infrastructure of the entire mobile Internet. This paper briefly analyzes the security issues and attack conjectures by analyzing WeChat's login protocol and the important parameters of the packet transmission in the protocol.

Keywords: Network protocol · WeChat · Login protocol

1 Research Background and Significance of the Project

WeChat started from the first quarter of 2012 with only about 59 million monthly active users. With the continuous advancement of China Mobile Internet, WeChat's active account has maintained steady growth. At the end of 2014–2017, the number of monthly active users of WeChat respectively It has reached 500 million, 697 million, 889 million and 989 million, and the overall user growth of WeChat with mobile Internet users has slowed down since the second quarter of 2017. The year-on-year growth rate in 2017 was 23% and 19.5% respectively. 15.8% and 11.2%. According to the first quarter earnings report released by Tencent in 2018, the first quarter of 2018, WeChat and WeChat combined monthly active accounts reached 1.04 billion, a year-on-year growth rate of 10.9%. WeChat became China's first month active users with more than 1 billion products. In the process of replacing the PC Internet with the largest number of users in the country, WeChat has become a new traffic hub and center in the process of replacing the Internet with the mobile Internet [1].

At the same time, the widespread use of IM software such as WeChat has aroused public concern about IM security issues. Based on the purpose of network information security, the analysis of communication protocols will play a positive role in maintaining network security. Communication protocol, which is a kind of mutually acceptable rule that different devices follow when completing information exchange and resource sharing through communication channels, is the principle that all

© Springer Nature Switzerland AG 2019
X. Sun et al. (Eds.): ICAIS 2019, LNCS 11635, pp. 288–297, 2019.
https://doi.org/10.1007/978-3-030-24268-8_27

communication parties follow in communication engineering and whole service engineering. It includes applications for data unit formats, various information that information units should contain, timing of information acceptance and transmission, and connection methods (Fig. 1).

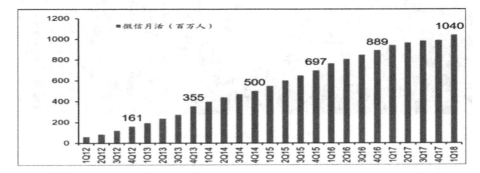

Fig. 1. Development process of WeChat monthly active users

However, the mainstream IM software on the market currently follows different communication protocols, and since the instant communication software companies have their own interests, they have always maintained a conservative and confidential attitude towards their respective protocol formats and related communication technologies. The inconsistency and non-disclosure have caused constraints and obstacles to the maintenance of network security by network security personnel and related departments [2]. Therefore, the relevant analysis of the communication protocol of IM software is of great significance.

By studying relevant literatures on the Internet and published, we find that there are few specific studies and analysis on WeChat communication protocols, and there are very few studies on information security and communication encryption modes in the login process and communication interaction process. WeChat's domestic influence and the number of users and the importance of communication protocols for network communication security, we believe that WeChat's communication protocol has great research potential [3].

2 Research Status and Trends

In the CSDN blog, a blogger uses HTTPAnalyzer to analyze the http/https protocol of WeChat. The blogger captures the authentication process of the WeChat scan code login on the webpage, and carries it in the data packet transmitted in each step. Key information is extracted and analyzed. The process of interacting between the client and the server when logging into the web version of WeChat is given. And use the program to implement WeChat WEB client that supports the function of getting friends list and sending and receiving messages (Fig. 2).

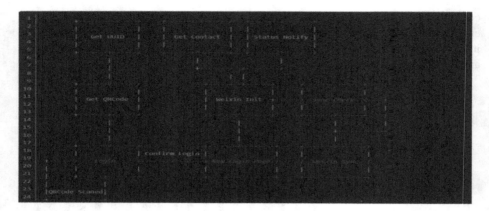

Fig. 2. Packet information

In the paper "WeChat interaction protocol and encryption mode research" by Wan Yuanchun et al., the Wireshark tool was used to analyze the login process of WeChat Android 4.5 and the data packet format for data interaction. Then, through reverse analysis and debugging technology, it was analyzed. The encryption mode of WeChat is comprehensively analyzed [4]. The security of WeChat encryption mode is analyzed from the aspects of encryption protocol, encryption algorithm and pseudo-random number used by WeChat. Finally, the insufficiency of WeChat AES session key is pointed out, and an improved method is proposed [5].

In the "WeChat Protocol Simple Research Notes", the author mainly analyzes the WeChat transmission protocol, and gives the process when WeChat acquires new data: 1. Server-side notification, client acquisition. 2. The client carries the latest SyncKey and initiates a data request. 3. The server generates the latest SyncKey along with the latest data and sends it to the client. 4. Based on the version number mechanism synchronization protocol, it can ensure data incremental and orderly transmission. 5. SyncKey, generated by the server serial number generator, will generate the latest SyncKey once a new message is generated. Similar to the version number. The server side notification has a status update, and the client actively obtains it since the last update. The author uses the Firefox + Firebug combination debugging method to analyze the data packets generated in the communication, and also confirms that WeChat roughly obtains new data by exchanging SyncKey [6].

The two ideas for WeChat login are similar to the method we selected. By extracting the data stream generated when the scan code is applied to the webpage, we extract the key information and analyze the authentication protocol of WeChat. The main reason is that WeChat as a commercial software does not encrypt the key information in the data packet when the data stream is transmitted, which also provides the possibility to analyze the authentication protocol by grabbing the data packet through the packet capture software. The difference is the object of analysis. Although the analysis is on WeChat, the operation to be performed when logging in to the WEB client and Android is different. When logging in to the WEB client, the server needs to return a QR code to the client. However, when the Android side logs in for the first time, it is necessary to enter the account password, so the login authentication protocol is also different. WeChat does not encrypt the key information in the transmitted data packet, which poses a great security risk. Future trends should focus on ensuring that critical information in the packet is not intercepted by the attacker, preventing the attacker from stealing the user's data.

3 Protocol Process Base on WeChat

For this experiment, the packet capture is performed by wireshark, but in order to combine the important parameters in the analysis protocol, the burst analysis is performed using the burst suit.

For a WeChat login on the web side, the usual process is to log in to the wx.qq.com website, and then log in through the mobile phone to log in. In this process, protocol interaction and important data transmission and exchange must be carried out. In this process, we first compare the two packets (one is the first time we access the WeChat web version of the interface, the other is the WeChat login successfully, the data packet when the data is initialized) to see the landing WeChat What kind of information is needed (Figs. 3 and 4).

```
POST /cgi-bin/mmwebwx-bin/webwxstatreport?fun=new&lang=zh_CN HTTP/1.1
Host: wx.qq.com
Connection: close
Content-Length: 1046
Accept: application/json, text/plain, */*
Origin: https://wx.qq.com
User-Agent: Mozilla/5.0 (Windows NT 6.1; WOW64) AppleWebKit/537.36 (KHTML, like Gecko) 37abc/2.0.4.4 Chrome/60.0.3112.113 Safari/537.36
Content-Type: application/json;charset=UTF-8
DNT: 1
Referer: https://wx.qq.com/?&lang=zh_CN
Accept-Language: zh-CN,zh;q=0.8
Cookie: RK=tYpkrwDRVb; o_cookie=825457110; pgv_pvi=8230618112; pgv_pvid=8791401760; ptcz=9b1c35dc3e03303af3fd30e9a2d78adee69dc8e54db72f6ba05b332c9e6f504a;
pt2gguin=o2268679265; mm_lang=zh_CN; MM_WX_NOTIFY_STATE=1; MM_WX_SOUND_STATE=1

{"BaseRequest":{"Uin":"","Sid":"","DeviceID":"e234080797257064"},"Count":2,"List":[{"Type":1,"Text":"{\"type\":\"[app-runtime]\",\"data\":{\"unload\":{\"listenerCount
\":117,\"watchersCount\":115,\"scopesCount\":30}}}"},{"Type":1,"Text":"{\"type\":\"[app-timing]\",\"data\":{\"appTiming\":{\"qrcodeStart\":1539331727444,\"qrcodeEnd\"
:1539331727709},\"pageTiming\":{\"navigationStart\":1539331726137,\"unloadEventStart\":1539331726462,\"unloadEventEnd\":1539331726468,\"redirectStart\":0,\"redirectEn
d\":0,\"fetchStart\":1539331726137,\"domainLookupStart\":1539331726162,\"domainLookupEnd\":1539331726220,\"connectStart\":1539331726220,\"connectEnd\":1539331726346,\
"secureConnectionStart\":1539331726252,\"requestStart\":1539331726347,\"responseStart\":1539331726457,\"responseEnd\":1539331726460,\"domLoading\":1539331726404,\"dom
Interactive\":1539331727278,\"domContentLoadedEventStart\":1539331727279,\"domContentLoadedEventEnd\":1539331727281,\"domComplete\":1539331727436,\"loadEventStart\":1
539331727436,\"loadEventEnd\":1539331727438}}}"}]}
```

Fig. 3. Packets when accessing the web version for the first time.

```
POST /cgi-bin/mmwebwx-bin/webwxinit?r=-1737518722&lang=zh_CN&pass_ticket=ZSRkOD%252BOqTtuv?sQtT517TjMEXNvYqKGhHTyOvwaRBbH7tpoKck^QoIcr%252Byzh%252ByICE HTTP/1.1
Host: wx.qq.com
Connection: close
Content-Length: 149
Accept: application/json, text/plain, */*
Origin: https://wx.qq.com
User-Agent: Mozilla/5.0 (Windows NT 6.1; WOW64) AppleWebKit/537.36 (KHTML, like Gecko) 37abc/2.0.4.4 Chrome/60.0.3112.113 Safari/537.36
Content-Type: application/json;charset=UTF-8
DNT: 1
Referer: https://wx.qq.com/?&lang=zh_CN
Accept-Language: zh-CN,zh;q=0.8
Cookie: RK=tYpkrwDRVb; o_cookie=825457110; pgv_pvi=8230618112; pgv_pvid=8791401760; ptcz=9b1c35dc3e03303af3fd30e9a2d78adee69dc8e54db72f6ba05b332c9e6f504a;
pt2gguin=o2268679265; ptui_loginuin=825457110; webwxuvid=c45b2ae025c32e452e6c5be770c3417bb2bbci9bac31bd543d20d43483bd019291d5e9a02212a74b447a0e65ae04635;
wxpluginkey=1539333962; MM_WX_NOTIFY_STATE=1; MM_WX_SOUND_STATE=1; wxuin=2284756364; wxsid=rDfBMjBhc431DyIC; wxloadtime=1539335817; mm_lang=zh_CN;
webwx_data_ticket=g9d5Fzq2HFn54DJ2sRXd4DJ4;
webwx_auth_ticket=CImBEN+7jO4agAGi5tjObqEA+FgVi79PCZ5mBNLz806M/Viwzi4zBxOCiONBAEVFqW3UmqLh0Lbo60rv9GQbk+1rAGujXURkRS9Kui1h+pECB42CmbH4UDSqES9dxWLc1PzZfVpyYVNtbYOnHMmA
H8IruEp2841GHGtCtialfR3sb+zGJqUV11j2Dv==; login_frequency=1; last_wxuin=2284756364

{"BaseRequest":{"Uin":"2284756364","Sid":"rDfBMjBhc431DyIC","Skey":"@crypt_ae348239_09cbddae0972171b245fc56e3c7fe9d9","DeviceID":"e599843517721379"}}
```

Fig. 4. Packets when WeChat is initialized

By comparing the two packets above, we can see that four important data are required for login: uin, sid, skey, pass_ticket. These four values have different meanings. Uin contains the information of the logged in user. As long as the same account is logged in, the value will not be changed. sid is a security identifier, which is issued by the server to the user to uniquely identify the user. For the same account. The value is also fixed; skey: similar to WeChat password, the same value will not change for the same account; pass_ticket: can understand the temporary password for this login, the value is random and time-sensitive.

Through the above four values, we will log in to WeChat, but how to obtain these four values, then we will analyze the WeChat login protocol.

In the first step, for the first time the user logs in, that is, the user who logs in to wx. qq.com for the first time, the client sends a packet as shown in Fig. 6 to the server. There is a line parameter in the packet as "BaseRequest":("Uin":"","Sid":"","DeviceID":"e234080797257064"), we initially guess that Uin, Sid and DeviceID are the few required to log in to WeChat. The item parameter, DeviceID, is used to mark the identity of the machine used for logging in, but it is random (Fig. 5).

Fig. 5. The first login packet

In the second step, we will capture a packet returned by the server to the client. As shown in Fig. 6, the content of the packet is basically the same as the content of the first packet, which is used to confirm the relevant information.

Fig. 6. Packet returned by the server

In the third step, the client sends a packet to the server. As shown in Fig. 7, we can see the word "appid = wx782c26e4c19acffb" from the packet. We think that the appid is like the username that needs to be logged in.

```
GET /jalogin?appid=wx782c26e4c19acffb&redirect_uri=http%3A%2F%2Fwx.qq.com%2Fcgi-bin%2Fmmwebwx-bin%2Fwebwxnewloginpage&fun=new&lang=zh_CN&_=1539332018485 HTTP/1.1
Host: login.wx.qq.com
Connection: close
User-Agent: Mozilla/5.0 (Windows NT 6.1; WOW64) AppleWebKit/537.36 (KHTML, like Gecko) 37abc/2.0.4.4 Chrome/60.0.3112.113 Safari/537.36
Accept: */*
DNT: 1
Referer: https://wx.qq.com/?&lang=zh_CN
Accept-Language: zh-CN,zh;q=0.8
Cookie: RK=tYpkrwDRVb; o_cookie=825457110; pgv_pvi=8230618112; pgv_pvid=8791401760; ptcz=9b1c35dc3e03303af3fd30e9a2d78adee89dc0e54db72f6ba05b332c9e6f504a;
pt2gguin=o22d8679D265; ptui_loginuin=825457110; mm_lang=zh_CN
```

Fig. 7. The third step packet

In the fourth step, after receiving the GET request of the data packet in the third step, the server returns a data packet to the client, as shown in Fig. 8 where one parameter in the BaseRequest is "AaPjGBneCg", and the related data is consulted. We know that this parameter is uuid, which is the unique identifier that identifies this session. Each uuid corresponds to a QR code. Moreover, uuid is time-sensitive, that is, when the next step is not performed for a long time, the value will be invalid, and the corresponding QR code will also be invalid.

```
POST /cgi-bin/mmwebwx-bin/webwxstatreport?fun=new&lang=zh_CN HTTP/1.1
Host: wx.qq.com
Connection: close
Content-Length: 235
Accept: application/json, text/plain, */*
Origin: https://wx.qq.com
User-Agent: Mozilla/5.0 (Windows NT 6.1; WOW64) AppleWebKit/537.36 (KHTML, like Gecko) 37abc/2.0.4.4 Chrome/60.0.3112.113 Safari/537.36
Content-Type: application/json;charset=UTF-8
DNT: 1
Referer: https://wx.qq.com/?&lang=zh_CN
Accept-Language: zh-CN,zh;q=0.8
Cookie: RK=tYpkrwDRVb; o_cookie=825457110; pgv_pvi=8230618112; pgv_pvid=8791401760; ptcz=9b1c35dc3e03303af3fd30e9a2d78adee89dc0e54db72f6ba05b332c9e6f504a;
pt2gguin=o22d8679D265; ptui_loginuin=825457110; mm_lang=zh_CN; MM_WX_NOTIFY_STATE=1; MM_WX_SOUND_STATE=1

{"BaseRequest":{"Uin":"","Sid":"","DeviceID":"e798f1412d6983085"},"Count":1,"List":[{"Type":2,"Text":"{\"type\":\"[pic-error]\",\"data\":{\"text\":\"qrcode can not
load.\",\"src\":\"https://login.weixin.qq.com/qrcode/AaPjGBneCg=="}}"}]}
```

Fig. 8. The fourth step packet

In the fifth step, after receiving the data packet containing the uuid information, the client sends a GET request packet as shown in Fig. 9 to the server, and sends related information such as uuid and timestamp to the server, and then the server provides the server. QR code. At the same time, we found that the timestamp in the data packet is to ensure the timeliness and freshness of the QR code. If the code is not scanned for a long time, the client will resend a packet containing the new uuid, that is, repeat the fourth and five steps.

```
GET /cgi-bin/mmwebwx-bin/login?loginicon=true&uuid=AaPjGBvECg==&tip=1&r=-1733771298&_=1539332018486 HTTP/1.1
Host: login.wx.qq.com
Connection: close
User-Agent: Mozilla/5.0 (Windows NT 6.1; WOW64) AppleWebKit/537.36 (KHTML, like Gecko) 37abc/2.0.4.4 Chrome/60.0.3112.113 Safari/537.36
Accept: */*
DNT: 1
Referer: https://wx.qq.com/?&lang=zh_CN
Accept-Language: zh-CN,zh;q=0.8
Cookie: RK=tYpkrwDRVb; o_cookie=825457110; pgv_pvi=8230618112; pgv_pvid=8791401760; ptcz=9b1c35dc3e03303af3fd30e9a2d78adee89dc0e54db72f6ba05b332c9e6f504a;
pt2gguin=o22d8679D265; ptui_loginuin=825457110; mm_lang=zh_CN
```

Fig. 9. Step 5 Packet

In the sixth step, after we scan the code, click on the mobile phone to confirm the login. During this period, the client sends the data packet as shown in Fig. 10 to the server. The important parameter information is login icon = true & uuid = QzbmxPo8Gw == & tip = 0 & r = 1736220100 &_ = 153933449334493549. We found that when the packet is sent for the first time, the default value of the tip is 0. After every few seconds, the client will send the same data packet to the server to ask if the user has confirmed the login on the mobile terminal. Both are 1. If the phone does not confirm the login for too long, the server will terminate the session.

Fig. 10. Step 6 packet

In the seventh step, after clicking and confirming the login on the mobile terminal, the server returns a ticket value, and the client sends the ticket value together with the uuid to the server through the GET request packet as shown in Fig. 11.

Fig. 11. Seventh step packet

In the eighth step, after receiving the data packet in the seventh step, the server returns the data packet as shown in FIG. Analyze the information in the data packet, we can find five important parameters: pass_ticket, sid, uin, skey, webwx_auth_ticket, where pass_ticket, sid, uin, skey are the parameters used by the client and server to initialize and transfer information. Webwx_auth_ticket is used for comparison authentication with the encrypted result of the first four parameters and for secondary login during the period when the cookie has not expired. At this point, the login interaction process ends (Fig. 12).

Fig. 12. The eighth step packet

The above WeChat protocol login process can be summarized by the following flow hart.

For the above picture, after scanning the code on the webpage, it needs to be authenticated on the mobile phone. During the period, the client will send the data packet to confirm whether the mobile phone terminal has confirmed it. Situation: The first one is too long to scan the code. At this time, a packet with window.code = 408 will be sent to indicate that it has timed out and needs to be rescanned. The second one is to scan the code, but no confirmation. At this time, window.code = 201, but if the time limit is exceeded, it will still become the first case; the third is to confirm the login. At this time, window.code = 200, the server will confirm the account. The information is sent to the client for the next steps (Fig. 13).

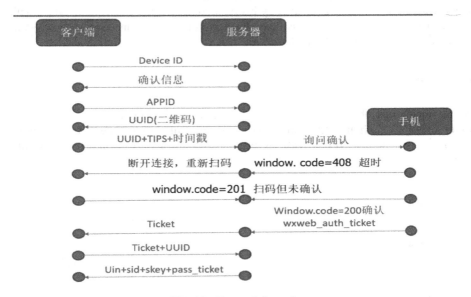

Fig. 13. Protocol flow chart

4   Analysis of Protocol Security

By analyzing the packets of the entire login process, we find that each packet has a timestamp, which is invalid when using a replay attack; and the values carrying important information are time-sensitive, such as uuid and pass_ticket are only in one segment. Time can be used, and it takes a new value to be retrieved after the time has elapsed, so the range that can be utilized if these values are stolen is small.

However, through many experiments, we found that after the successful login, if you quit the page and then visit the website in a short time, you will not need to scan the code to verify the login directly. This is what was said before. If the cookie of the above four logins is not invalid, the login can be directly logged in. According to this phenomenon, we try to input webwx_auth_ticket in the scan code interface, that is, record the data of uin, sid, skey, pass_ticket value, construct a data packet and send it to the server, and find that there is no need to scan the code successfully.

Does this mean that if the above value is leaked, it will be hacked by WeChat? After our analysis, it was found to be impossible. First of all, the timeliness of pass_ticket is very short. The successful login through the above method is also realized in a relatively short time from the last normal login. Secondly, for the device id at the beginning of the protocol, That is, to identify the value of the login machine, if the attacker wants to construct a data packet for malicious login, then how to set the value, use its own, or use the attacker's. No matter which one you use, an error occurs because it does not match. But the specific cause of the error, because the value is a random value, is still unclear. At present, our assumption is that all the values of the subsequent interactions, such as pass_ticket, contain information about the device id, so if the attacker uses the device id generated by his own computer, the subsequent values will be mismatched. Invalid. If you use the attacker, you will get an error because your computer has not generated this device id.

5   Work Outlook

As we mentioned above, the method of attacking eavesdropping, for example, the value of webwx_auth_ticket.but this is only a theory, still not implemented, so the next step is to use "itchat" API provide by wechat to build a web client with XSS vulnerability. To verify our guess

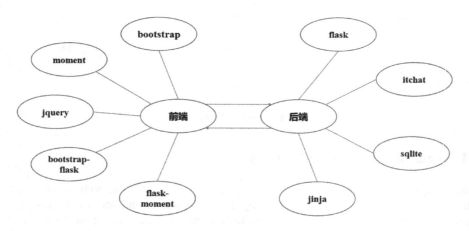

Fig. 14. Tool

The above Fig. 14 is the software and technology used by the client to implement the front-end and back-end. The front-end mainly uses bootstrap and jquery. The back-end uses flask for logic, sqlite for data, and itchat, which is WeChat. Provide a python-based library to complete the specific functions in WeChat. There is a message board section to steal cookies to verify our guess.

Acknowledgment. The authors would like to thank the anonymous reviewers for their helpful comments for improving this paper. This work is supported by the National Natural Science Foundation of China under grant (No. 61572153, No. 61871140, No. 61872100) and the National key research and development plan under Grant No. 2018YFB0803504.

References

1. https://wenku.baidu.com/view/ae65006a192e45361066f58e.html
2. Cheang, C.F., Wang, Y., Cai, Z., Xu, G.: Multi-VMs intrusion detection for cloud security using dempster-shafer theory. CMC: Comput. Mater. Continua **57**(2), 297–306 (2018)
3. Yang, W., et al.: A MPTCP scheduler for web transfer. CMC: Comput. Mater. Continua **57**(2), 205–222 (2018)
4. https://blog.csdn.net/avsuper/article/details/63678827
5. http://www.blogjava.net/yongboy/archive/2014/03/05/410636.html
6. Wan, Y., et al.: Research on WeChat interaction protocol and encryption mode. Microcomput. Appl. **31**(2), 31–34 (2015)

Bitcoin Network Size Estimation Based on Coupon Collection Model

Runnan Tan, Xiangyi Kong, Yu Zhang, Qingfeng Tan$^{(\boxtimes)}$, Hui Lu$^{(\boxtimes)}$, Mohan Li, and Yanbin Sun

Cyberspace Institute of Advance Technology, Guangzhou University,
Guangzhou 510006, China
{tqf528,luhui}@gzhu.edu.cn

Abstract. Bitcoin was originally proposed in 2009 and exists as a p2p digital currency that can be exchanged for currency in most countries and is uncontrollable. Moreover, the bitcoin network is unstable, so it is imperative to study the security of bitcoin, and estimating its network size is one of the basic and important links. Based on the coupon collector model, this paper uses active measurement to estimate the size of the Bitcoin network. Experiments show that the model can achieve an average coverage of 88%, so the model can be used to estimate the network size. At the end of the paper, the problems and improvement ideas of the model are put forward, and this is the direction and focus of future research.

Keywords: Bitcoin network · Estimation of network scale · Coupon collector problem

1 Introduction

Bitcoin is an important electronic and decentralized crypto currency system originally proposed by Satoshi Nakamoto [1] in 2009. Bitcoin adopts a P2P (peer-to-peer) network architecture based on the Internet. Each computer in the same network is equal to each other. Each node provides network services together, and there are no "special" nodes. And there are no servers, centralized services, or hierarchies in the P2P network. The nodes of the P2P network interact and cooperate with each other. Each node provides services to other nodes in the network while providing services externally.

For Bitcoin networks, if there is no data communication for the established connection, the node where it is located periodically sends a message to maintain the connection. If a node continues to have a connection for up to 90 min without any communication, it is considered to have been disconnected from the network and the network will begin to look for a new peer node. Therefore, the bitcoin network will be dynamically adjusted according to changing node and network problems at any time, and the organic adjustment of scale increase and decrease can be performed without centralization control. So bitcoin network scale estimation is a basic and important issue in calculating the dynamics of its network.

The bitcoin network is dynamic and unstable, and each node can go online or offline at any time, which causes trouble for the statistics of the current network size.

© Springer Nature Switzerland AG 2019
X. Sun et al. (Eds.): ICAIS 2019, LNCS 11635, pp. 298–307, 2019.
https://doi.org/10.1007/978-3-030-24268-8_28

This paper temporarily ignores this problem and assumes that no nodes are online or offline within a certain period of time. Therefore, this study can also analyze the number of bitcoin nodes in the network.

2   Related Work

The measurement research of the existing P2P system is generally divided into active measurement and passive measurement according to the measurement method. The passive measurement is mainly used to analyze the flow characteristics of the P2P system, such as the flow size, bandwidth and connection time. Active measurement is the ability to measure macroscopic features, such as topologies, by interacting with nodes. The purpose of this paper is to estimate the size of Bitcoin's network, so we use an active measurement approach.

For the study of P2P active measurement, Liu et al. [2] firstly used 8893 sub-clusters to obtain the required measurement data by continuously requesting the Tracker server. Each time the Tracker server is requested, the server will return several node information, and the current number of nodes in the cluster. They use the sum as the measurement result of the cluster size, but this method lacks the support of the theoretical model, and the result integrity is difficult to guarantee.

In recent years, Hobfeld [3] and Zhang have designed an active measurement model based on the coupon collector problem (CCP). According to the CCP model, for a BT cluster of n nodes, the expected $E(X_n^k)$ can be used to estimate the number of requests required. This model is supported by a theoretical model, so the integrity of the results is guaranteed.

Jia [4] has studied sampling collision based algorithms and sample distribution based algorithms, and proposed improvements to these two algorithms [5]. For the two scale estimation algorithms based on sampling theory, his improvement method is to randomly select x nodes by using the improved random walk strategy, and take all the neighbors of these nodes as random samples. Such algorithms are scalable and robust, and the improved algorithm can greatly reduce operating overhead.

The above methods provide theoretical basis and inspiration for this study. For the Bitcoin network, this paper proposes an active measurement model and estimation method based on the coupon collector problem to estimate the network scale.

3   Background

Bitcoin was originally proposed in 2009 and exists as a P2P digital currency that can be exchanged for currency in most countries and is uncontrollable. The blockchain was born from Bitcoin. Since the introduction of Bitcoin, there have been many digital currencies like Bitcoin, all based on public blockchains.

The Bitcoin network is based on a TCP connection and the 8333 is the default port. If a new Bitcoin node wants to join the Bitcoin network, it can be divided into two steps. The first step: obtaining a list of normal nodes in the current bitcoin network, that is, a list of seed nodes; and second step: communicating with other nodes in the bitcoin network according to the bitcoin protocol. The communication process between the Bitcoin nodes [6] can also be divided into two steps. The first step the handshake process (as shown in Fig. 1), the nodes exchange version information and complete the verification. Step 2: After the handshake is completed, in order to obtain the active node information around the other node, the getaddr message can be sent to the other node to obtain the active nodes around it, as shown in Fig. 2.

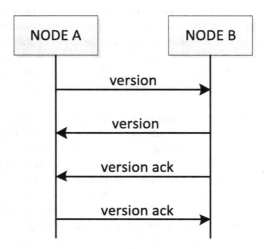

Fig. 1. Bitcoin node handshake process

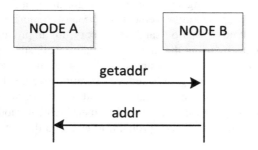

Fig. 2. Request to get a list of nodes

From this we can conclude that for the active measurement of the bitcoin network scale [7], the neighbor node can be obtained by connecting with its neighbor node, then the neighbor node is connected to obtain the neighbor node, and so on, so that many node lists are obtained. Since only a part of the node information can be obtained for each request, and there is a problem that the acquired node has duplicates, this is a random sampling process that is put back again, and is a coupon collector problem [8]. So this study will use the coupon collector model to estimate the scale of the Bitcoin network. Specific theories and experiments will be presented in subsequent chapters.

4 Theoretical Model

4.1 Network Scale Estimation Method

Bitcoin nodes are peer-to-peer, and any node can go online or offline at any time, so the bitcoin network is dynamic and unstable. Research on the Bitcoin network should not only study its micro features, such as node information, but also its macro features, such as network size and dynamics [9]. One aspect of research dynamics is to study the gap in the total of network nodes over a certain period of time, so network size estimation is a fundamental and important step.

At present, there are many methods to study the scale of P2P networks [10]. This paper proposes an estimation method based on coupon collectors model for Bitcoin networks. The coupon collector model is a random sampling method with a return. This model is supported by a theoretical model, so the integrity of the results is guaranteed.

Active measurement of the Bitcoin network can obtain a list of nodes by continuously obtaining information of neighbor nodes. However, only partial node information can be obtained for each request, and duplicate information may exist for any two returned results. So this is a random sampling process with a return, which satisfies the model of the coupon collector problem, that is: there are n different coupons in total, each coupon has the same probability and unlimited quantity. Take one coupon each time, how many experiments do you need to complete on average if you want to collect all the coupons?

4.2 Theoretical Modeling Analysis

This section details the modeling method based on the coupon collector problem and analyzes it.

Let p_i denote the probability that a new coupon will be obtained after collecting i coupons. p_i can be calculated by:

$$p_i = \frac{n-i}{n} \tag{1}$$

Let x_i indicate the number of experiments required to obtain a new coupon after collecting i different coupons, the probability of the number of experiments is z is:

$$p(x_i = z) = (1 - p_i)^{z-1} p_i \tag{2}$$

It can be seen that x_i obeys the geometric distribution and its expectation can be calculated by:

$$E(x_i) = \frac{1}{p_i} \tag{3}$$

Let X_n denote the number of experiments required to collect all n coupons, then:

$$X_n = \sum_{i=0}^{n-1} x_i \tag{4}$$

Based on the expectation's linear nature, it can be concluded that

$$E(X_n) = \sum_{i=0}^{n-1} E(x_i) = \sum_{i=0}^{n-1} \frac{1}{p_i} = \sum_{i=0}^{n-1} \frac{n}{n-i} = n \sum_{i=0}^{n-1} \frac{1}{i} = n \cdot H_n \tag{5}$$

Where H_n is the Harmonic series of n. When $n \to \infty$, $H_n \to \ln n + \gamma + O(1/n)$. γ is Euler-Mascheroni constant. $\gamma \approx 0.5772156649$. Equation 5 can be rewritten by:

$$E(X_n) \approx n(\ln n + \gamma) \tag{6}$$

Therefore, for the coupon collection model, the expected number of coupons required to obtain all types of coupons is $n(\ln n + \gamma)$, which can be used to estimate the number of coupons, that is, the number of coupons is $n(\ln n + \gamma)$.

5   Experiment and Analysis

5.1   Experiment Setup

The experiment was performed on the ubuntu14.04 operating system, and needed to design and implement a tool for long-term active measurement of the Bitcoin network based on the coupon collection model. The tool can enter the bitcoin network through a seed node built into the Bitcoin network, handshake with neighboring nodes, and request its node list to obtain the node's IP address and the status of the current bitcoin network. The tool is multi-threaded, saving some time. In addition, the tool can count the number of times a node is returned. If the number is greater than 0, the node is written to the dnsseed.dump file, so the tool completes the deduplication of collecting node. The tool can also count the number of new nodes discovered during runtime. When the number of new nodes becomes smaller, the collection is converging and fewer new nodes are getting smaller.

A total of six DNS domain names are included in the Bitcoin source code, as shown in Table 1. These seed nodes can be used to get a list of nodes around when a new node joins the bitcoin network.

The new node does not necessarily need to establish a connection with the seed node, but the advantage of connecting to the seed node is that a seed node can quickly discover other nodes in the network. In the Bitcoin core client, whether or not to use the seed node is controlled by "-dnsseed". By default, this option is set to 1, which means that the seed node is used. Alternatively, the IP address of at least one bitcoin node is initially provided to the node being started (the node does not contain any constituent information of the bitcoin network). After this, the initiating node can establish a new connection with subsequent instructions. The user can "refer" the boot node and connect to a node using the command line parameter "-seednode" and use that node as a DNS seed. After the initial seed node is used to form the "referral" information, the client disconnects from it and communicates with the newly discovered peer node.

A node must be connected to several different peer nodes to establish a variety of paths to the bitcoin network in the bitcoin network. Since nodes can join and leave at any time, the communication path is unreliable. Therefore, the node must continue to do two things: discover the new node when it loses an existing connection, and help it when other nodes start. A node only needs one connection when it starts, because the first node can refer it to its peers, which in turn provide referrals. A node, if connected to a large number of other peer nodes, is neither necessary nor a waste of network resources. After the boot is complete, the node remembers the peer node it has recently successfully connected to; therefore, it can quickly re-establish a connection with the previous peer network when it is restarted. If the peer of the previous network does not respond to the connection request, the node can use the seed node to restart.

In the experiment, the seed node, seed.bitcoin.sipa.be, is taken as an example to make native node join the entry point of the bitcoin network. The experiment collected new nodes every hour and collecting 8 times, calculating that the change trend of the number of new nodes found and the gap between actual network size and estimated value, with the increase of experiment times. In addition, the experiment compared the estimated values of connecting different seed.

Table 1. DNS of the Bitcoin seed node

DNS of seed node
seed.bitcoin.sipa.be
dnsseed.bluematt.me
dnsseed.bitcoin.dashjr.org
seed.bitcoinstatd.com
seed.bitcoin.jonasschnelli.ch
seed.btc.petertodd.org

5.2   Experiment Results and Analysis

According to our experimental data, m node information can be obtained for each experiment, that is, the number of nodes acquired is equal to the number of experimental data. It is conceivable that each experimental data must coincide with the previous experimental data, so the number of current experimental data minus the number of data repeated with the previous data is the number of newly discovered nodes in the current experiment.

Through further analysis, we can know that the sum of all newly discovered nodes until the current experiment is the value of n mentioned in Eq. (6).

It can be seen from Fig. 3 that as the number of collections is accumulated, the number of new nodes is found to be less and less. So the process is in line with the coupon collection problem model. The number of new nodes collected each time, and the number of difference sets of the two adjacent collection results can be used to estimate the scale of the Bitcoin network, according to the model mentioned in the previous section.

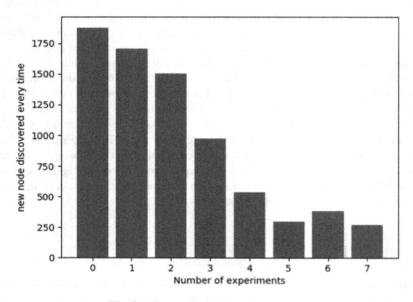

Fig. 3. New node discovered every time

Figure 4 illustrates the close relationship between the model and the experimental results. The model is smaller than the actual measured network size, which may be due to the instability of the Bitcoin network node. As the number of experiments increases, the gap between the two gradually disappears.

The experiment first connected one of the six seed nodes. Through analysis, if you first connect another seed node, the experimental results should be similar, because the difference between the two experiments is that the entry into the Bitcoin network is different, and the measured network size should be similar. Figure 5 shows the estimated network size when connecting two different seed nodes. The results show that the network size measured by connecting two different seed nodes is similar. The gap between the results is negligible.

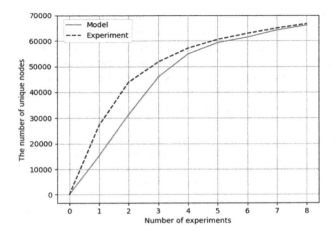

Fig. 4. The experimental number of nodes vs. the model's number

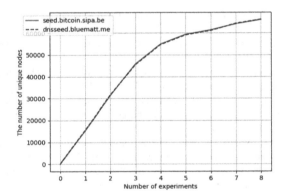

Fig. 5. Different results for connecting different seed nodes

6 Conclusion

This paper uses the coupon collector model to estimate the network size of the Bitcoin network using an active measurement tool. This paper first proposes a theoretical model, and uses this model to estimate the scale of the Bitcoin network, and then through experiments to verify that the model can indeed complete the scale statistics. Moreover, through the experimental results, the average coverage rate can be calculated, that is, the ratio of the number of new nodes estimated by the model to the number of new nodes obtained experimentally. By calculation, we can know that the average coverage can reach 88.21%, so the model can be used to estimate the network size.

Of course, there are still some problems in the model. For example, since every two requests receive repeated node information. The larger the scale is, the larger the information repetition rate will be. A large amount of duplicate data can increase the difficulty of analysis processing. Through further analysis, the repetition rate at the beginning of the experiment is low, and many new nodes are obtained for almost every request. At the end of the experiment, the number of new nodes is reduced. In order to acquire a new node, a large number of requests need to be sent, resulting in a sharp cost in the later stage of the experiment. So the model is not perfect and needs to be improved. This is the direction and focus of future research.

Acknowledgment. The authors would like to thank the anonymous reviewers for their helpful comments for improving this paper. This work is supported by the National Natural Science Foundation of China under grant (No. 61572153, No. 61871140, No. 61872100) and the National key research and development plan under Grant No. 2018YFB0803504.

References

1. Bitcoin is an innovative payment network and a new kind of money. https://bitcoin.org/en/. Accessed 17 Oct 2018
2. Bitcoin White Paper: A Peer-to-Peer Electronic Cash System. https://www.8btc.com/wiki/bitcoin-a-peer-to-peer-electronic-cash-system. Accessed 17 Oct 2018
3. Liu, J.C., Wang, H.Y., Xu, K.: Understanding peer distribution in the gloabal Internet. IEEE Netw. **24**(4), 40–44 (2011)
4. Habeld, T., Lehrieder, F., Hock, D., et al.: Characterization of BitTorent swarms and thire distribution in the Internet. Comput. Netw. **55**(5), 1197–1215 (2011)
5. Cui, Q., McIntosh, S., Sun, H.: Identifying materials of photographic images and photorealistic computer generated graphics based on deep CNNs. CMC Comput. Mater. Continua **55**(2), 229–241 (2018)
6. Xiong, Z., Shen, Q., Wang, Y., Zhu, C.: Paragraph vector representation based on word to vector and CNN learning. CMC Comput. Mater. Continua **55**(2), 213–227 (2018)
7. Tan, Q., Gao, Y., Shi, J., Wang, X., Fang, B., Tian, Z.: Towards a comprehensive insight into the eclipse attacks of tor hidden services. IEEE Internet Things J. (2018). https://doi.org/10.1109/jiot.2018.2846624
8. Zhang, H., Yi, Y., Wang, J., Cao, N., Duan, Q.: Network security situation awareness framework based on threat intelligence. CMC Comput. Mater. Continua **56**(3), 381–399 (2018)
9. Gao, Y., Tan, Q., Shi, J., et al.: Large-scale discovery and empirical analysis for I2P eepSites. In: IEEE Symposium on Computers and Communications, vol. 1, pp. 444–449 (2017)
10. Cao, J.: Research about size estimation methods in P2P network. Comput. Eng. Appl. **44**(20), 99–101 (2008)
11. Wang, X., Li, C., Shi, B., et al.: P2P cluster size estimation method based on random sampling process. Nanjing Normal Univ. **37**(1), 76–80 (2014)
12. Yang, Z., Li, L., Ji, Q., et al.: An optimized P2P cluster rapid measurement model. Chin. Comput. Syst. **35**(2), 296–302 (2014)
13. PeterNeal: The generalized coupon collector problem. Appl. Probab. **45**(3), 621–629 (2008)
14. Vasudevan, S., Towsley, D., Goeckel, D., et al.: Neighbor discovery in wireless networks and the coupon collector's problem. China (2009)
15. Bitcoin DNS Seed. https://bitcoin.org/en/glossary/dns-seed. Accessed 19 Oct 2018

16. Bitcoin Source Code. https://github.com/bitcoin/bitcoin. Accessed 19 Oct 2018
17. Ling, Z., Fu, X., Yu, W., Luo, J., Yang, M.: Extensive analysis and large-scale empirical evaluation of tor bridge discovery. Southeast University, Technical report (2011)
18. Liu, Q., Xu, P., Yang, H., et al.: Research on measurement of peer-to-peer file sharing system. J. Softw. **17**(10), 2131–2140 (2006)
19. Li, M., Sun, Y., Jiang, Y., Tian, Z.: Answering the min-cost quality-aware query on multi-sources in sensor-cloud systems. Sensors (2018). https://doi.org/10.3390/s18124486
20. Han, W., Tian, Z., Huang, Z., Li, S., Jia, Y.: Bidirectional self-adaptive resampling in imbalanced big data learning. Multimed. Tools Appl. (2018). https://doi.org/10.1007/s11042-018-6938-9
21. Wang, Z., et al.: Automatically traceback RDP-based targeted ransomware attacks. Wirel. Commun. Mob. Comput. (2018). https://doi.org/10.1155/2018/7943586
22. Tian, Z., Su, S., Shi, W., Yu, X., Du, X., Guizani, M.: A data-driven model for future internet route decision modeling. Future Gener. Comput. Syst. (2019). https://doi.org/10.1016/j.future.2018.12.054
23. Qiu, J., Chai, Y., Liu, Y., Gu, Z., Li, S., Tian, Z.: Automatic non-taxonomic relation extraction from big data in smart city. IEEE Access **6**, 74854–74864 (2018). https://doi.org/10.1109/ACCESS.2018.2881422
24. Sun, Y., Li, M., Su, S., Tian, Z., Shi, W., Han, M.: Secure data sharing framework via hierarchical greedy embedding in darknets. ACM/Springer Mob. Netw. Appl
25. Yu, X., Tian, Z., Qiu, J., Jiang, F.: A data leakage prevention method based on the reduction of confidential and context terms for smart mobile devices. Wirel. Commun. Mob. Comput. https://doi.org/10.1155/2018/5823439
26. Wang, Y., Tian, Z., Zhang, H., Su, S., Shi, W.: A privacy preserving scheme for nearest neighbor query. Sensors **18**(8), 2440 (2018). https://doi.org/10.3390/s18082440
27. Tian, Z., et al.: A real-time correlation of host-level events in cyber range service for smart campus. IEEE Access **6**, 35355–35364 (2018). https://doi.org/10.1109/ACCESS.2018.2846590
28. Chen, J., Tian, Z., Cui, X., Yin, L., Wang, X.: Trust architecture and reputation evaluation for Internet of Things. J. Ambient Intell. Humanized Comput. **2**, 1–9 (2018)
29. Wu, C., Zapevalova, E., Chen, Y., Li, F.: Time optimization of multiple knowledge transfers in the big data environment. CMC Comput. Mater. Continua **54**(3), 269–285 (2018)

A Survey of the Software Vulnerability Discovery Using Machine Learning Techniques

Jian Jiang[1(✉)], Xiangzhan Yu[1,2], Yan Sun[2], and Haohua Zeng[2]

[1] School of Computer Science and Technology, Harbin Institute of Technology,
Harbin, China
1356117066@qq.com, yxz@hit.edu.cn
[2] Institute of Electronic and Information Engineering of UESTC in Guangdong,
Dongguan, China
289917845@qq.com, zhh0769@foxmail.com

Abstract. Nowadays, the study of vulnerability discovery has been attracted the widespread attention and the experts have proposed many different approaches in the past decades. To optimize the efficiency of the method, machine learning techniques are introduced into this area. In this paper, we provide an extensive review of the work in the field of software vulnerability discovery that utilize machine learning techniques. For the three key technologies of static analysis, symbolic execution and fuzzing in vulnerability discovery field, we first explain the basic principles respectively. Afterward, we review the research situation of software vulnerability discovery using machine learning techniques. Finally, we discuss both advantages and limitations of the approaches reviewed in the paper, and point out challenges and some uncharted territories in the three categories. In this paper, a brief study of the software vulnerability discovery using machine learning techniques is given, which is helpful to carry out the follow-up research work.

Keywords: Vulnerability discovery · Machine learning · Static analysis ·
Deep learning · Symbolic execution · Fuzzing

1 Introduction

In the current cyberspace, the number of serious vulnerabilities discovered in software is on the rise. The severity of these vulnerabilities has varying degrees, depending on factors such as exploitation complexity and attack-surface [1]. Numerous vulnerabilities seriously undermine the security of computer systems and IT infrastructure of companies and individuals. For instance, a vulnerability in the server message block (SMB) protocol exploited by the WannaCry ransomware have affected a wide range of systems and millions of users worldwide [2].

There are many software vulnerability discovery techniques, and the classification methods are also various. It can be divided into manual, automatic and semi-automatic depending on the degree of automation. From the point of view of code execution, it can be divided into dynamic analysis, static analysis and hybrid analysis. It also can be divided into black box test, white box test and gray box test depending on whether the software is open source. There are crossovers between the various categories [12]. Now, the main vulnerability discovery techniques that the paper mentioned is static analysis, symbolic execution and fuzzing. Symbolic execution both belong to the software dynamic analysis under the operating angle and can also be White box test divided by code openness, fuzzing is both dynamic analysis and black box test.

No matter what kind of the vulnerability discovery techniques, machine learning provides a new opportunity for intelligent, effective, and efficient approach. In this paper, we present an extensive review about static analysis, symbolic execution and fuzzing that utilize machine learning techniques. First, we explain the basic principles of static analysis. Afterward, we particularly review the research using machine learning techniques. In the end, we discuss their advantages and limitations of the approaches the reviewed papers proposed, point out the challenges in the field and some uncharted domains to inspire future work in this emerging research area.

2 Static Analysis Using Machine Learning Techniques

2.1 Principles of Static Analysis

Static analysis is the process of evaluating a system or component based on its form, structure, content, or documentation, which does not require program execution [3]. Based on targets' type, static analysis can be classified as source code analysis and binary analysis. In practice, their methods are the same, but the latter is more difficult [12].

Static analysis techniques include rule matching, data-flow analysis, control-flow analysis, program dependence analysis, information-flow analysis, static slice, abstract interpretation, model checking and theorem provers [3]. Nowadays, many research work on the static analysis using machine learning techniques have been done, and the result is inspiring.

2.2 Summary of Recent Works

Scandariato et al. [4] treated a programming language as a native language and analyzed the source code by means of text mining techniques. The proposed method is mainly based on the Bag-of-Words technique, where software component is seen as a series of terms with associated frequencies. The paper analyzed 20 "apps" include 182 releases for the Android OS platform using five well known machine learning algorithm: Decision Trees, k-Nearest Neighbor, Naive Bayes, Random Forest and Support Vector Machine (SVM). The best results are obtained by Naive Bayes and Random Forest. The paper used a commercial program vulnerability analysis solution to provide the labels of training dataset and performed three experiments. In the first experiment, the authors built both Naive Bayes model and Random Forest model based on the first version of each application. The other two experiments built a prediction model with subsequent-version and cross-project applications. According to the reported results, the first and second experiment's prediction is acceptable, yet the prediction of the last experiment is not.

Shin et al. [5] first apply artificial neural networks to binary analysis and tackle the problem of function identification. The central challenge is the lack of high-level semantic structure within binaries, as compilers discard it from the source code. Therefore, to recognize functions is the most important step in binary analysis. The paper use "one-hot encoding" to convert a byte into a vector, push it as the input of the neural network and used bidirectional models with RNN hidden units. Besides that, the paper also optimize the result with stochastic gradient descent and "rmsprop" method. The paper shows that recurrent neural networks can solve recognizing functions more efficiently than the previous state-of-the-art method in binaries analysis.

Perl et al. [6] presented a new method to identify vulnerability contributing commits. The authors combine code-metric analysis with metadata contained in code repositories. To evaluate the effectiveness, the authors first conduct a dataset containing 66 C/C++ GitHub projects with 170860 commits including 640 vulnerability contributing commits mapped to relevant CVE IDs. The paper selected project, author, commit, file as GitHub rich meta-data, and extracted the code-churn and developer-activity as the code-metrics. Afterward, the paper created a generalized Bag-of-Words model using the above features and trained a classifier of vulnerability contributing commits using linear SVM. The authors trained the classifier on data up until 2010 and test it against data from 2011 to 2014, the result of precision is 60% while the Flaw-finder static analysis tool reaches only 1% at the same level of recall.

Grieco et al. [7] proposed an approach that utilize lightweight static and dynamic features to predict whether a binary program is likely to contain a software vulnerability. Both static features and dynamic features try to abstracted the use patterns of the C standard library, the difference is static features are the set of potential subsequences of function calls, while dynamic features are obtained by analyzing program execution traces containing concrete function calls augmented with its arguments. In the experiments the paper covered, the authors used Bag-of-Words and word2vec to process the different sets of features. To addressed the class imbalance issue, the paper used a well tested solution called random oversampling [13]. The authors trained several machine learning classifiers: logistic regression, MLP of single hidden layer and random forest. The result of this paper showed that the best performing model is a random forest trained with dynamic features, vectorized with 2- or 3- grams, achieving an average test error of 31%.

Li et al. [8] designed Vulnerability Deep Pecker, a deep learning-based vulnerability detection system. To address the problem that existing vulnerability detection system rely on human experts to define features and often incur high false negative, the paper first defined code gadgets which is a number of lines of code that are semantically related to each other, and used it to represent programs. The authors select Recurrent Neural Networks (RNN) model and use Long Short-Term Memory (LSTM) to address the Vanishing Gradient problem. Then the authors find Bidirectional LSTM is more suitable for the reason that the argument(s) of a program function call may be affected by earlier statements or the later statements. Vulnerability Deep Pecker has two phase: the learning phase and detection phase. In the learning phase, the system extract the library or API functions and the corresponding program slices, generate code gadgets and their corresponding labels, transform code gadgets to vector representation and train a BLSTM neural network. In the detection phase, the system first transform target programs into code gadgets and vectors, and then detected in the trained model. The authors collect 10791 programs related to vulnerabilities, and shows that Vulnerability Deep Pecker can achieve much lower false negative rate than other vulnerability detection system.

Lin et al. [9] proposed a data-driven method to address the shortage of high-quality training data and relying on the hand-crafted features in vulnerability discovery using machine learning [10]. First, the authors labeled 457 vulnerable functions and collected 32531 non vulnerable functions from six projects, and extracted the abstract syntax trees (ASTs) from source code using "CodeSensor", which is a robust parser implemented by [11]. Afterward, the authors converted the serialized ASTs to equal-length sequences while preserving the structural and semantic features. The paper proposed a BLSTM neural network, which takes the sequences above mentioned as input. The first layer of the network is word2vec embedding layer which maps each element of the sequence to a vector, and the second layer is an LSTM layer which contains 64 LSTM units in a bidirectional form. To accommodate large ASTs for extracting the latent sequential features in ASTs, the third layer of the network is a global max pooling layer. According to the reported results, the method of the paper proposed are more effective for predicting vulnerable functions, both within a project and across multiple projects compared with the traditional code metrics.

The following Table 1 gives a summary of recent works on static analysis using machine learning techniques.

Table 1. Summary of recent works on static analysis using machine learning techniques.

Paper	Approach summary	Advantages	Limitations	Future work
Scandariato et al. [4]	Bag-of-Words + Naive Bayes/Random Forest	Within-project	Cross-project	Expend to cross-project
Shin et al. [5]	Bidirectional models with RNN hidden units	Recognize functions of binaries code	Rely on training data	Explain the internal mechanics
Perl et al. [6]	Bag-of-Words + SVM	Precision and recall	Rely on the manual analysis before train	Minimize the likelihood
Grieco et al. [7]	Utilize static and dynamic features + Bag-of-Words/ Word2Vec + logistic regression/random forest	Accuracy	Test cases is small	Introduce 1D version of a CNN
Li et al. [8]	Code gadget + BLSTM of RNN	Lower false negative rate + not rely on hand-crafted features	Only contains buffer error and resource management error et al.	Solve the limitations
Lin et al. [9]	CodeSensor + BLSTM of RNN	More effective + not rely on training data and the hand-crafted features	Not apply to vulnerabilities involve multiple functions or files	Solve the limitations

2.3 Discussion

In the previous subsection, we reviewed and summarized several recent studies in the field of static analysis using machine learning techniques. A glance summary of all the articles reviewed in this section is also presented in Table 1. Some concluding points, challenges and possible future work could be drawn from the review of previous studies.

A statistical conclusion in the field of static analysis using machine learning techniques is the fact that Random Forest model can achieve the best result among the common used machine learning algorithm. However, as deep learning grow more and more mature, the technique has been used widely in this area and the results of the experiments using deep learning are more inspiring, especially the Bidirectional LSTM model of RNN algorithm. The features extracted from training data have to be processed before joined to the learning model, and the most widely used techniques are Bag-of-Words and word2vec.

Static analysis using machine learning techniques can find technical software vulnerabilities as well as logic vulnerabilities. In our opinion, this is a promising area, and more and more serious vulnerabilities will be discovered by this means. However, there are many limitations to static analysis using machine learning techniques. First, the approaches proposed by the papers reviewed earlier are not full-automatic and the results are unstable, because it rely on the quality of training data collected manual and the hand-crafted features selected by experts in a varying degrees. Second, all the methods the reviewed paper mentioned have to face the fact that the collected dataset suffers from a severe class imbalance. Last but not least, the experiments the reviewed paper implemented mostly aimed at source code, and the results to the binary code is not reasonable. However, the program we encountered in reality mostly have no source code.

It is clear that there is still room for much further progress in the field of static analysis using machine learning techniques. Some possible future works drawn from review of previous studies is as follows: introduce reinforcement learning to guide the learning of the training model and use transfer learning to address the problem of training data and test case vary significantly; combine static analysis with other vulnerability discover techniques, for instance, symbolic execution and fuzzing; conduct a learning model can achieve more reasonable result to binary code.

3 Symbolic Execution Using Machine Learning Techniques

3.1 Principles of Symbolic Execution

Symbolic execution [14] is a method for program reasoning that uses symbolic values as inputs instead of actual data, and it represents the values of program variables as symbolic expressions on the input symbolic values. No matter when a judgment and jump statement is encountered, the method will put the path constraints of the current execution path into the constraint set of the path. The path constraint refers to the value of the branch condition related to the input symbol and the path constraint set is used to store the constraints collected on each program path. We can obtain the accessibility of the path by constraint solver. If the result of the constraint solving has a solution, it means that the path is reachable, otherwise it means that the path is unreachable. In the ideal case of sufficient time and computing resources, the symbol execution can traverse all the paths of the target program and judge its accessibility.

3.2 Summary of Recent Works

Li et al. [15] utilize machine learning to address the major obstacle in applying symbolic execution to real world programs. The problem is the capability of constraint solving, which is closely related with the optimization problem: finding solutions to minimize the dissatisfaction degree. Unlike concolic testing and heuristic search, the authors proposed MLB, a new symbolic execution tool, driven by Machine Learning Based constraint solving. MLB encodes all the difficult operations as symbolic constraints and transforms the feasibility problems of the path conditions into optimization problems. Here, the paper adopt a machine learning based optimization method named RACOS (randomized coordinate shrinking) classification algorithm [16], which learns to discriminate good and bad solutions while trying to keep the error-target dependence and the shrinking rate small. According to the reported results, the method of the paper proposed are more effective and efficient with the instruction coverage reach to 89% and the instruction efficiency reach to 0.44%/s.

Meng et al. [17] proposed a new method combined symbolic execution with machine learning technique to discover vulnerability. Firstly, the authors collect vulnerable functions from CVE and NVD. Then they dig similar function set which have the most features in common in code base with the defined cosine distance. Secondly, vulnerable function call graphs can be extracted from source code base and it can be used to guide the symbolic execution engine to reach the target function. Finally, path constraint can be calculate through the constraint solver and then estimate the sink point according to vulnerability checking rules. The result of this paper showed that symbolic execution utilize machine learning can reach the vulnerable function of FFmpeg within 36 s while symbolic execution only need 8 h.

3.3 Discussion

In the previous subsection, we reviewed and summarized recent work in the field of symbolic execution using machine learning techniques. Symbolic execution is a promising approach to be used in vulnerability discovery, but previous works in this area suffer from some important limitations. In our opinion, path explosion and constrain solve are the two main challenges and machine learning techniques are introduced to address them in recent years. Researchers always concentrate on getting more valuable paths or optimizing constraint solver using machine learning techniques. The result is not inspiring and more efforts are needed in the future.

4 Fuzzing Using Machine Learning Techniques

4.1 Principles of Fuzzing

Fuzzing [18] is a highly automated testing technique that covers numerous boundary cases using invalid data (from files, network protocols, API calls, and other targets) as application input to better ensure the absence of exploitable vulnerabilities. It contains three aspects [19]: firstly, it generates semi-valid or random data; secondly, it sends the generated data into the target application; finally, it observes the application to see if it fails as it consumes the data. Semi-valid data is data that is correct enough to pass input examinations, but still invalid enough to cause problems.

The quality of the Semi-valid data is one of the most important factors that influence the effectiveness and efficiency of fuzzers. There are two main methods of data generation, including data-generation technique and data-mutation technique. Data-generation technique is usually based on specifications, such as file format specifications and network protocol specifications, to generate data. Data-mutation technique generates data by modifying some fields of valid inputs. When specifications are very complex, data-mutation is more appropriate, but the code coverage rate may be very low. So researchers introduced machine learning techniques to address the problems in this area.

4.2 Summary of Recent Works

Böhme et al. [20] model the American Fuzzy Lop (AFL) as a systematic exploration of the state space of a Markov chain and take the probability that fuzzing a seed which exercises program path i generates a seed which exercises path j as transition probability p_{ij}. The paper also improve the power schedules by assigning energy that is inversely proportional to the density of the stationary distribution. To fuzz the best seeds early on, the authors introduce a different search strategy that chooses seeds earlier exercise lower frequency paths and have been chosen less often. As evidenced by the experiments the paper mentioned, the method can exposes an order of magnitude more unique crashes than AFL in the same time budget.

Godefroid et al. [21] introduced neural-network-based learning techniques to fuzzing field and proposed Samplefuzz algorithm which leverages a learnt input probability distribution in order to intelligently guide where to fuzz well-formed inputs. The paper first presents an overview of the PDF format and pick up the "Objects" as the mutate element. To learn a generative model of PDF objects, the authors consider PDF objects as a sequence of characters and use a recurrent neural network based character-level language model (char-rnn). After the learnt char-rnn model has been created, the paper adopted SampleSpace as the sampling strategy. At last, the paper use Samplefuzz algorithm to create new PDF object instances, but at the same time introduce anomalies to exercise error-handling code.

Wang et al. [22] propose Skyfire, a novel data-driven seed generation approach, to improve the performance of the American Fuzzy Lop (AFL) fuzz testing framework. Firstly, the authors collect a vast amount of samples and abstract syntax trees (ASTs) based on the grammar. Secondly, Skyfire learns a probabilistic context-sensitive grammar (PCSG), which describes both syntax features and semantic rules for highly-structured inputs. Then, Skyfire leverage PCSG to generate seed inputs by iteratively selecting and applying a production rule on a non-terminal symbol until there is no non-terminal symbol in the resulting string. Finally, Skyfire randomly replace a leaf-level node in the AST with the same type of nodes to mutates the remaining seed inputs. According to the reported results, the method of the paper proposed can effectively improve the code coverage of fuzzers can significantly improve the capability of fuzzers to find bugs.

Nichols et al. [23] propose to use Generative Adversarial Network (GAN) models and Long Short Term Memory (LSTM) to increase the rate of unique code path discovery of AFL. Firstly, the authors run AFL on a target program for a fixed amount of time to produce the training data. As for the LSTM model, the authors use a 128 wide initial layer, an internal dense layer, a final softmax activation layer and a categorical cross-entropy loss function. The model takes in a seed sequence sampled from the training corpus and predicts the next character in the sequence. Then, the GAN [24] architecture the paper mentioned has two models. The generative model G is a fully connected 2 layer DNN with a ReLU non-linearity to generate realistic output and the discriminative model D is a 3 layer DNN to predict if the data is true or fake. The result of this paper showed that GAN was faster and more effective than the LSTM, and GAN helps AFL discover 14.23% more code paths, finds 6.16% more unique code paths, and finds paths that are on average 13.84% longer.

The following Table 2 gives a summary of recent works on fuzzing using machine learning techniques.

Table 2. Summary of recent works on fuzzing using machine learning techniques.

Paper	Approach summary	Use AFL	Future work
Böhme et. al. [20]	Markov chain	Yes	
Godefroid et al. [21]	char-rnn	No	Reinforcement learning
Wang et al. [22]	PCSG	Yes	Extend the method to more languages and complier
Nichols et al. [23]	GAN+LSTM	Yes	Reinforcement learning

4.3   Discussion

In the previous subsection, we reviewed and summarized several recent studies in the field of fuzzing using machine learning techniques. A glance summary of all the articles reviewed in this section is also presented in Table 2, where we have specified the key differentiating factors of each work.

In the field of fuzzing, machine learning techniques are introduced to guide the process of the input tests generating and mutating. Many researchers tend to extend AFL, the state-of-the-art coverage-based fuzzers, and adopted RNN, Markov, GAN and some algorithms of NLP to improve the performance of AFL. According to the papers, the result is inspiring, but there is still room for much further progress. Some possible future works drawn from review of previous studies is reinforcement learning.

5 Conclusion

Machine learning techniques have been successfully used in the domain of software vulnerability discovery. In this paper, we extensively reviewed previous work and organized the studies in three main categories. For each category, we provided a short yet sufficiently detailed summary of each work and discussed the concluding points, challenges and possible future work.

Acknowledgement. This work was supported by National Key Research & Development Plan of China under Grant 2016QY05X1000, National Natural Science Foundation of China under Grant No. 61771166, and Dongguan Innovative Research Team Program under Grant No. 201636000100038.

References

1. Nayak, K., Marino, D., Efstathopoulos, P., Dumitraş, T.: Some vulnerabilities are different than others. In: Stavrou, A., Bos, H., Portokalidis, G. (eds.) RAID 2014. LNCS, vol. 8688, pp. 426–446. Springer, Cham (2014). https://doi.org/10.1007/978-3-319-11379-1_21
2. Chen, Q.: Bridges, R.: Automated behavioral analysis of malware: a case study of WannaCry Ransomware. In: the 16th IEEE International Conference On Machine Learning And Applications, pp. 454–460, Cancun, Mexico (2017). https://dblp.uni-trier.de/pers/hd/c/Chen:Qian
3. Liu, B., Shi, L., Cai, Z., Li, M.: Software vulnerability discovery techniques: a survey. In: the 4th International Conference on Multimedia Information Networking and Security, Nanjing, China (2012)
4. Scandariato, R., Walden, J., Hovsepyan, A., Joosen, W.: Predicting vulnerable software components via text mining. IEEE Trans. Softw. Eng. **40**(10), 993–1006 (2014). https://ieeexplore.ieee.org/xpl/RecentIssue.jsp?punumber=32
5. Shin, E., Song, D., Moazzezi, R.: Recognizing functions in binaries with neural network. In: the 24th USENIX Security Symposium, Washington, D.C., USA (2015)
6. Perl, H., Dechand, S., Smith, M.: VCCFinder: finding potential vulnerabilities in open-source projects to assist code audits. In: Proceeding of the 22nd ACM SIGSAC Conference on Computer and Communications Security, pp. 426–437, Denver, Colorado, USA (2015)
7. Grieco, G., Grinblat, G., Uzal, L., Rawat, S., Feist, J., Mounier, L.: Toward large-scale vulnerability discovery using machine learning. In: Proceedings of the 6th ACM Conference on Data and Application Security and Privacy, pp. 85–96, San Antonio, TX, USA (2015)
8. Li, Z.: VulDeePecker: a deep learning-based system for vulnerability detection. In: the 25th Annual Network and Distributed System Security Symposium, NDSS, San Diego, California, USA (2018)
9. Lin, G., Zhang, J.: Cross-project transfer representation learning for vulnerable function discovery. IEEE Trans. Ind. Inf. **14**, 3289–3297 (2018). https://ieeexplore.ieee.org/xpl/RecentIssue.jsp?punumber=9424
10. Chen, L., Yang, C., Liu, F., Gong, D., Ding, S.: Automatic mining of security-sensitive functions from source code. CMC: Comput. Mater. Cont. **56**(2), 199–210 (2018)
11. Yamaguchi, F., Lottmann, M., Rieck, K.: Generalized vulnerability extrapolation using abstract syntax trees. In: Proceedings of the 28th Annual Computer Security Applications Conference, pp. 359–368 (2012)

12. Ghaffarian, S., Shahriari, H.: Software vulnerability analysis and discovery using machine-learning and data-mining techniques: a survey. ACM Comput. Surv. **50**(4) (2017)
13. He, H., Garcia, E.: Learning from imbalanced data. IEEE Trans. Knowl. Data Eng. **21**(9) (2009)
14. Chu, D.H., Jaffar, J., Murali, V.: Lazy symbolic execution for enhanced learning. In: the 5th International Conference on Runtime Verification, pp. 323–339, Toronto, ON, Canada (2014). https://link.springer.com/conference/rv
15. Li, X.: Symbolic execution of complex program driven by machine learning based constraint solving. In: Proceedings of the 31st IEEE/ACM International Conference on Automated Software Engineering, pp. 554–559, Singapore, Singapore (2016)
16. Yu, Y., Qian, H., Hu, Y.Q.: Derivative-free optimization via classification. In: Proceedings of the Thirtieth AAAI Conference on Artificial Intelligence, pp. 2286–2292 (2016)
17. Meng, Q., Wen, S., Zhang, B., Tang, C.: Automatically discover vulnerability through similar functions. In: 2016 Progress in Electromagnetic Research Symposium (PIERS), Shanghai, China (2016). https://ieeexplore.ieee.org/xpl/mostRecentIssue.jsp?punumber=7655139
18. Oehlert, P.: Violating assumptions with fuzzing. IEEE Secur. Priv. **3**(2), 58–62 (2005)
19. Liu, B., Shi, L., Cai, Z., Li, M.: Software vulnerability discovery techniques: a survey. In: Fourth International Conference on Multimedia Information Networking and Security (2012)
20. Böhme, M., Pham, V.T., Roychoudhury, A.: Coverage based greybox fuzzing as Markov Chain. In: Proceedings of the 2016 ACM SIGSAC Conference on Computer and Communications Security, NY, USA (2016)
21. Godefroid, P., Peleg, H., Singh, R.: Learn&Fuzz: machine learning for input fuzzing. In: Proceedings of the 32nd IEEE/ACM International Conference on Automated Software Engineering, pp. 50–59. Urbana-Champaign, IL, USA (2017)
22. Wang, J., Chen, B., Wei, L., Liu, Y.: Skyfire: data-driven seed generation for fuzzing. In: 2017 IEEE Symposium on Security and Privacy, San Jose, CA, USA (2017). https://ieeexplore.ieee.org/xpl/mostRecentIssue.jsp?punumber=7957740
23. Nichols, N., Raugas, M., Jasper, R., Hilliard, N.: Faster fuzzing: reinitialization with deep neural models. arXiv preprint arXiv:1711.02807 (2017)
24. Li, C., Jiang, Y., Cheslyar, M.: Embedding image through generated intermediate medium using deep convolutional generative adversarial network. CMC: Comput. Mater. Con. **56**(2), 313–324 (2018)

A Distributed Cryptanalysis Framework Based on Mobile Phones

Chaobin Wang, Le Wang$^{(\boxtimes)}$, Mohan Li, Yu Jiang, and Hui Lu

Cyberspace Institute of Advanced Technology, Guangzhou University,
Guangzhou 510006, Guangdong, China
18361265518@163.com, {wangle,jiangyu,
luhui}@gzhu.edu.cn, limohan.hit@gmail.com

Abstract. With the development of Internet, there have been many malicious attacks against information system vulnerabilities. Password brute cracking is a kind of classic scene on the condition of powerful processing capability nowadays. In the face of huge key space, a distributed operation mode is required for brute force password attack. We designed a mobile phone-based distributed password analysis system, that is, server serves as DES key fragmentation and encryption, as well as MD5 hashing; mobile terminals perform DES violence analysis and MD5 dictionary attack. At the end, the conclusion and prospect for this architecture are proposed.

Keywords: Password attack · Brute force · Distributed system · DES · MD5 · Android

1 Introduction

1.1 Research Significance

Nowadays, personal and corporate privacy data has been threatened with a variety of threats. The brute force cracking algorithm is a common research method to analyze the anti-aggression and security of cryptographic algorithms. The 56-bit DES password has been successfully brute-forced under distributed computing. Through the brute force experiment on the cryptographic algorithm, it can not only analyze how much attack strength the cryptographic algorithm can resist under the current computing resources, but also update the cryptographic algorithm according to the experimental results, for example, updating the 3DES based on the DES algorithm. Brute forcing of passwords requires powerful computing resources, so it can use idle computing resources to perform collaborative computing in a distributed manner, thus improving computing power and enhancing the efficiency of brute force cracking.

By analyzing the data of China Institute of Information and Communications Research, we can know that in 2016, the number of shipments of Android mobile phones in China was 560 million, and the number of shipments updated each year may reach 300 million. The number of Android phones eliminated per year is estimated to be between 3–4 billion. Therefore, if you can gather multiple idle Android phones, use the powerful computing resources combined by a large number of Android phones to

© Springer Nature Switzerland AG 2019
X. Sun et al. (Eds.): ICAIS 2019, LNCS 11635, pp. 318–331, 2019.
https://doi.org/10.1007/978-3-030-24268-8_30

perform distributed brute force password algorithm cracking, which can effectively improve the efficiency of brute force cracking and the probability of successful cracking.

From the perspective of scientific research, distributed cryptanalysis has great research value and good research prospects. First of all, the current information security research in China is developing very rapidly, and the threat of information security is also increasing. Password leakage will cause personal sensitive data to be stolen by hackers. Therefore, information security researchers can aggregate large-scale idle computing resources in a distributed mode and form powerful computing resources to implement brute force cracking research. Secondly, the domestic market has a large number of eliminated Android phones, and the current mainstream Android phones have powerful computing power. This provides an alternative to distributed crypt-analysis for personal and information security researchers.

1.2 The Development of Brute Force Cracking Algorithm

The brute force cracking algorithm is the most basic research method of cryptography research. A brute force password is an attacker who attempts to find a meaningful data or key by performing a ciphertext crack attempt by exhausting the key of the key space. Through brute password force, attackers steal private information and confidential data to gain illegal benefits.

In 1997, the Caronni group organized a successful 13-day experiment to success-fully hack the 48-bit RC5 algorithm. The distributed.net organization has also suc-cessfully brute-forced the 56bitRC5 algorithm and the 64bitRC5 algorithm in more than a month. The results of this experiment show that the longer the key length, the more time it takes to crack, and the lower the probability of successful cracking. Therefore, increasing the length of the key is the basic way to defend against brute force cracking algorithm attacks.

On January 18, 1999, under the cooperation of EFF organization and distributed. net, it took 22 h and 15 min to successfully brute the DES-III encryption algorithm through the combination of hardware and software. The results of this experiment show that the DES algorithm has security threats and needs to be improved to resist new technology attacks [1, 7].

On January 16, 2000, in collaboration with the Paul Ilardi team at the University of Chester and the distributed.net organization, the CSC algorithm for violently cracking the 56-bit key length was successfully hacked [3].

Through the research on the development of brute force cracking algorithm, we can see that the brute force cracking algorithm has evolved from the initial theoretical conjecture to the hardware-based brute force attack to the Internet-based distributed software brute force cracking. In this series of technology upgrades, the most important change is the limitation of a computer resource from the beginning, the cracking efficiency is slow, and the development to distributed network computing, combined with multiple computers to form powerful computing resources, quickly in the effective time Complete the brute force cracking of the cryptographic algorithm.

In the 21st century, Internet and computer technologies have been developed more maturely, and the computational complexity of cryptographic algorithms is getting larger and larger. The brute force cracking algorithm is mainly implemented in distributed computing. With the advancement of mass computer technology and the upgrade of computing devices, more and more individuals and groups have begun to study distributed password brute force cracking. This not only can detect the anti-aggressiveness of cryptographic algorithms, but also promote the development of cryptographic algorithms, making cryptographic algorithms more secure and reliable.

1.3   The Development of Distributed Computing

Centralized computing is the initial network architecture of the Internet. Centralized computing has the advantages of clear logical structure and convenient management. Based on the amount of computing on the Internet at the time, the network architecture of centralized computing can be well matched. However, with the rapid development and mass popularization of the Internet, the amount of computing generated by a large number of simultaneous online users and the huge amount of data processing brought by network applications such as large-scale online games and streaming media have resulted in data that the Internet needs to process in a unit of time. The exponential growth of the server makes it impossible for the server to process the data in a valid time and respond positively, resulting in a lag in operation. This situation has seriously impacted the network architecture of centralized computing. Therefore, researchers began research on distributed computing, trying to solve the problem of massive data processing.

Distributed computing technology is a collection of idle computer resources on the network, combined to form a powerful computing power, in the same local area network, to complete a variety of large-scale, complex computing tasks [2]. Distributed technology combines the Internet into a supercomputer to share resources such as computing resources and information resources. Since the beginning of research on distributed computing, technologies such as middleware technology, mobile Agent technology, Web technology, and network computing have been developed [9]. These technologies have effectively solved practical problems and have been widely used in corresponding fields. Among them, network computing is the key technology for large-scale distributed computing on the Internet. Network computing is to aggregate distributed software, hardware and other resources under the same local area network to complete large-scale distributed computing.

Review the development of distributed computing through the following examples:

In 1993, the RSA Institute of the United States held the RSA-129 password cracking competition. Lenstra and Manasse, researchers of the DEC System Research Center, combined with 500 staff members to complete password cracking in a very short time in a distributed computing environment. Crack the key. This cracking record shows the charm of distributed computing, and distributed computing has begun to gain the attention of researchers [2].

In 1995, the RSA-130 password cracking competition was held in the RSA Institute of the United States. The complexity of the cryptographic algorithm was improved. However, the challenge team used the distributed computing method to successfully crack the key. This has led to the attention of researchers based on the success of distributed network computing.

In 1996, American programmers Wartman and Kurwoski and others launched the GIMPS (Internet Mason Prime Search) project. If you want to verify whether a Mason number of a higher-order index is a prime number, you need a huge amount of calculation. Under the Internet-based distributed computing, combined with hundreds of computers, as of 2018, a total of 50 Mersenne primes were discovered. The largest Maison prime number is 23,249,925. Through the research of the GIMPS project, it not only helps the study of mathematical theory but also promotes the development of distributed computing.

On October 7, 2002, the Distributed.net organization dedicated to cryptographic algorithm cracking [2], combined with the world's 331,000 computer volunteers under the Internet-based distributed computing, succeeded after four years of joint research. Cracked the RC5-64 key developed by the US RSA Data Security Lab.

Based on the above development examples of distributed computing, we can conclude that under the condition that there are limitations on personal computer resources, we can use the distributed computing model to complete a huge computational research project. Therefore, the research of distributed computing mode and the development of distributed computing technology will be an important field of computer research in the future, and the primary research direction of scientific research institutions engaged in large-scale computing research around the world.

1.4   The Research Content

The paper designs a distributed brute force password cracking system based on mobile phone. This system is divided into servers and mobile terminals that participate in distributed computing. The main function of the server is to distribute and distribute tasks. The mobile terminal mainly performs calculation processing on tasks and returns the operation results to the server.

This paper designs a distributed password attack scheme for DES key violent exhaustion and MD5 dictionary attack and summary and prospect.

2   Overall Design of Password Analysis System Based on Mobile Phone

2.1   Requirement Analysis

The mobile phone-based cryptanalysis system consists of a server that distributes tasks and a mobile terminal that performs task calculations.

The distributed analysis mode is that the server distributes tasks to multiple Android phones on the same LAN, and the mobile end performs task processing and feeds the processing results back to the server.

The functions of the server are as follows:

1. Start the server, establish Socket communication, and bind the specified port.
2. DES algorithm encryption and MD5 value calculation. Enter the plain text and choose to encrypt the ciphertext using the DES encryption algorithm. Enter the

plain text and choose to use the MD5 algorithm to calculate the hash value of the message.

3. Key fragmentation processing. The server is mainly responsible for dividing the huge key space according to certain rules and storing it in the key database. The key database is divided into key blocks. The server can read the database and distribute the key block to the mobile terminal participating in the distributed operation. The server can update the state of the key block according to the processing result of the mobile terminal.

4. 4. Data exchange. After the Socket communication is established, the server can receive messages with the Android mobile client. The server can encrypt the DES encryption algorithm to obtain the ciphertext or use the hash value calculated by the MD5 algorithm to send it to the specified Android mobile client.

The function of brute force password analysis software on Android mobile phone is as follows:

1. Establish a Socket connection with the server to listen on the specified port.
2. Data exchange. Can receive messages with the server.
3. DES algorithm brute force processing. Receive the ciphertext and fragment number sent by the server. The fragment number is also part of the decryption key K. The two parts of the received data are brute-forced using the built-in DES decryption algorithm. If the fragmentation brute force fails, the failure message is fed back to the server, and the next task is requested. If the fragment is successfully brute-forced, the success message is fed back to the server, and the key K is decrypted and the crack task is completed.
4. MD5 dictionary attack. The Android password analysis software has built in MD5 values for several weak keys. If the MD5 hash value received from the server is the same as the built-in MD5 value, the collision is successful, the success message is fed back to the server, and the plaintext message is sent to the server together, if the MD5 hash value received from the server is built-in If the MD5 value is different, the collision fails and a failure message is fed back to the server.

2.2 Design of Working Mode of Password Analysis System

The cryptanalysis system works based on the working mode of distributed computing [5]. The working principle of distributed computing: in the face of a problem that only requires a lot of calculations, no other complicated operations are needed to solve the problem, the problem is divided by a server, divided into several subtasks, and then the subtasks are assigned to the computer. The calculation process is performed, and the computer feeds back the calculated result to the server. Finally, the server synthesizes the calculation results for analysis, and searches for the data to be acquired [6].

The working mode of distributed computing can effectively solve the problem of effective computing resources of a single computer. The server divides the problem of huge computation into several small computational tasks and distributes it to multiple computers for calculation. This working mode not only solves the problem of computing resource limitation, but also improves the computational efficiency. Advantages of the working mode of distributed computing [4]:

(i)   Reliability. Even if a mobile device fails, it will not affect other mobile devices, and the entire system can maintain normal operation [17].
(ii) Scalability. The computing power can be enhanced by adding new mobile devices. When the number of mobile devices participating in the calculation reaches a certain amount, the integrated data computing capability of the distributed system can be comparable to that of the supercomputer [18].
(iii) Implementing a balanced load on all nodes allows the task to be placed on the node that is most appropriate to handle it.
(iv) Flexibility. Mobile devices that participate in distributed computing are easy to install and operate.
(v)   Resource sharing. The server allocates data from the database to mobile devices participating in distributed computing.

For the mature development of industrial technology and the changing needs of consumers, Android mobile phones are not only rich in functions but also more powerful in performance. For example, Qualcomm Xiaolong processor, Huawei Kirin chip, MediaTek processor, these processors have powerful processing performance and excellent computing power. Every year, hundreds of millions of Android phones are eliminated, which is accompanied by the use of Android phones. In view of the rapid development of Android mobile phones and the Internet, the Android mobile phone used in this paper is used as a client for receiving tasks, and performs distributed calculation and feedback calculation results.

The working environment of this paper is to exchange data between the server and the Android phone in the same LAN [21]. The server sends the split subtask to the Android phone in the same LAN [22]. The brute force crack analysis software in the Android phone performs distributed brute force crack calculation and then feeds back the result. The distributed mode in the same LAN is (see Fig. 1).

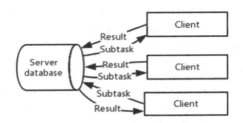

Fig. 1. Distributed structure within the same LAN

Socket Communication Design

In system design, the C/S network architecture mode [2, 4] is used, and the Android mobile terminal needs to communicate with the server [22]. The server issues a task, listens to the port, receives feedback from the client, and the client accepts the task and sends feedback. Therefore, the Socket method is selected for data communication [23].

The Android client and server can communicate in two ways: the first is based on the Http protocol, and the second is Socket communication [24]. Socket is not a protocol, Socket is a set of interfaces. Socket is an abstraction layer that acts between the TCP/IP protocol and the application layer for communication operations. In the Socket communication mode, after the server and the Android client are connected, the two parties can exchange information and transmit data to each other. The Socket communication flow is as follows.

The process of Socket communication of the server is as follows:

1. The server first needs to define a ServerSocket object, specify the IP address and bind the port to be listened to.
2. Open the listener by calling the accept method in ServerSocket to receive the client's request. When accept does not perform any data operation at the beginning, it defaults to the state of congestion.
3. The server creates the inputstream object, reads the data sent by the client to the server, gets the Socket stream, then loads the read character stream into the buffer through the BufferedReader object, and finally reads the data through the readLine() method.
4. The server creates an outputstream object, it sends the data to the connected client, then loads the written character stream into the cache through the BufferedWriter object, and finally writes the data to the data through the PrintWriter method.
5. Clear the buffer, close the stream, close the ServerSocket, and do the exception processing from the first step to the fourth step. If an error occurs during the execution, an IOException will be generated and processed accordingly, so that the code can be found in time error.

The process of Socket communication of the client is as follows:

1. Android client, first create a ServerSocket object, and specify the IP address of the server and bind the port that the server listens on.
2. The Android client sends data to the server by creating an outputstream object, writing the data to the cache via a BufferedWriter object, and then writing the data through the PrintWriter method.
3. The Android client accepts the data sent from the server by creating an inputstream object. The BufferedReader object loads the read data into the cache, and then reads the data through the readLine() method.
4. Clear the buffer, close the stream, close the ServerSocket, and do the exception processing from the first step to the third step. If an error occurs during the

execution, an IOException will be generated and processed accordingly, so that the code can be found in time error. Socket communication process is (see Fig. 2).

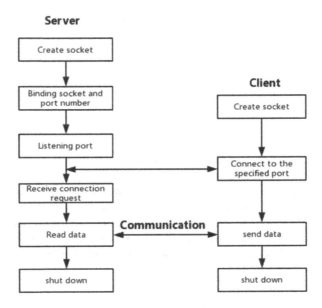

Fig. 2. Socket communication process

2.3   The Function Design of Password Analysis System

Architecture Design of Cryptographic Analysis System

In the development of distributed brute force cracking system, the C/S network architecture mode is adopted [19]. The cryptanalysis system consists of two parts, the server and the mobile phone. The mobile terminal and the server use Socket to establish a communication connection. For the DES brute force key K, first, the server reads the key block of the key database, and then the mobile phone downloads the corresponding key block to perform the crack calculation [20] of the current key block, and finally, sends the calculated result to the server. The server performs a corresponding update operation on the key block of the database according to the calculation result [19]. The architecture of the software is shown in (see Fig. 3).

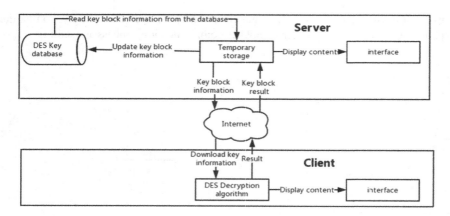

Fig. 3. Software architecture

For the collision of the MD5 value [8], the server first reads the hash value from the MD5 hash database, and then the mobile terminal downloads the corresponding hash value to perform the dictionary attack [26] of the current hash value, and finally, sends the calculated result to the server. The corresponding update operation is performed on the hash value of the hash database according to the calculation result. The architecture of the software is (see Fig. 4).

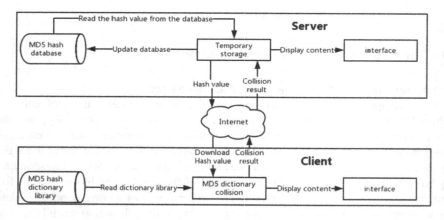

Fig. 4. Software architecture

Server Function Design

According to the overall architecture of the cryptanalysis software, the main functions of the server are: fragmentation and distribution processing of tasks. The specific functions are as follows [9]:

1. Key space fragmentation and allocation. The DES key database stores a small number of key blocks divided by a huge number of DES key spaces. The server

receives the task request from the client, and reads the key block from the DES key database and sends it to the corresponding client.

2. Update of the key block. There are three states in the key block: they are not distributed, have been distributed but have not yet received the processing result, and have been processed. When the server receives the task request from the client, it needs to check the key block in the database and send the key block of the first and second cases to the client.

In order to improve the efficiency of processing the key block, the state of the key block in process is set to 10 min, After the time has elapsed, the key block is set to unassigned and the key block is redistributed after the next client task request.

The server's database stores the key blocks that are partitioned. The record of each key block includes information such as code number, processing status, allocation time, start and end positions, and the like.

Client Function Design
According to the overall architecture of the cryptanalysis software, the main function of the mobile terminal is to apply for a task to the server, and perform corresponding processing according to the content of the task. The result of each task processing is sent to the server.

DES Brute Force Algorithm Design
The design idea of brute force DES key K is: the client knows a plaintext-ciphertext pair, and then uses the DES decryption algorithm to exhaust the key space [12]. When the original text decrypted by the key K is the same as the known original text, it finds the correct one. Key K. The design flow is (see Fig. 5).

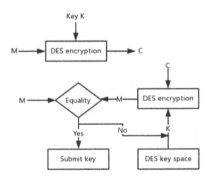

Fig. 5. DES decryption key algorithm design

MD5 Hash Collision Design
The design idea of the MD5 hash collision is that the client uses the MD5 dictionary library to receive the hash value for matching, and if the matching succeeds, the corresponding original text is returned [13, 14]. If the match fails, try another dictionary library [6, 15]. The design flow is (see Fig. 6).

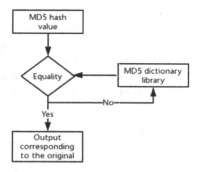

Fig. 6. MD5 collision design

Distributed Cryptanalysis Overall Workflow

The design and development of this paper uses the mainstream C/S (server/client) model for development [17–19]. The server plays a core role in sharding and task-distributing the task, i.e., the key space, and the Android mobile phone communicates with the server through Socket communication. The Android mobile terminal receives the ciphertext and fragmentation tasks that need to be cracked from the server, and then performs the crack calculation and feeds the result to the server. The working mode of the server and client in distributed cryptanalysis is (see Fig. 7).

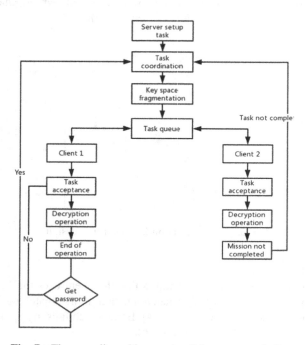

Fig. 7. The overall working mode of the server and client

As can be seen from Fig. 7., the server plays the role of task publishing, which implements fragmentation and distribution processing of tasks that need to be processed in the key space, and coordinates and manages the calculation and processing of tasks on different mobile terminals. detail [27]. The client is an Android mobile phone, and performs Socket communication with the server in the same local area network, thereby receiving the key fragmentation task and ciphertext that need to be processed, and feeding back the calculated result to the server [28, 29].

3 Conclusion and Prospect

3.1 Conclusion

Article studies the principle of distributed brute force cracking and related password attack technology, and designs a distributed brute force password cracking system based on mobile phone.

Based on the rapid development of mobile devices and the superiority of distributed computing mode, this paper designs a distributed cryptanalysis scheme based on Android mobile phone. The program mainly includes: the design of the working mode of the mobile phone-based cryptanalysis system, the overall design of the mobile phone-based cryptanalysis system, the design of the server task allocation and distribution, the design of the encryption algorithm, and the design of the mobile task processing function.

3.2 Prospect

With the popularization of mobile devices and the development of distributed computing models, the architecture design and working mode of the brute force cryptographic algorithm system have been further optimized and innovated. With the distributed computing model, the computing tasks can be distributed to the distributed computing resources in the local area network, thereby improving the computing efficiency and solving the centralized computing resource limitation. A distributed computing network consisting of mobile devices will be the preferred mode for future cryptanalysis.

Because of my limited level, this paper has many shortcomings.

(1) Research on distributed network computing models is not deep enough.
(2) The fragmentation design of the key space for brute force cracking is not mature enough, and the research on distributed brute force crack analysis is not thorough enough.

References

1. Curtin, M.: A brute force search of DES keyspace. USENIX (1998). http://www.usenix.org/publications/login/1998L5/curtin.html
2. Wattenhofer, R.: Principles of Distributed Computing (2014)
3. Shamir, A.: On the security of DES. In: Williams, Hugh C. (ed.) CRYPTO 1985. LNCS, vol. 218, pp. 280–281. Springer, Heidelberg (1986). https://doi.org/10.1007/3-540-39799-X_22

4. Zhang, L., Zhang, Y.: Brute force attack on block cipher algorithm based on distributed computation. Comput. Eng. **34**, 121–123 (2008)
5. Diffie, W., Hellman, M.E.: Special feature exhaustive cryptanalysis of the NBS data encryption standard. Computer **10**(6), 74–84 (2006)
6. Foster, I., Kesselman, C., Nick, J., et al.: Grid services for distributed system integration. Computer **1**, 37–46 (2002)
7. Patil, P., Narayankar, P., Narayan, D.G., et al.: A comprehensive evaluation of cryptographic algorithms: DES, 3DES, AES, RSA and Blowfish. Procedia Comput. Sci. **78**, 617–624 (2016)
8. Wang, X.: Collisions for hash functions MD4, MD5, HAVAL-128 and RIPEMD. Cryptology Eprint Archive Report 2004 (2004)
9. Marculescu, A.: Mobile architecture for distributed brute-force attacks. J. Mob. Embed. Distrib. Syst. **6**(1), 30–37 (2014)
10. Mamat, K., Azmat, F.: Mobile learning application for basic router and switch configuration on Android platform. Procedia Soc. Behav. Sci. **90**, 235–244 (2013)
11. Web Services Description Language (WSDL) Version 2.0 Part 1: Core Language. http://www.w3.org/TR/wsdl20/
12. Karame, G.O., Capkun, S., Maurer, U.: Privacy-preserving outsourcing of brute-force key searches. In: ACM Workshop on Cloud Computing Security Workshop, pp. 101–112. ACM (2011)
13. Bhattacharyya, R., Mandal, A., Nandi, M.: Security analysis of the mode of JH hash function. In: Hong, S., Iwata, T. (eds.) FSE 2010. LNCS, vol. 6147, pp. 168–191. Springer, Heidelberg (2010). https://doi.org/10.1007/978-3-642-13858-4_10
14. Aoki, K., Sasaki, Yu.: Preimage attacks on one-block MD4, 63-Step MD5 and more. In: Avanzi, R.M., Keliher, L., Sica, F. (eds.) SAC 2008. LNCS, vol. 5381, pp. 103–119. Springer, Heidelberg (2009). https://doi.org/10.1007/978-3-642-04159-4_7
15. Chang, D., Nandi, M.: Improved indifferentiability security analysis of chopMD hash function. In: Nyberg, K. (ed.) FSE 2008. LNCS, vol. 5086, pp. 429–443. Springer, Heidelberg (2008). https://doi.org/10.1007/978-3-540-71039-4_27
16. Dandass, Y.S.: Using FPGAs to parallelize dictionary attacks for password cracking. In: Proceedings of the Hawaii International Conference on System Sciences, pp. 485–485. IEEE (2008)
17. Li, M., Sun, Y., Jiang, Y., Tian, Z.: Answering the min-cost quality-aware query on multi-sources in sensor-cloud systems. Sensors (2018). https://doi.org/10.3390/s18124486
18. Han, W., Tian, Z., Huang, Z., Li, S., Jia, Y.: Bidirectional self-adaptive resampling in imbalanced big data learning. Multimedia Tools Appl. (2018). https://doi.org/10.1007/s11042-018-6938-9
19. Wang, Z.H., et al.: Automatically traceback RDP-based targeted Ransomware attacks. Wirel. Commun. Mob. Comput. (2018). https://doi.org/10.1155/2018/7943586
20. Tian, Z., Su, S., Shi, W., Yu, X., Du, X., Guizani, M.: A data-driven model for future internet route decision modeling. Future Gener. Comput. Syst. (2019). https://doi.org/10.1016/j.future.2018.12.054
21. Qiu, J., Chai, Y., Liu, Y., Gu, Z.Q., Li, S., Tian, Z.: Automatic non-taxonomic relation extraction from big data in smart city. IEEE Access **6**, 74854–74864 (2018). https://doi.org/10.1109/ACCESS.2018.2881422
22. Sun, Y., Li, M., Su, S., Tian, Z., Shi, W., Han, M.: Secure data sharing framework via hierarchical greedy embedding in darknets. Mobile Networks and Applications. ACM/Springer

23. Yu, X., Tian, Z., Qiu, J., Jiang, F.: A data leakage prevention method based on the reduction of confidential and context terms for smart mobile devices. Wirel. Commun. Mob. Comput. https://doi.org/10.1155/2018/5823439

24. Wang, Y., Tian, Z., Zhang, H., Su, S., Shi, W.: A privacy preserving scheme for nearest neighbor query. Sensors 18(8), 2440 (2018). https://doi.org/10.3390/s18082440

25. Tian, Z., et al.: A real-time correlation of host-level events in cyber range service for smart campus. IEEE Access 6, 35355–35364 (2018). https://doi.org/10.1109/ACCESS.2018.2846590

26. Tan, Q., Gao, Y., Shi, J., Wang, X., Fang, B., Tian, Z.: Towards a comprehensive insight into the eclipse attacks of tor hidden services. IEEE Internet Things J. (2018). https://doi.org/10.1109/jiot.2018.2846624

27. Chen, J., Tian, Z., Cui, X., Yin, L., Wang, X.: Trust architecture and reputation evaluation for internet of things. J. Ambient Intell. Humaniz. Comput. 2, 1–9 (2018)

28. Zhou, H., Sun, G., Fu, S., Jiang, W., Xie, T., Duan, D.: A distributed LRTCO algorithm in large-scale DVE multimedia systems. CMC: Comput. Mater. Continua 56(1), 73–89 (2018)

29. Wu, X., Zhang, C., Zhang, R., Wang, Y., Cui, J.: A distributed intrusion detection model via nondestructive partitioning and balanced allocation for big data. CMC: Comput. Mater. Continua 56(1), 61–72 (2018)

A Novel Threshold Signature Scheme Based on Elliptic Curve with Designated Verifier

Yu Liu[1]([⊠]) and Tong Liu[2]

[1] College of Computer Science and Technology,
Chongqing University of Posts and Telecommunications,
Chongqing 400065, China
1115864872@qq.com
[2] School of Cyber Security and Information Law,
Chongqing University of Posts and Telecommunications,
Chongqing 400065, China

Abstract. Aiming at the security threats and computationa complexity of existing threshold signature schemes, this paper proposes a threshold signature scheme based on elliptic curve. The scheme render no less than t legitimate and honest members to form a valid signature, where the signature is combined with the public key of the designated receiver, thus only the designated receiver can verify and decrypt the information by using his or her private key. According to the analysis, the proposed scheme has the characteristics of unforgeability, confidentiality and integrity of messages. Moreover, the scheme has good robusness, consumes less computing resources, and lower communication bandwidth.

Keywords: Elliptic curve · Threshold · Signature · Designated verifier

1 Introduction

The study of threshold signature is one of the hotspots in the field of cryptography. It combines threshold secret sharing with signature [1]. Desmedt and Frankel [2] first proposed a (t, n) threshold signature scheme in 1991. By decomposing signature key and handing it over to n members for secret management, no less than $t(t \leq n)$ members use the key they have mastered to sign together to generate a valid signature, thus increasing the difficulty for attackers to obtain the signature key, improving the reliability of the signature mechanism and better resisting forgery signature attack. In the existing threshold key sharing schemes, Lagrange interpolation theorem is often used to achieve secret sharing [3].

In 1994, Harn [4] combined Shamir secret sharing mechanism and ElGamal algorithm to propose a (t, n) threshold signature system of no letter center based on discrete logarithm to solve difficult problems. Nowadays, threshold signature has been applied to many fields of cryptography, which has improved the practical application value of threshold signature. Asaar et al. [5] proposed the first

© Springer Nature Switzerland AG 2019
X. Sun et al. (Eds.): ICAIS 2019, LNCS 11635, pp. 332–342, 2019.
https://doi.org/10.1007/978-3-030-24268-8_31

verifiable identity-based secure proxy ring signature scheme without bilinear pairings based on RSA hypothesis which improves security and has good efficiency. Karati et al. [6] proposed a new identity-based secure encryption scheme based on the bilinear Diffie-Hellman hypothesis, which has better acceptability and improved applicability. Meshram et al. [7] implemented a short signature scheme based on online/discrete identity in the wireless sensor network environment, which does not require any private key information in the discrete signature and has good practicability and feasibility. Gong et al. [8] proposed a node remote authentication mechanism. In order to reduce the computing resources of nodes and improve computing capacity, several nodes belonging to the same detection area are signed together with threshold signature technology. This scheme guarantees the security of data transmission. Liu [9] proposed a lightweight authentication communication scheme based on Lagrange interpolation, which combines Lagrange polynomial formula with message for sending authentication. Although the scheme has lower storage and communication cost, there are some security problems. Dragan et al. [10] proposed a scheme about distributed weighted threshold, in which participants are distributed at different levels and given the same weight at the same level. This scheme is based on the residual theorem, and there are a lot of multiplication and power multiplication operations in the signature process, so the calculation cost of the scheme is too large. Harn et al. [11] based on China's residual theorem proposed a threshold signature scheme, which the valid group signature must be signed by no less than t group members to generate, but this scheme is not traceable. Li et al. [12] based on the Lagrange interpolation of two variables constructed a group authentication scheme, but this scheme can only be executed once. Lin et al. [13] proposed a threshold secret sharing scheme, the scheme guarantees the confidentiality and integrity of messages in the partition and integration of messages, but the scheme of the platform computing power demand is high, and members of the private key is controlled by PKI VM, once the PKI VM has been attacked, the private key owned by all users are at risk of leaking. Xiong et al. [14] proposed two reversible data hiding schemes encrypted in cloud computing. The scheme guarantees the reliability of data security and can be operated in different stages of image encryption, but the cloud server takes up extra storage space. Tang et al. [15] proposed a new proxy re-encryption with keyword search scheme based on cloud computing, which improves the computational efficiency and practicality and can also resist the selected keyword attack.

This scheme uses elliptic curve to construct a threshold signature scheme which can verify and decrypt information signatures only if the designated receiver uses his or her own private key. The proposed scheme does not need a trusted center and can resist known partial message attack and known signature message attack. The proposed scheme has low computational complexity and the communication and time cost for information transmission are also small.

2   Preliminary Knowledge

2.1   Shamir Secret Sharing Scheme

Shamir threshold scheme divides secret s into n parts held by each participant, each part of the secret is called a sub-secret key or shadow, requirements: (1) The original secret s can be reconstructed by no less than k participants using part of the information they held; (2) Reconstructing the original secret s from less than k participants who cannot use part of the information they hold. Where k is called the threshold value of the scheme.

Based on polynomial Lagrange interpolation, Shamir threshold scheme is generally constructed as follows: suppose the finite field is $GF(q)$, where q is a large prime number, which satisfies the requirement that $q \geq n + 1$. Select a secret value s randomly in $GF(q)$, that is, $s \in GF(q)$. $k - 1$ coefficient $a_1, a_2, \cdots, a_{k-1}$ is randomly selected in $GF(q)$, that is, $a_i \in GF(q)(1, 2, \cdots, k - 1)$. Construct a polynomial $f(x) = a_0 + a_1 x + \cdots + a_{k-1} x^{k-1}$ of degree $k - 1$ in $GF(q)$.

The set of participants is $P = \{P_1, P_2, \cdots, P_n\}$, and the sub-secret key assigned by P_i is $f(i)$. Randomly select k participants $P_{i_1}, P_{i_2}, \cdots, P_{i_k} (1 \leq i_1 < i_2 < \cdots < i_k \leq n)$ want to construct the original secret s, Lagrange interpolation formula can be used to construct the polynomial as follows:

$$f(x) = \sum_{j=1}^{k} f(i_j) \prod_{l=1, l \neq j}^{k} \frac{(x - i_l)}{(i_j - i_l)} mod q$$

Hence the secrets $s = f(0)$.

However, participants don't have to know the whole polynomial $f(x)$, they just have to know the constant term $f(0)$, so only the following expression can be used to figure out s:

$$s = (-1)^{k-1} \sum_{j=1}^{k} f(i_j) \prod_{l=1, l \neq j}^{k} \frac{i_j}{(i_j - i_l)} mod q$$

2.2   Threshold Signature

A threshold signature scheme includes four algorithms: (1) Generate system parameters. (2) Threshold key generation algorithm: the system calculates the public key and the corresponding portion of the private key, and secret sharing between members. (3) Threshold signature generation algorithm: each member encrypts the message with the secret values it holds and parameters, generates part of the signature, and then the combination collects signature. (4) Signature verification algorithm: the receiver verifies the validity of the obtained signature.

2.3   Discrete Logarithmic Puzzle (DLP) and the Calculation of Diffie-Hellman Puzzle (CDHP)

Assuming that G is an additive group, the two mathematical problems on G are:

(1) DLP: given two $P, Q \in G$, it is difficult to find a positive integer $n \in Z_q^*$ and make it satisfy $Q = nP$.
(2) CDHP: for $a, b \in_R Z_q^*$, $P \in G$, given (P, aP, bP), it is difficult to calculate abP.

3 Threshold Authentication Scheme Based on Elliptic Curve

The proposed scheme does not need a trusted center, each participant has equal status, and none of the participants is credible. The proposed scheme uses elliptic curve to realize threshold signature, and t participants are selected from n participants in finite domain to generate the signature through cooperation. N participants all have one private key component. Valid signatures can be formed only if no fewer than t valid participants aggregate their private key components, which improves the confidentiality of the scheme. When at most $n - t$ participants are attacked, they will not be able to generate valid signatures and verify them. Moreover, it is difficult for attackers to obtain the key components of t participants at the same time, which improves the security of the scheme.

The proposed scheme consists of system initialization phase, threshold signature phase and signature information authentication phase. The notations require for this scheme are shown in Table 1.

Table 1. List of the notations used

Notation	Description
d_Q	Private key of group Q
Y_Q	Public key of group Q
d_i	Private key of the i participant (P_i)
Y_i	Public key of the i participant (P_i)
ID_i	Identity of the i participant (P_i)
d_u	Private key of the designated receiver (U_i)
Y_u	Public key of the designated receiver (U_i)

3.1 System Initialization Phase

(1) A secure elliptic curve $E(Fq)$ on the finite domain Fq is selected to ensure that the discrete logarithm problem on the elliptic curve is difficult to solve. A basis point P is selected on $E(Fq)$, whose order is q (q is a large prime number).

(2) Group $Q = \{p_1, p_2, \cdots p_n\}$ is the set of n participants, each participant $p_i (i = 1, 2, \cdots, n)$ has a different identity ID_i (ID_i is a positive integer and that $i \neq j$, $ID_i \neq ID_j$).

(3) The private key of $d_Q \in Z_q^*$ in group is randomly selected, and the public key of group Q is $Y_Q = d_Q \cdot P \in E(Fq)$, according to the polynomial:

$$f(x) = d_Q + a_1 x + a_2 x^2 + \cdots + a_{i-1} x^{i-1} mod q$$

The private key and public key components of participant $p_i \in Q$ in group Q are calculated respectively: $d_i = f(ID_i)$, $Y_i = d_i P$, and the public key and private key of the designated receiver U_i is (Y_u, d_u).

(4) Each participant publishes public parameters: $E(Fq)$, P, q, Y_Q, Y_i and $ID_i(i = 1, 2, \cdots, n-1)$.

3.2   Threshold Signature Phase

t participants is selected from group $Q = \{p_1, p_2, \cdots p_n\}$, denoted as $Q_t = \{p_1, p_2, \cdots, p_t\}$, the signature combination is p_c, the designated receiver U_i, and the signature steps are:

(1) Participants $p_i = \{p_1, p_2, \cdots, p_t\}$ randomly select $r_i \in Z_q^*$, calculate $V_{i_1} = r_i P$, $V_{i_2} = r_i Y_u$ and send (V_{i_1}, V_{i_2}) to p_c.
(2) p_c verifies V_{i_1} and V_{i_2} of different participants $p_i, p_j (i \neq j)$. If $V_{i_1} = V_{i_2}$, that indicates they chose the same random number, namely $r_i = r_j$, and p_c informes them to select new random number and them send new calculation results to p_c; otherwise, p_c calculates

$$V_1 = \sum\nolimits_{i=1}^{t} V_{i_1} \bmod q = (V_{1_x}, V_{1_y})$$

$$V_2 = \sum\nolimits_{i=1}^{t} V_{i_2} \bmod q = (V_{2_x}, V_{2_y})$$

and broadcasts to each participant p_i.
(3) Participant p_i calculates $f = m \cdot (V_{1_x} + V_{2_x}) \bmod q$, $s_i = r_i + d_i c_i \bmod q$, among

$$c_i = \prod\nolimits_{j=1, j \neq i}^{t} \frac{-ID_i}{(ID_j - ID_i)} \bmod q$$

send (f, s_i) to p_c.
(4) p_c verifies the validity of each information according to whether $V_{i_1} = s_i P - c_i Y_i$ is established. If equation is valid, then the p_c calculates

$$s = \sum\nolimits_{i=1}^{t} s_i \bmod q$$

sends a message pair (f, s) to the designated receiver U_i.

3.3   Signature Message Authentication Recovery Phase

The designated receiver U_i receives information pair (f, s), calculates $V_1' = sP - Y_Q \bmod q$, verifies if the equation $V_1' = V_1$ is true, if true, U_i calculates $V_2' = d_u \cdot V_1' \bmod q$, so that the original message can be effectively restored from the message: $m = f \cdot (V_{1_x}' + V_{2_x}')^{-1}$.

4 Analysis of Correctness and Security

4.1 Correctness

Theorem 1. *The proposed scheme is based on Shamir secret sharing. According to Lagrange formula:* $s = (-1)^{k-1} \sum_{j=1}^{k} f(i_j) \prod_{l=1,l\neq j}^{k} \frac{i_j}{(i_j - i_l)} mod q$, *that is, formula* $\sum_{i=1}^{t} d_i c_i - d_Q mod q = 0$ *in the proposed scheme is valid, where* $c_i = \prod_{j=1,j\neq i}^{t} \frac{-ID_i}{(ID_j - ID_i)} mod q$, *so the designated recipient verifies the signature is correct after receiving the signature.*

Proof.

$$V_1' = sP - Y_Q mod q$$
$$= \sum_{i=1}^{t} s_i P - Y_Q mod q$$
$$= \sum_{i=1}^{t} (r_i + d_i c_i) P - Y_Q mod q$$
$$= \sum_{i=1}^{t} r_i P + \sum_{i=1}^{t} d_i c_i P - Y_Q mod q$$
$$= V_1 + (\sum_{i=1}^{t} d_i c_i - d_Q mod q) P$$
$$because \sum_{i=1}^{t} d_i c_i - d_Q mod q = 0, \ so \ V_1' = V_1.$$

4.2 Unforgeability

Theorem 2. *If adversary A takes advantage of ε and asks the number of key generation and signature times to crack the signature, challenger B can use the advantage that cannot be ignored to save DL difficult problem.*

Type 1 adversary A_1: this type of adversary is a malicious system and therefore knows the master key, but cannot replace the public key of the participant;

Type 2 adversary A_2: this type of adversary is an external malicious user and therefore does not know the master key, but can replace the public key of any participant.

If there is an adversary A_1 who can win the game with the advantage of ε in probabilistic polynomial time, then there is a differentiable player B who can solve DL problem with the advantage of $\varepsilon' \geq (1 + \frac{1}{q_E})^{q_E + q_S}$ in probabilistic polynomial time.

Proof. Suppose B is the solver of DL difficulty problem, whose input is $cP \in G$, and for any unknown $c \in Z_q^*$, the aim of DL problem is to calculate c. Adversary A_1 knows the group manager key, but cannot replace the participant's public key. Suppose that A_1 performs the following operations in the attack experiment: q_S is the number of times A_1 accesses signature queries; q_E is the number of times that part of the key generates queries.

Initialization: Firstly, B generates public parameters Params = $<E(Fq), P, q, Y_Q, Y_i$ and $ID_i(i = 1, 2, \cdots, t)>$, where $Y_Q = cP$, then adversary

A_1 receives public parameters sent by B; at the same time, B respectively maintains list L_G, L_{PK}, L_{SK} and L_S to track partial key generation query, private key generation query, public key generation query and signature query for B. At the beginning, all lists are empty.

   Partial key generation query. When a part of $A_1's$ query about ID_i and public parameter Y_i is received, B performs the following operations:

(1) If $<ID_i,\ X_i,\ dID_i = (d_i, Y_i),\ Type_i> \in L_G$, B returns $dID_i = (d_i, Y_i)$ to A_1;
(2) Otherwise, B selects random numbers $Type \in \{0,1\}$, and $Pr[Type = 1] = \delta = \frac{1}{q_E}$; If $Type = 1$, B sets the tuple corresponding to ID to be $<ID, Y, \bot, \bot, 0>$. If $Type = 0$, then B randomly selects $d_i \in Z_q^*$, calculates $Y_i = d_i P$, and adds $<ID_i,\ dID_i = (d_i, Y_i),\ Type = 1>$ to L_G, and returns $dID_i = (d_i, Y_i)$ to A_1.

   Private key generation query. When receiving $A_1's$ private key generation query about ID_i, B performs the following operations:

(1) If there is for $<ID_i, d_i> \in L_{SK}$, B returns the corresponding d_i to A_1 in the tuple;
(2) Otherwise, B calculates polynomial $d_i = f(ID_i)$, and conducts the private key generation query to obtain the corresponding tuple $<ID_i, d_i>$, adds to L_{SK} and returns d_i to A_1; Meanwhile, B adds $<ID_i, Y_i>$ to L_{PK}.

   Public key generation query. When receiving $A_1's$ public key generation query about ID_i, B performs the following operations:

(1) If there is for $<ID_i, Y_i> \in L_{PK}$, B returns the corresponding Y_i to A_1 in the tuple;
(2) Otherwise, B calculates polynomial $d_i = f(ID_i)$ and $Y_i = d_i P$, and conducts the public key generation query to obtain the corresponding tuple $<ID_i,\ d_i,\ Y_i>$, adds to L_{PK}, and returns Y_i to A_1. At the same time, B adds $<ID_i, d_i>$ to L_{SK}.

   Signature query. When B receives $A_1's$ signature query on identity-public key pair $<ID_i, Y_i>$, B performs the following operations:
   If $Type = 1$, then B stops. Otherwise, B randomly selects $r_i \in Z_q^*$ and calculates $V_{i_1} = r_i P$, $s_i = r_i + d_i c_i mod q$. If all $ID_i (1 \le i \le t)$ are $ID_i \ne ID_j$. B calculates $V_1 = \sum_{i=1}^t V_{i_1} mod q$, $s = \sum_{i=1}^t s_i mod q$, generates signature $\sigma = (V_1, s)$ back to the adversary, while adding $<ID_i, s>$ to L_S.
   After a limited number of such inquiries, A_1 outputs the signature of identity-public key pair $<ID_i, Y_i>$ and signatures $\sigma = (V_1, s)$, and B queries the corresponding record values of identity ID_i in L_G, L_{PK}, L_{SK} and L_S, so the following equation is established

$$V_1 = sP - Y_Q$$
$$\sum_{i=1}^t r_i P = sP - cP$$

So B can be calculated successfully $c = s - \sum_{i=1}^{t} r_i$ to solve the DL problem. Its advantage is:

$$\varepsilon' \geq (1 + \frac{1}{q_E})^{q_E + q_S}$$

If there is an adversary A_2 who can win the game with the advantage of ε in probabilistic polynomial time, then there is a differentiable player B who can solve DL problem with the advantage of $\varepsilon' \geq (1 + \frac{1}{q_E})^{q_E + q_S}$ in probabilistic polynomial time.

Proof. Suppose B is the solver of DL difficulty problem, whose input is $cP \in G$, and for any unknown $c \in Z_q^*$, the aim of DL problem is to calculate c. Adversary A_2 does not know the system manager key, but can replace any participant's public key.

Initialization: Firstly, B generates public parameters $Params = <E(Fq),$ P, q, Y_Q, Y_i and $ID_i(i = 1, 2, \cdots, t)>$, where $Y_Q = d_Q P$, then B adversary A_2 receives public parameters sent by B; at the same time, B respectively maintains list L_G, L_{PK}, L_{SK} and L_S to track partial key generation query, private key generation query, public key generation query and signature query for B. At the beginning, all lists are empty.

A_2 can perform partial key generation query and Signature query mentioned above.

Public key generation query. When receiving $A_2's$ public key generation query about ID_i, B performs the following operations:

(1) If there is for $<ID_i, Y_i> \in L_{PK}$, B returns the corresponding Y_i to A_2 in the tuple;
(2) Otherwise, B randomly selects $c \in Z_q^*$, calculates $Y_i = cP$, and conductes public key generation query to obtain corresponding tuples $<ID_i, Y_i>$, adds $<ID_i, Y_i>$ to L_{PK}, and returns Y_i to A_2; At the same time, B adds $<ID_i, c>$ to L_{SK}.

After a limited number of such inquiries, A_2 outputs the signature of identity-public key pair $<ID_i, Y_i>$ and signatures $\sigma = (V_1, s)$, and B performs the following operations:

(1) If $Type = 1$, B abandons and terminates the simulation;
(2) Otherwise, B queries the corresponding record values of identity ID_i in L_G, L_{PK}, L_{SK} and L_S, so the following equation is established:

$$V_1 = sP - Y_Q$$

$$\sum_{i=1}^{t} r_i P = sP - d_Q P$$

So B can be calculated successfully $c = d_Q \cdot (\sum_{i=1}^{t} c_i)^{-1}$ to solve the DL problem.

Its advantage is:

$$\varepsilon' \geq (1 + \frac{1}{q_E})^{q_E + q_S}$$

4.3 Confidentiality

(1) Known partial message attack. The attacker can obtain some information about the encryption algorithm through this process, so that the attacker can crack the encrypted information more effectively in the future. The attacker obtains the message (V_{i_1}, V_{i_2}) and (f, s_i) through eavesdropping. Due to the assumption of discrete problems, the attacker cannot obtain r_i, and the participant's private key d_i cannot be obtained from the equation $s_i = r_i + d_i c_i mod q$. Therefore, the security of the algorithm is mainly determined by the difficulty of solving discrete logarithm problems on elliptic curves in finite fields, while is secure.

(2) Known signature message attack. The attacker obtains the signature encrypted information and uses public parameters to crack the encrypted information. The attacker obtains signature encrypted information (f, s) by eavesdropping. In this scheme, the signature is combined with the public key of the designated receiver to jointly encrypt and form a message, and the attacker attempts to calculate the private key of the designated receiver by combining the signature information with the public key of the system or the public key of the designated receiver, thereby obtaining the original text is as difficult as solving the discrete logarithm problem, so the encrypted information is secure.

4.4 Robustness

The designated receiver U_i can determine whether some of the participants have tampered with the sub-key to cheat by calculating and comparing $V_1' = V_1$. In the threshold signature scheme, the whole system can still generate complete valid signatures when there are less than $n - t$ non-cooperators, so it has good robustness.

5 Performance Analysis

Compared with some other schemes based on threshold signature of elliptic curve, the time complexity of other operations such as module addition, exclusive OR and so on are relatively small compared with modular exponentiation and modular multiplication, which are ignored here. Where T_m represents the modular multiplication operation, T_p represents the bilinear pairing operation and T_e represents the modular exponentiation operation. Comparing the computational time of this scheme with other similar schemes, as shown in Table 2.

Table 2. Comparison between our scheme and other schemes

Scheme	Signature algorithm	Verification algorithm
Meshram et al. [7]	$T_m + T_p + T_e$	$T_m + T_p$
Barreto et al. [16]	$T_m + T_e$	$T_m + T_p + T_e$
Xu [17]	$T_m + T_e$	$T_m + T_e$
Our scheme	$2T_m$	T_e

Although in a signature scheme based on Shamir threshold, it takes a lot of time for t members to generate partial signatures, it is far less than the time consumed by bilinear pairing and power exponential operation. The proposed scheme avoids using bilinear and power exponential operations, and greatly reduces the amount of calculation and consumption time. Moreover, the proposed scheme has less data transmission, which reduces the time and resources required for transmission. Therefore, compared with other schemes, the proposed scheme consumes the least time and resources and has better performance.

6   Conclusion

The elliptic curve based threshold signature scheme proposed in this paper, in which only no less than t valid participants can cooperate to form a valid signature, and only the designated receiver can verify and decrypt messages, so as to meet the requirements of unforgeability, message confidentiality and transmission security, etc. The proposed scheme greatly reduces the computational complexity and the communication and time cost required for secure transmission of messages, and it also has good robustness.

References

1. Shamir, A.: How to share a secret. Commun. ACM **22**(11), 612–613 (1979)
2. Desmedt, Y., Frankel, Y.: Shared generation of authenticators and signatures. In: Feigenbaum, J. (ed.) CRYPTO 1991. LNCS, vol. 576, pp. 457–469. Springer, Heidelberg (1992). https://doi.org/10.1007/3-540-46766-1_37
3. Ding, K., Ding, C.: A class of two-weight and three-weight codes and their applications in secret sharing. IEEE Trans. Inf. Theory **11**(61), 5835–5842 (2015)
4. Harn, L.: Group-oriented threshold signature scheme and digital multisignature. IEEE Proc. Comput. Digit. Tech. **141**(5), 307–313 (1994)
5. Asaar, M.R., Salmasizadeh, M., Susilo, W.: A short identity-based proxy ring signature scheme from RSA [EB/OL] (2015)
6. Karati, A., Biswas, G.P.: Efficient and provably secure random oracle-free adaptive identity-based encryption with short-signature scheme. Secur. Commun. Netw. **9**(17), 4060–4074 (2016)
7. Meshram, C.Y., Powar, P.L., Obaidat, M.S.: An UF-IBSS-CMA protected online/offline identity-based short signature technique using PDL [EB/OL] (2017)
8. Gong, B., Zhang, Y., Wang, Y.: A remote attestation mechanism for the sensing layer nodes of the internet of things. Future Gener. Comput. Syst. **78**(3), 867–886 (2018)
9. Liu, Y., Cheng, C., Gu, T., et al.: A lightweight authenticated communication scheme for smart grid. IEEE Sens. J. **16**(3), 836–842 (2016)
10. Dragan, C.C., Tiplea, F.L.: Distributive weighted threshold secret sharing schemes. Inf. Sci. **339**, 85–97 (2016)
11. Harn, L., Wang, F.: Threshold signature scheme without using polynomial interpolation. IJ Netw. Secur. **18**(4), 710–717 (2015)

12. Li, S., Doh, I., Chae, K.: A group authentication scheme based on Lagrange interpolation polynomial. In: Proceedings of the 10th International Conference on Innovative Mobile and Internet Services in Ubiquitous Computing (IMIS16), pp. 386–391. IEEE (2016)
13. Lin, H.Y., Hsieh, M.Y., Li, K.C.: Secured map reduce computing based on virtual machine using threshold secret sharing and group signature mechanisms in cloud computing environments. Telecommun. Syst. 60(2), 303–313 (2015)
14. Xiong, L., Shi, Y.: On the privacy-preserving outsourcing scheme of reversible data hiding over encrypted image data in cloud computing. CMC: Comput. Mater. Continua 55(3), 523–539 (2018)
15. Tang, Y., Lian, H., Zhao, Z., Yan, X.: A proxy re-encryption with keyword search scheme in cloud computing. CMC: Comput. Mater. Continua 56(2), 339–352 (2018)
16. Barreto, P.S.L.M., Libert, B., Mccullagh, N., et al.: Efficient and provably-secure identity-based signatures and signcryption from bilinear maps [EB/OL] (2017)
17. Xu, F.: Proactive threshold RSA signature scheme based on polynomial secret sharing. J. Electron. Inf. Technol. 38(9), 2280–2286 (2016)

A Congestion Control Methodology with Probability Routing Based on MNL for Datacenter Network

Renhui Hou[1,4], Dongbin Wang[2,3(✉)], Yao Wang[2], and Zhouyi Zhu[2]

[1] School of Software Engineering,
Beijing University of Posts and Telecommunications, Beijing, China
627107350@qq.com
[2] School of Cyberspace Security,
Beijing University of Posts and Telecommunications, Beijing, China
{dbwang,wangyao613,iezhuzhouyi}@bupt.edu.cn
[3] National Engineering Laboratory for Mobile Network Security (BUPT),
Beijing, China
[4] Key Laboratory of Trustworthy Distributed Computing and Service (BUPT)
Ministry of Education, Beijing, China

Abstract. The burst traffic is one of the most important reasons that cause congestion in the data centers. One way to reduce network congestion is to reroute elephant flows on new paths. Most of the current researches focus on the scheme of detecting elephant flows and a few such as Offline Increasing First Fit (OIFF) considers the routing algorithm, which chooses the path with the max remaining bandwidth when scheduling elephant flows. OIFF may relieve the network congestion, but it may also put several elephant flows on the same links which results in new congestions. In this paper, we present Max Probability Fit Algorithm (MPF), a new routing methodology which is based on multinomial logit model (MNL). MPF chooses the rerouting path for each flow with probability, and it's less likely to distribute the traffic to the same links. The experiment shows that MPF can increase performance of throughput by 3.6% and bring down packet loss rate by 26.84% over OIFF.

Keywords: Congestion · Rerouting · Probability

1 Introduction

From small enterprises to large scale cloud providers, most of the existing IT systems and services are strongly dependent on highly scalable and efficient data centers [1]. Since the traffic in data centers vary time to time, when the capacity of network resource and node cannot withstand current network loads, it causes network congestion in datacenter, following with the decrease of network performance, even the crashes of system, thus improving robustness of datacenter network against network congestion is a challenging but considerable problem.

© Springer Nature Switzerland AG 2019
X. Sun et al. (Eds.): ICAIS 2019, LNCS 11635, pp. 343–352, 2019.
https://doi.org/10.1007/978-3-030-24268-8_32

There have been two types of solutions of congestion control:

(1) One is deployed on the terminal from the end-to-end system. If the destination end detects congestion, it sends signal resembling congestion to the source end, thus the source end adjusts the amount of sending packets to relieve the network congestion, such as DCTCP, D^3, D^2TCP. In the methods above, through modifying the congestion window or receiving window, the sender can slow down the rate of TCP flows, reduce the amount of data packets in the network and the length of queue in switches.

(2) The other one considers when congestion occurs, the forwarding device schedules data flows in the network or manage the queue in the port, under the view of surrounding network information, to eliminate congestion, such as Open Shortest Path First (OSPF) and Equal-cost multi-path (ECMP [2]). OSPF selects the path with the least hops for each source/destination pair through which all packets are arranged to go. ECMP is a routing method for routing packets along multiple paths to the same destination of equal cost. When a packet with multiple alternative paths arrives, it is forwarded on the one that corresponds to a hash of selected fields of that packet's headers modulo the number of paths, splitting load to each subnet across multiple paths.

However, all the solutions above are restricted because of the limited surrounding information, thus they cannot make adjustment according to the global information such as network status and traffic patterns.

Software-defined network (SDN) is a novel network architecture. The network architecture can be decoupled into two parts: control plane and data plane. Furthermore, SDN controllers in the control plane give the network control decisions, and SDN switches in the data plane only accomplish the data forwarding function according to these decisions [3]. SDN provides with a global view and the ability to centrally manage the network through decoupling the controlling and forwarding.

There have been researches in various terms of SDN, for example, [4] is proposed to deal distributed denial-of-service attacks in SDN networks. The emergence of SDN is expected to change the current state of congestion control:

(1) In terms of traffic measurement, it deploys flexible, scalable and global task, collects the network status information in real time, monitors and analyzes the traffic accurately.

(2) In terms of traffic management, it comprehensively considers the network status and network application requirements, and carries out flow schedule in a dynamic, flexible and fine-grained way, thus it improves the network load-balancing.

(3) In terms of resource utilization and maintenance, it dynamically allocates the network resources including bandwidth and storage based on the centralized network state feedback, thus it achieves effective and reasonable resource utilization.

Although there have been a lot of researches, the data centers still suffer from severe congestion, especially on the links in the core layer, meanwhile, there are also a large number of idle links in the core layer. Bensons et al. pointed that 75% of the links in the core layer are underutilized [5]. Therefore, it's reasonable to schedule flows on the congested link to the links with low load when congestion occurs.

Datacenter measurements show that a large fraction of datacenter traffic is carried in a small fraction of flows [6]. The authors report that 90% of the flows carry less than 1 MB of data (mice flows) and more than 90% of bytes transferred are in flows greater than 100 MB (elephant flows). Al-Fares et al.'s Hedera [7] shows that managing elephant flows effectively can yield as much as 113% higher aggregate throughput compared to ECMP which works well only for large numbers of mice flows and no elephant flows. Therefore, it's reasonable to only manage the elephant flows on the congested links.

Currently, most research against congestion in data center work focuses on analyzing the traffic flows and finding the elephant flows while only a few research focuses on scheduling algorithm:

Hedera [7] is a scalable, dynamic traffic management system. The edge switches, which are connected with the egress ports of end hosts, probe and mark the elephant flows. Hedera estimates the bandwidth requirements of elephant flows, and then chooses reasonable paths for these flows. In terms of routing algorithm, Hedera proposed Global First Fit Algorithm. For any path belonging to the set of the alternative paths of a flow, if the minimum remaining bandwidth of the link on this certain path can satisfy the demand of flow, then the first satisfied path is chosen as the new path the flow should be forwarded on. However, it's easily to lead to unreasonable bandwidth allocation without fully considering all satisfied paths.

Curtis et al.'s Mahout [8] also proposed to optimize the management of elephant flows. A shim layer, which is abstracted by the operating system in the end host, monitors flows generated by the host through the socket buffer. If the buffer exceeds a predetermined threshold, the specified flow is marked as an elephant flow. Mahout used Offline increasing first fit Scheduling Algorithm to calculate paths for elephant flows. All satisfied paths are compared and the path with the max remaining bandwidth are chose. The experimental results show that it can effectively increase the utilization of path bandwidth and throughput in the network. But it may put several flows on the same links which may result in severe convergence to same low-loaded links and congestion may occur on these links.

In this paper, we present a congestion control methodology that when congestion occurs, we schedule the elephant flows on other reasonable paths. Especially, we present Max Probability Fit Algorithm (MPF), a new routing methodology which is based on multinomial logit model (MNL [9]). MNL is a classical model of random utility theory, which is used to assess the individual's choosing behavior. Since the behavior of "choosing a path" is caused by various factors, it is difficult to estimate exactly what to be selected. Hence, in random utility theory, we estimate the "probability" to be chose toward each alternative path.

When scheduling several flows simultaneously, since MPF chooses the rerouting path for each flow with probability, it's less likely to lead to the convergence to same links. Furthermore, MPF makes for ensuring the network performance such as ensuring the throughput of the network after congestion occurs.

2 Routing Algorithm of MPF

2.1 Multinomial Logit Model

Let us suppose a situation where i is going to choose an alternative j from an alternative set $N = \{1, 2, \ldots, n\}$. We assume the utility when i chooses alternative j U_{ij}, which is composed of observable utility V_{ij} and random utility ε_{ij} as follow

$$U_{ij} = V_{ij} + \varepsilon_{ij} \tag{1}$$

V_{ij} is a function estimated by a researcher which depends on the observed characteristics of the alternative j or i. ε_{ij} is a random function, representing the utility that cannot be observed. According to the maximum utility theory, the purpose of the choice is to maximize the utility, therefore i only chooses j when U_{ij} exceeds all the utilities of other alternatives as follow

$$V_{ij} + \varepsilon_{ij} > V_{ik} + \varepsilon_{ik}, \forall j \neq k, j, k \in N \tag{2}$$

The probability P_{ij} that i chooses j is as follow

$$P_{ij} = \Pr(V_{ij} + \varepsilon_{ij} > V_{ik} + \varepsilon_{ik}, \forall j \neq k) = \Pr(\varepsilon_{ik} < \varepsilon_{ij} + V_{ij} - V_{ik}, \forall j \neq k) = F(V_{ij}) \tag{3}$$

$F(V_{ij})$ is in different formats when ε_{ij} is from different distributions. In the MNL, random factors in the utilities are assumed to be independent random variables from the identical Gumbel distribution, therefore, the probability P_{ij} that the individual i chooses the alternative j is as follow

$$P_{ij} = \frac{exp[\gamma * V_{ij}]}{\sum_{j \in N} exp[\gamma * V_{ij}]} \tag{4}$$

2.2 Routing Based on MNL

Let us consider a flow f_i at the rate φ_i from the source s to the destination d. $W = \{s_1, s_2, \ldots, s_m\}$ is the set of all satisfied paths. Any satisfied path $s = \{l_1, l_2, \ldots, l_n\}(s \in W)$ starts from s and ends with d, and the minimum remaining bandwidth of the link on this certain path can satisfy the demand of flow as follows

$$RB_{s_j} = RB_{l_a} = min\{RB_{l_1}, RB_{l_2}, \ldots, RB_{l_n}\} \tag{5}$$

$$Capacity_{l_a} - RB_s + \varphi_i < Threshold_{l_a} \tag{6}$$

RB_{s_j} above symbols the rest bandwidth of the path s_j. $Capacity_{l_a}$ above is a determined value, which means the max load of the link l_a. $Threshold_{l_a}$ above is a predetermined value which represents congestion if current load exceeds it. In general, when a flow chooses a routing path, the smallest cost path should be used most often, and the higher the path cost of the path becomes, the less the path is used. To incorporate this feature, let us define the probability P_{ij} that flow f_i chooses the path s_j as follow

$$P_{ij} = \frac{exp\left[-\gamma * C_{ij}\right]}{\sum_{j \in N} exp\left[-\gamma * C_{ij}\right]} \tag{7}$$

C_{ij} above means the cost that f_i chooses s_j. In Mahout, Curtis proposes Offline increasing first fit Scheduling Algorithm which points out that the path with max remaining bandwidth should be chose. If f_i suddenly grows in a rapid rate, the path with max remaining bandwidth may has the least probability to be congested among all satisfied paths. Here, we define the cost that f_i chooses s_j as follows:

$$C_{ij} = \frac{\varphi_i}{RB_{s_j}} \tag{8}$$

Finally, we get the set of probability of all the satisfied paths for f_i $P_i = \{P_{i1}, P_{i2}, \ldots, P_{im}\}$. Every time MPF chooses the routing path for f_i according to the computed set P_i.

3   System Architecture of MPF

3.1   Architecture

MPF system consists of three modules, the Monitor, the Network State and the Routing Engine.

Monitor implemented in the controller, queries the statistics from each switch by polling them at fixed intervals. Every time the Monitor sends a request, it would receive the response messages from the switches. Once congestion is detected, the Monitor would locate where the congestion occurs and inform the Routing Engine. Meanwhile, the Network State updates the current statistics of the network state, then sends the statistics to the Routing Engine. The Routing Engine queries the information of elephant flows on the congested link, computes the fit rerouting paths for these elephant flows, and installs rules of the new routing paths on the corresponding switches.

3.2   Monitor

The purpose of this module is to query the statistics from all switches and detect whether congestion occurs. This module collects statistics by polling each switch at fixed intervals. If the queue length in a port exceeds the predetermined threshold, congestion is considered to be occur, and the connected link is regarded as the congested link.

3.3 Network State

The purpose of this module is to store the state information of the network. It stores the all the links in the network, which are denoted by the corresponding pairs of the source point and the destination point connected by the link, the max load and the current load of the links. Table 1 shows an example of the links stored in this module if there are only three links in the network.

Table 1. Link information in the Network State

Link	Max load	Current load
of:000/1-of:010/3	100M	20M
of:002/1-of:010/1	80M	50M
of:010/2-of:001/1	100M	70M

The Network State also stores all flow information in the network, including the current track and rate of the flow. As defined in Hedera, flows are packet streams with the same 10-tuple of <src MAC, dst MAC, src IP, dst IP, EtherType, IP protocol, TCP src port, dst port, VLAN tag, input port> . Here, we denote a flow by its 10-tuple. Table 2 shows an example of the flows stored in this module if there are only two flows in the network.

Table 2. Flow information in the Network State

Flow	Track	Rate
Tuple_1	AA-of:000/1-of:001/2-of:001/1-of:002/2-BB	20Mbits/s
Tuple_2	CC-of:003/1-of:002/2-of:002/1-of:001/2-DD	50Mbits/s

3.4 Routing Engine

As the core of the whole system, this module is responsible for rerouting functions. It chooses which flows should be scheduled and decides which paths it should forward the flows on.

As stated above, Hedera shows that managing elephant flows effectively can yield as much as 113% higher aggregate throughput compared to ECMP which works well only for large numbers of mice flows and no elephant flows. Thus we need to detect elephant flows and schedule them. Generally, if the transfer bytes of a flow reach the predetermined threshold, we consider this flow as an elephant flow. DevoFlow [10] assigns the threshold to be 1 MB–100 MB while Mahout considers it should be 100 KB. Hedera sets the threshold to be 10% of the bandwidth of the network interface card and we follow it.

After getting the elephant flows, we calculate a rerouting path for each flow using the methodology proposed in Sect. 2.

4 Evaluation

4.1 Experimental Environment

In the absence of real OpenFlow switches, we evaluated the performance of our method on Mininet, a lightweight simulation tool, widely used to formulate a self-defined network topology connected composed by some virtual end-hosts, switches and routers. We implement MPF on an open source controller called ONOS, one of the most popular SDN controllers at present.

4.2 Experiment Topology

In this experiment, we use the fat-tree topology, which is commonly used in the datacenter network. Fat-tree is stable, scalable and can be easily deployed with simple architecture. For a fat-tree network built from n-port switches, there are k pods, each consisting of two layers: lower pod switches (edge switches), and the upper pod switches (aggregation switches). Each edge switch manages $\left(n/2 \right)$ hosts. The k pods are interconnected by $\left(n/2 \right)^2$ core switches. In our experiment, we set 16 hosts corresponding to n = 4 and assign the capability of every link as 100Mbits/s.

4.3 Experiment Pattern

In the absence of commercial data center network traces, for both the testbed and the simulator evaluation, we first create a communication pattern called Stride (i) which is commonly used in datacenter network. In this pattern, a host with index i sends a UDP flow with 5Mbits/s to the host with index $(x + i) mod(num\_hosts)$ as the background flows. Here, we set i = 8. Each experiment lasts for 60 s. At the time of 10 s, we send k bust flows with 45Mbits/s between two random hosts as source and destination. We test when k range from 1 to 10.

4.4 Result

To evaluate the effectiveness of MPF, we implement simple network with no methods for congestion control and OIFF, which reroutes the elephant flows to the path with the max remaining bandwidth when congestion is detected, and then compare them with MPF.

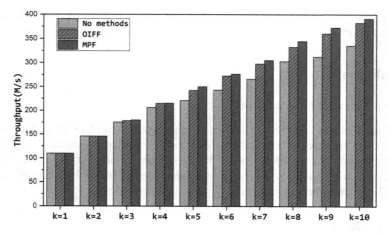

Fig. 1. Throughput of No methods, OIFF and MPF

Figure 1 shows how throughput varies when the amount of burst flows k ranges from 1 to 10. As is commonly known, the larger throughput represents the better performance of the network.

From Fig. 1, when k = 1 and 2, the throughput of three algorithms are identical. We can consider that no congestion occurs in this case. When k ranges from 3 to 10 and congestion occurs, MPF performs better than OIFF and both they increase the throughput than with no methods. For instance, when k = 8, we find that MPF can yield as much as 13.82% higher throughput compared to no methods, and increase performance of throughput by 3.6% over OIFF as well. What's more, when the value of k grows, the network went into more severe congestion, and we observe that MPF and OIFF show greater advantages than no methods. However, there was little difference in the performance gap between MPF and OIFF when we vary k after its value exceeds 5.

Figure 2 shows how packet loss rate varies when the amount of burst flows k ranges from 4 to 8. The metric packet loss rate means the ratio of the number of lost packets to the number of sent packets in a test. Therefore, the smaller packet loss rate represents the better performance of the network.

From Fig. 2, MPF performs better than OIFF and no methods. For instance, when k = 7, MPF obviously brings down the packet loss rate by 26.84% and 41.57% compared with OIFF and no methods, respectively.

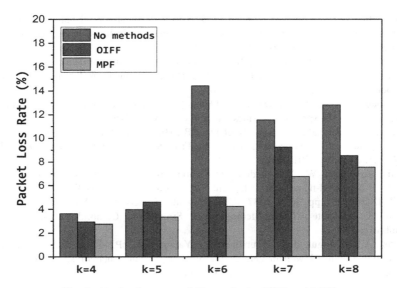

Fig. 2. Packet loss rate of No methods, OIFF and MPF

5 Conclusion

This paper proposes MPF, a congestion control methodology which reroutes for flows with probability based on MNL. In MPF, the Monitor queries the statistics from each switch by polling them at fixed intervals. Once congestion is detected, the Monitor would locate where the congestion occurs. The Routing Engine queries the information of elephant flows on the congested link, computes the fit rerouting paths for these elephant flows, and installs rules of the new routing paths on the corresponding switches. MPF chooses the rerouting path for each flow with probability based on MNL. The path with more remaining bandwidth has more probability to be chosen.

To evaluate the performance of MPF, we compare MPF to network with no methods for congestion control and OIFF on the performances on throughput and packet loss rate. We simulated the topology and traffic pattern of datacenters. The results show that MPF can increase performance of throughput by 3.6% and bring down packet loss rate by 26.84% over OIFF.

References

1. Kreutz, D., Ramos, F.M., Verissimo, P., Rothenberg, C.E., Azodolmolky, S., Uhlig, S.: Software-defined networking: a comprehensive survey. Proc. IEEE **103**(1), 14–76 (2015)
2. Hopps, C.: Analysis of an Equal-Cost Multi-Path Algorithm. RFC 2992, IETF (2000)
3. Wan, M., Yao, J., Jing, Y., Jin, X.: Event-based anomaly detection for non-public industrial communication protocols in SDN-based control systems. CMC: Comput. Mater. Continua **55**(3), 447–463 (2018)

4. Cheng, R., Xu, R., Tang, X., Sheng, V.S., Cai, C.: An abnormal network flow feature sequence prediction approach for DDoS attacks detection in big data environment. CMC: Comput. Mater. Continua **55**(1), 95–119 (2018)
5. Benson, T., Akella, A., Maltz, D.: Network traffic characteristics of data centers in the wild. In: Proceedings of the 10th ACM SIGCOMM Conference on Internet Measurement, Melbourne, Australia, pp. 267–280 (2010)
6. Greenberg, A., et al.: VL2: a scalable and Hexible data center network. In: SIGCOMM 2009. LNCS. http://www.springer.com/lncs. Accessed 21 Nov 2016
7. Al-Fares, M., Radhakrishnan, S., Raghavan, B., Huang, N., Vahdat, A. Hedera: dynamic flow scheduling for data center networks. In: Proceedings of the NSDI, vol. 10, pp. 19–33. USENIX, Berkeley (2010)
8. Curtis, A.R., Kim, W., Yalagandula, P.: Mahout: low-overhead datacenter traffic management using end-host-based elephant detection. In: Proceedings of the 2011 IEEE INFOCOM, pp. 1629–1637. IEEE Computer Society Press, Washington (2011)
9. Train, K.: Discrete Choice Methods with Simulation. Cambridge University Press, Cambridge (2003)
10. Curtis, A.R., Mogul, J.C., Tourrilhes, J., Yalagandula, P., Sharma, P., Banerjee, S.: Devoflow: scaling flow management for high performance networks. ACM SIGCOMM Comput. Commun. Rev. **41**(4), 254–265 (2011)

Fast Failover for Link Failures in Software Defined Networks

Zilong Yin[1,4], Dongbin Wang[2,3(✉)], Yinxing Zhao[2], Yaoyao Guo[2], and Shuwen Han[5]

[1] School of Software Engineering,
Beijing University of Posts and Telecommunications, Beijing, China
zilongYin@bupt.edu.cn
[2] School of Cyberspace Security,
Beijing University of Posts and Telecommunications, Beijing, China
{dbwang,gyl}@bupt.edu.cn, 642661489@qq.com
[3] National Engineering Laboratory for Mobile Network Security (BUPT),
Beijing, China
[4] Key Laboratory of Trustworthy Distributed Computing and Service (BUPT)
Ministry of Education, Beijing, China
[5] Article Numbering Center of China, Beijing, China
hanshw@ancc.org.cn

Abstract. Although Software-Defined Networking and its implementation facilitate networks management and dynamic network configuration, recovering from network failures in time remains non-trivial. In this paper, we present a fast failover mechanism called CombinePR to deal with link failure problem. In the fast failover mechanism, the controller established multiple paths for each source-destination pair in the related OpenFlow-enabled switches. In Fat-Tree, one link called origin link in the selected path can be replaced by other three links which are not in the selected path and can connect the same two switches connected by the that origin link. CombinePR randomly selects a links set as alternative links set for each source-destination link pair when considering a failure in each link of the active path. When a link becomes broken, OF switches are able to distributed the affected flows to alternative three links. The experiments show the CombinePR can reduce 43.6% loss packet rate compared to FFS.

Keywords: Software Defined Networks · Link failure · Fast failover

1 Introduction

In recent years, software-defined network (SDN) has received increasing attention in both academia and industry. Based on the SDN technology, the network architecture can be decoupled into two parts: control plane and data plane. Furthermore, SDN controllers in the control plane give the network control decisions, and SDN switches in the data plane only accomplish the data forwarding function according to these decisions [1]. The controller supports any kinds of control software to manager underlying network devices via an open and standardized application programming interface (API). OpenFlow [2, 3] is a well-known example of such an API. An OpenFlow-enabled

© Springer Nature Switzerland AG 2019
X. Sun et al. (Eds.): ICAIS 2019, LNCS 11635, pp. 353–361, 2019.
https://doi.org/10.1007/978-3-030-24268-8_33

switch supports one or more flow table and communicates with the controller through a secure channel. The controller can manage the packets traffic by reactively or proactively installing flow entries in the flow table. In each flow entry, certain instructions are specified to handle the matched packets. Therefore, an OpenFlow-enabled switch can perform different functionalities according to the flow entries installed by applications. In the last years, numerous efforts exploited SDN flexibility and programmability to cope with increasingly stringent network requirements of many technology trends. For example DDOS [4] and Secure Video Streaming [5].

Due to its centralized control paradigm, SDN is being adopted in the various types of networks such as data center, mobile networks, transport networks, and enterprise networks. Network resilience is crucial to SDN networks [6]. In this paper, we focus on link failure. To cope with link failure, there are two typical approaches: restoration [7, 8] and protection [8, 9]. In restoration, when a switch detects a link failure, a notification message is sent to the controller. For each affected flow, the controller computes another path and writes an alternative flow entry into the related switches. Since the controller needs to handle a large number of affected flows simultaneously, this approach would yield a long latency to recover all the affect flows. In protection, the controller computes multiple paths for each flow and install flow entries into the related switches in advance. In cases of link failure, the switch can directly forward the affected flows to another path without waiting for the response from the controller.

Dar Lin et al. [9] use fast-failover group type to provide protection and reduce recovery time in data plane. However, the controller computes backup paths (From the selected switch to destination switch) based on Dijkstra's algorithm, so the switch forward all affected flows to the same path. Much packet will lose when the total flow rates of the affected flows is large.

Gonçalves et al. [10] discuss the trade-off between two link recovery approaches, a routing algorithm called algorithm 1 that prioritizes disjoint paths and the other one called algorithm 2 that allows overlapping between primary and backup routes. On the algorithm 1 it was taken into consideration that, in order to prevent a disruption when a link is removed from the topology, it's necessary to have two disjont paths. When a link becomes faulty, source switch is able to failover the affected flows to backup path. The experiment shows algorithm 1 has higher packet loss rate than algorithm 2. The algorithm proposed by Dar Lin and algorithm 2 are the same algorithm.

Ramos et al. [11] propose SlickFlow, a link protection approach that leverages OpenFlow to support encoding of alternative paths in packet header. van Adrichem et al. [12] propose a failure protection mechanism that handles single-link failure with precomputed backup paths installed using OpenFlow fast failover group type. Sgambelluri et al. [13] propose a mechanism where the controller precomputes backup paths, installs flow rules with low priority along primary path to redirect traffic. These three methods are just some ways to install backup path. They are not better fast failover mechanism.

Li Jian et al. [14] present a scalable failover method. They adopt Fat-Tree as the reference DCN topology and design their failover method using an OpenFlow-based approach. Further, to provide scalability, they design their failover algorithm in a local optimal manner, with which only three switches must be modified for handling a single fault, regardless of the size of the target network. Also according to the proposed failover algorithm, no matter how large the topology is, the sum of failure detection time and flow setup time is more or less the same and the time is about 36 ms. But the number of affected flow is only one in experiment. This failover method is a restoration method. The average recovery time of the fast restoration mechanism will grows exponentially as the number of affected flows increases [9].

We observed that restoration method needs long latency to recover all the affected flows. Previous protection methods ignored the characteristics of the Fat-Tree. In this research, we aim to lessen loss packet rate and shorten recovery time.

In this work, we present a fast failover mechanism called CombinePR to deal with link failure problem. CombinePR is a protection method. In CombinePR, the controller pre-establishes multiple paths for each source-destination pair in the related OpenFlow-enabled switches. In Fat-Tree [14], one link called origin link can be replaced by many links sets when links in this set can be connected from the source switch of origin link to destination switch of origin link and the size of links set is three. CombinePR randomly selects a link set as alternative links set for each source-destination pair when considering a failure in each link of the active path. When a link becomes faulty, OF switches are able to failover the affected flows to alternative links set. The emulation on ONOS controller and MININET emulator shows the CombinePR can yield as much as 43.6% lower loss packet rate compared to FFS [9] when the network takes heavy loads. The recovery time of the two methods is roughly the same.

The remainder of this paper is organized as follows. Section 2 presents fast failover mechanisms. Section 3 demonstrates experimental results. Finally, the conclusion is given in Sect. 4.

2   Fast Failover Mechanisms

2.1   Fat-Tree and Alternative Link Set

Among recently proposed DCN topologies, Fat-Tree is known as one of the most promising topologies for future DCNs. Fat-Tree originated from the Clos switching network and was adopted and introduced as a candidate for future DCNs in [14].

In our research work, we use the Fat-Tree topology. Fat-Tree is stable, scalable, easily deployed with simple architecture. For a Fat-Tree network built for k-port switches, there are k pods, each consisting of two layers: lower pod switches (edge switches), and the upper pod switches (aggregation switches). The k pods are inter-connected by $(k/2)^2$ core switches. We set $k = 4$ in experiment. Figure 1 depicts a 4-port switch built as a Fat-Tree with $k = 4$.

Figure 1 illustrates an example of the alternative links sets. For example, three alternative links sets <A1C2A3C1>, <A1C2A5C1> and <A1C2A7C1> for link <A1C1>. There are two flows in figure. For the flow from h1 to h16 and the flow from h2 to h16, the controller computes the same path <E1A1C1A7E8>. Then, three backup paths <E1A1C2A3C1A7E8>, <E1A1C2A5C1A7E8> and <E1A1C2A7E8> are also computed for a potential failure in link <A1C1>. CombinePR will randomly selects an alternative links set for each source-destination pair in corresponding link. For example, for flow from h1 to h16, alternative links set is <A1C2A3C1>. For flow from h2 to h16, alternative links set is <A1C2A5C1>.

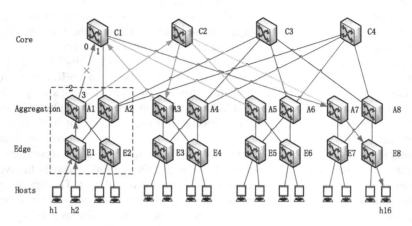

Fig. 1. Example of the alternative link set

2.2   Fast Failover Mechanism

Figure 2 shows the flowchart of the fast failover mechanism. In the beginning, the controller performs topology discovery to acquire global topology information. Then, the edge switches of Fat-Tree are formed into a switch set N_{se}. For a OF switch i in the switch set N_{se}, the controller computes $|N_{se}| - 1$ active paths (From the selected switch to other OF switches) based on Dijktra's algorithm. Then, for an active path j, the controller also computes $|Lj|$ backup paths considering a failure in each link traversed by the active path. Then, for a link k in higher-layer links (between core switches and the aggregation), controller computes n − 1 (n is the number of pods in Fat-Tree) alternative links sets (From the source switch of link k to destination switch of link k) based on Dijktra's algorithm. For a link k in lower-layer links, controller computes $n/2 - 1$ (n is the number of pods in Fat-Tree) alternative link set. Each host in source hosts sets (the hosts attach to source switch) and each host in destination hosts sets (the hosts attach to destination switch) form a pair, and then all pairs formed into a source-destination pair sets N_{sd}. Each source-destination pair in N_{sd} randomly selected an alternative links set. Finally, the controller proactively establishes an active path by installing a flow entry with high priority and establishes a backup path by installing a flow entry with low priority. When a link failure affects active path, active flow entries are removed and the related backup flow entry is automatically used.

Algorithm 1 Framework of the failover mechanism for our system

Input: Network topology

Output: an alternative links set for each flow in each link in active path

1: $N_{es} \leftarrow$ number of edge switches

2: **for** $i = 1; i <= N_{es}; i + +$ **do**

3:      Active path computation(form switch i to other switches);

4:      $N_{ap} \leftarrow$ number of Active paths

5:      **for** $j = 1; j <= N_{ap}; j + +$ **do**

6:          $L_j \leftarrow$ number of Links of j-th active path

7:          **for** $k = 1; k <= L_j; k + +$ **do**

8:              Alternative links sets computation

9:              $N_{sd} \leftarrow$ number of source destination pairs

10:              **for** $m = 1; m <= N_{sd}; m + +$ **do**

11:                  Randomly select an alternative links set

12:                  Install flow entries in related switches

13:              **end for**

14:          **end for**

15:      **end for**

16: **end for**

Fig. 2. Framework of the failover mechanism

3 Performance Evaluation

3.1 Emulation Environment

We investigate the performance of proposed mechanisms through emulation of real implementation. We use Ubuntu version 16.04 for the installation of ONOS version 12 and MININET version 2.3.0. The proposed mechanisms are implemented on ONOS controller. We use MININET to emulate the Fat-Tree topology. In the fast failover mechanism, packet loss rate, average recovery time are adopted as performance metrics.

3.2 Experiments

Figure 3 shows that the packet loss rate of the fast failover mechanism on different flow rate. In this experiment, we randomly select ten pairs hosts. The rate of flow in host pairs is random, and the number of affected flows is greater than 3. As shown on the figure, the performance of these two strategies is similar when the range of flow rate is within the range of 0 to 20 or within the range of 10–30. But the CombinePR can yield as much as 43.6% lower loss packet rate compared to FFS when the range of flow rate is within the range of 20 to 40.

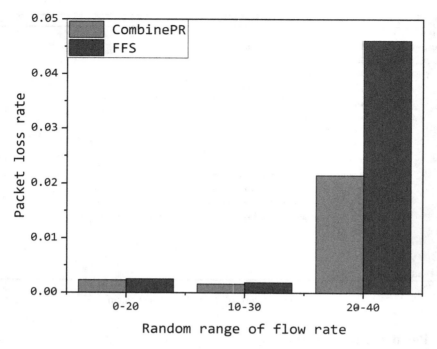

Fig. 3. Packet loss rate

The reason is that the affected flows will be returned to the active path after through different alternative links set when the CombinePR is adopted. However when the FFS is adopted, the affected flows will be switched to the same backup path which is the shortest path from the source switch of fault link to destination switch. When flow rate is within the range of 0 to 20 or within the range of 10 to 30, the remaining bandwidth of backup path is large enough to route all affected flows. So the packet loss rate is small for two methods. Some packets were lost during the period when the affected flows was rerouted to backup path. Because the total packets of network When flow rate is within the range of 0 to 20 is less than the total packets of network When flow rate is within the range of 10 to 30. So the packet loss rate of former is greater than latter. When flow rate is within the range of 20 to 40, the remaining bandwidth isn't large. The backup path can't fit all affected flows' bandwidth demand, therefore the network has high packet loss rate when the FFS is adopted. Due to each affected flow selected the one of alternative links sets, so the network has low packet loss rate when the CombinePR is adopted.

Figure 4 illustrates the average recovery time of CombinePR and FFS varying with different number of affected flows. In this experiment, we select one, two, four of four pairs hosts (h1->h31, h2->h31, h3->h31, h4->h31). The rate of flow in host pairs is selected randomly within range of 0 to 20. In Fig. 4, the average recovery time of two strategies only sightly increases as the number of affected flows increases. The figure show that the recovery time of the two strategies is short and difference of the result of the two strategies is within 10 ms.

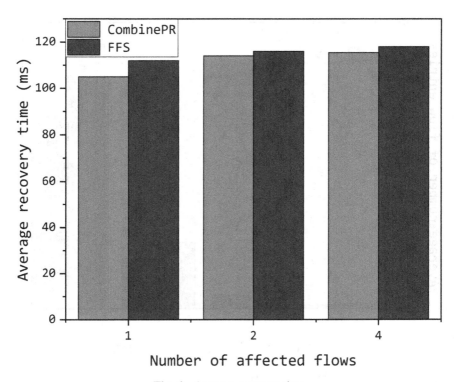

Fig. 4. Average recovery time

Because both strategies are protection, controller needn't to handle affected flows when a link becomes faulty. Therefore, the recovery time is short and no related to the num of affected flows. Throught the experiment, we observed that time for delecting a link failure is relatively long (greater than 110 ms) due to the inefficiency of current implementation of ONOS topology discovery application.

Figure 5 show that the average number of flow entries of two fast failover mechanisms on different num of host per switch. The average number of fast failover grows exponentially as the number of affected flows increases. It is because, the controller needs to compute multiple paths for each source-destination pair and proactively installs flow entries and group entries in related OF switches. We can observe that the average number of flow entries of CombinePR is 1.5 times to FFS. The number of backup entries for each link is three when the CombinePR is adopted, as the backup path is from source of this link to the destination of this link. But the backup path is from source of this link to destination of active path when the FFS is adopted. So the number of flow entries when the CombinePR is adopted is larger than the FFS is adopted when we use the Fat-Tree topology whose number of pods is 4.

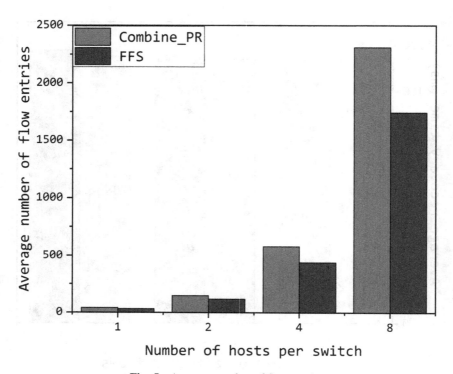

Fig. 5. Average number of flow entries

4 Conclusion

Network resilience is crucial to SDN networks. The research works of the predecessors in the fast failover mechanism can be divided into two typical approaches: restoration and protection. But restoration methods need longer latency. Since the controller needs to handle a large number of affected flows simultaneously, this approach would cause longed latency to recover all the affected flows. Protection has higher packet loss rate, as traffic of all affected flows is larger than the remaining capacity of backup path. And previous protection methods ignored the characteristics of the Fat-Tree.

To minimum loss packet rate and short recovery time, we present a fast failover mechanism called CombinePR to deal with link failure problem. CombinePR is a protection method based on the characteristics of the Fat-Tree. That randomly selects three links set for as the backup of each link in the active path as its alternative links set. When a link becomes broken, OF switches are able to distribute the affected flows in the link to the alternative links set. The experiment shows the CombinePR can reduce 43.6% loss packet rate compared to FFS.

Acknowledgment. This work was supported in part by national science and technology major project of the ministry of science and technology of China No. 2012BAH45B01.

References

1. Wan, M., Yao, J., Jing, Y., Jin, X.: Event-based anomaly detection for non-public industrial communication protocols in SDN-based control systems. CMC: Comput. Mater. Continua **55**(3), 447–463 (2018)
2. Mckeown, N., et al.: OpenFlow: enabling innovation in campus networks. ACM SIGCOMM Comput. Commun. Rev. **38**(2), 69–74 (2008)
3. ONF. OpenFlow Switch Specification version 1.3.2, 25 April 2013
4. Cheng, R., Xu, R., Tang, X., et al.: An abnormal network flow feature sequence prediction approach for DDoS attacks detection in big data environment. CMC Comput. Mater. Continua **55**(1), 95–463 (2018)
5. Liu, P., Wang, X., Chaudhry, S.R., Javeed, K., Ma, Y., Collier, M.: Secure video streaming with lightweight cipher PRESENT in an SDN testbed. CMC Comput. Mater. Continua **57** (3), 353–363 (2015)
6. da Rocha Fonseca, P.C., Mota, E.S.: A survey on fault management in software-defined networks. IEEE Commun. Surv. Tutorials **19**, 2284–2321 (2017)
7. Staessens, D., Sharma, S., Colle, D., Pickaver, M., Demeester, P.: Software defined networking: meeting carrier grade requirements. In: Proceedings of the 18th IEEE Workshop on Local and Metropolitan Area Networks, pp. 1–6, October 2011
8. Sharma, S., Staessens, D., Colle, D., Pickavet, M., Demeester, P.: OpenFlow: meeting carrier-grade recovery requirements. Comput. Commun. **36**(6), 656–665 (2013)
9. Lin, Y., Ieng, H., Hsu, C., Liao, C., Lai, Y.: Fast failover and switch over for link failures and congestion in software defined networks. In: IEEE International Conference on Communication, pp. 1–6 (2016)
10. Gonçalves, P., Martins, A., Corujo, D., Aguiar, R.: A fail-safe SDN bridging platform for cloud networks. In: 2014 16th International Telecommunications Network Strategy and Planning Symposium (Networks), pp. 1–6. IEEE (2014)
11. Ramos, R.M., Martinello, M., Rothenberg, C.E.: Slickflow: resilient source routing in data center networks unlocked by openflow. In: 2013 IEEE 38th Conference on Local Computer Networks (LCN), pp. 606–613. IEEE (2013)
12. van Adrichem, N.L., Van Asten, B.J., Kuipers, F.A.: Fast recovery in software-defined networks. In: 2014 Third European Workshop on Software Defined Networks (EWSDN), (Budapest, Hungary), pp. 61–66. IEEE, September 2014
13. Sgambelluri, A., Giorgetti, A., Cugini, F., Paolucci, F., Castoldi, P.: Effective flow protection in OpenFlow rings. In: National Fiber Optic Engineers Conference, Optical Society of America (2013)
14. Al-fares, M., Loukissas, A., Vahdat, A.: A scalable, commodity data center network architecture. In: Proceedings ACM SIGCOMM Conference Data Communication, pp. 63–74 (2008)

Steady-State Topology Discovery of Target Networks Based on Statistics Method

Di Yang, Yan Liu[✉], and Jing Chen

China State Key Laboratory of Mathematical Engineering
and Advanced Computing, Zhengzhou, China
ms_liuyan@aliyun.com

Abstract. The progress of target network topology discovery research is slow due to the uncertainty of the target network range, and large-scale network measurement activities lead to a large accumulation of "false links" in the results, it is difficult to obtain a relatively accurate network topology. In this paper, we proposed a statistical-based target network steady-state topology discovery method. By statistical analyzing the characteristics of the measured data, we have proposed corresponding solutions to network boundary recognition, "false links" deletion and network steady-state topology construction, so that a relatively complete and accurate target network steady-state topology can be obtained. We also use this method to probe the HK (Hong Kong) and TW (Tai Wan) network and compare it with the data of CAIDA in the same period. Not only do the number of nodes and edges found are increased by two or three orders of magnitude, but also the number of "false links" in the results is greatly reduced.

Keywords: Target network · Steady-state network topology · Network delay · Boundary recognition

1 Introduction

The Internet can be seen as a network alliance of about 50,000 networks or inter-connected Autonomous Systems (AS) [1]. Most of these interconnected networks are owned and managed by different operators, build their own physical infrastructures and serve different purposes. Network type and business diversity and self-management lead to the heterogeneity of the Internet and the imbalance of regional development [2]. With the continuous development and its large scale, it is unrealistic to obtain the entire Internet topology. Fortunately, the network topology in a target area can be obtained through scientific and reasonable measurements.

In order to ensure the pertinence and accuracy of the target network topology discovery, we must not only distinguish which IP nodes belong to the target network and accurately identify the target network boundary, but also effectively delete the "false links" in the measurement process. However, due to various limitations of the network infrastructure and probing methods, this problem has been lacking in effective progress for decades [3]. In order to solve those problems, based on the existing traceroute network measurement method, this paper has done a lot of research to

X. Sun et al. (Eds.): ICAIS 2019, LNCS 11635, pp. 362–374, 2019.
https://doi.org/10.1007/978-3-030-24268-8_34

improve the integrity and accuracy of the target network topology discovery. Mainly from the following aspects to improve:

- Reasonably selects the probing source and target points inside and outside the target network, strive to initiate detection from different locations of the Internet, so that the probing data will enter the target network from different paths, which can discover more nodes and links.
- A network boundary recognition method based on path delay is proposed. It can reasonably determine the range and boundary of the target network, delete nodes that do not belong to the target network and improve the accuracy of topology discovery.
- A method for constructing a steady-state topology of the target network based on fixed-link node pair mining is proposed, which can effectively filter the "false link" phenomenon in the topology measurement process.

The rest of this article is organized as follows: Sect. 2 describes the challenges of network topology discovery. Section 3 gives the solution to this paper. Section 4 gives a detailed description of our method. Section 5 introduces the target network boundary recognition method based on path delay. Section 6 introduces the steady-state topology construction method of the target network. Section 7 design experiments to verify the effectiveness of our approach. Section 8 summarize the full text and point out the next research direction.

2   Related Work and Challenges

Network topology discovery is a major research branch of network measurement. The focus of this research is the Internet physical topology, where nodes represent meaningful network entities and links represent relations between those entities. Large-scale network topology discovery, mainly for entities at the network layer. Depending on the granularity of node, we can classify network topologies into four categories: AS (Autonomous System) level, POP (Point of Presence) level, Router level, and IP interface level [4], where IP interface level network topology discovery is the basis. IP interface level network topology, depicting network layer connection for network IP interfaces. The node is represented by the IP interface of the router, and there is a one-to-one mapping relationship between the node and IP [5]. The edge between them shows the direct connection in the network layer.

Traceroute is the most widely used tool for discovering IP interface level topologies. It uses a limited time-to-live (TTL) probe message, sends it from the probe source to the destination node, and then increases the TTL value in turn. In this way, the probe message continuously returns the IP address of the passing router interface to the probe source along the forward path of the packet, and also reports the RRT value at each hop. Eventually, a topology path will be formed from the source point to the target node. Based on the probe principle of Traceroute technology, it is mainly used in active measurement methods in practical applications [6]. V. Jacobson first implemented the tooling of traceroute, which uses ICMP packets as probe messages [7]. There are also traceroute variants that use other types of probe messages, such as UDP and TCP packets [8].

Target network topology discovery faces at least the challenge of integrity and accuracy at the operational level. The first reason is the Internet network architecture. The basis of the Internet composition - TCP/IP protocol, has no notion of interdomain boundaries at the network layer [9, 10]. In addition, for the sake of security or commercial competition, network owners often hide their own networks, this also creates difficulties for network topology discovery. The second reason is how to recognize the target network boundary and how to distinguish which IP is inside the target network, this has never been a definitive conclusion [11]. In all public IP geodata-bases, the IP information is inconsistent [12]. The third reason is the limitation of probing technology based on traceroute. In the process of measurement, due to the widespread load balancing factors in routers, the "false links" will accumulate in large amounts, resulting in an error in the network topology discovery [1].

3   Our Countermeasures

How to completely and accurately obtain the target network topology is the focus of this paper. Based on the network distributed measurement, we have adopted the appropriate strategies below.

3.1   Measurement Integrity

To ensure the integrity of the measurement, required us to discover more nodes and links. The studies have found that it is impossible to find more nodes and links by simply increasing the number of probing source, target or detection, it must be adopted with a reasonable probing strategy. We proposed a public data fusion method and a network comprehensive measurement method to solve this problem.

Public data fusion is to know which IP nodes are really located in the target network, not only to provide a basis for probe source and target detection but also can mark some IP nodes. Komosný [13] comprehensively evaluated the accuracy of six worldwide IP geodatabase (including MaxMind, IP2Location, Ipligence, HostIP, Netacuity, and Geobytes), found that the best-performing database can only achieve a 50% correct rate at the regional level, while the city-level correct rate is only 30%. The study by Gharaibeh [12] found that use IP database information to locate entities in the network topology is not reliable. But they also point out that if an IP has consistent results across multiple geolocation databases, then the credibility of this result is very high. We take the HK network as an example. Figure 1 indicates the number of IPs marked as HK in different databases.

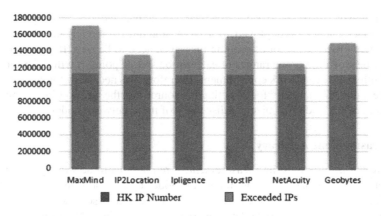

Fig. 1. Coverage of IP addresses marked as HK in databases.

From the figure we can see that the number of IP addresses marked as HK in the six IP geodatabases is varied. However, by querying the APNIC, we find that the total number of IPs currently allocated to HK is 11,213,056.

We selected the IPs with locations all marked in target network from six IP geodatabases as a candidate for internal probing source and targets.

The comprehensive measurement method, based on the idea of distributed probing, adopts three probing strategies from the outside to the inside, from the inside to the inside and from the inside to the outside, which can ensure the integrity of the topology discovery. It requires us to reasonably select the source and targets within and outside the target network. Figure 2 shows a schematic diagram of the integrated measurement method.

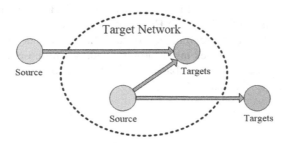

Fig. 2. Schematic diagram of the integrated measurement method.

We know that the distributed network measurement method is essentially a collection of multiple single-point measurements. Using a single point for traceroute, the topology of the discovery is tree-like, which is a spanning tree rooted at the probe source. It can only find a portion of the network IP which is closest to the probe source [3]. If only simply increase the number of probe source points, although the detected network range can be increased, they will also have intersecting parts with each other, which will cause repeated probe. However, in order to save overhead, in actual network topology discovery, probing nodes cannot be deployed in a large amount. Moreover, in a large scale of measurement processes, a lot of probing messages need to be sent. If there is too much crossover between the probe ranges of each probe source point, it will definitely have a negative effect on the network environment. Therefore, it is necessary for us to reasonably formulate a selection strategy for detecting the source and the target point to improve the probing efficiency and maximize the discovery of more network nodes.

3.2   Measurement Accuracy

To ensure the accuracy of the measurement, it requires us to accurately recognize the target network boundary and avoid doping the nodes that are outside the target network. Research shows that the accuracy of the existing IP geodatabase is not satisfactory [12]. Therefore, we believe that it is a bit sloppy to rely solely on the DNS information and the Whois information of the IP to determine the network range. By analyzing a large amount of network delay obtained by traceroute, we find that network delay presents different characteristics at the boundary. Therefore, we propose a boundary recognition method based on network delay, which can reasonably determine the range and boundary of the target network, improve the accuracy of topology discovery.

Another problem that cannot be ignored is the false connections that occurs during a large scale of measurement processes caused by network load balancing. The more number of the measurements, the more the false connections accumulates. Usually, the path through which data packets arrive at a specified node in the network is relatively fixed. But due to factors such as sudden changes in the network environment or router traffic balancing policies, the paths of the probe packets before and after is different. Assume that there is a network topology as showed in Fig. 3, node A is the source of the probe, and node I is the target. The node found in each hop of the probe packet is also identified in the figure. Determining the topology based on the feedback information will result in a non-existent path such as A-B-F-D-H-I. Among them, the two connection relationships of F-D and D-H do not actually exist.

In order to avoid a large accumulation of false links, by analyzing the frequency characteristics of fixed link nodes in the probing data, we propose a steady-state network topology construction method based on fixed-link node pair mining, which can effectively remove the "false links".

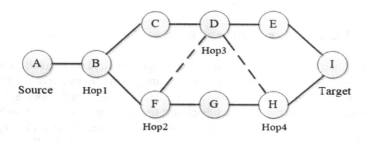

Fig. 3. Impact of router load balancing policy on measurement results.

4   Target network Comprehensive Measurement

4.1   The Summary of Our Methods

We adopt the distributed comprehensive measurement method to discover the target network topology. The first step is public data fusion, aims to provide a basis for select the probing source and target points within the network. The second step is to reasonably select the probing source and target points and develop a scientific probing strategy to improve the integrity of the topology discovery. The third step is to recognize the target network boundary based on path delay to improve the accuracy of topology discovery. The final step is to construct a steady-state topology of the network based on the fixed-link node pair mining, effectively remove the "false link".

4.2   Public Data Fusion

We chose the same six global IP geodatabases as Komosný [13]. Studies have shown that if the IP data have consistent results across all databases, the credibility of this result is very high [12, 13]. So we select the IP which locations are all marked in target network from these six geodatabases, as a candidate set for the inside network source and target points.

4.3   Selection Strategy for Probing Source and Target

We know that the distributed network measurement method is essentially a collection of multiple single-point measurements. If only simply increase the number of probing source points, although the detected network range can be increased, the intersection parts of the detections are also increased. In a large-scale measurement process, a lot of probing packets need to be sent, If there are too many intersections between the probing ranges of each source point, it will definitely have a negative effect on the network environment. It is necessary to reasonably formulate a selection strategy for the probing source and target points.

Through the summary analysis of relevant research, we use the following three simple but effective strategies for the selection of probing source and target points:

- The probing source points inside and outside the target network is deployed in different AS. As it shown in Fig. 4.
- Select target points evenly across different network segments in the target network.
- When selecting the outside target points, select the IP which is not in the same AS with the outside probing source point.

For specific technical details of the measurement process, we directly use previously matured research results. In order to avoid packet filtering, we use Wang Gu's various packet combination detection schemes [14], In terms of reducing detection redundancy, the "Doubletree" algorithm is used.

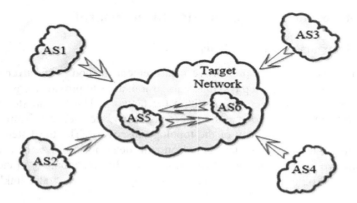

Fig. 4. Probing source selection diagram.

5 Boundary Recognition

5.1 Probing Data Analysis

Based on the probing strategy in part IV, we conducted multiple large-scale measurements for target networks.

Hops Analysis. By analyzing the probing results, we find that even if the probing source and target belongs to different countries or regions, the total number of hops in the most probing result will not exceed 20, most are concentrated between 4 and 16. Figure 5 shows the distribution of the total hops when the target network is successfully detected.

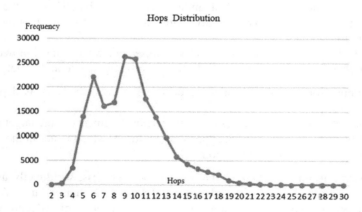

Fig. 5. Distribution of total hops.

We believe this phenomenon may be related to the layered architecture of the Internet. In order to facilitate management and save costs, the hierarchical relationship of the router is generally related to the geographical or administrative division, because the consequences of the geographical distribution of the router are the waste of cable laying and the huge routing table. By analyzing the traceroute probing result, it can be seen that after the packet is sent from the probe source, it is transmitted to a higher-level router (AS or ISP) through the egress router of the unit or region to which the host belongs. That is, packets are transmitted from a city-level network to the national backbone network and then to other regional networks. The number of hops from the end host to the top-level national backbone routers generally do not exceed 10, so the hops between the two end hosts are generally no more than 20. Usually, there is also a connection between the peer backbone routers in the adjacent area, so the data packets can communicate directly without being forwarded by the public upper-level routers of the two, which further reduces the distance between the two nodes in the network.

Network Delay Analysis. Liu discovered in their research that there is a "low-high-low" distribution characteristic of single-hop delays between network nodes in different cities [15]. The reason they believe is that the data packets transmitted over different network paths have different delays (packets are transmitted slow between ISP backbone routes, and fast between urban internal routes). In the previous section, we found that when packets are forwarded across regions, they will inevitably pass through the national/regional backbone network. Therefore, we can further to infer that the packet will also have a "low-high-low" phenomenon when transmitted between different countries network.

We randomly select 300 active IPs as the target nodes in HK, and use the probe points distributed outside HK to detect them, then select the data with the successful probe to analyze the delay characteristics. Although in general, 10 hops will enter the target network, for the sake of insurance, we intercept the first 18 hop data delay information in the probe data for analysis, and the final results are given in Fig. 6.

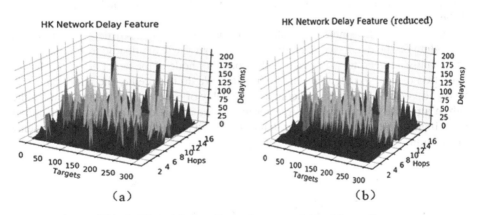

Fig. 6. Time delay profile in the successful probing path.

Figure 6(a) shows the delay distribution of the nodes in the network. We can find that although the network delay will have high and low changes before 8 hops, but between the 8 and 10 hop nodes, the delay of the nodes is obviously very high, and after 10 hops the delay has become undulating. The data indicate that there is a "low-high-low" phenomenon between the nodes from the source point to the target. In order to show this change more clearly, in Fig. 6(b), we reduce the delay between the first 8 hop nodes, and the phenomenon of "low-high-low" delay distribution on the probe path is more obvious.

The reason we analyze this phenomenon may still be related to the hierarchical structure of the Internet. The network delay is mainly comprised of two parts: the transmission delay and the routing delay. The transmission delay is the time to forward a packet over a network link, usually proportional to the link length. The route delay refers to the delay caused by forwarding packets in routers, mainly the queue delay and the router processing delay. which is generally related to the number of messages and router performance. In the hierarchical architecture of the Internet, networks within the same area are connected to the Internet through several common gateway nodes (the gateway nodes are the boundaries of the regional network). This leads to a large amount of data being transmitted through the backbone network when people are doing network activities, it will definitely cause certain congestion and increasing the routing delay. In addition, the distance between the backbone network routes in different areas is relatively long, so the transmission delay will increase accordingly. Reflected from the probing data, the delay between the backbone routing nodes is high, and the delay inside the network border gateway is low, so the delay on the entire probe path may have a significant "low-high-low" phenomenon.

5.2   Network Boundary Recognition

In the previous section, we found that the delay inside the regional network is low, but between the boundary is high. The entire path delay exhibits a significant "low-high-low" phenomenon, so we can recognize the network boundary by analyzing the change of the network delay.

We calculate the single-hop delay by measuring the returned delay information. Depending on the delay characteristics of "low-high-low", the first node with the delay significantly descending is selected as the boundary node of the target network. Here is a question of how to determine the high delay. We do this: center the nodes pair with the highest delay of the path and compare the delay of nodes pair to the two ends of the path in turn. If the larger delay is greater than twice of the lower and not less than half of the highest in the path, the larger delay is deemed to be a high delay. The path delay information is shown in Fig. 7.

Fig. 7. Delay diagram in a successful probing path.

T_{max} is the maximum value of the delay, then centered on T_{max}, compared the delay to the two segments of the path in turn. We take the calculation on the right path as an example to illustrate its calculation process: Compare the values of T_{max} and t2, If $2 * t2 < T_{max}$, IP6 is the target network boundary, ends; If $2 * t2 > T_{max}$, it is considered that t2 is also a high delay, and then compared t2 with t4, until finding a node that meets the requirements.

To further verify the accuracy of this method, we use the traceroute reverse measurement to verify. Take the high delay nodes pair as the target nodes, detecting them with sources inside the target network, then observing the change of delay on the path. We also found that the delay shows an obviously "low-high" changes.

6   Steady-State Topology Construct of Network Based on Fixed-Link Node Pair Mining

Due to the influence of "load balancing" in the network, the "false links" obtained in different batch measurement processes are different. Although we can relatively reduce the occurrence of "false links" by choosing to measure during the periods which network is used less. But this does not completely avoid the accumulation of "false links" during large-scale measurements. To construct a steady-state target network topology, it requires us to remove the "false links", otherwise it may cause a large deviation between the obtained network topology and the real network topology.

The "false link" is mainly caused by the widespread "load balancing" strategy in the network, the location of it in the network is random, and the node pairs that constitute it are also relatively random. Therefore, in the process of measurements, fixed "false link" node pairs will certainly appear little. In comparison, the location and node pairs of the "real links" in the network are fixed, so it will certainly be discovered many times. We counted the number of all fixed-link occurrences in the probing data and found that some fixed-link appeared significantly less frequently in the network. As shown in Fig. 8, we give the distribution characteristics of the first 500 fixed-link node pairs whose appearance frequency is arranged from small to large. The abscissa represents the number of the fixed link node pair, which is numbered from small to large according to the occurrence frequency.

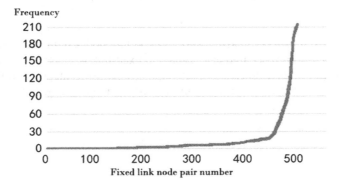

Fig. 8. Frequency statistics of fixed link nodes in the probing topology.

From the figure, we can find that when the occurrence frequency of fixed-link is around 20, there is a significant upward turning point. For the sake of insurance, we take 30 as the threshold and regard the link with occurrence frequency less than 30 as the possible "fake link". Of course, these phenomena can only indicate that they are likely to be "fake links". In order to further prove the "true or false" of these links, we regard these nodes as the target nodes and measure separately. In the final probing results, they did not form the fixed link., so we infer that these links are "false links" and need to be removed in the steady-state network topology construction.

The reason we do like this is that when we calculate the occurrence frequency of fixed-link in each measurement result, we find that the frequency increased sharply before the first 500 pairs of fixed-link nodes, that is there is an inflection point (This inflection point is different in the results of each round of measurements, depending on the total number of measurements).

7 Experimental Comparison

We selected HK and TW as the target network and use the probing strategy of Sect. 4 to perform 50 rounds of detections, finally obtained the steady-state topology of the target network based on our method. Then compared it with the data of CAIDA in the same period in terms of both integrity and accuracy. The standard is: the more nodes and links are discovered. The network topology more complete; the fewer number of "false links" in the topology, the topology more accurate.

The results of the integrity comparison are shown in Table 1, the number of nodes and links we have found are considerably improved.

Table 1. Comparison of nodes and links findings.

Target network	Statistical indicators	CAIDA	Our method	The rate of over discovery
HK	Nodes	215,665	260,534	20.80%
	Links	251,722	348,587	38.48%
TW	Nodes	320258	377351	17.83%
	Links	357294	467855	30.94%

In terms of accuracy comparison, sort all fixed link nodes in the network topology according to their occurrence frequency, and 500 fixed-link with the lowest, middle and highest frequency were extracted respectively, then measure them as probing target. Regard the link that cannot constitute the fixed-link as the "false link", the specific results are shown in Table 2.

Table 2. Comparison of nodes and links findings.

Target network	Statistical indicators	Frequency of occurrence	CAIDA	Proportion	Our method	Proportion
HK	False Links	Lowest	374	74.8%	11	2.2%
		Middle	7	1.4%	3	0.6%
		Highest	0	0	0	0
TW		Lowest	411	82.2%	17	3.4%
		Middle	4	0.8%	1	0.2%
		Highest	0	0	0	0

We can also find that the number of "false links" in the middle and highest fixed-link, is significantly lower than that in the lowest, this further validates the correctness of the steady-state topology construction method of the target network in Sect. 6.

8 Conclusion

For the target network topology discovery task, we propose a statistical-based target network steady-state topology discovery method, which can obtain the target network topology relatively completely and accurately. The next step will be to take appropriate measures to further improve the integrity and accuracy of network topology discovery, such as increasing the number of measurements or improving the measurement methods.

Acknowledgment. This work was supported by the National Key R&D Program of China (No. 2016YFB0801303, 2016QY01W0105), the National Natural Science Foundation of China (No.61309007, U1636219, 61602508, 61772549, U1736214, 61572052) and Plan for Scientific Innovation Talent of Henan Province (No. 2018JR0018).

References

1. Motamedi, R., Rejaie, R., Willinger, W.: A survey of techniques for internet topology discovery. IEEE Commun. Surv. Tutorials **17**, 1044–1065 (2014)
2. Floyd, S., Paxson, V.: Difficulties in simulating the Internet (2001)
3. Claffy, K., Luckie, M., Dhamdhere, A., et al.: Bdrmap: inference of borders between IP networks. In: ACM on Internet Measurement Conference, pp. 381–396 (2016)
4. Donnet, B., Friedman, T.: Internet topology discovery: a survey (2007)
5. Shavitt, Y., Shir, E.: DIMES: let the internet measure itself. ACM SIGCOMM Comput. Commun. Rev. **35**(5), 71–74 (2005)
6. Beverly, R., Berger, A., Xie, G.G.: Primitives for active internet topology mapping: toward high-frequency characterization. In: ACM SIGCOMM Conference on Internet Measurement, pp. 165–171 (2010)
7. "Traceroute": ftp://ftp.ee.lbl.gov/traceroute.tar.gz
8. Toren, M.C.: Tcptraceroute: an implementation of traceroute using TCP SYN packets. Man page (2001). http://michael.toren.net/code/tcptraceroute/

9. Surhone, L.M., Tennoe, M.T., Henssonow, S.F., et al.: TCP/IP Model (2010)
10. Yang, W., Dong, P., et al.: A MPTCP scheduler for web transfer. CMC: Comput. Mater. Continua **57**(2), 205–222 (2018)
11. Wang, J., Ju, C., et al.: A PSO based energy efficient coverage control algorithm for wireless sensor networks. CMC: Comput. Mater. Continua **56**(3), 433–446 (2018)
12. Gharaibeh, M., Shah, A., Huffaker, B., et al.: A look at router geolocation in public and commercial databases. In: Internet Measurement Conference, pp 463–469 (2017)
13. Komosný, D., Vozňák, M., Rehman, S.U., et al.: Location accuracy of commercial IP address geolocation databases. Inf. Technol. Control **46**(3), 333–344 (2017)
14. Wang, G., et al.: Topology discovery of backbone network based on multi-message combination. Comput. Eng. Sci. **29**(8), 4–6 (2007)
15. Liu, S., Liu, F., Zhao, F., et al.: IP city-level geolocation based on the PoP-level network topology analysis. In: International Conference on Information Communication and Management, pp 109–114. IEEE (2016)

A Novel Method for Weighted Throughput Fairness in Contention-Based WLANs with Multiple Priority Levels

Chun Shi[1], Zhi-qun Zheng[1], Zheng-jie Deng[1], Yu-juan Wang[2], and Shu-qian He[1(✉)]

[1] Hainan Normal University, Haikou 571158, People's Republic of China
76005796@qq.com
[2] Xinhua College of Sun Yat-Sen University, Guangzhou 510520, People's Republic of China

Abstract. Focus on the weighted throughput fairness in IEEE 802.11e networks, we propose an adaptive and full-distributed access mechanism. We define a new parameter of Detection Window (DW) that has the same sizes for all nodes. During the process of DW, nodes detect messages of CSI and estimate active node number to set sizes of CW according to itself priority level. We set optimal CW sizes for nodes with the highest priority level and increase CW sizes for nodes with lower priority levels. The selected CW determines sizes of backoff windows and attempt probability of channel access, which can be reflected weighted throughput fairness corresponding to multiple priority levels. The simulation results confirm the validity and good scalability of the proposed access mechanism among multiple priority levels.

Keywords: IEEE 802.11e · Medium access control · EDCA · Weighted throughput fairness

1 Introduction

THESE applications of different traffic types, such as voice, video or data traffic, need multiple Quality of Service (QoS) levels. The weighted throughput fairness corresponding to multiple priority levels (MPLs) is one of the main research directions to improve the QoS performance of network. The IEEE 802.11 family provides the most popular usage in wireless networks. The methods in IEEE 802.11 cannot solve the multiple transmission times of the same nodes during one transmission cycle, which results in the bad fairness.

In this work, we focus on contention-based methods (DCF mechanism and EDCA mechanism) for detail analyses of CSI measurement. We propose an Access Mechanism with Multiple Priority Levels (AMMPL) to analyze performance of weighted throughput fairness.

© Springer Nature Switzerland AG 2019
X. Sun et al. (Eds.): ICAIS 2019, LNCS 11635, pp. 375–384, 2019.
https://doi.org/10.1007/978-3-030-24268-8_35

2 State of the Art

There are two main contention-based methods: DCF mechanism and EDCA mechanism in [1]. Except for some access parameters, these two methods have the same processes of data transmission like Fig. 1.

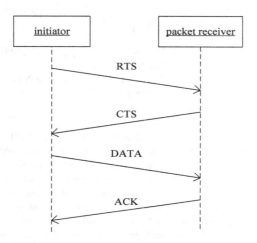

Fig. 1. RTS/CTS/DATA/ACK mode

In Fig. 1, the initiator detects the status of channel. If the channel is idle, the initiator sends RTS frame to reserve the channel for the next data transmission. If the packet receiver gets the RTS frame and analyzes that it is the destination receiver of the RTS frame, the packet receiver sends a CTS frame to the initiator, which means that the packet receiver is ready to accept data frame and announces the occupation of the shared channel for the later data transmission. After receiving the CTS frame, the initiator sends a data frame and waiting the ACK frame. If the packet receiver gets the accurate data frame, it sends ACK frame back to the initiator that means it has gotten the accurate data frame. And then, the full transmission is done.

If the initiator cannot receive the ACK frame during certain time, it judges the failed data transmission. The length of the data packet and the waiting time for ACK frame are the total time for the initiator to determine the collision of data transmission. To reducing the waste time of judgment process of collision, the RTS/CTS frames are used for the large length of data packet due to the large collision judgment time.

If the length of data packet is small, however, nodes can exchange messages without RTS/CTS frames. There is a threshold to determine the usage of RTS/CTS frames to reserve the channel. The usage of RTS/CTS frames, however, increases the overhead of throughput due to the exchange time especially in networks with large nodes.

With the data transmissions of the initiator and the receiver, other nodes detect the activities of the shared channel and defer their data transmissions according to the status of the channel.

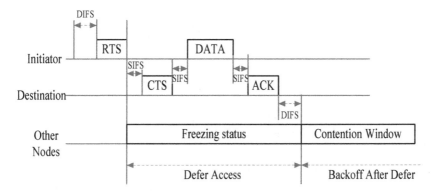

Fig. 2. Access status of other nodes

As shown in Fig. 2, other nodes get into a freezing status if they receive the accurate RTS frame of the initiator. And other nodes stop backoff processes or activities of data sending for avoiding data collisions with the initiator and the destination. After the data transmission between the initiator and the destination, other nodes begin the backoff processes again for reserving the shared channel.

During these processes of data transmission, there are some transmission collision events among two nodes and more transmitting at the same time. If nodes judge the transmission collision event, they normally adjust access parameters for next retransmission. In this work, we focus on the adjustment rules of CW and show the rules of CW in Fig. 3.

As shown in Fig. 3, the adjustment rule of CW can be described as

$$CW_{i+1} = MIN\{(CW_i + 2) * 2 - 1, \ CW_{max}\} \tag{1}$$

In (1), $i (i \in (0, 1, 2, \bullet \bullet \bullet))$ means the transmission times. And we have $CW_0 = CW_{min}$. In IEEE 802.11, both methods of DCF and EDCA have the fixed sizes of CW $\{CW_{min}, CW_{max}\}$. Nodes select sizes of backoff window randomly in CW and begin decrement processes of backoff window. If sizes of backoff window reach to zero, nodes begin to send data. If there is a successful data transmission, nodes reset CW sizes. If there are collisions, nodes will double CW sizes.

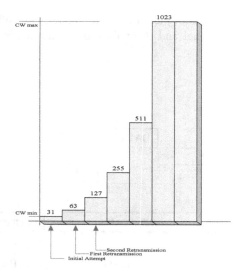

Fig. 3. Adjustment rules of CW

The DCF mechanism uses the same set of access parameter for all nodes, and the EDCA mechanism uses different sets of access parameter for multiple priority levels. In EDCA mechanism, nodes with higher priority level have smaller sizes of CW than that of nodes with lower priority level. Without knowledge of channel status information (CSI), fixing range of CW sizes for nodes with multiple priority levels cannot obtain the expected results as analyses in [2, 3] and [4].

Some works focus on the proportional fairness in multiple priority levels or multi rates WLANs in [5] and [6]. A game theoretic approach is used to analyze model of DCF for tuning CW dynamically in [7]. Collided packets are used to adjust next transmission time for collision-free access in [8]. Some nodes are dependent on itself statuses of data transmission (successful transmission or collision) in [1]. Some nodes adjust CW sizes based on messages detected from decrement processes of backoff window in [3] and [9].

In above adaptive optimizations, the key problem is the calculation of CSI and estimation algorithm of dynamic network conditions (active node numbers in this paper). The idle slot intervals are analyzed when nodes have different CW sizes in [10]. The estimation algorithm with multiple functions is used to track the node number in [2], which is complicated and should be simplified. A searching algorithm is used to find the node number in [11]. An extended Kalman filter is used to obtain the numbers of active queues in [12]. Some optimizations can be found in [13] and [14].

To obtain messages of CSI in homogeneous network with DCF mechanism, the normal window used by adaptive access mechanisms is the backoff window that nodes select in CW in [2]. During their decrement processes of backoff window, nodes detect events of data transmission and calculate message of CSI (for example, idle slot intervals, slot utilization or collision rate). These mechanisms can improve the throughput and fairness of each node with adaptive adjustment rules between access parameters and message of CSI in homogeneous networks. For networks with QoS requirements, the EDCA mechanism presents an application mode. A node itself generates all data with different priority levels. The node sets different sizes of CW for every type of traffics according to priority levels in its transmission queues. It's the number of packets with multiple priority levels that has the important effect on weighted throughput fairness. And it's not easy to add some traffic loads of special priority level. Some adaptive mechanisms of [2, 3] and [9] overlap detection processes on backoff processes, which mean that nodes normally sense messages of CSI during their decrement processes of backoff window. These detection processes work well in DCF mechanism and lost their advantage in EDCA mechanism.

In QoS networks, nodes with MPLs have different sizes of backoff windows and obtain different messages of CSI by overlapping detection processes of CSI on decrement processes of backoff window. Nodes with high priority levels usually use small sizes of CW and select small backoff window to access channel quickly. Nodes with low priority levels, however, use large sizes of CW and select large backoff window, which means more accurate status of CSI than nodes with higher priority levels due to long sensed window. It's unfit to detect messages of CSI during the decrement processes of backoff window in QoS networks. Due to lack of accurate messages of CSI, there are less contention-based mechanisms to analyze throughput performance of three and more priority levels.

In this paper, we propose the AMMPL mechanism and the method can have the main contributions:

- We present a new adjustment rule of CW, in which nodes with the highest priority levels are set the optimal CW sizes and nodes with lower priority levels according to their priority levels have been increased the sizes of CW.
- We define a new parameter of Detection Window (DW) and propose an adjustment rule of DW sizes, which separates detection processes from processes of backoff window.

3 Adaptive Access Mechanism with Multiple Priority Levels

In this section, we focus our interest on the analyses on network with two WPLs, which can be verified in three WPLs. Firstly, we introduce some main results of AMOCW mechanism in [2]; and then, we define a parameter of Detection Window (DW) that has an adjustment rule of Binary Increase and Binary Decrease, which can be used for QoS networks; lastly, we develop adjustment rules of CW in network with two priority levels.

3.1 Throughput Ratios of Priority Levels

Before presenting adjustment rules of CW sizes, we assume that there are two types of WPLs (Class high (H) and Class Low (L)) corresponding to the higher throughput S_H and the lower one S_L for the convenience of analysis. Each node in network is belonged to only one priority level. We obtain

$$S_H : S_L = \rho_H : \rho_L \tag{2}$$

where ρ_H and ρ_L are throughput ratios among nodes with the higher priority level (nodes$_H$) and nodes with the lower priority level (nodes$_L$) ($\rho_H \geq \rho_L$).

Normally, we set $\rho_L = 1$. For case of $\rho_H > \rho_L$, throughput of nodes$_H$ (ρ_H) is larger than that of nodes$_L$ (ρ_L). If nodes$_L$ finish one data transmission, nodes$_H$ should send ρ_H/ρ_L traffic loads for given the same length of packets.

3.2   AMOCW Mechanism

AMOCW mechanism in [2] is fit for homogeneous WLANs and can reach high throughput and fairness. By introducing a parameter of CW index (CWI (θ)), the mechanism builds approximately linear relationship between CW sizes (W for short) and active node number (N) in the network.

$$W \approx \theta \cdot (N - 1) \tag{3}$$

And it further designs a calculation of idle slot intervals n as:

$$n = E_{SLOT} \Big/ \Big(E_C + E_S - \sum_{i=1}^{m} (E_{Si} - 1) \Big) \tag{4}$$

where E_{SLOT} is the values of idle slot time. E_S and E_C are successful data transmission times and collision times detected in the channel, respectively. m is the active node number in the networks that the tagged node detects.

3.3   Definition of Adjustment Rules of DW

In networks with multiple priority levels, nodes should have the same results of CSI although multiple access parameters.

We introduce a new parameter of DW, which sets the same sizes for all nodes. We define a Binary Increase/Binary Decrease adjustment rule of DW as follow,

$$\begin{cases} DW_{new} = \alpha \cdot DW_{cur} & (n \leq n_{opt}) \\ DW_{new} = \beta \cdot DW_{cur} & (n > n_{opt}) \end{cases} \tag{5}$$

where DW_{cur} and DW_{new} mean parameter that nodes are using and predicted values, respectively. n_{opt} is the optimal idle slot intervals between two data transmissions, which can be calculated in advance with the determined parameters. α and β are coefficients used to adjust values of DW (in this paper, we set $\alpha = 2$ and $\beta = 1.5$). The adjustment rules of DW have the simple function that is independent from the adjustment rules of CW. During the process of DW, the tagged node can detect the status of CSI and calculate the idle slot intervals between two data transmissions.

3.4 Estimation Algorithm of Node Number

Based on (4) and (5), we can obtain values of CSI. And then, we further give the estimation algorithm of node number with values of CSI. For simplicity, we present a linear estimation algorithm of node number as follow,

$$N_{new} = \frac{n}{n_{opt}} N_{cur} \tag{6}$$

where N_{cur} and N_{new} are values of node number that the tagged node is using and predicted values, respectively. Compared with estimation algorithm in [2], this estimation algorithm is simply and has the same effective.

3.5 Adjustment Rules of CW Sizes

The throughput can be connected with parameter τ that means attempt probability of data transmission in a slot. During one data transmission cycle, nodes with multiple priority levels should send packets according to their throughput ratios (as like, ρ_H, ρ_L), which can be seen as probability of channel access.

$$\rho_H : \rho_L \approx \tau_H : \tau_L \tag{7}$$

Based on $\tau = 2/W$, we obtain

$$\rho_H : \rho_L \approx 2/W_H : 2/W_L \tag{8}$$

We select an adjustment that nodes$_H$ have the optimal CW sizes (W_{opt}), which is the smallest values of CW than nodes with other priority levels.

$$W_H = W_{opt} \approx \theta_{opt} \cdot (N - 1) \tag{9}$$

where θ_{opt} has been analyzed in [2]. With the optimal parameter W_{opt}, nodes can hold the fitful channel status that has low collision probability and high throughput. Based on (7) and (9), we develop CW sizes for nodes with other priority levels as

$$W_L \approx (\rho_H/\rho_L) \cdot \theta_{opt} \cdot (N - 1) \tag{10}$$

According to (8)–(10), nodes with multiple priority levels have different CW sizes to meet weighted throughput fairness. Nodes$_H$ have the smaller CW sizes and nodes$_L$ have the larger CW sizes. These CW sizes determine backoff window to access the channel. And then, the backoff window of nodes$_H$ is smaller than that of nodes$_L$, which means that the calculated results of CSI will be different if nodes detect the messages of CSI during backoff window.

We define some main functions of DW as follows:

- **Calculation:** Nodes detect status of CSI and count events of data transmissions to calculate idle slot intervals between two data transmissions;

- **Estimation:** Nodes estimate active node number in the channel, in which nodes should eliminate the bad impact of multiple transmission times of the same node.
- **Adjustment:** Nodes adjust sizes of DW based on the estimated node number and keep the values of estimated node number for adjustments of CW. With determined CW sizes, nodes select backoff window randomly in CW and begin decrement process as normal work like EDCA mode.

4   Computer Simulation and Analysis

In this section, we use the OPNET (version 14.5) modeler to verify the proposed mechanism and mainly compare with EDCA mechanism. Each node is in saturation state and uses RTS/CTS frames to reserve the ideal channel. According to [2], we simply set $\theta_{opt} = 10$ for nodes$_H$ and throughput ratios of three priority levels are defined as $\rho_H : \rho_M : \rho_L = 3 : 2 : 1$ ($\rho_L = 1$) corresponding to the highest priority level, the middle priority level and the lowest priority level. The CW sizes are determined according to (8)–(10). The ranges of EDCA mechanism are W_H ([16, 64]), W_M ([24, 96]) and W_L ([48, 192]). Other main simulation parameters are the same listed in [2].

As shown in Fig. 4, the simulated throughput ratios of AMMPL mechanism are around theoretic values, which confirm the validity and good scalability of the proposed mechanism. Due to reasonable division of functions between DW process and CW process, the mechanism provides the accurate measurement of CSI and estimation algorithm of active node number in an independent DW process. Based on estimated node number, the linear adjustment rules of CW guarantee throughput ratios according to multiple priority levels. Compared with AMMPL mechanism, the EDCA mechanism cannot hold the throughput ratios between nodes with higher priority levels (nodes$_H$ or nodes$_M$) and nodes$_L$. Due to lack of accurate CSI in EDCA mechanism, both throughput ratios (High : Low and Middle : Low) increase with increment of node number, which means that nodes with higher priority levels have more throughput than that of nodes$_L$. The throughput ratios between nodes$_H$ and nodes$_M$ are near the theoretic values both in AMMPL mechanism and EDCA mechanism.

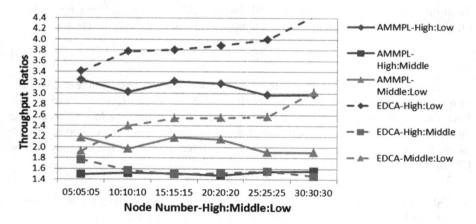

Fig. 4. Throughput ratios

5 Conclusion

By defining a new parameter of DW to calculate events of data transmission, we obtain the accurate values of CSI for better estimation algorithm of node number. And then, we adjust the optimal CW sizes for nodes with the highest priority levels and increase CW sizes for nodes with low priority levels corresponding to their throughput ratios based on the estimated node number.

In the future work, we will study the history data of DW for better estimation algorithm of active node number. These access parameters and more performance in networks with multiple priority levels will be gotten further analysis.

Acknowledgement. This work is supported by National Natural Science Foundation of China (61362016, 61562023, 61502127) National special project of international cooperation in science and technology (2014DFA13140).

References

1. IEEE Standard for Information Technology-Telecommunications and Information Exchange between Systems-Local and Metropolitan area Networks-Specific Requirements-Part 11: Wireless LAN Medium Access Control (MAC) and Physical Layer (PHY) Specifications, IEEE Std. 802.11 (2012)
2. Shi, C., Dai, X., Liang, P., Zhang, H.: Adaptive access mechanism with optimal contention window based on node number estimation using multiple thresholds. IEEE Trans. Wirel. Commun. **11**(6), 2046–2055 (2012)
3. Gao, Y., Sun, X., Dai, L.: Throughput optimization of heterogeneous IEEE 802.11 DCF networks. IEEE Trans. Wirel. Commun. **12**(1), 398–411 (2013)
4. Krishnan, M.N., Yang, S., Zakhor, A.: Contention window adaptation using the busy-idle signal in 802.11 WLANs. In: Global Communications Conference, pp. 4794–4800. IEEE (2014)
5. Su, W.U., Yan, M., Feng, G.: 802.11 MAC optimization mechanism based on throughput proportional fairness. Radio Commun. Technol. (2016)
6. Champati, J.P., Chaporkar, P.: Proportionally fair resource allocation in multi-rate WLANs. IEEE Trans. Control Netw. Syst. **PP**(99), 1 (2017)
7. Ghazvini, M., Movahhedinia, N., Jamshidi, K.: GCW: A Game Theoretic Contention Window Adjustment Approach for IEEE 802.11 WLANs. Kluwer Academic Publishers, Dordrecht (2015)
8. Zhao, H., Wei, J., Sarkar, N.I., et al.: E-MAC: an evolutionary solution for collision avoidance in wireless ad hoc networks. J. Netw. Comput. Appl. **65**, 1–11 (2016)
9. Nassiri, M., Heusse, M., Duda, A.: A novel access method for supporting absolute and proportional priorities in 802.11 WLANs. In: Proceedings of INFOCOM 2008, April, pp. 1382–1390 (2008)
10. Wan, H.W.H., King, H., Ahmed, S., et al.: WLAN fairness with idle sense. IEEE Commun. Lett. **19**(10), 1794–1797 (2015)
11. Sanada, T., Tian, X., Okuda, T., et al.: Estimating the number of nodes in WLANs to improve throughput and QoS. IEICE Trans. Inf. Syst. **E99.D**(1), 10–20 (2016)

12. Kadota, I., Baiocchi, A., et al.: Kalman filtering: estimate of the numbers cf active queues in an 802.11e EDCA WLAN (2014)
13. Liu, W., Luo, X., Liu, Y., et al.: Localization algorithm of indoor Wi-Fi access points based on signal strength relative relationship and region division. CMC: Comput. Mater. Continua **55**(1), 071–093 (2018)
14. Wang, J., Ju, C., Gao, Y., et al.: A PSO based energy efficient coverage control algorithm for wireless sensor networks. CMC: Comput. Mater. Continua **56**(3), 433–446 (2018)

Bitcoin Node Discovery: Large-Scale Empirical Evaluation of Network Churn

Yu Zhang[1], Runan Tan[1], Xiangyi Kong[1], Qingfeng Tan[1,2], and Xiangtao Liu[1,2(✉)]

[1] Guangzhou University, Guangzhou, China
liuxt@gzhu.edu.cn
[2] Cyberspace Institute of Advanced Technology, Guangzhou University, Guanghzhou, China

Abstract. Bitcoin was founded by Nakamoto Satoshi on January 3, 2009, based on a borderless peer-to-peer network, founded with consensus initiative open source software. There are many nodes in the Bitcoin network. By discovering and analyzing these nodes, we can summarize some of the characteristics of Bitcoin and blockchain networks. In this paper, the following work was completed: (1) Explain the communication process and related protocols of Bitcoin nodes. (2) Large-scale discovery of bitcoin nodes. (3) Analyze and summarize the dynamic of the nodes.

Keywords: Bitcoin node · Blockchain · Communication protocol · Node identification

1 Introduction

Since Satoshi Nakamoto proposed the concept of Bitcoin for the first time in 2009 in [1]. Until now, Bitcoin has become the earliest ancestor of the blockchain and has affected the whole world. The total market value of bitcoin is now between $5 billion and $10 billion. Although the price of Bitcoin has been fluctuating, but always at a higher exchange rate, at the time of this paper, the exchange rate of Bitcoin against the US dollar is about 6329:1 [2]. Compared to traditional currencies, Bitcoin is decentralized, anonymity, tax-free, free of supervision, robustness and borderlessness. As more and more people began to pay attention to Bitcoin, Bitcoin has also attracted widespread attention in various countries and China has become the world's largest bitcoin trading market. About 70% of bitcoin transactions are generated from China [3]. Analysis of bitcoin nodes allows us to make a prediction and analysis of Bitcoin's operating mechanism and future development.

Bitcoin is the first blockchain technology application. Blockchain as a disruptive technology in the Internet is valued by more and more countries, enterprises and the public [4]. It can be applied in many fields such as finance, logistics, medical care, etc. Blockchain and artificial intelligence are also the hottest Internet technologies in recent years. Known as the "next Internet", will bring enormous changes to society, the application of the block chain will be extended with all aspects of social life, improve the overall efficiency of society and promote social collaboration.

X. Sun et al. (Eds.): ICAIS 2019, LNCS 11635, pp. 385–395, 2019.
https://doi.org/10.1007/978-3-030-24268-8_36

Blockchain it is a dynamic network, the number of nodes is constantly changing and the dynamics of bitcoin nodes is an important feature of Bitcoin. The characteristics of Bitcoin refer to the on-line and offline time of Bitcoin and the dynamics of nodes and others. Through statistics and analysis of relevant knowledge, we can predict the future size and node status of Bitcoin nodes and summarize the law and development trend of Bitcoin network [5]. This paper applies a model to the processing of data on the basis of previous scholars to carry out a quantitative analysis of dynamics, and puts forward a summary.

2   Related Work

Although Satoshi proposed the concept of Bitcoin in [1] in 2009, but many people are studying in the direction of Bitcoin network, p2p network and blockchain for many years. Juan Eduardo Pazmiño & Carlo Kleber da Silva Rodrigues think simply dividing's bitcoin network may reduce transaction verification time in [6], and Andreas M. Antonopoulos elaborates on the principles of Bitcoin, the characteristics of trading and bitcoin networks, and knowledge of Bitcoin network security and blockchain in [7].

Brighten Godfrey et al. proposed an equation for evaluating network dynamics in 2006 in [8]. Phillip Winter and others at Princeton University improved their equations on P. Brighten Godfrey on a 2016 basis. Solved the problem that excessive volatility and excessive volatility offset each other [9]. In May 2017, Li Pengfei et al. proposed a node identification method based on network connectivity and node deletion. In April 2018 [10], Chen et al. showed that 90% of the new unstable nodes continue to jitter during the evolution process, and only 10% of the nodes grow into large, high nodes in the AS-level network topology [11].

In summary, although there are many related researches on p2p networks, for p2p networks, the crawling work and related analysis of bitcoin network nodes are few, and as a representative of p2p networks, the analysis of bitcoin nodes can help. We have a deep understanding of the characteristics of the p2p network, and can also summarize the rules of the Bitcoin network, so it is necessary to capture and analyze the Bitcoin nodes.

3   Background

Bitcoin is series of concept and technology as the foundation to build digital currency state system. Bitcoin agreement in the form of a variety of open source software implementation. Anyone can participate in Bitcoin activities and can be distributed through computer operations called mining. The maximum number of Bitcoin agreements is 21 million to avoid inflation, Bitcoin does not rely on central agencies to issue new money and maintain transactions. Instead, it is completed by blockchain. It uses digital encryption algorithms and the entire network to defend against 51% computing power to ensure the security of assets and transactions. As the originator of the blockchain, this concept is proposed in [1]. The basic bitcoin node includes the following four functions can be see in Fig. 1.

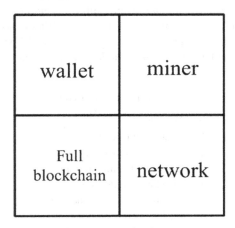

Fig. 1. Bitcoin core node

1. Wallet: those node can support Bitcoin transactions, query and other functions.
2. Miner: those node can compete for the task of creating a new block by resolving the workload proof Hash operation to obtain new bitcoin and charge transaction fees.
3. Full Blockchain: Those nodes store complete blockchain complete data, allowing all transactions to be verified independently without external reference.
4. Network: All basic bitcoin nodes have routing capabilities, and nodes with routing networks can help forward transactions and block data, discover and maintain connections between nodes [7].

Blockchain is a string of data generated by cryptographic methods. Blockchain is a group of scattered client nodes. The core advantage of the blockchain is decentralization. It can solve high cost, inefficiency and insecure data storage in the centralization mechanism by implementing peer-to-peer transactions in distributed systems, which with nodes without mutual trust by using data encryption, time-stamp distributed consensus and other methods.

Before analyzing the Bitcoin node, we need to understand how the Bitcoin client node communicates. In order to join the Bitcoin network, the Bitcoin client will do the following things: when we start a bitcoin client, the bitcoin node remembers the node that has recently been connected to it, and when we restart the client, it can connect with the previous nodes as soon as possible. when it lose the previous nodes, the client will try to find new nodes, The original node will send a message containing its own IP to the new node. The new node forwards it to its own neighbor too. After established a connection with a node, the node will do the same things again. Through the above steps to forming a bitcoin network. To find the first node, Several fixed seed nodes are compiled on the source code of Bitcoin. Each time the Bitcoin client starts, the Bitcoin client discovers other nodes through these seed nodes.

The Bitcoin network is based on the TCP protocol. The default port is 8333. If a new Bitcoin node wants to join the Bitcoin network, it needs to obtain the normal contact list of the network in the current Bitcoin network in the first, and then run the Bitcoin protocol stack. Finally, communicate with other nodes in Bitcoin. In order to solve the problem of how the initial node is found, the Bitcoin source code contains 6 seed nodes. when the Bitcoin client is started, other nodes will be traversed from the 6 seed nodes in default model. The six seed nodes can be in the Table 1.

Table 1. Seed node

No	Seed node
1	seed.bitcoin.sipa.be
2	dnsseed.bluematt.me
3	dnsseed.bitcoin.dashjr.org
4	seed.bitcoinstats.com
5	seed.bitcoin.jonasschnelli.ch
6	seed.btc.petertodd.org
7	seed.bitcoin.sprovoost.nl

Eight ways to find Bitcoin discovery nodes on Wikipedia [12]:

1. Nodes discover their own external address by various methods.
2. Nodes receive the callback address of remote nodes that connect to them.
3. Nodes makes DNS request to receive IP addresses.
4. Nodes can use addresses hard coded into the software.
5. Nodes exchange addresses with other nodes.
6. Nodes store addresses in a database and read that database on startup.
7. Nodes can be provided addresses as command line arguments.
8. Nodes read addresses from a user provided text file on startup.

We will use the third method to find the nodes and analyze information about these nodes.

As the initiator of the communication, node A first completes the handshake process with node B. When a handshake is performed between nodes, if there is a problem with the handshake packet sent by one party, the other node does not respond. After the handshake is correct, Node B will send a large number of data packets to Node A, such as obtaining the packet of node A's header and block information.

If the node A wants to obtain the information of the node B, the corresponding message is sent. After receiving the message, the node B will continue to send a message to the node A to obtain the desired information. The information obtained, after a while, responds to the result of node A sending a message.

When the Bitcoin network establishes a connection, the node sends out a version message containing the basic request command to start communication. The version contains the following contents (Table 2):

Table 2. Version content

No	Version content
1	Protocol version
2	Define the communication protocol version used by the communication end
3	Local service
4	List of local services supported by this node
5	IP address of other nodes visible to this node
6	Local node's native IP address
7	The minor version number of the software type on which the current node is running
8	The block height of the current node (the creation node is 0)

After receiving the version packet, the other node returns a Vera confirmation and connection. Similarly, if the node wants to connect to other nodes, the same method is used (Fig. 2).

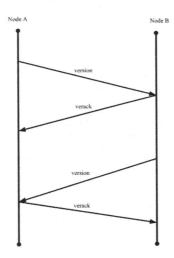

Fig. 2. Node connection

After the connection is established, the node sends an address message containing its own IP to the neighboring node. The neighboring nodes use the same method to forward, and the accessed node can actively send getaddress information to the neighboring nodes, asking them to return the IP list address of the peer node.

In a bitcoin network, the node is always in dynamic change. If the connected node has no data communication, other nodes will periodically send information to maintain the connection. If a node does not communicate for 90 min, it will be considered disconnected from the network. The road will start to find a new node, so the Bitcoin network will dynamically adjust according to the network conditions, which is the premise of this paper.

4 Traffic Packet and Nodes Discovery

Bitcoin belongs to the p2p network. Based on the understanding of the Bitcoin protocol, it is necessary to use the packet capture software to perform packet capture analysis on the bitcoin node communication. In this paper, Wireshark is used for packet capture analysis. Wireshark is an excellent packet capture tool that can capture and analyze traffic in the network communication process in real time [13]. The environment used in this article is the Ubuntu 64-bit virtual machine. The Bitcoin client is run on the Ubuntu system. At the same time, the Wireshark tool is opened, the crawl port is set as 8333, and the packet capture process of the node communication process is performed. After the program runs for a period of time, a list of traffic packets will appear. This is required to filter, select the traffic package with "bitcoin", and then focus on the "Version" package. Click on the relevant content and we can see the bitcoin communication process and important information in the list.

First, the wireshark software is used to capture the traffic packet of the bitcoin node communication process, and then analyze the bitcoin handshake protocol. The following figure is the captured traffic packet (Fig. 3).

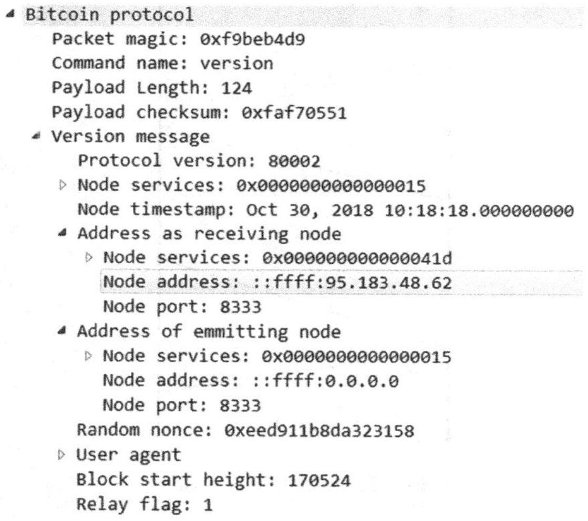

```
◢ Bitcoin protocol
      Packet magic: 0xf9beb4d9
      Command name: version
      Payload Length: 124
      Payload checksum: 0xfaf70551
   ◢ Version message
        Protocol version: 80002
      ▷ Node services: 0x0000000000000015
        Node timestamp: Oct 30, 2018 10:18:18.000000000
      ◢ Address as receiving node
         ▷ Node services: 0x000000000000041d
           Node address: ::ffff:95.183.48.62
           Node port: 8333
      ◢ Address of emmitting node
         ▷ Node services: 0x0000000000000015
           Node address: ::ffff:0.0.0.0
           Node port: 8333
        Random nonce: 0xeed911b8da323158
      ▷ User agent
        Block start height: 170524
        Relay flag: 1
```

Fig. 3. Traffic packet

From the captured packets we know that the packet structure is as follows (Table 3):

Table 3. Some fields of version package

Description	Features
Services	Node service
Timestamp	Stanrdard UNIX timestamp in seconds
Node port	Always 8333
Node address	IP of the node
Height	To determine the height of the node

4.1 Node Acquisition

Large-scale discovery of nodes using an open source project called "bitcoin-seeder" in Github [14]. This project is a crawler for the bitcoin network, which exposes a list of reliable nodes via a built-in DNS server. Crawlers run in parallel (by default 24 threads simultaneously. This project can specify a seed node, and implement automatic grabbing of the node and deduplicate, record the height and version of the node and other information, so that we can work next. The running idea of this program is as follows:

First, Obtain an IP seed list from the DNS seed, then start 24 threads, scan the list of seed nodes via 'GetAddr' and save, then establish a TCP connection with all nodes in the IP seed list to complete the handshake. After that, obtain the cache node around the seed node and store it in the cache node list. In the next, the node will communicate with other nodes in the cache node list to obtain a new cache node, add them to the current cache node list and deduplicate it. The project will repeat above four steps until all cached node lists have been processed.

The obtained node needs to be twice-confirmed. This is because the characteristics of the p2p network are unstable. For the stored address, most of them will display timeout or connection rejection. The project will record the corresponding reason for the node with the wrong connection. If it succeeds, it will filter out the version package, and then parse the version package, which has the specific information of the bitcoin node.

5 Evalution

In the experiment of this paper, the system environment is Ubuntu64 bit 18.04 virtual machine installed in windows7 environment, programming language is Python2.6, using matplotlib library for visual analysis.

By large-scale crawling the bitcoin nodes, we can analyze the dynamics of the bitcoin nodes. In order to increase the reliability of the experiment, we take a time-sharing and multi-sample crawling in the way of seed nodes. The project climbs these nodes every two hours and each time crawling 8000–9000 nodes of information, We repeated the step for 7 times, and the Crawled nodes number separately is 9006, 8995, 8891, 8806, 8599 and 8884. This data is closer to the number 9905 of the Bitnode website which indicating that the data obtained by the open source project has high reliability [15]. The information of nodes including block height, version, etc. and then based on this information, we completed the following analysis.

As mentioned above, the dynamics of a node is an important feature of evaluating a bitcoin network. The dynamics of the network is the different states of the network at different times (t1 and t2), the bitcoin network is composed of many changing nodes. Therefore, in order to evaluate the dynamics of the nodes, we need to make a quantitative evaluation of the network node information. In order to describe the dynamics of the network, we use the formula (2) (3) to consider both the newly added nodes and the left nodes. However, since too low quantity fluctuations may offset excessive quantity fluctuations, it is necessary to adopt the optimization of this formula, which is to divide into two formulas to evaluate the newly added nodes and the nodes leaving the network.

$$\alpha_n = \frac{|C_t \backslash C_{t-1}|}{|C_t|} \tag{1}$$

$$\alpha_l = \frac{|C_{t-1} \backslash C_t|}{|C_{t-1}|} \tag{2}$$

In the above equation, C_t is the network state at time and C_{t-1} is the network state at another time. A complement of two time elements is defined as \, which is the elements in the previous collection and not the elements in the latter collection. In the equation, the values of and are both in the range of [0,1]. The closer the value is to 1, the larger the change in the nodes in the network, which means many nodes leave the network, and new nodes are added. The closer to 0, the fewer nodes in the network change, or even almost no changes.

According to the 6 times of data crawled, and using Python program analysis, the following data is obtained (Table 4).

Table 4. α_n and α_l

Times	1	2	3	4	5	6
α_n	0.0121	0.0134	0.0119	0.2359	0.0425	0.2207
α_l	0.01100	0.0025	0.0026	0.2106	0.0594	0.2346

As can be seen from the above figure, although the Bitcoin network is a p2p network, the stability of the nodes is still very good. Most of the nodes remain connected during the test period, and the value of the sum remains between 0.0025 and 0.23. This shows that the Bitcoin network is a relatively stable p2p network.

Bitcoin nodes can be online at any time and can be offline at any time [16]. However, for a Bitcoin client, it is not easy to go online and offline under normal circumstances. Therefore, in the Bitcoin network, some nodes are always online. These nodes are called stable [31]. The proportion of nodes and stable nodes in the bitcoin network determines the stability of the entire network. Therefore, statistical analysis of the time when the network nodes go online within a certain period of time is also an important aspect of analyzing the stability of the bitcoin network, in order to analyze more accurately [32]. For stable nodes, the past 2 h, 8 h, one day, one week and one month are selected as the metrics. The figure below shows the proportion of nodes in the node list that have 80% of the time scale on the corresponding time scale in different time scales in the past [33] (Fig. 4).

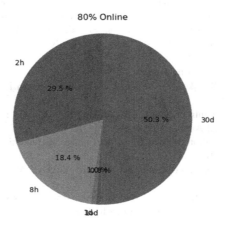

Fig. 4. 80% online ratio

Through the above analysis, we can know that there are a certain number of nodes in the Bitcoin network. These nodes have strong stability and remain online for different time periods. As a p2p network, Bitcoin is dynamic. But for other reasons, still maintain a certain degree of stability, limited by space, no longer repeat.

6 Conclusion

This paper introduces the overview of Bitcoin and blockchain, analyzes the contents of the handshake process in the bitcoin node communication process and communication process, uses the wireshark tool to capture the bitcoin traffic packet, and implements bitcoin using open source tools. Large-scale crawling of node-related information, and then statistically analyzing the dynamics of the nodes through the captured content, using the existing formula to quantitatively describe the dynamics, and repeatedly crawling the experimental data reduces the occurrence of accidental errors and obtains The more accurate results, and finally summarized the characteristics of Bitcoin.

Acknowledgement. This work is supported by the National Natural Science Foundation of China under Grant NO. 61572153, NO. 61702220, and NO. 61702223, China Grants U1636215, and the National Key research and Development Plan (Grant NO. 2018YFB0803504).

References

1. Nakamoto, S.: Bitcoin: a peer-to-peer electronic cash system. In: Proceedings of the Conference on Social Computing (SocialCom) (2011). (Reid, F., Harrigan, M., Donet, J.A.D.)
2. https://coinmarketcap.com/zh/currencies/bitcoin/. Accessed 9 Nov 2018
3. Liping, J.: Bitcoin: theory, practice and effect. Stud. Int. Finance **12**, 002 (2013)
4. Swan, M.: Blueprint for a New Economy, p. 152. O'Reilly Media, Inc., Sebastopol (2015)
5. Tapscott, D., Tapscott, A.: Blockchain Revolution: How the Technology Behind Bitcoin Is Changing Money, Business, and the World. Penguin, City of Westminster (2016)
6. Pazmiño, J.E., da Silva Rodrigues, C.K.: Simply dividing a bitcoin network node may reduce transaction verification time. SIJ Trans. Comput. Netw. Commun. Eng. (CNCE) **3**(2), 17–21 (2015)
7. Antonopoulos, A.M.: Mastering Bitcoin (2014)
8. Brighten Godfrey, P., Shenker, S., Stoica, I.: Minimizing churn in distributed systems. In: SIGCOMM. ACM (2006)
9. Winter, P., Ensafi, R.: Identifying and characterizing Sybils in the Tor network. In: USENIX Security Symposium, 12 August (2016)
10. Li, P., Lei, Y.: Identification method for critical nodes in dynamic Ad hoc network. Appl. Res. Comput. **34**(5) (2017)
11. Chen, L., Liu, P.: Analysis on dynamic evolution of nodes of AS-level topology. J. Beijing Univ. Technol. **44**(4) (2018)
12. https://en.bitcoin.it/wiki/Satoshi_Client_Node_Discovery. Accessed 9 Nov 2018
13. Orebaugh, A., Ramirez, G., Beale, J.: Wireshark & Ethereal Network Protocol Analyzer Toolkit. Elsevier, Amsterdam (2006)
14. https://github.com/sipa/bitcoin-seeder. Accessed 9 Nov 2018
15. https://bitnodes.earn.com/. Accessed 9 Nov 2018
16. https://en.wikipedia.org/wiki/Bitcoin. Accessed 9 Nov 2018
17. Li, M., Sun, Y., Jiang, Y., Tian, Z.: Answering the min-cost quality-aware query on multi-sources in sensor-cloud systems. Sensors **18**, 4486 (2018)
18. Han, W., Tian, Z., Huang, Z., Li, S., Jia, Y.: Bidirectional self-adaptive resampling in imbalanced big data learning. Multimedia Tools Appl. (2018). https://doi.org/10.1007/s11042-018-6938-9
19. Wang, Z., et al.: Automatically traceback RDP-based targeted ransomware attacks. Wirel. Commun. Mobile Comput. (2018). https://doi.org/10.1155/2018/7943586
20. Tian, Z., Su, S., Shi, W., Yu, X., Du, X., Guizani, M.: A data-driven model for future internet route decision modeling. Future Gener. Comput. Syst. (2018). https://doi.org/10.1016/j.future.2018.12.054
21. Qiu, J., Chai, Y., Liu, Y., Gu, Z., Li, S., Tian, Z.: Automatic non-taxonomic relation extraction from big data in smart city. IEEE Access **6**, 74854–74864 (2018). https://doi.org/10.1109/access.2018.2881422
22. Sun, Y., Li, M., Su, S., Tian, Z., Shi, W., Han, M.: Secure data sharing framework via hierarchical greedy embedding in darknets. ACM/Springer Mobile Networks and Applications
23. Yu, X., Tian, Z., Qiu, J., Jiang, F.: A data leakage prevention method based on the reduction of confidential and context terms for smart mobile devices. Wirel. Commun. Mobile Comput. https://doi.org/10.1155/2018/5823439
24. Wang, Y., Tian, Z., Zhang, H., Su, S., Shi, W.: A privacy preserving scheme for nearest neighbor query. Sensors **18**(8), 2440 (2018). https://doi.org/10.3390/s18082440

25. Tian, Z., et al.: A real-time correlation of host-level events in cyber range service for smart campus. IEEE Access **6**, 35355–35364 (2018). https://doi.org/10.1109/access.2018.2846590
26. Tan, Q., Gao, Y., Shi, J., Wang, X., Fang, B., Tian, Z.: Towards a comprehensive insight into the eclipse attacks of tor hidden services. IEEE IoT J. (2018). https://doi.org/10.1109/jiot.2018.2846624
27. Chen, J., Tian, Z., Cui, X., Yin, L., Wang, X.: Trust architecture and reputation evaluation for internet of things. J. Ambient Intell. Humaniz. Comput. **2**, 1–9 (2018)
28. Wang, B., Gu, X., Yan, S.: STCS: a practical solar radiation based temperature correlation scheme in meteorological WSN. Int. J. Sens. Netw. **28**(1), 22 (2018). https://doi.org/10.1504/ijsnet.2018.10015978
29. Wang, B., Gu, X., Zhou, A.: E2S2: a code dissemination approach to energy efficiency and status surveillance for wireless sensor networks. J. Internet Technol. **8**(4), 877–885 (2017). https://doi.org/10.6138/jit.2017.18.4.20160815
30. Wang, B., Gu, X., Ma, L., Yan, S.: Temperature error correction based on BP neural network in meteorological WSN. Int. J. Sens. Netw. **23**(4), 265–278 (2017). https://doi.org/10.1504/ijsnet.2017.083532
31. Tan, Q., et al.: Towards a comprehensive insight into the eclipse attacks of Tor hidden services. IEEE IoT J., 1 (2018)
32. Zhang, H., Yi, Y., Wang, J., Cao, N., Duan, Q.: Network security situation awareness framework based on threat intelligence. In: CMC, vol. 56, no. 3, pp. 381–399 (2018)
33. Hou, M., Wei, R., Wang, T., Cheng, Y., Qian, B.: Reliable medical recommendation based on privacy-preserving collaborative filtering. In: CMC, vol. 56, no. 1, pp. 137–149 (2018)

DDoS Attack Situation Information Fusion Method Based on Dempster-Shafer Evidence Theory

Wei Guo[1], Xiangyan Tang[1(✉)], Jieren Cheng[1,2], Jinying Xu[3], Canting Cai[1], and Yulong Guo[1]

[1] Key Laboratory of Internet Information Retrieval of Hainan Province, Hainan University, Haikou 570228, China
tangxy36@163.com
[2] College of Information Science and Technology, Hainan University, Haikou 570228, China
[3] Zhejiang Science and Technology Information Institute, Hangzhou 310006, China

Abstract. Distributed Denial of Service (DDoS) attacks have caused great damage to the network environment and its services. However, the currently existing single point detection methods for DDoS attack cannot achieve satisfying results. This paper proposes a DDoS attack situation information fusion method based on Dempster-Shafer evidence theory (DS). Firstly, according to the statistics of IP traffic packet, destination IP address data packet, and destination port, the traffic threat value and the traffic weight value based on the target IP address are respectively calculated to indicate the possibility of being attacked and the impact on the network when the attack is performed. Then, the above values were fused to obtain the DDoS attack fusion feature Network Flow Combination Relevance, CR) to accurately provide an evaluable network situation before and after the attack. Finally, based on the above CR values, a DDoS attack feature fusion model was developed. Combined with DS evidence theory, the network security situation value was given to evaluate the probability of DDoS attack. The experimental results show that compared with similar methods, the proposed method can provide evaluable forecast for potential DDoS attack threats, improve the situational awareness of DDoS attacks, and reduce false alarm rate, missing alarm rate and total error rate.

Keywords: DDoS attack · Network flow feature extraction · Dempster-Shafer evidence theory · Information fusion

1 Introduction

With the rapid development of new technologies, such as cognitive communication, cloud computing, quantum computing and big data [1], the network has infiltrated into all aspects of human society and is inseparable from the whole human society. A distributed denial of service (DDoS) attack uses a large number of botnets to launch a large number of normal or abnormal requests to the target, exhausting the target host

© Springer Nature Switzerland AG 2019
X. Sun et al. (Eds.): ICAIS 2019, LNCS 11635, pp. 396–407, 2019.
https://doi.org/10.1007/978-3-030-24268-8_37

resources or network resources, so that the host under attack cannot provide services to legitimate users. The botnet is a network platform for attackers to launch DDoS attacks, which can not only improve the attack efficiency, but also help hide the identity of the attacker. Its attacks varied in ways that are difficult to capture, leaving victims facing huge economic losses.

The report of Arbor Networks [2] shows that in recent years, DDoS attacks have been up to one-third of all cyber threats. Apparently, DDoS attacks have become the major cyber-crimes in today's society. Although we try to minimize the number of DDoS attacks, they have rapidly expanded the frequency and scale of targeted networks and computers, and are also evolving to exploit flash memory proxies, low-rate attacks, and exploit vulnerabilities in DNS servers for extended attacks. DDoS attacks continue to threaten today's network environments, and these threats have grown significantly in terms of the size and impact of Internet service providers and governments. Therefore, it is urgent to use information fusion method to accurately and efficiently perceive DDoS attacks and reduce economic losses and negative social impacts.

As an important part of situation fusion, information fusion plays an irreplaceable role. It is a multi-level and multi-faceted process, which can complete the detection, correlation, estimation and combination of information or data from multiple information sources.

2 Related Work

There has been a lot of research in the academic community on methods and techniques for multi-source information fusion. Khaleghi and Yager et al. [3, 4] outlined multi-source data fusion, including the concept, value, difficulty and existing methods of data fusion, and proposes a framework for multi-source data fusion. Naumann et al. [5] considered that it is necessary to solve the inconsistency of multi-source data and its data conflict through three steps of "pattern matching, repeated detection, and data fusion". Snidaro and Golestan et al. [6, 7] proposed different information fusion frameworks, through which specific entities and their relationships are modeled.

The essence of information fusion is to identify the data influencing the development of network from a large amount of data. Lin and Esposito et al. [8, 9] proposed different multi-sensor information fusion algorithms to solve the problem of multi-sensor information fusion. Chen et al. [10] proposed a new mathematical model of compensation strategy to characterize replay attacks and bandwidth constraints, and designed a recursive distributed Kalman fusion estimator, which improved the overall accuracy and robustness. Müller et al. [11] proposed the method of transforming the information contained in the world object oriented model into the ontology of logical reasoning or the Markov Logic Networks for probabilistic reasoning, and designed an advanced data fusion component. Aleroud et al. [12] reviewed intrusion detection technologies and introduced new research classifications, and created the attack prediction model by analyzing several dimensions of computational data mining techniques. Guo et al. [13] proposed a method for analyzing consumers' demand for e-commerce recommendation system by using multi-source information. In order to realize the recognition of false alarm events, the literature [14, 15] adopts the DS evidence theory algorithm to obtain the security situation of the network and reduce the uncertainty by integrating the previous and current network security conditions. Wu et al. [16] studied heterogeneous network security detection methods based on multi-source fusion, and proposed a game theory analysis method related to detection strategy. Pereira Junior et al. [17] proposed a new fusion method using data quality and semantic concepts to enhance and improve the problem of collaborative information association.

Above all, the DDoS attack has the characteristics of simple operation, multiple attack method, difficult defense, and great destructiveness. At the same time, the large-scale, massive and complex network flow in the new network environment makes the current single-point detection for DDoS attack cannot achieve good results, and there is no effective multi-source situation information fusion for DDoS attacks. Therefore, this paper proposes a DDoS attack situation fusion method based on DS evidence theory, which can effectively detect abnormal traffic and has a good discrimination.

3   DDoS Attack Feature Fusion Model

3.1   DDoS Attack Feature Analysis

In the actual network environment, there are external factors such as noise, delay and congestion, to effectively detect DDoS attacks, choose can comprehensively reflect the characteristics of the attack is to reduce computational complexity and improve the core element of the accuracy and stability [18, 19]. Cheng et al. [20] proposes a DDoS attack detection method based on time series prediction, this sequence is then used in network traffic prediction and calculation error. Hoque et al. [21] proposed a real-time detection method to identify DDoS attacks using correlation measures. Cheng et al. [22] proposed a DDoS attack detection method based on anomaly network flow feature sequence prediction in big data environment. Mehmood et al. [23] proposed A new method to apply naive Bayesian classification algorithm in intrusion detection system (IDS) to perceive abnormal or irregular traffic and actions of nodes.

Through the research on various DDoS attack detection, it is concluded that DDoS attacks have the characteristics of wide distribution of attack sources, high attack intensity and strong concealment of attack sources. The basic characteristics of DDoS attacks can be summarized as follows [24]:

(1) The attack source is widely distributed. (2) High attack power. (3) The attack source is concealed. (4) The destination address of abnormal traffic is centralized, and there is no congestion control. (5) Abnormal flow flows to more or less destination ports. (6) When a flood attack occurs, the number of requests to a flag bit of the target machine increases significantly.

3.2   Method for Calculating Traffic Threat Value

Combined with previous work, this paper proposes the method for calculating traffic threat value [25].

Definition 1: For the destination port of the network traffic and the number of packets received by the port, the sampling statistics are $\Delta t = 0.1$ s per unit time, and they are used as the fusion calculation to define and define the threat value characteristics of the network flow (T_i):

$$T_i(t) = p_i(t) \cdot 1000 \cdot lg(a_i(t))/\Delta t \tag{1}$$

Where $p_i(t)$ is the access range, which is expressed by the ratio between the destination port and the total port number. Suppose the destination port number is $dp_i(t)$, $p_i(t) = dp_i(t)/2^{16}$. $a_i(t)$ is the access intensity, represented by the number of packets received per port, assuming that the total number of packets is $b_i(t)$, $a_i(t) = b_i(t)/dp_i(t)$. The delta Δt is unit time. During the DDoS attack, the access intensity was larger than normal, and the attack probability was higher.

Formula (1) is expressed in logarithmic form, which can keep the treatment of access intensity within a reasonable range and not fluctuate too much. Using Δt as a divisor reduces the impact of the time interval on the threat value, and 1000 is the amplification of the threat value, which is beneficial to the comparison of the final value.

During the period of DDoS attack, the number of ports may increase greatly in a short time, resulting in the increase of threat value. The higher the threat value, the higher the possibility of attack.

3.3 Method for Calculating Traffic Weight Value

The threat value of the traffic cannot fully represent the specific situation of the node, and the importance of the destination IP in the entire network should also be considered, which is represented by the traffic weight value based on the destination IP address. Based on the traffic weight value of the destination IP address, the ratio between the total number of all traffic in the destination IP and the total network traffic is expressed, as shown in formula (2):

Definition 2: The destination IP data packet of the network traffic is subjected to sampling statistics with a unit time of $\Delta t = 0.1$, and the statistical characteristics (Q_i) of the traffic weight value based on the destination IP address are defined and calculated:

$$Q_i(t) = b_i(t)/N \tag{2}$$

In formula (3), $Q_i(t)$ represents the IP weight, $b_i(t)$ represents the total number of packets of the corresponding destination IP address, and N represents the total number of IP packets in the entire network. The time interval is not introduced in the calculation because the weight value of the traffic should be an objective condition, regardless of the selected time interval. The greater the proportion of the destination IP traffic weight in the total traffic, the greater the weight, the greater the impact on the network when the node is attacked. Therefore, the stronger the node is, the larger the corresponding weight is.

3.4   DDoS Attack Fusion Feature

No single feature can completely describe the DDoS attack period combined with the two-part feature extraction rules in Sects. 3.2 and 3.3. Within the sampling time Δt, $T_i(t)$ and $Q_i(t)$ extraction and two features are calculated respectively to construct the correlation degree of binary group feature network flow combination (Network flow combination relevance, CR).

$$CR = \; <T_i(t), Q_i(t)> \tag{3}$$

First, the two-part statistic in the two-group is based on the characteristics of the attack characteristics of the DDoS attack; Secondly, $T_i(t)$ feature extracts the total number of network traffic data packets and the statistics of ports, which can better reflect the correlation between the attack flow and normal flow in the network, while $Q_i(t)$ feature extracts the statistics of IP of network traffic purpose, and can more accurately depict the sharp increase of data packets when the network is attacked by DDoS. The combination of these two aspects can accurately describe the attack flow at the victim end and can directly affect the normal traffic changes, and the partially aggregated attack flow is mixed with a large number of normal flows, so as to provide relevant information of the network before and after the attack timely and accurately. More complete distinction between network conditions before and after the attack.

4   DDoS Attack Situation Information Fusion Method Based on DS Evidence Theory

DS theory was born in Harvard University in the 1960s, and the introduction of trust function marked the formal emergence of evidence theory as a complete theory for dealing with uncertainty. Its greatest feature is the use of "interval estimation" rather than "point estimation" for the description of uncertainty information, showing a great deal of flexibility in distinguishing the unknown from the uncertain and accurately reflecting evidence collection.

4.1   DS Evidence Theory

DS evidence theory is an effective method for inferring uncertain events, and can use synthetic formulas to fuse multi-source data [26].

Frame of Discernment. The frame of discernment is also called the sample space. If θ is used to represent the sample space, the set consisting of all the subsets in θ is called the power set, which is denoted as 2. When there are n elements in θ, 2^n is the number of elements of the power set. If the variable x represents the corresponding letter, x = {G, Y, L}, then A = {G} means "x is G", if A = {G, Y}, then "x could be G Or Y".

Basic Probability Assignment Functions. Basic Probability Assignment (BPA), assuming the function m: $2^\theta \rightarrow [0, 1]$, and satisfying $m(\emptyset) = 0$ and $\sum_{A \subseteq \theta} m(A) = 1$, then m is the BPA on 2^θ. m(A) is called the basic probability number, which indicates the degree of trust of the current environment to the A set.

Belief Function. The belief function is also abbreviated as Bel. Bel: $2^\theta \rightarrow [0, 1]$, for any $A \subseteq \theta$ has $Bel(A) = \sum_{B \subseteq A} m(B)$, Bel(A) represents the total trust level of A.

Plausibility Function. The plausibility function is also abbreviated as Pl. Pl: $2^\theta \rightarrow [0, 1]$, for any $A \subseteq \theta$ has $Pl(A) = 1 - Bel(\bar{A})$ and $\bar{A} = \theta - A$. The plausibility function is also called irrefutable function or upper limit function, and Pl(A) represents a non-false trust degree to A. The relevant inference for Pl(A) is $Pl(A) = \sum_{A \cap B \neq \emptyset} m(B)$, and the likelihood of an event is based on distrust of its opposite event.

Confidence Interval. For a certain hypothesis A of the frame of discernment θ, its belief function Bel(A) and the plausibility function Pl(A) are calculated according to the basic probability assignment function, Bel(A) and Pl(A) are the lower limit and upper limit of the trust to A respectively, and the confidence interval is denoted as: [Bel(A), Pl(A)]. Pl(A) − Bel(A) indicates the uncertainty of A, that is, whether A is true or false.

The Combinatorial Function of Evidence. When DS evidence theory is used to solve practical problems, different probability assignment functions are obtained when faced with evidence from different data sources.

Orthogonal Sum. $m = m1 \oplus m2$, $m(\emptyset) = 0$
    Among them:

$$K = 1 - \sum_{x \cap y = \emptyset} m_1(x) \times m_2(y) = \sum_{x \cap y \neq \emptyset} m_1(x) \times m_2(y) \qquad (4)$$

K is called the normalization factor and is used to reflect the degree of conflict of evidence.

4.2   Network Security Situation Value

In this paper, each binary group is taken as a piece of evidence, and each binary group provides the probability of being attacked. The network security situation value is given after combining multiple evidences by DS evidence theory, that is, the probability of the network being attacked by DDoS, which is used to represent the situation of the entire network.

The frame of discernment selected in this paper is $\theta = \{T, F\}$, where T Indicates that DDoS attacks have occurred and F indicates that no DDoS attacks have occurred. The power set $2^\theta = \{\emptyset, T, F, U\}$, which $\emptyset$ means both attack occurred and no attack occurred, U means that unable to judge. Let $p(T)$ be the probability of an attack occurring, and $p(T) \in [0, 1]$, then $p(F) = 1 - p(T)$. The probability assignment functions in this paper are $m_i(T) = p_i(T)$, $m_i(F) = p_i(F)$. In the power set of this paper, $m(\emptyset) + m(T) + m(F) + m(U) = 1$, where $m(\emptyset) = 0, m(U) = 0$.

In the first stage, two different evidences, m_1 and m_2, were obtained from the data source.

Then, use DS evidence theory to fuse m_1 and m_2:

(1) First, calculating the normalization constant:

$$K = 1 - \sum_{x \cap y = \emptyset} m_1(x) \times m_2(y) \qquad (5)$$

(2) Calculating the combined function of "T":

$$m_1 \oplus m_2(\{T\}) = K^{-1} \times \sum_{x \cap y = \{T\}} m_1(x) \times m_2(y) \qquad (6)$$

(3) Calculating the combined function of "F":

$$m_1 \oplus m_2(\{F\}) = K^{-1} \times \sum_{x \cap y = \{F\}} m_1(x) \times m_2(y) \qquad (7)$$

(4) Calculating the belief function and plausibility function:

Evidence judgment is achieved by two functions. For any $A \subseteq \theta$, $2^\theta \to [0, 1]$, there is a belief function $Bel(A) = \sum_{B \subseteq A} m(B)$, plausibility function $Pl(A) = \sum_{A \cap B \neq \emptyset} m(B)$. Let bel_1, bel_2, ..., bel_n be the belief function corresponding to n different evidences on the frame of discernment θ, so the plausibility function $Pl(A)$ corresponding to different evidence can also be obtained. The belief function is the minimum limit of possibility, while the plausibility function is the maximum limit of possibility.

Using DS evidence theory to fuse $m_i(T)$ of n binary groups to obtain $m(T)$, and compare the obtained value with the set threshold. If it is less than the threshold, it is judged to be normal, and it is judged to be under attack if it is not less than.

DS evidence theory can combine multiple evidences to obtain an integrated probability value. The security situation value obtained by DS evidence theory fusion can be used to judge whether the network is attacked or not. The calculated probability can effectively judge whether the network is subject to DDoS attack.

5 Experimental Results and Analysis

5.1 Experimental Environment

The experimental data set selected in this paper uses the CAIDA "DDoS Attack 2007" dataset [27] and runs on the computer with 2.80 GHz, Intel Core i7-7700HQ processor and 8G memory based on PyCharm, Matlab, Eclipse and other platforms.

5.2   Comparative Experiment and Analysis of Three Characteristics

In order to achieve good experimental results, this experiment conducted a preliminary analysis of the data. 2600 and 1500 sample records (with unknown attacks in the test set) were randomly sampled from the training set and test set containing multiple types of DDoS attacks, with sampling time $\Delta t = 0.1$ s. In order to compare the DDoS attack fusion feature and traffic threat value better, the accuracy, missing report rate (MR), and false alarm rate (FR) were obtained with normal. The calculation formula of evaluation standards define as follows:

$$MR = \frac{FN}{TN + FN} \tag{8}$$

$$FR = \frac{FP}{TN + FP} \tag{9}$$

assuming that TN is the number of attack samples that are correctly marked, FN is the number of attack samples that are incorrectly marked, and FP is the number of normal samples that are incorrectly marked.

Known attacks and unknown attacks of mixed traffic in a random sample size of 100, 300, 500, 1000, 1500 samples as test set based on the destination IP address. Through five sets of experiments with different sample sizes, comparing the classification effects of T_i, Q_i and CR proposed in this paper of different classifiers C-Support Vector Machine (C-SVM) and Convolutional Neural Network (CNN) different classifiers in C-Support Vector Machine (C-SVM) and Convolutional Neural Network (CNN), the experimental results are shown in Figs. 1 and 2.

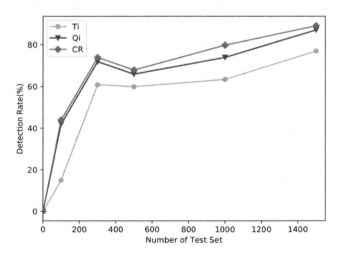

Fig. 1. Comparison of detection rates of three features in CNN.

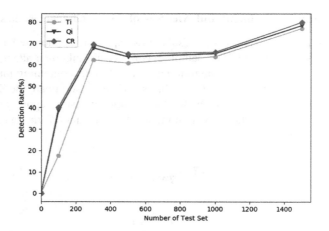

Fig. 2. Comparison of detection rates of three features in C-SVM.

According to Figs. 1 and 2, the detection rate of *CR* in the fused binary group proposed in this paper is higher than that of T_i and Q_i. Finally, this paper summarizes the performance of the three features, and the results under different classifiers are shown in Tables 1 and 2. It can be seen from Tables 1 and 2 that with the increase of training samples, *CR* still has higher classification accuracy than T_i and Q_i, and the detection effect on pre-attack is relatively better. Although the C-SVM and CNN classifiers have higher missing report rate when the number of samples is small, this is related to the higher proportion of the pre-attack period and the lower eigenvalue, which affects the effective identification of the classifier. In summary, the DDoS attack feature fusion model proposed in this paper effectively improves the overall accuracy and detection rate, and reduces the missing report rate and total error rate.

Table 1. Results of three features in CNN.

		100	300	500	1000	1500
T_i	Accuracy (%)	41	77	76.2	78.1	84
	MR (%)	85	38.4	39.5	36.5	22
	FR (%)	0	0	0	0	0
Q_i	Accuracy (%)	60	83	80	85.3	90
	MR (%)	58	27.2	33.3	24.5	14
	FR (%)	0	0	0	0	0
CR	Accuracy (%)	44	84	82	88	91
	MR (%)	39	26.2	32.7	20.6	11
	FR (%)	0	0	0	0	0

Table 2. Results of three features in C-SVM.

		100	300	500	1000	1500
T_i	Accuracy (%)	40	76	75.8	78	83.7
	MR (%)	82.3	37.8	39.4	36.2	22.5
	FR (%)	0	0	0	0	0
Q_i	Accuracy (%)	57	80.7	78.2	79.1	84.5
	MR (%)	61.5	32.3	36.4	34.9	21.6
	FR (%)	0	0	0	0	0
CR	Accuracy (%)	58	81.7	79	79.5	85.6
	MR (%)	60	30.6	35	34.2	20.2
	FR (%)	0	0	0	0	0

The overall network security situation value is obtained by DS evidence theory, and the probability of being attacked by DDoS is given.

(1) By combining DS evidence theory with information fusion, DDoS attacks can be better perceived.
(2) The flow rate with a safety situation value exceeding 0.6 can be judged as abnormal.
(3) By combining the characteristics of DDoS attack and experimental analysis, it can be determined that the network is attacked when the probability of being detected to be attacked by DDoS is greater than 0.6.
(4) The security situation value obtained after DS evidence theory fusion can be used to judge whether the network is attacked.

6   Conclusion

In view of the fact that the current single-point detection DDoS attack can not achieve good results, this paper proposes a DDoS attack situation information fusion method based on DS evidence theory. Firstly, the data is analyzed, and the destination address, the destination port number, the total number of IPs per unit time, and the number of ports of an IP are obtained, and then the traffic threat value and the traffic weight based on the destination IP address are calculated and analyzed. Based on this, a DDoS attack fusion feature CR is proposed, and a DDoS attack feature fusion model is presented. In addition, DS evidence theory method is combined with information fusion to obtain the overall network security situation value and the probability of network being attacked by DDoS. Experimental results show that the proposed method can effectively perceive DDoS attacks, effectively distinguish abnormal traffic from normal traffic, effectively reduce alarm failure and total error rate, and improve the overall accuracy and detection rate.

Acknowledgment. This work was supported by the Hainan Provincial Natural Science Foundation of China [617048,2018CXTD333]; National Natural Science Foundation of China [61762033, 61702539]; Hainan University Doctor Start Fund Project [kyqd1328]; Hainan University Youth Fund Project [qnjj1444]; Social Development Project of Public Welfare Technology Application of Zhejiang Province [LGF18F020019].

References

1. Shi, C.: A novel ensemble learning algorithm based on D-S evidence theory for IoT security. CMC: Comput. Mater. Continua **57**(3), 635–652 (2018)
2. Arbor Networks: Arbor Networks, 13th Worldwide Infrastructure Security Report. https://pages.arbornetworks.com/rs/082-KNA087/images/13th_Worldwide_Infrastructure_Security_Report.pdf
3. Khaleghi, B., Khamis, A., Karray, F.O., et al.: Multisensor data fusion: a review of the state-of-the-art. Inf. Fusion **14**(1), 28–44 (2013)
4. Yager, R.R.: A Framework for Multi-source Data Fusion, 1st edn. Elsevier, Amsterdam (2004)
5. Naumann, F., Bilke, A., Bleiholder, J., et al.: Data fusion in three steps: resolving inconsistencies at schema, tuple-, and value-level. Bull. Tech. Committee Data Eng. **29**(2), 21–31 (2006)
6. Snidaro, L., Visentini, I., Bryan, K.: Fusing uncertain knowledge and evidence for maritime situational awareness via Markov logic networks. Inf. Fusion **21**(1), 159–172 (2015)
7. Golestan, K., Khaleghi, B., Karray, F., et al.: Attention assist: a high-level information fusion framework for situation and threat assessment in vehicular ad hoc networks. IEEE Trans. Intell. Transp. Syst. **17**(5), 1271–1285 (2016)
8. Lin, L.: Multi-sensor information fusion method based on BP neural network. Int. J. Online Eng. **12**(5), 53 (2016)
9. Esposito, C., Castiglione, A., Palmieri, F., et al.: Event-based sensor data exchange and fusion in the internet of things environments. J. Parallel Distrib. Comput. **118**(2), 328–343 (2018)
10. Chen, B., Ho, D.W.C., Hu, G., et al.: Secure fusion estimation for bandwidth constrained cyber-physical systems under replay attacks. IEEE Trans. Cybern. **48**(6), 1862–1876 (2017)
11. Müller, W., Kuwertz, A., Muhlenberg, D., et al.: Semantic information fusion to enhance situational awareness in surveillance scenarios. In: 2017 IEEE International Conference on Multisensor Fusion & Integration for Intelligent Systems, pp. 397–402. IEEE, Korea (2017)
12. Aleroud, A., Karabatis, G.: Contextual information fusion for intrusion detection: a survey and taxonomy. Knowl. Inf. Syst. **52**(3), 563–619 (2017)
13. Guo, Y., Yin, C., Li, M., Ren, X., et al.: Mobile e-commerce recommendation system based on multi-source information fusion for sustainable e-business. Sustainability **10**(1), 147 (2018)
14. Shi, B., Xie, X.Q.: Research on network security situation forecast method based on D-S evidence theory. Comput. Eng. Des. **34**(3), 821–825 (2013)
15. Li, F.J., Qian, Y.H., Wang, J.T., et al.: Multigranulation information fusion: a Dempster-Shafer evidence theory based clustering ensemble method. In: International Conference on Machine Learning and Cybernetics, pp. 58–63. IEEE, Florence (2015)
16. Wu, H., Wang, Z.: Multi-source fusion based security detection method for heterogeneous networks. Comput. Secur. **74**, 55–70 (2018)

17. Pereira Junior, V.A., Sanches, M.F., Botega, L.C., Coneglian, C.S., Oliveira, N., Araújo, R. B.: Using semantics to improve information fusion and increase situational awareness. In: Arezes, P., et al. (eds.) Advances in Safety Management and Human Factors. AISC, vol. 491, pp. 101–113. Springer, Cham (2016). https://doi.org/10.1007/978-3-319-41929-9_11
18. Iglesias, F., Zseby, T., et al.: Analysis of network traffic features for anomaly detection. Mach. Learn. **101**, 59–84 (2015)
19. Usha, M., Kavitha, P.: Anomaly based intrusion detection for 802.11 networks with optimal features using SVM classifier. Wirel. Netw. **23**(8), 1–16 (2016)
20. Cheng, J., Zhou, J., Liu, Q., et al.: A DDoS detection method for socially aware networking based on forecasting fusion feature sequence. Comput. J. **61**(7), 959–970 (2018)
21. Hoque, N., Kashyap, H., Bhattacharyya, D.K.: Real-time DDoS attack detection using FPGA. Comput. Commun. **110**, 48–58 (2017)
22. Cheng, J., Xu, R., Tang, X., et al.: An abnormal network flow feature sequence prediction approach for DDoS attacks detection in big data environment. Comput. Mater. Continua **55** (1), 95–119 (2018)
23. Mehmood, A., Mukherjee, M., Ahmed, S.H., et al.: NBC-MAIDS: Naïve Bayesian classification technique in multi-agent system-enriched IDS for securing IoT against DDoS attacks. J. Supercomput. **74**(10), 5156–5170 (2018)
24. Cheng, J., Zhang, C., Tang, X., Sheng, V.S., Dong, Z., Li, J.: Adaptive DDoS attack detection method based on multiple-kernel learning. Secur. Commun. Netw. **2018**, 19 p. (2018). Article ID 5198685. https://doi.org/10.1155/2018/5198685
25. Li, F., Zhang, X., Zhu, J., et al.: Network security situation awareness model based on information fusion. J. Comput. Appl. **35**(7), 1882–1887 (2015)
26. Bogler, P.: Shafer-Dempster reasoning with applications to multisensor target integration system. IEEE Trans. Syst. Man Cybern. **17**(6), 968–977 (1987)
27. The Cooperative Association for Internet Data Analysis: The CAIDA UCSD "DDoS Attack 2007" Dataset [EB/OL], 05 August 2007

Webshell Detection Model Based on Deep Learning

Fangjian Tao[1,3], Chunjie Cao[1,2,3(✉)], and Zhihui Liu[1,3]

[1] Key Laboratory of Internet Information Retrieval of Hainan Province,
Hainan University, Haikou 570228, China
xxaq66@gmail.com, chunjie_cao@126.com, 835554057@qq.com
[2] State Key Laboratory of Marine Resource Utilization in the South China Sea,
Hainan University, Haikou 570228, China
[3] School of Information Science and Technology,
Hainan University, Haikou 570228, China

Abstract. Aiming at the problem that the existing Webshell detection method relies on manual extraction of features, low automation and easy to bypass, a Webshell detection algorithm based on deep learning is proposed. Some methods to escape the detection of deep learning model and the solution is proposed. Through the noise reduction and malicious payload reduction of Webshell and normal web pages, the features are automatically extracted in the deep learning model. The experimental results show that the recognition accuracy of the model is 99.56%. The detection range is wide and can cope with many kinds of bypass strategies.

Keywords: Deep learning · Webshell detection ·
Adversarial machine learning · Malicious code detection

1 Introduction

Now, people's work and life have been closely related to the Internet. Because of its easy updating and convenient use, web applications are greatly facilitating people's lives but at the same time facing many threats. Webshell is a kind of backdoor script that runs on the web server. During the hacking process, Webshell often plays a very important role. Once the Webshell is successfully uploaded, the web server will be controlled by the hacker very likely. Further, it may cause the server to be inserted shadow links, become slaves for mining or DDoS, and even lead to more serious consequences.

Supported by National Natural Science Fund Project No. 61661019; Major Science and Technology Project of Hainan province No. ZDKJ2016015-2; Hainan Education Reform Project No. Hnjg2017ZD-1; NSFC under Grant No. 61662021; NSF of Hainan No. ZDYF2017128 and No. 20156243.

X. Sun et al. (Eds.): ICAIS 2019, LNCS 11635, pp. 408–420, 2019.
https://doi.org/10.1007/978-3-030-24268-8_38

There are too many ways to upload a Webshell through various web application vulnerabilities, and it is extremely easy to be deformed to escape the current detection method, which is very harmful.

This paper studies the application of deep learning in the field of Webshell detection, analyzes the vulnerability of the Webshell detection model and possible attack methods and security enhancement methods. Three Webshell detection models are compared in this paper.

2 Related Work

Webshell usually contains a series of attack functions such as file upload and download, database operation, command execution, and privilege escalation. It is a malicious dynamic script, which is often mixed in many normal files or inserted in normal files. For Webshell detection methods, there are currently several types of methods:

1. Static detection: Use regular expression matching, feature string, blacklist, etc. to detect whether the script has malicious features. This method has a fast detection speed and requires manual extraction of features, which is easily bypassed by the kill operation.
2. Dynamic detection: The script file is executed in a sandbox, and the change of the system state is detected to determine whether the script file is malicious. Need to execute script files and maintain system state table, which consumes a lot of resources and is inefficient. And for some special Trojans can not detect any course, this Trojan need to perform after passing certain information, such as: Webshell with special request headers by expanding encrypted Webshell.
3. Method based on log analysis: The normal script files in the web application form a complete system, so they are often linked to each other. The Webshell as a malicious script file appears in the web application system, which almost no contact with the normal script file, and therefore behave as a "island." The method of log analysis is severely lazy and not very practical. It is powerless for Webshells that insert normal script files, and hackers often clean up logs after using Webshell.
4. Statistical methods: Extract statistical features such as information entropy, longest words, coincidence index, key function, file compression ratio, the percentage of uppercase letters and special characters in the document. This method to detect malicious scripts has better recognition effect on some deformed scripts, but the false positive rate and false negative rate are higher.
5. Attribute judgment: Webshell file attributes, such as file creation time, modification time, owner, etc., may be inconsistent with normal files. Since this method does not check the file itself, it can only be used as a reference.

Most of the above methods rely on manual extraction of features, low degree of automation, and are easily bypassed by deformation.

3   Deep Learning Based Webshell Detection Model

Deep learning algorithm has the ability to extract features automatically, to find the relationship between the data which is difficult to find manually, largely avoided the feature engineering. Compared to traditional Webshell detection methods, deep learning detection model has less manual intervention, strong adaptability, low hysteresis, low false positives rate and false negatives rate. But there is also a certain vulnerability. The model will be attacked by harmful data, if a valid noise filter is missing.

This paper analyzes the ways in which the detection model may be attacked and the method of model security enhancement. A feature enhancement method is proposed to improve the security of the model. The detection models based on DNN, CNN and LSTM are designed and compared (Fig. 1).

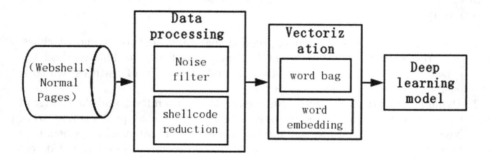

Fig. 1. Webshell detection model based on deep learning

3.1   Data Processing

Process raw data to make it suitable for deep learning algorithms. This process is mainly divided into the following three points:

(1) Malicious payload restoration: Since most Webshell use encryption, confusion, etc. to evade detection, it is necessary to restore malicious payloads as much as possible. Otherwise, a lot of information will be lost in the vectorization in the next step.
(2) Vectorization: Convert text information into vectors.
(3) Enhanced algorithm security: Take appropriate action against the possible attacks on the model.

Malicious Load Restoration. Due to the special nature of Webshell script, may through the "confusion", "encryption", or use the "local file containing", "remote loading a malicious payload," and other ways to evade detection. These operations can result in loss of information during vectorization. As follows.

Remote Payload. The malicious payload exists on the remote server and is disguised as an image.

```
<?php@file_put_contents(
'_',@file_get_contents('http://139.199.220.37/b1.jpg'));
@include('_');@delete('_');?>
```

Local Payload. The malicious payload is not in the Webshell itself.

```
<?php include "./b1.jpg"?>
```

Confuse Payload. Malicious features are hidden by methods such as encoding, compression, custom encryption, string splitting, shifting operations, and the like.

```
<?eval(
  gzinflate(
    base64\_decode('7P37ehq58igM/73zPLkHhWENMLE5+RAf... ' )
  )
)?>
```

After being confused, the malicious features in the execution function are hidden.

Therefore, we should try to restore malicious payloads before vectorization. For cases where the malicious payload is not in this file, we should load the malicious payload firstly. If the malicious payload has been confused, we should attempt to reverse the payload.

Vectorization. The goal of vectorization is to convert text to vectors, which should minimize information loss. Webshell text can be vectorized by character or word granularity. If the original script is vectorized at the character level granularity, there will be no overflow of the word bag. But character-level granularity can lead to dimensionality disasters. Therefore, this paper uses word granularity to study.

Word Bag Model. The document is first segmented, and then the number of occurrences of each word in the document is counted to obtain the vector corresponding to each document.

N-gram. The main idea of the N-gram algorithm is that the nth occurrence of a word is only related to the word that appeared before. This is similar to the Restricted Boltzmann Machine reconstructed training, state is only related to time t and time t-1. In this paper, 1-gram and 2-gram are used to sample the original data to obtain the word bag. 1-gram does not consider the word relationship before and after, 2-gram takes into account the two words before and after. Such a vectorized document retains some timing information to some extent (Fig. 2).

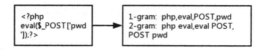

Fig. 2. Word bag extracted by 1,2-gram

Tf-idf. The importance of a word increases proportionally with the number of times it appears in the file, but it also decreases inversely with the frequency it appears in the corpus. Vectors that have been weighted by tf-idf can better highlight keyword information.

Tf-idf = $tf * idf$, *tf* and *idf* are calculated as:

$$tf_{i,j} = \frac{n_{i,j}}{\sum_k n_{k,j}} \tag{1}$$

$$idf_i = \log \frac{|D|}{|j : t_i \in d_j| + 1} \tag{2}$$

$n_{i,j}$ represents the times of word in the document d_j, $\sum_k n_{k,j}$ is the total number of words in the document d_j, $|D|$ represents the total number of documents in the corpus, $|j : t_i \in d_j| + 1$ represents the number of documents which containing the word.

Deep Learning Model Security Enhancement. Webshell requires further data processing after a malicious payload restore operation. Because the word bag-based model has the problem of the upper limit of the word bag capacity, and the words in the word bag are often ordered by default. This may cause some attack scenarios.

Word Bag Overflow Attack. During the model training phase, an attacker can construct a Webshell that contains many words that are meaningless to the classification to pollute the data set, causing the word bag to overflow, and many words that are meaningful for the classification are squeezed out of the word bag. This affects the result of vectorization, causing the model to shift in the direction desired by the attacker.

Special Construction Attacks. An attacker may be able to bypass the detection model by simply Webshell structure. Similar to the anti-image recognition system: by superimposing a specially constructed noise image on the original image, although the superimposed image looks similar to the original, the image recognition system recognizes it as another image.

Similarly, an attacker can change the result of a vectorization by constructing words in a Webshell script. In the multi-layer perceptron model experiment designed below, the accuracy of the model in the test set detection reached 99.5%. Use this trained model to scan a typical one-word Webshell:

```
<?php assert($_REQUEST["c"]);?>
```

Webshell probability is derived as follows: 99.7%. However, by adding some specially constructed annotation information to the Trojan script, you can bypass the detection model. As follows:

```
<?/*WP_USER_ADMIN,true,require_once,admin,login,If,
is_multisite,wp_redirect,admin_url,blog,domin,Filters,whether,to,
redirect,the,request,the User,Multisite*/
Php assert($_REQUEST["c"]);?>
```

At this point, the model concludes that the probability of Webshell is reduced to: 40.5%, which is recognized as a normal file (Fig. 3).

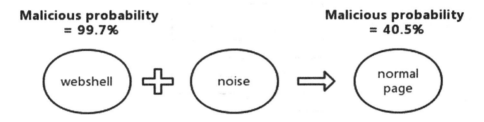

Fig. 3. Special construction attack

Manual analysis makes it easy to determine that this script is a typical Webshell, but the deep learning model recognizes it as a normal file because the Webshell detection model lacks background knowledge. The model automatically extracts the characteristics of the entire content of the document, but common sense is that the content of annotation should not be considered as a factor. In addition, to change the result of vectorization, we can bypass the model detection by constructing redundant variables, constants, etc..

Model Security Enhancement Method. The test model needs to have a certain professional background knowledge. One way is to not sample the part of document which is useless information such as comment information. If a variable, constant, or function is not called in the document, it can be filtered.

3.2 Deep Learning Detection Model Design

MLP Detection Model. A deep feedforward network, or multi-layer perceptron (MLP), is a typical deep learning model. The feedforward network is organized into a chain structure, which in turn contains an input layer, hidden layers, and an output layer. It can learn a nonlinear relationship, which is equivalent to a universal function approximator.

For input x , a model with three hidden layers can be described as:

$$f(x) = f_1(f_2(f_3(x))) = w_1(w_2(w_3(x) + b_3) + b_2) + b_1 \qquad (3)$$

The original data is vectorized by a word bag of size 25000, and the input data dimension is 25000, so its input layer has 25,000 nodes. Hidden layer designed three layers, respectively, each of nodes 20, 10, 5, activation function of each layer uses a rectifier linear unit (ReLU), cross entropy loss function selected as the objective function (Fig. 4).

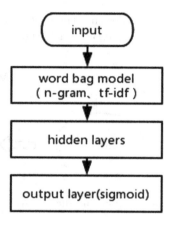

Fig. 4. MLP model

CNN Detection Model. Convolutional neural network (CNN), the neural network is designed to handle data having a grid-like structure. The convolution operation uses three concepts of "sparse connection", "parameter sharing", and "equal representation" to improve the machine learning system. Time series data can be regarded as one-dimensional grid data that is regularly sampled on the time axis. Therefore, in dealing with the problem of time-series text, the convolution operation has a translational invariance in time series, that is, inputs at different positions on the time axis have the same feature output. A typical convolutional network consists of three stages. The first stage is a parallel extraction feature of multiple convolution kernels, and the second stage uses a rectifying linear function to generate nonlinear activation. The third stage uses a pooling function for downsampling.

Applicability of Convolutional Networks. The convolution operation has an infinitely strong a priori, that is, the object being operated contains only local connection relationships and has translational variability. The pooling operation has an infinitely strong a priori, that is, the object being manipulated must have invariance to a small amount of translation. Convolution and pooling operation apply only when the a priori assumptions are reasonable and correct.

Webshell is a kind of time-series text, which is a script program itself. The program content has local context, and there are some less global contexts, which largely satisfy the prior of convolution local connection. Although convolution cannot extract global features, the characteristics of local connections are often sufficient to produce better Webshell classification effects. After the local data is translated a small amount on the local time axis, the semantics it contains should be unchanged. Obviously, Webshell also satisfies the prioritization of pooling operations.

Model Design. Unlike the depth feedforward network (DNN), which uses the vectorization of the n-gram word bag model, the input of the convolutional network cannot lose the timing information, otherwise it will not satisfy the a priori of the convolution operation and the pool operation.

(1) Embedded layer
   The learning process of word embedding is similar to the learning process of an autoencoder. Dimension reduction can be achieved by word embedding.
(2) Convolution layer
   A convolution operation is a mathematical operation of two real-valued functions. Let 'X' be a one-dimensional input vector, 'a' is the time interval, where integer is taken, 't' is the time window, and 'w' is the convolution kernel. The convolution process for the input vector can be described by the following formula.

$$s(t) = (x * w)(t) = \sum_{a=0}^{\text{len}(X)-1} x(a)w(t-a) \tag{4}$$

Considering that Webshell itself is a kind of program, one-dimensional convolution kernels with lengths of 3, 4, and 5 are used for neighborhood filtering on one-dimensional input signals. This sampling method is equivalent to adding an infinitely strong prior: respectively, assuming that the vocabulary is related to the surrounding 3–5 vocabulary, which is roughly consistent with the vocabulary correlation feature in the programming language. The number of convolution kernels is designed to be 256.

(3) Pooling layer
   The maximum pooling operation is used to further reduce dimensions. After the pooling layer, the data dimension is reduced to 64.
(4) Convolution feature classification
   After convolutionalization, the data is merged and flattened into feature vectors, and then classified by the fully connected layer (Fig. 5).

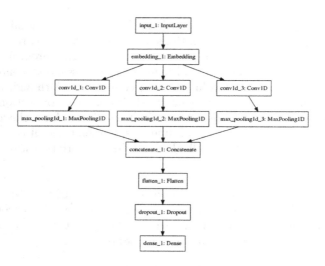

Fig. 5. CNN model

LSTM Detection Model. Recurrent neural network (RNN) is a type of network that specializes in processing sequence information. The multi-layer perceptron model assigns a separate parameter to each point in time, thus learning all the features of each location in the timing information. The convolutional network uses a one-dimensional convolution kernel to slide on the time axis to share parameters across time, which is shallow. Its parameter sharing is reflected in the use of the same convolution kernel at different time steps. RNN parameters are shared in a different way. It shares parameters in several time steps, in a deeper way. Each item of output is a function of the previous item, and this looping mode allows parameters to be shared in a deeper way. As described in Eq. 5:

$$a^{(t)} = f(a^{(t-1)}, x^{(t)}, \theta) \tag{5}$$

Current application results in the best model is the long short-term memory (LSTM), which controls whether to remember information through three gates: updating gate, forgetting and output gates. Equations 6–7 are the expressions for these three gates, respectively.

$$G_u = \text{sigmoid}(w_u[a^{(t-1)}, x^{(t)}] + b_u) \tag{6}$$

$$G_f = \text{sigmoid}(w_f[a^{(t-1)}, x^{(t)}] + b_f) \tag{7}$$

$$G_o = \text{sigmoid}(w_o[a^{(t-1)}, x^{(t)}] + b_o) \tag{8}$$

'A' represents the transfer of information on the time axis, 'c' is a memory cell, and its expression is Eq. 9–11.

$$c_n^{(t)} = \tanh(w_c[a^{(t-1)}, x^{(t)}] + b_c) \tag{9}$$

$$c^{(t)} = G_u * c_n^{(t)} + G_f * c^{(t-1)} \tag{10}$$

$$a(t) = G_o * \tanh c^{(t)} \tag{11}$$

Like the convolution model, RNN needs to retain timing information. Therefore, the same quantitative method is used and word embedding training is performed.

The experiment designed two layers of LSTM. The first layer LSTM outputs the 256- dimensional feature vector and passes it to the second layer LSTM. The output of the second LSTM layer is connected to the classification layer (Fig. 6).

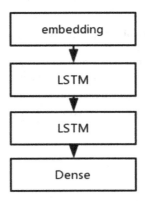

Fig. 6. LSTM model

LSTM Detection Model. Evaluation standard

The dataset uses the webshell open source collection project on GitHub, which marks the webshell as '1' and the normal web document as '0'. The dataset is randomly divided into training and test sets according to 4:1 (Table 1).

Table 1. Confusion matrix

	Predict: 0	Predict: 1
True: 0	TN	FP
True: 1	FN	TP

Formulas 12–15 is the performance index

$$\text{accuracy} = \frac{TP + TN}{TP + TN + FN + FP} \tag{12}$$

$$\text{precision} = \frac{TP}{TP + FP} \tag{13}$$

$$recall = \frac{TP}{TP + FN} \quad (14)$$

$$F = \frac{2 * precision * recall}{precision + recall} \quad (15)$$

The CNN and LSTM models converge better than the MLP model because they can process timing information. As shown in Fig. 7. The MLP model has the highest accuracy in the test set. As shown in Table 2. This also has a certain relationship with the way of retaining timing information, the loss convergence is faster and it is more likely to lead to over-fitting.

Table 2. Model evaluation

Model	Accuracy	Precision	Recall	F
MLP	99.57%	100%	99%	99.5%
CNN	97.93%	96.13%	99.34%	97.7%
LSTM	97.12%	95.89%	98.13%	96.99%

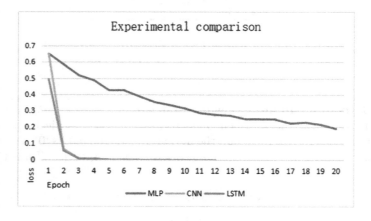

Fig. 7. Experimental comparison

4   Conclusion

Based on the deep learning Webshell detection model, MLP, CNN and LSTM networks can achieve better detection results. The deep learning detection model avoids feature engineering and can discover abstract features that are difficult to understand by humans. Webshells that use multiple strategies to avoid killing are difficult to bypass the detection of this model.

References

1. Cheng, R., Xu, R., Tang, X., Sheng, V.S., Cai, C.: An abnormal network flow feature sequence prediction approach for DDoS attacks detection in big data environment. Comput. Mater. Continua **55**(1), 095–095 (2018)
2. Choi, Y.H., Kim, T.G., Choi, S.J., Lee, C.W.: Automatic detection for JavaScript obfuscation attacks in web pages through string pattern analysis. In: Lee, Y., Kim, T., Fang, W., Ślęzak, D. (eds.) FGIT 2009. LNCS, vol. 5899, pp. 160–172. Springer, Heidelberg (2009). https://doi.org/10.1007/978-3-642-10509-8_19
3. Cova, M., Kruegel, C., Vigna, G.: Detection and analysis of drive-by-download attacks and malicious JavaScript code. In: Proceedings of the 19th International Conference on World Wide Web, pp. 281–290. ACM (2010)
4. Curtsinger, C., Livshits, B., Zorn, B., Seifert, C.: Zozzle: Low-overhead mostly static JavaScript malware detection. In: Proceedings of the USENIX Security Symposium, pp. 3 (2011)
5. Deng, L.Y., Lee, D.L., Chen, Y.H., Yann, L.X.: Lexical analysis for the webshell attacks. In: 2016 International Symposium on Computer, Consumer and Control (IS3C), pp. 579–582. IEEE (2016)
6. Hou, Y.T., Chang, Y., Chen, T., Laih, C.S., Chen, C.M.: Malicious web content detection by machine learning. Expert Syst. Appl. **37**(1), 55–60 (2010)
7. Huang, W., Stokes, J.W.: MtNet: a multi-task neural network for dynamic malware classification. In: Caballero, J., Zurutuza, U., Rodríguez, R.J. (eds.) DIMVA 2016. LNCS, vol. 9721, pp. 399–418. Springer, Cham (2016). https://doi.org/10.1007/978-3-319-40667-1_20
8. Ma, J., Saul, L.K., Savage, S., Voelker, G.M.: Identifying suspicious URLs: an application of large-scale online learning. In: Proceedings of the 26th Annual International Conference on Machine Learning, pp. 681–688. ACM (2009)
9. Meng, Z., Mei, R., Zhang, T., Wen, W.P.: Research of Linux webshell detection based on SVM classifier. Netinfo Secur. **5**, 4 (2014)
10. Meyerovich, L.A., Livshits, B.: ConScript: specifying and enforcing fine-grained security policies for JavaScript in the browser. In: 2010 IEEE Symposium on Security and Privacy, pp. 481–496. IEEE (2010)
11. Mingkun, X., Xi, C., Yan, H.: Design of software to search ASP web shell. Procedia Eng. **29**, 123–127 (2012)
12. Moshchuk, A., Bragin, T., Deville, D., Gribble, S.D., Levy, H.M.: SpyProxy: execution-based detection of malicious web content. In: USENIX Security Symposium, pp. 1–16 (2007)
13. Provos, N., McNamee, D., Mavrommatis, P., Wang, K., Modadugu, N., et al.: The ghost in the browser: analysis of web-based malware. HotBots **7**, 4–4 (2007)
14. Behrens, S., Hagen, B.: Web Shell Detection Using NeoPI (2012). http://resources.infosecinstitute.com/web-shell-detection/. Accessed 6 Nov 2017
15. Sun, X., Lu, X., Dai, H.: A matrix decomposition based webshell detection method. In: Proceedings of the 2017 International Conference on Cryptography, Security and Privacy, pp. 66–70. ACM (2017)
16. Tu, T.D., Guang, C., Xiaojun, G., Wubin, P.: Webshell detection techniques in web applications. In: 2014 International Conference on Computing, Communication and Networking Technologies (ICCCNT), pp. 1–7. IEEE (2014)

17. Wang, Y.M., Beck, D., Jiang, X., Roussev, R.: Automated web patrol with strider HoneyMonkeys: finding web sites that exploit browser vulnerabilities. In: NDSS. Citeseer (2006)
18. Zhang, H., Yi, Y., Wang, J., Cao, N., Duan, Q.: Network security situation awareness framework based on threat intelligence. CMC-Comput. Mater. Continua **56**(3), 381–399 (2018)

A Security-Sensitive Function Mining Framework for Source Code

Lin Chen[1,2], Chunfang Yang[1,2(✉)], Fenlin Liu[1,2], Daofu Gong[1,2], and Shichang Ding[3]

[1] Zhengzhou Science and Technology Institute, Zhengzhou 450001, China
chunfangyang@126.com
[2] State Key Laboratory of Mathematical Engineering and Advanced Computing, Zhengzhou 450001, China
[3] University of Göttingen, Goldschmidtstr. 7, 37077 Göttingen, Germany

Abstract. The security-sensitive functions can be effectively used to improve the efficiency of vulnerability mining techniques, but mining security-sensitive functions of the large-scale code base is difficult. An automatic mining framework for security-sensitive functions is proposed. Firstly, a class of high-resolution code features is used to extract suspected security-sensitive function sets, and then a class of code features is applied to measure the sensitivity of each suspected security-sensitive function. Ultimately, the final security-sensitive function set is ensured based on the measurement result. Established along the framework, a mining algorithm for a type security-sensitive function is proposed. Through the mining experiments on three well-known open source codes, the performance of this algorithm is better than the existing methods.

Keywords: Code feature · Security-sensitive function · Code mining · Software defect

1 Instruction

Software vulnerability discovery methods are primarily classified as automated mining technique and manual auditing. Automated mining techniques have developed rapidly in recent years. Common mining techniques include: fuzzing tests [2], model checking [6], symbolic execution [3, 8, 9], machine learning [13, 15] and so on, these techniques have greatly improved the efficiency of vulnerability discovery. However, in reality, the structure of the software is more and more complex and the scale is getting bigger. The above techniques are faced with such paths explosion and state explosion when dealing with large software. In order to meet the vulnerability mining needs of large software, researchers often split the problem into some smaller problems.

The first, the size of the target software was reduced by a decomposition process. For example, [2, 11] decomposed the whole source codebase into many corresponding sub-libraries by the slicing process. Then, a bug mining process was performed on every smaller sub-library. [7, 10] proposed a guided fuzzing test. The dangerous operation is the starting point of the fuzzing, which effectively improves the efficiency of the fuzzing test. The second, a small range of vulnerability was focused only every

© Springer Nature Switzerland AG 2019
X. Sun et al. (Eds.): ICAIS 2019, LNCS 11635, pp. 421–432, 2019.
https://doi.org/10.1007/978-3-030-24268-8_39

time. For example, Yamaguchi et al. [14] automatically generated detection script, which traversed along the code property graph of the target software, for only one given sink function rather than the entire vulnerability type such as buffer overflow.

These splitting methods above usually applied a security-sensitive function or a type of security-sensitive function. Also, in the actual manual auditing process, experienced analysts often use security-sensitive functions of key modules as an entry point of analysis to improve audit efficiency. In summary, the application of security-sensitive functions is very important to both automated vulnerability mining techniques and manual auditing.

Mining security-sensitive function manually has two drawbacks: first, the work is tedious and time-consuming; second, the judgment is not objective. So, it cannot meet the current requirements of high-efficiency vulnerability mining techniques. The techniques of automatic mining security-sensitive functions had gradually attracted the researchers' attention. At present, the specialized research on the automatic mining of security-sensitive functions is limit. Some preliminary exploratory researches are carried out on argument-sensitive [4] and sequence-sensitive functions. The argument-sensitive function attributes their security to the validity of their arguments, the arguments of the invocation instance need to meet specific legal requirements. Liang et al. [2, 11] proposed a mining method for bug-prone functions in the process of detecting bugs. By counting the proportion of invocation instances whose argument is protected by conditional statements, they judged whether the function is a bug-prone function or not. The performance of the mining method is not evaluated directly, and the effectiveness of the method is verified by the final bug detection results. Chen et al. [4] improved the method of [2, 11] by increasing the detection of the implicit check of the argument, which reduced the false negative of mining result. The sequence-sensitive function must be paired with another function. Otherwise, it may cause a bug. [5] mined a type of sequence-sensitive function that "<a> must be paired with <b> in pairs" and found bugs that deviated the specification.

In order to improve the scalability of the security-sensitive function mining method, this paper proposed an automatic mining framework for security-sensitive functions. The framework mainly consists of two steps. Firstly, for different types of security-sensitive functions, the code features that reflect the security specification of the security-sensitive functions to be extracted, which are used to screen out the suspected security-sensitive functions from the code base. Secondly, the code features related to the security characters such as specification, code idioms et al. are used to measure the sensitivity of each suspected security-sensitive function, and then the suspected security-sensitive function with high sensitivity is identified as a true security-sensitive function. Based on the mining framework proposed, an argument-sensitive function mining algorithm was designed and performed better than [4, 11] in the experiment.

2 Mining Framework for Security-Sensitive Functions

2.1 Security-Sensitive Function

Chen et al. [4] described security-sensitive function as a function with security specifications. And failure to satisfy any of the specifications to call the function may result in bugs in the program. The description of the security-sensitive function in this paper is the same as it in [4].

Each security-sensitive function F contains one or more security specifications, and the security specification set of F is denoted as SP_F. According to different types of security specification set, security-sensitive functions can be classified. For the set of security-sensitive functions $sstvF = \{F_1, F_2 \ldots F_n\}$, if these functions have the same security specification sets between each other, that Eq. (1) is exact, then they are considered to belong to the same type of security-sensitive functions.

$$\forall F_i, F_j \in sstv\ F,\ SP_{F_i} = SP_{F_j} \tag{1}$$

If they have different sets of security specifications, but there is a non-empty security specification intersection among them, that Eq. (2) is exact, then they are considered to be a type of security-sensitive function under the constraint of the security specification set SP_Δ. The $sstvF$ can be denoted as $sstvF^{SP_\Delta}$.

$$SP_\Delta = \bigcap_{i=1}^{n} SP_{F_i} \neq \emptyset \tag{2}$$

Obviously, for a function F' and a known security-sensitive function set $sstvF^{SP_\Delta}$, if $SP_\Delta \subseteq SP_{F'}$, then $F' \in sstvF^{SP_\Delta}$, that means the function F' is a security-sensitive function under constraints of the security specification set SP_Δ, in order to express easily and conveniently, let $SP_{F'} = pubSP_{F'} \cup pvtSP_{F'}$, where $pubSP_{F'}$ is the common-specification set, which contains the same security specifications as them in $sstvF^{SP_\Delta}$, so $pubSP_{F'} = SP_\Delta$; and $pvtSP_{F'}$ is personality-specification set, which contains the different specifications from SP_Δ, so $pvtSP_{F'} = SP_{F'} - SP_\Delta$.

To determine whether a function belongs to a certain type of security-sensitive function, we need to identify whether it contains the corresponding security specifications. In actual programming development, when a programmer calls a security-sensitive function, the security specification is embodied in the semantics of the calling code, and show as a certain code form. Therefore, in the mining process of the security-sensitive function, the appropriate code features could be extracted from the calling code to identify whether the function has a corresponding security specification. However, due to different programming habits, background knowledge, and execution context, the same security specification can be implemented differently, and be showed as different code forms, which may lead to feature extraction failure, then affecting the accuracy of automatic mining.

In order to improve the accuracy of mining technique for security-sensitive function, this paper proposed a mining framework, which applies the security features corresponding to common-specification to mine the set of suspected security-sensitive functions, and applies auxiliary code features extracted from personality-specifications, coding idioms, software metrics and so on to measure the sensitivity of every suspected security-sensitive functions and then identify the final security-sensitive function.

2.2   The Framework

As shown in Fig. 1(a), the security-sensitive function mining framework mainly consists screening process and measurement process.

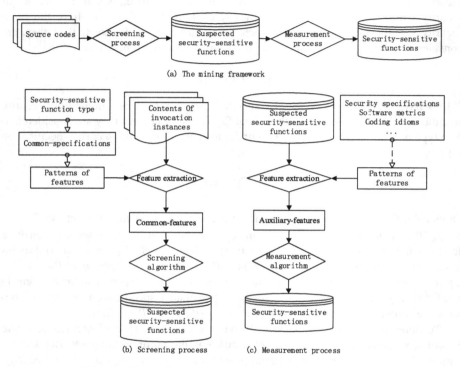

(a) The mining framework

(b) Screening process   (c) Measurement process

Fig. 1. Mining framework for security-sensitive functions

The screening process is shown in Fig. 1(b) in detail. First, according to the types of security-sensitive functions that need to be mined, select the common-specification set, and convert each common-specification into a corresponding feature pattern; then, according to the feature patterns, extract corresponding common-features from the content of each invocation instance; According to the statistical results of all the common features to determine whether the function is a suspected security-sensitive function or not.

The measurement process is shown in Fig. 1(c) in detail. First, select security-related information from the security specifications, coding idioms, software metrics et al., convert the information into the corresponding feature patterns; extract the auxiliary-features of each suspected security-sensitive function invocation instance according to the feature patterns; finally, according to the statistics result measures the security sensitivity of each suspected function, and determines the function whose metric value is higher than the preset threshold as a security-sensitive function.

2.3   Feature Extraction

Code features extracted will be applied in the screening process and measurement process. The quality of the features directly affects the accuracy of mining result, but depending on the feature selection mainly.

The process of feature selection is converting abstract security specifications into concrete feature patterns. For example, a security specification is "some arguments need validity check", and then the corresponding feature can be "Arguments are checked by a conditional statement directly or indirectly. If the check fails, the function will not be executed" proposed in [11], or can be "Arguments are checked with an explicit or implicit style" proposed in [4]. Different features will lead to different mining results.

In this framework, the selection of common-features has a great impact on the final mining accuracy: on the one hand, selected features may cause the loss of part of the semantics of the security specification, which would result in false positives, so it needs a measurement process to reduce false positives. On the other hand, if the selected features are difficult to extract, features extraction from some invocation instances possibly failing, which would result in false negatives.

The auxiliary-features are used to measure the security sensitivity of the function. If the function has more features related to code security, it indicates that the security sensitivity of the function is higher. Therefore, the source of the auxiliary-features includes can be not only security specifications, but also code restrictions, code idioms, software metrics, and so on. Different auxiliary-features play different roles for different types of security-sensitive functions. Therefore, different features should be given different weights to indicate their impact on security sensitivity measurements.

By arranging the existing literature, Table 1 lists some frequently-used code features for bug detection and specification mining, which can be selected as common-feature or auxiliary-feature according to the type of security-sensitive function.

Table 1.   Frequently-used code features

Feature source	Samples of feature	Location
Security specifications	Argument checking	[4, 11]
	Error handling	[1]
Sensitive objects	Argument type	
	The argument comes from user input	
Coding idioms	Function name contains special substring	
Software metrics	Code complexity	

For the feature extraction in the mining framework, whether the feature is used as a common-feature or as an auxiliary-feature is closely related to the type of security-sensitive function, For example, for the feature "handles sensitive objects (such as handles, memory)", it is best suited for mining security-sensitive functions related to resource leak vulnerability as one of common-features, and it is more suitable for mining sensitive functions related to race conditions as one of auxiliary-features.

2.4 Screening Process

The purpose of the screening process is to filter out the set of suspected security-sensitive functions from the source code repository. According to the above process, if a function contains all defined common-features, it is called a suspected security-sensitive function; if any of the common-features are missing, it is classified as a regular function. However, for some special invocation instances of a target function, the extraction of common-features has the following two problems: First, during the programming process, due to the negligence of the developer, some of the invocation instances may not implement a certain security specification, so that the common-features cannot extract from these invocation instances; Secondly, due to the diversification of the implementation of security specifications, for an unknown implementation, the common-security features may extracted failed. The failure of common-features extraction in some special instances would influence the screening result on the target function.

In order to avoid the impact of special invocation instances, the screening process uses a statistical method. If most of the invocation instances contain a common-feature, the function is considered to contain the common-feature, which means that the target function has a corresponding security specification. If the target function contains all the common-features of the common-feature set, then the target function is considered to be a suspected security-sensitive function. The formal description of the process is as follows:

Let $sstvF^{SP_\Delta}$ is a security-sensitive function set under the constraint of security specification set SP_Δ. $Feature_{SP_\Delta} = \{a_1, a_2 \ldots a_m\}$ is a code feature set corresponding to SP_Δ. Let $InsSet_{F'} = \{Ins_1, Ins_2 \ldots Ins_n\}$ is the instance set of target function F'.

For any invocation instance Ins_i, its confidence value of the feature a_i is calculated by calculation formula (3)

$$v_{(Ins_i, a_i)} = \begin{cases} 1, & Ins_i \ contains \ a_i \\ 0, & others \end{cases} \tag{3}$$

Then, for the target function F', its confidence value of the feature a_i is calculated by calculation formula (4)

$$V_{(F', a_i)} = \begin{cases} true, & if \ \frac{\sum_{j=1}^{n} v_{(Ins_j, a_i)}}{n} > \lambda_{a_i} \\ false, & others \end{cases} \tag{4}$$

Where λ_i is the confidence threshold of a_i. If Eq. (5) is satisfied, then the function F' is considered to be a suspected security-sensitive function, otherwise F' is a regular function.

$$\bigcap_{i=1}^{m} V_{(F', a_i)} = true \tag{5}$$

In the screening process, the threshold λ_{a_i} has an important influence on the screening result, and the setting of the threshold λ_{a_i} is related to the code quality and the accuracy of common-feature extraction.

First of all, for a mature reality program, it is usually tested repeatedly by developers and testers. Moreover, during the long-term use, the developer will continuously fix the discovered security issues. After repeated iterations, the code quality of the program can be considered to be enhanced gradually. For a project with high code quality, it can be assumed that most of the invocation instances of the security-sensitive function implement its security specifications, and the code has a good coding style, which makes the special invocation instance less. For these projects with high code quality, a higher threshold λ_{a_i} can be set, which can reduce the false positive rate of the final mining result.

Secondly, if the selected features are too complex, the difficulty of extraction may cause the feature extraction of some invocation instances failed. For example, in order to extract the feature "Argument comes from the user input", complicated inter-process data analysis or even dynamic analysis is required, the extraction is difficult and the ratio of successful extraction would be small; if the feature is "The argument name contains the string 'str'", the extraction is simple. Therefore, the setting of the threshold λ_{a_i} should also take account of the difficulty of feature extraction.

2.5   Measurement Process

In order to reduce false positives of security-sensitive function, the suspected security sensitive function set needs to be verified. The sensitivity of each suspected security sensitive function is measured. The function with high-level measurement is confirmed as a security sensitive function.

The measurement process uses auxiliary-features to measure the security sensitivity of suspected security-sensitive functions. The method of judging whether a function contains an auxiliary-feature is similar to the method of judging whether a function contains a common-feature in the screening process. First, the auxiliary-feature of each invocation instance is extracted, if the ratio of invocation instances containing the auxiliary-feature is greater than the confidence threshold of the auxiliary-feature, the target function has this auxiliary-feature.

This framework uses auxiliary-features to describe the sensitivity of the suspected function. Because different auxiliary-features have different ability to describe the sensitivity, so every auxiliary-feature has a corresponding weight. According to the extraction results and weights of all the auxiliary-features, the sensitivity measurement of the suspected security-sensitive function is calculated, and then the final security-sensitive functions are determined by the sensitivity measurement. The specific identification method is described as follows:

Let $Feature_{aux} = \{b_1, b_2 \ldots b_m\}$ is selected auxiliary-feature set, $InsSet_{F'} = \{Ins_1, Ins_2 \ldots Ins_n\}$ is the invocation instance set of the suspected security-sensitive function F'.

For any invocation instance Ins_i, its confidence value of the feature b_i is calculated by calculation formula (6).

$$v_{(Ins_i,b_i)} = \begin{cases} 1, & \text{if } Ins_i \text{ cotans } b_i \\ 0, & \text{others} \end{cases} \tag{6}$$

Then, for the target function F', its confidence value of the feature $b_.$ is calculated by calculation formula (7).

$$V_{(F',b_i)} = \begin{cases} 1, & \text{if } \dfrac{\sum_{j=1}^{m} v_{(Ins_j,b_i)}}{n} > \lambda_{b_i} \\ 0, & \text{others} \end{cases} \tag{7}$$

Where λ_{b_i} is the confidence threshold of b_i. Then the sensitivity measurement of the target suspected function F' is calculated by calculation formula (8).

$$W_{F'} = \frac{\sum_{i=1}^{m} V_{(F',b_i)} * \omega_{b_i}}{\sum_{i=1}^{m} \omega_{b_i}} \, 0 \leq W_{F'} \leq 1, \tag{8}$$

Where ω_{b_i} is the measure weight representing the ability of b_i, and the higher the measurement value $W_{F'}$, the higher sensitivity of the target suspect function F'. If $W_{F'} > W_\Omega$ is satisfied, the suspected security-sensitive function F' is determined to be a security-sensitive function, that $F' \in sstvF^{SP_\Delta}$. The W_Ω is the measurement threshold, its value is decided by the quality of source code, the type of security-sensitive function, auxiliary-feature set et al.

3   Experiment and Analysis

In order to verify the validity of the proposed framework, this paper will construct an argument-sensitive function mining algorithm based on the framework and compare it with the existing methods AntMiner [11] and [4].

3.1   Argument-Sensitive Function Mining Algorithm

The security-sensitive function mining algorithm based on mining framework needs to select common-features and auxiliary-features, set the confidence threshold of each common-feature and auxiliary-feature, set the measured weight of every auxiliary-feature and the measurement threshold. In order to be as fair as possible compared to existing methods, in general, this paper selects features and algorithm parameters similar to them.

When mining argument-sensitive functions, the feature used in [11] was "there is an argument protected by conditional statements", which was named "explicit check" in [4]. Besides, [4] proposed a new check style named "implicit check" and selected {"there is an argument protected by explicit or implicit check"} as its code feature. In this paper, we also select it as the only common-feature and select {"there is an argument of pointer type"} as the only auxiliary-feature.

As analyzed before, the algorithm parameters are decided by code quality, the type of security-sensitive function, the difficulty of feature extraction and so on. In order to compare fairly, simply, we directly set some algorithm parameters the same as [11] and [4]. The features and parameters of the proposed mining algorithm are shown in Table 2.

Table 2. Parameters of the proposed argument-sensitive function mining algorithm

Mining process	Feature type	Feature set	Confidence threshold	Measured weight	Measurement threshold
Screening process	Common-feature	{"there is an argument protected by explicit or implicit check"}	$\lambda_{a_1} = 0.7$	None	None
Measurement process	Auxiliary-feature	{"there is an argument of pointer type"}	$\lambda_{b_1} = 0.7$	$\omega_{b_1} = 1$	$W_\Omega = 0.5$

3.2 Sample Selection

In order to compare with [4], three well-known open source software, chosen as samples in [4], was selected as experiment samples. The details of these programs are shown in Table 3. OpenSSL is a widely used open source software library package, including SSL (Secure Socket Layer) protocol and TLS (Transport Layer Security) protocol toolkit and numerous password libraries; Libtiff is an open source code base for manipulating Tag Image File Format (TIFF). SQLite is a self-contained, embedded, full-featured, public-domain, SQL database engine.

Table 3. A dataset of the three open-source projects.

Project	Version	Size (M)
OpenSSL	1.1.0f	8.2
Libtiff	4.0.7	8.6
SQLite	3.18.0	74

3.3 Mining Argument-Sensitive Functions

In order to verify the validity of the framework, the argument-sensitive functions of the three open source software are mined separately. The mining results are shown in Table 4.

It can be seen from Table 4 that the number of suspected security-sensitive functions mined by the proposed algorithm is equal to the number of security-sensitive functions mined by [4], and the number of confirmed security-sensitive functions is less than [4]. That is because the common-feature selected in this paper is the same as the feature used in [4], and the same confidence thresholds were adopted, that means the algorithm of our screening process is equivalent to the mining algorithm in [4].

Since the proposed method has a measurement process more than the method of [11] and [4], using the auxiliary-feature "there is an argument of pointer type" to measure the sensitivity of the suspected security-sensitive function, the suspected security-sensitive function with sensitivity measurement lower than the measurement threshold W_Ω were excluded to reduce the false positive rate, so the number of argument-sensitive functions finally determined in this paper is less than mined by [11] and [4].

Most of the functions mined in this experiment are project-specific functions, which are unique to the project. Only by manual analysis can confirm whether the argument-sensitive functions mined are correct, but the number of sensitive functions mined is too large to perform manual analysis on every result, so the performance of the three algorithms cannot be compared clearly in this experiment. In order to accurately evaluate the performance of the three mining algorithms, the known argument-sensitive functions will be mined.

Table 4. The number of argument-sensitive functions

Project	AntMiner [11]	Chen [4]	Proposed		Total number
			Suspected argument-sensitive functions	Argument-sensitive functions	
OpenSSL	2063	2401	2401	1540	6226
Libtiff	575	633	633	415	1239
SQLite	1804	2081	2081	1400	4926

3.4   Comparison with Existing Algorithms

In order to evaluate the performance of this method better, this paper redoes the relevant experiments [4], 28 argument-sensitive functions and 32 regular functions were selected from the well-known glibc library as the benchmarks. Glibc is the GNU Project's implementation of the C standard library. It was widely used by many software projects. Since the selected functions are used frequently and widely, their security specifications are well known, and it is easy to confirm which functions are argument-sensitive.

The source code of the three open-source software was combined, and AntMiner [11], Chen [4] and the proposed algorithm were used to identify 60 Glibc functions. The receiver operating characteristics (ROC) curves of the results are shown in Fig. 2, where the curve of the proposed algorithm is above that of AntMiner [11] and Chen [4]. This indicates that our method yielded the best performance of all.

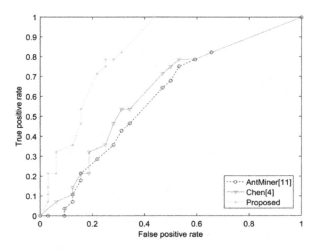

Fig. 2. ROC curves of the three methods

The above experiments' results show that the mining algorithm based on the proposed mining framework can mine security-sensitive functions effectively. And only one auxiliary-feature is used to measure the sensitivity of the function in this measurement process, obviously, the performance of the mining algorithm proposed can be improved better, such as adding more auxiliary-features to reduce false negatives.

4 Summary

The security-sensitive function is important for software defect detection, which can help to reduce the level of difficulty and improve detection efficiency. However, it is difficult to identify security-sensitive functions in large programs accurately. At present, the research on the automatic mining of security-sensitive functions is still on an exploratory stage, and the accuracy of automatic mining techniques needs to be greatly improved. In this paper, a security-sensitive function mining framework is proposed. Firstly, a screening process is used to obtain the suspected security-sensitive functions. Then a measurement process is used to measure the sensitivity of these functions to determine the final security-sensitive function. Based on the framework, an argument-sensitive function mining algorithm is constructed. The experimental results show that the algorithm can mine the argument-sensitive function effectively and get a better performance than the existing algorithms.

Acknowledgments. This study was supported in part by the National Natural Science Foundation of China (Nos. 61401512, 61602508, 61772549, U1636219, and U1736214), the National Key R&D Program of China (Nos. 2016YFB0801303 and 2016QY01W0105), the Key Technologies R&D Program of Henan Province (No. 162102210032), and the Key Science and Technology Research Project of Henan Province (No. 152102210005).

References

1. Acharya, M., Xie, T.: Mining API error-handling specifications from source code. In: Chechik, M., Wirsing, M. (eds.) FASE 2009. LNCS, vol. 5503, pp. 370–384. Springer, Heidelberg (2009). https://doi.org/10.1007/978-3-642-00593-0_25
2. Bian, P., Liang, B., Zhang, Y., Yang, C., Shi, W., Cai, Y.: Detecting bugs by discovering expectations and their violations. IEEE Trans. Softw. Eng. 1 (2018)
3. Cadar, C., Dunbar, D., Engler, D.: KLEE: unassisted and automatic generation of high-coverage tests for complex systems programs. In: Proceedings of the 8th USENIX Conference on Operating Systems Design and Implementation, pp. 209–224. USENIX Association, Berkeley (2008)
4. Chen, L., Yang, C., Liu, F., Gong, D., Ding, S.: Automatic mining of security-sensitive functions from source code. CMC **56**, 199–210 (2018)
5. Engler, D., Chen, D.Y., Hallem, S., Chou, A., Chelf, B.: Bugs as deviant behavior: a general approach to inferring errors in systems code. In: Proceedings of the Eighteenth ACM Symposium on Operating Systems Principles, pp. 57–72. ACM, New York (2001)
6. Engler, D., Musuvathi, M.: Static analysis versus software model checking for bug finding. In: Steffen, B., Levi, G. (eds.) VMCAI 2004. LNCS, vol. 2937, pp. 191–210. Springer, Heidelberg (2004). https://doi.org/10.1007/978-3-540-24622-0_17
7. Ganesh, V., Leek, T., Rinard, M.: Taint-based directed whitebox fuzzing. In: Proceedings of the 31st International Conference on Software Engineering, pp. 474–484. IEEE Computer Society, Washington, DC (2009)
8. Godefroid, P., Klarlund, N., Sen, K.: DART: directed automated random testing. In: Proceedings of the 2005 ACM SIGPLAN Conference on Programming Language Design and Implementation, pp. 213–223. ACM, New York (2005)
9. Godefroid, P., Levin, M.Y., Molnar, D.A.: Automated whitebox fuzz testing. In: Proceedings of the Network and Distributed System Security Symposium, NDSS 2008, San Diego, California, USA, 10–13 February 2008, p. 16 (2008)
10. Haller, I., Slowinska, A., Neugschwandtner, M., Bos, H.: Dowsing for overflows: a guided fuzzer to find buffer boundary violations. In: Proceedings of the 22nd USENIX Security Symposium, Washington, DC, USA, 14–16 August 2013, pp. 49–64 (2013)
11. Liang, B., Bian, P., Zhang, Y., Shi, W., You, W., Cai, Y.: AntMiner: mining more bugs by reducing noise interference. In: 2016 IEEE/ACM 38th International Conference on Software Engineering (ICSE), pp. 333–344. ACM Press, New York (2016)
12. Majumdar, R., Wang, Z.: BBS: a phase-bounded model checker for asynchronous programs. In: Kroening, D., Păsăreanu, C.S. (eds.) CAV 2015. LNCS, vol. 9206, pp. 496–503. Springer, Cham (2015). https://doi.org/10.1007/978-3-319-21690-4_33
13. Malhotra, R.: A systematic review of machine learning techniques for software fault prediction. Appl. Soft Comput. **27**, 504–518 (2015)
14. Yamaguchi, F., Maier, A., Gascon, H., Rieck, K.: Automatic inference of search patterns for taint-style vulnerabilities. In: 2015 IEEE Symposium on Security and Privacy, pp. 797–812. IEEE (2015)
15. Xi, X., Sheng, S., Sun, B., Wang, L., Hu, F.: An empirical comparison on multi-target regression learning. CMC **56**, 185–198 (2018)

Abstraction of Operations in Trusted Components Based on OR-Transition Colored Petri Net

Yong Yu[1], Ming Jing[1], Detao Ji[1], Yuanyuan Wang[1],
Zhongwen Xie[1(✉)], and Shudong Li[2(✉)]

[1] School of Software, Key Laboratory in Software Engineering
of Yunnan Province, Yunnan University, Kunming 650091, China
xiezw56@126.com
[2] Cyberspace Institute of Advanced Technology, Guangzhou University,
Guangzhou 510006, China
lishudong@gzhu.edu.cn

Abstract. In this paper, research is carried out with a hot issue in current trusted software research as the main content – component-based trusted software construction and its key theory and technology. In this paper, based on characteristics of trusted components, we analyze the related properties of trusted components on the basis of our proposed OR-transition Petri net-based component description and modeling work, and on this basis, propose benign concept of component, and put forward method of abstracting operation in trusted component.

Keywords: Trusted component · Component network · Petri net · Component abstraction

1 Introduction

"Credibility" of software means that dynamic behavior of software system and its results are always in line with people's expectations and continuous service can still be provided when it is disturbed. Wherein, "credibility" emphasizes predictability and controllability of behavior and results, while "disturbance" includes operational errors, environmental impact and external attacks [1]. Trusted software, as one of the most valuable and challenging core issues in the field of computer software research, has aroused great concern of domestic and foreign government organizations, scientific and industrial circles with targeted research projects successively put forward.

The field of software engineering provides abstraction and refinement mechanisms to understand and handle complexity of software. The idea of abstraction technology is to map a large number of specific states or operations in the system to a much less abstract state or operation based on one aspect of the characteristics in order to facilitate analysis and processing of the software system model.

In the process of modeling and designing components, it is an important technique to construct hierarchical models by means of abstract means. This paper will construct a hierarchical trusted component model by abstracting operation in trusted component based on the component model of OR-transition colored Petri net in previous work [2].

© Springer Nature Switzerland AG 2019
X. Sun et al. (Eds.): ICAIS 2019, LNCS 11635, pp. 433–442, 2019.
https://doi.org/10.1007/978-3-030-24268-8_40

2 Related Work

In recent years, scholars at home and abroad begin to study trusted components-related issues from different perspectives:

Literature [3] discusses that traditional software fault-tolerant method is based on the idea of redundancy and diversity, and there is need for programmers to design multiple fault-tolerant versions in advance. The adaptive software system can adapt to the changes of the operating environment, user's requirements and correct the defects in operation through adjustment of its own structure and behavior, and finally improve credibility of the software system.

Literature [4] holds that, in the early stage of software development, due to constraints of hardware and software conditions, plus essentially unchanged environment, needs and functions of software after it is put into operation, in software design and development, architecture is only a static description of software development stage which rarely takes into account its dynamic changes. Literature [5, 6] discusses that evolvability is an important feature of trusted components.

In order to prove that formalization method combined with software process is an effective way to ensure software security, and meanwhile, support the software development team in integrating security into software development life cycle in early stage, literature [7] proposes CLASP (Comprehensive, Lightweight Application Security Process), which builds activity-based, role-based process component sets based on formal best practices. In literature [8], a structural algebraic model of internetware architecture is proposed. Six kinds of network connection operations are defined, and algebraic model is used to represent the components, which enhances the abstraction ability of the architecture description. Literature [9] reports research results to improve the traditional trust model with consideration of cooperation effects.

Literature [10] describes components, connectors and configuration constraints, and describes the relationship between connector and component. Reliability of components is analyzed in literature [11–13], and trusted component modeling and algorithm efficiency are discussed. Literature [14–17] studies the relationship between component evolution and reliability evaluation. The parameters in trusted component Model are discussed in literature [18–20]. Literature [21] presents a scheme named SecDisplay for trusted display service, it protects sensitive data displayed from being stolen or tampered surreptitiously by a compromised OS.

3 Benignness Definition of Trusted Component Subnet

Definition 1. For internal subnet $N_t = <P'_t, T'_t, F'_t, S'_t, A'_{Pt}, A'_{Tt}, A'_{Ft}>$ of trusted component $C_t = <P_t, T_t, F_t, S_t, A_{Pt}, A_{Tt}, A_{Ft}, IP_t, OP_t>$, $B_t(N_t) = \{y \in P'_t \cup T'_t | \exists x \notin P'_t \cup T'_t, x \in loc(y)\}$ is the boundary of the subnet N_t.

Definition 2. In internal subnet $N_t = <P'_t, T'_t, F'_t, S'_t, A'_{Pt}, A'_{Tt}, A'_{Ft}>$ of trusted component $C_t = <P_t, T_t, F_t, S_t, A_{Pt}, A_{Tt}, A_{Ft}, IP_t, OP_t>$, for subset $IB_t(N_t) \subseteq B_t(N_t)$ of boundary $B_t(N_t)$ of subnet N_t, if $\forall y \in IB_t(N_t), \exists x \in (P_t \cup T_t) \backslash (P'_t \cup T'_t)$, so that $<x, y> \in F_t$, then $IB_t(N_t)$ is insert boundary of subnet N_t; for subset $OB_t(N_t) \subseteq B_t(N_t)$

of boundary $B_t(N_t)$ of subnet N_t, if $\forall y \in OB_t(N_t), \exists x \in (P_t \cup T_t) \backslash (P'_t \cup T'_t)$, so that $<y, x> \in F_t$, then $OB_t(N_t)$ is exit boundary of subnet N_t.

Definition 3. For internal subnet $N_t = <P'_t, T'_t, F'_t, S'_t, A'_{Pt}, A'_{Tt}, A'_{Ft}>$ of trusted component $C_t = <P_t, T_t, F_t, S_t, A_{Pt}, A_{Tt}, A_{Ft}, IP_t, OP_t>$, if boundary $B_t(N_t) \subseteq P_t$, then subnet N_t is state boundary subnet of trusted component C_t; if boundary $B_t(N_t) \subseteq T_t$, then subnet N_t is operation boundary subnet of trusted component C_t.

Definition 4. For internal subnet $N_t = <P'_t, T'_t, F'_t, S'_t, A'_{Pt}, A'_{Tt}, A'_{Ft}>$ of trusted component $C_t = <P_t, T_t, F_t, S_t, A_{Pt}, A_{Tt}, A_{Ft}, IP_t, OP_t>$, if subnet N_t is state boundary subnet of trusted component C_t and for every insert boundary $p \in IB_t(N_t)$, $\forall x \in (P'_t \cup T'_t) \backslash \{p\}$ of subnet N_t, $xF^*_{R}p$ is false, then subnet N_t is strict state boundary subnet of trusted component C_t; if subnet N_t is operation boundary subnet of trusted component C_t and for every insert boundary $t \in IB_t(N_t)$, $\forall x \in (P'_t \cup T'_t) \backslash \{t\}$ of N_t, $xF^*_{R}t$ is false, then subnet N_t is strict operation boundary subnet of trusted component C_t.

The definition requires that the subnet is not cycling relative to exit/insert boundary, but circulation can exist within the subnet.

Definition 5. Suppose internal subnet $N_t = <P'_t, T'_t, F'_t, S'_t, A'_{Pt}, A'_{Tt}, A'_{Ft}>$ of trusted component $C_t = <P_t, T_t, F_t, S_t, A_{Pt}, A_{Tt}, A_{Ft}, IP_t, OP_t>$ is strict operation boundary subnet, if $\forall p \in {}^{\cdot}IB_t(N_t)$, then $|p^{\cdot} \cap IB_t(N_t)| = 1$, and if $\forall p \in OB_t(N_t)^{\cdot} \cap (P_t \backslash P'_t)$, then $|{}^{\cdot}p \cap OB_t(N_t)| = 1$, then subnet N_t is benign strict operation boundary subnet of trusted component C_t.

Note: For benign strict operation boundary subnet N_t of trusted component C_t, number of outgoing arc of any element in the pre-set of insert boundary $IB_t(N_t)$ is 1 relative to the subnet N_t (i.e., selected branch is nonexistent); and the number of incoming arc of any element in post-set of exit boundary $OB_t(N_t)$ and outside subnet N_t is also 1 relative to the subnet N_t (i.e., there is no conflict). The purpose of this is to avoid multiple arcs after abstraction.

The operation boundary subnet is also a subnet with operation as a boundary. In trusted component $C_t = <P_t, T_t, F_t, S_t, A_{Pt}, A_{Tt}, A_{Ft}, IP_t, OP_t>$, the benign strict operation boundary subnet N_t can be replaced by an operating element, so as to achieve abstraction. If trusted component C_t is benign, the benign nature of trusted component C_t remains unchanged after benign strict operation boundary subnet N_t is replaced with an operating element.

4   Abstraction of Operations in Trusted Components

Definition 6. Suppose subnet $N_t = <P'_t, T'_t, F'_t, S'_t, A'_{Pt}, A'_{Tt}, A'_{Ft}>$ is a non-empty, benign strict operation boundary subnet of trusted component $C_t = <P_t, T_t, F_t, S_t, A_{Pt}, A_{Tt}, A_{Ft}, IP_t, OP_t>$, then trusted component $C[t_N \to N_t]_t = <P_{[N]t}, T_{[N]t}, F_{[N]t}, S_{[N]t}, A_{[N]Pt}, A_{[N]Tt}, A_{[N]Ft}, IP_{[N]t}, OP_{[N]t}>$ is a simple abstraction of trusted component C_t with respect to subnet N_t. Wherein:

(1) $P_{[N]t} = P_t \backslash P'_t$;

(2) $T_{[N]t} = (T_t \backslash T'_t) \cup \{t_N\}$, wherein, t_N represents a new operation;

(3) $F_{[N]t} = \{<x,y> \,|x \in (P_t \cup T_t)\backslash(P_t' \cup T_t') \wedge y \in (P_t \cup T_t)\backslash(P_t' \cup T_t') \wedge <x,y> \in F_t\} \cup \{<x,t_N> \,|x \in (P_t\backslash P_t') \wedge \exists y \in T_t' \text{ so that } <x,y> \in F_t\} \cup \{<t_N,x> \,|x \in (P_t\backslash P_t') \wedge \exists y \in T_t' \text{ so that } <y,x> \in F_t\};$

(4) $S_{[N]t} \subseteq S_t;$

(5) $A_{[N]Pt} : \forall p \in P_{[N]t}, A_{[N]Pt}(p) = A_{Pt}(p);$

(6) $A_{[N]Tt} : \forall t \in T_{[N]t}\backslash\{t_N\}, A_{[N]Tt}(t) = A_{Tt}(t); A[N]Tt(tN) = \sum\limits_{x \in IB(N)} ATt(x);$

(7) $A_{[N]Ft} : \forall <x,y> \in \{<x,y> \,|x \in (P_t \cup T_t)\backslash(P_t' \cup T_t') \wedge y \in (P_t \cup T_t)\backslash(P_t' \cup T_t') \wedge <x,y> \in F_t\}$, then $A_{[N]Ft}(<x,y>) = A_{Ft}(<x,y>); \forall <x,t_N> \in \{<x, t_N> \,|x \in (P_t\backslash P_t') \wedge \exists y \in T_t' \text{ so that } <x,y> \in F_t\}$, then $A_{[N]Ft}(<x,t_N>) = A_{Ft}(<x,y>); \forall <t_N,x> \in \{<t_N,x> \,|x \in (P_t\backslash P_t') \wedge \exists y \in T_t' \text{ so that } <y,x> \in F_t\}$, then $A_{[N]Ft}(<t_N,x>) = A_{Ft}(<y,x>);$

(8) $IP_{[N]t} = IP_t; OP_{[N]t} = OP_t.$

Note: If N_t is a non-strict operation boundary subnet, since there may be an internal arc connected to N_t's insert boundary operation t, i.e. $p \in P_t'$ so that $<P_t', t> \in F_t'$, then $A_{[N]Tt}(t_N)$ value has a problem.

Note: Because of abstraction of benign strict operation boundary subnet in trusted component $C_t = <P_t, T_t, F_t, S_t, A_{Pt}, A_{Tt}, A_{Ft}, IP_t, OP_t >$, the access interface of trusted component is maintained, i.e. $IP_{[N]t} = IP_t, OP_{[N]t} = OP_t.P_{[N]t}$ contains all states that are not in N_t, while $T_{[N]t}$ also contains a new operation t_N in addition to all operations that are not in N_t, which represents abstraction of operation boundary subnet N_t. $F_{[N]t}$ is obtained by union set of three arcs, wherein, the first set is made by two arcs with endpoints not in N_t, the second set consists of those arcs connecting outer edge of set N_t to operation t_N, and the third set consists of those arcs connecting operation t_N to outer edge of set N_t. After a simple abstraction, function of the arc in trusted component $C_{t\,[N]t}$ should be the same as the original, and guard function that operates t_N is the sum of guard function of operation in insert boundary $IB(N)_t$ of N_t.

Theorem 1. Suppose trusted component $C_t = <P_t, T_t, F_t, S_t, A_{Pt}, A_{Tt}, A_{Ft}, IP_t, OP_t >$ is benign, subnet N_t is a non-empty benign strict operation boundary subnet within trusted component C_t. If trusted component $C[t_N \to N]_t = <P_{[N]t}, T_{[N]t}, F_{[N]t}, S_{[N]t}, A_{[N]Pt}, A_{[N]Tt}, A_{[N]Ft}, IP_{[N]t}, OP_{[N]t} >$ is a simple abstraction of trusted component C_t with respect to N_t, then trusted component $C[t_N \to N_t]_t$ is also benign.

Demonstration: As can be known from definition of benign nature of trusted component, it is necessary to prove that trusted component $C[t_N \to N]_t$ is benign from the following aspects: (1) t_N is completely structurally active and $\forall p \in t_N', t_N$ is type matching with p; (2) $\forall t \in T_{[N]}, \exists ip \in IP_{[N]t}$ so that ipF_R^*t; (3) $\forall t \in T_{[N]t}, t \in ET_{[N]t}$ or $\exists x \in OP_{[N]t} \cup ET_{[N]t}$, so that tF_R^*x; (4) $\forall ip \in IP_{[N]t}, \exists t \in T_{[N]t}$ so that $<ip, t> \in F_t$, and t is structurally active for ip; (5) $\forall op \in OP_{[N]t}, \exists t \in T_{[N]t}$ so that $<t, op> \in F_t$, and t is type matching with op; (6) $\forall t \in T_{[N]t}$, operation t is completely structurally active.

Suppose non-empty benign strict operation boundary subnet $N_t = <P_t', T_t', F_t', S_t', A_{Pt}', A_{Tt}', A_{Ft}' >$ of trusted component C_t, insert boundary $IB(N)_t = \{t_1, t_2, \ldots, t_k\}$ of subnet N, then:

(1) Prove that t_N is completely structurally active:

a. $\forall p \in P_{[N]t}, A_{[N]Pt}(p) = A_{Pt}(p)$,

b. $A[N]T_t(tN) = \sum\limits_{x \in IB(N)} AT_t(x)$,

c. $\forall <x, t_N> \in \{<x, t_N> | x \in (P_t \backslash P_t') \wedge \exists y \in T_t' \text{ so that } <x, y> \in F_t\}$,

From $A_{[N]Ft}(<x, t_N>) = A_{Ft}(<x, y>)$, it can be known that $\forall p \in \cdot t_N$, t_N and p are type matched.

Since subnet N_t is a non-empty benign strict operation boundary subnet, it can be abstracted with operation t_N, and trusted component C_t becomes trusted component C $[t_N \rightarrow N]_t$ after abstraction. In trusted component $C[t_N \rightarrow N]_t$, if $\forall p' \in \cdot IB(N)_t$, then $<p', t_N> \in F_{[N]t}$, so $\cdot IB(N)_t = \cdot t_N$.

Since trusted component C_t is benign, each operation $t \in IB(N)_t$ in insert boundary $IB(N)_t$ of subnet N_t is completely structurally active, i.e. $\forall t \in IB(N)_t$, $\forall p' \in \cdot t$. There exists a state subset $P_t \subseteq \cdot t$ in trusted component C_t that makes $p' \in P_t$ and $\sum A_{Ft}(<p', t>) = A_{Tt}(t)(p' \in P_t)$ satisfy.

Thus, for any state $p \in \cdot t_N$ in pre-set of operation t_N in trusted component C $[t_N \rightarrow N]_t$, there exists a unique operation $t_i \in IB(N)_t$ in the insert boundary of subnet N that makes $<p, t_i> \in F_t$ and $p \in P_{ti} \wedge \sum\limits_{p' \in P_{ti}} <p_t', ti> = AT_t(ti)$ satisfy.

Thus, for any state p in pre-set $\cdot t_N$ of operation t_N, there exist operation $t_i \in IB(N)_t$ and k state subsets P_{t1}, P_{t2}, ..., P_{tk}, that make

$$p \in P_{ti} \wedge \sum\limits_{p' \in P_{t1}} <p', t1> + \ldots + \sum\limits_{p' \in P_{ti}} <p', ti> + \ldots + \sum\limits_{p' \in P_{tk}} <p', tk>$$

$$= AT_t(t1) + \ldots + AT_t(ti) + \ldots + AT_t(tk) = AT_t(tN)$$

satisfy.

Hence, t_N is completely structurally active.

At the same time, trusted component C_t is benign. According to $\forall p \in P_{[N]t}, A_{[N]Pt}(p) = A_{Pt}(p)$ and $\forall <x, y> \in \{<t_N, x> | x \in (P_t \backslash P_t') \wedge \exists y \in T_t' \text{ so that } <y, x> \in F_t\}$ in the definition, $A_{[N]Ft}(<t_N, x>) = A_{Ft}(<y, x>)$, so operation t_N is not terminating operation, then t_N is type matching with p.

(2) $\forall t \in T_{[N]t}, \exists ip \in IP_{[N]t}$ so that ipF_R^*t

For any operation $\forall t \in T_{[N]t}$ in trusted component $C[t_N \rightarrow N]_t$, if $t_N F_R^* t$ is false, then abstraction of subnet N_t by operation t_N does not affect structure reachability relation between operation t and input interface. Therefore, as trusted component C_t is benign, $\exists ip \in IP_t = IP_{[N]t}$ so that ipF_R^*t.

If $t_N F^* t$ is true, then it can be seen from (1) that operation t_N is type matching with state in pre-set $\cdot t_N$ and post-set $t_N\cdot$, and operation t_N is also structurally active. Thus, since trusted component C_t is benign, for any state in pre-set $\cdot t_N$ of operation t_N, $\exists ip \in IP_t = IP_{[N]t}$ so that ipF_R^*p satisfy. Also, p and t_N, t_N and state in post-set $t_N\cdot$ are type matched, $t_N F^* t$, then $pF_R^* t$ is true, so that $\exists ip \in IP_t = IP_{[N]t}$ and $ipF_R^* t$ are true.

(3) $\forall t \in T_{[N]t}$, then $t \in ET_{[N]t}$ or $\exists x \in OP_{[N]t} \cup ET_{[N]t}$, so that tF_R^*x;

For any operation $\forall t \in T_{[N]t}$ in trusted component $C[t_N \rightarrow N]_t$, if tF^*t_N is false, then abstraction of subnet N_t by operation t_N does not affect structure reachability relation between operation t and terminating operation or output interface. Therefore, as trusted component C_t is benign, then $t \in ET_{[N]t}$ or $\exists x \in OP_t = OP_{[N]t} \cup ET_{[N]t}$, so that tF_R^*x.

If tF^*t_N is true, it can be seen from (1) that operation t_N is terminating operation, i.e. $t_N \in ET_{[N]t}$ or operation t_N and state in post-set t_N' are type matched, and operation t_N is structurally active. Therefore, as trusted component C_t is benign, then for any state p in post-set t_N' of operation t_N, $\exists x \in OP_t \cup ET_{[N]t} = OP_{[N]t} \cup ET_{[N]t}$, then tF_R^*x satisfy. As $\exists ip \in IP_t = IP_{[N]t}$, ipF_R^*p is true.

Then, $\forall t \in T_{[N]t}, t \in ET_{[N]t}$ or $\exists x \in OP_{[N]t} \cup ET_{[N]t}$, so that tF_R^*x.

At the same time, as trusted component C_t is benign, subnet N is a non-empty benign operation boundary subnet and operation t_N in trusted structure $C[t_N \rightarrow N]_t$ is completely structurally active, we can easily prove (4) $\forall ip \in IP_{[N]t}, \exists t \in T_{[N]t}$ so that $<t, ip> \in F_t$ and t is structurally alive with respect to ip; (5) $\forall op \in OP_{[N]t}, \exists t \in T_{[N]t}$ so that $<t, op> \in F_t$, and t and op are type matched; (6) $\forall t \in T_{[N]t}$, operation t is completely structurally active.

5   Examples of Operational Abstractions in Trusted Components

For trusted component $C_t = <P_t, T_t, F_t, S_t, A_{Pt}, A_{Tt}, A_{Ft}, IP_t, OP_t>$, if:

$P_t = \{p_1, p_2, p_3, p_4, p_5, p_6, p_7, p_8, ip_1, ip_2, op_1, op_2\}$;

$T_t = \{t_1, t_2, t_3, t_4, t_5, t_6, t_7, t_8\}$;

$F_t = \{<ip_1, t_1>, <ip_2, t_4>, <p_1, t_1>, <p_2, t_2>, <p_3, t_3>, <p_4, t_5>, <p_5, t_6>, <p_6, t_7>, <p_7, t_8>, <p_8, t_4>, <t_1, p_2>, <t_2, p_3>, <t_3, p_8>, <t_3, op_1>, <t_4, p_4>, <t_5, p_5>, <t_6, p_6>, <t_6, op_2>, <t_7, p_7>, <t_8, p_1>\}$;

$S_t = \{a_2, a_3, a_5, b_2, b_3, b_5, b_6, d_4, f_4, r, u_3, w_1, w_2\}$;

A_{Pt}: $\{A_{Pt}(ip_1) = \{a_2, b_2\}, A_{Pt}(ip_2) = b_5, A_{Pt}(p_1) = f_4, A_{Pt}(p_2) = r, A_{Pt}(p_3) = w_1, A_{Pt}(p_4) = r, A_{Pt}(p_5) = w_2, A_{Pt}(p_6) = u_3, A_{Pt}(p_7) = r, A_{Pt}(p_8) = d_4, A_{Pt}(op_1) = \{a_3, b_3\}, A_{Pt}(op_2) = \{a_5, b_6\}\}$;

A_{Tt}: $\{A_{Tt}(t_1) = a_2 + b_2 + f_4, A_{Tt}(t_2) = r, A_{Tt}(t_3) = w_1, A_{Tt}(t_4) = b_5 + d_4, A_{Tt}(t_5) = r, A_{Tt}(t_6) = w_2, A_{Tt}(t_7) = u_3, A_{Tt}(t_8) = r\}$;

A_{Ft}: $\{A_{Ft}(<ip_1, t_1>) = a_2 + b_2; A_{Ft}(<ip_2, t_4>) = b_5; A_{Ft}(<p_1, t_1>) = f_4; A_{Ft}(<p_2, t_2>) = r; A_{Ft}(<p_3, t_3>) = w1; A_{Ft}(<p_4, t_5>) = r; A_{Ft}(<p_5, t_6>) = w_2; A_{Ft}(<p_6, t_7>) = u_3; A_{Ft}(<p_7, t_8>) = r; A_{Ft}(<p_8, t_4>) = d_4; A_{Ft}(<t_1, p_2>) = r; A_{Ft}(<t_2, p_3>) = w_1; A_{Ft}(<t_3, p_8>) = d_4; A_{Ft}(<t_3, op_1>) = a_3 + b_3; A_{Ft}(<t_4, p_4>) = r; A_{Ft}(<t_5, p_5>) = w_2; A_{Ft}(<t_6, p_6>) = u_3; A_{Ft}(<t_6, op_2>) = a_5 + b_6; A_{Ft}(<t_7, p_7>) = r; A_{Ft}(<t_8, p_1>) = f_4\}$;

$IP_t = \{ip_1, ip_2\}$;

$OP_t = \{op_1, op_2\}$。

The graphical representation of trusted component C_t is shown in Fig. 1:

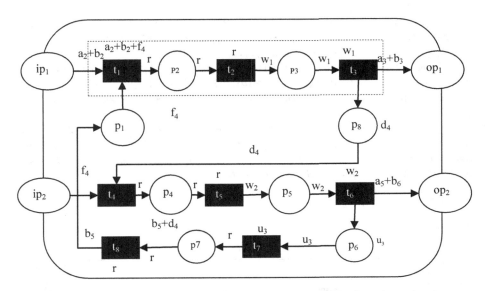

Fig. 1. Graphical representation of trusted component C_t before abstraction.

For non-empty benign strict operation boundary subnet $N_t = <P'_t, T'_t, F'_t, S'_t, A'_{Pt}, A'_{Tt}, A'_{Ft}>$ of trusted component C_t, as shown in the dashed box in Fig. 1:

$P_t' = \{p_2, p_3\}$;
$T_t' = \{t_1, t_2, t_3\}$;
$F_t' = \{<p_2, t_2>, <p_3, t_3>, <t_1, p_2>, <t_2, p_3>\}$;
$S_t' = \{a_2, b_2, f_4, r, w_1\}$;
A_{Pt}': $\{A_{Pt}(p_2)=r, A_{Pt}(p_3)=w_1\}$;
A_{Tt}': $\{A_{Tt}(t_1)=a_2+b_2+f_4, A_{Tt}(t_2)=r, A_{Tt}(t_3)=w_1\}$;
A_{Ft}': $\{A_{Ft}(<p_2, t_2>)=r; A_{Ft}(<p_3, t_3>)=w_1; A_{Ft}(<t_1, p_2>)=r; A_{Ft}(<t_2, p_3>)=w_1\}$.

In trusted component C_t, subnet $N_t = <P'_t, T'_t, F'_t, S'_t, A'_{Pt}, A'_{Tt}, A'_{Ft}>$ satisfies the abstraction condition, so after it is abstracted by operation t_N, trusted component C_t becomes trusted component $C[t_N \rightarrow N]_t = <P_{[N]t}, T_{[N]t}, F_{[N]t}, S_{[N]t}, A_{[N]Pt}, A_{[N]Tt}, A_{[N]Ft}, IP_{[N]t}, OP_{[N]t}>$ as shown in Fig. 2, wherein:

$P_{[N]t} = \{p_1, p_4, p_5, p_6, p_7, p_8, ip_1, ip_2, op_1, op_2\}$;

$T_{[N]t} = \{t_N, t_4, t_5, t_6, t_7, t_8\}$;

$F_{[N]t} = \{<ip_1, t_N>, <ip_2, t_4>, <p_1, t_N>, <p_4, t_5>, <p_5, t_6>, <p_6, t_7>, <p_7, t_8>, <p_8, t_4>, <t_N, p_8>, <t_N, op_1>, <t_4, p_4>, <t_5, p_5>, <t_6, p_6>, <t_6, op_2>, <t_7, p_7>, <t_8, p_1>\}$;

$S_{[N]t} = \{a_2, a_3, a_5, b_2, b_3, b_5, b_6, d_4, f_4, r, u_3, w_1, w_2\}$;

$A_{[N]Pt}$: $\{A_{Pt}(ip_1)=\{a_2, b_2\}, A_{Pt}(ip_2)=b_5, A_{Pt}(p_1)=f_4, A_{Pt}(p_4)=r, A_{Pt}(p_5)=w_2, A_{Pt}(p_6)=u_3, A_{Pt}(p_7)=r, A_{Pt}(p_8)=d_4, A_{Pt}(op_1)=\{a_3, b_3\}, A_{Pt}(op_2)=\{a_5, b_6\}\}$;

$A_{[N]Tt}$: $\{A_{Tt}(t_N)=a_2+b_2+f_4, A_{Tt}(t_4)=b_5+d_4, A_{Tt}(t_5)=r, A_{Tt}(t_6)=w_2, A_{Tt}(t_7)=u_3, A_{Tt}(t_8)=r\}$;

$A_{[N]Ft}$: $\{A_{Ft}(<ip_1, t_N>)=a_2+b_2; A_{Ft}(<ip_2, t_4>)=b_5; A_{Ft}(<p_1, t_N>)=f_4; A_{Ft}(<p_4, t_5>)=r; A_{Ft}(<p_5, t_6>)=w_2; A_{Ft}(<p_6, t_7>)=u_3; A_{Ft}(<p_7, t_8>)=r; A_{Ft}(<p_8, t_4>)=d_4; A_{Ft}(<t_N, p_8>)=d_4; A_{Ft}(<t_N, op_1>)=a_3+b_3; A_{Ft}(<t_4, p_4>)=r; A_{Ft}(<t_5, p_5>)=w_2; A_{Ft}(<t_6, p_5>)=u_3; A_{Ft}(<t_6, op_2>)=a_5+b_6; A_{Ft}(<t_7, p_7>)=r; A_{Ft}(<t_8, p_1>)=f_4\}$;

$IP_{[N]t} = \{ip_1, ip_2\}$;

$OP_{[N]t} = \{op_1, op_2\}$。

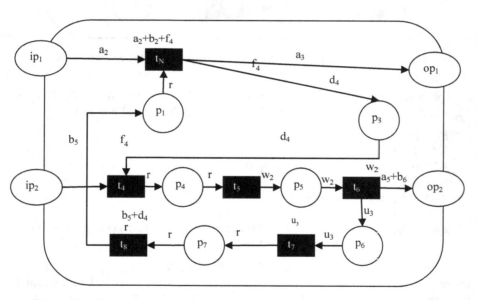

Fig. 2. Graphical representation of trusted component $C[t_N \rightarrow N]_t$ after abstraction.

6   Summary

Component is an important composition element of software architecture. In this paper, based on characteristics of trusted components, we analyze the related properties of trusted components on the basis of OR-transition colored Petri net-based component model defined by our previous work and on this basis, propose benign concept of trusted component, put forward method of abstracting operation in trusted component, and prove that the abstraction carried out under this method can keep benign nature of trusted components unchanged.

Acknowledgments. Project funded by the National Science Foundation of China under Grant (No. 61462091, U1803263, 61672020, 61866039), by the Data Driven Software Engineering innovation team of Yunnan province (No. 2017HC012); by China Postdoctoral Science Foundation (No. 2013M542560, 2015T81129), A Project of Shandong Province Higher Educational Science and Technology Program (No. J16LN61).

References

1. Liu, K., Shan, Z., Wang, J., He, J., Zhang, Z., Qin, Y.: Overview on major research plan of trustworthy software. Bull. Natl. Nat. Sci. Found. China **22**(3), 145–151 (2008)
2. Yu, Y., Li, T., Liu, Q., Dai, F., Zhao, N.: OR-transition colored petri net and its application in modeling software system. In: Proceedings of 2009 International Workshop on Knowledge Discovery and Data Mining, January 2009, Moscow, Russia, pp. 15–18 (2009)
3. Bernstein, L., Yuhas, C.: Trustworthy Systems Through Quantitative Software Engineering. Quantitative Software Engineering. Wiley-IEEE Computer Society Press, New York (2005). Silver Spring MD
4. Ding, B., Wang, H.M., Shi, D.X., Li, X.: Component model supporting trustworthiness-oriented software evolution. J. Soft. **22**(1), 17–27 (2011). http://xueshu.baidu.com/s?wd= author%3A%28LI%20Xiao%29%20School%20of%20Computer%20National% 20University%20of%20Defense%20Technology&tn=SE_baiduxueshu_c1gjeupa&ie=utf-8&sc_f_para=sc_hilight%3Dperson
5. Yang, H.J., Zheng, S.: Software evolution for moving into and moving within internetware paradigm. Int. J. Softw. Inf. **7**(1), 41–61 (2013)
6. Jia, Y.H., Zheng, S.: Software evolution based on service-oriented requirement in internetware. In: 4th International Conference on Computer Research and Development, pp. 20–25. IACSIT Press, Singapore (2012)
7. Secure Software, Inc. The CLASP Application Security Process (2005). http://www.ida.liu. se/~TDDC90/papers/clasp_external.pdf
8. Zhao, H., Sun, J.: An algebraic model of internetware software architecture. Sci. Sinica **43** (1), 161 (2013)
9. Xie, X., Yuan, T., Zhou, X., Cheng, X.: Research on trust model in container-based cloud service. CMC: Comput. Mater. Continua **56**(2), 273–283 (2018)
10. Chen, X.: New system based on event-driven and service-oriented business activity monitoring design and implementation. Appl. Res. Comput. **29**(3), 977–980 (2012)
11. Panwar, P., Garg, A.: Analysis of reliability and cost tradeoffs in architecture based software applications using a genetic algorithm. Int. J. Comput. Appl. **72**(1), 33–37 (2013)
12. Qiuying, L., Haifeng, L., Guodong, W.: Sensitivity analysis on the influence factors of software reliability based on diagnosis reasoning. Adv. Intell. Syst. Comput. **180**, 557–566 (2013)
13. Shanmugapriya, P., Suresh, R.M.: Software architecture evaluation methods—a survey. Int. J. Comput. Appl. **49**(16), 19–26 (2012)
14. Franco, J.M., Barbosa, R., Zenha-Rela, M.: Reliability analysis of software architecture evolution. In: Sixth Latin-American Symposium on Dependable Computing (LADC), Rio de Janeiro, Brazil, pp. 11–20 (2013)

15. Rathod, H., Parmar, M.: Study of genetic approach in estimating reliability of component based software. PARIPEX - Indian J. Res. **1**(11), 17–19 (2012)
16. Wang, J., Chen, W.R.: A reliability-oriented evolution method of software architecture based on contribution degree of component. J. Softw. **7**(8), 1744–1750 (2012)
17. Han, W., Tian, Z., Huang, Z., Li, S., Jia, Y.: Bidirectional self-adaptive resampling in imbalanced big data learning. Multimedia Tools Appl. (2018). https://doi.org/10.1007/s11042-018-6938-9
18. Liu, Y.P., Xu, C., Cheung, S.C.: diagnosing energy efficiency and performance for mobile internetware applications. IEEE Softw. **32**(1), 67–75 (2013)
19. Chargo, J.T.: Automated software architecture extraction using graph-based clustering. Graduate Theses and Dissertations, Iowa State University (2013)
20. Li, S., Wu, X., Zhao, D., Li, A., Tian, Z., Yang, X.: An efficient dynamic ID-based remote user authentication scheme using self-certified public keys for multi-server environments. PLoS ONE **13**(10), e0202657 (2018)
21. Cui, J., Zhang, Y., Cai, Z., Liu, A., Li, Y.: Securing display path for security-sensitive applications on mobile devices. CMC: Comput. Mater. Continua **55**(1), 017–035 (2018)

Trusted Component Decomposition Based on OR-Transition Colored Petri Net

Na Zhao[1,2], Min Cao[1], Chenming Song[2], Shuang Shi[2], Yong Yu[2(✉)], and Shudong Li[3(✉)]

[1] Electric Power Research Institute of Yunnan Power Grid Co. Ltd., Kunming 650217, China
[2] Key Laboratory in Software Engineering of Yunnan Province, School of Software, Yunnan University, Kunming 650091, China
Yuy1219@163.com
[3] Cyberspace Institute of Advanced Technology, Guangzhou University, Guangzhou 510006, China
lishudong@gzhu.edu.cn

Abstract. Since software evolution has become ineluctable for many trusted systems, the research works in this paper will be focused on a hot topic in the present trusted software researches-key theories and technologies of component-based trusted software evolution. In this paper, we analysed the evolution of trusted software architecture on the basis of the characteristics of trusted component, and proposed the cohesion-based trusted component decomposition algorithm on the basis of trusted component description and modelling based on OR-transit Petri Net in our previous works.

Keywords: Trusted component · Component net · Component decomposition · Petri Net

1 Introduction

For software, "being trusted" means that the dynamical behaviors and results of software system always conform to people's expectation, and the software system can provide continuous service when it's interfered. Predictability and controllability are emphasized for system to be trusted. And interference includes errors, environment impacts, outside attacks, and so on [1].

In recent years, as the development of computer technology and enterprises' businesses, enterprise applications usually encounter the following problem: soon after the software development and operation, or even during the design process, the system fails to meet users' demands due to the change of outside environment, adjustment of users' requirements and improvement of technologies. So, it is necessary to reconstruct the software or develop a new software, that is to say, the software needs evolution. Evolution has been inevitable in many systems [2]. It pays attention to the whole life circle of software, and observes the changes of software from the angle of system's functional behaviors. However, the evolution of the software architecture must go in advance of the evolution of component-based trusted software system. And the

X. Sun et al. (Eds.): ICAIS 2019, LNCS 11635, pp. 443–451, 2019.
https://doi.org/10.1007/978-3-030-24268-8_41

evolution of the software architecture is the base and core of the evolution of the whole trusted software system.

In our previous works [3], according to the relevant definition and principles of trusted software architecture and component, we extended Petri net to OR-transit colored Petri net, thus to effectively use the transitions in OR-transit colored Petri net to describe the operations in trusted component. This paper analyzed the evolution of trusted software architecture on the basis of the characteristics of trusted component, and proposed the cohesion-based trusted component decomposition algorithm on the basis of trusted component description and modeling based on OR-transit Petri Net in our previous works.

2 Related Work

As one of the most valuable and challenging core topics in the computer software research field, trusted software has attracted enormous attention from government organizations, science field and industry field at home and abroad. Scholars all over the world have studied relevant problems of trusted software from different perspectives:

Literature [4] introduced the architecture and technology classification framework centering on reliability, and made classified comments on the following six aspects: reliability modeling, reliability growth model, assessment, test resource allocation and optimal distribution, reliability process simulation, and then conducted in-depth analysis and normalized classification on typical models. Literature [5] proposed the reliability evaluation model based on software behavior trace after fully considered software's operation flow and background. Aiming at the dynamical reliability in software's operating process, literature [6] put forward the software dynamical reliability evaluation model based on check point grading attributive. Literature [7] presents a scheme named SecDisplay for trusted display service, it protects sensitive data displayed from being stolen or tampered surreptitiously by a compromised OS.

Literature [8–11] also did some work on the problem of component evolution. To ensure the reliability of software management in the whole life circle, literature [12] integrated reliability theory and methods on the basis of ICEMDA architecture, and brought forward a reference method of model driven architecture of trusted software. Literature [13, 14] analyzed the reliability of components and discussed the modeling of trusted component and efficiency of algorithm.

Literature [15–17] discussed the architecture of internetware and analyzed how to unify, coordinate and scientifically handle the discovery and selection of components in internet environment. From its point of view, it's necessary to study and design a comprehensive reliability evaluation and processing system, and even to design better reliability computing method according to different impact factors such as node delay, bandwidth, processing capacity and so on. In this way higher solving speed and more functions can be achieved. There have been some works [18–21] on the research of evaluation and evolution of trusted component. Literature [22] introduced the thought of trust chain model in reliability computation, and came up with an internetware intelligent physical model. Literature [23–27] discussed the performance parameters in the component modeling. Literature [28] reports research results to improve the traditional trust model with consideration of cooperation effects.

3 Analysis on Evolution of Trusted Software Architecture

In trusted software architecture, the cohesion of trusted component refers to the closeness of the relationship among the elements in the trusted component. A trusted component of high cohesion possesses some basic functions and can hardly be separated.

And coupling is applied to test the connection force between two or among many connected components. It's a measurement to assess the correlation among the components in the trusted software architecture. Whether the coupling is strong or weak depends on the complexity of the interfaces between components, the position and way of entering and calling components, and the amount of data transmission via interfaces. We should pursue loose coupling system as possible in our design of trusted software, in that the design, test and maintenance of any of the components in this kind of system are independent. In addition, the possibility of error propagation among components will decrease due to rare connections among components. The coupling between components will directly influence the intelligibility, testability, reliability and maintainability of the system, therefore, in the trusted architecture based on trusted components, the coupling between trusted components is an important attributive of software architecture.

The purpose of trusted software development is to develop a high-cohesion and low-coupling system. Cohesion and coupling are important attributives of trusted software system which is based on trusted software architecture. And in the analysis and design of trusted software system, only when we produce a high-cohesion and low-coupling trusted software architecture can we lay a foundation for later achievement of high-quality trusted software system.

As mentioned before, as environment and requirements in trusted software change, trusted software needs constant evolution. The present software technologies are not intelligent enough to automatically adapt to all kinds of unpredictable changing requirements. Hence, to keep up with the changing requirements, the architecture of trusted software system also needs endless evolution.

To obtain high-cohesion and low-coupling trusted software architecture, we need to conduct evolution on the existing trusted software architecture according to its cohesion and coupling to meet our requirements on cohesion and coupling. In the evolution of trusted software architecture based on OR-transit colored Petri net, the evolution is actually the operations of decomposition, adding, deleting, merging, revising and so on for the elements in OR-transit colored Petri net. In this paper, we will discuss the cohesion-based trusted component decomposition under the description of OR-transit colored Petri net.

4 Cohesion-Based Trusted Component Decomposition

In the design of trusted software architecture, we should try the best to achieve high cohesion of trusted components. Thus, it's necessary to carry out cohesion-based decomposition for the low-cohesion trusted components in the trusted software architecture, thus to enable the cohesion of decomposed trusted component to meet the requirement.

In addition, in starting state of the development of trusted software architecture, we should make efforts to control the amount of trusted components, in that smaller amount of trusted components will make relation among trusted components to be simpler, and the design, realization and maintenance of trusted components to be easier. However, with the increase and refinement of requirements, a trusted component may realize more and more functions, and relevant development and maintenance also becomes harder and harder.

4.1   Principle of Decomposition

In the evolution of trusted software architecture, usually we need to decompose some trusted components in trusted software architecture into two or more components on the basis of cohesion, thus to get two or more high-cohesion components. Meanwhile, the good trusted software architecture after decomposition [1] will remain unchanged, in other words: if the original trusted software architecture is good, then the trusted software architecture obtained after the decomposition of trusted components is good as well.

In the decomposition of trusted components, the connectivity of the trusted components to be decomposed should be considered first of all. If a trusted component is unconnected, then according to connectivity it can be decomposed into two components; if a component is connected, then find the cutting arc set in the component and choose a proper cutting arc as the base to decompose the component into two. If the component cohesion still fails to satisfy the requirements after decomposition, the aforementioned steps can be repeated to decompose the component again.

Therefore, before introducing the component decomposition method, we first provide the component connectivity and its relevant definition.

Definition 1: For trusted component $C_t = <P_t, T_t, F_t, S_t, A_{Pt}, A_{Tt}, A_{Ft}, IP_t, OP_t>$, for random $x, y \in P_t \cup T_t, x(F_R \cup F_R^{-1})^* y$ is always true, so C_t is connected; otherwise C_t is unconnected. (Here F_R^{-1} is the converse to F_R, namely $yF_R^{-1}x$ exists for xF_Ry.)

Definition 2: For the sub trusted component $C_t' = <P_t', T_t', F_t', S_t', A_{Pt}', A_{Tt}', A_{Ft}', IP_t', OP_t'>$ of trusted component $C_t = <P_t, T_t, F_t, S_t, A_{Pt}, A_{Tt}, A_{Ft}, IP_t, OP_t>$, if C_t' is connected, then C_t' is called the connected sub trusted component of C_t.

Definition 3: Sub trusted component $C_t' = <P_t', T_t', F_t', S_t', A_{Pt}', A_{Tt}', A_{Ft}', IP_t', OP_t'>$ is the connected sub connected trusted component of trusted component $C_t = <P_t, T_t, F_t, S_t, A_{Pt}, A_{Tt}, A_{Ft}, IP_t, OP_t>$. If after adding a random arc which is in Ct but not in Ct' and its relevant status and operations in Ct', Ct' is unconnected, then C_t' is called the maximum connected sub trusted component of Ct; and the amount of all the maximum connected sub trusted components in Ct is remarked as $\delta(Ct)$.

Definition 4: After deleting a random arc $<x, y> \in Ft$ in trusted component Ct = <Pt, Tt, Ft, St, APt, ATt, AFt, IPt, OPt>, the trusted component changes into Ct' = <Pt', Tt', Ft', St', APt', ATt', AFt', IPt', OPt'>, where:

(1) $P_t' = P_t$;
(2) $T_t' = T_t$;
(3) $F_t' = F_t \backslash \{ <x, y> \}$;

(4) $S'_t = S_t$;

(5) $\forall p \in P'_t$ then $A'_{Pt}(p) = A_{Pt}(p)$;

(6) $t \in T'_t$ then $A'_{Tt}(t) = A_{Tt}(t)$;

(7) $f \in F'_t$ then $A'_{Ft}(f) = A_{Ft}(f)$;

(8) $IP'_t = IP_t$;

(9) $OP'_t = OP_t$.

Definition 5: In trusted component $C_t = <P_t, T_t, F_t, S_t, A_{Pt}, A_{Tt}, A_{Ft}, IP_t, OP_t>$, the obtained trusted component after deleting an arc $f = <x, y> \in F_t$ in trusted component $C'_t = <P_t, T_t, F_t/\{f\}, S_t, A_{Pt}, A_{Tt}, A_{Ft}, IP_t, OP_t>$. If $\delta(C'_t) = \delta(C_t) + 1$, then arc $f \in F_t$ is called the cutting arc of Ct.

Definition 6: The sub trusted component $C'_t = <P'_t, T'_t, F'_t, S'_t, A'_{Pt}, A'_{Tt}, A'_{Ft}, IP'_t, OP'_t>$ in trusted component $Ct = <Pt, Tt, Ft, St, APt, ATt, AFt, IPt, OPt>$ is called the projection sub trusted component of C_t based on set N ($N \subseteq Pt \cup Tt$), when and only when:

(1) $P'_t = P_t \cap N$;

(2) $T'_t = T_t \cap N$;

(3) $F'_t = (P'_t \times T'_t \cup T'_t \times P'_t) \cap F_t$;

(4) $IP'_t = IP_t \cap N$;

(5) $OP'_t = OP_t \cap N$;

(6) $S'_t = S^N_t \subseteq S_t$; (where S^N_t is the sum of the corresponding types of all the elements in N);

(7) $p \in P'_t$ then $A'_{Pt}(p) = A'_{Pt}(p)$;

(8) $t \in T'_t$ then $A'_{Tt}(t) = A_{Tt}(t)$;

(9) $f \in F'_t$ then $A'_{Ft}(f) = A_{Ft}(f)$.

the projection sub trusted component of trusted component $C'_t = <P'_t, T'_t, F'_t, S'_t, A'_{Pt}, A'_{Tt}, A'_{Ft}, IP'_t, OP'_t>$ based on set N ($N \subseteq P_t \cup T_t$) can be expressed as C^N_t, namely $C'_t = C^N_t$.

4.2 Decomposition of Unconnected Trusted Component in Trusted Software Architecture

In trusted software architecture, if the trusted component to be decomposed is unconnected, we can draw the dependency graph of the trusted component. From the definition of dependency graph of trusted component [1] it can be known that because the trusted component is unconnected, its dependency graph is unconnected too and can be divided into a number of maximum connected sub graphs. Then divide these maximum connected sub graphs into two groups as evenly as possible according to the amounts of their element nodes. And calculate the cohesion of the dependency sub graphs constructed by each group according to the cohesion measurement of trusted component. If the cohesion of both groups is higher than the original trusted component cohesion, decompose the trusted component with the above mentioned method; if it's not higher than the original trusted component cohesion, then regroup the maximum connected sub graphs until the cohesion meets the requirements.

During decomposition process, some elements of trusted software architecture also needs to be modified accordingly. The specific decomposing method is as Algorithm 1 shows:

Algorithm 1 Non-connectivity-based trusted component decomposition method *Decomposition*-$1(SA_t,\ C_{ti})$

Input: good trusted software architecture SA_t=<CN_t, LN_t, D_t, G_t, A_{Lt}, A_{Gt}> and its non-connected trusted component C_{ti} = <P_{ti} ={p_{i1}, p_{i2}, ..., p_{im}}, T_{ti} ={t_{i1}, t_{i2}, ..., t_{in}}, F_{ti}, S_{ti}, A_{Pti}, A_{Tti}, A_{Fti}, IP_{ti}, OP_{ti}>

Output: decompose the non-connected trusted component C_{ti} and get trusted software architecture SAt'=<CNt', LNt', Dt', Gt', ALt', AGt'>.

BEGIN

FOR j=1 TO m DO

N_j={p_{ij}};

FOR j=1 TO n DO

N_{m+j}={t_{ij}};

FOR for all the arcs <x, y>∈ F_t in trusted component C_t, DO

IF x∈ N_i, y∈ N_j and i≠j, THEN

BEGIN

N_i=N_i ∪ N_j;

N_j=Φ;

END;

Group set N_1, N_2, ..., N_k which is obtained by merging into two groups, N_{11} and N_{22}, as evenly as possible, and calculate the cohesion among the elements in each group's corresponding dependency graph according to dependency. If the cohesion meets the requirements, carry out the next steps; otherwise, regroup set N_1, N_2, ... , N_k until the cohesion meets the requirements.

C_{ti1}= C_{ti}^{N11};

C_{ti2}= C_{ti}^{N22}; /*construct the project sub components C_{ti}^{N11} and C_{ti}^{N22}* of trusted component C_{ti} which are based on N_{11} and N_{22}/

CN_t= CN_t ∪ C_{ti1} ∪ C_{ti2}; /*add the two project sub components C_{ti1} and C_{ti2} of trusted component C_{ti} into SA_t. In that project sub components C_{ti1} and C_{ti2} are irrelevant to the other trusted components and connectors in architecture SA_t at this time, the other elements in SA_t stay unchanged.*/

FOR for every connector L_t (L_t∈ LN_t) in trusted software architecture SA_t DO

FOR for every input interface ip of trusted component C_{ti} DO

BEGIN

IF ip∈ N_{11}, THEN

BEGIN

G_t=G_t ∪ {<L_t, $C_{ti1}.ip$>}; /*add arc <L_t, $C_{ti1}.ip$> into G_t*/

A_{Gt} (<L_t, $C_{ti1}.ip$>)=A_{Gt} (<L_t, $C_{ti}.ip$>);

G_t=G_t \{<L_t, $C_{ti}.ip$>}; /*delete arc <L_t, $C_{ti}.ip$>from G_t*/

END;

ELSE

BEGIN

G_t=G_t ∪ {<L_t, $C_{ti2}.ip$>}; /*add arc <L_t, $C_{ti2}.ip$> into G_t*/

A_{Gt} (<L_t, $C_{ti2}.ip$>)=A_{Gt} (<L_t, $C_{ti}.ip$>);

G_t=G_t\{<L_t, $C_{ti}.ip$>}; /*delete arc<L_t, $C_{ti}.ip$> from G_t*/

END;

END; /*end of FOR */

FOR for every output interface op of trusted component C_{ti} DO
BEGIN
  IF $op \in N_{11}$, THEN
  BEGIN
    $G_t = G_t \cup \{<C_{ti1}.op,\ L_t>\}$; /*add arc $<C_{ti1}.op,\ L_t>$ into G_t*/
    $A_{Gt}\,(<C_{ti1}.op,\ L_t>) = A_{Gt}\,(<C_{ti}.op,\ L_t>)$
    $G_t = G_t \backslash \{<C_{ti}.op,\ L_t>\}$; /*delete arc $<C_{ti}.op,\ L_t>$ from G_t;
  END;
  ELSE
  BEGIN
    $G_t = G_t \cup \{<C_{ti2}.op,\ L_t>\}$; /*add arc $<C_{ti2}.op,\ L_t>$ into G_t*/
    $A_{Gt}\,(<C_{ti2}.op,\ L_t>) = A_{Gt}\,(<C_{ti}.op,\ L_t>)$
    $G_t = G_t \backslash \{<C_{ti}.op,\ L_t>\}$; /*delete arc $<C_{ti}.op,\ L_t> G_t$*/
  END;
  END; /*end of IF */
 END; /*end of FOR */
END; /*end of FOR /*
$CN_t = CN_t \backslash \{C_{ti}\}$; /*delete isolate trusted component C_{ti}*/
END.

The comparison between trusted software architecture $SA_t' = <CN_t',\ LN_t',\ D_t',$ $G_t',\ A_{Lt}',\ A_{Gt}'>$ after decomposing trusted component C_{ti} and the original architecture:
  $CN_t' = CN_t \cup C_{ti}^{N11} \cup C_{ti}^{N22} \backslash \{C_{ti}\}$;
  $LN_t',\ D_t',\ A_{Lt}'$ are unchanged;
  $G_t',\ A_{Gt}'$ need to be changed accordingly.

5   Conclusion

As the requirements of trusted software and its environment change all the time, trusted software needs continuous evolution. In the phase of system evolution, any expansion and modification of trusted software needs to be carried out in the guidance of architecture to keep the rationality and correctness of overall design and the analyzability of its performance and also to underlie the complexity of maintenance and upgrade and the analysis of costs. Thus the quality and evolution costs of trusted software can be better controlled.

In our previous works, we utilized component to expand OR-transit Petri net. In the trusted software architecture evolution based on OR-transit Petri net, the evolution of trusted software architecture is actually the operations of decomposing, adding, deleting, merging and revising for the elements in Or-transit Petri net.

On the basis of trusted component model based on OR-transit colored petri net which was defined in our previous works, according to the characteristics of trusted component, this paper analyzed the influence of cohesion and coupling of trusted component on the evolution of trusted software architecture, and provided cohesion-based trusted component decomposition algorithms on that basis.

Acknowledgments. This work has been supported by the National Science Foundation of China under Grant (No. 61462091, U1803263, 61672020, 61866039), by the Data Driven Software Engineering innovation team of Yunnan province No. 2017HC012, by the Science Foundation of Key Laboratory in Software Engineering of Yunnan Province under Grant No. 2017SE205, by the eighteenth batch of Yunnan Province in the young academic and technical leaders reserve personnel training project under Grant No. C614300.

References

1. Liu, K., Shan, Z., Wang, J., He, J., Zhang, Z., Qin, Y.: Overview on major research plan of trustworthy software. China Science Fund. **22**(3), 145–151 (2008)
2. Tokuda, L., Batory, D.: Automating three modes of evolution for object-oriented software architectures. In: Proceedings of COOTS 1999, San Diego, pp. 189–202 (1999)
3. Yu, Y., Li, T., Liu, Q., Dai, F., Zhao, N.: OR-transition colored Petri Net and its application in modeling software system. In: Proceedings of 2009 International Workshop on Knowledge Discovery and Data Mining, Moscow, Russia, January 2009, pp. 15–18 (2009)
4. Zhang, C., Cui, G., Liu, H.W., Meng, F.C.: Component-based software reliability process technologies. Chin. J. Comput. **37**(12), 2586–2612 (2014)
5. Tian, J., Han, J., Du, R., Wang, Y.: Creditability evaluation model based on software behavior trace. J. Comput. Res. Dev. **49**(7), 1514–1524 (2012)
6. Li, Z., Tian, J., Yang, X.: Dynamic trustworthiness evaluation model of software based on checkpoint's classification attributes. J. Comput. Res. Dev. **50**(11), 2397–2405 (2013)
7. Cui, J., Zhang, Y., Cai, Z., Liu, A., Li, Y.: Securing display path for security-sensitive applications on mobile devices. CMC: Comput. Mater. Continua **55**(1), 017–035 (2018)
8. Franco, J.M., Barbosa, R., Zenha-Rela, M.: Reliability analysis of software architecture evolution. In: Sixth Latin-American Symposium on Dependable Computing (LADC), Rio de Janeiro, Brazil, pp. 11–20 (2013)
9. Rathod, H., Parmar, M.: Study of genetic approach in estimating reliability of component based software. PARIPEX - Indian J. Res. **1**(11), 17–19 (2012)
10. Shanmugapriya, P., Suresh, R.M.: Software architecture evaluation methods – a survey. Int. J. Comput. Appl. **49**(16), 19–26 (2012)
11. Wang, J., Chen, W.R.: A reliability-oriented evolution method of software architecture based on contribution degree of component. J. Softw. **7**(8), 1744–1750 (2012)
12. Zhan, D., Feng, J., Nie, L., Xu, X.F.: Construction approach of confidence management software based on layered verification. J. Harbin Inst. Technol. **44**(5), 75–80 (2012)
13. Li, Q.Y., Li, H.F., Wang, G.D.: Sensitivity analysis on the influence factors of software reliability based on diagnosis reasoning. Adv. Intell. Syst. Comput. **180**, 557–566 (2013)
14. Liu, Y.P., Xu, C., Cheung, S.C.: Diagnosing energy efficiency and performance for mobile internetware applications. IEEE Softw. **32**(1), 67–75 (2015)
15. Yue, Y.: Multi-factor decision making for software reliability evaluation. Appl. Res. Comput. **32**(4), 1110–1113 (2015)
16. Yang, H.J., Zheng, S.: Software evolution for moving into and moving within internetware paradigm. Int. J. Softw. Inform. **7**(1), 41–61 (2013)
17. Jia, Y.H., Zheng, S.: Software evolution based on service-oriented requirement in internetware. In: 4th International Conference on Computer Research and Development, IACSIT Press, Singapore, pp. 20–25 (2012)

18. Panwar, P., Garg, A.: Analysis of reliability and cost tradeoffs in architecture based software applications using a genetic algorithm. Int. J. Comput. Appl. **72**(1), 33–37 (2013)
19. Secure Software, Inc.: The CLASP Application Security Process (2005). http://www.ida.liu.se/~TDDC90/papers/clasp_external.pdf
20. Chargo, J.T.: Automated software architecture extraction using graph-based clustering. Graduate thesis and dissertations, Iowa State University (2013)
21. SecureChange Project (2009–2012). http://www.securechange.eu/
22. Xu, J., Si, G., Yang, J., Wen, S., Zhang, B.: An internetware dependable entity model and trust measurement based on evaluation. Chin. Sci. Inf. Sci. **43**(1), 108–125 (2013)
23. Kumar, P.S., Karsai, G.: Integrated analysis of temporal behavior of component-based distributed real-time embedded systems. In: International Symposium on Object Component Service Oriented Real Time Distributed Computing, pp. 50–57 (2015)
24. Liu, J., Liu, L.: A coloured Petri Net approach to the functional and performance analysis of SIP Non-INVITE transaction. In: Koutny, M., Haddad, S., Yakovlev, A. (eds.) Transactions on Petri Nets and Other Models of Concurrency IX. LNCS, vol. 8910, pp. 147–177. Springer, Heidelberg (2014). https://doi.org/10.1007/978-3-662-45730-6_8
25. Long, S.: Analysis of concurrent security protocols using colored Petri Nets. In: International Conference on Networking, pp. 227–230 (2009)
26. Han, W., Tian, Z., Huang, Z., Li, S., Jia, Y.: Bidirectional self-adaptive resampling in imbalanced big data learning (2018). Multimedia Tools Appl. https://doi.org/10.1007/s11042-018-6938-9
27. Choosang, S., Gordon, S.R.: A coloured Petri Net methodology and library for security analysis of network protocols. J. Comput. **9**(2), 243–256 (2014)
28. Xie, X., Yuan, T., Zhou, X., Cheng, X.: Research on trust model in container-based cloud service. CMC: Comput. Mater. Continua **56**(2), 273–283 (2018)

High-Speed File Transferring Over Linux Bridge for QGA Enhancement in Cyber Range

Jiajun Xie[1], Chunrui Zhang[1], Fang Lou[1], Yu Cui[2], Lun An[3],
and Le Wang[4(✉)]

[1] Institute of Computer Application, China Academy of Engineering Physics,
Mianyang 621900, China
xiejiajun_caep@163.com
[2] School of Cyberspace Security,
Hunan Heetian Information Technology Co., Ltd., Changsha 410000, China
[3] Beijing University of Posts and Telecommunications, Beijing 100876, China
[4] Guangzhou University, Guanghzou, China
wangle@gzhu.edu.cn

Abstract. Cyber Range has become an import infrastructure in current cyber
security development which is used to systematically improve related abilities
such as talent cultivation, cyberwarfare drilling and advanced technology testing. In cyber range, communications and controls between host and guest
system is a very important function to monitor and manage the procedures of a
task, such as traffic analyzing, guest forensics, configuration transfer and data
transfer. QGA is a daemon program running inside the guest system which is
designed to support this requirement through a virtual serial device. As the
limitations of serial devices, the performance is poor, especially in large file
transferring. To overcome this limitation, a new mechanism named HSFT is
proposed. It uses virtual NIC which bonded on Linux bridge and provides
network connections to communicate with guest system. The experiments
results show that HSFT is much faster than QGA in both file reading and writing
processes.

Keywords: Cyber range · OpenStack · KVM · QGA · File transfer

1 Introduction

A cyber range is a virtual platform which can be used for cyber talent cultivation,
cyberwarfare drilling, advanced technology testing and cybertechnology development.
It is used for the security event and topology simulation on specified environments such
as enterprises, governments, organizations and militaries. In addition, elements in an
environment like staffs, operations systems, software, and applications should be
embedded into the cyber range to make the virtual environment more realistic [1].

In cyber range, a safe, isolated and legal environment can be constructed for each
project. For basic usage, college students can study cyber security knowledge and make
practice to enhance their skills. For advanced users, like government and military
agencies, the stability, security and performance of cyberinfrastructures and IT systems

© Springer Nature Switzerland AG 2019
X. Sun et al. (Eds.): ICAIS 2019, LNCS 11635, pp. 452–462, 2019.
https://doi.org/10.1007/978-3-030-24268-8_42

can be strengthened. Thus, cyberwarriors and IT professionals employed by various agencies could train, develop and test cyber range technologies to ensure consistent operations and readiness for real world deployment [2].

To construct a cyber range platform, virtualization techniques and services like QEMU-KVM & Libvirt, virtualization platforms like OpenStack, are widely used. OpenStack is a cloud operating system that controls large pools of compute, storage, and networking resources throughout a data center. A dashboard that gives administrators control while empowering their users to provision resources through a web interface. QEMU-KVM is a fast processor emulator using dynamic translation to achieve good emulation speed. QEMU can run independently, but due to the emulation being performed entirely in software it is extremely slow. To overcome this, QEMU allows you to use KVM as an accelerator so that the physical CPU virtualization extensions can be used. In summary, QEMU is a hypervisor that runs within user space and performs virtual hardware emulation, whereas KVM is a hypervisor that runs in kernel space, that allows a user space program access to the hardware virtualization features of various processors [3].

Different from virtualization systems, cyber range is requested to provide more monitoring and controlling functions on guest machines, such as traffic analyzing, guest forensics, configuration transfer and data transfer. As a result, related components are usually embedded into the platform and provide functions, acting as an entry point. For guest forensics in cyber range, configurations and data transferring between guest and host are usually important for the running a program. While, the tool of QEMU Guest Agent (QGA) is usually used to satisfy this purpose through a serial device mounted on the virtual machine [4, 5].

Relationships between Cyber Range, OpenStack [6, 7], QEMU-KVM [8], Libvirt and QGA are shown in Fig. 1.

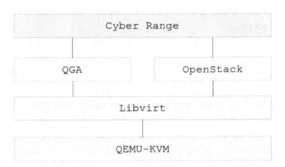

Fig. 1. Relations for Cyber Range, OpenStack, QEMU-KVM, Libvirt and QGA

2   File Transferring in QGA

QGA is a daemon program running inside the guest system which is designed to help management on status, processes, networks of the guest system. It could execute multi-functions to check or modify the guest system, such as get or set CPU status, read or write files. Currently, the communication between guest and host system is via VIRTIO serial device. In the guest system, a serial device is plugged-in. While in the host system, a socket is created. The process of reading and writing on the socket will be mapped to the serial device with a format of QMP protocol. This process is shown in Fig. 2.

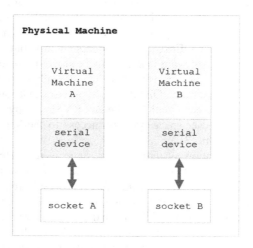

Fig. 2. Communications between host and guest system

QGA provides more than 20 functions, such as guest-set-vcpus, guest-get-vcpus, guest-network-get-interfaces, guest-suspend-hybrid, guest-suspend-ram, guest-fstrim, guest-fsfreeze-freeze guest-file-flush, guest-file-seek, guest-file-write, guest-file-read, guest-file-close and so on.

For cyber range, the ability to monitor and control every aspect like networks and guest systems is significant. And the manager of a virtual environment usually needs to monitor or control a specified virtual machine to make the simulation process running as expected or scripted. To support these requirements, QGA is widely used to write configurations from host to guest and read status data from guest for host. In which, configurations are often used configure, start, restart the monitoring services running in the guest system, while data are often used to analyze the running status of a guest system. Usually, data reading needs to transfer massive data, such as operation logs, connection logs, file reading and writing logs, processes logs. To transfer these logs from guest to host, high-speed transfer links are needed. However, for serial device, the transferring speed is limited to a low speed which dissatisfy the speed requirements. As a result, we proposed the method of file transferring over Linux bridge, and demonstrated in details in next section.

3   High-Speed File Transferring Over Linux Bridge

As QGA has limits on the speed of uploading and downloading files, we proposed an ethernet-based method 'High-Speed File Transferring over Linux Bridge' (HSFT for short) to solve this problem. For guest systems with network configured, the network link can be utilized to transfer data logs and the process will be discussed in this section.

3.1   Network Architectures

HSFT is based on current OpenStack network architecture in VLan [9] mode, and the current architecture is shown in Fig. 3. In this figure, the physical network interface 'eth1' is at bottom and linked on an OVS [10] bridge 'br-vlan' to connect physical networks. OVS bridges 'br-vlan' and 'br-int' are used to control and modify the VLan IDs between physical networks and inner network of this host. In addition, ethernet of Layer 2 can be insulated. For a virtual machine, there is a serial of virtual NICs. Take VM A for example, VM A has two cards, eth0 and eth1. Eth0 is connected to tapXXX, qbrXXX, qbvXXX and qvoXXX. Finally, qvoXXX is linked on br-int to make VLan and traffic controls. While, eth1 is the same. Eth0 and tapXXX are tap devices and eth0 is used in VM A, tapXXX is linked on qbrXXX, which is a Linux Bridge. QvbXXX and qboXXX are veth pairs which transfer packets form one side to another side. For a virtual machine, communications with other virtual machines can be divided into 2 types. If the destination virtual machine is on the same physical machine, then the traffic will arrive at br-int and being forwarded to the related 'qvo' devices. While, if the destination virtual machine is on other physical machines, the route will be form br-int to br-eth1 and forward the packets into physical networks.

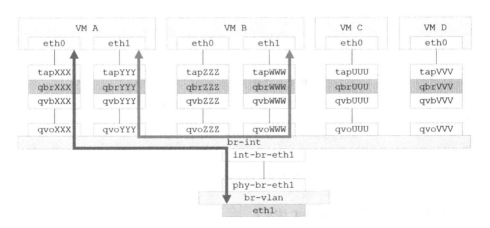

Fig. 3. Network architecture in OpenStack for VLan

3.2   HSFT Architecture

To transfer files through networks, the most significant task is to construct a channel to make connections between guest system and host systems with little infections on the OpenStack Traffic links [11]. This means that we need to use separate NICs and separate links. As a result, a proxy node is needed. As shown in Fig. 4, 'Service A' with a tap device is deployed to satisfy this requirement. Tap1 is a tap device and linked to the bridge belongs to VM A which makes VM A and Service A in the same ethernet. In this way, Service A could communicate with VM A through TAP0 and TAP1 linked to Linux Bridge 0. In addition, as Linux Bridge has mac table, the traffic will not be forwarded to br-int and further infect other networks. To communicate with file server, Service A will use a different network interface, such as eth1, to avoid the interferences to eth0 used by br-vlan. As shown in Fig. 4, ETH0 connects to Data Link, while ETH1 connects to OP Link. The 'Service A' proxy program can be constructed to support multiple virtual machines with multiple TAP devices that bounded to different Linux Bridges belonged to different virtual machines. Or it can be constructed to be multiple 'Service A's, which means each virtual machine has its own 'Service A', and this 'Service A' only service this guest system.

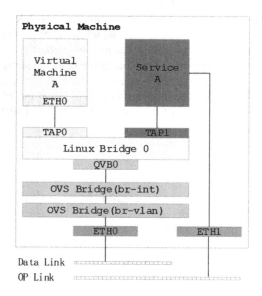

Fig. 4. HSFT architecture

3.3   Modules and Processes for HSFT

HSFT contains 3 modules: GSer, TSer and HSer. GSer runs in the guest system as a daemon process. It listens on a UDP port and receive commands and data for writing files. Also, GSer can send status and data when reading file, while this is done by sending raw packet with ethernet header. HSer is used for receiving commands and send status to the file server. TSer is the communication module for GSer and will send and receive commands and data to GSer in VM A. In addition, the status and data will be forwarded to HSer and further be forwarded to HSer.

Currently, reading a file from VM A and writing a file to the VM A is supported. And this process is usually accomplished in 5 steps, as shown in Fig. 5.

– Step 1: File server sends file reading request to HSer.
– Step 2: HSer schedules this request and forward the request to TSer.
– Step 3: TSer communicates with GSer through UDP packets and sends reading request.
– Step 4: GSer executes the commands and continuously sends file data to TSer.
– Step 5: TSer will make the file fragments integrated and inform HSer to send it to file server.

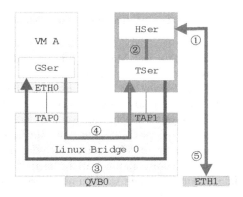

Fig. 5. Modules and Processes for HSFT

3.4   Service Constructions and Monitoring for HSFT

For services running in a virtual machine or in overall platform, a TCP port is assigned to each service to receive file tasks. And a fixed TCP port is configured into each service representing the file server. This process is called registration and used in service constructions. Another important process is called heartbeat and used for service monitoring.

In registration, a schedule service will be loaded first on each host. This schedule service will connect to the file server as the TCP port configured. When file transfer task is needed, the schedule service will receive a task requirement and setup a new Service X and bond to the dedicated VM if needed. The Service X will be assigned a free TCP port and listen on it. In addition, the TCP port of the file server is also configured to Service X. At this time, Service X will connect to and communicate with the file server. This registration is shown in Fig. 6.

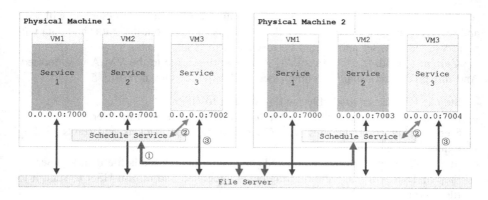

Fig. 6. Registration for HSFT

As shown in Fig. 6, 3 main steps are needed to establish a dedicated file transfer task.

- Step 1: Schedule Service in Physical Machine 1 is up and register itself to File Server to notify that Physical Machine 1 is up and ready. Meanwhile, Schedule Service in Physical Machine 2 is up and register itself to File Server to notify that Physical Machine 2 is up and ready. File Server receive these messages and maintains the up status for physical machines.
- Step 2: When a file transfer task is configured, the File Server will look for the physical machine running the target VM and check related status. If it is in up status, then the file transfer configuration will be sent to the related Schedule Service. The Schedule Service will then set up a new Service X (such as Service 3 in Fig. 6).
- Step 3: After the Service X set up, Service X will directly connect to File Server and do file transfer. Get transfer tasks or transfer data.

As each Service X communicates with File Server, the File Server needs to manage the status for each Service X. This is done by Heartbeats. Every 30 s, a Service X sends a Heartbeat to the File Server and notifies the UP status of itself. If a Service X is timeout and lost in the File Server, the File Server will send a CHECK request to the related Schedule Service to check the status of the lost Service X. After receiving this message, the Schedule Service will check the related Service X process and restart it if needed. This is shown in Fig. 7.

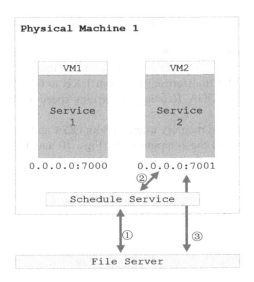

Fig. 7. Monitoring for HSFT

As shown in Fig. 7, 3 main steps are needed to monitor the status for each service for HSFT.

- Step 1: If File Server lost the status of a Service X, File Server will request the related Schedule Service to check Service X.
- Step 2: Schedule Service checks the status of the lost Service X. Locate the problem and fix it or restart it.
- Step 3: The fixed Service X connect to File Server and start communications.

4 Experiments

To test the performance of HSFT, we create a simple OpenStack testing environment in physical servers. Each server is with 24 cores & 2.6 GHz CPU, 64 GB Memory, 1 TB Hard Disk and 4 GE NICs. In OpenStack, we allocated a computing zone with one compute node configured and we deployed a centos 7.3 virtual machine on this server.

The test is divided into 2 steps: reading performance test and writing performance test. In each test, we transfer 8 files with a size of 1 KB, 16 KB, 256 KB, 4 MB, 16 MB, 32 MB and 64 MB. And each file will be transferred 3 times, the average time used is computed and recorded.

As shown in Fig. 6, performance in reading and writing in QGA differs a lot when file size increases. The average speed is shown in Fig. 7, when file size increases over 4 MB, the speed become to stable. The speed for QGA-Read is about 230 KB/s, while QGA-Write is about 2200 KB/s, which is an abnormal result with huge difference. We checked the QGA program and found only 4 KB data can be read one time, while

80 KB data can be written one time. This caused the huge difference in performance on reading and writing process.

Second, performance of HSFT in reading and writing is tested with the same files. As shown in Figs. 8 and 9, the performance of HSFT is much better than QGA in file transferring. Time used for transferring files from 1 KB to 64 KB is no more than 2 s compared to over 250 s in QGA. Reading and writing speed in HSFT is over 30 MB/s when stabled.

In addition, the CPU and memory usage in both QGA and HSFT is low which will not bring much pressure on the compute node (Figs. 10 and 11).

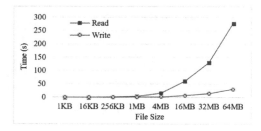

Fig. 8. Average time used for QGA

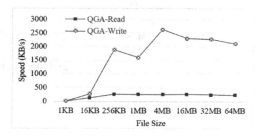

Fig. 9. Average speed for QGA

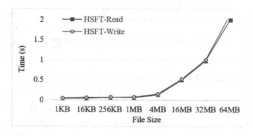

Fig. 10. Average time used for HSFT

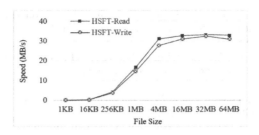

Fig. 11. Average speed for HSFT

5   Conclusions and Future Work

HSFT provides a new mechanism for the communicating and controlling between host and guest system beyond QGA in a cyber range. It uses networks in HSFT compared to VIRTIO serial device in QGA, and the file transfer speed raised a lot to over 30 MB/s in reading and writing.

Currently, HSFT is only a prototype system, as only file reading and writing functions are accomplished. Many functions provided in QGA has not been integrated and this can be done in future. The security aspect is the second part that need to be considered. In HSFT design, a service program is running and can be connected through network on the private bridge. This exposes an entry to connect to our management network. As a result, access control mechanisms are needed to prevent vulnerabilities exploited by malicious users.

Acknowledgment. This work is supported by CAEP Foundation (NO. CX2019040), and Defense Industrial Technology Development Program (NO. JCKY2018212C020, JCKY2016212C005).

References

1. NIST. https://www.nist.gov/sites/default/files/documents/2018/02/13/cyber_ranges.pdf. Accessed 03 Mar 2018
2. Binxing, F., Yan, J., Aiping, L., Weizhe, Z.: Cyber ranges: state-of-the-art and research challenges. J. Cyber Secur. **1**(3), 1–9 (2016)
3. Hu, Y., Jin, H., Yu, Z., et al.: An optimization approach for QEMU. In: 2009 1st International Conference on Information Science and Engineering (ICISE), pp. 129–132. IEEE (2009)
4. Bushouse, M., Reeves, D.: Hyperagents: migrating host agents to the hypervisor. In: Proceedings of the Eighth ACM Conference on Data and Application Security and Privacy, pp. 212–223. ACM (2018)
5. Holler, A., Krieg, A., Rauter, T., et al.: QEMU-based fault injection for a system-level analysis of software countermeasures against fault attacks. In: 2015 Euromicro Conference on Digital System Design (DSD), pp. 530–533. IEEE (2015)
6. OpenStack Community. https://www.openstack.org/. Accessed 10 Nov 2018
7. Corradi, A., Fanelli, M., Foschini, L.: VM consolidation: a real case based on OpenStack cloud. Future Gener. Comput. Syst. **32**, 118–127 (2014)

8. Kim, T., Choi, S., No, J., et al.: HyperCache: a hypervisor-level virtualized I/O cache on KVM/QEMU. In: 2018 Tenth International Conference on Ubiquitous and Future Networks (ICUFN), pp. 846–850. IEEE (2018)

9. Madjed, B., Mohamed, B.: Flexibility of managing VLAN filtering and segmentation in SDN networks. In: International Symposium on Networks, Computers and Communications (ISNCC) (2017)

10. Yipeng, W., Tsung-Yuan, C., Ren, W.: Optimizing open vSwitch to support millions of flows. In: GLOBECOM, pp. 1–7 (2017)

11. Robert, M., Nicole, T.: Space link extension (SLE) emulation for high-throughput network communication. In: 32nd AIAA International Communications Satellite Systems Conference (2014)

12. Tian, Z., Wang, Y., Sun, Y., Qiu, J.: Location privacy challenges in mobile edge computing: classification and exploration. IEEE Netw. (2019)

13. Tian, Z., et al.: Real time lateral movement detection based on evidence reasoning network for edge computing environment. IEEE Trans. Ind. Inform. (2019)

14. Tian, Z., Shen, S., Shi, W., Xiaojiang, D., Guizani, M., Xiang, Yu.: A data-driven model for future internet route decision modeling. Future Gener. Comput. Syst. **95**, 212–220 (2019). https://doi.org/10.1016/j.future.2018.12.054

15. Tian, Z., et al.: A real-time correlation of host-level events in cyber range service for smart campus. IEEE Access. **6**, 35355–35364 (2018). https://doi.org/10.1109/access.2018.2846590

16. Tan, Q., Gao, Y., Shi, J., Wang, X., Fang, B., Tian, Z.H.: Towards a comprehensive insight into the eclipse attacks of tor hidden services. IEEE Internet Things J. (2018). https://doi.org/10.1109/jiot.2018.2846624

17. Xiao, Y., Rayi, V., Sun, B., Du, X., Hu, F., Galloway, M.: A survey of key management schemes in wireless sensor networks. J. Comput. Commun. **30**(11–12), 2314–2341 (2007)

18. Du, X., Xiao, Y., Guizani, M., Chen, H.H.: An effective key management scheme for heterogeneous sensor networks. Ad Hoc Netw. (Elsevier) **5**(1), 24–34 (2007)

19. Xiao, Y., Du, X., Zhang, J., Guizani, S.: Internet protocol television (IPTV): the killer application for the next generation internet. IEEE Commun. Mag. **45**(11), 126–134 (2007)

20. Du, X., Chen, H.H.: Security in wireless sensor networks. IEEE Wirel. Commun. Mag. **15**(4), 60–66 (2008)

21. Du, X., Guizani, M., Xiao, Y., Chen, H.H.: Transactions papers, "a routing-driven elliptic curve cryptography based key management scheme for heterogeneous sensor networks". IEEE Trans. Wirel. Commun. **8**(3), 1223–1229 (2009)

22. Hou, M., Wei, R., Wang, T., Cheng, Y., Qian, B.: Reliable medical recommendation based on privacy-preserving collaborative filtering. CMC **56**(1), 137–149 (2018)

23. Zhang, H., Yi, Y., Wang, J., Cao, N., Duan, Q.: Network security situation awareness framework based on threat intelligence. CMC - Comput. Mater. Continua **56**(3), 381–399 (2018)

Playing First-Person-Shooter Games with A3C-Anticipator Network Based Agents Using Reinforcement Learning

Yibo Sun[2], Adil Khan[1,5(✉)] [iD], Kai Yang[3,4(✉)], Jiang Feng[1], and Shaohui Liu[1]

[1] School of Computer Science, Harbin Institute of Technology,
Harbin 150001, People's Republic of China
adil.adil25@yahoo.com
[2] Harbin No. 6 High School, Harbin 150001, Heilongjiang,
People's Republic of China
[3] Army Air Force College, Beijing 100000, People's Republic of China
kaiyang266@gmail.com
[4] Post-Doctoral Scientific Research Station,
Nanjing General Hospital of Former Nanjing Military Region,
Nanjing 210000, People's Republic of China
[5] Department of Computer Science, University of Peshawar,
Peshawar, Khyber Pakhtunkhwa, Pakistan

Abstract. Common built-in bots act upon pre-written scripts to make decisions and actions where sometimes they acquire and take advantage of unfair information, instead of acting flexibly like human players, who make decisions only based on game screens. This paper mainly focuses on studying the applications of deep learning and reinforcement learning in the field of computer game agents. The goal is to create agents that make decisions in human's way and gets rid of relying on unfair information. A game agent is implemented in line to the A3C algorithm. This agent takes the original real-time game screen as an input to the network and then outputs the corresponding discrete actions. The agent can interact with Viz and read the real-time game screen to make decisions for controlling the characters. This paper made an improvement to the A3C algorithm by adding an anticipator network to the original model structure. The goal of doing this is to make the agent act more like human players. It generates anticipation before making decisions, and then combines the real-time game screen with anticipation images together as an input to the network defined by the A3C algorithm. The result shows, that the A3C algorithm with Anticipation performs better than the original A3C algorithmd.

Keywords: Artificial intelligence (AI) · Artificial neural networks · Computational intelligence · Game-AI · Machine learning · Reinforcement learning

Y. Sun and A. Khan—The authors contributed equally to this work.

X. Sun et al. (Eds.): ICAIS 2019, LNCS 11635, pp. 463–475, 2019.
https://doi.org/10.1007/978-3-030-24268-8_43

1 Introduction

One of the applications that artificial intelligence is closest to our lives is to be a human opponent in computer games. Anyone who has had a game experience knows that most players in the game of confrontation and strategy can play against other players online, or they can directly choose to compete with the computer, that is, against the built-in scripted robot. At present, almost all of the game's built-in scripting robots on the market are hard-coded [1]. What they do, how to do it, etc., will be written into the code in advance, and then in actual combat, they only need to be based on the proposed rules. In addition to the game information that can be legally acquired (such as own blood volume, own weapons or resource information), such scripted robots may also obtain some extra unfair game information (for example, the status of the opponent, the location of the invisible opponent in the game, the invisible materials in the game, etc.) to complete the entire decision process. Although scripting robots take advantage of unfair information when taking action, because they are hard-coded [2], the vast majority of decision-making methods are like traversing a decision tree. It is difficult to make effective use of information to make more informed decisions and is extremely dependent. In addition, from another angle, the scripting robot is more like a low-level player who uses the plug-in. At present, many game manufacturers are looking for ways to make the built-in robots, like humans, only play games based on the information they can obtain, simulating human players to make decisions and battles without relying on the additional unfair information. They can, like human players, make decisions based on game screens, game sound effects, etc. [3].

Since the recent past, Artificial intelligence has shown awesome potential in multiple military fields [4–6]. In the current tide of globalization, the importance of developing artificial intelligence technology is even more obvious. In the foreseeable future, artificial intelligence will have a huge impact on the global political and economic landscape. Therefore, the research on this topic is of great strategic significance.

2 Analysis of the Problem and Related Research

The existing research work has greatly promoted the research application of deep learning and reinforcement learning in artificial intelligence [7], however, ignored a very important factor. A key factor in the ability of top human players to perform at a high level in many games is to predict before taking any action and to take precautions in advance for what may happen soon. When making decisions, they consider the current game situation and their own predictions about the future game situation. So, in this regard, the research work proposed in this paper is based on the A3C algorithm model [8], adding the prediction part of the future game picture to its structure, and combining the prediction result with the current game picture as a complete input for the decision network. Currently, the methods that are considered to be the most likely to approach or implement artificial intelligence are deep learning and reinforcement learning.

The traditional DQN has an overestimation problem when calculating the target Q-value, that is, the max operation is used in selecting and measuring the action which causes the Q-value to result in high estimation. Google DeepMind then improved it and introduced Double-DQN in 2015 [9]. It decomposes the selection and measurement of actions and is independently responsible for the two DQNs, which alleviates the overestimation problem to some extent. One of the Double-DQN networks is used to make decisions, select actions, and another network is used for the calculation of target Q-values [10]. Each training is performed only on the network responsible for decision making. When the DQN responsible for the decision converges to a certain extent, the two network tasks are exchanged, and the DQN network that performs the target Q-value calculation before the training is looped until the model converges. In the use of training data, random sampling is usually used to break the correlation between data, but in doing so, some important data may be ignored and discarded. Google DeepMind proposed the Prioritized Replay DQN [11]. In this paper, a new weighted sampling method is proposed, which uses the error of the loss function of the DQN network corresponding to each sample as the priority level to improve the sampling frequency of the larger error data. This approach is similar to the AdaBoost method in machine learning. In 2016, Google DeepMind proposed the Dueling-DQN algorithm [12]. The previous DQN and its variants directly estimate the action state value function, but in practice, the value of the state is independent of the action, so the final output of the DQN network model in Dueling-DQN is changed to two branches, one to estimate the value of the action-independent state, another branch is used to estimate the relative value of each action in that state, and then the results of the two branches are summed as an estimate of the value function of the original action state. This improvement has greatly improved the performance of DQN, and the changes are relatively simple, becoming one of the three best papers in ICML 2016. In addition, Google DeepMind also proposed a method of asynchronous training DQN [13], which is used to speed up model training. The above are the main improvements and variants of the current DQN. The Actor-Critic algorithm is more straightforward in solving the reinforcement learning problem. It directly looks for the strategy and then uses the value function to evaluate the adjustment strategy. Since its output is a probability distribution, it can be used to solve continuous problems [14]. One of the most common and widely used variants of the Actor-Critic algorithm is the A3C algorithm, which is an asynchronously trained Actor-Critic algorithm, which was proposed by Google DeepMind in 2016 to improve the training speed of the model. In addition, in 2017, Google DeepMind improved the A3C algorithm and proposed the UNREAL model [15].

3   Implementation Tools, Environment, and Settings

The model is implemented and experimented using OpenCV 3.3, Ubuntu Server 16.04 LTS operating system, Intel(R) Core(TM) i7-7700 CPU @ 3.60 GHz processor, NVIDIA GeForce GTX1080/PCIe/SSE2 GPU for processing CNN's, 32 GB memory, pycharm professional 2017.2 editor, Python 3.6 as a development language, Tensorflow-GPU 1.3.0 as a development framework and VizDoom 1.1.4 [16] as an AI research platform. The whole training (learning) and the testing process is calculated in time. The game scenario(s) used for training and testing are both D3_battle and CIG on VizDoom. Usually, it takes about 3–7 days or more for the model to train until the convergence is stable.

4 Model Design (Network Structure) and Implementation Details

The network structure diagram of the A3C algorithm model designed and used in the research is shown in Fig. 1. Input 4 + 1 (prediction) in the input part indicates that the input of the basic Actor-Critic model is the closest to the current game time. The history of 4 frames, followed by the plus 1 represents the input structure when the additional predicted picture is inputted as input, that is, 4 + 1 represents the input of Actor-Critic in the Anticipator-A3C model since the structure of the two parts is completely identical. Since the input structure of the network represented by Actor and Critic is exactly the same, only the output dimension is different in structure, so in practice, the convolution layer is usually shared by both, so as to reduce the amount of network training and speed up the training. In addition, in order to allow the agent to obtain more legitimate information, relevant game information (such as blood volume, ammunition number, etc.) can be added at the full connection layer. Moreover, the initial model of the study is very difficult to converge in these more complex environments, basically not in line with expectations, and later adjusted the network size, increased the number of convolution kernels, and added the maximum pooling after the convolution layer. By making this change, the model can be more easily converged. After analysis, the convolution kernel is added to extract more image features. The most important thing is that the addition of the maximum pooling layer reduces the feature dimension obtained by the convolution layer and retains the significant features. The maximum pooling layer introduces invariance. Since the motion is relatively random during the initial training of the model, the probability of successfully killing the target is small, and many targets in the game. The distance from the agent varies greatly. The size and position of the target in the picture may vary widely. In addition, the initial training may be more likely to be punished because of the possibility of accidental opening of the gun, so that the model is no longer shot, even if it can. The ability to shoot is also lost when killing the target. The invariance of the largest pooling layer allows the model to extend this capability to the extent of the target distance and position after successful killing of the target.

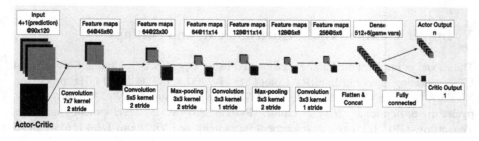

Fig. 1. Actor-critic convolutional neural network structure

The network structure of the Actor-Critic part of the Anticipator-A3C model has been introduced above. Next, the network structure of the Anticipator part is introduced. The Anticipator network inputs the frame corresponding to the current game screen, and the output predicts the frame corresponding to the next game screen. The input and output structures are identical. Therefore, the design uses the first convolution, the pooled extraction feature, and then the deconvolution to generate the prediction Image, but in order to make the Anticipator part also use the legal game information, the full connection layer is added in the middle of the network, and then the relevant game information is added in the full connection layer. So, in these ways, the network structure of the Anticipator designed can be seen in Fig. 2.

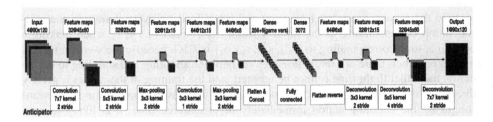

Fig. 2. Anticipator convolutional neural network structure

In this paper, the models are trained using RMSProp for gradient descent to optimize the model. The Actor-Critic partial learning rate is set to 1e−6, the Anticipator partial learning rate is set to 5e−5, the γ is set to 0.99, and the batch size is set to 128. The thread performs asynchronous training at the same time. The legal game information game_variables added in the model's full connection layer is a vector of length 6: [remaining blood volume, remaining bullets, remaining armor durable, 50 if blood volume <30 else-50, 50 if Bullet <5 else-50, 50 if armor durability = = 0 else-50].

The training data is generated by the model to be trained in real time and is directly used for training. It is easy to occur and has a fit for a specific game process. In order to reduce the correlation between data sequences and to improve the stability of training, multi-threading is adopted. Asynchronous training is used to train the model. The basic idea is to create several threads, each thread has a private model, and the main thread has a shared model. Before each game starts, the child thread requests the main thread to update the network weight of the private model to make it. The network weights are consistent. After the update is completed, the game starts. Then, when each set of training data is obtained, the corresponding gradient value is calculated, the gradient value is gradient-decided on the main model, and the network weight of the main model is updated until the game ends. The above operation is repeated until the child thread enters the next game. Multi-threaded asynchronous training can effectively reduce the correlation of training data and also make full use of computing resources.

Usually, the two adjacent frames in the game are almost identical, which means that there are many redundant calculations if the model is to process the game picture frame by frame. And although in training, due to the asynchronous game mode (i.e., the game will wait for the model to make decisions and then refresh the game screen, enter the next game screen, and then wait for the model to make decisions, loop back and forth until the game is over), do frame-by-frame processing, but the actual experimental test uses asynchronous game mode (that is, the game does not wait for the model to make decisions, only constantly update the game screen over time, and continuously push the game progress), so It is not always possible to do frame-by-frame processing. Moreover, the game itself requires a certain number of frames for each action, especially the action required for shooting and shooting requires more frames to complete. Moreover, the model uses historical 4 frames as the model input. If it is a continuous 4 frames, some of the movement trends contained in the picture are not obvious because the picture is almost the same, and the corresponding historical content is too short, which makes the memory ability of the model weak. Therefore, in order to make the model closer to the human operating frequency and set a decision every 4 frames, the real-time stamp corresponding to the input 4 frames is {t-12, t-8, t-4, t} when making a decision at time corresponding to $\{s_{t-3}, s_{t-2}, s_{t-1}, s_t\}$ in CIG, because the weapon used is a rocket launcher, there is a large time interval between shooting and shooting to hit the enemy, the bullet flight time cannot be ignored, and the training of the model is greatly affected by the instant reward, if the model cannot effectively capture the real reward brought by the shooting action immediately or in extreme time, it is likely to mistakenly think that the shooting action will only cause the loss of the bullet to bring punishment and the model will lose the ability to kill. This allows the model to better converge in complex scenarios. In addition, in order to make the model's target value and the real value closer to the training, and let the action get better and there are rewards and punishments with a large delay (such as in the CIG game scene from shooting to killing the enemy) the time interval is more closely related. The algorithm takes the n-step time difference (where n is determined by the batch size and the game duration) to calculate the target value. Although the target value obtained in this way is a biased estimate, the value depends on for a specific game sequence, but doing so can reduce the amount of training required so that the convergence speed is greatly improved.

5 Model Experimentations (Model Training Process)

Take the Anticipator-A3C model as an example to analyze the relevant statistical data in the actual training process in the D3_battle game scene. The model training process itself is an asynchronous multi-threaded execution. Each chart contains the same number of data curves as the number of threads. For the convenience of display, each graph only shows the data curve obtained by one of the threads. The values for each point in the graph are plotted by the performance calculations of the agent in five consecutive games during training. Judging the training state of the model is mainly based on the game performance of the agent rather than the change of the loss function. Figure 3 shows the change in the loss value of the network when the Anticipator-A3C model is trained in the D3_battle scenario. The horizontal axis represents the number of game stations in the training. Analysis of the curves in the graph, they cannot visually and effectively indicate whether the model has converged, and it is not used as the main reference for the training state in the training process. Figure 4 is used to describe the survival of the agent in the game during training, and the horizontal axis represents the number of games in the training. From (a) in Fig. 4, during the training process, the average number of deaths per game in the 5th game is reduced from 1 at the beginning (almost every time it is killed) to 0 (almost every time being able to Survive) indicates that the agent has evolved from being easily killed to being difficult to kill. The average residual blood volume curve in (b) of Fig. 4 also confirms this point. The average blood volume of the agent at the end of each 5 games is rising, and it can even stay close to full blood at the end of the game. Figure 5 shows the killing situation of the agent in the game during training and its own ammunition. The horizontal axis represents the number of games in the game. From (a) in Fig. 5, during the training process, the average number of kills per game of the 5th game increased from 0 to 30 from the initial stage, indicating that the ability of the agent to find and kill the target is greatly improved. The average residual ammunition number curve in (b) of Fig. 5 shows that the ammunition of the agent is not enough from the initial stage of training to the end, indicating that it will not only shoot the gun but also search for ammunition, which also confirms the agent explores the improvement of map capabilities.

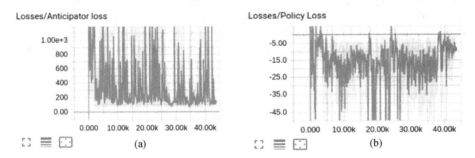

Fig. 3. Anticipator and Actor loss change graph

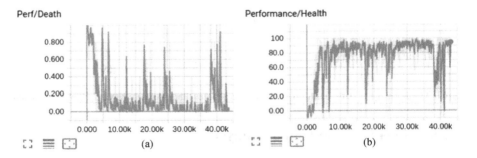

Fig. 4. Change in the average number of deaths and average residual blood volume of the agent

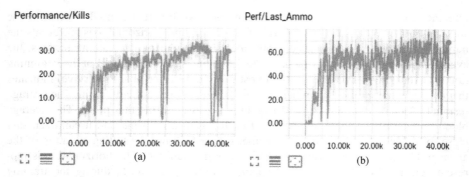

Fig. 5. Change in the Average no of kills and the Average number of remaining ammunition

Figure 6 shows the average number of execution actions per agent during training and the average change in total rewards per game. The horizontal axis represents the number of games in training. In the game, as long as the agent is still alive; it will perform the action. Since the total duration of each game is limited; the total number of actions that the agent can perform in each game is limited. (a) in Fig. 6 shows that the total number of actions performed by the agent in each round continues to rise until the upper limit is reached, indicating that its lifetime has increased to the upper limit, and its trend and the left graph in Fig. 4 (average number of deaths) the curve of change is just upside down. (b) in Fig. 6 shows that the total reward that the agent can get in each game is increasing until it no longer increases.

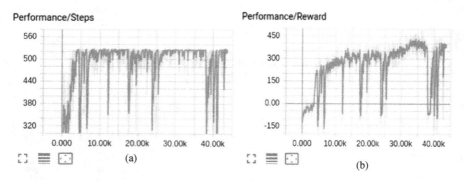

Fig. 6. The Average no of execution actions per agent and the Average reward change per game

6   Experimental Results and Analysis

The A3C model and the Anticipator-A3C model were tested several times in the prepared game scene. The first two models are trained in the D3_battle scenario. The reward mechanism settings for training are shown in Table 1. The D3_battle scene is a game scene created by the Intel team participating in the VizDoom competition. It is a rectangular maze in which monsters, medical kits, and ammunition are randomly refreshed. The target of the agent is as far as possible without being killed. The training and testing time of the D3_battle scene is 1 min per game. If the game duration becomes 1 min or the agent is killed, the game ends. The game screen update frequency is 35 frames per second, which are 2100 frames per minute. The experimental test results of the model in the D3_battle scenario are shown in Table 3. The experimental data is based on the average performance of 100 games. The DFP model in Table 2 is proposed by the Intel team participated in the VizDoom competition. The experimental data is from the paper [17]. As can be seen from the data in the table, the average number of kills per game and the average number of remaining ammunition in the proposed model is obviously better than the DFP model and the A3C model, which means, the performance of our proposed model is better in the game than DFP and A3C.

Table 1. Game scene D3_battle rewards and punishment settings

Element	Description	Reward/penalty factor
Survival punishment	Punish only to survive longer and do nothing	−0.1/action
Blood loss	Punish the blood loss (hit)	−0.4/point
Ammunition loss	Punishment of ammunition reduction (shooting)	−2/piece
Blood reward	Increase blood volume (pick up medical kit)	0.4/point
Ammunition reward	Increase in reward ammunition (pick up ammunition)	0.5/piece
Stagnation penalty	Punishment stays in place or stuck in the corner can't move forward	−0.5/action
Kill reward	Reward kill monster	20 times
Death penalty	Punishment killed by monsters	−30 times
Stagnation penalty effective threshold	Stop penalty occurs when the movement distance is less than the threshold	10
Number of monsters	Number of monsters included in the game scene	15

Table 2. Game scenario(s) D3_battle experimental test results

Game scene D3_Battle	Avg no. of game frames (upper limit 2100)	Avg residual blood volume (upper limit 100)	Max/Avg/Min remaining ammunition	Max Avg/Min no. of kills per game	Avg no. of deaths
DFP	–	–	-/-/-	-/13.8/-	–
A3C	2050.39	92.30	115.00/39.21/0.00	41.00/29.53/9.00	0.05
Anticipator-A3C	2057.64	90.23	130.00/65.72/0.00	42.00/31.98/11.00	0.06

The 'CIG scene' is a game scene officially used in the VizDoom competitions. It is a polygonal maze. The map size is larger than D3_battle. There are steps in the map, that is, there is a vertical gap. In the maze, the armor, medical kit, ammunition, explosive barrels, and built-in scripting robots are refreshed at fixed positions, which can acquire and utilize some unfair information. The goal of the agent is to find and kill the scripted robots as much as possible without killing or suicide. The necessary materials, the weapons used by each individual are rocket launchers, with AOE damage, high damage, and close fire can cause damage to them. If the Agent or scripting robot dies during the game, it will be randomly reborn at a resurrection point on the map. The reward mechanism settings for training the two models in the CIG scenario are shown in Table 3. The training time of the CIG scenario(s) is 1 min per game. If c 1 min or the agent is killed, the game ends. The test time is 2 min per game. When the game duration reaches 2 min, the game ends. If the agent is killed or suicide, the game can be revived to continue. The experimental test results of the model in the CIG scenario(s) are shown in Table 4. The experimental data is based on the average performance of 100 games. The F1 model in Table 4 is proposed by the Facebook team participated in the VizDoom competition. The experimental data is from the paper [18]. In addition, 'Anticipator-A3C with fake prediction' in the table indicates that the predicted frame supplied to the Actor-Critic model is forged.

Table 3. Game scenario(s) CIG rewards and punishment settings

Element	Description	Reward/penalty factor
Survival punishment	Punish only to survive longer and do nothing	−0.1/action
Blood loss	Punish the blood loss (hit)	−0.1/point
Ammunition loss	Punishment of ammunition reduction (shooting)	−3/piece
Blood reward	Increase blood volume (pick up medical kit)	0.2/point
Ammunition reward	Increase in reward ammunition (pick up ammunition)	3/piece (each limit is 5)
Stagnation penalty	Punishment stays in place or stuck in the corner can't move forward	−0.5/action
Kill reward	Reward kill monster	20 times
Suicide punishment	Punish the death caused by oneself	−20 times
Death penalty	Punish the death caused by the opponent or himself	−5 times
Increased armor	Reward armor for increased durability (pick up armor)	0.025/durability
Armor loss	Punish armor durability reduction (hit)	−0.025/durability
Stagnation penalty effective threshold	Stop penalty when moving distance is less than the threshold	10
Number of built-in bots	Number of monsters included in the game scene	15

Table 4. Game scene CIG experiment test results

Game scene CIG	Avg residual blood volume (upper limit 100)	Max/Avg/Min remaining ammunition	Max/Avg/Min kills (deducted suicides)	Max/Avg/Min deaths (including suicides)
F1	–	–	17.00/10.34/5.00	–
A3C	74.05	15.00/9.78/0.00	22.00/11.40/2.00	15.00/9.21/6.00
Anticipator-A3C with the fake prediction	74.47	18.00/10.09/0.00	20.00/11.09/2.00	14.00/9.19/4.00
Anticipator-A3C	74.82	18.00/10.23/0.00	23.00/13.15/3.00	14.00/9.19/4.00

From the data in Table 2 above, the performance of the proposed model is better than F1 and basic A3C. In addition, when using forged prediction frames, the performance of the proposed model will be reduced, proving that the predicted frames do contain some useful information. The number of deaths in the model is still high, and improvements in this area are needed in the future.

The image data collected by the experiments is analyzed, and it is found that the predicted frame can indeed contain some useful information intuitively. When the opponent has an open fire, the picture in the predicted frame is whitened, and the corresponding position of the spot in the predicted frame is the brightest in the predicted frame, making the model more concerned with the opponent's attack. Making it more closely linked to the reward and punishment mechanism. The model finds that it has made a shooting action based on the information of the historical frame and the current frame, so the position of the hand is raised in the predicted frame, and the muzzle has a flare, which coincides with the future frame. The model can effectively distinguish the difference between the flare caused by the fire and the fire caused by the opponent's fire. It seems that adding the prediction module is reasonable and effective. From another point of view, the prediction part is actually a single-step simulation of the future. It predicts the state to be transferred to the future based on the current frame and the historical frame. Usually, when solving such problems, Monte Carlo cannot be solved like the problem of Go.

7   Conclusion and Future Work

A game agent based on an A3C algorithm with prediction is proposed, and the anticipator module is added in combination with the game characteristics of human players. The anticipator module predicts the next screen change according to the game screen currently available to the agent, predicts the upcoming change in the screen, and generates the predicted game screen as one of the inputs of the A3C algorithm model. The agent continuously interacts with the environment (game engine), reads and implements the game screen and makes decisions, takes actions to influence the environment, adjusts its own strategy according to the feedback of the environment, and finally finds the optimal strategy to achieve end-to-end learning process. To be more specific and short, the overall research results are ideal.

Acknowledgment. The authors would like to thank the school of computer science and technology, Harbin Institute of Technology, Harbin, Heilongjiang 150001, PR China, and NVIDIA for powerful GPU machine donation. This work is partially funded by the Higher Education Department KPK, Pakistan, the MOE–Microsoft Key Laboratory of Natural Language Processing and Speech, Harbin Institute of Technology, the Major State Basic Research Development Program of China (973 Program 2015CB351804) and the National Natural Science Foundation of China under Grant No. 61572155, 61672188 and 61272386.

Conflict of Interest. The authors declare that they have no conflicts of interest.

References

1. Khan, A., Feng, J., Liu, S., Jifara, W., Tian, Z., Fu, Y.: State-of-the-art and open challenges in RTS game-AI and StarCraft. (IJACSA) Int. J. Adv. Comput. Sci. Appl. **8**(12), 9 (2017). https://doi.org/10.14569/ijacsa.2017.081203

2. Kot, B., et al.: Information visualization utilizing 3D computer game engines case study. In: Proceedings of the 6th ACM SIGCHI New Zealand Chapter's International Conference on Computer-Human Interaction Making CHI Natural - CHINZ 2005, p. 53–60 (2005). https://doi.org/10.1145/1073943.1073954

3. Mnih, V., et al.: Human-level control through deep reinforcement learning. Nature **518** (7540), 529–533 (2015)

4. Khan, A., et al.: A competitive combat strategy and tactics in RTS games AI and StarCraft. In: Zeng, B., Huang, Q., El Saddik, A., Li, H., Jiang, S., Fan, X. (eds.) PCM 2017. LNCS, vol. 10736, pp. 3–12. Springer, Cham (2018). https://doi.org/10.1007/978-3-319-77383-4_1

5. Zhou, S., Liang, W., Li, J., Kim, J.-U.: Improved VGG model for road traffic sign recognition. CMC: Comput. Mater. Continua **57**(1), 11–24 (2018)

6. Kan, X., et al.: Snow cover mapping for mountainous areas by fusion of MODIS L1B and geographic data based on stacked denoising auto-encoders. CMC: Comput. Mater. Continua **57**(1), 49–68 (2018)

7. Khan, A., Jiang, F., Liu, S., Grigoriev, A., Gupta, B.B., Rho, S.: Training an agent for FPS doom game using visual reinforcement learning and VizDoom. (IJACSA) Int. J. Adv. Comput. Sci. Appl. **8**(12) (2017). https://doi.org/10.14569/issn.2156-5570

8. Babaeizadeh, M., et al.: Reinforcement learning through asynchronous advantage actor-critic on a GPU (2016)

9. Silver, D., et al.: Mastering the game of Go with deep neural networks and tree search. Nature **529**(7587), 484–489 (2016). https://doi.org/10.1038/nature16961

10. Van Hasselt, H., Guez, A., Silver, D.: Deep reinforcement learning with double Q-learning. In: AAAI (2015)

11. Schaul, T., et al.: Prioritized experience replay. arXiv preprint arXiv:1511.05952 (2015)

12. Wang, Z., et al.: Dueling network architectures for deep reinforcement learning. arXiv preprint arXiv:1511.06581 (2015)

13. Mnih, V., et al.: Asynchronous methods for deep reinforcement learning. In: International Conference on Machine Learning (2016)

14. Grondman, I., et al.: A survey of actor-critic reinforcement learning: standard and natural policy gradients. IEEE Trans. Syst. Man Cybern. Part C (Appl. Rev.) **42**(6), 1291–1307 (2012)
15. Jaderberg, M., et al.: Reinforcement learning with unsupervised auxiliary tasks. arXiv preprint arXiv:1611.05397 (2016)
16. Kempka, M., et al.: ViZDoom: a Doom-based AI research platform for visual reinforcement learning. arXiv preprint arXiv:1605.02097. (2016) arXiv:1605.02097 [cs.LG]
17. Dosovitskiy, A., Koltun, V.: Learning to act by predicting the future. arXiv preprint arXiv: 1611.01779 (2016)
18. Wu, Y., Tian, Y.: Training agent for first-person shooter game with actor-critic curriculum learning. In: Conference Paper at ICLR 2017 (2017)

Identify Influentials Based on User Behavior Across Different Topics

Yong Quan[1]([⊠]), Yichen Song[1], Lu Deng[1], Yan Jia[1], Bin Zhou[1], and Weihong Han[2]

[1] College of Computer, National University of Defense Technology, Changsha, China
qy8801@nudt.edu.cn
[2] Cyberspace Institute of Advanced Technology, Guangzhou University, Guangzhou, China

Abstract. With the rapid development of Internet technology and the widespread use of social networks in daily life, a large amount of information is propagated on the Web through various interactions among users. Researches on measuring users' influence are becoming a hot spot, but the traditional methods are not suitable enough for identifying influential individuals in large-scale social networks. According to users' time series behavior patterns of publishing information and their interested topics, we propose a TBRank model for mining individual influence of uses in different topics. Compared to other methods, our method can distinguish the difference of influence across different topics, and measure the influence of users more accurately. The experimental results on real dataset validate the effectiveness of our work.

Keywords: Social influence · Behavior analysis · Social network

1 Introduction

With the popularity of social networking services, a large number of users are widely involved in the discussion of related content while publishing information on the network, resulting in the rapid spread of information. The spread of information in social networks is mainly driven by user behavior, and the interaction between users determines the effect of information dissemination. It is of great practical significance to study the dissemination effect of information in the network, such as brand promotion or new product sales [1] and public opinion monitoring [2].

How to accurately locate high-influence users is a hot research topic in social influence analysis. The mainstream idea to solve this problem is to quantitatively calculate an influence score for each user in a social network through influence measurement technology, and rank the scores to select influence individuals [3]. The main idea of traditional measurement technologies is building the relationship network and influence weight matrix between users, and calculating the influence of users by mining relational networks and users' features. These methods are not suitable for identifying influence individuals in social networks across different topics.

X. Sun et al. (Eds.): ICAIS 2019, LNCS 11635, pp. 476–487, 2019.
https://doi.org/10.1007/978-3-030-24268-8_44

Information has different topical attributes, and different users pay attention to different topics, especially in social network. Measuring user influence at topic level is a more fine-grained approach in social influence analysis, which is a research trend for influential individual discovery. In addition, how to construct an effective relationship network and accurately calculate the weight coefficient in the network for social platforms where the social relationship between users changes with time is a big challenge in social network analysis.

The external factors that affect users' social behavior are mainly the topics of information and the users' interests. Therefore, the influence is rooted in the interaction process between users, and the degree of association between behavior patterns among users is foundation of individual influence calculating. Most existing methods focus on the propagation probability of influence between users in different topics and calculating influence with the random walk method; or construct a complex probability generative model and infer user topical influence by fitting the loss function based on the observed social networking data. Since users' social behavior is driven by both influence and information, which can represent the changes of influence. Hence, we can measure the influence of users in different topics from the aspects of behavior patterns and information content [4].

Based on the intuitions above, this paper designs a topic-related influence measurement TBRank, which considers the influence propagation coefficients related to social behavior and information in social networks. Through calculating the influence weight coefficient, the accuracy of user influence algorithm will be improved. The experiments carried out on real dataset confirm the effectiveness of the proposed method in measuring user topical influence.

2 Related Work

Early work mainly studies the influence users within social networks in a qualitative analysis way, and demonstrates the existing and difference of user influence. Other existing methods of mining influential individuals with the network structure constructed by users and their social relationships can discover key nodes in social networks. However, the topics in information that meet users' interests can be discussed enthusiastically, and forming information cascade propagation at last [5]. In addition to the network structure, the text content generated by users can reflect the influence of users. The novel topic information can quickly attract the public's attention and enhance the publisher's influence. This topic-related influence is more suitable for applications such as information retrieval or social recommendation in social networks.

Quantitative calculation of influence in different topics has become the mainstream trend of users' influence analysis in social networks. Using information content to analyze the influence of users in a fine-grained way can distinguish the influence individuals in different topics. Haveliwala [6] proposed a topic-sensitive PagerRank method that uses the same transition probability matrix to calculate influence, and believed that users have same influence diffusion probability in different topics. Weng et al. [7] proposed an influence measurement method based on network link structure and topic similarity. By constructing the transfer matrix of user influence in different topics, the validity of the method was verified in the Twitter dataset. Tang et al. [8] proposed the topic factor graph (TAP) model to calculate the influence transition probability among users and mining the influence individuals based on the random walk model in different topics. Silva et al. [9] believed that a correlation exists between influential users and popular information, and proposed Profile-Rank model, which is a random walk based propagation model in user-information map and identifying influential users and hot spot information at the same time. Ding et al [10] proposed a Multi-Rank method to locate influential users in multi-relation network. The method considers the jump probabilities of users within or between different networks, calculating the influence of user in different topics based on the random walk model.

There are also ways to integrate influence calculation and topic discovery into a same model. For example, Liu et al. [11] proposed a method to measure the influence of user and mining topics in heterogeneous networks, using text content and link relationships to mine the influence of different topics. Bi et al. [12] proposed an FLDA model that integrates information topic discovery with social influence analysis in a probabilistic generative process, which is essentially a Bernoulli polynomial hybrid model, and designed a distributed Gibbs sampling solution method.

3 Definition

In this section, the problem of user influence measurement at topic level in social networks is defined and formally described. Before defining the problem, we firstly introduce the involved concepts and symbols (Table 1).

Table 1. Symbol definition and description

Symbol	Description
G	Relational network
B	Weibo text
T^u	Topic Distribution Vector of user u
C^k	Topic circle
$P_u(t)$	Probability density function of publishing information by user u
$R_u(t)$	Delay probability density function of forwarding information by user u
$\Lambda_{u,v}^A$	Influence propagation coefficient related to behavior
$\Lambda_{u,v}^k$	Influence propagation coefficient related to topic k
$W_{u,v}^k$	Influence propagation coefficient
I_u^k	The influence of user u on topic k

Definition 3.1 (User topic distribution): In social networks, users are often interested in a plurality of topics. T^u is the topic distribution function of user u, and it is a K-dimension vector $T^u = \left(T_1^u, T_2^u, \ldots, T_K^u\right)$, where T_k^u represents the user's interest degree of topic k, $0 \leq T_k^u \leq 1$.

Definition 3.2 (Topic circle): The information disseminated in social networks contains a variety of topics. The topic circle refers to a user collection related to a specific topic, which is represented by $C^k \subseteq V$. The necessary and sufficient condition for the user u to be a member of the topic circle C^k is that T_k^u is greater than a certain threshold, indicating that the user is interested in the topic k.

Definition 3.3 (Probability of user posting a blog): The behavior of users in social networks to post information is related to time t. $P_u(t)$ is used as the time probability density function of posting blogs for user u.

Define 3.4 (Probability of user forwarding delay): In social networks, the time of user's behavior about forwarding a blog is always late than the blog's posting time. $R_u(t)$ is used to represent the probability density function of the time difference t between the time when the user u forwards the information and the time when the transmitted information is published.

With the above definitions, the research questions in this paper will be formally described as follows: how to calculate the influence of relevant users on different topics by using the influence measurement techniques at the topic level with social networking data, including relationship structure $G = (V, E)$, information text and user behavior. In different topic categories, a real-valued scalar is given to the influence of the user, representing the amount of influence the user has in the topic.

4 Modeling

Based on user behavior, we propose the topical level influence measurement model TBRank, which can identify influential users in different topic circles. For the data such as user behavior and interaction information in social networks, the weight coefficient between the user links in the network structure is calculated, thereby the accuracy of the user influence measurement will be improved.

The TBRank model consists of three parts: the first part is to calculate the behavior-related influence propagation coefficient through the time series mode of user behavior; the second part is based on the topic mining technology to calculate the topic-related influence propagation coefficient; the third part combines the behavior-related and topic-related influence propagation coefficient to measure user influence in a specific topic circle.

4.1 Behavior Correlation

Similar to the work done in [13], the statistical analysis of the time series features of the Sina Weibo dataset from August 1 to September 30, 2014 was taken, and the results are shown in Fig. 1. It is worth noting that the correlation between the forwarding and posting behavior of uses in a coarse-grained way proves that users' behaviors such as posting or forwarding have a certain law. The social behavior between influential users may have some consistency of time series characteristics. The stronger the consistency, the higher the influence propagation intensity between users.

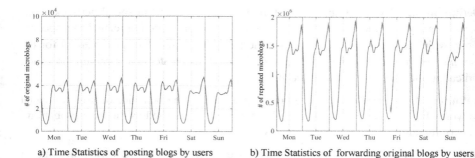

a) Time Statistics of posting blogs by users   b) Time Statistics of forwarding original blogs by users

Fig. 1. User time series feature statistics

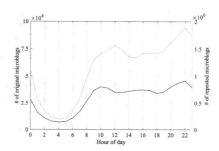

Fig. 2. Statistics on the time of original blogs posting and forwarding within a day

According to Fig. 2, we can see that there is a certain correlation in the temporal pattern between the original information posting behavior and the information forwarded behavior, which can effectively reflect the influence propagation intensity between users. Therefore, the following assumptions are made: user's forwarding behavior in social networks is directly influenced by other users. The influence can be measured as:

$$\Lambda_{u,v}^{A} = \int P_u(\tau) \int P_v(\tau + \epsilon) R_v(\epsilon) d\epsilon d\tau \tag{1}$$

where $\Lambda_{u,v}^{A}$ represents the behavioral coefficient that the influence spreads from the user u to v. The intuitive meaning of Eq. (1) is that when the user u posts the information at time τ, if user v can always forward the information within the time interval ϵ after the time τ, the influence of user u on user v is greater, and vice versa.

The integral solution for the probability density function is not simple. In order to facilitate the application in practice, we use the discretization method to solve the integral term. By dividing 24 h into disjoint time intervals, the probability distributions of the user's posting and forwarding time delays in different time intervals are obtained, can be calculated and presented as follows:

$$\Lambda_{u,v}^{A} = \sum_{i} \hat{P}_u(t_i) \sum_{j} \hat{P}_v(t_{i+j-1}) \cdot \hat{R}_v(t_j) \tag{2}$$

where $\hat{P}_u(t_i)$ indicates the probability of user posting blogs in the i-th time interval, and $\hat{R}_v(t_j)$ indicates the probability of user forwarding delay in the j-th time interval. For the convenience of calculation, the time interval of $\hat{P}_u(t_i)$ and $\hat{R}_v(t_j)$ is set to be the same.

4.2 Topic Correlation

Users who focus on common topics are similar, and related information is more likely to spread between them [14]. To explore the usage of topic attribute in influence measurement, it is necessary to determine the topic category involved in the information, calculating the user's tendency in different topics, and quantify the influence propagation intensity of the topic relevance between users. In order to mine topic information in large-scale untagged text content, this paper adopts a classic LDA model proposed by Blei [15]. Formula as shown in (3).

$$p(\mathbb{C}|\alpha, \beta) = \prod_{m=1}^{M} p(\theta_m|\beta) \prod_{n=1}^{N_m} p(z_{m,n}|\theta_m) \cdot p(s_{m,n}|\phi_{z_{m,n}}, \alpha) \tag{3}$$

Given a document collection $\mathbb{C}$, the word $s_{m,n}$ in the document is a known variable. α and β are hyperparameters that can be pre-specified, and the implied variables θ_m, ϕ_k and $z_{m,n}$ are all unknown. The variational-EM method for solving hidden variable parameters based on LDA model is given in [15], while Gibbs Sampling is used to estimate the hidden variable parameters of the model [16].

Since users with the same hobbies tends to share or pay attention to the same topical information, the topic-related influence will spread more strongly between them. By measuring the similarity between the topic distributions of users, it is possible to capture the propagation probability of influence between users from the topic level. Thereby the accuracy of user influence calculation method can be improved. It is known that the topic distribution of user u is set as $T^u = (T_1^u, T_2^u, \ldots, T_K^u)$, and Eq. (4) is a measure of the topic-related influence propagation coefficient by measuring the similarity between users on a specific topic.

$$\Lambda_{u,v}^{k} = \frac{1}{1 + \exp(1 + |T_k^u - T_k^v|)} \tag{4}$$

4.3 TBRank Model

Digging into the influence of users in a specific topic circle can not only find out the influential users in different topics, but also narrow the scope of users in social influence analysis. The user's attention to different topics is known to be $T^u = (T_1^u, T_2^u, \ldots, T_K^u)$, for a given threshold value ε_k related to the topic k, the topic circle will be $C^k = \{u \in V | T_k^u \geq \varepsilon_k\}$.

In order to improve the efficiency and simplify the calculation, we sort the user's topic distribution T^u by value, and obtain $\tilde{T}^u = \left(T^u_{1'}, T^u_{2'}, \ldots, T^u_{K'} \right)$, $\forall i', j'$, if $i' < j'$, then $T^u_{i'} \geq T^u_{j'}$. Because the user is not interested in all topics and has influence in each topic, the user u is only can be interested in γ_u topics at most and the topic circle can be determined by the following formula.

$$C^k = \left\{ u \in V \middle| \exists i', i' \leq \gamma_u \cap i' = k \cap T^u_{i'} > 0 \right\}$$ (5)

The same user may appear in different topic circles, and different topical circles contain different users. With the random walk model mining user influence in different topic circle C^k, it is also necessary to calculate the transfer probability of influence between users, which is related to the behavioral and topical influence between users.

$$W^k_{v,u} = \omega \Lambda^A_{u,v} + (1 - \omega) \Lambda^k_{u,v}$$ (6)

where Ω is a linear weighting factor. The $W^k_{v,u}$ indicates the probability that the influence is passed from the user v to u, representing the probability that the user will browse the information to select the walking path in social networks.

TBRank: Topical influence calculation method

Input: Social network structure $G = (V, E)$, time and content of users' blogs, μ, γ, K, α, β, ω ;

Output : Influence at the topic level, π^k, $k = 1, 2, \ldots, K$;

```
1: Based on LDA Model, mining user's topic Distribu-
tion T^u, u ∈ V
2: foreach k ∈ K do
3:      Based on Eq. (5) constructing topicC^k
4: end
5: foreach G^k = (C^k, E^k) do
6:    foreach (v, u) ∈ E^k do
7:       calculate  Λ^A_{u,v}, Λ^k_{u,v}, W^k_{v,u}
8:    end
9: end
11:calculating U^k based on Eq. (8)
12:repeat
13:    π^k_{t+1} = μW^kπ^k_t + (1 − μ)U^k ;
14:until convergence ;
15:return π^k ;
```

For the topic k, the network structurere presented by the topical circle $G^k = (C^k, E^k)$, $E^k \subseteq E$ is a collection of related users. The transition probability matrix W^k of influence between users is the weight coefficient matrix associated with the network structure G^k. Therefore, the user influence calculation method TBRank based on the random walk model in a specific topic circle is proposed, and the calculation formula is:

$$\pi^k = \mu W^k \pi^k + (1 - \mu) U^k \tag{7}$$

where μ is the jump factor. The $\pi^k = \left(\pi_1^k, \pi_2^k, \ldots, \pi_{N^k}^k\right)$ indicates the influence of users, and $N^k = |C^k|$ is the number of users involved in the topical circle. U^k is used to prevent situations in which only one user is concerned in G^k [7].

$$U^k = \frac{1}{\sum_i T_k^i} \left(T_k^1, T_k^2, \ldots, T_k^{N^k}\right) \tag{8}$$

The detailed process of computing user influence at the topic level based on user behavior is shown in Algorithm 1.

5   Experiment

5.1   Date Set

The original Sina Weibo dataset contains a total of 23,125,584 blog posts from August 10 to September 20, 2014, of which 1,024,996 original blog posts and 285,127 users.

Table 2. Introduction of data sets

Data set	Sina Weibo
Number of users	243,872
Number of following relations	10,352,184
Number of original blogs	861,437
Number of forwarding blogs	21,832,915

The original data was processed as follows: we used HanLP tools for word segmentation [17], deleting blogs with less than 10 valid terms and related users, and further discarded users with less than 20 postings (originating or forwarding), which will ensure that meaningful time series patterns for users or blogs are obtained. After the pre-processing, 22,694,352 blogs from 243,872 users were included. The specific statistical characteristics are shown in Table 2.

5.2   Comparisons

In order to verify the effectiveness of the TBRank model, the following methods were selected as control methods for experimental performance comparison.

Followers: Recorded as M1, refers to the number of fans of the user during the observation period, and the number is used as the basis for ranking the user's influence.

TSPR: Recorded as M2, is a topic-sensitive PageRank method [6], which extends the classic PageRank method by constructing a bias vector.

TwitterRank: Recorded as M3, in the topic circle C^k, the method considers the similarity and link structures between users to measure the influence of users [7].

ProfileRank: Recorded as M4, this method identifies influential users and popular information in the information dissemination dataset [9].

TBRank: Our work is recorded as M5 during the experiment.

The parameters involved in all comparison methods are set to the values with which the results in the original paper are optimal. All experiments were performed on a single-node server with a 64-bit CentOS 6.6 system configured as follows: 2 quad-core Intel Xeon E5-2403 CPU@1.80 GHz, 64 GB RAM, 2.0 TB hard drive.

5.3   Results Analysis

With the selected parameters, the text content of the blogs published by users is aggregated. This experiment constructs 243,872 large documents to mine the topic distribution for each user, and calculates their interests for 50 topics. Every user can only appear in 10 topic circles at most. Figure 3 shows the user distribution in different topic circles. It can be seen that the user distribution in 50 topic circles is not balanced. The largest topic circle is Topic28 which contains 106,795 users, and the smallest is Topic50 which contains 18,257 users.

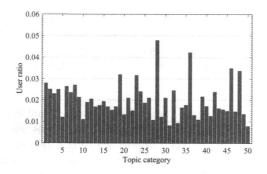

Fig. 3. Distribution of users in different topical circles

Due to the lack of standard test data sets, the results of the influence algorithms will be analyzed by voting method in the experiment, as used in [10]. For example, assuming that M1 gives a ranking result of user set R1 and all five algorithms vote for a user set R_{vote} vote as a reference correct result, then M1's accuracy is defined as follows:

$$\text{Accuracy} = \frac{|R1 \cap R_{vote}|}{|R1|} \tag{9}$$

This accuracy rate is a coarse-grained evaluation criterion, which represents the extent to which the user influence rank calculated by the method is acceptable by other methods.

Figure 4 shows the accuracy of all methods in Top-10, Top-20, Top-50 and Top-100. To illustrate the problem, only the performance of the methods in the five topic circles with the largest number of users is given. As can be seen from the Fig. 4, in all the topic circles, the performance of all methods shows the same trend. M5 has the best performance, and the accuracy rate is the highest among the four types of rankings. It can be indicated that the calculation of user influence with TBRank model can be accepted by other algorithms.

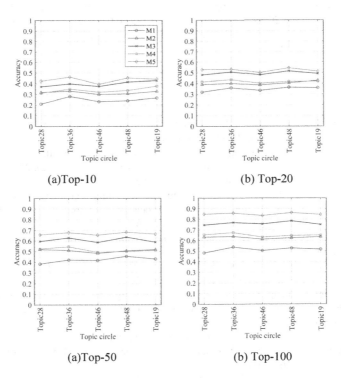

Fig. 4. Algorithms' accuracy in different user influence rankings

To analyze Fig. 4 in a detailed way, as the number of users in the ranking of users for comparison increases, the accuracy of all methods increases. Because in a larger ranking list, it is approved by more than three methods, which the correct result set is larger. Compared to other methods, the accuracy of M3 and M5 is relatively close, as both methods fully use the topic information of the blogs.

6 Conclusions

This paper proposes a method to measure the influence of users at the topic level in social networks. The proposed method comprehensively considers the characteristics of user behavior and topics, and mines influential users based on random walk model. The essence of this method is to construct a novel calculation method of transition probability, considering the influence propagation mechanism from the two perspectives of behavioral relevance and topic relevance. The future work can explore how to integrate more accurate topic discovery technology into the user influence measurement algorithm, and combine the user emotion and other attributes to make the user influence more fine-grained.

Acknowledgment. The work is supported by the National Key Research and Development Program of China (No. 2016QY03D0601, No. 2016QY03D0603), National Natural Science Foundation of China (No. 61732022, No. 61732004, No. 61472433, No. U1636215, No. 61672020, No. 61502517).

References

1. Senecal, S., Nantel, J.: The influence of online product recommendations on consumers' online choices. J. Retail. **80**(2), 159–169 (2004)
2. Bae, Y., Lee, H.: Sentiment analysis of Twitter audiences: measuring the positive or negative influence of popular twitterers. J. Am. Soc. Inform. Sci. Technol. **63**(12), 2521–2535 (2012)
3. Rogers, E.: Diffusion of Innovations. The Free Press, New York (1962)
4. Kim, D., Lee, J., Lee, B.: Topical influence modeling via topic-level interests and interactions on social curation services. In: Proceedings of the IEEE 32nd International Conference on Data Engineering, pp. 13–24 (2016)
5. Leskovec, J., Adamic, L., Huberman, B.: The dynamics of viral marketing. ACM Trans. Web **1**(1), 5 (2007)
6. Haveliwala, T.: Topic-sensitive PageRank. In: Proceedings of the 11th International Conference on World Wide Web, pp. 517–526 (2002)
7. Weng, J., Lim, E., Jiang, J., He, Q.: Twitterrank: finding topic-sensitive influential twitterers. In: Proceedings of the 3rd ACM International Conference on Web Search and Data Mining, pp. 261–270 (2010)
8. Tang, J., Sun, J., Wang, C., Yang, Z.: Social influence analysis in large-scale networks. In: Proceedings of the 15th ACM International Conference on Knowledge Discovery and Data Mining, pp. 807–816 (2009)
9. Silva, A., Guimarães, S., Meira Jr., W., Zaki, M.: ProfileRank: finding relevant content and influential users based on information diffusion. In: Proceedings of the 7th Workshop on Social Network Mining and Analysis, pp. 2 (2013)

10. Ding, Z., Jia, Y., Zhou, B., Han, Y.: Mining topical influencers based on the multi-relational network in micro-blogging sites. China Commun. **10**(1), 93–104 (2013)
11. Liu, L., Tang, J., Han, J., Jiang, M., Yang, S.: Mining topic-level influence in heterogeneous networks. In: Proceedings of the 19th ACM International Conference on Information and Knowledge Management, pp. 199–208 (2010)
12. Bi, B., Tian, Y., Sismanis, Y., Balmin, A., Cho, J.: Scalable topic-specific influence analysis on microblogs. In Proceedings of the 7th ACM International Conference on Web Search and Data Mining, pp. 513–522 (2014)
13. Spasojevic, N., Li, Z., Rao, A., Bhattacharyya, P.: When-to-post on social networks. In: Proceedings of the 21st ACM International Conference on Knowledge Discovery and Data Mining, pp. 2127–2136 (2015)
14. McPherson, M., Smith-Lovin, L., Cook, J.: Birds of a feather: homophily in social networks. Ann. Rev. Sociol. **27**(1), 415–444 (2001)
15. Blei, D., Ng, A., Jordan, M.: Latent Dirichlet allocation. J. Mach. Learn. Res. **3**, 993–1022 (2003)
16. Porteous, I., Newman, D., Ihler, A., Asuncion, A., Smyth, P., Welling, M.: Fast collapsed gibbs sampling for latent Dirichlet allocation. In: Proceeding of the 14th ACM International Conference on Knowledge Discovery and Data Mining, pp. 569–577 (2008)
17. HanLP. http://hanlp.linrunsoft.com/. Accessed 28 Dec 2018

Taylor Series Localization Algorithm Based on Semi-definite Programming

Jianfeng Lu$^{(\boxtimes)}$ and Xuanyuan Yang

Institute of Information Technology,
Taizhou Polytechnic College, Taizhou, Jiangsu, China
13801436812@163.com, 1392786661@qq.com

Abstract. In order to improve the positioning accuracy of time difference of arrival, a Taylor series algorithm based on semi-definite programming is proposed in this paper. Firstly, base on the squared distance difference model, a semi-positive programming method is used to obtain the coarse location of the target node. Then, based on the distance difference model, the location of the target node is formulated as a linear least square problem by Taylor series expansion. Finally, the refined location is obtained by iteration. simulation results show that when the target node locates in the inner area surrounded by anchor nodes, the estimated values obtained by Taylor series algorithm are more concentrated and the center is more closer to the actual location of the target node than that obtained by semi-definite programming algorithm, and the superiority of Taylor series algorithm will be more obvious when the target node is far away from the center of the inner area.

Keywords: Positioning · Taylor series · Semi-definite programming · Time difference of arrival · CRLB

1 Introduction

Nowadays, ranging-based wireless positioning plays an increasingly important role in many fields. For example, in navigation, detection, rescue, intelligent transportation, Internet of Things and other systems, it is necessary to use wireless technology to accurately estimate the location of the target node [1].

The existing positioning technologies based on range can be divided into four basic types: Received Signal Strength Indicator (RSSI) [2], Angle of Arrival (AOA) [3], Time of Arrival (TOA) [4] and Time Difference of Arrival (TDOA) [5]. Further, according to the different estimation models, TDOA localization algorithm can be divided into two categories: the first is to minimizing the sum of squared error of the squared range differences (SRD) from the target node to different anchor nodes, in which a linear least square problem is constructed, and it could be resolved by positive semi-definite programming method [6, 7], Lagrange method [8], constrained total least squares localization method [9, 10], etc. This kind of algorithm can obtain the global optimal solution under the general least squares criterion or the local optimal solution under the total least squares criterion, but it is only suitable for the case of small measurement error. The second kind is to minimizing the sum of error of the range differences (RD) from the target

X. Sun et al. (Eds.): ICAIS 2019, LNCS 11635, pp. 488–497, 2019.
https://doi.org/10.1007/978-3-030-24268-8_45

node to different anchor nodes, in which a non-linear square problem is constructed, and it could be resolved by Taylor series method [11], heuristic algorithm [12], traditional optimization algorithm [13, 14], and etc. Although these algorithms could achieve superior location precision, the computation complex is huge for heuristic algorithm, and it is easily felled into non-convergent state when the measurement noise is large.

This paper concentrates on the Taylor series localization algorithm. For this kind of algorithm, it is important to select an initial coordinate point which directly affects the performance of the algorithm. Considering that semi-definite programming (SDP) can obtain the optimal solution under the SDR model, we propose a Taylor series localization algorithm (Taylor) based on semi-definite programming. Firstly, coarse location of the target is acquired using SDP based on the SRD model, then the location of the target is formulated as a linear least square problem using the Taylor series expansion based on the RD model, and finally iterative process is utilized to get the refined location. The simulation results show that when the node locates inside the area surrounded by the anchors, the estimated coordinates obtained by Taylor algorithm are more centralized than those obtained by semi-definite programming, and the center point is closer to the actual location of the target node; and when the target node is far away from the center of the area, the performance superiority of Taylor series algorithm will be more obvious.

2 Problem Statements

For the sake of simplicity, we only take the two-dimensional coordinate system into consideration; it should be noted that the algorithm is also applicable to the three-dimensional coordinate system. Suppose that in the two-dimensional coordinate system, there are N anchor nodes not on the same line with coordinates (x_i, y_i), and a reference anchor 0 at the origin. We also assume that there is a target node with unknown coordinates (x, y).

The true distance difference between the target node arriving at the anchor node i and the reference anchor node is:

$$g_{i0}(x, y) = \sqrt{(x - x_i)^2 + (y - y_i)^2} - \sqrt{x^2 + y^2} \tag{1}$$

However, the actual value is difficult to obtain. But fortunately, we could acquire the measurement distance d_{i0}:

$$d_{i0} = g_{i0}(x, y) + n_{i0}, \quad i = 1, \cdots, N \tag{2}$$

where n_{i0} is the measurement error. Our task is to estimate the location of the target node based on the measurement value.

After we replace the g_{i0} in (1) by d_{i0}, move $\sqrt{x^2 + y^2}$ to the left side of equation, square the two sides and arrange them, the following results can be obtained:

$$A_2 \theta = b_2 \tag{3}$$

$$\text{where } A_2 = \begin{bmatrix} x_1 & y_1 & d_{10} \\ x_2 & y_2 & d_{20} \\ \vdots & \vdots & \vdots \\ x_N & y_N & d_{N0} \end{bmatrix}, \quad \theta = \begin{bmatrix} x \\ y \\ d_0 \end{bmatrix} \text{ and } b_2 = \frac{1}{2} \begin{bmatrix} x_1^2 + y_1^2 - d_{10}^2 \\ x_2^2 + y_2^2 - d_{20}^2 \\ \vdots \\ x_N^2 + y_N^2 - d_{N0}^2 \end{bmatrix}. \quad d_0 \text{ is the}$$

distance between the target node and the reference anchor. Because of the square operation, (3) essentially estimates the location based on the square difference of the distance between the target node and the different anchor nodes.

Based on the principle of minimizing the sum of squares of measurement errors, according to (2), the estimated value of the location $(\hat{x}, \hat{y})$ of the target node can be expressed as a minimization problem shown in (4):

$$(\hat{x}, \hat{y}) = \min_{(x,y)} \sum_{i=1}^{N} (g_{i0} - d_{i0})^2 \qquad (4)$$

$$= \min_{(x,y)} \left\| \begin{matrix} d_{10} - \sqrt{(x - x_1)^2 + (y - y_1)^2} + \sqrt{x^2 + y^2} \\ d_{20} - \sqrt{(x - x_2)^2 + (y - y_2)^2} + \sqrt{x^2 + y^2} \\ \vdots \\ d_{N0} - \sqrt{(x - x_N)^2 + (y - y_N)^2} + \sqrt{x^2 + y^2} \end{matrix} \right\|_2^2 \qquad (5)$$

where $\|\cdot\|_2$ represents the 2-norm of the vector.

3   Localization Algorithm

(4) is a non-linear optimization problem. However, Taylor series decomposition can make linear approximation possible, and the semi-positive definite algorithm can obtain the global optimal solution of (3). Therefore, we propose a Taylor series localization algorithm based on semi-positive definite programming, which includes two aspects: one is the linear approximation of the original problem using Taylor series, and the other is the selection of an initial coordinate so as to search the optimal solution.

3.1   Taylor Series Linear Approximation

Let (x_0^o, y_0^o) be an initial point, then the first order Taylor series expansion expression is:

$$g_{i0}(x, y) \approx g_{i0}(x_0^o, y_0^o) + a_i(x - x_0^o) + b_i(y - y_0^o) \qquad (6)$$

where $a_i = \frac{\partial g_{i0}(x,y)}{\partial x}\big|_{x=x_0^o}$ and $b_i = \frac{\partial g_{i0}(x,y)}{\partial y}\big|_{y=y_0^o}$. Although Taylor series expansion is not related to the (x_0^o, y_0^o), (6) ignores the higher order terms, so only when (x, y) is close to (x_0^o, y_0^o), can a better approximation be achieved.

Let $\Delta x = (x - x_0^o)$ and $\Delta y = (y - y_0^o)$, substituting (6) into (5), we obtain:

$$(\hat{x}, y) \approx \min_{(x,y)} \left\| \begin{array}{c} d_{10} - g_{10}(x_0^o, y_0^o) - a_1\Delta x - b_1\Delta y \\ d_{20} - g_{20}(x_0^o, y_0^o) - a_2\Delta x - b_2\Delta y \\ \vdots \\ d_{N0} - g_{N0}(x_0^o, y_0^o) - a_N\Delta x - b_N\Delta y \end{array} \right\|_2^2 \tag{7}$$

(7) is equivalent to solving the optimal solution of a linear Eq. (8) under the ULS criterion:

$$A_1 X = b_1 \tag{8}$$

where $A_1 = \begin{bmatrix} a_1 & b_1 \\ a_2 & b_2 \\ \vdots & \vdots \\ a_N & b_N \end{bmatrix}$, $X = \begin{bmatrix} \Delta x \\ \Delta y \end{bmatrix}$ and $b_1 = \begin{bmatrix} d_{10} - g_{10}(x_0^o, y_0^o) \\ d_{20} - g_{20}(x_0^o, y_0^o) \\ \vdots \\ d_{N0} - g_{N0}(x_0^o, y_0^o) \end{bmatrix}$. When the

measured noises n_i are independent and the same distribution, the optimal solution is $(A_1^T A_1)^{-1} A_1^T b$.

3.2   Initial Coordinate Selection of the Target Node

It can be seen from (6) that Taylor series method needs an initial point. The closer the initial point is to the optimal solution of (5), the better the positioning accuracy of this algorithm can be improved. Since the semi-definite programming algorithm [6] can obtain the global optimal solution based on the ULS criterion, we apply it to the acquisition of initial coordinate.

Based on the criterion of minimizing the sum of squares of errors, the optimal solution of (3) can be expressed as:

$$(x, y) = \arg\min_{\theta} \left((A_2\theta - b_2)^T (A_2\theta - b_2) \right) \tag{9}$$

where $d_0^2 = x^2 + y^2$ if the reference node locates at the origin point of the coordinate systems. We now rearrange (9) and can get:

$$(x, y) = \arg\min_{X,x} \left(Tr(A_2^T A_2 X) - 2b_2^T A_2 X + b_2^T b_2 \right)$$

$$s.t. \begin{cases} d_0^2 = x^2 + y^2 \\ \begin{bmatrix} X & x \\ x & 1 \end{bmatrix} \geq 0 \\ X = \theta\theta^T \\ \mathrm{rank}\left(\begin{bmatrix} X & x \\ x & 1 \end{bmatrix} \right) = 1 \end{cases} \tag{10}$$

where $Tr(\bullet)$ represent the trace, and $rank(\bullet)$ is the rank of matrix. Obviously, (10) is equivalent to (9) and is a non-convex optimization problem because the constraint $rank\left(\begin{bmatrix} X & x \\ x & 1 \end{bmatrix}\right) = 1$ is non-convex. So we ignore the constraint $rank\left(\begin{bmatrix} X & x \\ x & 1 \end{bmatrix}\right) = 1$ and get:

$$(x, y) = \arg \min_{X, x} \left(Tr(A_2^T A_2 X) - 2b_2^T A_2 X + b_2^T b_2\right)$$

$$s.t. \quad \begin{cases} d_0^2 = x^2 + y^2 \\ \begin{bmatrix} X & x \\ x & 1 \end{bmatrix} \geq 0 \\ X = \theta \theta^T \end{cases} \tag{11}$$

Obviously, (11) is a semi-definite convex programming problem, and the global optimal solution could be obtained by the interior point method.

3.3 Localization Algorithm Based on SDP

The general principle of Taylor series localization algorithm and the process of semi-positive definite programming are introduced. And now, we give the complete process of Taylor series (Taylor) localization method based on the SDP algorithm:

Step 1: the initial location $\begin{bmatrix} x_0^o \\ y_0^o \end{bmatrix}$ of the target node is obtained by solving (11).

Step 2: using (8), we obtain $\begin{bmatrix} \Delta x \\ \Delta y \end{bmatrix}$, and then let $\begin{bmatrix} x_0^n \\ x_0^n \end{bmatrix} = \begin{bmatrix} x_0^o \\ y_0^o \end{bmatrix} + \begin{bmatrix} \Delta x \\ \Delta y \end{bmatrix}$;

Step 3: if $\sqrt{\Delta x^2 + \Delta y^2} \geq \varepsilon$, then replacing $\begin{bmatrix} x_0^o \\ y_0^o \end{bmatrix}$ by $\begin{bmatrix} x_0^n \\ x_0^n \end{bmatrix}$ and go to Step 2;

otherwise taking the $\begin{bmatrix} x_0^n \\ x_0^n \end{bmatrix}$ as the final coordinates of the target node, where ε is a small preset value.

3.4 CRLB

CRLB is the abbreviation of Cramer Rao Lower Bound. It is the theoretical limit of the minimum variance that all unbiased estimators can achieve. That is, there is no unbiased estimator with its minimum variance smaller than CRLB. For many reasons, some problems are difficult or even impossible to obtain its unbiased estimator arriving at CRLB. If we find that the effect of an estimator is better than that of CRLB, then the estimator must be biased, but this does not mean that the all the biased estimator can reach the CRLB bound. It has been proved that there is no unbiased estimator which can reach the lower bound of CRLB in the TDOA model itself [15].

The CRLB is related to the Fisher Matrix, and when the measurement error follows Gaussian distribution, the Fisher Matrix F is [16]:

$$F = F_M^T F_M \qquad (12)$$

where

$$F_M = \begin{bmatrix} \frac{x}{\sqrt{(x-a_2)^2+(y-b_2)^2}} + \frac{y}{\sqrt{(x-a_2)^2+(y-b_2)^2}} & \frac{x}{\sqrt{(x-a_1)^2+(y-b_1)^2}} + \frac{y}{\sqrt{(x-a_1)^2+(y-b_1)^2}} \\ \frac{x}{\sqrt{(x-a_3)^2+(y-b_3)^2}} + \frac{y}{\sqrt{(x-a_3)^2+(y-b_3)^2}} & \frac{x}{\sqrt{(x-a_1)^2+(y-b_1)^2}} + \frac{y}{\sqrt{(x-a_1)^2+(y-b_1)^2}} \\ \vdots & \vdots \\ \frac{x}{\sqrt{(x-a_2)^2+(y-b_N)^2}} + \frac{y}{\sqrt{(x-a_2)^2+(y-b_N)^2}} & \frac{x}{\sqrt{(x-a_1)^2+(y-b_1)^2}} + \frac{y}{\sqrt{(x-a_1)^2+(y-b_1)^2}} \end{bmatrix}$$

In this paper, we compare our algorithm with CRLB. The purpose is to show the performance of the algorithm from a more perspective. We can see from the simulation results that the performance of the SDP and Taylor algorithms are better than CRLB, which means that the estimators of the two algorithms are both biased.

4 Simulations

The simulation environment is MATLAB 7.0. The simulation circumstance is shown in Fig. 1, and the parameters are as follows: in a two-dimensional coordinates system, there are eight anchor nodes with coordinates (0, 0) m, (0, 20) m, (0, 40) m, (20, 40) m, (40, 40) m, (40, 20) m, (40, 0) m, (20, 0) m. They form a square area, in which the anchor with coordinates of (0, 0) m is the reference node; the measurement noise of TDOA follows gauss distribution with the mean value 0 and the variance δ^2. We evaluate the performance of the algorithm from two perspectives: deviation and

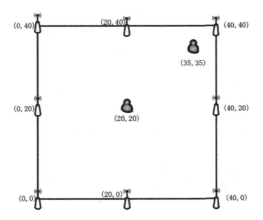

Fig. 1. Simulation Circumstance with 8 Anchor Nodes and One Target Node with coordinates (20, 20) m or (35, 35) m

variance. The deviation is the root of the sum of the squared errors between the estimated coordinate and the actual coordinate, and the variance is the root of the sum of
squared errors between the coordinate estimation value and the average value. We
compare our algorithm with the SDP and the CRLB.

Figures 2 and 3 show the positioning deviation and variance under different
measurement noises when the coordinates of the target node are (20, 20) m, where the
target node is located in the center of the area surrounded by anchors. From the two
figures, we can see that the performance of Taylor series algorithm is better than that of
semi-definite programming algorithm both in deviation and variance. This shows that
the coordinate estimated by Taylor series algorithm are more centralized, and the center
of Taylor series algorithm is closer to the actual location of the target node.

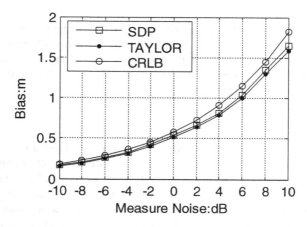

Fig. 2. The location of the Bias under Different Measure Noise with Target coordinates (20, 20) m

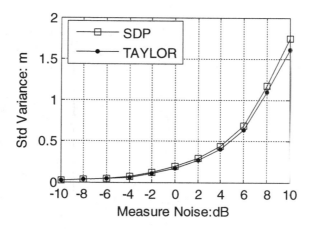

Fig. 3. The location of the Variance under Different Measure Noise with Target coordinates
(20, 20) m

Figures 4 and 5 show the location deviation and variance under different measurement noises when the coordinates of the target node are (35, 35) m, where the target node is located in the boundary area. From the two figures, we can see that the performance of Taylor series algorithm is also better than that of semi- definite programming algorithm both in deviation and variance. This shows that the coordinate positions estimated by Taylor series algorithm are more centralized, and the center of Taylor series algorithm is closer to the actual location of the target node.

In addition, by comparing Fig. 4 with Fig. 2 and Fig. 5 with Fig. 3, we can find that as the target node leaves the center of the area, the performance of Taylor series algorithm will gradually becomes more superior.

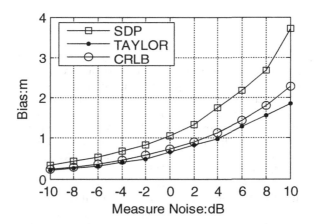

Fig. 4. The Location of the Bias under Different Measure Noise with Target coordinates (35, 35) m

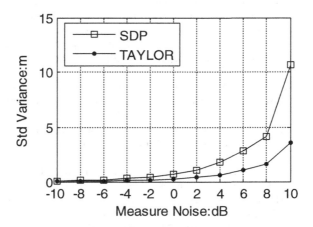

Fig. 5. The location of the Standard Variance under Different Measure Noise with Target coordinates (35, 35) m

5 Conclusions

This paper combines Taylor series method with semi-definite programming, and proposes a Taylor series location algorithm based on semi-definite programming. The algorithm uses the SDP to obtain the course estimate of the coordinate of the target, and takes the value as an initial point of Taylor series expansion. The simulation results show that when the node locates inside the area surrounded by anchors, the estimated values obtained by Taylor series algorithm are more centralized and the center point is closer to the actual location of the target than those obtained by SDP, and as the target node is far away from the center, the performance of Taylor series algorithm will gradually becomes more superior.

References

1. Zhou, T.Y., Lian, B.W., Yang, S.Q., et al.: Improved GNSS cooperation positioning algorithm for indoor localization. Comput. Mater. Continua **56**(2), 225–245 (2018)
2. Wang, Z., Zhang, H., Lu, T., et al.: A grid based localization algorithm for wireless sensor networks using connectivity and RSS rank. IEEE Access **6**(2), 8426–8439 (2018)
3. Zheng, Y., Sheng, M., Liu, J.Y., et al.: Exploiting AoA estimation accuracy for indoor localization: a weighted AoA-based approach. IEEE Wirel. Commun. Lett. **8**, 65–68 (2018)
4. Takayuki, A., Masanori, S., Hiromichi, H.: Time of arrival based smartphone localization using visible light communication. In: 2017 International Conference on Indoor Positioning and Indoor Navigation (IPIN), pp. 1–7 (2017)
5. Vahid, H., Mohsen, A., Khosrow, S., et al.: Exact solutions of time difference of arrival source localisation based on semi-definite programming and lagrange multiplier: complexity and performance analysis. IET Sig. Process. **8**(8), 868–877 (2014)
6. Xu, E.Y., Ding, Z., Dasgupta, S.: Reduced complexity semidefinite relaxation algorithm for source localization based on time difference of arrival. IEEE Trans. Mob. Comput. **10**(9), 1276–1282 (2011)
7. Zou, Y.B., Wan, Q., Liu, H.P.: Semidefinite programming for TDOA localization with locally synchronized anchor nodes. In: 2018 IEEE International Conference on Acoustics, Speech and Signal Processing (ICASSP), pp. 3254–3258 (2018)
8. Huang, Y.T., Benesty, J., Gary, W.E., et al.: Real-time passive source localization: a practical linear correction least squares approach. IEEE Trans. Speech Audio Process. **9**(8), 943–956 (2001)
9. Zhao, Y.S., Zhao, Y.J., Sun D.H., et al.: Constrained total least squares localization algorithm for multistatic passive radar using bistatic range measurements. In: 2018 19th International Radar Symposium (IRS), pp. 1–8 (2018)
10. Yang, K., An, J.P., Bu, X.Y., et al.: Constrained total least squares location algorithm using time difference of arrival measurements. IEEE Trans. Veh. Technol. **59**(3), 1558–1562 (2010)
11. Wu, H., Su, W.M., Hong, G.: A novel Taylor series method for source and receiver localization using TDOA and FDOA measurements with uncertain receiver positions. IN: Proceedings of 2011 IEEE CIE International Conference on Radar, pp. 24–27 (2011)
12. Jiang, Y.L., Liu, M.N., Chen, T., et al.: TDOA passive location based on Cuckoo search algorithm. J. Shanghai Jiao Tong Univ. **23**(3), 368–375 (2018)

13. Xie, S.D., Hu, A.Q., Huang, Y.: Nonlinear least square localization algorithm based on time difference of arrival. Appl. Mech. Mater. **411–414**, 903–906 (2013)
14. Zhou, Y.J., Kou, X.J., Zhu, J.J., et al.: A Newton algorithm for weighted total least squares solution to a specific error in variable model with correlated measurements. Stud. Geophys. Geod. **58**(3), 349–375 (2014)
15. Anders, H.M.: On the existence of efficient estimators. IEEE Trans. Sig. Process. **48**(11), 3028–3031 (2000)
16. Zhang, M., Xie, S., Liu, Q., et al.: Research on the least square source localization algorithm. J. Comput. Inf. Syst. **8**(1), 1–8 (2012)

Research on Pedestrian Attribute Recognition Based on Semantic Segmentation in Natural Scene

Xin Feng[1], Yangyang Li[2], Haomin Du[1], and Hongbo Wang[1(✉)]

[1] State Key Laboratory of Networking and Switching Technology,
Beijing University of Posts and Telecommunications, Beijing 100876, China
xfeng@bupt.com, {duhaomin, hbwang}@bupt.edu.cn
[2] National Engineering Laboratory for Public Safety
Risk Perception and Control, CAEIT, Beijing 100041, China
liyangyang@cetc.com.cn

Abstract. Smart city is a new term given to society by technology, and cameras are important infrastructure for building a smart city. How to use camera information efficiently and effectively plays an important role in people's daily life and maintain social order. Pedestrian information accounts for a large proportion of camera information, so we hope to make good use of pedestrian information. Previous works use traditional machine learning methods and neural network to identify pedestrian attributes, mainly judge the existence of pedestrian attributes in natural scenes. However, it's not enough to judge whether an attribute exist or not, getting the position of an attribute often gives you more information. In this paper, we propose to use semantic segmentation to obtain the position information of pedestrian attributes. We first propose pedestrian attribute semantic dataset in natural scene called PASD (Pedestrian attribute semantic dataset), which select 27 visualized pedestrian attributes. Deeplabv3+ is used to perform experiments on PASD, which obtain the mIoU (mean intersection over union) baseline of 27 pedestrian attributes. For getting useful conclusion, we conduct data analysis about mIoU from three aspects: attribute distribution, accuracy and resolution.

Keywords: Pedestrian attribute · Location information ·
Semantic segmentation

1 Introduction

With the development of artificial intelligence like image classification [18] and internet of things technology, Smart cities have been well developed. Urban cameras have become more and more popular, and the analysis of camera information is significant to public safety. Pedestrian attribute is an important information type in camera information and can be applied to pedestrian search [1], pedestrian recognition [2, 3], and pedestrian re-recognition [4].

Hence, pedestrian attribute recognition has important practical significance. Previous work used traditional machine learning methods and neural network to identify

© Springer Nature Switzerland AG 2019
X. Sun et al. (Eds.): ICAIS 2019, LNCS 11635, pp. 498–509, 2019.
https://doi.org/10.1007/978-3-030-24268-8_46

pedestrian attributes, mainly judge the existence of pedestrian attributes in natural scenes.

However, it's not enough to judge whether an attribute exist or not, getting the position of an attribute often gives you more information. For example, the position information of pedestrian helps to improve the ability of pedestrian re-recognition. As we know, human view the position of attributes as supplementary information to judge whether two pedestrians are same person, as shown in Fig. 1. We can conduct pedestrian re-recognition by using hair, tops and pant in different position. So, when machine get this information, it will improve the pedestrian re-recognize task. On the other hand, if obtaining the location of attributes, we can do further research for some attributes with known location information, like analyzing the brand of bag, the size of shoes and so on.

Fig. 1. Re-identification of attributes by attribute location information (Color figure online)

There is a challenge in getting pedestrian attribute position: The diversity of pedestrian postures leads to the diversity of pedestrian attributes. For example, the regional information of pedestrian clothes may change with the pedestrian's swing. Therefore, if you obtain the position information of the pedestrian attribute, you need to consider how to express the pedestrian attribute location information. First, we con-sidered the general target detection algorithm, mainly researching an improved method based Faster R-CNN [6] and YOLO (You only look once). During the investigation, it was found that the general target detection algorithm detects the object by marking the object in the form of a rectangular frame, which will cause a lot of repetitive areas and can't represent the location information of attributes accurately. To solve upon prob-lem, we turn our attention to semantic segmentation.

Semantic segmentation is a pixel-level image classification method. By classifying each pixel of a picture, the position information of each category in the picture can be obtained. Taking Fig. 1 as an example, the pixels belonging to the hair should be classified into hair and signed with blue, the pixels belonging to the pants will be signed with bright green to represent pants. Different classifications are signed with different colors. At the moment, we can see that no matter how the pedestrian attribute changes, semantic segmentation can clearly distinguish the outline of the attribute.

This paper proposes to use the method of semantic segmentation to obtain the pedestrian attributes and their position information in natural scenes. We will verify its feasibility, explore the problems and valuable rules that need to be paid attention to when use this method. In this paper, mIoU (mean intersection over union) is used to measure the performance of semantic segmentation model.

The main contributes of this paper is: (1) we proposed the first pedestrian attribute semantic dataset in natural scene called PASD (Pedestrian Attribute Semantic Dataset). (2) We use semantic segmentation framework deeplabv3+ to conduct experiment and get the mIoU reference value of pedestrian attributes, which can provide reference for the work afterwards. (3) In this paper, mIoU is analyzed from three aspects: accuracy, percentage of PASD pedestrian attribute categories, and resolution of the image. The factors influencing mIoU of pedestrian attributes are summarized.

2   Related Work

2.1   The Research of Pedestrian Attribute Recognition

With the development of neural network, the neural network method achieves higher accuracy in pedestrian attribute recognition than traditional machine learning. There are three research directions based on neural network research: the first research direction is based on traditional neural networks. Mainly through the neural network itself to identify attribute features. DeepSAR and DeepMAR [7] can make better use of the correlation between various attributes; the second research direction is to transform attribute gender into serialization model. Neural PAR [8] transforms attribute recognition problem into attribute generation problem, and uses LSTM for attribute recognition. The model of JRL [15] based on the RNN network model explicitly explores a sequential prediction constraint; the third research direction is to apply the attention mechanism to attribute recognition. Sarafianos [16] and HydraPlus-Net [17] both use the multi-level features to better identify pedestrian attributes.

2.2   Semantic Segmentation

Semantic segmentation is the pixel-level classification of images. By classifying each pixel of an image, the position information of each category in the picture can be obtained. With the success of convolution network, the convolution network is quickly applied to semantic segmentation.

Recently, the encoder-decoder network structure is very common in semantic segmentation. The encoder-decoder consists of two parts: (1) the spatial dimension of the feature map will gradually decrease in the encoder part, while the longer range information is easier to capture. (2) The decoder part will gradually restore the object details and spatial dimensions. For example, SegNet [13] uses encoder's pooling indices to learn additional convolutional layers. U-Net [14] added a skip connection between the encoder and the corresponding layer of decoder. Deeplab [9, 10] use Atrous convolution, proposing Atrous Spatial Pyramid Pooling and combining with the latest network structure, which further improved the accuracy of semantic segmentation.

In the use of semantic segmentation for attribute recognition, Kalayeh et al. [11] proposed an encoder-decoder based SSP and SSG structure to achieve recognition of face attributes. This paper focuses on the semantic segmentation of pedestrian attributes in natural scenes. Compared with face attribute segmentation, pedestrian attribute categories have more complexity and therefore have greater challenges.

3   Method

3.1   The Choice of Semantic Segmentation Framework

When judge to select a semantic segmentation model, we mainly consider two factors: accuracy and efficiency. In terms of accuracy, this paper uses the mIoU of each model in the PASCAL VOC2012 test set as the benchmark. Deeplabv3+ [10] get the best mIoU with 87.8.

In terms of model efficiency, many semantic segmentation models do not study the efficiency problem. The author mainly considers the use of deep separable convolution. The depth separable convolution can reduce the number of convolution parameters while maintaining the effect of extracting features. All convolutions in the Xception model used by deeplabv3+ use deep separable convolution, which greatly reduces the size of the model and greatly increases the computational efficiency of the model.

Based on the above factors, we use deeplabv3+ as a basic model to analyze pedestrian attributes. This model combines the advantages of deeplabv3 and encoder-decoder.

3.2   The Introduction of Deeplab Structure

Deeplabv3 contains key structures with Atrous convolution and ASPP (Atrous Spatial Pyramid Pooling). Deeplabv3+ adds Xception [12] to the basic model, which greatly improves the training efficiency.

Atrous Convolution. Atrous convolution is an improvement to ordinary convolution. For an input of 9 * 9, if use ordinary convolution, you will lose a lot of spatial information. Atrous convolution preserves the spatial information of the image without adding parameters by inserting zero into the convolution kernel. Atrous convolution can predict any precision in the final convolution layer, which can more easily control the size of input and output in the convolution network then ordinary convolution.

Consider a two-dimensional case, assuming that the input size is m * m, the size of convolution kernel is k, and the step size is s. A new parameter r has been introduced in Atrous convolutions, assume that the output size is n * n. There are following formulas:

$$n = (m + (k - 1)(r - 1) - k)/(2 * s) \tag{1}$$

ASPP. In semantic segmentation, the size of each category is different. In order to solve this problem, deeplab draws on the success of spatial pyramiding in the visual field, using Atrous Spatial Pyramid Pooling. The special of ASPP is to use multiple Atrous convolutions with different rates in parallel and concat the results of each branch to get the final result. Atrous Spatial Pyramid Pooling is shown in Fig. 2.

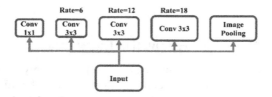

Fig. 2. The structure of Atrous Spatial Pyramid Pooling

In addition, deeplabv3+ adds an image-level feature. Image pooling construct of three part: First, a global average pooling operation is performed on the input of the final feature matrix, and then the result of pooling passes a 1 * 1 convolution with 256 channels followed by a batch normalization. Finally, the feature is restored to the desired size by bilinear upsampling.

Depthwise Separable Convolution. Depthwise separable convolution separate original convolution into depthwise convolution and pointwise convolution. The structure of depthwise separable convolution is shown as Fig. 3. Deeplabv3+ also uses depthwise separable convolution in Atrous Spatial Pyramid Pooling, which gain better computation efficiency with guaranteed accuracy.

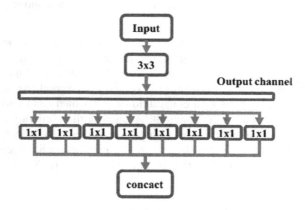

Fig. 3. Depthwise separable convolution

Xecption. The original Xception uses 36 convolution layers. This network is divided into three parts: entry flow, middle flow and exit flow. Deeplabv3− use an improved version of Xception and made the following three changes: (1) Deeper Xception same as in [12] except do not modify the entry flow network structure for fast computation and memory efficiency. (2) All max pooling operations are replaced by depthwise separable convolution with striding, which enables network to extract feature maps at an arbitrary resolution. (3) Adding ReLU and batch normalization after each 3 * 3 depthwise convolution.

Encoder-Decoder. Deeplabv3+ uses deeplabv3 as encoder. Deeplabv3 uses Atrous convolution to extract feature maps at an arbitrary resolution. There introduces a new parameter output stride to represent the ratio of the input picture size to the output size. For example, the final feature map is usually 1/32 of the input and the value of output stride is 32. In semantic segmentation, output stride is often set as 16 or 8. Deeplabv3+ uses an improved Atrous Spatial Pyramid Pooling, which add an image level feature (implemented by an avgpool) and concat with Atrous convolution with different rates. This concentrated value is as the output of encoder.

In the part of decoder, deeplabv3+ proposes a decoder structure suitable for semantic segmentation. First, the output of encoder is upsampled with factor of 4, then it is merged with the low-level features in the encoder containing the same space size and use 1 × 1 convolution to reduce the number of channel which make training easily as the low-level feature of encoder always contains a lot of channels.

Loss function. Deeplabv3+ use cross-entropy softmax as loss function. Deeplabv3+ model used by our experiment is shown as Fig. 4.

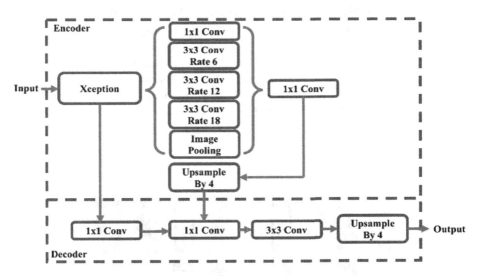

Fig. 4. The structure of deeplabv3+

4   Dataset

So far, there is no available dataset for semantic annotation of pedestrian attributes in natural scenes for experimental. Therefore, we created the first pedestrian attribute dataset with semantic annotations in natural scenes called PASD (Pedestrian attribute semantic dataset). First of all, we select 1461 pedestrian images from the PETA [5] for semantic annotation. PETA is a dataset in the field of pedestrian recognition in natural scenes accepted by academy. It contains 19000 images with 35 pedestrian attribute categories. In selecting image, we consider the following factors: (1) Image resolution, we select semantically segmented images based on human recognition and ignore images that are not recognized by human. (2) The balance of categories. For some categories have few number (such as stripe, grid), we try to maintain the balance of this categories.

In order to analyze the effect of resolution on pedestrian attribute recognition using semantic segmentation. In addition to selecting images from PETA, we also selected 250 pedestrian images taken by city surveillance cameras in real life scenarios. The resolution of these images are higher than those in PETA.

For classification selection, we first refer to the pedestrian attribute selection method of the PETA. PETA divides the pedestrian attributes into 35 categories which are based on attributes that is selected by anthropologists to represent human characteristics, and the attribute categories of the dataset itself. We consider the distribution of attributes in the training set, and certain attributes (such as age, gender, etc.) cannot be separated and visualized by semantic segmentation. Finally, the author selects 27 pedestrian attributes. The attribute values are shown in Table 1.

Table 1. The pedestrian attributes we finally selected

Sunglasses	Jeans	Sneaker	Leather shoes
Shorts	Stripes	Logo	Trousers
ShortSleeve	Tshirt	Skirt	Backpack
Hat	Casual upper	Hair	Sandals
Plaid	Suitcase	Bag	Muffler
Formal upper	Long hair	Shoes	Jacket
Plastic bag	CarryingOther	V-Neck	

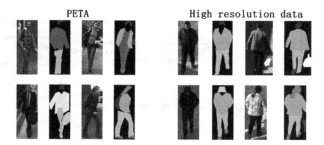

Fig. 5. Some images in our dataset, which is consist of parts of PETA and some high resolution images.

PASD consist of 1,711 semantic segmentation annotations, of which there are 1461 PETA datasets and 250 datasets of our own. Some images in PASD are shown in Fig. 5.

5 Experiment

5.1 Experiment Setup

For the input data, no additional operation is performed on the picture except resize the picture to 513. The initial weight, we set the basic learning rate to 0.001, and the learning rate is reduced using poly strategy. We use momentum and set the number of iterations to 900000. The batch norm layer is not trained. The value of output stride that we train and test is set to 8. The corresponding ASPP parameters are set to 6, 12 and 18 respectively. To prevent overfitting, the dropout's keep value is set to 0.3. At the same time, we adopt the early stop strategy. GPU is 1080ti.

5.2 Experiment Results

We randomly selected 1273 images as training data. The test data selected 288 images containing 188 low resolution images and 100 high resolution images. The mIoU of 288 test set images is shown in Table 2.

Table 2. mIoU of 288 test set images

Attribute	mIoU	Attribute	mIoU
Sunglasses	0	Jeans	0.378738642
Sneaker	0.354543	Leather shoes	0.184471875
Formal upper	0.603124	Shorts	0.346722752
Stripes	0.519705	Logo	0
Trousers	0.832277	Long hair	0.6549505
ShortSleeve	0.473253	Tshirt	0.26975289
Skirt	0.563472	Backpack	0.233864143
Shoes	0.390536	Hat	0.229438677
Casual upper	0.444053	Hair	0.66051203
Sandals	0.196731	Jacket	0.731595635
Plaid	0.458361	Suitcase	0.731545508
Bag	0.416399	Muffler	0.159364507
Plastic bag	0.350488	CarryingOther	0.142766684
V-Neck	0.022614		
Average	0.31996		

6 Data Analysis

It can be seen that the overall mIoU is still relatively low, and there is a severe overfitting in the training phase. We analyzed the mIoU value from the following three aspects.

6.1 The Relationship Between mIoU and Each Category Ratios

Firstly, we give a line chart of the relationship between mIoU and category ratios, as shown in Fig. 6.

It can be seen that when the number of samples is small, the change trend of mIoU and category ratios is same basically. After analyzing the pictures and the Table 2, the following factors affect the category mIoU: (1) A relatively high mIoU can be obtained if the category profile is fixed or has unique visualization features. Such as Suitcase, strips, Jacket. Conversely, a relatively low mIoU is obtained for categories with more category diversity. Such as shoes, which has variability and uncertainty in the natural scene, that is, the human eye can't tell which kind of shoes it is. (2) Image resolution, such as sunglasses, most of the sunglasses in the data set are difficult to identify clearly. (3) The proportion of categories still plays a key role. We have calculated the correlation coefficient between the proportion of mIoU and category ratios is 0.492077145, so the proportion of mIoU and category ratios is still positively correlated.

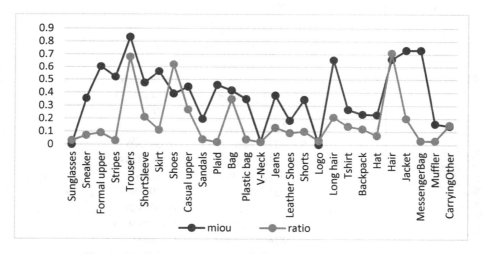

Fig. 6. The relationship between mIoU and each category ratios

6.2 The Relationship Between mIoU and Accuracy

In addition to mIoU, we also output 27 types of prediction accuracy. The method for calculating the accuracy here is that if the number of accumulated pixels of a certain category in the image is greater than 10, this image is considered to contain the category. The calculated accuracy of the 288 test set images is shown in Table 3.

We see that the accuracy rate of only one of the Trousers exceeded the result in [8]. In order to analyze the reasons, we plotted the relationship between mIoU and accuracy, as shown in the Fig. 7.

Table 3. The accuracy of pedestrian attributes

Attribute	mIoU	Attribute	mIoU
Sunglasses	0	Jeans	0.457143
Sneaker	0.770992	Leather Shoes	0.346154
Formal upper	0.692308	Shorts	0.636364
Stripes	0.535714	Logo	0
Trousers	0.985294	Long hair	0.803571
ShortSleeve	0.728571	Tshirt	0.512821
Skirt	0.833333	Backpack	0.527778
Shoes	0.666667	Hat	0.56
Casual upper	0.692308	Hair	0.936893
Sandals	0.538462	Jacket	0.875
Plaid	0.384615	Suitcase	0.461538
Bag	0.747573	Muffler	0.4
Plastic bag	0.636364	CarryingOther	0.537037
V-Neck	0.2		

We calculated the correlation coefficient between mIoU and accuracy to be 0.78534118, which obtain a positive correlation between mIoU and accuracy. That is, mIoU directly affects accuracy, so you can improve accuracy by raising mIoU.

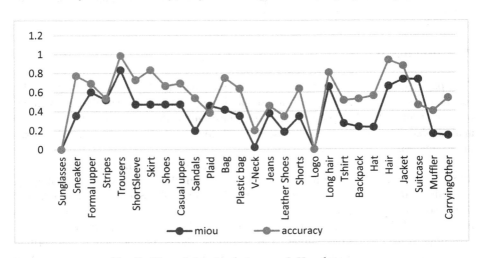

Fig. 7. The relationship between mIoU and accuracy

6.3 The Relationship Between mIoU and Resolution

Finally, in order to test the effect of different resolution on mIoU. We selected 100 high resolution images from the surveillance screen for testing. Note that the selected high resolution dataset contains only 12 categories. We draw low resolution images and high resolution images mIoU relationship table, as shown in the Fig. 8.

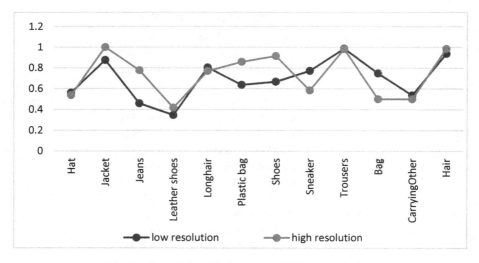

Fig. 8. The relationship between mIoU and resolution

As you can see, the high resolution mIoU is generally higher than the low resolution mIoU. For Longhair and Sneaker, there are special circumstances. We analyzed that class diversity leads to poorly recognized issues that make Long hair recognized as a hair and Sneaker recognized as shoes.

7   Conclusion

This paper focus on obtaining the location information of pedestrian attributes by semantic segmentation. We prove that semantic segmentation is feasible for obtaining pedestrian attributes. We propose the first pedestrian attribute semantic dataset PASD and use deeplabv3+ to get mIoU baseline with low resolution images and high resolution images.

In addition, we analyzed the experimental data and draw some conclusion. Firstly, mIoU is proportional to the number of samples when there are few data samples. In particular, attributes with variability are not well divided. The Second is the problem of data resolution: as the society develops, the resolution of the camera will continue to increase, and the low resolution images in the PETA are not applicable in reality. Therefore, some images of relatively high resolution should be obtained. It was verified in experiments that semantic segmentation yields better results on high resolution images.

Acknowledgement. This work was supported by CETC Joint Research Program under Grant 6141B08020101, 6141B0801010a, and the National Natural Science Foundation of China under Grant 61002011.

References

1. Sami, J.E., Nixon, M.: Analysing soft clothing biometrics for retrieval. In: International Workshop on Biometric Authentication, pp. 234–245 (2014)
2. Martinson, E., Lawson, W., Trafton, J.G.: Identifying people with soft-biometrics at fleet week. In: IEEE International Conference on Human-Robot Interaction, pp. 49–56 (2013)
3. Reid, D., Nixon, M., Stevenage, S.: Soft biometrics: human identification using comparative descriptions. IEEE Trans. Pattern Anal. Mach. Intell. **36**(6), 1216–1228 (2014)
4. Li, A., Liu, L., Wang, K., Liu, S., Yan, S.: Clothing attributes assisted person re-identification. TCSVT **25**, 869–878 (2015)
5. Deng, Y., Luo, P., Loy, C.: Learning to recognize pedestrian attribute. arXiv preprint arXiv: 1501.00901 (2015)
6. Meng, R., Rice, S.G., Wang, J., Sun, X.: A fusion steganographic algorithm based on faster R-CNN. CMC: Comput. Mater. Continua **55**(1), 001–016 (2018)
7. Li, D., Chen, X., Huang, K.: Multi-attribute learning for pedestrian attribute recognition in surveillance scenarios. In: IEEE Asian Conference on Pattern Recognition, pp. 111–115 (2015)
8. Ji, Z., Zheng, W., Pang, Y., Deep pedestrian attribute recognition based on LSTM. In: IEEE International Conference on Image Processing (2017)
9. Chen, L.-C., Papandreou, G., Schroff, F., Adam, H.: Rethinking Atrous convolution for semantic image segmentation. In: CVPR (2017)
10. Chen, L.-C., Zhu, Y., Papandreou, G., Schroff, F., Adam, H.: Encoder-decoder with atrous separable convolution for semantic image segmentation. In: CVPR (2017)
11. Kalayeh, M.M., Gong, B., Shah, M.: Improving facial attribute prediction using semantic segmentation. In: CVPR (2017)
12. Qi, H., et al.: Deformable convolutional networks – COCO detection and segmentation challenge 2017 entry. In: ICCV COCO Challenge Workshop (2017)
13. Badrinarayanan, V., Kendall, A., Cipolla, R.: SegNet: a deep convolutional encoder-decoder architecture for image segmentation. arXiv:1511.00561 (2015)
14. Ronneberger, O., Fischer, P., Brox, T.: U-Net: convolutional networks for biomedical image segmentation. In: Navab, N., Hornegger, J., Wells, W.M., Frangi, A.F. (eds.) MICCAI 2015. LNCS, vol. 9351, pp. 234–241. Springer, Cham (2015). https://doi.org/10.1007/978-3-319-24574-4_28
15. Wang, J., Zhu, X., Gong, S., et al.: Attribute recognition by joint recurrent learning of context and correlation. In: IEEE International Conference on Computer Vision, pp. 531–540 (2017)
16. Sarafianos, N., Xu, X., Kakadiaris, I.A.: Deep imbalanced attribute classification using visual attention aggregation. In: European Conference on Computer Vision (2018)
17. Liu, X., Zhao, H., Tian, M.: HydraPlus-Net: attentive deep features for pedestrian analysis. In: IEEE International Conference on Computer Vision, pp. 350–359 (2017)
18. Fang, W., Zhang, F., Sheng, V.S., Ding, Y.: A method for improving CNN-based image recognition using DCGAN. CMC: Comput. Mater. Continua **57**(1), 167–178 (2018)

An Evolving Network Model Based on a Triangular Connecting Mechanism for the Internet Topology

Tao Tang and Guangmin Hu[(✉)]

University of Electronic Science and Technology of China,
Chengdu 611731, China
hgm@uestc.edu.cn

Abstract. Modeling the Internet topology is the basis for developing and utilizing the Internet in a deeper level. Scale-free feature and small-world effect are two most significant characteristics of the Internet. Most existing models make reasonable jobs at catching the former, while they do less well in matching the latter one. For this issue, an evolving network model with a new triangular connecting mechanism was presented. Numerical simulations show that networks generated by the model are consistent with the Internet in many topological properties. This model is suitable for modeling other complex networks as well.

Keywords: Internet topology · Scale-free feature · Small-world effect

1 Introduction

In the past few decades, we have witnessed the Internet born and develop into a large complex ecosystem. The Internet is one of the most significant inventions in the last century since it makes all the difference in the world. A great number of efforts have been made to characterize the topology of the Internet, which could be of great significance in routing protocols, searching algorithms and even the virus spreading on the Internet [1–4].

Scale-free feature is one of the most crucial properties of the Internet. It means that the degree distribution $P(k)$ of the Internet graph obeys a power law from $P(k) \propto k$ for node degree k, where $P(k)$ denotes the probability that a node is connected to k other nodes exactly and is called the degree exponent. This phenomenon was first observed by Faloutsos et al. in [5]. Barabási and Albert proposed an evolving network model (BA model) to explain the origin of the scale-free power-law degree distribution [6]. The BA model considers that the power law is a consequence of two evolving mechanisms: growth and preferential attachment, which are common to numerous complex networks [7–9]. Though networks produced by the BA model have a power-law degree distribution, they are far from the Internet topology graph. For making them closer to the real Internet, quite a few models were proposed by means of modifying the two evolving mechanisms [10–15].

© Springer Nature Switzerland AG 2019
X. Sun et al. (Eds.): ICAIS 2019, LNCS 11635, pp. 510–519, 2019.
https://doi.org/10.1007/978-3-030-24268-8_47

Another significant character of the Internet is small-world effect [16], which implies that the Internet has a small characteristic shortest path length L and a large clustering coefficient C. The characteristic shortest path L is defined to be the average length of the shortest paths of all possible node pairs in a network:

$$L = \frac{1}{N(N-1)} \sum_{i \neq j} d_{ij} \tag{1}$$

where N is the number of nodes in the network and d_{ij} is the shortest path length between the node i and the node j. The local clustering coefficient C_i of a node i quantifies the extent its neighbors are linked. For a node i in a network, we use $\Gamma(i)$ to denote the subgraph that consists of all the nodes adjacent to the node i. Since the node i has a degree k_i, the total number of possible edges in $\Gamma(i)$ equals to $k_i(k_i - 1)/2$. And the local clustering coefficient C_i is given as:

$$C_i = \frac{|E(\Gamma(i))|}{k_i(k_i - 1)/2} \tag{2}$$

where $E(\Gamma(i))$ is the actual number of edges in the subgraph $\Gamma(i)$. The clustering coefficient C of a network is the average value of all the local clustering coefficients:

$$C = \frac{1}{N} \sum_{i=1}^{N} C_i \tag{3}$$

Bu and Towsley have pointed out that these two metrics (L and C) should be taken into consideration when modeling the Internet topology in [10]. Nevertheless, most models do not good enough in conforming the characteristic path length and the clustering coefficient to the Internet topology simultaneously.

2 The Evolving Models

2.1 The Barabási-Alert Model

The Barabási-Alert (BA) model proposed in 1999 is the first scale-free model, and it has a great influence in the field of network modeling. It considers that growth and preferential attachment are the most two critical features of the real networks. In past network models such as Erdős-Rényi (ER) model [17] and Watts-Strogatz (WS) model [18] the number of vertices is usually fixed and the change of the nodes is ignored. But in many real networks, the number of nodes varies equably throughout a lifetime. For instance, from Fig. 1 it appears that the number of AS (Autonomous System)es in the Internet almost grows linearly. Besides, the probability that two nodes are connected in the past models are assumed to be random and uniform. While in reality, most networks exhibit preferential connectivity. At the inter-domain level Internet topology, the newly added ASes prefer to connect to a popular AS due to the fact that popular ASes tend to peer with each other. In that case the Internet can have better connectivity.

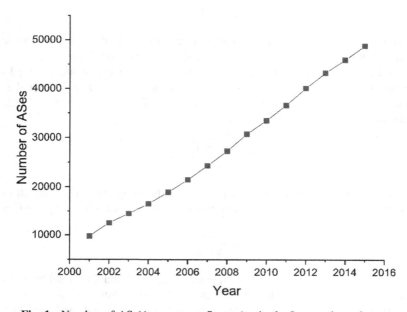

Fig. 1. Number of AS (Autonomous System)es in the Internet in each year

The generation algorithm of the BA model is as follows:

- *Growth*: Starting with a small network constructed with m_0 nodes and n_0 edges. At each time step, a new node is added and connected to $m(m \leq m_0)$ existing nodes in the network.
- *Preferential attachment (PA)*: The probability Π that a new node will be connected to node i dues to the degree k_i of that node, i.e., $\Pi(i) = k_i / \sum_j k_j$.

From Fig. 2 we can see that the number of links between ASes in the Internet almost increases uniformly just as the number of ASes. Therefore, we can assume that when a new node is added to the Internet, a fixed number m links is attached to the Internet.

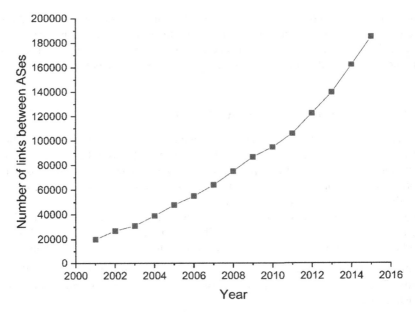

Fig. 2. Number of links between AS (Autonomous System)es in the Internet in each year

Though the mechanisms of the BA model are very simple, both numerical simulations and theoretical analysis show that the BA model yields networks with scale-free feature [6]. However, the degree distribution $P(k)$ of the BA model follows a power law with degree exponent $\gamma = 3$, while γ is about 2.1 for the real Internet topology. In addition, the clustering coefficient C of networks generated by the BA model is approximated to 0, which is far from true.

2.2 The Generalized Linear Preference Model

In the BA model, the extension of networks all derived from the addition of new vertices, and the connections between existing nodes are unaltered. This does not apply to many networks including the Internet. New connections between existing ASes could be added in order to have better connectivity to the Internet.

To capture this phenomenon in the networks, Bu and Towsley presented the Generalized Linear Preference (GLP) model [10]. Staring with m_0 nodes connected through $m_0 - 1$ edges, at each time step, the two operations are performed in the GLP model:

- With probability $p(0 < p < 1)$ we add a new node with m new links. Each link is connected to an existing node. And node i with degree k_i is chosen by the newly added node with probability $\Pi(i) = k_i / \sum_j k_j$.
- With probability $1 - p$, m new links are added between the existing nodes. For each end of each link, node i is chosen with probability $\Pi(i) = (k_i - \beta) / \sum_j (k_j - \beta)$, where β is a tunable parameter and $\beta < 1$.

Likewise, the GLP model can produce networks with a degree power law. And the degree exponent can be closer to the real Internet than the BA model by adjusting the parameter β. Moreover, the clustering coefficient is high of the generated networks, which shows the small-world property of real networks. That is what the BA model fails to do.

2.3   The Positive-Feedback Preference Model

In the actual Internet, when a new node is added and connected to several host nodes, new traffic load is brought to the host nodes. This leads to both the increase of traffic volume and the change of traffic pattern around the host nodes. In order to balance network traffic and optimize network performance, addition of new links connecting host nodes to peer nodes may be triggered.

Based on this, Zhou and Mondragón proposed the Positive-Feedback Preference (PFP) model to fit the Internet topology. The PFP model starts with a small random network, and one of the following operations is performed at each time step:

- With probability $p(0 < p < 1)$, add a new node, and connect it to an existing host node. Then one new internal link appears between the host node and another existing peer node.
- With probability $q(0 < q < 1)$, add a new node, and connect it to a host node. Then two new internal link appears between the host node and two peer nodes.
- With probability $1 - p - q$, add a new node, and connect it to two host nodes. Then a new internal link appears between one of the host nodes and one peer nodes.

When we have to choose a host node or a peer node to connect, a nonlinear preferential attachment mechanism is used. A node i with degree k_i is chosen with probability $\Pi(i) = k_i^{1 + \delta \log_{10} k_i} / \sum_j k_j^{1 + \delta \log_{10} k_j}$, while $\delta \in [0, 1]$. Besides the degree distribution and the small-world feature, networks generated by the PFP model match in the Internet topology in many other aspects such as maximum degree and so on.

2.4   A Tunable Triangular Connecting Model

The Internet shows a high clustering. A great number of triangles can be observed in the Internet [18–21]. This is easy to make sense. In the Internet, an AS would like to link with ASes nearby for a more stable routing. For modeling this characteristic, we proposed a triangular connecting mechanism as follows:

- Triangular Connecting (TC): Considering node v intending to add an edge. $M(v)$ represents the set of nodes who possess common neighbors with node v but are not adjacent to node v. Then node v picks one node u from $M(v)$ using a preferential attachment mechanism $\Pi(u) = k_u / \sum_j k_j$ to establish a connection.

A semblable work was done by Holme and Kim to model the similar feature in social networks [22]. A triad formation (TF) mechanism was presented by them. Except for the different ways of connecting, the TF step is always following with a preferential attachment (PA) step, while our TC step is independent.

Now we apply the TC mechanism to an evolving model. In this Tunable Triangular Connecting (TTC) model, the network evolves from an initial network consisting of m_0 nodes and n_0 edges. The initial network is connected without isolated nodes. At every time step, one of the following operations is performed:

- With probability $p(0 < p < 1)$, add a new node, and connect it to an existing node i with degree k_i chosen by a preferential attachment with probability $\Pi(i) = k_i / \sum_j k_j$.
- With probability $q(0 < q < 1)$, randomly choose a node n from the existing network, and connect it to another existing node i chosen by a preferential attachment with probability $\Pi(i) = k_i / \sum_j k_j$.
- With probability $1 - p - q$, randomly choose a node n from the existing network, and perform a TC step, i.e., connect it to a node i chosen by a preferential attachment with probability $\Pi(i) = k_i / \sum_j k_j$ from set $M(n)$.

The TTC model just gives an explanation of how the Internet topology evolves. As time goes on, new ASes join into the Internet and bring new links constantly. Furthermore, new connections would also be created between existing ASes. And with a reasonable probability an existing AS prefers to connect with a near one for the reason we referred above.

Besides, this model is proper for modeling other complex networks. For instance, in a friendship network, new members enter the network continually by building friendships with the old members [23–25]. And some of the old members become friends as well. In general, two members are likely to become friends if they have a common friend (or more), because they can know each other via their common friend (s). Of course, any two members can be friends for some other reasons. Hence, the TTC model would be good at simulating a friendship network, too.

3   Model Validation

The validation was done by comparing the Internet AS-level graph with networks generated by the BA model, the GLP model, the PFP model and our TTC model. The Internet topology data was obtained from the archives of the Internet AS-level Topology Archive [26], which combined the data from BGP data collected by Route Views [27], RIPE RIS [28], PCH [29] and Internet2 [30]. Such this data can be considered as the most complete AS-level Internet topology data. To my regret, it stopped updating the AS-level topology at 2015. We adopted the snapshot token on Jan. 2015, which including 48921 nodes and 152815 links. Networks generated by the models have equal nodes and approximate links with the Internet AS graph. Our TTC model is grown with parameters $m_0 = 600$, $n_0 = 600$, $p = 0.32$, $q = 0.84$. In the cases of the other models, we take the parameters recommended by their authors [6, 10, 11].

As we mentioned before, degree distribution $P(k)$ is one of the most important statistical characteristics of the Internet topology. So we first gave the degree distributions of the networks generated by the models and compared them with the Internet AS graph, as shown in Fig. 3. And Fig. 4 illustrates the power law more directly for giving the empirical complementary distribution $F(k) = \sum_{i=k}^{\infty} P(k)$, i.e., the fraction of nodes with degree greater than or equal to k. It is obvious that the TTC model, by contrast, is much closer to the real Internet AS graph.

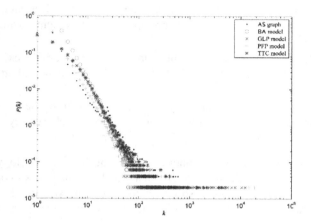

Fig. 3. Comparisons of the degree distributions between the real Internet and the models

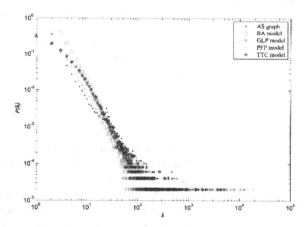

Fig. 4. Comparisons of the empirical complementary distribution between the real Internet and the models

The characteristic shortest path length L and the clustering coefficient C are the primary metrics to measure the small-world effect of networks. Generally, there is a negative correlation between them. Thus, most models are unable to coordinate the two metrics to be consistent with the Internet topology simultaneously. From Table 1, we can see our TTC model performs well in this issue, while other models are ordinary or even worse (the BA model does not show small-world effect at all).

Table 1. Comparisons of the parameters between the real Internet and the models

	AS graph	BA model	GLP model	PFP model	TTC model
Number of nodes (N)	48921	48921	48921	48921	48921
Number of links (E)	152815	146713	152418	132185	151203
Average degree ($\bar{k}$)	6.2	6.0	6.2	5.4	6.2
Characteristic path length (L)	3.79	4.82	3.09	2.79	3.82
Clustering coefficient (C)	0.40	0.00	0.61	0.58	0.41
Node with degree 1 ($P(\text{degree}) = 1$)	35.5%	0%	31.4%	26.7%	30.0%
Maximal degree (k_{max})	4535	532	12287	18819	5041

Nodes with degree 1 account for a third of the whole Internet, which are quite important components of the Internet. They represent the edge of the Internet. Table 1 indicates that the TTC model and the GLP model give closer results to the Internet graph at this point. There is not any node with degree 1 in the networks generated by the BA model.

The maximal degree k_{max} of networks is defined as the maximal value of connections a node owns. The maximal degree reflects the inhomogeneity of networks in some extent. And Table 1 shows the maximal degree of our TTC model is approximate to the Internet, while other models are too low or too high.

4 Conclusion

Review at the previous Internet topology models, almost all the models failed in matching the scale-free feature and small-world effect synchronously. In this paper, we proposed a new evolving network model with a triangular connecting mechanism. The model explains how the ASes interact with other ASes in the Internet in a simplified and generalized way.

Simulations show that this model accurately reproduces many of the topological characteristics of the Internet, which is better than those classical, representative models. And this model can also be applied to modeling other complex networks by adjusting the parameters. The model has advantages of simplicity, flexibility and easy extensibility, we consider it to be a step for a further understanding of the Internet topology.

Acknowledgments. The authors would like to thank the members of our research group. Personally, Tao Tang would like to thank Huangyu Hu, Xuemeng Zhai, and Binwei Wu for correcting our paper and other help.

References

1. Su, J., Wen, G., Hong, D.: A new RFID anti-collision algorithm based on the Q-ary search scheme. Chin. J. Electron. **24**(4), 679–683 (2015)
2. Su, J., Zhao, X., Hong, D., Luo, Z., Chen, H.: Q-value fine-grained adjustment based RFID anti-collision algorithm. IEICE Trans. Commun. **99**(7), 1593–1598 (2016)
3. Su, J., Hong, D., Tang, J., Chen, H.: An efficient anti-collision algorithm based on improved collision detection scheme. IEICE Trans. Commun. **99**(2), 465–470 (2016)
4. Zhang, J., Xie, N., Zhang, X., Yue, K., Li, W., Kumar, D.: Machine learning based resource allocation of cloud computing in auction. Comput. Mater. Continua **56**(1), 123–135 (2018)
5. Faloutsos, M., Faloutsos, P., Faloutsos, C.: On power-law relationships of the internet topology. In: ACM SIGCOMM Computer Communication Review, pp. 251–262. ACM (1999)
6. Barabási, A.L., Albert, R.: Emergence of scaling in random networks. Science **286**(5439), 509–512 (1999)
7. Arthur, W.B.: Complexity and the economy. Science **284**(5411), 107–109 (1999)
8. Banavar, J.R., Maritan, A., Rinaldo, A.: Size and form in efficient transportation networks. Nature **399**(6732), 130 (1999)
9. Amaral, L.A.N., Scala, A., Barthelemy, M., Stanley, H.E.: Classes of small-world networks. Proc. Natl. Acad. Sci. **97**(21), 11149–11152 (2000)
10. Bu, T., Towsley, D.: On distinguishing between internet power law topology generators. In: Proceedings Twenty-First Annual Joint Conference of the IEEE Computer and Communications Societies 2002, pp. 638–647. IEEE (2002)
11. Zhou, S., Mondragón, R.J.: Accurately modeling the Internet topology. Phys. Rev. E **70**(6), 066108 (2004)
12. Fan, Z., Chen, G., Zhang, Y.: A comprehensive multi-local-world model for complex networks. Phys. Lett. A **373**(18–19), 1601–1605 (2009)
13. Shakkottai, S., Fomenkov, M., Koga, R., Krioukov, D., Claffy, K.C.: Evolution of the internet as-level ecosystem. Eur. Phys. J. B **74**(2), 271–278 (2010)
14. Wang, X., Loguinov, D.: Understanding and modeling the Internet topology: economics and evolution perspective. IEEE/ACM Trans. Netw. **18**(1), 257–270 (2010)
15. Wen, G., Duan, Z., Chen, G., Geng, X.: A weighted local-world evolving network model with aging nodes. Phys. A **390**(21–22), 4012–4026 (2011)
16. Watts, D.J., Strogatz, S.H.: Collective dynamics of 'small-world' networks. Nature **393** (6684), 440 (1998)
17. Erdős, P., Rényi, A.: On random graphs I. Publ. Math. Debrecen **6**, 290–297 (1959)
18. Bianconi, G.: Number of cycles in off-equilibrium scale-free networks and in the internet at the autonomous system level. Eur. Phys. J. B **38**(2), 223–230 (2004)
19. Su, J., Ren, Y., Yang, Y., Han, Y., Wen, G.: A collision arbitration protocol based on specific selection function. Chin. J. Electron. **26**(4), 864–870 (2017)
20. Su, J., Sheng, Z., Xie, L.: A collision-tolerant-based anti-collision algorithm for large scale RFID system. IEEE Commun. Lett. **21**(7), 1517–1520 (2017)
21. Holme, P., Kim, B.J.: Growing scale-free networks with tunable clustering. Phys. Rev. E **65** (2), 026107 (2002)
22. Li, Y., Li, J., Chen, J., Lu, M., Li, C.: Seed selection for data offloading based on social and interest graphs. Comput. Mater. Continua **57**(3), 571–587 (2018)
23. Su, J., Sheng, Z., Hong, D., Wen, G.: An effective frame breaking policy for dynamic framed slotted Aloha in RFID. IEEE Commun. Lett. **20**(4), 692–695 (2016)

24. Su, J., Sheng, Z., Xie, L., Li, G., Liu, A.X.: Fast splitting based tag identification algorithm for anti-collision in UHF RFID System. IEEE Trans. Commun. **67**, 2527–2538 (2018)
25. Su, J., Sheng, Z., Leung, V.C., Chen, Y.: Energy efficient tag identification algorithms for RFID: survey, motivation and new design. IEEE Wirel. Commun. (2019)
26. Internet AS-level Topology Archive. http://irl.cs.ucla.edu/topology/
27. University of Oregon Route Views project. http://archive.routeviews.org/
28. RIS Raw Data—RIPE Network Coordination Centre. http://data.ris.ripe.net/
29. Packet Clearing House. https://www.pch.net/resources/Routing_Data/
30. Internet2. http://ndb7.net.internet2.edu/bgp/

A New Quantum Private Query Protocol with Better Performance in Resisting Joint-Measurement Attack

Xi Chen[1]([✉]), Shangjun He[1], Gonghua Hou[1], Lifan Yang[1], Lin Lin[1], Ruyi Chen[2], and Ningcheng Yuan[3]

[1] Fuzhou Power Supply Branch, State Grid Fujian Power Co., Ltd., Fuzhou, Fujian, China
{chen_xi9, he_shangjun, hou_gonghua, yang_lifan, lin_lin24}@fj.sgcc.com.cn
[2] State Grid Xintong Yili Technology Co., Ltd., Fuzhou, Fujian, China
chen_ruyin@sgitg.sgcc.com.cn
[3] Beijing University of Posts and Telecommunications, Beijing, China
yuanningcheng@bupt.edu.cn

Abstract. Quantum private query (QPQ) as a kind of protocol with strong practicability, its research depth is deepening. However, joint measurement (JM) attack poses a threat to the security of databases in protocol. Specifically, a malicious user can illegally obtain entries more than the average number of honest users from the database. Taking Jakobi et al.'s protocol as an example, a malicious user can obtain up to 500 bits from a database of 104 bits in one query instead of the expected 2.44 bits. In order to prevent JM attack, we design a new quantum private query protocol which has the similar procedure of raw oblivious key generation with Wei Chunyan et al.'s and Jakobi et al.'s. In our protocol, we add a step that Alice has to send back the measured qubits after some operation which ensures she must measure honestly. Therefore, our protocol can protect database security in theoretically, and the protocol can also improve the communication transmission distance because the photons Alice returns to Bob is re-prepared by her. Moreover, our protocol keeps the good peculiarities of QKD-based QPQs, e.g., its loss tolerant and robust against quantum memory attack.

Keywords: Quantum private query · Joint measurement attacks · Database security

1 Introduction

Secure communication is the science of researching information security technology in communication, and private query is an effective means to protect information security of both parties in the process of information access. With the development of science and technology, people's wisdom has improved, and classic private queries have become more and more incapable of satisfying enough security. More rapid development of cloud services, etc., people in the process of querying information will only

X. Sun et al. (Eds.): ICAIS 2019, LNCS 11635, pp. 520–528, 2019.
https://doi.org/10.1007/978-3-030-24268-8_48

increasingly worry about the security of their information. Classical secret communication, including public key encryption system and private key encryption system, relies on the security of key, encryption algorithm, password transmission, decryption and decryption algorithms to ensure its security. However, due to the inevitable existence of eavesdroppers in the communication process, all the transmissions in the classical secure communication are binary strings, which leads to the distribution of keys will always be eavesdropped in a large probability without the detection of legitimate users. With the rapid development of the information industry, people are increasingly demanding the integrity and privacy of information protection. In the process of communication, we not only require the information not to be obtained by external eavesdroppers, but also to protect the privacy of correspondents. In cryptography, SPIR [1] is one such problem. That is, a user Alice, wants to retrieve an entry x_i from a database $X = x_1 x_2 \ldots x_N$, the database holder Bob does not want Alice to get any information except x_i, and Alice does not want Bob to know which entry she wants to query. In order to solve these problems, many protocols based on mathematical problems have been proposed and we called classical cryptosystem. However, these cryptosystem becomes vulnerable with the introduction of quantum computer [3, 4]. Different with the classical cryptography, quantum cryptography is based on the physical principles [5] like no-cloning theorem, the principle of superposition states and the principle of parallel computation which make it unconditionally secure. Immediately, a lot of hot topics in quantum cryptography have been proposed, including Quantum Key Distribution (QKD) [17, 18, 20–26], Quantum Private Query (QPQ) [2, 6–16], Quantum Secret Sharing (QSS) [27–34], Quantum Secure Direct Communication (QSDC) [35–41] and Quantum Signature [42–48].

Quantum Key Distribution [18] in quantum cryptography is already a very mature protocol and its security is unconditional. By using the basic principles of quantum mechanics, it is easy to achieve one-time and one-time confidentiality, and it can ensure the key distribution process is absolutely safe, it is a secret communication that is unconditionally secure in principle. In order to solve the SPIP problem, QKD-based quantum private query came into a research hotspot. Ideally, Alice retrieves only one entry from Bob. But the truth is that this situation is difficult even in the quantum version. So the QPQ protocol relaxed this condition. Usually Alice can get a few entries from Bob (not just 1 bit). And user privacy is guarded in the sense of cheat sensitivity (that is, Alice has a nonzero probability to discover Bob's attack if he tries to infer the retrieval address).

Some of the previous QPQs [6–8] represented the database as a unitary operation. Although these QPQs have a good performance in theory, they are of poor practicality in practical applications. They are not loss tolerant and the dimensions of the unitary operation would be very high when the dimensions of the database are large. In 2011, Jakobi et al. [16] presented a QPQ protocol based on the SARG04 QKD [17] protocol. And with many QKD protocols have been experimentally realized, QKD-based QPQ is more practical. Generally in such QPQs, the generate of an oblivious raw key are in the same way and the procedure are as follows. First (1) Bob knows K^r entirely, (2) Alice knows only part of its bits, and (3) Bob does not know which bits are known to Alice. Then, they divide K^r into several substrings with equal length and add them bitwise to obtain a final key K^f. As a result, Alices knowledge on K^f is reduced to roughly one bit. Finally, Bob uses K^f to encrypt the database according to a shift claimed by Alice in order that she can extract the wanted bit correctly from the encrypted database.

QKD-based QPQ has become a research hotpot today and its practicality is also getting higher and higher. In 2012, Gao et al. [9] proposed a flexible generalization about Jakobi et al.'s protocol. After this, Panduranga Rao et al.'s [10] gave two more efficient modifications of the classical postprocessing about Jakobi et al.'s protocol. In 2013, Zhang et al.'s [11] presented a QPQ protocol based on a counterfactual QKD scheme. Then, Wei et al.'s [12] gave a QPQ of blocks which allows the user to retrieve a multibit block from the database in one query. Considering the real noisy channel, Chan et al.'s [13] presented a fault tolerant QPQ protocol in which an error-correction method for the oblivious key used in QKD-based QPQs is presented, then they gave a proof-of-concept demonstration of this protocol over a deployed fiber. Moreover, Gao et al.'s [14] studied the classical postprocessing of QKD-based QPQs deeply. They exhibited effective attacks on several postprocessings and presented an error-correction method for the oblivious QKD as well. In 2015, Liu et al.'s [15] designed a stable QPQ protocol, in which the failure probability is always zero. Recently, Wei et al.'s [2] proposed a protocol which can resist the JM attack, which propose a QPQ protocol based on a two-way QKD scheme.

The above progress has achieved a great breakthrough in the development of cryptography, but there are still some security issues. That is, joint measurement (JM) attack, which will cause considerable damage to the security of database Bob. For example, in the Jakobi et al.'s [16] protocol, Alice can acquire each final key bit with probability $\frac{1}{2}$ by jointly measuring the six qubits contributing to it (see Fig. 2 in Ref. [16]), hence she can obtain as many as 500 bits from the database when $N = 10^4$. Worse yet, JM attack, which would be conducted at the very end of the protocol (when Alice knows which qubits should be measured jointly), can escape being detected because Bob would not check Alices honesty after that. This problem would arise with the development of quantum memories.

The first one that proposed to resist the JM attack is Wei et al.'s [2] protocol. Based on the reference to this protocol, we propose a new protocol which also can resist joint measurement attack and our protocol is more simple. Specifically our protocol adds a step that Alice has to send back the measured qubits after some operation which ensures Bob can judge whether Alice makes measurement honestly. Bob will detect the particles randomly which returned from Alice to determine whether Alice has made an honest measurable. In this way if Alice still saves the raw key for joint measurement Bob would have a high probability (about $\frac{1}{2}$) to discover her attack then terminate the protocol. Therefore, our protocol has a high level of security in resisting joint measurement attack.

2 Protocol

Here, all quantum channels are public and all the classical channels are authenticated in this protocol. The security task can be realized by the following steps.

(1) The database holder Bob sends the user Alice a long random sequence of qubits (e.g., photons) in states $|0\rangle$, $|1\rangle$, $|+\rangle$ and $|-\rangle$. Here

$$|+\rangle = \frac{1}{\sqrt{2}}(|0\rangle + |1\rangle), \quad |-\rangle = \frac{1}{\sqrt{2}}(|0\rangle - |1\rangle)$$

States $|0\rangle$ and $|1\rangle$ represent bit 0, while $|+\rangle$ and $|-\rangle$ represent bit 1.

(2) Alice measures each state in the basis of $\{|0\rangle, |1\rangle\}$ or the basis of $\{|+\rangle, |-\rangle\}$ randomly. After measuring, then Alice chose to send the measurement result to Bob directly or send the measurement result after pass the measurement result to H gate (i.e. $H \equiv \frac{1}{\sqrt{2}} \begin{bmatrix} 1 & 1 \\ 1 & -1 \end{bmatrix}$), and the probability of each operation is equal, i.e., $\frac{1}{2}$.

(3) Here, Alice declares which qubits were successfully detected. As for the missing or undetected photons, she discards. This item that discards photons does not allow Alice to deceive, because after step 2, Alice still has no information whatsoever on the sent bit values. Therefore, the protocol is completely loss tolerant.

(4) Bob declares two quantum states for each bit successfully measured by Alice. Here one of them is the aum state that Bob actually sends, and the other is one of the other pairs of orthogonal basis. Generally, $\{|0\rangle, |+\rangle\}$, $\{|1\rangle, |-\rangle\}$, $\{|+\rangle, |1\rangle\}$ or $\{|-\rangle, |0\rangle\}$. That is if Bob send $|0\rangle$, then he could announce, for example, $\{|0\rangle, |+\rangle\}$. This process is identical to that described in the SARG04 QKD protocol.

(5) Now, Alice can determine her measurements after step 4 to a certain extent. Specifically, Alice has a certain probability to decrypt the bit value actually sent by Bob according to the base she uses and the pair of quantum states obtained by Bob. For example, if Bob has been sent the state $|0\rangle$, and the probability that Alice used $\{|0\rangle, |1\rangle\}$ basis or $\{|+\rangle, |-\rangle\}$ basis to measured is 1/2. Then if Bob announced $\{|0\rangle, |+\rangle\}$, only if Alice measured it with $\{|+\rangle, |-\rangle\}$ and obtained the result $|-\rangle$, she can conclude that Bob sent the state $|0\rangle$. In other words, Alice can successfully determine the probability of the bit value sent by Bob is $\frac{1}{4}$. Both conclusive and inconclusive results are kept.

(6) At this point, Bob announces the checking bit to Alice. Let Alice declares the measurement result and the operation she has chosen. Bob determines whether Alice has made an honest measurement though the Alice's announcement with a certain probability, and if Alice is honest, the protocol continues, if not, the protocol terminates.

(7) Both Alice and Bob discard all these detection bits. And the string created in the protocol must be $k \times N$ in length. Here k is the number of divided substrings, and N is the size of the database and is also the size of each substring. Then, in order to reduce Alice's information on the key to roughly one bit, these string are bitwise after step 6. The specific example is given below in Fig. 1 to make the explanation more clearly.

0	1	?	1	?	?	0	0	?	1

+

?	0	1	1	0	?	1	0	0	?

?	1	?	0	?	?	1	0	?	?

Fig. 1. Alice only gets the information of each bit in the substring. After bitwise, the value of this bit can be obtained. As long as she has one who can't judge, she won't get the final key. In fact, Alice can accurately get the probability that each bit is greatly reduced. Here question marks symbolize bits whose value is unknown to Alice.

(8) If Alice does not get any bit information after the operation of bitwise substring in step 7, the protocol must be started over. Certainly, this probability is very small. The discussion of this probability is given later in the part of security analysis for a detailed description.

(9) If the protocol completion, K^f has been correctly confirmed. Alice will know at least 1 bit of information of it. Suppose she knows the j_{th} bit K_j^f and wants the i_{th} bit of the database X_i. She then announces the number $s = j - i$ in order to allow Bob to encode the database by bitwise adding K^f, shifted by s. So, Bob announces N bits $C_n = X_n \oplus K_{n+s}^f$ where Alice can read $C_i = X_i \oplus K_j^f$ and thus obtain X_i. The shift will hence make sure that Alices bit of interest is encoded with a key element she knows so that the task of private query can be achieved completely.

3   Security Analysis

In this part we will analyze the security of our protocol. The design of the protocol mainly analyzes the database security and user security in the communication process.

3.1   Database Security

We discuss the database security in our protocol first. Imagine, a user spending a dollar to buy a message in the database. If this user is malicious, then the message he wants to get is not just this one, but the more the better, then he will find ways to destroy the database's ban and get multiple messages. Because the process of generating a raw key in our protocol is similar to J protocol [16]. The raw key generation process is also briefly introduced in our introduction. So the simple attack method mentioned in the J protocol can also resist in our protocol. And our protocol is mainly for the joint measurement attack problem which occurs in the J protocol. So we just focus on the security of the protocol against joint measurement attack.

　　If Alice wants to attack Bob, she is likely to proceed in the following steps. First in step 2, Alice can use a quantum memory to store the photons sent by Bob instead of making honest measurements, so that Alice can perform joint measurement. But in the step 2, Alice must to send some photons to Bob. So she can return a fake particle. For the sake of generality, we assume that the fake particles returned by Alice are $\frac{|00\rangle + |11\rangle}{\sqrt{2}}$. When Bob announced the checking particles in step 6, Alice made an honest measurement to these particles. Then she performs joint measurement to the remaining particles which may contribute to the final key. But even so, Bob still has $\frac{1}{2}$ probability to discover Alice's attack.

Suppose Bob sends the $|0\rangle$, after Alice measures it in the $\{|0\rangle, |1\rangle\}$ or the $\{|+\rangle, |-\rangle\}$ basis randomly, she may get $|+\rangle, |-\rangle$ or $|0\rangle$, the probability of each is $\frac{1}{4}, \frac{1}{4}$, and $\frac{1}{2}$ respectively. When the measurement result is $|0\rangle$, after two operations Alice will obtain $|0\rangle$ or $|+\rangle$, and the probability of each is $\frac{3}{8}$ respectively. The same is when the measurement result is $|+\rangle$ or $|-\rangle$, by two operations Alice will obtain $|0\rangle, |+\rangle$ or $|-\rangle$, $|1\rangle$, and the probability of each is $\frac{1}{8}$ respectively. At this point, if Alice wants to successfully cheat Bob, she wants to turn the fake particles she sent to Bob into the result which her honest measurement and via the corresponding gate operation. That is, when Alice obtain $|0\rangle$ by honest measurement, she wants to turn the fake particles she sent to Bob into the $|0\rangle$ or $|+\rangle$. Then Alice will chose the $\{|0\rangle, |1\rangle\}$ or the $\{|+\rangle, |-\rangle\}$ basis to measure the entangled particles in her hand. Suppose she chose the $\{|0\rangle, |1\rangle\}$ basis to measure, then the fake particles in Bob's hand have a $\frac{1}{2}$ probability of collapsing to $|0$, and there is also a $\frac{1}{2}$ probability of collapsing to $|1\rangle$. If the fake particles in Bob's hand collapsing to $|1\rangle$, Bob will find the dishonest of Alice. Similarly, if Alice chooses the $\{|+\rangle, |-\rangle\}$ basis, Bob also has a $\frac{1}{2}$ probability of finding that Alice is dishonest.

In summary, $P_{Bobfind} = \frac{1}{2}$. That is to say our protocol has higher security against joint measurement attack.

3.2   User Security

User privacy, i.e., the protocol can make sure that Bob does not know the address of the entry Alice will retrieve. Similar with the J protocol, our protocol also can resist intermediate attack and entangled attack in terms of user privacy. In our protocol, Alice's process of returning particles will bring some information leakage [19], but the impact is small. Then we will analyze it in detail.

Suppose if Bob want to get the retrieval entry address of Alice, he will measure the photons that Alice returns to him. Since Bob knows exactly what state (such $|0\rangle$) he sent to Alice, he can choose the appropriate basis ($\{|0\rangle, |1\rangle\}$) to measure the photons that Alice returns to him. At this point, Bob may get some information of Alice through his measurement results. According to our protocol process, Bob can guess the selection of the Alice raw key basis at a certain probability, not knowing Alice's conclusive results. Assume that Bob send the $|0\rangle$ to Alice, then Alice returns to him with $|0\rangle, |1\rangle, |+i, |-i$. Bob use the $\{|0\rangle, |1\rangle\}$ basis to measure the photons Alice returns to him. Then he may obtain $|0\rangle$ or $|1\rangle$, and the probability of each is $\frac{5}{8}, \frac{3}{8}$ respectively. If he get $|0\rangle$, through our protocol we can know that Bob has 40% probability to determine that Alice chose the wrong basis. The same is if he get $|1\rangle$ Bob has 66.6% probability to determine that Alice chose the wrong basis. But even so, Bob only gets the raw key basis information selected by Alice at this time. For a final key,

Bob needs to guess k conclusive results of Alice in a row. That is to say, the probability changes into $(40\%)^k$ or $(66\%)^k$. With the increase of the parameter k, Bob's guesses probability will decrease by the exponential power and tend to zero.

In summary, our protocol can guarantee the security of Alice's privacy (i.e., the final query address).

4 Conclusion

This paper mainly discusses a new QPQ protocol based on SARG04 QKD. This protocol can resistant to the impact of joint measurement attack on the database. First, in our protocol, user Alice returns the measurement results to Bob directly or returns after the measurement results through a H gate operation. Bob announces the checking particles to determine whether Alice is making an honest measurement in step 2. And this step can effectively distinguish Alice's honesty, prevent its preservation of the raw key and jointly measure it, and get more information about the final key. In addition, Alice uses these two operations to prevent Bob from obtaining its basis information, thereby stealing Alice's retrieval address. In other words, Alice will be able to steal Bob's more entries in any way, and Bob will find it with a high probability. Bob can't get Alice's retrieval address information in the process. In addition, compared to the previous protocol, since the photon returned by Alice to Bob in our protocol is re-prepared by her, the protocol can also improve the communication transmission distance.

Acknowledgments. This paper is supported by Development of quantum cryptography equipment and terminal modules for distribution of electricity business (536800170042).

References

1. Gentner, Y., Ishai, Y., Kushilevitz, E., Malkin, T.: Protecting data privacy in private information retrieval schemes. J. Comput. Syst. Sci. **60**, 592 (2000)
2. Wei, C.Y., Wang, T.Y., Gao, F.: Practical quantum private query with better performance in resisting joint-measurement attack. Phys. Rev. A **93**, 042318 (2016)
3. Shor, P.W.: Polynomial-time algorithms for prime factorization and discrete logarithms on a quantum computer. In: Proceedings of the 35th Annual Symposium on the Foundations of Computer Science, Santa Fe, New Mexico, p. 124. IEEE, Piscataway (1994)
4. Grover, L.K.: A fast quantum mechanical algorithm for database search. In: Proceedings of the 28th Annual ACM Symposium on Theory of Computing, p. 212. ACM, New York (1996)
5. Gisin, N., Ribordy, G., Tittel, W., Zbinden, H.: Quantum cryptography. Rev. Mod. Phys. **74**, 145 (2002)
6. Giovannetti, V., Lloyd, S., Maccone, L.: Quantum private queries. Phys. Rev. Lett. **100**, 230502 (2008)
7. Giovannetti, V., Lloyd, S., Maccone, L.: Quantum private queries: security analysis. IEEE Trans. Inf. Theory **56**, 3465 (2010)

8. Olejnik, L.: Secure quantum private information retrieval using phase-encoded queries. Phys. Rev. A **84**, 022313 (2011)
9. Gao, F., Liu, B., Wen, Q.Y., Chen, H.: Flexible quantum private queries based on quantum key distribution. Opt. Express **20**, 17411 (2012)
10. Panduranga Rao, M.V., Jakobi, M.: Towards communication-efficient quantum oblivious key distribution. Phys. Rev. A **87**, 012331 (2013)
11. Zhang, J.L., Guo, F.Z., Gao, F., Liu, B., Wen, Q.Y.: Private database queries based on counterfactual quantum key distribution. Phys. Rev. A **88**, 022334 (2013)
12. Wei, C.Y., Gao, F., Wen, Q.Y., Wang, T.Y.: Practical quantum private query of blocks based on unbalanced-state Bennett-Brassard-1984 quantum-key-distribution protocol. Sci. Rep. **4**, 7537 (2014)
13. Chan, P., Lucio-Martinez, I., Mo, X., Simon, C., Tittel, W.: Performing private database queries in a real-world environment using a quantum protocol. Sci. Rep. **4**, 5233 (2014)
14. Gao, F., Liu, B., Huang, W., Wen, Q.Y.: Postprocessing of the oblivious key in quantum private query. IEEE. J. Sel. Top. Quant. **21**, 6600111 (2015)
15. Liu, B., Gao, F., Huang, W.: QKD-based quantum private query without a failure probability. Sci. China-Phys. Mech. Astron. **58**, 100301 (2015)
16. Jakobi, M., et al.: Practical private database queries based on a quantum-key-distribution protocol. Phys. Rev. A **83**, 022301 (2011)
17. Scarani, V., Acin, A., Ribordy, G., Gisin, N.: Quantum cryptography protocols robust against photon number splitting attacks for weak laser pulse implementations. Phys. Rev. Lett. **92**, 057901 (2004)
18. Bennett, C.H., Brassard, G.: Quantum cryptography: public-key distribution and coin tossing. In: Proceedings of the IEEE International Conference on Computers, Systems and Signal Processing, p. 175. IEEE, New York (1984)
19. Lo, H.K.: Insecurity of quantum secure computations. Phys. Rev. A **56**, 1154 (1997)
20. Deng, F.G., Long, G.L.: Bidirectional quantum key distribution protocol with practical faint laser pulses. Phys. Rev. A **70**, 012311 (2004)
21. Gao, F., Guo, F.Z., Wen, Q.Y., Zhu, F.C.: On the information-splitting essence of two types of quantum key distribution protocols. Phys. Lett. A **355**, 172–175 (2006)
22. Huang, W., Guo, F.Z., Huang, Z., Wen, Q.Y., Zhu, F.C.: Three-particle QKD protocol against a collective noise. Opt. Commun. **284**(1), 536–540 (2011)
23. Salas, P.J.: Security of plug-and-play QKD arrangements with finite resources. Quantum Inf. Comput. **13**(9–10), 861–879 (2013)
24. Liu, B., et al.: Choice of measurement as the secret. Phys. Rev. A **89**(4), 042318-1–042318-7 (2014)
25. Lo, H.K., Ma, X.F., Chen, K.: Decoy state quantum key distribution. Phys. Rev. Lett. **94**, 230504 (2005)
26. Hwang, W.Y.: Quantum key distribution with high loss: toward global secure communication. Phys. Rev. Lett. **91**, 057901 (2003)
27. Cleve, R., Gottesman, D., Lo, H.K.: How to share a quantum secret. Phys. Rev. Lett. **83**(3), 648–651 (1999)
28. Hillery, M., Buzek, V., Berthiaume, A.: Quantum secret sharing. Phys. Rev. A **59**(3), 1829–1834 (1999)
29. Karlsson, A., Koashi, M., Imoto, N.: Quantum entanglement for secret sharing and secret splitting. Phys. Rev. A **59**(1), 162–168 (1999)
30. Xiao, L., Long, G.L., Deng, F.G., Pan, J.W.: Efficient multiparty quantum secret sharing schemes. Phys. Rev. A **69**(5), 052307-1–052307-5 (2004)
31. Lu, H., et al.: Secret sharing of a quantum state. Phys. Rev. Lett. **117**(3), 030501-1–030501-5 (2016)

32. Xiang, Y., et al.: Multipartite Gaussian steering: monogamy constraints and quantum cryptography applications. Phys. Rev. A **95**, 1–6 (2017)
33. Kogias, I., et al.: Unconditional security of entanglement-based continuous-variable quantum secret sharing. Phys. Rev. A **95**, 012315-1–012315-6 (2017)
34. Massoud, H.D., Elham, F.: A novel and efficient multiparty quantum secret sharing scheme using entangled states. Sci. China Phys. Mech. Astron. **55**, 1828–1831 (2012)
35. Boström, K., Felbinger, T.: Deterministic secure direct communication using entanglement. Phys. Rev. Lett. **89**(18), 187902-1–187902-4 (2002)
36. Gao, F., Qin, S.J., Wen, Q.Y., Zhu, F.C.: Cryptanalysis of multiparty controlled quantum secure direct communication using Greeberger-Horne-Zeilinger state. Opt. Commun. **283**(1), 192–195 (2010)
37. Huang, W., et al.: Fault tolerant quantum secure direct communication with quantum encryption against collective noise. Chin. Phys. B **21**(10), 100308-1–100308-9 (2012)
38. Wang, C., Deng, F.G., Li, Y.S., Liu, X.S., Long, G.L.: Quantum secure direct communication with high-dimension quantum superdense coding. Phys. Rev. A **71**, 044305 (2005)
39. Deng, F.G., Long, G.L.: Secure direct communication with a quantum one-time pad. Phys. Rev. A **69**, 052319 (2004)
40. Wang, J., Zhang, Q., Tang, C.J.: Quantum secure direct communication based on order rearrangement of single photons. Phys. Rev. Lett. **358**(4), 256–258 (2006)
41. Wang, C., Deng, F.G., Long, G.L.: Multi-step quantum secure direct communication using multi-particle Green–Horne–Zeilinger state. Opt. Commun. **253**(1–3), 15–20 (2005)
42. Zeng, G.H., Keitel, C.H.: Arbitrated quantum-signature scheme. Phys. Rev. A **65**, 042312 (2002)
43. Li, Q., Chan, W.H., Long, D.Y.: Arbitrated quantum signature scheme using Bell states. Phys. Rev. A **79**, 054307 (2009)
44. Gao, F., Qin, S.J., Guo, F.Z., Wen, Q.Y.: Cryptanalysis of the arbitrated quantum signature protocols. Phys. Rev. A **84**, 022344 (2011)
45. Dunjko, V., Wallden, P., Andersson, E.: Quantum digital signatures without quantum memory. Phys. Rev. Lett. **112**, 040502 (2014)
46. Lee, H.Y., Hong, C.H., Kim, H.S., Lim, J.G., Yang, H.Y.: Arbitrated quantum signature scheme with message recovery. Phys. Rev. Lett. **321**(5–6), 295–300 (2004)
47. Zou, X.F., Qiu, D.W.: Security analysis and improvements of arbitrated quantum signature schemes. Phys. Rev. A **82**, 042325 (2010)
48. Choi, J.W., Chang, K.Y., Hong, D.: Security problem on arbitrated quantum signature schemes. Phys. Rev. A **84**, 062330 (2011)
49. Tang, X., Chen, Z., Zhang, H., Liu, X., Shi, Y., Shahzadi, A.: An optimized labeling scheme for reachability queries. CMC: Comput. Mater. Continua **055**(2), 267–283 (2018)
50. Zhang, X., Wang, P., Sun, W., Badler, N.I.: A novel twist deformation model of soft tissue in surgery simulation. CMC: Comput. Mater. Continua **55**(2), 297–319 (2018)

PPCSB: A Privacy-Preserving Electricity Consumption Statistics and Billing Scheme in Smart Grid

Chenyang Li[1], Yuling Chen[2(✉)], Yu Yang[1], Chaochao Li[1],
and Yang Zeng[1]

[1] School of Cyberspace Security,
Beijing University of Posts and Telecommunications, Beijing, China
[2] State Key Laboratory of Public Big Data, GuiZhou University,
Guiyang, Guizhou, China
61997525@qq.com

Abstract. Research on the privacy protection of smart grids mostly stays in fixed electricity prices or electricity aggregation. Aiming at the problem of real-time pricing and privacy data protection of smart grid, this paper proposes a privacy-preserving electricity consumption statistics and billing scheme in smart grid (PPCSB). In this scheme, the techniques of additive homomorphic encryption and mixed multiplicative homomorphic encryption are used to ensure the security of the data communication; Batch verification is used to improve the efficiency of signature verification. In addition, the proposed scheme does not require a trusted third party in order to improve the usability of the scheme. Through performance analysis of the scheme, it shows that the scheme has better security and better functions.

Keywords: Smart grid · Privacy-preserving · Meter billing ·
Homomorphic encryption

1 Introduction

As a next-generation power grid, the smart grid has received more and more attention. Its rapid development has brought huge impact on the traditional fixed price, and thus proposed a real-time electricity price strategy. PU modifies the electricity price in real time according to the user's electricity information, and feeds the electricity price back to users so that they can adjust the electricity consumption [1].

The interaction of real-time power consumption provides great convenience for PU, but uncontrolled access to fine-grained electricity consumption data may threaten users' privacy. In the process of collecting, transmitting and storing the power information of the smart grid, personal information that was not easily available before, such as identity information of electrical equipment and behavioral habits of using electrical equipment, may be leaked. This information can be used by third parties to provide targeted marketing promotions, and also can be used by malicious people to commit illegal activities such as burglary. Therefore, the privacy protection of information collection and transmission in smart grid has become an important issue.

© Springer Nature Switzerland AG 2019
X. Sun et al. (Eds.): ICAIS 2019, LNCS 11635, pp. 529–541, 2019.
https://doi.org/10.1007/978-3-030-24268-8_49

1.1   Related Work

On the privacy protection issue of smart grid, relevant experts and scholars mainly study in two aspects: data aggregation technology and data anonymity technology. In the previous research, researchers used the trusted computing platform to secure the privacy data such as power consumption. This method requires additional hardware devices, which increases the system overhead and lowers the practicability. Li et al. [2] proposed a smart grid security data aggregation scheme based on homomorphic encryption, which uses homomorphic encryption technology to aggregate user' power consumption and provide aggregated data to power utility. Chen et al. [3] also designed an aggregation scheme for protecting private data based on homomorphic encryption. The scheme distributes the relevant keys for smart meters and servers through trusted third parties, and obtains the regional aggregated ciphertext from the concentrator. Zhang et al. [4] proposed an improved certificateless ring signature scheme that achieves privacy protection by disrupting the association between user identity and electricity data. Shen et al. [5] designed a smart grid secondary power aggregation control scheme taking the geographical situation into consideration. The scheme uses the homomorphic encryption technology to aggregate the user's power, so that the trusted control center can only obtain the regional power consumption data, thereby ensuring the security of the user's private information.

Although the above schemes guarantee the security of user' privacy information to a certain extent, most of them do not consider billing functions and real-time pricing requirements, as well as privacy issues that may arise in these requirements and functions.

1.2   Contribution

In this paper, we propose a privacy-preserving electricity consumption statistics and billing scheme (PPCSB) in smart grid based on homomorphic encryption, signature batch verification and Horner's rule. Compared with the previous work, the advantages of this paper are:

- The scheme supports secure charging based on real-time electricity price. PU determines and sends the real-time electricity price to the user so that the user can reasonably adjust the power consumption, then PU extracts the power ciphertext of each SM from the aggregated ciphertext sent by GW through the Horner's law, and obtains the total electricity bill ciphertext in the billing period by using the hybrid multi-state homomorphic encryption technology. Finally, PU feeds back the total electricity bill ciphertext to CC to obtain the electricity fee.
- Other system nodes other than SM will not get meter's fine-grained data. The data received by GW is the meter's electricity data after the second homomorphic encryption. The finest data that the PU can access is data ciphertext through homomorphic encryption; CC is exposed to the electricity bills data of each meter within a billing period.
- The scheme improves the execution efficiency through batch verification technology, and is more practical which does not require trusted third parties and additional hardware devices.

The paper is organized as follows: in Sect. 2, we introduce the preliminaries including Signature verification, homomorphic encryption, Horner's rule and real-time pricing. Then, our PPCSB scheme is proposed in Sect. 3, including the system model and detailed scheme design. System performance analysis, including safety analysis, functional analysis and performance analysis, is given in Sect. 4. The conclusion is drawn in Sect. 5.

2   Preliminaries

2.1   Bilinear Pairing and Signature Verification

The bilinear pair generation algorithm is a probability algorithm. The algorithm takes the safety parameter k as input and outputs a quintuple (q, P, G_1, G_2, e), where q is a large prime with length k, G_1, G_2 is a cyclic addition group of q order, P is a generator of G_1, and $e : G_1 \times G_1 \rightarrow G_2$ is a bilinear pair map. Bilinear pair mapping has good properties such as linearity, non-degenerate, and computability.

Digital signatures guarantee the integrity of information transmission and prevent repudiation in transactions. Digital signature means that the abstract information is encrypted by the sender's private key and transmitted to the receiver along with the original text. After receiving, the receiver decrypts it with the sender's public key and gets the abstract information from it. The receiver then uses the hash function to process the original text and compare it with the decrypted abstract information. If it is the same, the verification is passed.

In the BLS signature, the system randomly selects $x \in Z_q^*$ as the private key and calculates xP as the public key. The process of signing and signature verification is as follows:

$$sig(m) = x \cdot H(m) \tag{1}$$

$$e(P, sig(m)) = e(xP, H(m)) \tag{2}$$

2.2   Homomorphic Encryption

Homomorphic encryption enables data processing without revealing any raw information. In homomorphic encryption, the result that is decrypted after algebraic operations on ciphertext data is the same as the result of algebraic operations directly on plaintext. The Paillier encryption algorithm is a homomorphic encryption algorithm consisting of three parts: key generation, encryption and decryption.

Key Generation. Select a security parameter k; determine the large prime numbers p, q of length k; calculate the RSA coefficients N and λ; define the function L(x); select the generator $g \in Z_{N^2}^*$, and calculate μ.

$$N = pq \tag{3}$$

$$\lambda = lcm(p - 1, q - 1) \tag{4}$$

$$L(x) = (x - 1)/N \tag{5}$$

$$\mu = (L(g^\lambda \bmod N^2))^{-1} \tag{6}$$

Then the public key is (N, g) and the private key is (λ, μ).

Encryption. Suppose m is plaintext data, c is encrypted data, and E($\cdot$) stands for encryption function. The encryption process is as follows:

$$c = E(m) = g^m \cdot r^N \bmod N^2 \tag{7}$$

Decryption. Decrypting ciphertext c can obtain plaintext m, D($\cdot$) represents the decryption function, and the decryption process is as follows:

$$m = D(c) = L(c^\lambda \bmod N^2) \cdot \mu \bmod N \tag{8}$$

Algorithm Characteristics. The Paillier encryption system has the properties of additive homomorphism and mixed multiplication homomorphism, and the property of additive homomorphism is as follows:

$$D(E(m_1) \cdot E(m_2) \bmod N^2) = m_1 + m_2 \bmod N \tag{9}$$

The property of mixed multiplicative homomorphic are as follows:

$$D(E(m)^y \bmod N^2) = D(g^{m_1 y} \cdot r_1^{Ny} \bmod N^2) = m_1 y \bmod N \tag{10}$$

2.3 Horner's Rule

Horner's rule is a polynomial evaluation algorithm that converts the evaluation of a unary n-degree polynomial into multiple one-time evaluations. Our scheme uses it to realize data aggregation at the regional gateway and data analysis at the power utility.

Horner's rule makes the polynomial $P(x) = a_n x^n + a_{n-1} x^{n-1} + \cdots + a_1 x + a_0$ depressed with x as the common factor, and transform it into a new representation: $P(x) = (\ldots(a_n x + a_{n-1})x + \cdots)x + a_0$. Given P(x) and x, solve for the coefficients $a_n, a_{n-1}, \ldots, a_0$ can be done by n divisible operations and n modular operations.

2.4 Real-Time Pricing

The fixed electricity price can't really reflect the relationship between the user's power demand and supply. When the power demand fluctuates, the power utility can't change the power supply accordingly, which causing a lot of waste of resources. In response to it, a real-time price strategy is proposed. Real-time electricity price refers to the process of estimating current electricity consumption and determining pricing based on the electricity consumption in the previous period within a given period of time, such as 1 h or a shorter period. Through the change of the real-time electricity price, the user can adjust the power consumption to improve the utilization of resources. The scheme is designed on the basis of real-time electricity price, and no specific pricing process is given. It is assumed that the power utility can estimate the current electricity information through the previous power consumption, and then determine the unit price.

3 PPCSB Scheme

3.1 Overall Scheme

This paper proposes a privacy-preserving electricity consumption statistics and billing scheme in smart grid (PPCSB), including six parts.

1. System initialization. This part mainly completes the generation and distribution of system parameters and the registration of system entities.
2. Real-time electricity price determination. This part mainly refers to that the power utility sends the real-time electricity price of this period to the user, so that the user can adjust their electricity consumption in this period. The real-time electricity price at this part is determined by the power utility according to the electricity consumption in the previous period.
3. Meter data generation. This part mainly completes the generation of the meter's electricity ciphertext and digital signature, and transmits them to the regional gateway.
4. Regional data aggregation. This part mainly completes the verification of electricity data, and sends data aggregated for a region to the power utility.
5. Calculate the electricity charge ciphertext for the current period. In this part, the verification of the regional gateway data is mainly completed, and the power ciphertext of single meter is analyzed from data sent by the regional gateway. On this basis, the electricity charge ciphertext of a single meter in this period is calculated.
6. Bill generation and distribution. In this part, the electricity price ciphertext of each meter within a billing cycle is calculated and sent to the control center together with the signature. The control center verifies the data, calculates each meter bill, and sends it to user bound to the meter.

3.2 System Model

As shown in Fig. 1, the system model for smart grid contains a smart meter (SM), a regional gateway (GW), a control center (CC), a power utility (PU), and a user (User) bound to the meter.

- Smart Meter (SM): The terminal device installed on the user side, which has the function of collecting, encrypting, and uploading power data.

- Regional Gateway (GW): The bridge between SMs and PU that collects and aggregates all meter data in its jurisdiction and uploads it to PU, which has the function of receiving, calculating and forwarding.
- Power Utility (PU): It is responsible for collecting, parsing and storing the meter data uploaded by GW, and uploading the data parsed to CC at the end of a billing cycle. In addition to the functions of collecting, parsing, calculating and forwarding, power utility is also responsible for the interaction with users.
- Control Center (CC): Decipher the electricity bill ciphertext uploaded by PU and forward it to PU. CC has functions such as calculating and forwarding. The purpose of setting up CC is to separate the permissions for data processing.
- User (User): Electricity bill inquiry.

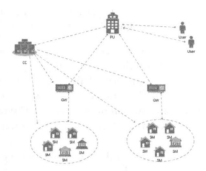

Fig. 1. System model for smart grid.

3.3 Scheme Design

System Initialization. In this part, CC generates the relevant parameters required by the homomorphic encryption algorithm and the signature algorithm. The specific steps are as follows:

- CC selects the security parameter k, determines the large prime number q with length k, the additive cyclic group G_1, G_2 of order q, a generator P of G_1, and a bilinear pair mapping $e : G_1 \times G_1 \rightarrow G_2$ through the bilinear pair parameter generation algorithm.
- CC selects a safe hash function $H_1 : \{0, 1\}^* \rightarrow G_1$.
- CC selects another security parameter k1, large primes p1 and q1 with length k1, and calculates the public key $pk_1 = (N_1, g_1)$ and private key $sk_1 = (\lambda_1, \mu_1)$. of the homomorphic encryption.
- CC uses $s \in Z_q^*$ as the system private key and $y = xs$ as the public key.
- CC publishes system parameters $\{q, P, G_1, G_2, e, N_1, g_1, H_1, y\}$.

System Entity Registration. Suppose the whole region is divided into m communities, and each community has n users. GW_k represents the kth regional gateway, namely the regional electricity data aggregation gateway, where k = 1, 2... m; SMi represents the ith smart meter in a community, where i = 1, 2... n. The process of PU registration is as follows:

- PU randomly selects x ∈ Z_q^* as its own private key and calculates the public key Y.
- PU randomly selects D as a constant of the polynomial, and D is greater than the product of the number of communities and the maximum amount of electricity collected by a meter in a collection period.
- PU sends the registration request to CC, and meanwhile sends id information ID_PU and public key Y to CC.
- CC returns its identity information ID_CC to PU.
- PU selects a security parameter k2 to calculate the public key pk = (N, g), and the private key sk = (λ, μ) for the quadratic homomorphic encryption algorithm.

The process of GW_k registration is as follows:

- GW_k randomly selects $x_k \in Z_q^*$ as its own private key and calculates the public key Y_k.
- GW_k sends the registration request to PU, and meanwhile sends id information ID_GW_k and public key Y_k to PU.
- PU calculates the encryption parameter $g_k = \{g_{k1}, g_{k2}, \ldots, g_{kn}\}$ of meters under the jurisdiction of GW_k, where the calculation process of the encryption parameter is:

$$g_{ki} = g^{D^i} \tag{11}$$

- PU returns the encryption parameter g_k and the identity information ID_PU to GW_k.

The process of SMi registration is as follows:

- SMi randomly selects $x_i \in Z_q^*$ as its own private key and calculates the public key Y_i.
- SMi sends the registration request to GW_k, and meanwhile sends id information ID_SMi and public key Y_i to GW_k.
- GW_k returns the encryption parameter g_{ki} and the identity information ID_GW_k to SMi.

Real-Time Pricing Determination. Fixed electricity prices cannot change the supply of electricity when power demand fluctuates, resulting in a large amount of waste of resources. In real-time electricity price, users can adjust electricity consumption independently and improve the resources utilization hrough the adjustment of electricity price. The determination of real-time electricity price refers to that the PU determines the electricity price for this period according to the electricity usage in the previous region and sends the unit electricity price to the user. In this scheme, PU can only obtain the ciphertext of regional electricity, and the determination of electricity price requires PU to analyze the ciphertext.

Electricity Ciphertext Generation. The scheme supposes that each time period is 1 h, then at the end of the current period, the smart meter performs secondary homomorphic encryption on the power consumption l_i to obtain the power ciphertext $E(l_i)$. Meanwhile, Smart meters use information such as the private key x_i, meter identity ID_SMi and timestamp TS generated in the registration part to generate the signature σ_i, in which timestamps are added to prevent replay attacks. Finally, the message M_{SM_i} composed of ciphertext and signature is sent to GW_k.

$$l_i = g_1^{dij} r_1^N \bmod N^2 \tag{12}$$

$$E(l_i) = g_{ki}^{l_i} r^N \bmod N^2 \tag{13}$$

$$\delta_i = x_i H_1(E(l_i)||ID\_SM_i||TS) \tag{14}$$

$$M_{SM_i} = E(l_i)||ID\_SM_i||TS||\delta_i \tag{15}$$

Regional Electricity Aggregation. After receiving n pieces of electricity meter data, GW_k firstly verifies the data to ensure that the received data comes from legal electricity meter in the community and the electricity meter data has not been tampered with. Due to the large number of electricity meters, single verification needs to consume too much time and resources. This scheme adopts the batch verification method proposed in [5] to reduce the calculation times of bilinear pairings.

If the signature verification is passed, GW_k aggregates the ciphertext of n electric meters to obtain C_k, and Uses the private key x_k, regional gateway identity ID_GW$_k$ and timestamp TS to generate the signature δ_k. Finally, the message M_{GW_k} composed of ciphertext and signature is sent to PU.

$$C_k = \prod_{i=1}^{n} E(l_i) \bmod N^2 \tag{16}$$

$$\delta_k = x_k H_1(C_k||ID\_GW_k||TS) \tag{17}$$

$$M_{GW_k} = C_k||ID\_GW_k||TS||\delta_k \tag{18}$$

Electricity Fee Ciphertext Calculation in a Period. After receiving the aggregated data from the GWs, PU firstly verifies the data to ensure that the data comes from the legal regional gateway and the data has not been tampered with. If the signature verification is passed, PU analyzes the aggregated data in GW_k according to Horner's rule, and obtains the power ciphertext M_{ki} of the single meter during the period (M_{ki} represents power information of the ith smart meter in the kth aggregation gateway), the parsing process is as follows:

$$C_k = \prod_{i=1}^{n} E(l_i) \bmod N^2 = \prod_{i=1}^{n} g^{D^i l_i} \cdot r^N \bmod N^2 = g^{D^1 l_1 + D^2 l_2 + \cdots + D^n l_n} \cdot (r^n)^N \bmod N^2$$

$$\tag{19}$$

Let $M_k = D^1 l_1 + D^2 l_2 + \cdots + D^n l_n$ and $R = r^n$, then

$$C_k = g^{M_k} \cdot R^N \bmod N^2 \qquad (20)$$

PU uses the homomorphic encryption private key sk $= (\lambda, \mu)$ to decrypt and obtain M_k. According to horner's rule, M_{ki}, or l_i, the electricity ciphertext for each meter at this period, can be obtained by means of modular calculation. Then, PU can get the charge ciphertext P_{kij} (j stands for the jth period) of each meter in this period according to M_{ki} and the unit price of the electricity for this period. The calculation process is as follows:

$$P_{kij} = M_{ki}^{B_j} \qquad (21)$$

Bill Generation and Distribution. Assume that a billing period is composed of v periods. At the end of a billing period, PU adds the charge ciphertexts of each meter for v periods to obtain the charge ciphertext P_{ki} of each meter in a billing period. At the same time, PU combines the private key x, the power utility identity ID_PU and the timestamp TS to generate a signature δ_{PU}. Finally, the message M_{PU} composed of ciphertext and signature is sent to CC.

$$P_{ki} = \prod_{j=1}^{v} P_{kij} \bmod N^2 \qquad (22)$$

$$\delta_{PU} = x H_1(P_{ki} || ID\_PU || TS) \qquad (23)$$

$$M_{PU} = P_{ki} || ID\_PU || TS || \delta_{PU} \qquad (24)$$

After receiving the message, CC verifies it. After the verification is passed, the message is decrypted by using the private key $sk_1 = (\lambda_1, \mu_1)$ to obtain the total electricity bill B of each meter in the billing period. Then PU receives the bill sent by the CC and forwards it to the user bound to the meter.

$$P_{ki} = \sum_{j=1}^{v} M_{ki} \cdot B_j = \sum_{j=1}^{v} (g_1^{d_{ij}} r_1^N)^{B_j} \bmod N^2 = \sum_{j=1}^{v} g_1^{d_{ij} B_j} r_1^{N B_j} \bmod N^2 \qquad (25)$$

4   Scheme Analysis

4.1   Security Analysis

Fine-Grained Electricity Data Privacy Protection. What the user sends to the regional gateway is the power ciphertext with homomorphic encryption. Even if the adversary obtains the power ciphertext through eavesdropping and other means in the communication process, he cannot get any information about the user's power consumption.

The aggregation operation of the regional gateway is based on ciphertext. Even if the adversary intrudes into the regional gateway, he can't obtain the fine-grained electricity data. PU collects and processes the electricity ciphertext aggregated by the regional gateway, and obtains the electricity ciphertext of each meter after analysis. There is no relevant decryption key in the regional gateway and power utility. This part uses the method of separating private ciphertext and secret key to protect the privacy data. As for CC, what it receives is the ciphertext of electricity charge in one billing cycle uploaded by the power company. The electricity charge in one billing cycle can be obtained by CC through decryption, but the real-time electricity or electricity charge cannot be obtained. Based on the above, CC also cannot obtain the user's fine-grained power consumption data.

Data Integrity and Non-repudiation. Each entity in the scheme adds a signature to the message packet to be sent. The receiver only receives the message after the verification so as to ensure the integrity of relevant data and prevent tampering. In addition, each entity's private key is in its own custody, and they cannot deny the information sent and signed by itself, so as to detect dishonesty in time.

4.2   Functional Analysis

Dynamic User. User joins and exits are almost transparent to CC. When a new meter is applied for joining, it is no longer necessary to interact with the control center. Firstly, the power company binds the meter to the user and the regional gateway. Then, the regional gateway distributes the encryption parameter g_{ki} for it. The process of joining dynamically does not require all configuration information to be initialized. If the meter is applied to exit, it will be revoked at the regional gateway and the power company.

Electricity Billing. After the real-time electricity price is modified, the smart meter sends the ciphertext of the previous period to the regional gateway. The regional gateway aggregates the ciphertext sent by the meter under its jurisdiction and forwards it to the power company. The power company analyzes the ciphertext of each meter, and calculating the electricity charge ciphertext of the previous period according to the mixed multiplication homomorphic encryption algorithm. In this way, the electricity charge ciphertext of each meter for a billing cycle is calculated and fed back to the control center to get the electricity charge for a billing cycle.

Bill Verification. When the user disputes the electricity bill, he can apply to the power company for a detailed bill. The power company will send the detailed electricity charge ciphertext (not the total electricity charge ciphertext in a billing cycle) in the billing cycle to the control center. The control center decrypts the detailed electricity charge ciphertext to get the detailed bill and returns it to the power company, which sends the detailed bill to the user for verification.

Table 1. Functional comparison between different schemes

Scheme	Trusted third party	Dynamic user	Electricity billing	Bill verification
[3]	YES	NO	NO	NO
[4]	YES	NO	NO	NO
[5]	NO	YES	NO	NO
PPCSB	NO	YES	YES	YES

Table 1 shows the functional comparison between the scheme proposed in this paper and some other existing schemes. Through the comparison, it is found that the proposed scheme has more comprehensive functions, supporting electricity pricing, bill verification, and does not need a trusted third party.

4.3   Performance Analysis

This part will analyze the computing cost and communication cost of each entity in the system.

Computing Cost. Assume that the cost of an exponential operation on $Z_{N^2}^*$ is T_e, the cost of one multiplication operation on G_1 is T_m, the cost of one exponential operation on G_2 is T_G, and the cost of one bilinear pair operation is T_P. The cost of the multiplication operation on $Z_{N^2}^*$ and the Horner's analytic operation are small and negligible compared with the above four kinds of operations. The calculation costs of different entities in the scheme are shown in Table 2:

Table 2. Computing cost of different entity in the scheme

Entity	Operation	Computing cost
SM	1. Electricity ciphertext generation 2. Signature generation	$\approx 4T_e + T_m$
GW	1. Signature verification 2. Aggregate ciphertext generation 3. Signature generation	$\approx (n + 2)T_P + T_m$
PU	1. Signature verification 2. Decrypt C_k and get M_k 3. Analyze and calculate real-time electricity charge ciphertext (ignored) 4. Electricity charge ciphertext aggregation in a billing cycle 5. Signature generation	$\approx (m + 2)T_P + T_m + T_e$
CC	1. Signature verification 2. Decrypting the electricity charge ciphertext in a billing cycle	$\approx T_P + mnT_e$

Communication Cost. Assuming that the ciphertext length after homomorphic encryption is L_1 and the signature length is L_2.

Communication cost sent by the meter to the regional gateway: $L_1 + |ID\_SM| + |TS| + L_2$

Communication cost sent by the regional gateway to the power company: $L_1 + |ID\_SM| + |TS| + L_2$

Communication cost sent by the power company to the control center: $L_1 + |ID\_SM| + |TS| + L_2$.

5 Conclusion

This paper proposes a smart grid system model without trusted third parties. Based on this, a privacy-preserving electricity consumption statistics and billing scheme (PPCSB) in smart grid is proposed. Based on real-time electricity price, the scheme realizes the functions of electricity collection and meter billing through homomorphic encryption and Horner's rule, so as to ensure that each entity in the system cannot obtain fine-grained power data. Through the analysis of security and function for the scheme, it shows that the scheme has better security and comprehensive function.

Acknowledgments. This work is supported by the National Natural Science Foundation of China grant (U1836205), Major Scientific and Technological Special Project of Guizhou Province (20183001), Open Foundation of Guizhou Provincial Key Laboratory of Public Big Data (2018BDKFJJ014), Open Foundation of Guizhou Provincial Key Laboratory of Public Big Data (2018BDKFJJ019) and Open Foundation of Guizhou Provincial Key Laboratory of Public Big Data (2018BDKFJJ022).

References

1. Allcott, H.J.: Rethinking real-time electricity pricing. Resour. Energy Econ. **33**(4), 820–842 (2011)
2. Li, F., Luo, B., Liu, P.C.: Secure information aggregation for smart grids using homomorphic encryption. In: Proceedings of the 1st IEEE International Conference on Smart Grid Communications (2010)
3. Chen, L., Lu, R., Cao, Z.J.: MuDA: multifunctional data aggregation in privacy-preserving smart grid communications. Peer-to-Peer Netw. Appl. **8**(5), 777–792 (2015)
4. Zhang, S., Zhao, Y., Wang, B.J.: Certificateless ring signcryption scheme for preserving user privacy in smart grid. Autom. Electr. Power Syst. **42**, 118–123 (2017)
5. Shen, H., Zhang, M.J.: A privacy-preserving multilevel users' electricity consumption aggregation and control scheme in smart grids. J. Cryptol. Res. **3**, 171–191 (2016)
6. Li, H., Lin, X., Yang, H.J.: EPPDR: an efficient privacy-preserving demand response scheme with adaptive key evolution in smart grid. IEEE Trans. Parallel Distrib. Syst. **25**(8), 2053–2064 (2014)
7. Zhang, Y., Zheng, D., Zhao, Q.C.: PADA: privacy-aware data aggregation with efficient communication for power injection in 5G smart grid slice. In: International Conference on Networking & Network Applications (2017)

8. Leontiadis, I., Molva, R., Onen, M.C.: Privacy preserving statistics in the smart grid. In: IEEE International Conference on Distributed Computing Systems Workshops (2014)
9. Ge, S., Zheng, P., Lu, R.J.: FGDA: fine-grained data analysis in privacy-preserving smart grid communications. Peer-to-Peer Netw. Appl. **3**, 1–13 (2017)
10. Lu, R., Liang, X., Li, X.J.: EPPA: an efficient and privacy-preserving aggregation scheme for secure smart grid communications. IEEE Trans. Parallel Distrib. Syst. **23**(9), 1621–1631 (2012)
11. Xu, W., Xiang, S., Vasily, S.J.: A cryptograph domain image retrieval method based on Paillier Homomorphic block encryption. CMC: Comput. Mater. Continua **55**(2), 285–295 (2018)
12. Xiong, L., Shi, Y.J.: On the privacy-preserving outsourcing scheme of reversible data hiding over encrypted image data in cloud computing. CMC: Comput. Mater. Continua **55**(3), 523–539 (2018)

Blockchain Private Key Storage Algorithm Based on Image Information Hiding

Ning Wang[1], Yuling Chen[2(✉)], Yu Yang[1], Zigang Fang[1], and Yizhe Sun[1]

[1] School of Cyberspace Security,
Beijing University of Posts and Telecommunications, Beijing, China
[2] State Key Laboratory of Public Big Data, GuiZhou University,
Guiyang, Guizhou, China
61997525@qq.com

Abstract. The private key is the unique credential of the blockchain asset and can be used to sign and authenticate transactions. Losing the private key also loses the control of the account, so the leakage of the private key is one of the major factors affecting the security of the blockchain. In order to improve the security of blockchain private key storage technology in transactions, this paper proposes a blockchain private key storage algorithm based on image information hiding. In order to improve the camouflage ability and reduce the bit error rate, the algorithm adds random numbers and error correction code to the original private key to provide double protection. After generating the watermark information, the watermark information is embedded into the digital image by means of discrete wavelet transform and quantized index modulation to realize the process of information hiding. Finally, it is proved that this algorithm has good transparency and robustness, can hide the private key information visually, and extract it accurately.

Keywords: Blockchain private key storage · Image information hiding · RoBustness

1 Introduction

Essentially, the blockchain is an integrated distributed database of various computer technologies, such as peer-to-peer networks, consensus mechanisms, encryption algorithms, and smart contracts [1]. The core of blockchain to build a secure, trusted storage and transaction system is cryptography [2]. For each node, the private key is the only key to prove identity [3].

From user's point of view, the private key is a messy, irregular string, which makes it difficult to store the private key. The blockchain private key is generally stored in a blockchain wallet. According to [4], the wallets are divided into several types, such as cold wallet, a local wallet, online wallet, etc., but there are some deficiencies in terms of security, ease of use, cost and so on; [5] audited the security risks of digital currency wallets, summed up the current common types of wallet vulnerabilities, and the widely used mnemonic mode has security problems; [6] analyzed and compared six blockchain private key storage methods in detail, for example, local storage, password protection, offline mode, offline computable mode, autonomous key generation method and hosting mode. After analysis, and the author believed that these methods also have various problems.

In order to apply to the blockchain application with higher security requirements, this paper proposes a blockchain private key storage algorithm based on image information hiding, using the spread transform dither modulation watermark algorithm based on discrete wavelet transform to convert the blockchain private key into watermark information, and store it in the digital image in an invisible manner. After many tests and verifications, the algorithm is available to the storage and use of the blockchain private key, and has excellent transparency and robustness.

2   The Theory of Information Hiding

This paper proposes a storage algorithm of blockchain private key based on image information hiding. Private keys is used as text watermark information, and a suitable watermark algorithm is selected to embed watermark into the carrier image for storage. The general process is shown in Fig. 1. Firstly, watermark information is generated according to the content of the blockchain private key, and then the watermark information is embedded into the carrier image according to the embedding algorithm to obtain a watermark image. The watermark extraction algorithm corresponds to the embedding process to a certain extent. According to the reverse process of the embedded algorithm, the watermark information in the watermark image is extracted, and finally the blockchain private key is extracted.

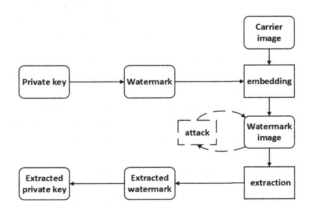

Fig. 1. Information hiding algorithm

3   The Proposed Scheme

3.1   Watermark Generation

Although the existence and content of the blockchain private key can be hidden by the image information hiding technology, in order to enhance the security of the private key storage, the original private key needs to be further processed. In the process of blockchain trading, if an attacker intercepts a carrier image containing a watermark and notices that the image appears to contain hidden information, he may attempt to perform a steganographic analysis to verify the existence of the secret information and extract the specific content. Therefore, before generating the watermark, the random number is added on the basis of the original private key, and convert it into a binary matrix format, so the private key is camouflaged, and an error correction code is also added to reduce the error in the transmission process. The application of random numbers and error correction codes provides double protection for the original private key.

3.2   Watermark Embedding

Watermark Embedding Position. The choice of watermark embedding location needs to consider security and the impact on the quality of the carrier. The security issue means that the embedded watermark cannot be easily extracted by an illegal user or erased easily. The quality problem means that the embedding of the watermark causes the distortion of carrier image to be undetectable to human senses. Therefore, for the watermark information with a private key hidden, a suitable position or layer of the carrier image should be selected to embed watermark without affecting the sensory effect, thereby hiding the existence of the private key information, for example, in terms of the YUV mode of image, since people are more sensitive to brightness than to color, watermark information can be embedded in the color layer.

Embedding Algorithm. This algorithm is mainly applied to blockchain private key storage. Therefore, it is necessary to choose a transform domain algorithm with good robustness—Discrete Wavelet Transform (DWT) [7].

After the first-level discrete wavelet transform image, four wavelet coefficient matrices are generated, which are horizontal component, vertical component, diagonal component and low-frequency component, which are generally recorded as HL1, LH1, HH1, LL1, "1" represents a first-level discrete wavelet transform [8]. The energy of the image is mainly concentrated in the low frequency approximation part, so embedding the watermark information in the low frequency part will have better robustness. In order to reduce the amount of data processed, the next step of wavelet decomposition can be performed on the low frequency approximate part of the image. The algorithm will perform three-level discrete wavelet decomposition on the carrier image, and finally obtain the coefficient matrix LL3 of the low-frequency approximate part.

Quantized Index Modulation (QIM) is robust to common signal processing attacks. The principle is to quantify the watermark information and the original information of the carrier according to different quantizers. The calculated result is an image containing watermark information. The QIM algorithm has significant advantages in computational complexity and algorithm implementation, so it has been widely used, but the robustness against some common signal processing attacks (such as random noise, compression, image enhancement, etc.) needs to be improved [9].

Spread Transform Dither Modulation (STDM) is an important extension of the QIM digital watermark series [10].

It does not need to consider the physical effects such as printing and cropping. It only considers the case where small probability occurs, including image scaling, JPEG compression, noise attack, etc. In these cases, STDM has better robustness [11].

The specific algorithm process is as follows:

1. The selected embedded layer is segmented according to the length of the watermark, and each image matrix is embedded with a part of the watermark using DWT and STDM algorithm.
2. Each segmented matrix is used as a three-level discrete wavelet transform to obtain a matrix LL3 of low-frequency coefficients $a \times b$, a is the number of rows of the matrix, b is the number of columns of the matrix, and LL3 is converted into an N-dimensional row vector, and the packet size is taken as n, thereby get the $[N/n]$ group of n-dimensional row vectors $\{u1, u2, \cdots, u_{[N/n]}\}$. Where $N = a \times b$, $uk = \{u1, u2, \cdots, un\}, k \in [1, [N/n]]$.
3. The even term in the vector u is denoted as vector x, and the odd term is denoted as vector y, set lx and ly be the modules of vector x and vector y:

$$lx = \left(\frac{2}{n}\sum\nolimits_{i=1}^{\frac{n}{2}} |u2i|^2\right)^{\frac{1}{2}} \tag{1}$$

$$ly = \left(\frac{2}{n}\sum\nolimits_{i=1}^{\frac{n}{2}} |u2i - 1|^2\right)^{\frac{1}{2}} \tag{2}$$

4. In the process of jitter modulation, the amount of jitter $d(m)$ is determined according to different watermark bits (0 or 1). Set $z = \frac{lx}{ly}$, substitute $z + d(m)$ as the STDM quantization factor into the STDM quantization function $Q_{d(m)}(z)$, the formula is as follows, $d(m) \in \{-1, 1\}$, Δ is the quantization step size, and the function $round(\bullet)$ is responsible for rounding $\bullet$.

$$z_q = Q_{d(m)}(z) = \Delta round\left(\frac{z + d(m)\Delta/2}{\Delta}\right) - d(m)\frac{\Delta}{2} \tag{3}$$

5. Set $\theta = \frac{z_q}{z}$, therefore $z_q = \frac{lx \cdot \theta^{1/2}}{ly \cdot \theta^{-1/2}}$, then the quantized vector x' and vector y' are as follows:

$$x' = x \cdot \sqrt{\theta} \tag{4}$$

$$y' = y \cdot \sqrt{\theta} \tag{5}$$

6. The unpacked N mod n coefficients and the quantized $[N/n]$ group vector x' and vector y' are subjected to discrete wavelet inverse transform to obtain a new low-frequency component containing watermark information. Finally, the processed color layer and the two unprocessed layers are combined into an RGB watermark image.

Obviously, according to the STDM principle, if the STDM quantization factor changes less after signal processing, the lower the bit error rate, the better the robustness of the algorithm. The algorithm uses the ratio of the Euclidean distance of the n-dimensional vector's odd and even terms, and the jitter amount as the quantization factor. The quantization factor is only affected by the scaling, noise, JPEG compression and other attacks that may be encountered in the watermark image. Therefore, the algorithm has good robustness.

Embedding Process. The overall embedding process of the watermark is shown in Fig. 2. First, the private key is preprocessed, and a random number and an error correcting code are added to the private key to generate watermark information. An appropriate watermark embedding layer is selected in the original carrier image, and the embedded layer matrix is segmented according to the length of the watermark, and each segmented matrix stores partial watermark information. The segmented matrixs are subjected to three-level discrete wavelet transform to obtain four wavelet transform coefficients of HL3, LH3, HH3 and LL3. Then, the watermark is embedded in the LL3 low frequency coefficient matrix according to the above algorithm. Then, the layer after embedding the watermark is subjected to discrete wavelet inverse transform, and the newly generated low frequency part and the original high frequency part are combined to generate a watermarked carrier layer, and a complete watermark image is synthesized with the unprocessed layer.

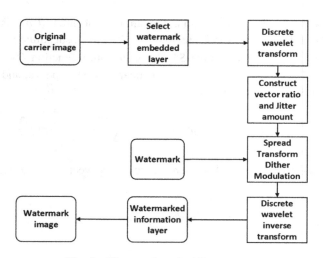

Fig. 2. Watermark embedding process

3.3 Watermark Extraction

The process of extracting the blockchain private key from the watermark image is the inverse transformation of the embedded private key. It is also necessary to perform a three-level discrete wavelet transform on the carrier layer, construct an odd-numbered vector $\hat{x}$, an even-numbered vector $\hat{y}$ and calculate their respective modes $l\hat{x}$, $l\hat{y}$.

Set $\hat{z} = \frac{l\hat{x}}{l\hat{y}}$, and enter the minimum distance detection decoding process. The jitter amount d_0 d_1, corresponding to 0, 1 bits are used to process $\hat{z}$, and obtain the quantization factors $\hat{z} + d_0$, $\hat{z} + d_1$. According to the STDM principle, the quantization factor is substituted into the STDM quantization function $Q_{d(m)}(\hat{z})$ to obtain the quantized value $\hat{z}_q$, and finally decoded according to the minimum distance formula to determine the output watermark information.

$$\hat{m} = \arg \min_{d(m)\in\{-1,1\}} \left| \hat{z} - Q_{d(m)}(\hat{z}) \right| \qquad (6)$$

However, at this time, the watermark information extracted is masqueraded, not the final extracted private key, and the error correction code of the watermark information needs to be decoded, converted from the matrix form to the original private key information format. At last, the added random numbers should be removed. The process is shown in Fig. 3.

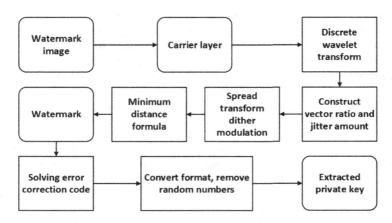

Fig. 3. Watermark extraction process

4 Performance Analysis

4.1 Performance Evaluation Standard

Security analysis: By embedding the watermark information of the hidden blockchain private key into the picture, not only the content of the private key information is well hidden, but also the imperceptibility and non-perceivedness of the blockchain private key storage are greatly enhanced. In addition, in order to prevent malicious stegano-graphic analysis, the algorithm adds random numbers to the original private key information for camouflage, and adds error correction code [12], which greatly improves the difficulty of steganographic analysis.

Transparency analysis [13]: The primary characteristic of information hiding is transparency. Transparency refers to the degree to which the quality of the carrier signal changes after embedding secret information. Watermark images are often dif-ficult to detect abnormalities in human visual systems. Therefore, the evaluation of algorithm transparency is mainly determined by the Peak Signal to Noise Ratio (PSNR) of the original image and the watermark image. In general, a PSNR value higher than 35 dB indicates that the transparency of the algorithm is good. The Mean Squared Error (MSE) and PSNR are defined as follows:

$$PSNR = 10 \cdot \lg(\frac{MAX^2}{MSE})$$ (7)

$$MSE = \frac{1}{mn}\sum_{i=0}^{m-1}\sum_{j=0}^{n-1}||I(i,j) - K(i,j)||^2$$ (8)

In the formula, MAX represents the maximum value of the color of the image point. Generally, each sample point uses 8 bits, then $MAX = 2^8 - 1$; MSE represents the mean square error of two monochromatic images. If it is a color image, MSE represents the mean square error of the three channels R, G, and B. I and K represent two monochromatic images, one of which is the noise approximation of the other.

Robustness analysis [14]: The robustness is determined by the bit error rate. The *ber* is defined as follows, where *ErrorSum* is the total number of bit errors of the watermark information, and *Len* is the length of the watermark information.

$$ber = \frac{ErrorSum}{Len}$$ (9)

In general, if the watermark image is not modified, the extracted private key will be complete and correct, that is, the bit error rate is zero. However, after the watermark image is affected by image scaling, noise attack, etc., the algorithm uses discrete wavelet transform and the improved STDM algorithm, the tested *ber* is extremely low. So the algorithm has good robustness.

Practicality analysis: By hiding the private key information of the blockchain in the image, it is difficult to detect the abnormality by relying only on the human visual system, so it has strong security and makes up for the security defects of the blockchain wallet. Moreover, the algorithm is easy to store and retrieve the private key, and can accurately recover the private key in a short time, and has strong resistance to possible scaling attacks and noise attacks. Therefore, this algorithm has a certain degree of practicability in blockchain private key storage with high security requirements.

4.2   Experimental Results

In order to test the performance of this algorithm, this paper simulates the embedding effect and extraction effect of blockchain private key information.

Combined with the actual application, three sets of samples are selected here, and each set of ten pictures is used as the test carrier image. Sample1 is processing photo, Sample2 is network download photo, and Sample3 is mobile phone photo.

The blockchain private key is generated by a random seed and is essentially a 256-bit random binary number, usually expressed in hexadecimal. In this paper, we selected 64-bit hexadecimal number as the blockchain private key information "a25cd8e6b2f-f512d5e2a025d806dc08a33f44e97e2abd21d57e2f1af3c8d9e1e" for simulation test and embed it in test images. In the specific practice, firstly, the image resolution is uniformly adjusted to 960 * 720 before embedding the watermark, and at the same time, in order to achieve the best robustness, after several tests, it was determined that the packet size in the watermark embedding and extraction algorithm is set to 32, and the quantization step size is set to 0.15.

The Efficiency of Embedding and Extraction. The embedding effect of the algorithm is tested by three sets of test carrier images. Sample1, Sample2, and Sample3 are carrier images in different scenarios that may occur during actual application. The test results of the three groups of samples are shown in Table 1. Without signal attack, the average bit error rate of each group of samples is 0, and the private key extracted from the watermark image is complete and no-error; The embedding time is improved with the complexity of the image texture, but the embedding time can be limited to 3.0 s; private key information extraction time is faster than the embedding time, but also more stable, the extraction speed is about 1.2 s. This shows that the algorithm is robust without any processing on the watermark image, and can accurately and quickly extract the blockchain private key information. At the same time, the private key extraction time about 1.2 s is in line with the practical application in the transaction process.

Table 1. Sample test results

Samples	Sample1	Sample2	Sample3
Average embedding time/s	2.8027	2.8336	2.9408
Average bit error rate%	0.0000	0.0000	0.0000
Average extraction time/s	1.1856	1.1963	1.2312

Transparency Analysis. In Fig. 4, (a)–(c) are images before the watermark information is embedded, and the watermark information is embedded into each block of the image according to the algorithm proposed here, thereby obtain the watermark images (d)–(f). Subjectively, We can see that it is difficult for the naked eye to perceive the hidden information content and hidden position in the watermark image. Therefore, from the human visual point of view, storing the blockchain private key through this algorithm is safe and reliable, which greatly reduces the risk of private keys being stolen and tampered with.

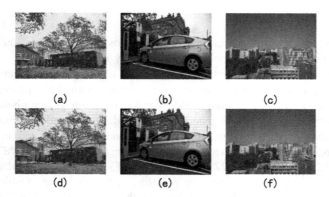

Fig. 4. Comparison of carrier images before and after embedding watermark

Subjective evaluation is a more accurate method for evaluating image quality, but it is often affected by factors such as observer's mood and fatigue. The objective evaluation is to evaluate the quality of the image based on the machine. It is to process and analyze the image signals input and output in the system. Objectively, The test of algorithm transparency is mainly based on the PSNR of the original image and the watermark image. The transparency test results of the three groups of samples are shown in Table 2. The PSNR of each group of samples is higher than 35 dB, which indicates that the transparency of the algorithm is better. The difference between the watermark image and the original image can not be noticed by the naked eye, therefore, the algorithm can well hide the existence of the blockchain private key.

Table 2. Transparency test results

Samples	Sample1	Sample2	Sample3
Average PSNR/dB	38.1587	36.3259	37.1346

Robustness Analysis. Then test these attacks that the watermark image may encounter, such as image scaling, Poisson noise, salt and pepper noise, Gaussian noise, and JPEG compression. The result of the tailoring attack was also added as a comparison. The ber value of the watermark image after attack is used as a verification index of the robustness of the algorithm [15]. Table 3 shows the results of the robust test.

According to the test results in Table 3, the algorithm is robust to image attacks such as image scaling, Poisson noise, JPEG compression, etc., and can accurately recover the blockchain private key information. However, if processed by printing, trimming, etc., the watermark information will be lost to a certain extent, and it is difficult to completely recover the accurate private key information. Therefore, when using the algorithm to save the blockchain private key, the watermark image of the hidden private key information cannot be printed, trimmed, etc., otherwise the private key information will be lost, resulting in irreparable blockchain asset loss.

Table 3. Robustness test results

Image attack	Average ber		
	Sample1	Sample2	Sample3
Scale 0.5 times	0.0000	0.0000	0.0000
Scale 2 times	0.0000	0.0000	0.0000
Poisson attack	0.0000	0.0000	0.0000
Salt and pepper attack	0.0000	0.0000	0.0000
Gaussian noise 30 dB	0.0000	0.0000	0.0000
JPEG compression QF = 60	0.0000	0.0000	0.0000
Tailoring attack	0.4158	0.4412	0.5317

5 Conclusions

The preservation of the blockchain private key has high requirements for transparency, robustness and security [15]. Therefore, this paper proposes a blockchain private key storage algorithm based on image information hiding, which hides the private key in the watermark information, and protects the watermark information by adding random numbers and adding error correcting codes. At last, watermark information is embedded into the carrier image using a watermarking algorithm based on DWT and STDM. This method not only hides the existence but also the content of the private key. Without any signal attack, hiding the private key of the blockchain in the image is highly robust, and can quickly and accurately extract the private key. In order to improve the robustness of this method to common image attacks, the algorithm uses the ratio of the Euclidean distance of the n-dimensional vector's odd and even terms, and the jitter amount as the STDM quantization factor, which can effectively resist image attacks such as image scaling, JPEG compression, poisson noise, etc. In most cases, the private key can be accurately extracted and the algorithm can adapt to the blockchain domain with high security requirements.

Acknowledgement. This work is supported by the National Natural Science Foundation of China grant (U1836205), Major Scientific and Technological Special Project of Guizhou Province (20183001), Open Foundation of Guizhou Provincial Key Laboratory of Public Big Data (2018BDKFJJ014), Open Foundation of Guizhou Provincial Key Laboratory of Public Big Data (2018BDKFJJ019) and Open Foundation of Guizhou Provincial Key Laboratory of Public Big Data (2018BDKFJJ022).

References

1. Zou, Y., Yu, B., Zhuang, P.: Blockchain core technology and application, pp. 99–102. Mechanical Industry Press (2018)
2. Xie, H., Wang, J.: Research on blockchain technology and its application. Netinfo Secur. 192–195 (2016)
3. Liang, J., Jin, X., Qi, W., et al.: Key management scheme for wireless sensor networks in advanced measurement system. Autom. Electr. Power Syst. **40**(19), 119–126 (2016)

4. Kingo. Classification and Comparative Analysis of Bitcoin Wallets. https://www.8btc.com/article/30431. Accessed 17 Sept 2014
5. 360 Information Security Department. Digital Money Wallet Security White Paper. https://www.anquanke.com/post/id/146233. Accessed 26 May 2018
6. Eskandari, S., Barrera, D., Stobert, E., et al.: A first look at the usability of bitcoin key management. In: Workshop on Usable Security (USEC), San Diego, USA (2015)
7. Shensa, M.J.: The discrete wavelet transform: wedding the a trous and Mallat algorithms. IEEE Trans. Signal Process. **40**(10), 2464–2482 (1992)
8. Yang, Y., Lei, M.: Information hiding and digital watermarking, pp. 15–18. Beijing University of Posts and Telecommunications Press (2017)
9. Feng, X., Zhu, X., Tang, Z.: Research progress on multimedia digital watermarking technology. Comput. Eng. Appl. (13), 6–10 (2017)
10. Chen, B., Wornell, G.: Quantization index modulation: a class of provably good methods for digital watermarking and information embedding. IEEE Trans. Inf. Theory **47**(4), 1423–1443 (2001)
11. Qu, Z., Li, Z., Xu, G., Wu, S., Wang, X.: Quantum images steganography protocol based on quantum image expansion and grover search algorithm. IEEE Access **7**, 50849–50857 (2019)
12. Liu, W., Chen, Z., Liu, J., Su, Z., Chi, L.: Full-blind delegating private quantum computation. CMC: Comput. Mater. Continua **56**(2), 211–223 (2018)
13. Tong, Y., Zhang, Q., Qi, Y.: Image quality evaluation model based on PSNR and SSIM. Chin. J. Image Graph. **11**(12), 1758–1763 (2006)
14. Yuan, Z., Zhang, Q., Chen, N.: Robustness analysis and research of digital watermarking. Comput. Eng. Des. **26**(3), 614–616 (2005)
15. Qu, Z., Zhu, T., Wang, J., Wang, X.: A novel quantum stegonagraphy based on brown states. CMC: Comput. Mater. Continua **56**(1), 47–59 (2018)

Heuristic-Q: A Privacy Data Pricing Method Based on Heuristic Reinforcement Learning

Xi Chen[1], Jingjie Chen[1], Yuling Chen[2(✉)], Jinglan Yang[1],
and Deyin Li[1]

[1] School of Cyberspace Security,
Beijing University of Posts and Telecommunications, Beijing, China
[2] State Key Laboratory of Public Big Data, Guizhou University,
Guiyang, Guizhou, China
61997525@qq.com

Abstract. With the development of big data applications in recent years, the value of personal data has received more and more attention. How to balance the conflict between data value development and personal privacy protection is an urgent problem to be solved. In response to the above contradictions, the market proposed a private data transaction mechanism to realize the commercial use of private data. However, existing private data transaction mechanisms still have deficiencies in some respects. In order to seek pricing strategies that maximize total revenue, this paper designs and constructs a privacy data dynamic pricing model from the perspective of data collectors, introduces heuristic reinforcement learning ideas, and proposes a pricing strategy algorithm based on heuristic functions. Finally, the simulation experiment of the proposed pricing model and strategy learning algorithm is carried out, and its performance is analyzed. The simulation results confirm that the algorithm can help data collectors get higher returns in the process of limited private data transactions.

Keywords: Reinforcement learning · Heuristic function · Data pricing · Privacy protection

1 Introduction

Personal data is an important property of an individual and its value can be reflected by data transactions or data mining [1]. Whether it's data trading or data mining, the process of developing the value of personal data generally involves multiple participants. Each participant can benefit from the use of personal data at a certain cost. In the process of using personal data, each participant wants to get the highest possible return at the lowest possible cost, and each participant's decision may have an impact on the earnings of other participants. To solve the conflict between the development of personal data value and personal privacy protection, the key is to achieve a certain equilibrium state through the rational decision of each participant.

The key step to establishing a data market is to set a reasonable price for the data. This paper analyzes the game relationship among multiple participants in data collection and uses the heuristic reinforcement learning method to solve effective pricing

X. Sun et al. (Eds.): ICAIS 2019, LNCS 11635, pp. 553–565, 2019.
https://doi.org/10.1007/978-3-030-24268-8_51

strategies. Relevant research results can provide some constructive opinions for the formulation of privacy pricing strategies in practical applications.

2   Related Work

2.1   Data Pricing

In current research on data pricing, data collectors' demand for personal data is often expressed as a query condition on the dataset. For example, literature [2] proposed a pricing mechanism for query results, literature [3, 4] discusses the properties that query pricing function needs to satisfy. In addition to pricing queries, some scholars have studied how to price data directly. Literature [5] studied the pricing problem in the following scenarios: multiple data collectors purchase data from multiple data providers, and the rewards paid by the data collector are related to the data provider's attitude toward privacy. Literature [6] studied the data pricing mechanism from the perspective of data providers. The proposed mechanism considers the purpose of data usage and the degree of privacy of data.

Literature [7] studies how to set data prices from the perspective of data collectors. In that paper, scholars have proposed the use of reinforcement learning to develop dynamic pricing strategies and achieved some certain results. However, the traditional reinforcement learning method has a time-consuming problem in the iterative solution process. In order to solve this problem, this paper introduces the heuristic reinforcement learning idea, and increases the heuristic function to improve the performance of the algorithm and speed up the learning of the algorithm.

2.2   Heuristic Reinforcement Learning

Heuristic reinforcement learning [8] is mediated by heuristic functions: $H : S \times A \rightarrow R$, it affects the action selection of the agent in the learning process of the agent. $H_t(s_t, a_t)$ indicates the importance of performing a_t actions in state s_t. The algorithm can accelerate the learning of agents by combining prior knowledge, adding additional returns or limiting the exploration scope. An important feature of the heuristic reinforcement learning algorithm is that the heuristic function can realize online self-adjustment and update as the learning process advances and the new heuristic information is enhanced.

In the framework of the heuristic reinforcement learning algorithm, different heuristic functions can be defined according to different known prior knowledge. A priori knowledge can be derived from information collected during the process of learning and exploration, as well as historical experience. The strategy has a strong correlation with the heuristic function. When a heuristic occurs, it indicates that other actions should be ignored in the current state. The heuristic function defines a tentative strategy for the acceleration of learning.

In general, adding heuristics is a very important way to improve reinforcement learning. Through the heuristic function, the learning process can be accelerated to a favorable state. Therefore, in the following work, this paper will construct a privacy data dynamic pricing model, and propose a heuristic function-based pricing strategy algorithm for the model to help data collectors maximize the total revenue.

3   System Model and Problem Formulation

3.1   Privacy Pricing

In the data transaction scenario constructed in this paper, one data collector sequentially trades with multiple data providers, and each data provider owns one data record. To compensate for the loss that data providers may suffer from privacy disclosure, data collectors need to pay a certain amount of compensation to the data provider. This article uses g represents the price that the data collector paid for a data record.

When the data collector's quotation is received, the data provider can decide whether to sell its data [9]. Because different data providers have different attitudes toward privacy, this article uses parameters $\sigma \in [0, 1]$ to quantify the attitude of data providers to privacy. The higher the value of parameter σ is, the higher the data provider attaches importance to privacy. The σ value for each data provider can be treated as a random variable. Parameter σ can be understood as the privacy cost of the data provider "generating" a data record. The data provider will sell the private data only if the data collector's offer is higher than this cost. In other words, if and only if $g \geq \sigma$, the transaction between the two will succeed. In the following discussion, this article sometimes refers to σ as the "type" of the data provider.

In the built model, we assume that the data collector transacts with T data providers in turn, the type of data provider participating in the transaction at time $t \in \{1, 2, 3, \ldots, T\}$ is σ_t. At the beginning of the transaction, the data collector selects a price from set $G \triangleq \{g_i | g_i = \frac{i}{M}, i = 1, 2, \ldots, M\}$ as the quote, then the data provider decides whether to accept the offer and provide the data based on its type σ. This model treats each price in set G as a quote state for the data collector. If the data collector selects the quote state g_i at time t, the corresponding revenue it can obtain is $p(g_i; \sigma_t)$. To protect the privacy of data providers, data collectors first anonymize the collected data. Next, data collectors can mine data or sell data to the third parties. Regardless of the route, data collectors can profit from the data they purchase. If v is used to represent the value created by a data record to the data collector, given any quotation state $g_i \in G$, then by trading with a data provider of type σ_t, the revenue that the data collector can obtain in this transaction is as follows:

$$p(g_i; \sigma_t) = \begin{cases} v - g_i, g_i \geq \sigma_t \\ 0, 0 \leq g_i \leq \sigma_t \end{cases} \tag{1}$$

Further, given the distribution of σ and the quote of the data collector g, the expected return of the data collector is as follows:

$$E[p(g; \sigma)] = F_\sigma(g)(v - g) \tag{2}$$

Among them, $F_\sigma(g)$ represents the probability that the data provider will accept quote g. In the case of $F_\sigma(g)$ unknown, the data collector needs to apply a learning policy to determine the optimal quotation state with the highest expected revenue $S_t^* = \underset{i=1,\ldots,M}{argmax} \, p_i$.

Learning strategies can be understood as a set of mappings from historical information to quotation status $\{\psi_t\}$, in which ψ_t maps the historical information before time t (including the quotation of the data collector, the transaction result, etc.) to the ordinal number S_t of the quotation state selected at time t. The performance of the learning strategy can be assessed with a "regret" [10]. In short, the regret value represents the difference between the cumulative return of the strategy to be evaluated and the cumulative return of a benchmark strategy. The so-called benchmark strategy refers to the strategy of always selecting the optimal quotation status. Since the choice of the quotation status and the return from each quotation status are random, the regret value is usually calculated by the following formula:

$$R(T) = \sum_{t=1}^{T} p_{s_t^*} - \sum_{t=1}^{T} p_{s_t} \tag{3}$$

Among them, T is called the time range.

3.2   Data Anonymization

As mentioned earlier, before using the data, the data collector will first anonymize the collected raw data. In the privacy data dynamic pricing model constructed in this paper, the data collector uses K-anonymity [11] to process the privacy data of the data provider, so as to achieve the purpose of privacy protection.

In a data set, if each record has at least the same quasi-identifier as the other $k - 1$ records, the data set is said to be k-anonymous. If the data set satisfies the k-anonymity condition, the probability that each individual's identity is accurately recognized by the privacy attacker is not higher than $\frac{1}{k}$. The higher the value of the parameter k, the more secure the privacy of the data provider. To achieve k-anonymity, a common practice is to generalize the data. Generalization can result in loss of information, resulting in a decline in data utility. For a given k value, as the total amount of data collected by the data collector increases, the degree of generalization required to achieve the k-anonymity condition decreases, and the corresponding information loss is also reduced.

As can be seen from Eq. (2), given the σ distribution and the quote g, the expected return of the data collector is determined by the value of the data v. It should be noted that v represents the value that a data record can create for a data collector after anonymization. If v_{ori} represents the value of the original data record, then $v < v_{ori}$. As discussed above, the difference between v and v_{ori} depends on the total number of data records collected by the data collector. The total number of data records collected by the data collector before time $t + 1$ is represented by N_t. After k-anonymity processing of a data set composed of N_t records, the value of each data record can be defined as:

$$v_t = \begin{cases} v_{\min}, & \text{if } N_t < k \\ (1 - \rho(N_t; k))v_{ori}, & \text{otherwise} \end{cases} \tag{4}$$

Among them, the meaning of constant variable v_{min} is: when the total number of data records is lower than k, because the condition of k-anonymity cannot be met, the data collector cannot use the data under the premise of ensuring privacy and security, and at this time, the value that each data record can create for the data collector is extremely low. In the above formula, function $\rho(N_t; k)$ represents the average information loss caused by k-anonymity, and this function is a monotone non-increasing function of N_t.

Due to the time-varying nature of the income distribution, the optimal offer state is not fixed, so the regret value defined in formula (3) cannot be used to evaluate the performance of the learning strategy. In the subsequent simulation analysis, the "weak regret" value proposed in literature [12] was used as the evaluation index in this paper. Given the time range T, the calculation method of the weak regret value is as follows:

$$R(T) = \max_{i=1,\dots,M} \sum_{t=1}^{T} \mathrm{p}(g_i; \sigma_t) - \sum_{t=1}^{T} p(g_{s_t}; \sigma_t) \tag{5}$$

4 Learning Policy

The Q-learning algorithm was first proposed by C.Watkins in his doctoral thesis "Learning from delayed rewards" [13] in 1989, it is one of the classic algorithms for reinforcement learning. In this paper, the Heuristic-Q algorithm is proposed to improve the traditional Q-learning algorithm by designing and adding Heuristic function.

Figure 1 shows the framework diagram of the Heuristic-Q algorithm. It can be seen that compared with the original algorithm, Heuristic-Q algorithm has added the feature module. In the feature module, two important features of additional reward and harmonic function are obtained based on existing prior knowledge and environmental information. The original immediate return and the additional return together constitute a new reward function, hereinafter referred to as the heuristic reward function; the harmonic function guides the action selection of the agent, hereinafter referred to as the heuristic strategy selection function.

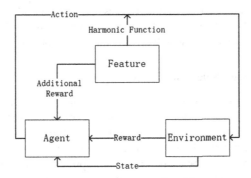

Fig. 1. The framework diagram of the Heuristic-Q algorithm

4.1 Heuristic Reward Function

The Heuristic-Q algorithm's heuristic reward function is derived by adding the original immediate reward function to the additional reward function, written as follows:

$$R_H = R_L + R_F \tag{6}$$

Among them, R_H is the heuristic reward function, R_L is the immediate reward function, and R_F is the additional reward function. In the original algorithm, the original immediate return function is as follows:

$$R_L = \begin{cases} v - g, g \geq \sigma \\ 0, 0 \leq g < \sigma \end{cases} \tag{7}$$

Considering the actual data transaction scenario in reality and the privacy data dynamic pricing model constructed in this paper, we can use the difference between the price g of data collector's bid at each round and the expected price σ of the data provider as a feature. On the premise that the data collector's bid g is greater than the expected price σ of the data provider, the closer the value is to 0, the better the situation. Based on this feature, the additional return function R_F is set as follows:

$$R_F = \begin{cases} \frac{1}{g-\sigma} * w, g - \sigma > 0.1 \\ 10 * w, 0 \leq g - \sigma \leq 0.1 \\ g - \sigma, g - \sigma < 0 \end{cases} \tag{8}$$

Among them, ω should be a small positive number, so as not to disturb the existing reward value too much. In the above formula:

1. When $g - \sigma > 0.1$, the closer the price offered by the data collector to the expected price of the data provider, the larger the heuristic reward given by the algorithm I s;
2. When $0 \leq g - \sigma \leq 0.1$, the algorithm determines that the price offered by the data collector is in the most ideal state and gives the highest additional return value;
3. When $g - \sigma < 0$, the data collector fails the transaction due to underbidding, and R_F value is negative at this time, which reflects the punishment for this pricing strategy.

4.2 Heuristic Strategy Selection Function

In order to solve the problem of "exploration-exploitation", data collectors can use effective heuristic strategy selection function as an exploration strategy to guide action selection to improve the learning efficiency of the algorithm. The basic idea of the UCB algorithm [14] is to estimate the expected return of each offer using a linear combination of previously observed benefits. This paper applies this idea to heuristic strategy selection functions π_H. This function maintains two variables during the learning process. The formula of heuristic strategy selection function π_H is given below:

$$\pi_H = \bar{r}_i + \beta * \sqrt{\frac{\ln t}{n}} \tag{9}$$

Among them, the first variable n_i is defined as:

$$n_i \triangleq \sum_{\tau=1}^{t-1} \amalg(g_\tau \geq \sigma_\tau) \tag{10}$$

This variable represents the number of times the quoted state g_i is selected from the initial time to time t; The second variable $\bar{r}_i$ represents the average of the historical return of the quote status g_i. Variable $\bar{r}_i$ is taken as the estimate of expected return corresponding to quotation state g_i, the upper bound on the confidence of this estimate is $\bar{r}_i + \beta * \sqrt{\frac{\ln t}{n_i}}$, among them the parameter β is used to control the width of the confidence interval. After each iteration of the Q empirical value, the action corresponding to the current quote state with the highest revenue confidence upper bound is selected.

In the heuristic strategy selection process, if the selected quote state corresponds to a higher value $\beta * \sqrt{\frac{\ln t}{n_i}}$, that is, the n_i value selected in the history of this quotation state is small, it indicates that the data collector makes a decision of "exploration", and at this time, $\bar{r}_i$ is unreliable as an estimate of expected revenue. On the contrary, if the selected quotation state corresponds to a high $\bar{r}_i$ value, it indicates that the data collector has made a decision of "exploitation", in which case, the data collector mainly uses historical returns to estimate expected returns. As the number of times this quote state is selected increases, the value of $\beta * \sqrt{\frac{\ln t}{n_i}}$ decreases rapidly, so the number of times the data collector makes "exploratory" decisions is limited. As $\beta * \sqrt{\frac{\ln t}{n_i}}$ value decreases, the average historical return $\bar{r}_i$ is closer to the real expected return, which means that the quotation state corresponding to the maximum $\bar{r}_i$ value is more likely to be the real optimal quotation.

To sum up, the Heuristic strategy selection function π_H can effectively solve the balance problem of "exploration-exploitation" in the learning process of data collectors, and act on the Heuristic-Q algorithm together with the Heuristic reward function, which significantly optimizes the learning and guidance process of the algorithm.

5 Simulation

5.1 Dataset and Anonymization Method

The data used in the simulation was from the Adult [15] dataset, which is one of the most commonly used datasets in data anonymization research. The raw Adult data set contains 32,561 records from the census database, each consisting of 15 attribute values. After removing the records with incomplete information, this article takes the remaining 30,000 records as the data provider's data, and each record corresponds to a data provider. Referring to the existing research on anonymization [16], this paper develops a Java program by using the open source software ARX [17]. ARX implements a variety of anonymization algorithms and information Loss measurement methods. K-anonymity is selected here and Loss index proposed in literature [18] is used to measure information loss. The value of information loss is between 0 and 1. The higher the value is, the greater the information loss is.

In the subsequent experiments, k-anonymity parameter k was set as 10. To obtain the quantitative relationship between information loss and the total number of data records, during the simulation, the data fitting toolbox provided by MATLAB was used to fit the experimental results. Given k = 10, the parametric function $\rho(N_t; k)$ in formula (3–4) can be expressed as follows:

$$\rho(N_t; k) = 1.193(N_t)^{-0.1104} \tag{11}$$

5.2   Parameter Setting of Learning Policies

To simulate a private data pricing scenario, we need to determine the type of each data provider first. Here, a normally distributed random number $\tilde{\sigma}_i$ with mean 0.6 and standard deviation $\frac{1}{6}$ is generated. Since $\tilde{\sigma}_i$ may fall outside the interval $[0, 1]$, this paper defines σ_i as follows:

$$\sigma_i = \begin{cases} 0, & if\ \tilde{\sigma}_i < 0 \\ 1, & if\ \tilde{\sigma}_i > 1 \\ \tilde{\sigma}_i, & otherwise \end{cases} \tag{12}$$

The data collector selects the price from set $G \triangleq \{g_i | g_i = \frac{i}{M}, i = 1, 2, \ldots, M\}$. In this paper, M = 10 is set in the simulation. Other parameters related to the learning algorithm are set as follows:

1. v_{ori}: This paper tests two v_{ori} values, namely $v_{ori} = 2$ and $v_{ori} = 8$. Since the price range is $[0, 1]$, if $v_{ori} = 2$, it can ensure that the data collector can still get non-negative benefits when the anonymization causes a 50% decline in data value. The larger the value of v_{ori} is, the more obvious the influence of information loss on data value will be. Therefore, the expected return corresponding to each price will be more sensitive to the change of the total number of data records.
2. γ, β, ω: In this paper, the values of learning parameters γ, β, ω are simulated. Among the multiple results obtained, the optimal results are reserved for the comparison of different algorithms.
3. k: In all simulations, k - the anonymous parameter $k = 10$.
4. T: In subsequent experiments, the total number of data transactions $T = 30000$.

5.3   Simulation Results and Evaluation

In order to evaluate the performance of the Heuristic-Q algorithm proposed in this paper, the UCB algorithm and the Q-learning algorithm in literature [6] were simultaneously used in the simulation process to carry out experiments and analyze and compare the results.

The goal of a data collector is to collect as much data as possible at a lower price. Therefore, this paper measures the performance of the learning algorithm by the actual total revenue of the data collector. If the data collection process terminates after time t, the total benefit to the data collector is as follows:

$$P(t) = N_t v_t - \sum_{\tau=1}^{t} g_\tau \, \mathrm{II}(g_\tau \geq \sigma_\tau) \tag{13}$$

Among them, v_t is calculated according to formula (4), and the information loss $\rho(N_t; k)$ in formula (4) is obtained by running the anonymization algorithm on the data set generated by the algorithm. The second item on the right of the above equation represents the total price paid by the data collector in the process of data collection.

Given the type $\{\sigma_i\}_{i=1}^{30000}$ of the data provider, the parameters and the learning algorithm, the data collection process is simulated. In order to reduce the influence of randomness, the entire data collection process is repeated for 10 times under the given same setting. Finally, the average value obtained from the 10 simulations is used as the simulation result of each learning algorithm.

Figures 2 and 3 respectively show the cumulative total benefits of the Heuristic-Q algorithm, Q-learning algorithm and UCB algorithm when v_{ori} value is 2 and 8 respectively.

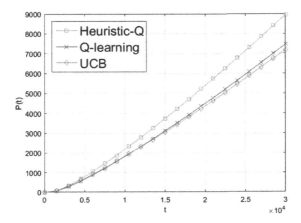

Fig. 2. Cumulative total revenue of each algorithm when $v_{ori} = 2$

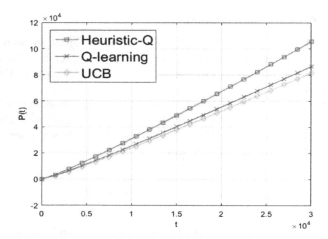

Fig. 3. Cumulative total revenue of each algorithm when $v_{ori} = 8$

As can be seen from Figs. 2 and 3, when the types of data providers are normally distributed, the Heuristic-Q algorithm, whether $v_{ori} = 2$ or $v_{ori} = 8$, performs better than the other two algorithms. The experimental results show that, with Heuristic-Q algorithm as the pricing guiding strategy of data collectors, data collectors can obtain higher cumulative benefits in the process of data transaction.

In order to further analyses the performance of the proposed learning algorithm, this paper not only calculates the total return of the data collector in the transaction process through simulation, but also calculates the weak regret value of the three algorithms above Figs. 4 and 5 show the variation of weak regret values of the three algorithms when v_{ori} values 2 and 8 respectively.

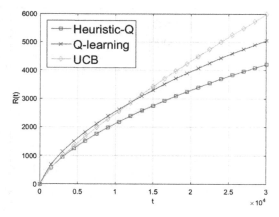

Fig. 4. Results of weak regret values of each algorithm when $v_{ori} = 2$

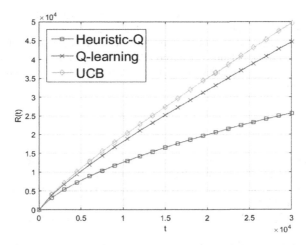

Fig. 5. Results of weak regret values of each algorithm when $v_{ori} = 8$

Simulation results on real data sets show that when v_{ori} values 2 and 8 respectively, the weak regret value curves of the Heuristic-Q algorithm converge the most, and the weak regret value grows the slowest with time, which reflects the superiority of the Heuristic-Q pricing strategy algorithm proposed in this paper over the other two algorithms. The evaluation result of the weak regret value also indicates that the data collector can find the optimal price with a high probability by executing the Heuristic-Q algorithm.

In addition to calculating the weak regret value, this paper also counted the times when the Heuristic-Q algorithm selected different offers. The statistical results show that the price most frequently selected by Heuristic-Q algorithm is consistent with the optimal price selected afterwards. This result once again proves the validity of the proposed algorithm.

6 Conclusion

For the data trading market, pricing privacy data scientifically and rationally is very important. In order to balance the conflict between data value development and personal privacy protection, this paper constructs a privacy data dynamic pricing model from the perspective of data collectors. Then, Heuristic reinforcement learning is introduced, and Heuristic-Q pricing strategy algorithm is proposed by designing and adding Heuristic function to accelerate the learning speed of strategy algorithm. Finally, the pricing model and strategy learning algorithm are simulated. Simulation results prove that the proposed algorithm can help data collectors to obtain higher returns in the limited privacy data transaction process.

Acknowledgments. This work is supported by the National Natural Science Foundation of China grant (U1836205), Major Scientific and Technological Special Project of Guizhou Province (20183001), Open Foundation of Guizhou Provincial Key Laboratory of Public Big Data (2018BDKFJJ014), Open Foundation of Guizhou Provincial Key Laboratory of Public Big Data (2018BDKFJJ019) and Open Foundation of Guizhou Provincial Key Laboratory of Public Big Data (2018BDKFJJ022).

References

1. Xiao, B., Wang, Z., Liu, Q., et al.: SMK-means: an improved mini batch k-means algorithm based on mapreduce with big data. CMC **56**(3), 365–379 (2018)
2. Li, C., Li, D.Y., Miklau, G., et al.: A theory of pricing private data. ACM Trans. Database Syst. **39**(4), 34:1–34:28 (2014)
3. Koutris, P., Upadhyaya, P., Balazinska, M., et al.: Query-based data pricing. J. ACM **62**(5), 43:1–43:44 (2015)
4. Lin, B.R., Kifer, D.: On arbitrage-free pricing for general data queries. Proc. VLDB Endow. **7**(9), 757–768 (2014)
5. Gkatzelis, V., Aperjis, C., Huberman, B.A.: Pricing private data. Electron. Markets **25**(2), 109–123 (2015)
6. Li, X.B., Raghunathan, S.: Pricing and disseminating customer data with privacy awareness. Decis. Support Syst. **59**, 63–73 (2014)
7. Chen, X., Yang, Y., Xu, L., et al.: Dynamic privacy pricing based on reinforcement learning. In: Proceedings of 2018 International Conference on Big Data and Computing, pp. 59–64. Association for Computing Machinery (2018)
8. Bianchi, R.A.C., Ribeiro, C.H.C., Costa, A.H.R.: Heuristically accelerated Q–learning: a new approach to speed up reinforcement learning. In: Bazzan, A.L.C., Labidi, S. (eds.) SBIA 2004. LNCS (LNAI), vol. 3171, pp. 245–254. Springer, Heidelberg (2004). https://doi.org/10.1007/978-3-540-28645-5_25
9. Chuanrong, W., Zapevalova, E., Chen, Y., et al.: Time optimization of multiple knowledge transfers in the big data environment. CMC **54**(3), 269–285 (2018)
10. Bubeck, S., Cesa-Bianchi, N.: Regret analysis of stochastic and nonstochastic multi-armed bandit problems. arXiv preprint arXiv:1204.5721 (2012)
11. Sweeney, L.: Achieving k-anonymity privacy protection using generalization and suppression. Int. J. Uncertainty, Fuzziness Knowl.-Based Syst. **10**(05), 571–588 (2002)
12. Auer, P., Cesa-Bianchi, N., Freund, Y., et al.: The nonstochastic multiarmed bandit problem. SIAM J. Comput. **32**(1), 48–77 (2002)
13. Watkins, J.C.H.: Leaning from delayed rewards. Ph.D. thesis. University of Cambridge, England (1989)
14. Auer, P., Cesa-Bianchi, N., Fischer, P.: Finite-time analysis of the multiarmed bandit problem. Mach. Learn. **47**(2/3), 235–256 (2002)
15. Bache, K., Lichman, M.: UCI machine learning repository. University of California, Irvine, School of Information and Computer Sciences (2013). http://archive.ics.uci.edu/ml
16. LeFevre, K., DeWitt, D.J., Ramakrishnan, R.: Incognito: efficient full-domain k-anonymity. In: Proceedings of the 2005 ACM SIGMOD International Conference on Management of Data, SIGMOD 2005, pp. 49–60. ACM, New York (2005). http://doi.acm.org/10.1145/1066157.1066164

17. Kohlmayer, F., Prasser, F., Eckert, C., et al.: Flash: efficient, stable and optimal k-anonymity. In: 2012 International Conference on Privacy, Security, Risk and Trust (PASSAT), 2012 International Conference on Social Computing (SocialCom). [S.l.: s.n.], pp. 708–717 (2012)
18. Iyengar, V.S.: Transforming data to satisfy privacy constraints. In: Proceedings of the Eighth ACM SIGKDD International Conference on Knowledge Discovery and Data Mining, KDD 2002, pp. 279–288. ACM, New York (2002). http://doi.acm.org/10.1145/775047.775089

JPEGCNN: A Transform Domain Steganalysis Model Based on Convolutional Neural Network

Lin Gan[1], Jingjie Chen[1], Yuling Chen[2(✉)], Zhujun Jin[1], and Wenxi Han[1]

[1] School of Cyberspace Security,
Beijing University of Posts and Telecommunications, Beijing, China
[2] State Key Laboratory of Public Big Data, GuiZhou University, Guizhou, China
61997525@qq.com

Abstract. Convolutional Neural Network (CNN) has gained an overwhelming advantage in many fields of pattern recognition. Both excellent data learning ability and automatic feature extraction ability of CNN are urgently needed in image steganalysis. However, the application of CNN in image steganalysis is still in its infancy, especially in the field of JPEG steganalysis. In this paper, a steganalysis model based on CNN in gray image transform domain is proposed, which is called JPEGCNN. At the same time, on the basis of JPEGCNN, JPEGCNN is extended to the transform domain of color image by researching and designing different methods of feature extraction. RGBMERGE-JPEGCNN and RGBADD-JPEGCNN are proposed respectively, which make up for the lack of research on steganalysis model based on convolution neural network in the transform domain of color image. Experiments show that JPEGCNN, RGBMERGE-JPEGCNN and RGBADD-JPEGCNN proposed in this paper have good detection ability for steganography algorithm in transform domain.

Keywords: Steganalysis · Convolutional Neural Network · Transform domain

1 Introduction

Steganalysis is a technique to determine whether additional information is hidden in the cover or not by analyzing the statistical characteristics of the carrier, and even to estimate the amount of information embedded in the carrier, and to obtain the content of the hidden information. At present, steganalysis is usually regarded as a two-class problem in the field of steganalysis. The goal is to distinguish between cover and stego. Under this circumstance, the existing methods mainly construct steganalysis detectors through the following two steps: feature extraction and classification. In the feature extraction step, a series of hand-crafted features are extracted from the image to capture the effects of the embedding operation. The effectiveness of steganalysis depends heavily on feature design. However, this work is complicated due to the lack of an accurate natural image model. At present, the most reliable characteristic design paradigm is to calculate the noise residuals and then model the residuals using the conditions of adjacent elements or joint probability distribution. With the increasing

© Springer Nature Switzerland AG 2019
X. Sun et al. (Eds.): ICAIS 2019, LNCS 11635, pp. 566–577, 2019.
https://doi.org/10.1007/978-3-030-24268-8_52

complexity of steganography, the more complex statistical characteristics of images need to be considered in the design process of the steganalysis domain, and the characteristics are gradually moving towards complexity and high dimensionality. For example, the representative steganalysis methods such as SRM (Spatial Rich Model) [1], PSRM (Projection Speciation Rich Model) [2] and other feature dimensions all exceed 10,000 dimensions. In the classification step, classifiers such as SVM or ensemble classifier learn the extracted features and use them for classification. Because the steps of feature extraction and classification are separated, they can't be optimized uniformly, which means that the classifier may not make full use of the useful information in feature extraction.

In order to solve the aforementioned problems, researchers have introduced deep learning theory into steganalysis in recent years. At the same time, according to the domain of steganography information extraction, image steganalysis can be divided into two categories: spatial domain steganalysis and transform domain steganalysis. There are many research results for spatial domain steganalysis, but few for transform domain steganalysis [3]. In 2016, Zeng et al. [4] applied the deep learning framework to transform do-main steganalysis for the first time and proposed a JPEG steganalysis model with three CNN subnetworks, which is called Hybrid CNN (HCNN). The final experimental results show that the accuracy of HCNN is higher than DCTR [5] and PHARM [6]. Zeng et al.'s findings demonstrate the feasibility of applying a deep learning framework for transform domain steganalysis. However, the HCNN is more complex than the previous deep learning based steganalysis model in spatial domain. The reasons are as follows: (1) The network has two additional steps quantitative and truncated. (2) The feature extraction module contains three paths, whereas the previous model only contains one path. In view of the vacancy of applying CNN theory to steganalysis in transform domain and the shortcomings of previous research results, an efficient steganalysis model based on CNN in transform domain is proposed, which is called JPEGCNN. Compared with HCNN, the proposed model has the following advantages: (1) The core of HPF layer in the preprocessing module is simpler. (2) Operation without quantization and truncation. (3) Parallel subnetwork structure is not required. These three points make the network proposed in this paper easier to implement and less computational overhead. In addition, on the basis of JPEGCNN, the general steganalysis model JPEGCNN for gray image transformation domain is extended to color image transformation domain by studying and designing different feature extraction methods. RGBMERGE-JPEGCNN and RGBADD-JPEGCNN are proposed respectively, which make up for the lack of research on steganalysis model based on convolution neural network in color image transformation domain.

The following contents are as follows: The second part mainly describes the structure of JPEGCNN proposed in this paper. The third part is the experiment of JPEGCNN. The fourth and fifth parts elaborate the color extended version of JPEGCNN and related experiments. The last part is conclusion and prospect.

2 JPEGCNN Model

2.1 Preprocessing Module

The preprocessing module usually has a HPF layer. The HPF layer is a special con-volutional layer that is at the forefront of the entire network. In this layer, a pre-defined high-pass filter is usually used for filtering. the kernel used by the HPF layer in JPEGCNN is still from the SRM and size is 3 × 3. The absolute values of the weights in the kernel are distributed between 0 and 1, as follows.

$$\frac{1}{4} \begin{pmatrix} -1 & 2 & -1 \\ 2 & -4 & 2 \\ -1 & 2 & -1 \end{pmatrix} \tag{1}$$

The use of the filter described above is based on the following reasons: (1) Pixel residuals, rather than quantized DCT coefficients, are more conducive to steganalysis. The steganography algorithm usually has a small modification range for JPEG quan-tized coefficients, mostly plus or minus one. Therefore, the influence on the statistical characteristics of JPEG quantized coefficients is not significant. Using a filter similar to HCNN, there is no significant advantage in learning the difference between the two types of sample data from the transform domain. For spatial domain, although the quantization coefficient is only changed by 1 unit, the interference of the stegano-graphic operation on the spatial pixels is further amplified by the amplification step of the quantization step, which is advantageous for the steganographic analysis. In addition, SRM has given a neighborhood pixel correlation model. There is a clear model in the spatial domain analysis as a guide. Pix-el residuals suppress the inter-ference of image content. However, the correlation of neighborhood pixel correlation in the DCT domain is not modeled. The direct analysis of the DCT coefficients is inevitably affected by the image content, which further demonstrates the rationality of analyzing the residuals in the spatial domain. (2) A reasonably sized filter kernel function is more conducive to steganalysis. Research indicates that for complex ima-ges, neighborhood pixel correlation will decrease dramatically as the distance between the boundary and the center increases. The 5 × 5 filter used by GNCNN contains too many pixels with a distance from the center pixel greater than 2, and its ability to capture the neighborhood pixel correlation will decrease. Therefore, JPEGCNN uses a 3 × 3 size filter.

2.2 Feature Extraction Module

After residual is extracted by the preprocessing module, image is input into the feature extraction module composed of several convolutional layers.

Feature extraction module usually consists of multiple convolutional layers. Con-volutional layer's input and output are a set of arrays called feature map, and each convolutional layer typically produces feature map in three steps, convolution, non-linear activation, and pooling operation. The first step uses k convolutional kernels for filtering, resulting in k new feature maps. $F^n(X)$ denotes the feature map of the nth layer output. Weight^n denotes the nth layer convolutional kernel and Bias^n denotes the offset. The convolutional layer can be expressed as follow:

$$F^n(X) = P\left(A^n\left(F^{n-1}(X) * Weight^n + Bias^n\right)\right) \tag{2}$$

In the formula, $F^0(X) = X$ represents input data and $A^n(\cdot)$ represents the nonlinear activation function. Nonlinear activation function is applied to each input element. Typical activation functions are sigmod, TanH, and ReLU. $P(\cdot)$ represents pooling operation, including average pooling operation and maximum pooling operation. In general, nonlinear activation function and pooling operation are optional in a specific layer, and a convolutional layer can also be set as untrainable.

In convolutional layer, each output feature map combines the features of multiple input feature maps by convolution. The structure of the convolutional layer involves the concepts of local perception and weight sharing. For local perception, each low-dimensional feature is only calculated from a subset of the inputs, such as the area of the pixel at a given location in the image. The local feature extractor shares the same parameters when applied to different adjacent input positions, which corresponds to the convolution of the image pixel values with the kernel containing the weight parameters. Weight sharing generates a shift-invariant operation, which also reduces the number of free variables, thereby increasing the generalization of the network.

The feature extraction module of JPEGCNN has 5 layers. Each of layer contains 16 convolution kernels of size 3×3 or 5×5. Compared to HCNN, the number of convolutional layers in JPEGCNN has been reduced by nearly half. The first convolutional layer of the feature extraction module uses the Gaussian activation function, and the deeper layers use ReLU activation function. Combined with the experimental results of ICNN, it is known that using ReLU as an activation function at a deeper level of CNN is a better choice. The average pooling operation is used at the end of each convolutional layer. The purpose of the pooling operation is to convert low-level feature representation into more useful feature identifier, thereby saving important information and discarding irrelevant detail. In general, deeper feature representation requires information from progressively larger input regions. The role of pooling is to merge information into a small set of local regions while reducing computational overhead, which is similar to the purpose of quantifying and truncating operations to aggregate useful features and discarding useless information.

2.3   Classification Module

The features extracted by the feature extraction module are input into the classification module for classification. The classification module finally outputs the category of image which is cover or stego. The classification module usually contains several fully-connected layers and a classifier [7].

Ye et al. [8] proposed that the fully-connected layer usually contains more training parameters. When the training set is not large enough, it easily leads to overfitting. One solution is to use only one fully-connected layer during training. There is another way to solve the problem of overfitting that is to use the dropout to regularize the fully-connected layer. When using dropout for training, the neuron output in the corresponding layer is set to 0 with a certain probability. This technology can improve CNN's generalization ability to some extent.

The classification module has two 128-dimensional fully-connected layers and a softmax classifier. Dropout layers are added after each fully-connected layer to prevent overfitting. The dropout parameter is set to 0.5.

2.4 The Overall Structure

Combining the above three modules, the structure of JPEGCNN is shown in the Fig. 1. Taking the 256 × 256 size image as input. The input size of each layer is marked in the upper left corner.

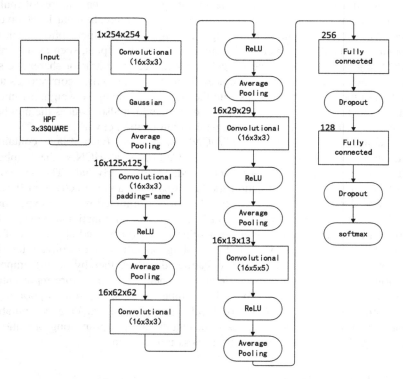

Fig. 1. The overall structure of JPEGCNN

3 Experiments and Analysis of JPEGCNN Model

3.1 The Data Set and Parameter

The data set used in this paper's experiment is the standardized data set BOSSBase 1.01 [9]. BOSSBase 1.01 contains 10,000 images. Each of image's size is 512 × 512. Due to limitation in computing resource, this paper resized the size of BOSSBase 1.01 images to size 256 × 256 in the experiment. 5 transform domain steganography algorithms were used to evaluate the steganalysis ability of the JPEGCNN. These transform domain steganography algorithms were Jsteg, nsf5, MB1, MB2, and J-UNIWARD [10].

In experiment, steganography algorithms and cover were used to generate the corresponding stego. These 10,000 cover images and 10,000 stego images together formed the data of one experiment (10,000 pairs of cover-stego images). The training set, verification set, and test set used a ratio of 8:1:1, that was, the training set was 8000 pairs of cover-stego images, the verification set was 1000 pairs of cover-stego images, and the test set was 1000 pairs of cover-stego images.

The network learning rate in this paper was mostly set to 0.05 (occasionally 0.005 depending on experimental results). Adadelta [11] gradient descent algorithm was used during training. The size of mini-batch was 64. In the pre-processing module, the HPF layer initialization weight has been described in the second section and was set to non-trainable. The parameter of the Gaussian activation function was $\sigma^2 = 0.2$. In the feature extraction module, the convolutional kernel of each layer was initialized using a "Xavier" [12] initializer. The pooling size of each layer was 3×3 and the step size was 2. The total number of parameters of JPEGCNN is 63,212, and the number of parameters that could be trained is 63,202, while the number of parameters of HCNN is one million. JPEGCNN greatly reduces the number of parameters and improves computational efficiency.

3.2   The Experimental Results

The experimental result is shown in Fig. 2. The horizontal axis represents the steganography algorithms used, and each steganography algorithm uses three embedding rates. The vertical axis represents the accuracy of the JPEGCNN model on the test set. The embedding rate is calculated based on the bpn-zac (bits per nonzero AC DCT). It can be seen that JPEGCNN has good detection ability for five steganography algorithms.

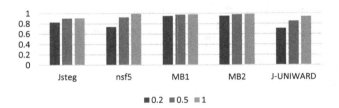

Fig. 2. The performance of JPEGCNN

4   JPEGCNN Color Extension Model

4.1   JPEGCNN Steganalysis Model Based on RGB Three-Channel Merge

According to the two strategies of steganalysis of color image, the most direct way of steganalysis of color image is to transform the three-channel color image directly into a single-channel gray image, and then use the gray image steganalysis model JPEGCNN for steganalysis. This JPEGCNN model based on RGB three-channel merge is called RGBMERGE-JPEGCNN in this paper.

When transforming color image into gray image, it is necessary to consider the perception ability of human eyes to different colors and give appropriate weights to different channels in order to effectively retain useful information in each channel and reduce information loss. In this paper, the brightness equation is used to fuse the three channels of color image into a single channel gray image. The brightness equation is shown in Eq. 3 below.

$$y = 0.299R + 0.587G + 0.144B \tag{3}$$

Where y denotes the gray value of the pixel, R denotes the value of the red channel, G denotes the value of the green channel, and B denotes the value of the blue channel. The values before R, G and B are the conversion coefficients designed according to the sensitivity of human eyes to different colors of light.

Therefore, in the preprocessing module of RGBMERGE-JPEGCNN, besides HPF layer, an operation module of color channel fusion is needed. On the basis of JPEGCNN, the operation of color channel fusion is added to the preprocessing module, and the summary structure of RGBMERGE-JPEGCNN as shown in Fig. 3 below can be obtained.

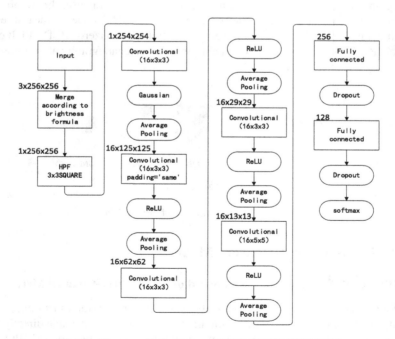

Fig. 3. The overall structure of RGBMERGE-JPEGCNN

4.2   JPEGCNN Steganalysis Model Based on RGB Three-Channel Superposition

R, G and B channels are merged by brightness formula, which may lose some useful information when fusing. In addition to the idea mentioned above, there is another way of thinking. For the three color channels R, G and B, each color channel can be regarded as a gray image. Therefore, the residual can be calculated on three color channels separately, then the residual can be superimposed, and then input into the network for feature extraction. The advantage of this method is to retain all residual information contained in the three color channels.

This JPEGCNN model based on RGB three-channel superposition is called RGBADD-JPEGCNN. In order to stack the residuals on the three color channels, the high-pass filter in the preprocessing module of RGBADD-JPEGCNN is extended to the size of 3x3x3, that is to say, the high-pass filter of JPEGCNN is expanded to a three-channel version. As shown in Formula 4 below.

$$
\begin{aligned}
\text{Layer 1 } \frac{1}{4} &\begin{pmatrix} -1 & 2 & -1 \\ 2 & -4 & 2 \\ -1 & 2 & -1 \end{pmatrix} \\
\text{Layer 2 } \frac{1}{4} &\begin{pmatrix} -1 & 2 & -1 \\ 2 & -4 & 2 \\ -1 & 2 & -1 \end{pmatrix} \quad (4) \\
\text{Layer 3 } \frac{1}{4} &\begin{pmatrix} -1 & 2 & -1 \\ 2 & -4 & 2 \\ -1 & 2 & -1 \end{pmatrix}
\end{aligned}
$$

When the color image is inputted into RGBADD-JPEGCNN, the residuals of R, G and B channels can be extracted separately by three-dimensional high-pass filter and three-dimensional convolution operation of the inputted color image, and the results can be superimposed to the output of only one channel. The calculation process is as follows: (1) Two-dimensional convolution between the first layer and R channel, two-dimensional convolution between the second layer and G channel, and two-dimensional convolution between the third layer and B channel. (2) The final three-dimensional convolution results are obtained by adding the convolution result matrices of the first and third channels according to their corresponding positions.

After preprocessing the input image with the extended high-pass filter, the dimension of the data is reduced from three-dimensional to two-dimensional, and the operation can follow the idea of JPEGCNN to deal with the two-dimensional matrix. The summary structure of RGBADD-JPEGCNN is shown in Fig. 4 below.

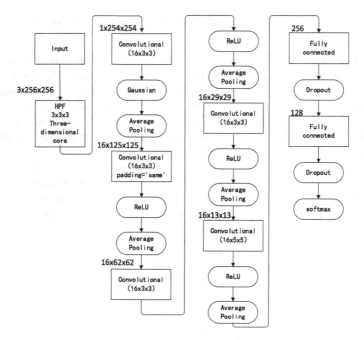

Fig. 4. The overall structure of RGBADD-JPEGCNN

5 Experiments and Analysis of JPEGCNN Color Extension Model

5.1 The Data Set and Parameter

The data set used in the experiment is the color version of the standardized data set BOSSBase v1.0. The content of the image includes people, scenery, architecture, dolls and other contents. The format of the image is cr2. In this paper, 2000 original images in cr2 format are used to make data sets. Firstly, the image in cr2 format is converted into uncompressed JPEG format. Then, the JPEG image is cut into four sub-images at the center. Finally, the four sub-images are scaled to 256 × 256, which is used as the carrier image of the steganography algorithm in the color transform domain. The carrier image is expanded to 8000 pieces by using enhanced data sets. Five steganalysis algorithms in transform domain are used to evaluate the steganalysis effect of the proposed network. They are: Jsteg, nsf5, MB1, MB2 and color-extended version of J-UNIWARD: Color-Jsteg, Color-nsf5, Color-MB1, Color-MB2 and Color-J-UNIWARD.

5.2 The Experimental Results

The results of RGBMERGE-JPEGCNN model analysis for five color image steganography algorithms in transform domain are shown in Fig. 8. The horizontal axis represents the steganography algorithm used, and each steganography algorithm uses three embedding rates. The vertical axis represents the accuracy of RGBMERGE-JPEGCNN model on the test set after training.

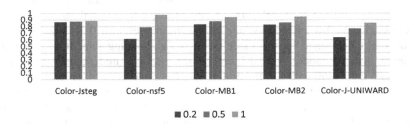

Fig. 5. The performance of RGBMERGE-JPEGCNN

From Fig. 5, we can see that RGBMERGE-JPEGCNN model has good analysis ability for five color image steganography algorithms in transform domain. When the embedding rate is 1.0, RGBMERGE-JPEGCNN model has a good analysis effect on the three algorithms of Color-nsf5, Color-MB1 and Color-MB2, with the accuracy of more than 90%. As the embedding rate decreases, the analysis accuracy of Color-Jstep algorithm decreases slightly, which indicates that RGBMERGE-JPEGCNN model is insensitive to the embedding rate transformation of the algorithm. At the low embedding rate of 0.2, RGBMERGE-JPEGCNN model still maintained more than 80% analysis accuracy for Color-Jsteg, Color-MB1 and Color-MB2. Generally speaking, the strategy of transforming color image into gray image by using brightness formula and steganalysis is feasible, and it has the potential of optimization from the results shown in the figure above.

Using RGBADD-JPEGCNN model, the analysis results of five steganography algorithms in the transform domain of color maps are shown in Fig. 6.

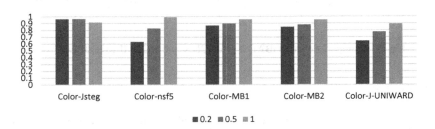

Fig. 6. The performance of RGBADD-JPEGCNN

From Fig. 6, we can see that RGBADD-JPEGCNN model has good analysis ability for five color image steganography algorithms in transform domain. When the embedding rate is 1.0, RGBADD-JPEGCNN model can analyze four steganography algorithms: Color-Jsteg, Color-nsf5, Color-MB1 and Color-MB2 with an accuracy of more than 90%.

At the same time, we can see that with the decrease of embedding rate, the accuracy of RGBADD-JPEGCNN model for color-Jstep algorithm increases. The reason is that the RGBADD-JPEGCNN model with 0.5 embedding rate is initialized and fine-tuned by the model with 1.0 embedding rate, while the model with 0.2 embedding rate is initialized and fine-tuned by the model with 0.5 embedding rate. It can be roughly considered that the model with 0.5 embedding rate has undergone 400 rounds of training, and the model with 0.2 embedding rate has undergone 600 rounds of training. Although the embedding rate decreases, the difference of image modification degree between color-Jstep algorithm and high embedding rate is not obvious. The increase of training rounds brings more benefits than the loss of embedding rate. The experimental results show that although the embedding rate of steganography algorithm is decreasing, the accuracy of steganalysis is increasing.

From the analysis accuracy, although the RGBADD-JPEGCNN model is slightly superior to the RGBMERGE-JPEGCNN model in terms of channel characteristics. The comparison is shown in Fig. 7 below. The horizontal axis represents the steganography algorithm used, and each steganography algorithm uses three embedding rates. The vertical axis represents the difference between the analysis accuracy of RGBADD-JPEGCNN model and that of RGBMERGE-JPEGCNN model. It is speculated that the use of brightness equation in channel fusion results in the loss of some steganalysis features, while channel superposition preserves the steganalysis features in each channel.

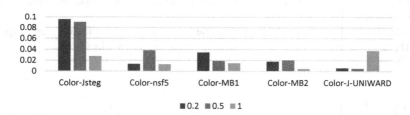

Fig. 7. Comparison of RGBADD-JPEGCNN and RGBMERGE-JPEGCNN

6   Conclusion

In view of the vacancy of applying convolutional neural network to steganalysis in transform domain, this paper proposes a gray image steganalysis model JPEGCNN based on convolutional neural network and two color image steganalysis models RGBMERGE-JPEGCNN and RGBADD-JPEGCNN based on convolutional neural network. In this paper, the related validation and testing are carried out on BOSSBase 1.01 data set. Experiments show that the proposed steganalysis model in transform domain has good analysis ability for steganography algorithm in transform domain.

Future research directions will focus on the following two points: First, the proposed network model still has to improve the accuracy of Steganalysis for various steganography, especially in the case of low embedding rate. Second, the current generic steganalysis models are often limited to a specific domain, such as gray image spatial domain and color image transformation domain. Steganalysis between different domains may not be compatible. This is closely related to the design of steganalysis features. One of the trends of future general steganalysis research is whether we can design a more abstract steganalysis feature, which can span different domains and make the steganalysis model more general without domain restriction.

Acknowledgments. This work is supported by the National Natural Science Foundation of China grant (U1836205), Major Scientific and Technological Special Project of Guizhou Province (20183001), Open Foundation of Guizhou Provincial Key Laboratory of Public Big Data (2018BDKFJJ014), Open Foundation of Guizhou Provincial Key Laboratory of Public Big Data (2018BDKFJJ019) and Open Foundation of Guizhou Provincial Key Laboratory of Public Big Data (2018BDKFJJ022).

References

1. Fridrich, J., Kodovsky, J.: Rich models for steganalysis of digital images. IEEE Trans. Inf. Forensics Secur. **7**, 868–882 (2012)
2. Holub, V., Fridrich, J.: Random projections of residuals for digital image steganalysis. IEEE Trans. Inf. Forensics Secur. **8**, 1996–2006 (2013)
3. Chen, J., Wei, L., Yeung, Y., Xue, Y., Liu, X., Lin, C., Zhang, Y.: Binary image steganalysis based on distortion level co-occurrence matrix. CMC: Comput. Mater. Continua **055**(2), 201–211 (2018)
4. Zeng, J., Tan, S.: Large-scale JPEG steganalysis using hybrid deep-learning framework. IEEE Trans. Inf. Forensics Secur. **13**(5), 1200–1214 (2016)
5. Holub, V., Fridrich, J.: Low-complexity features for JPEG steganalysis using undecimated DCT. IEEE Trans. Inf. Forensics Secur. **10**(2), 219–228 (2015)
6. Holub, V., Fridrich, J.: Phase-aware projection model for steganalysis of JPEG images. In: Proceedings of SPIE, Electronic Imaging, Media Watermarking, Security, and Forensics XVII, vol. 9409 (2015)
7. Fang, W., Zhang, F., Sheng, V.S., Ding, Y.: A method for improving CNN-based image recognition using DCGAN. CMC: Comput. Mater. Continua **57**(1), 167–178 (2018)
8. Ye, J., Ni, J., Yi, Y.: Deep learning hierarchical representations for image steganalysis. IEEE Trans. Inf. Forensics Secur. **12**(11), 2545–2557 (2017)
9. Bas, P., Filler, T., Pevný, T.: "Break our steganographic system": the ins and outs of organizing BOSS. In: Filler, T., Pevný, T., Craver, S., Ker, A. (eds.) IH 2011. LNCS, vol. 6958, pp. 59–70. Springer, Heidelberg (2011). https://doi.org/10.1007/978-3-642-24178-9_5
10. Qu, Z., Cheng, Z., Wang, X.: Matrix coding-based quantum image steganography algorithm. IEEE Access **7**, 35684–35698 (2019)
11. Zeiler, M.D.: ADADELTA: an adaptive learning rate method arXiv:1212.5701 (2012)
12. Glorot, X., Bengio, Y.: Understanding the difficulty of training deep feedforward neural networks. In: Proceedings of Aistats, vol. 9, pp. 249–256 (2016)

Quantum Algorithm for Support Vector Machine with Exponentially Improved Dependence on Precision

Xiao Feng[1(✉)], Jincheng Li[1(✉)], Changgui Huang[1(✉)], Jinze Li[1(✉)], Ruyin Chen[1(✉)], Jinfa Ke[1(✉)], and Zhenjiang Ma[2(✉)]

[1] State Grid Xintong Yili Technology Co., Ltd., Beijing, China
{fengxiao,lijincheng,huangchanggui,lijinze,chenruyin, kejinfa}@sgitg.sgcc.com.cn
[2] Beijing University of Posts and Telecommunications, Beijing, China
mzj36900@bupt.edu.cn

Abstract. Supervised machine learning is the classification of new data on the basis of already classified training data, from which support vector machine is one of the most significant model. In 2014, Rebentrost, Mohseni and Lloyd showed that for a suitable specified $N \times M$ data set, there is a quantum algorithm that constructs a support vector machine model in quantum settings. If the data set is well-defined, their algorithm runs in time poly(logMN, $1/\varepsilon$), where ε is the desired precision of the output state. We in this paper present an improved quantum support vector machine model whose running time is polynomial in $\log(1/\varepsilon)$, exponentially improving the dependence on precision while keeping essentially the same dependence on other parameters.

Keywords: Quantum algorithm · Supervised machine learning · Quantum supremacy

1 Introduction

Dating back to the 1980s, quantum computing has been shown to be more computationally powerful in solving certain kinds of problems than classical computing. In the past decades, to achieve computational advantages, quantum computing has been brought into the field of machine learning. This gives birth to a new disciplinary research field, quantum machine learning. It is a cross-field of computer science and quantum physics on studying how to learn from training data and make predictions on new data in quantum settings [1–5, 16, 17]. Since its inception, quantum machine learning has become a hot topic that attracting world wide attentions, and a number of efficient quantum algorithms have been proposed for various machine learning tasks [6–9].

Quantum mechanics is well known to produce atypical patterns in data. Classical machine learning methods such as deep neural networks frequently have the feature that they can both recognize statistical patterns in data and produce data that possess the same statistical patterns: they recognize the patterns that they produce. This observation

X. Sun et al. (Eds.): ICAIS 2019, LNCS 11635, pp. 578–587, 2019.
https://doi.org/10.1007/978-3-030-24268-8_53

suggests the following hope. If small quantum information processors can produce statistical patterns that are computationally difficult for a classical computer to produce, then perhaps they can also recognize patterns that are equally difficult to recognize classically. The realization of this hope depends on whether efficient quantum algorithms can be found for machine learning. A quantum algorithm is a set of instructions solving a problem, such as determining whether two graphs are isomorphic, that can be performed on a quantum computer. Quantum machine learning software makes use of quantum algorithms as part of a larger implementation. By analysing the steps that quantum algorithms prescribe, it becomes clear that they have the potential to outperform classical algorithms for specific problems (that is, reduce the number of steps required). This potential is known as quantum speedup. The notion of a quantum speedup depends on whether one takes a formal computer science perspective—which demands mathematical proofs—or a perspective based on what can be done with realistic, finite size devices—which requires solid statistical evidence of a scaling advantage over some finite range of problem sizes [18–25]. For the case of quantum machine learning, the best possible performance of classical algorithms is not always known. This is similar to the case of Shor's polynomial-time quantum algorithm for integer factorization: no sub-exponential-time classical algorithm has been found, but the possibility is not provably ruled out. Determination of a scaling advantage contrasting quantum and classical machine learning would rely on the existence of a quantum computer and is called a 'benchmarking' problem. Such advantages could include improved classification accuracy and sampling of classically inaccessible systems. Accordingly, quantum speedups in machine learning are currently characterized using idealized measures from complexity theory: query complexity and gate complexity Query complexity measures the number of queries to the information source for the classical or quantum algorithm. A quantum speedup results if the number of queries needed to solve a problem is lower for the quantum algorithm than for the classical algorithm. To determine the gate complexity, the number of elementary quantum operations (or gates) required to obtain the desired result are counted [26–31].

The most fundamental examples of supervised machine learning algorithms are linear support vector machines (SVM) and perceptions. The task of these methods is to find an optimal separating hyperplane between two classes of data such that all training examples of one class are found only on one side of the hyperplane with high probability. When the margin between the hyperplane and the data are maximized, the most robust classifier could be obtained. The SVM model can be solved in time $\mathcal{O}(\log 1/\varepsilon \, poly(N, M))$ [10], where N is the dimension of feature space, M is the number of training vectors and ε is the accuracy. However, classical computing cannot solve this problem if the handling data sets extend to million level.

Similar to the classical counterpart, the quantum SVM is a paradigmatic example of quantum machine learning [8]. The first quantum SVM algorithm was proposed in the early 2000s, using a variant Grover's search for function minimization, which can find s support vectors out of N vectors consequently takes $\sqrt{N/s}$ iterations [11]. Recently, Rebentrost et al. showed that a quantum SVM can be implemented in $\mathcal{O}(poly(1/\varepsilon \log MN))$ for training and classification. In this paper, we present an improved quantum SVM algorithm with $\mathcal{O}(poly(\varepsilon^{-1} \log 1/\varepsilon \log MN))$ running time.

Specifically, we handle the dimension M, N by matrix inverse algorithm, and reduce the dependency of precise $1/\varepsilon$ by quantum Fourier transformation [12]. In case when a low-rank approximation is appropriate, our quantum SVM operates on the full training set in logarithmic runtime.

2   Review of SVM

The fundamental mission for the SVM is to classify a vector into one of two classes, given M training data points of the form $\{(\mathbf{x_j}, y_j) : \mathbf{x_j} \in R^N, y_j = \pm 1, j = 1, \ldots, M\}$, where label variable $y_j = 1$ or -1 indicates the class that x_j belongs. For the classification, the SVM finds a maximum-margin hyperplane with normal vector w that divides the data set into two classes. The task of SVM aims to find two parallel hyperplanes whose maximum possible distance is $2/\|\mathbf{w}\|$ with each side of the hyperplane $y_j = 1$ and -1. Adjusting the fact which part $\mathbf{x_j}$ belongs depends on two constraints s.t. $\mathbf{wx_j} + b \geq 1$ for $y_j = 1$ and $\mathbf{wx_j} + b \leq -1$ for $y_j = -1$. Therefore, finding the maximum margin hyperplane consists of minimizing $\|\mathbf{w}\|^2/2$ subject to the inequality constraints $y_j(\mathbf{wx_j} + b) \geq 1$ f for all index j. This is the fundamental formulation of the problem. The dual formulation is maximizing over the Karush-Kuhn-Tucker multipliers $\alpha = (\alpha_1, \ldots, \alpha_M)^T$ the function:

$$L(\alpha) = \sum_{j=1}^{M} y_j \alpha_j - \frac{1}{2} \sum_{j,k=1}^{M} \alpha_j K_{j,k} \alpha_k$$

The constraints can be expressed as

$$\sum_{j=1}^{M} \alpha_j = 0 \text{ and } y_j \alpha_j \geq 0.$$

The hyperplane parameters w, b are decomposed of $\mathbf{w} = \sum_j \alpha_j \mathbf{x_j}$ and $b = y_j - \mathbf{wx_j}$ for all the $j = 1, \ldots, M$. We then introduce the kernel matrix, a central quantity for supervised machine learning problems, $K_{j,k} = k(\mathbf{x_j}, \mathbf{x_k})$. We in this paper present how to prepare the quantum kernel matrix, whose kernel function is inner products $k(\mathbf{x_j}, \mathbf{x_k}) = \mathbf{x_j} \mathbf{x_k}$ or Gaussian distance $k(\mathbf{x_j}, \mathbf{x_k}) = \exp(\|\mathbf{x_j^2}\| + \|\mathbf{x_k^2}\|)$. Solving the kernel matrix approximately takes O(M^3) complexity. As each kernel product takes $\mathcal{O}(N)$ overhead, the classical support vector machine algorithm takes running time $\mathcal{O}(\log 1/\varepsilon M^2(M+N))$ with accuracy ε. The classification result can be computed as

$$y(\mathbf{x}) = sign(\sum_{j=1}^{M} \alpha_j k(\mathbf{x_j}, \mathbf{x}) + b)$$

3 Quantum Kernel Matrix

3.1 Construct Quantum Inner-Product Kernel Matrix

In the quantum setting, assume that there exists the mechanism supporting classical data encoding into quantum states:

$$|\mathbf{x_j}\rangle = \frac{1}{\|\mathbf{x_j}\|} \sum_{k=1}^{N} (\mathbf{x_j})_k |k\rangle$$

Here the notation $(\mathbf{x_j})_k$ denotes the k-th components of the vector $\mathbf{x_j}$. For the quantum mechanical preparation, we utilize QRAM mechanism obtaining the quantum state

$$|\chi\rangle = \frac{1}{\sqrt{N_\chi}} \sum_{i=1}^{M} \|\mathbf{x_i}\| |i\rangle |\mathbf{x_i}\rangle$$

where normalized factor $N_\chi = \sum_{i=1}^{M} \|\mathbf{x_i}\|^2$ with the $\mathcal{O}(\log MN)$ running time. Discard the second register, we obtain the quantum inner-product kernel matrix

$$\frac{K}{tr(K)} = tr_2(|\chi\rangle\langle\chi|) = \frac{1}{N_\chi} \sum_{i,j=1}^{M} \langle \mathbf{x_j} \mid \mathbf{x_i}\rangle \|\mathbf{x_i}\mathbf{x_j}\| |i\rangle\langle j|$$

3.2 Construct Quantum Gaussian Kernel Matrix

Suppose the data set $\mathbf{x} = \mathbf{x_1}, \ldots, \mathbf{x_M}$ is stored in the structure of a special designed binary tree [13], thus we can assume there existing a pair of oracle U_1, U_2, s.t.

$$U_1 |j\rangle |0\rangle |0\rangle = |j\rangle |\mathbf{x_j}\rangle |0\rangle$$

$$U_2 |j\rangle |\mathbf{x_j}\rangle |0\rangle = |j\rangle |\mathbf{x_j}\rangle |\|\mathbf{x_j}\|\rangle$$

Perform the oracle $U_1^\dagger U_2 U_1$ onto the state $|\chi'\rangle = |\chi\rangle |0\rangle$, the system becomes to

$$\frac{1}{\sqrt{N_\chi}} \sum_{i=1}^{M} |i\rangle |\|\mathbf{x_i}\|\rangle$$

Add an ancilla qubit and perform controlled rotation, we obtain

$$|G\rangle = \frac{1}{\sqrt{C}} \sum_{i=1}^{M} \exp\left(\|\mathbf{x_i}\|^2 |i\rangle |\|\mathbf{x_i}\|\rangle\right)$$

Uncompute the second system by invoking $U_2^\dagger$, the system finally turns to our destination

$$\frac{K}{tr(K)} = |G\rangle\langle G| = \frac{1}{C}\sum_{i,j=1}^{M}\exp\left(\|\mathbf{x_i}\|^2 + \|\mathbf{x_j}\|^2\right)|i\rangle\langle j|$$

4   Quantum Least-Squares SVM

The main idea of this work is to adopt the least-squares reconstruction of the SVM that rounds the quadratic programming and gets the parameters from the solution of the linear equation system. The principal simplification is to draw into the lax variables e_j and replace the inequality constraints with equality constraints:

$$y_j(\mathbf{wx_j} + b) \geq 1 \rightarrow \mathbf{wx_j} + b = y_j - y_je_j.$$

Besides the constraints, the implied Lagrange function contains a penalty term $\frac{\gamma}{\sum_{i=1}^{M}e_i^2}$, where user-specified parameter γ determines the relative derivatives of training error and SVM objective. Taking partial derivatives of the Lagrange function and eliminating the variables $\mathbf{w}$, e_j into consideration, the least-squares approximation of the problem is introduced:

$$F\begin{pmatrix} b \\ \alpha \end{pmatrix} = \begin{pmatrix} 0 & \mathbf{1}^T \\ \mathbf{1} & K + \gamma^{-1}\mathbf{1} \end{pmatrix}\begin{pmatrix} b \\ \alpha \end{pmatrix} = \begin{pmatrix} 0 \\ y \end{pmatrix}$$

Here K is the kernel matrix we have constructed above, $y = (y_1, \cdots y_M)^T$ denotes the classier label and $1 = (1, \cdots, 1)^T$. The matrix F is a $(M+1) \times (M+1)$ dimensional matrix. Thus the quantum SVM parameter (b, α) are determined by

$$(b, \alpha^T) = F^{-1}(0, y^T)^T.$$

To inverse the matrix F, we now describe the Fourier approach, which is based on an approximation of $1/F$ as a linear combination of unitaries e^{-iFt_i}, $t_i \in R$. These unitaries can be implemented by using some Hamiltonian simulation methods [7, 14, 15]. Our quantum algorithm establishes the following Fourier expansion of the function $1/x$ on the domain D_k:

Theorem 1: Let the function $h(x)$ be defined as

$$h(x) = \frac{i}{\sqrt{2\pi}}\sum_{j=1}^{J-1}\Delta_y\sum_{k=-K}^{K}\Delta_z z_k e^{-z_k^2/2}e^{-ixy_jz_k},$$

where $y_j := j\Delta_y, z_k := k\Delta_z$, for some fixed $J = \Theta\left(\frac{k}{\varepsilon}log(k/\varepsilon)\right)$, $K = \Theta(klog(k/\varepsilon))$, $\Delta_y = \Theta\left(\varepsilon/\sqrt{log(k/\varepsilon)}\right)$ and $\Delta_z = \Theta\left(\left(k\sqrt{log(k/\varepsilon)}\right)^{-1}\right)$. Then $h(x)$ is "ε - close to $1/x$ on the domain D_k.

Based on the above theorem, the matrix F^{-1} can be expressed as the linear combination of some unitaries:

$$\frac{1}{F} = \frac{i}{\sqrt{2\pi}} \sum_{j=1}^{J-1} \Delta_y \sum_{k=-K}^{K} \Delta_z z_k e^{-z_k^2/2} e^{-ixy_jz_k}.$$

To implementing this equation, we need the following theorem.

Theorem 2: Let A be a Hermitian operator with eigenvalues in a domain $D \subseteq R$. Suppose the function $f : D \to R$ satisfies $|f(x)| \geq 1$ and all $x \in D$. And f is ε - close to $\sum_i \alpha_i T$ on D for some $\varepsilon \in (0, 1/2)$, coefficients $\alpha_i > 0$, and functions $T_i : D \to C$. Let U_i be a set of unitaries such that

$$U_i|0\rangle|\varphi\rangle = |0\rangle T_i(A)|\varphi\rangle + |\varphi^\perp\rangle$$

for all states $|\varphi\rangle$, where $(|0\rangle\langle 0| \otimes 1)|\varphi^\perp\rangle = 0$. Given an algorithm for creating a quantum state $|b\rangle$, there is a quantum algorithm that prepares a quantum state 4ε-close to $f(A)|b\rangle/\|f(A)|b\rangle\|$, succeeding with constant probability, that makes an expected $O(\alpha/\|f(A)|b\rangle\|)$ uses of the algorithm, U and V, where

$$U = \sum_i |i\rangle\langle i| \otimes U_i,$$

$$V|0\rangle = \frac{1}{\sqrt{\alpha}}\sum_i \sqrt{\alpha_i}|i\rangle, \alpha = \sum_i \alpha_i.$$

According to the Theorem 2, we introduce a signal quantum state and signal operator corresponding to $1/F$ under the Fourier expansion. Suppose there exists a unitary V that maps the initial state $|0\rangle$ to the quantum state

$$V|0\rangle = \frac{1}{(2\pi)^{\frac{1}{4}}\sqrt{\alpha}} \sum_{j=0}^{J-1} \sqrt{\Delta_y} \sum_{k=-K}^{K} \sqrt{\Delta_z|z_k|} e^{-z_k^2/2}|j, k\rangle,$$

where the parameter α is the L_1 norm of the coefficients of this linear combination

$$\alpha = \frac{1}{\sqrt{2\pi}} \sum_{j=0}^{J-1} \Delta_y \sum_{k=-K}^{K} \Delta_z|z_k| e^{-z_k^2/2} = \Theta(yJ).$$

Theorem 2 also requires the unitary

$$U = i \sum_{j=0}^{J-1} \sum_{k=-K}^{K} |j,k\rangle\langle j,k| \otimes sign(k) e^{-iF_{y_j z_k}}.$$

The term $e^{-iF_{y_j z_k}}$ can be implemented utilizing the Qubitization method [14] in running time

$$O\left(y_j z_k + log(1/\varepsilon)\right) = \Theta\left(\kappa\, log(\kappa/\varepsilon)\right) + log(1/\varepsilon).$$

Thus we can decompose the $1/F$ under the spectrum of F:

$$F^{-1} = \sum_{j=1}^{M+1} \frac{1}{\lambda_j} |\lambda_j\rangle\langle\lambda_j|.$$

Perform F^{-1} on the label sequence state $|y\rangle$, we obtain the SVM parameters:

$$|b,\alpha\rangle = \sum_{j=1}^{M+1} \frac{\langle\lambda_j \mid y\rangle}{\lambda_j} |\lambda_j\rangle.$$

According to the training set labels, the expansion coefficient of the new state are the desired SVM parameters:

$$|b,\alpha\rangle = \frac{1}{\sqrt{C}} \left(b|0\rangle + \sum_{k=1}^{M} \alpha_k |k\rangle \right),$$

where $C = b^2 + \sum_{k=1}^{M} \alpha_k^2$.

5   Classification

Here, we have trained the quantum SVM model and would like to classify a query state $|x\rangle$ now. From the computed state $|b,\alpha\rangle$, add a register and perform the QRAM mechanism for encoding $|x\rangle$ in the entangle state:

$$|u\rangle = \frac{1}{\sqrt{N}} \left(b|0\rangle|0\rangle + \sum_{k=1}^{M} \alpha_k |x_k| |k\rangle |x_k\rangle \right)$$

with the factorized factor $N = b^2 + \sum_{k=1}^{M} \alpha_k^2 |x_k|^2$. Then, after constructing the query state $|x\rangle$

$$|x\rangle = \frac{1}{\sqrt{N_x}} \left(|0\rangle|0\rangle + \sum_{k=1}^{M} |x| |k\rangle |x\rangle \right)$$

utilizing QRAM again, we can finally take swap test to invoke the classification mission. Suppose the axillary state $|\psi\rangle = \frac{1}{\sqrt{2}}(|0\rangle|u\rangle + |1\rangle|x\rangle)$ and measure another ancilla in the state $|\phi\rangle = \frac{1}{\sqrt{2}}(|0\rangle - |1\rangle)$. The measurement has the success probability $P = \frac{1}{2}(1 - \langle u \mid x\rangle)$. Thus if $P < 1/2$, the new vector x belongs to $+1$, otherwise -1.

6 Complexity Analysis

We now show that quantum matrix inversion substantially performs the operator e^{-iFt} and analyze the running time of our algorithm. The matrix F contains the kernel matrix K and an additional row and column owing to the offset consideration b. From literature [14], we know that the gate complexity of simulating the Hamiltonian F for time t with error ε is $\mathcal{O}(t + \log 1/\varepsilon)$. Noting that time $t = y_j z_k$, then F can be efficiently simulation in time $\Theta(\kappa \log \kappa/\varepsilon + \log 1/\varepsilon)$. It is interesting to note that the maximum absolute eigenvalue of $F/(tr(F))$ is ≤ 1 and the minimum absolute eigenvalue is $\leq O(1/M)$. Therefore, the condition number κ is $O(M)$ in this case. To solve such an eigenvalue would require exponential time. Considering the relationship $\varepsilon \leq \max(\lambda) \leq 1$, thus $\kappa = \mathcal{O}(1/\varepsilon)$ holds. In consideration of the preparation of the kernel matrix in $\mathcal{O}(\log MN)$, the run time is thus

$$\mathcal{O}(\log(\frac{1}{\varepsilon})\varepsilon^{-1} \log MN).$$

Compared to Rebentrost's algorithm, we achieve exponentially improved dependence on precision ε.

7 Conclusion

In this work, we have shown that the support vector machine can be implemented by quantum mechanics, and the complexity of proposed algorithm is logarithmic in the feature size and the amount of training data. Besides, the presented algorithm also improves dependence on precision ε. When the training data kernel matrix is controlled by the optimal Hamiltonian simulation method, the speed of the quantum algorithm is maximized. Furthermore, our algorithm also avoids the complexity caused by phase estimation and controlled rotation. In summary, quantum SVM is an important machine learning algorithm that can be efficiently implemented. It also provides advantages in data privacy and could be one important composition in quantum neural networks.

Acknowledgments. This paper is supported by development of power quantum security chip.

References

1. Yu, C.H., Gao, F., Wen, Q.Y.: An improved quantum algorithms for ridge regression. arXiv preprint arXiv:1707.09524 (2017)
2. Schuld, M., Sinayskiy, I., Petruccione, F.: Prediction by linear regression on a quantum computer. Phys. Rev. A **94**, 022342 (2016)
3. Wiebe, N., Kapoor, A., Svore, K.: Quantum deep learning. Computer Science (2014)
4. Rebentrost, P., Mohseni, M., Lloyd, S.: Quantum support vector machine for big data classification. Phys. Rev. Lett. **113**(13), 130503 (2014)
5. Rebentrost, P, Schuld, M, Wossnig, L., Petruccione, F., Lloyd, S.: Quantum gradient descent and Newton's method for constrained polynomial optimization. arXiv preprint arXiv:1612.01789 (2016)
6. Lloyd, S., Mohseni, M., Rebentrost, P.: Quantum algorithms for supervised and unsupervised machine learning. arXiv preprint arXiv:1307.0411 (2013)
7. Lloyd, S., Mohseni, M., Rebentrost, P.: Quantum principal component analysis. Nat. Phys. **10**(9), 108–113 (2013)
8. Harrow, W.A., Hassidim, A., Lloyd, S.: Quantum algorithm for linear systems of equations. Phys. Rev. Lett. **103**(15), 150502 (2009)
9. Wittek, P., Lloyd, S.: Quantum machine learning. Nature **549**(7671), 195 (2017)
10. Boyd, S., Vandenberge, L.: Convex Optimization. Cambridge University Press, Cambridge (2004)
11. Anguita, D., Ridella, S.: Quantum optimization for training support vector machines. Neural Netw. **16**(5–6), 763–770 (2003)
12. Childs, A.M., Kothari, R., Somma, R.D.: Quantum algorithm for systems of linear equations with exponentially improved dependence on precision. SIAM J. Comput. **46**(6), 1920–1950 (2015)
13. Kerenidis, I., Prakash, A.: Quantum recommendation systems. arXiv preprint arXiv:1603.08675 (2016)
14. Low, G.H., Chuang, I.L.: Hamiltonian simulation by qubitization. arXiv preprint arXiv:1610.06546 (2016)
15. Low, G.H., Chuang, I.L.: Optimal hamiltonian simulation by quantum signal processing. Phys. Rev. Lett. **118**(1), 010501 (2017)
16. Yu, C.H., et al.: Quantum algorithm for association rules mining. Phys. Rev. A **94**(4), 042311 (2016)
17. Yu, C.H., et al.: Quantum algorithm for visual tracking. Phys. Rev. A **99**(2), 022301 (2019)
18. August, M., Ni, X.: Using recurrent neural networks to optimize dynamical decoupling for quantum memory. Preprint at https://arxiv.org/abs/1604.00279 (2016)
19. Amstrup, B., Toth, G.J., Szabo, G., Rabitz, H., Loerincz, A.: Genetic algorithm with migration on topology conserving maps for optimal control of quantum systems. J. Phys. Chem. **99**, 5206–5213 (1995)
20. Hentschel, A., Sanders, B.C.: Machine learning for precise quantum measurement. Phys. Rev. Lett. **104**, 063603 (2010)
21. Lovett, N.B., Crosnier, C., Perarnau-Llobet, M., Sanders, B.C.: Differential evolution for many-particle adaptive quantum metrology. Phys. Rev. Lett. **110**, 220501 (2013)
22. Palittapongarnpim, P., Wittek, P., Zahedinejad, E., Vedaie, S., Sanders, B.C.: Learning in quantum control: high-dimensional global optimization for noisy quantum dynamics. Neurocomputing (in press). https://doi.org/10.1016/j.neucom.2016.12.087
23. Carrasquilla, J., Melko, R.G.: Machine learning phases of matter. Nat. Phys. **13**, 431–434 (2017)

24. Broecker, P., Carrasquilla, J., Melko, R.G., Trebst, S.: Machine learning quantum phases of matter beyond the fermion sign problem. Preprint at https://arxiv.org/abs/1608.07848 (2016)
25. Carleo, G., Troyer, M.: Solving the quantum many-body problem with artificial neural networks. Science **355**, 602–606 (2017)
26. Brunner, D., Soriano, M.C., Mirasso, C.R., Fischer, I.: Parallel photonic information processing at gigabyte per second data rates using transient states. Nat. Commun. **4**, 1364 (2013)
27. Cai, X.-D., et al.: Entanglement-based machine learning on a quantum computer. Phys. Rev. Lett. **114**, 110504 (2015)
28. Hermans, M., Soriano, M.C., Dambre, J., Bienstman, P., Fischer, I.: Photonic delay systems as machine learning implementations. J. Mach. Learn. Res. **16**, 2081–2097 (2015)
29. Tezak, N., Mabuchi, H.: A coherent perceptron for all-optical learning. EPJ Quantum Technol. **2**, 10 (2015)
30. Neigovzen, R., Neves, J.L., Sollacher, R., Glaser, S.J.: Quantum pattern recognition with liquid-state nuclear magnetic resonance. Phys. Rev. A **79**, 042321 (2009)
31. Pons, M., et al.: Trapped ion chain as a neural network: error resistant quantum computation. Phys. Rev. Lett. **98**, 023003 (2007)
32. Chen, J., et al.: Binary image steganalysis based on distortion level co-occurrence matrix. CMC: Comput. Mater. Continua **055**(2), 201–211 (2018)
33. Xiong, Z., Shen, Q., Wang, Y., Zhu, C.: Paragraph vector representation based on word to vector and CNN learning. CMC: Comput. Mater. Continua **055**(2), 213–227 (2018)

Reliability-Based and QoS-Aware Service Redundancy Backup Method in IoT-Based Smart Grid

Yunmei Luo, Yuping Luo, Xueping Ye, Jun Lu, and Shuqing Li[✉]

Huizhou Power Supply Bureau of Guangdong Power Grid Co., Ltd.,
Guangzhou, China
13928317601@139.com, 13829958669@163.com,
13923611985@139.com, bluejune@163.com,
13502230332@139.com

Abstract. Network Function Virtualization (NFV) and Edge Computing have become key technologies to support flexible scheduling of resources and guarantee service QoS in IoT-based smart grid. Network operators provide users with low-latency, highly reliable network services by placing an ordered set of Virtual Network Functions (VNFs) in edges cloud network. Due to the chaining nature and distributed placement, the failure of a single VNF will directly affect the normal operation of the service. But the existing redundancy backup scheme ignores the QoS requirements and resource sharing. In this paper, we propose a reliability-based and QoS-aware service redundancy backup method in edge clouds. The algorithm considers the sharing of backup network functions and the QoS requirements of services, and maximizes the cost of sharing resources while selecting the backup solution with the delay and reliability. Simulation experiments show that our algorithm can get a backup solution in a shorter time, and greatly reduce the cost while meeting the QoS requirements of the service.

Keywords: Network Function Virtualization · Edge Computing · IoT · Smart grid · Redundancy backup

1 Introduction

In the traditional service provision architecture of IoT-based smart grid, network functions and hardware devices are coupled to each other to form a vertically integrated network structure [1–5]. This rigid structure is not conducive to resource sharing and flexible deployment of services. NFV technology utilizes IT virtualization technology to enable flexible loading and instantiation of network function software and reduce the complexity of service deployment by using a large number of industrialized high-capacity servers, memories and switches carrying a variety of software-based network functions (NF). At the same time, the distributed edge cloud is deployed in the network, which can provide CPU and memory resources closer to the user than the centralized cloud. This not only ensures the mobility and QoS requirements of the user, but also reduces the transmission consumption of computationally intensive or delay-sensitive service [6].

© Springer Nature Switzerland AG 2019
X. Sun et al. (Eds.): ICAIS 2019, LNCS 11635, pp. 588–598, 2019.
https://doi.org/10.1007/978-3-030-24268-8_54

In an NFV-based network, the faults of the VNF may be caused by various reasons, one is that the physical host (PM) hardware that carries the network function generates faults, and the other is the virtual machine (VM) or software related to the function generates faults. A single VNF fault will affect the normal execution of the entire service chain, resulting in serious data loss and resource waste. Redundancy backup is a common method to improve system reliability, but backup VNF inevitably increases resource consumption. At the same time, redundancy VNF increases service chain length, and additional links further increase service end-to-end transmission delay. This is unacceptable for delay-sensitive services. Therefore, how to use the limited resources to efficiently meet the reliability and QoS requirements of the service is an urgent problem to be solved. The current backup method in [7] and [8] continue to iterate through the VNF backup process until the reliability of the service chain meets the requirements. In order to choose the right backup. Authors in [9] and [10] offer two different options. The VNF with low backup reliability is preferred, and the service delay requirement is neglected, which may result in the backup solution not meeting the QoS requirements of the service. [11] combine latency and reliability to ensure end-to-end transmission delay in the service chain, but ignore the sharing of backup functions, which creates unnecessary resource waste.

Aiming at the above problems, the sharing of network functions and the delay requirement of extended links in the backup process have become factors that must be considered. Since the possibility of VNF failure is mostly low, sharing multiple network functions with one backup network function becomes a feasible solution for improving resource utilization. At the same time, latency is an important indicator of whether a backup solution is reasonable. In addition, in the process of extending the link, it is necessary to consider the load balancing of the link to avoid partial defects caused by excessive load on some links.

Therefore, this paper proposes a reliability-based and QoS-aware service redundancy backup algorithm in IoT-based smart grid. In the terminal of IoT-based smart grid, proposed algorithm combines QoS requirements with the backup process, and considers the sharing of backup network functions. Improve the resource utilization efficiency and reliability of the service chain. The technical contributions of this paper are summarized as follows:

Considering the delay requirement of the service, in the terminal of IoT-based smart grid, we designed a algorithm of QoS-aware redundancy scheme for backup to ensure that the extended link meets the delay requirement and improves the rationality of the backup.

We have focused on the sharing of backup network functions to reduce excessive backup VNF, and at the same time propose a fault handling mechanism to solve the problem of simultaneous faults of multiple VNF sharing a backup.

The choice of the extended link takes the load balancing of the link into account, and the link with a smaller load is preferentially selected to avoid local congestion.

The remainder of this paper is organized as follows. The second part introduces the relevant research progress of service chain backup. The third part introduces our redundancy backup model. The fourth part introduces our backup scheme. The fifth part introduces the simulation experiment of our algorithm. The last part summarizes the full text.

2   Related Work

Specifically, to improve the reliability of the service chain, [12] proposes a reliability-aware and delay-limited service chain joint optimization framework, which combines the iterative backup selection and routing process, combined with single routing and multi-routing strategies to ensure reliability and ensure the timeliness of end-to-end response. [13] considers the physical layer and hypervisor layer for network availability, improves reliability by backing up the entire service chain, which results in low resource utilization; [14] proposes through cost-awareness importance measurement (CIM) to select the appropriate VNF for backup, and the server nodes with high reliability are selected for bearer, and the reliability is maximized at the minimum cost. However, the above solutions lack the consideration of service QoS requirements, and it is difficult to guarantee the quality of service.

3   System Model and Problem Description

In this section, we first establish a physical network and service chain model, and then introduce the QoS indicators considered in the backup process.

3.1   A Subsection Sample

The underlying physical network in IoT-based smart grid shown in Fig. 1 is represented by a weighted undirected graph $G = (N, L)$. N and L are the physical network node set and the link set. We specifically consider two types of nodes: (i) used as a server node hosting a VNF, the number of which is expressed as N, (ii) A switch node for traffic forwarding between VNFs. For any server node n_i, its capacity to carry VNF is $Cap(n_i)$, which can represent physical resources for CPU processing capacity, memory and storage space. For physical link $l_{ij} \in L$ of any connected node n_i with n_j, its bandwidth is B_{ij}, transmission delay is D_{ij}.

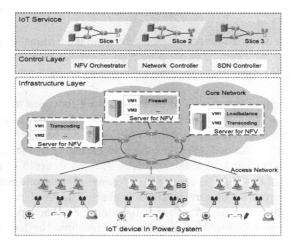

Fig. 1. IoT-based smart grid

Every service request contains a series of service chain s composed of VNF v. $V = \{v_1, v_2, \ldots v_k\}$ represents a collection of network functions. K indicates the number of VNF, $S = \{s_1, s_2, \ldots s_m\}$ represents a collection of service chains, M indicates the number of service chains. VNF v_i requires server node hosting while consuming server-side physical resources $Cap(v_i)$ With processing delay D_i, reliability r_i. Similarly, the virtual link between VNF l_{uv}^v, which mapping to physical link l_{ij}, need to consume the corresponding bandwidth resources. A service chain with minimal bandwidth requirements B_{req}, maximum tolerance delay D_{req} and minimum reliability R_{req} three attributes.

3.2 Delay and Reliability

Services have differentiated QoS requirements and typically include metrics such as minimum bandwidth requirements, maximum end-to-end latency, and service reliability. The end-to-end delay of a service consists of two parts: the transmission delay of the traversal link and the processing delay of the node:

$$D_S = \sum_{l \in S} D_l + \sum_{n \in S} D_n \tag{1}$$

After completing the backup of VNF, the additional link will increase the end-to-end delay of the service. When the delay of the backup service chain exceeds the maximum tolerance delay, the existence of the backup service chain will become meaningless, so it must be guaranteed.

The reliability of a single network function is estimated by its mean time between failure and average repair time, expressed as:

$$r = \frac{MTBF}{MTBF + MTTR} \tag{2}$$

$MTBF$ with $MTTR$ indicates the mean time between faults and the average time to repair. The reliability of a service is expressed as the product of the reliability of all network functions in the service chain, so the reliability of the service chain is expressed as:

$$R_S = \Pr[\text{all VNFs are reliable}]$$
$$= \prod r \tag{3}$$

In the case of faults of complex network functions, the reliability of the service is difficult to guarantee, and the traditional network function one-to-one backup will introduce additional overhead. Therefore, our proposed backup strategy considers the sharing of backup network functions. As shown in Fig. 2, comparing the two backup methods, we consider sharing for backup, which can save one VNF related cost while ensuring the reliability of the service.

Fig. 2. Backup scheme

3.3   Service Chain Queuing Model

The core of the VNF backup problem is to study how to improve the reliability of services efficiently and reliably. In the actual network, the user's service request is a dynamically generated process. Therefore, real-time performance must be considered in the study of VNF backup. At the same time, different services have different reliability and QoS requirements. We propose a service chain queuing model based on time window control, which sorts the services arriving within the same time window according to their different characteristics. We use the formula to accurately measure the characteristics of the service, which is a normalized value represented by Q.

$$Q_i = pro + (1 - pro)/D_i \tag{4}$$

Among them, *pro* is a binary number indicating whether the service is a protection class service. A value of 1 indicates that the service is a protection class service, otherwise it is a non-protection class service. D_i is the end-to-end delay requirement of the service. The larger the value, the bigger Q_i.

We will follow the services that arrive within the same time window by the value of the Q, VNF backup is performed according to the queue, so that the protection service and the service with high delay are preferentially backed up. The significance of this is that when the service behind the queue selects the shared backup, it should consider whether it can tolerate the queuing delay on the backup, so as to ensure that when the VNF sharing the backup fails simultaneously, each VNF can be processed within the allowed range.

3.4   Fault Handling Mechanism

Multiple shared VNFs sharing a backup network function can prevent excessive backup and greatly improve network resource utilization. However, when multiple VNFs fail at the same time, there is a problem that the backup network function is insufficient, which causes multiple VNFs to generate queuing delay when using the backup. In addition, different types of services have different priorities for fault handling due to their different reliability levels and QoS requirements. Therefore, in the process of fault handling, it must be ensured that the faulty service obtains backup for its the network function within the allowable delay range.

We process them following their values from large to small, namely:

(1) When multiple network functions sharing a backup fail at the same time, the protection service is prioritized;
(2) When multiple services are non-protected, priority is given to services with small latency requirements.

Through the above-mentioned processing mechanism, all the faults of protection services are processed, and the faults of the non-protection services are processed within the allowable range of the delay.

4   QoS-Aware Service Chain Redundancy Backup Model

We define the following binary auxiliary variables to describe redundancy backups of the service chain:

(1) $x_{i,j}$ indicates whether network function v_j is backup of network function v_i
(2) $y_{ij,uv}$ is a virtual link representing the service chain l_{uv}^v whether to map to a physical link l_{ij}
(3) $z_{i,j}$ Indicates backup network function v_j whether to map to a server node n_i

The goal of the problem is to minimize the network operator's capital expenditures and operating expenses while completing the VNF backup, meanwhile meeting QoS constraints (bandwidth, latency, and reliability). The objective function can be expressed as:

$$\min\{c_1 \sum_{i \in N} \sum_{j \in K} x_{i,j} + c_2 \sum_{i,j \in N} \sum_{u,v \in K} y_{ij,uv} \cdot B_r\} \tag{5}$$

The first item considers the installation cost of the network function; the second item represents the cost of consuming the link bandwidth.

Redundancy backups of VNF have the following limitations:

(1) The available capacity of the server node must be no less than the capacity consumed by the backup network function it carries.

$$\sum_{j \in K} b_{i,j} cap(v_j) \leq cap(n_i), \; \forall i \in N \tag{6}$$

(2) Considering that one node embedding too many backup network functions does not help improve the reliability of the service, we set up a server node to carry a limited number of network functions.

$$1 \leq \sum_{j \in K} z_{i,j} \leq z_0, \ \forall i \in N \tag{7}$$

(3) The available bandwidth of the physical link must be no less than the bandwidth consumed by the virtual link it carries.

$$\sum_{u,v \in K} y_{ij,uv} B_{req} \leq B_{ij}, \ \forall i,j \in N \tag{8}$$

(4) In the virtual link mapping process, except for the source node and the destination node, the sum of the directed traffic of other physical nodes is 0.

$$\sum_{i,j \in N} y_{ij,uv} - \sum_{i,j \in N} y_{ji,uv} = \begin{cases} 1, & \text{if } z_{i,u} = 1 \\ -1, & \text{if } z_{j,v} = 1 \\ 0, & \text{otherwise} \end{cases} \tag{9}$$

$$\forall u, v \in K$$

The redundancy backup of VNF has the following constraints:

(1) Any network function may have a network function for its backup.

$$\sum_{j \in K} x_{i,j} \leq 1, \forall i \in K \tag{10}$$

(2) The same backup VNF bearing too many VNF backup jobs also does not help to improve the reliability of the service chain. Therefore, we have set a limited number of network functions that any backup network function can support.

$$\sum_{i \in K} x_{i,j} \leq d_0, \forall j \in K \tag{11}$$

The service chain also satisfies the following QoS constraints:

(1) The additional delay caused by the service chain backup cannot be greater than its maximum additional tolerance delay requirement.

$$\sum_{i \in N} \sum_{j \in K} z_{i,j} D_i + \sum_{i,j \in N} \sum_{u,v \in K} y_{ij,uv} D_{ij} \leq D_{req} - D_s = D_{add} \tag{12}$$

(2) The reliability of the service chain cannot be less than its minimum reliability requirement.

$$R_s = \prod r_i \geq R_{req} \tag{13}$$

5 Simulation Experiment

We selected a 100-node physical network in the simulation experiment, which consisted of 30 server nodes and 70 switch nodes. The capacity of the server node and the link bandwidth are set to a fixed value. Each service chain consists of 2–6 VNFs, and the reliability of different VNFs is randomly selected from [0.9, 0.99]. According to the SLA requirements in Google Apps, the reliability requirements of each service chain are selected from [0.95, 0.98, 0.99, 0.995, 0.999], and the delay requirements vary from milliseconds to seconds. In the experiment, 1000 service chain requests were initially set.

To demonstrate the superiority of our algorithm, the following three redundancy backup algorithms were chosen for comparison. (1) MinCost algorithm: In the iterative backup of VNF, each time the VNF with the smallest resource consumption is selected for backup until the reliability of the service chain reaches the requirement. (2) Single-path algorithm: The algorithm performs backup on the original link, and the backup VNF is placed downstream of the same link of the backed up VNF to avoid the link cost and delay of the accessory.

We choose four indicators to evaluate:

(1) redundancy backup cost;
(2) backup cost-effectiveness ratio: ratio of backup cost to reliability improvement;
(3) link load balancing degree: variance of used bandwidth of all links;

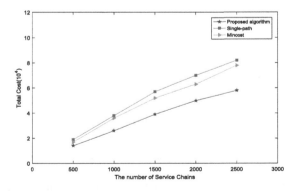

Fig. 3. Redundancy backup costs for different algorithms

Figure 3 shows costs of three algorithms to orchestrate different number of service chains. The cost of service chain orchestration includes VNF installation and link lease. Single-path only saves cost by not adding additional links. Such measures have limited effects. Mincost backs up by choosing the primary VNFs with the lowest cost, which reduces the total cost to some extent. Compared with the other two algorithms, proposed algorithm shows an excellent cost efficiency. Taking the number of chains 2000 as examples, proposed algorithm saves 17.1% and 22.2% of cost compared to Mincost and Single-path, respectively. When the number of services reaches 2500, cost of proposed algorithm is still lower than that of Mincost and Single-path.

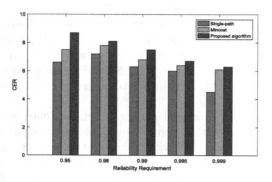

Fig. 4. Backup cost-effectiveness ratio of different algorithms

Figure 4 shows the cost-effectiveness ratio of three algorithms based on different reliability requirements. When the reliability requirement changes from 0.98 to 0.999, CER of the proposed algorithm is always higher than that of Single-path and Mincost. Taking the requirement 0.999 as examples, proposed algorithm's CER is 40% and 3% higher than Single-path and Mincost, respectively (Fig. 5).

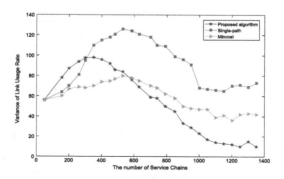

Fig. 5. Link load balancing degree of different algorithms

Link usage rate variance: This indicator is used to measure load state of entire network. Since link bandwidth is set to different values, so variance of three algorithms is not 0 at the beginning. In the early stages of algorithms, the three variances are not significantly different. Because Single-path places backups only downstream of orchestration path, as the number of service chains increases, network becomes more plugged and variance becomes large. On the contrary, proposed algorithm considers avoiding the above situation and chose free links as much as possible, so the variance will become smaller. Orchestrating 800, 1000, 1200 of services, link usage rate variance of proposed algorithm is 27%, 61%, 56% lower than that of Mincost, and 63%, 57%, 76% lower than that of Single-path.

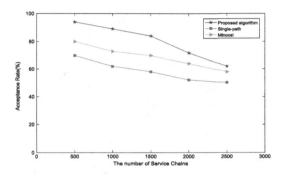

Fig. 6. Service acceptance rate of different algorithms

As shown in Fig. 6, orchestrating service chains with different quantities and availability requirements, proposed algorithm consistently maintains higher acceptance rate than the other two algorithms. Taking availability 0.99 and quantity 1000 as examples, acceptance rate of proposed algorithm is 3.3% and 7.2% higher than that of Mincost and Single-path, respectively. Even if availability requirement and quantity reach 0.999 and 2000, acceptance rate of proposed algorithm is still 4.4%, 6.9% higher than the other two.

6   Conclusion

In this paper, we study the scheme of improving the reliability of the service chain through redundancy backup. In the IoT-based smart grid, a reliability-based and QoS-aware service redundancy backup algorithm is proposed, focusing on the sharing of backup network functions, and optionally select shared backup VNF to improve resource utilization. At the same time, to ensure the reasonableness of the backup, the additional delay of the link is used as an indicator to measure the backup scheme. Our proposed scheme can select the backup scheme with the delay and reliability meeting the requirements while maximizing the shared resources to reduce the cost, and improve the reliability of the service quickly and effectively.

Acknowledgments. This paper is supported by research on ubiquitous business communication technology and service mode in smart grid distribution and consumption network-Topic 2: Development on smart grid distribution and consumption network communication terminal with high adaptability (GDKJXM20172919).

References

1. Zhen, Y., Zeng, L., Chen, X., Li, X., Liu, J.: Study of architecture of power Internet of Things. In: IET International Conference on Communication Technology and Application (ICCTA 2011), Beijing, pp. 718–722 (2011)
2. Chen, M., et al.: Wearable 2.0: enable human-cloud integration in next generation healthcare system. IEEE Commun. Mag. **55**(1), 54–61 (2017)
3. Afolabi, I., Taleb, T., Samdanis, K., Ksentini, A., Flinck, H.: Network slicing & softwarization: a survey on principles, enabling technologies & solutions. IEEE Commun. Surv. Tutor. **20**, 2429–2453 (2018)
4. Kaur, J., Kaur, K.: A fuzzy approach for an IoT-based automated employee performance appraisal. CMC: Comput. Mater. Continua **53**(1), 23–36 (2017)
5. Shi, C.: A novel ensemble learning algorithm based on D-S evidence theory for IoT security. CMC: Comput. Mater. Continua **57**(3), 635–652 (2018)
6. Foukas, X., Patounas, G., Elmokashfi, A., Marina, M.K.: Network slicing in 5G: survey and challenges. IEEE Commun. Mag. **55**(5), 94–100 (2017)
7. Kaloxylos, A.: A survey and an analysis of network slicing in 5G networks. IEEE Commun. Stand. Mag. **2**(1), 60–65 (2018)
8. Ordonez-Lucena, J., Ameigeiras, P., Lopez, D., Ramos-Munoz, J.J., Lorca, J., Folgueira, J.: Network slicing for 5G with SDN/NFV: concepts, architectures, and challenges. IEEE Commun. Mag. **55**(5), 80–87 (2017)
9. Hao, Y., Tian, D., Fortino, G., Zhang, J., Humar, I.: Network slicing technology in a 5G wearable network. IEEE Commun. Stand. Mag. **2**(1), 66–71 (2018)
10. Wang, G., Feng, G., Tan, W., Qin, S., Wen, R., Sun, S.: Resource allocation for network slices in 5G with network resource pricing. In: 2017 IEEE Global Communications Conference, GLOBECOM 2017, Singapore, pp. 1–6 (2017)
11. Guerzoni, R., Despotovic, Z., Trivisonno, R., Vaishnavi, I.: Modeling reliability requirements in coordinated node and link mapping. In: 2014 IEEE 33rd International Symposium on Reliable Distributed Systems, Nara, pp. 321–330 (2014)
12. Huin, N., Jaumard, B., Giroire, F.: Optimization of network service chain provisioning. In: 2017 IEEE International Conference on Communi-cations (ICC), Paris, pp. 1–7 (2017)
13. Ayoubi, S., Zhang, Y., Assi, C.: RAS: reliable auto-scaling of virtual machines in multi-tenant cloud networks. In: 2015 IEEE 4th International Conference on Cloud Networking (CloudNet), Niagara Falls, ON, pp. 1–6 (2015)
14. Ding, W., Yu, H., Luo, S.: Enhancing the reliability of services in NFV with the cost-efficient redundancy scheme. In: 2017 IEEE International Conference on Communications (ICC), Paris, pp. 1–6 (2017)

A Privacy-Preserving Electricity Trading Scheme Based on Blockchain

Yu Xu[1,2,3], Zhoubin Liu[4], Lili Li[1,2,3], and You Sun[5,6(✉)]

[1] State Grid Electronic Communication Co., LTD.
(State Grid Xiongan Financial Technology Group Co., LTD.),
Xuchang, China
[2] State Grid Power Finance and Electronic Commerce Laboratory,
Beijing, China
[3] State Grid Huitong (Beijing) Information Technology Co., LTD.,
Beijing, China
[4] State Grid Zhejiang Power Research Institute, Quzhou, China
[5] State Key Laboratory of Information Security,
Institute of Information Engineering, Chinese Academy of Sciences,
Beijing, China
sunyou@iie.ac.cn
[6] School of Cyber Security, University of Chinese Academy of Sciences,
Beijing, China

Abstract. Traditionally, transactions on the Internet need to be handled by trusted third-party credit agencies. As a new technology for the encrypted transmission of transaction information, blockchain technology is based on the principle of cryptography, so that it does not require the participation of third parties. Blockchain technology can be widely used in many fields, such as the power industry. On the one hand, blockchain technology can greatly reduce the system cost in electricity trading because it can be independent of the central organization and ensure the authenticity and non-tampering of data. On the other hand, in electricity trading, the user's personal information and transaction information need to be encrypted and protected, and a fine-grained access control scheme is provided to ensure the security of the transactions. In our paper, we propose a privacy-preserving electricity trading scheme which applies blockchain technology to electricity trading and combined with the decentralized policy-hiding attribute-based encryption scheme to achieve fine-grained access control and protect users' private information.

Keywords: Blockchain · Attribute-based encryption ·
Decentralized policy-hiding attribute-based encryption ·
Electricity trading management

Supported by the Science and Technology Project of State Power Grid Corp (SAP No. 52110417000G).

X. Sun et al. (Eds.): ICAIS 2019, LNCS 11635, pp. 599–611, 2019.
https://doi.org/10.1007/978-3-030-24268-8_55

1   Introduction

Since Satoshi Nakamoto proposed the concept of blockchain in his published paper "Bitcoin: A peer-to-peer electronic cash system" in 2008 [1], this technology has been widely used in various fields. The core functions of blockchain technology do not rely on the center or third-party organizations to ensure the authenticity of data, break the barriers to trust, and based on rules rather than trust transactions, greatly reduce the trust cost of business development and promote the efficient development of the business. With the support of blockchain technology, the grid system can realize self-service processing of all business processes, and users can also implement resource information processing, transmission, and transactions in the system.

However, in a traditional blockchain system, the user identity is marked by a public key belonging to him, which is not anonymization in the strict sense. Because the adversary may attack the system through the transaction graph analysis [2] to reveal the user's true identity. Second, in the electricity trading blockchain, transactions should be encrypted and stored in the block, and not all users have permission to view all transaction data. So, in this paper, we propose an electricity trading blockchain that combines attribute-based encryption schemes to achieve fine-grained access control while protecting user identity information.

We propose a solution to solve the electricity trading problem using blockchain technology. We store electricity trading data in the blockchain so that each transaction can be independent of third parties. In addition, we combine decentralized policy-hiding attribute-based encryption with blockchain technology to enable fine-grained access control without exposing user identity information, while user attributes can be managed by multiple authorities.

First, our solution uses blockchain technology for power trading and uses blockchain to store transaction records and make the data in the system non-tampered, unforgeable and verifiable. Second, the attribute-based cryptographic scheme is used to encrypt the data and store it in the corresponding block, and only the users who meet the specific attribute requirements can decrypt the data, realize fine-grained access control, and do not disclose the user's personal information. Third, a decentralized policy-hiding attribute-based encryption is used in our scheme, so that the user's attributes are no longer only issued by a central authority, but can be distributed by a number of different authority agencies. This mode is more in line with the actual application scenario. Finally, we conducted a security analysis of the proposed scheme and explained the security of the system applied to electricity trading from multiple perspectives.

2   Related Work

At present, many scholars have studied the privacy-preserving problem around the blockchain. Ricardo [3] proposed a management and control method based on blockchain which supports data accountability and source tracking. The method relies on the use of the Publicly Auditable Contracts deployed on the blockchain, adds the data control strategy into the smart contract [4], and automatically tracks the data source and logs the data usage process, thus increasing the transparency of data usage and access. Document [5] proposed a method for guaranteeing the authenticity of sensor data based on blockchain and applied in the microbial sampling robot system. Document [6] uses blockchain to implement non-tampered security audit logs. Document [7] applies blockchain to the authenticity protection of medical data to prevent data from being tampered with. Document [8] aiming at the problem of the limited computing power of wearable devices, using Bloom Filter to optimize the block data management and improve the spatial and temporal efficiency of the algorithm. Kosba et.al. have developed a blockchain contract development platform based on cryptography, Hawk [9], to address the privacy and security issues of intelligent contracts on blockchains. Hawk compilers automatically generate efficient zero knowledge proof based encryption protocols to interact with the blockchain. Greenspan proposed a homomorphic encryption technology to ensure the confidentiality of the data in the blockchain [10]. The Elements blockchain [11] allows the use of additive homomorphism commitment [12] to achieve confidential transactions. Aiming at the problem of limited storage capacity and computing resources of blockchains, document [13] realizes data sharing under the premise of protecting data privacy and security based on blockchain technology, realizes data storage by combining on-chain and off-chain storage, stores hash values of signatures on the blockchain, and encrypts data in the database that trusted by users off-chain in order to ensure the safety of data. Reference [14] proposes a distributed computing framework, Enigma, which separates data management from storage, manages data by storing data indexes in a blockchain via a Distributed Hash-Table (DHT) [15] and stores data with off-chain computational nodes which have stronger computing and storage capabilities.

However, there are still some problems in the existing methods: (1) Most of the schemes do not protect the data stored in the blockchain, and the management of the data relies on the security mechanism of the blockchain itself. If the blockchain encounters a consensus attack (such as 51% attack), the security of the data on the blockchain will not be discussed; (2) Although homomorphism encryption can realize the confidentiality of data very well, but due to noise problems, the computation depth of homomorphic encryption is limited and the key space is too large. So there is still a long way to go from practical application. There are few applications of partial homomorphic encryption (i.e. homomorphic encryption which only supports addition or multiplication). (3) User identity is unique to the public key address in the blockchain, user privacy is easy to leak, if the user's private key is lost, it will not be retrieved, and the user-related data resources will all be lost. Therefore, how to ensure transaction information and data security of the blockchain still needs further study.

3   Core System Components

In this section, we will introduce the core system components used in our electricity trading scheme.

Ciphertext-Policy Attribute-Based Encryption (CP-ABE): Amit and Brent first put forward the concept of attribute-based encryption (ABE) [17], and Vipul later made a further definition of ABE [18]. ABE schemes are mainly divided into two kinds: Key-Policy Attribute-Based Encryption (KP-ABE) [18] and Ciphertext-Policy Attribute-Based Encryption (CP-ABE) [19]. CP-ABE can be seen as binding each ciphertext to a predicate P, and each receiver's private key to a set of attributes, which can be decrypted only if the attributes of the key satisfy the predicate of the ciphertext. A CP-ABE scheme ABE consists of four algorithms for system setup, encryption, key generation, and decryption.

Decentralized Policy-Hiding ABE: Decentralized Policy-Hiding ABE is an attribute-based encryption scheme proposed by Yan Michlevsky et al. in 2018 [20]. In their scheme, there are five main stages, and it has shown as below. The first stage is *Setup* stage, it takes the security parameter λ as input, and it out put a master key MK. There are two group $\mathbb{G}_1$ and $\mathbb{G}_2$, which generator is g_1 and g_2. Choose two random matrix $A \in \mathbb{Z}_p^{(k+1)\times k}$ and $U \in \mathbb{Z}_p^{(k+1)\times(k+1)}$, the master key MK is calculated as $MK = \{g_1, g_2, g_1{}^A, g_1{}^{U^T A}\}$. The next stage is *AuthSetup*, the input of this algorithm is the master key MK and the index of the authority agency i, then it outputs the authority agency i's public key PK_i and private key SK_i as $PK_i = \{g_1{}^{W_i{}^T A}, \widehat{e}(g_1, g_2)^{\alpha_i{}^T A}, y = g_2{}^{\sigma_i}\}, SK_i = \{W_i, \alpha_i, \sigma_i\}$, where W_i is a matrix which randomly chooses in $\mathbb{Z}_p^{((k+1)\times(k+1))}$, α_i is a vector which length is $k+1$ and σ_i is a random number in $\mathbb{Z}_p$. At the Encrypt stage, construct a vector x, and choose a random vector s, the ciphertext CT is divided into three parts: $C_0 = g_1{}^{As}, C_1 = g_1{}^{(x_i U^T + W_i^T)As}$ and $C' = M \cdot \prod_{i=1}^n \widehat{e}(g_1, g_2)^{\alpha_i{}^T As} = M\widehat{e}(g_1, g_2)^{\alpha_i{}^T A}$ where M is the plaintext and $\alpha = \sum_{i=1}^n \alpha_i$. The next stage is *KeyGen*, the input of *KeyGen* is the master key MK, the index of the authority agency i, the authority agency's private key SK_i, other authority agencies' public key PK_j the user's global identifier GID and an attribute vector v, and it output the secret key based on the attribute vector v of the user whose global identifier is GID and issued by authority agency i, it consists of $K_i = g_2{}^{\alpha_i - v_i W_i h + \mu_i}$, where $\mu_i = \sum_{j=1}^{i-1} \mathcal{H}(y_j{}^{\sigma_i}, GID, v) - \sum_{j=i+1}^n \mathcal{H}(y_j{}^{\sigma_i}, GID, v)$. The last algorithm is *Decrypt*. It takes the ciphertext CT, and the secret key based on the attribute vector v of the user as input. The algorithm recovers plaintext through the following formula: $M = \frac{C'}{\widehat{e}(C_0, \prod_{i=1}^n K_i) \cdot \widehat{e}(\prod_{i=1}^n C_i{}^{v_i}, H(GID, v))}$.

4   Attribute-Based Blockchain

In this section, we will describe an attribute-based blockchain used in electricity trading.

Roles: There are several different roles in our scheme, they have different responsibilities and authorities in the system.

Energy Service Provider: They are responsible for selling electricity generated in various ways to the Electricity Companies.

Electricity Company: Electricity company sells electricity as the core business. It buys electricity from the Energy Service Providers and then retails to the end user to earn the difference.

Purchaser: Purchasers include ordinary residents, commercial users, industrial users, etc. They buy electricity from the Electricity Company to use.

Regulatory Authority: The Regulatory Authority is responsible for supervising the operation of the electricity market and the power dispatching transactions, supervising the implementation of the electricity policy, and supervising and inspecting the relevant electricity prices.

User: Users in our scheme is composed of Energy Service Provider, Electricity Company, Purchaser and Regulatory Authority.

Authority Agency: The Authority Agency is responsible for assigning attributes to users as they enter the system. In our scheme, different attributes of a user can be issued by one or more authorities.

Administrator: They are responsible for managing the system's data and assigning them global identities as they enter the system. The administrator is also responsible for generating global parameters when the system is initialized.

Blocks: In the electricity trading blockchain, the Company Transaction Block (CTB) stores transaction records of the electricity company purchasing energy from the energy service provider. Each CTB contains the unique transaction identifier, seller, purchaser, energy type, unit price, and some transaction information such as trading volume, total transaction amount, transaction date, etc. Energy service providers and electricity companies can add transactions to CTBs. The Purchaser Transaction Block (PTB) is similar to CTB, but it stores the transaction records of purchasers purchasing electricity from electricity companies. The CTB contains the unique transaction identifier, seller, purchaser, energy type, unit price, and some transaction information just like CTB. Electricity companies and purchasers can add transactions to PTBs. The regulatory authorities publish relevant information such as power policy and electricity price as transactions to Transaction Management Block (TMB). All users in the system have permission to read relevant information from TMBs to ensure the legality of the transactions. The System Management Block (SMB) storage system management information and the access control policy. Users can view these data before accessing the blockchain so that they don't have to constantly try to match their own policy to certain transactions. Each block in our scheme is consist of two parts: the block header and the main block. The block header contains the current block hash, the previous block hash, a timestamp and the signature of the publisher of this block. The main block stores transactions. The transaction type is depended on the block type as mentioned above. The main block of each block can contain one or more transactions of the same type.

Nodes: There are two types of nodes in our scheme: backup node and primary node. Backup nodes can create new transactions of different types and publish these transactions to the network with their signature. They can also access the transactions in blocks on the blockchain if they have corresponding access policy. Primary nodes are responsible for collecting transactions from the network, create new blocks and put the transactions to corresponding blocks. Primary nodes should publish the new blocks to the network with their own signature. Each node in this system has one or more attributes. When users enter the system for the first time, the authority agencies will issue a set of attributes to the users. These attributes can be issued by one or more different authority agencies. One attribute of the user is legal as long as it has the signature of the corresponding authority agency. When a user needs to publish a transaction to a block, he needs to encrypt the transaction with a specific set of attributes. In the data access stage, the data can be decrypted only if the intersection of the user's attributes and the ciphertext policy attributes exceeds a certain threshold. This process enables our system to achieve fine-grained access control without revealing user identity information. In addition, each node has its own global identity (GID). When they enter the system, the administrator gives the GID to users, which can bind keys issued by different authoritys to the same user.

Data Structures: There are mainly six different kinds of data structures in our scheme: *Cert, AttCert, ProposalRecord, BlockHeader, MianBlock,* and *Block.* Next, we will introduce this data structure in detail.

Cert: Every user come to the system will be issued a pair of keys used for the signature. They will be distributed to users in the form of *Cert.* The construction of *Cert* is as: $Cert = SIG_{SIK}(h_{cert}, CT_{sik||nonce}, vk, timestamp)$, where SIK is the signature key of administrator, h_cert is the hash value of this message, $CT_{sik||nounce}$ is the ciphertext of sik, and a $nonce$ encrypted using the user's public key. The sik is the signature of the user and vk is a verification key to verify the digital signature.

AttCert: In our scheme, a user has one or more attributes. Users need to use the private key corresponding to the attribute when decrypting a message. Authority agencies issue these attributes to users in the form of attribute certificates *AttCert.* The construction of *AttCert* is as $AttCert = SIG_{SIK}(h_{AttCert}, CT_{SK_{att}||nonce}, timestamp)$, where SIK is the signature key of the authority agency, $h_{AttCert}$ is the hash value of this message, SK_{att} is the private key corresponding to this attribute, $CT_{SK_{att}||nounce}$ is the ciphertext of SK_{att} and a $nonce$ encrypted using the user's public key.

ProposalRecord: When a user wants to add a transaction to a block in the blockchain, he posts the message to the network in the form of *ProposalRecord.*

It is shown as $ProposalRecord = (CT_{message||nonce}, timestamp, \sigma_{sik})$, where sik is the signature key of the user who publish the message, $CT_{message||nonce}$ is the ciphertext of the message and a *nonce* encrypted with attribute-based encryption, and σ_{sik} is calculate as $Sig_{sik}(CT_{message||nonce}, timestamp)$.

BlockHeader: A *BlockHeader* contains the current block's hash value, the previous block's hash value, a timestamp, and the signature and its structure is as follow $BlockHeader_i = (H_{Block_i}, H_{Block_{i-1}}, timestamp, SIG_{sik})$, where H_{Block_i} is the hash value of the current block, $H_{Block_{i-1}}$ is the hash value of the previous block, sik is the signature key of the publisher.

MainBlock: The main block stores transactions. It consists of n *Proposal-Record* as $MainBlock_i = \{ProposalRecord_{i1}, ..., ProposalRecord_{in}\}$, where i is the identity of the block and n is the number of the transactions in this block.

Block: A Block consist of a *BlockHeader* and its corresponding *MainBlock*, that is: $Block_i = (BlockHeader_i, MainBlock_i)$, where i is the identity of the block.

5 The Scheme

In this section, we will introduce our scheme in detail. Figure 1 shows the work pattern of the Electricity Trading Blockchain, it is mainly divided into six stages, in which the specific workflow of each stage will be introduced later.

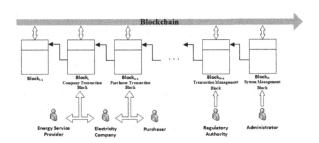

Fig. 1. Electricity trading blockchain.

5.1 System Setup

At the system setup phase, the Electricity Trading Blockchain is installed. It runs when the system is first started. The input of system setup phase is the security parameter λ. First, choose two group $\mathbb{G}_1$ and $\mathbb{G}_2$, which generators are g_1 and g_2. $A \in \mathbb{Z}_p^{((k+1)\times k)}$ and $U \in \mathbb{Z}_p^{(k+1)\times(k+1)}$ are two random matrixes, where k means it is based on k-*linear* computational hardness assumption. Finally, it output the master key MK and the master key MK is consists of $MK = \{g_1, g_2, g_1{}^A, g_1{}^{U^T A}\}$. It can be expressed as $Setup(\lambda) \to MK$.

5.2   Authority Setup

Each authority agency needs to run the Authority Setup algorithm when entering the system. The Authority Setup algorithm generates a public-private key pair $\{PK_i, SK_i\}$ belonging to them for each authority agency for use in subsequent key generation and encryption algorithms in the system. It takes the master key MK and the identifier of the authority agency i as input, randomly choose a matrix $W_i \in \mathbb{Z}_p^{(k+1) \times (k+1)}$ and a vector α_i which length is $k+1$, then choose a random number σ_i in $\mathbb{Z}_p$. This algorithm output the authority agency i's public key PK_i and private key SK_i as $PK_i = \{g_1^{W_i^T A}, \widehat{e}(g_1, g_2)^{\alpha_i^T A}, y = g_2^{\sigma_i}\}$, $SK_i = \{W_i, \alpha_i, \sigma_i\}$. The Authority Setup algorithm can be expressed as $AuthSetup(MK, i) \to PK_i, SK_i$.

5.3   User Setup

Each user enters this system need to run the User Setup algorithm. Through this algorithm, the users will get their own $Cert$ which contains the user's signature key and his verification key. On the other hand, this algorithm will also generate the $AttCert$ for the user which contains the user's attribute-based key used in data access. $AttCerts$ are issued by different authority agencies, and the user has the attribute only if the user has the private key corresponding to this attribute. The input of User Setup is the master key MK, the index of the authority agency which issue the attribute i, the authority agency's private key SK_i, other authority agencies' public key PK_j, the user's global identifier GID and an attribute vector v. We set A be the collection of all attributes in the system, which has l elements. The length of the attribute vector v is $l + 1$, and the first l elements of v are set as: if $i \in R$, $v_i = 1$, otherwise $v_i = 0$. Where R is the attribute set that the user own and the $(l + 1)$th element v_{l+1} is 1. The algorithm outputs the secret key based on the attribute vector v of the user whose global identifier is GID and issued by authority agency i, it consists of $K_i = g_2^{\alpha_i - v_i W_i h + \mu_i}$, where $\mu_i = \sum_{j=1}^{i-1} \mathcal{H}(y_j^{\sigma_i}, GID, v) - \sum_{j=i+1}^{n} \mathcal{H}(y_j^{\sigma_i}, GID, v)$. $\mathcal{H}$ is a random oracle which shown as $\mathcal{H} : \mathbb{G}_2 \times \{0,1\}^{\lambda} \times \mathbb{Z}_p^{l+1} \to \mathbb{Z}_p^{k+1}$. g_2^h is generated by $H_1(GID, v)$ to $H_{k+1}(GID, v)$, h is in $\mathbb{Z}_p^{k+1}$ and $H(GID, v) = (H_1(GID, v), ..., H_{k+1}(GID, v))^T$. Note that h is unknown. The User Setup algorithm in our scheme can be expressed as $UserSetup(MK, i, SK_i, \{PK_j\}_{j \neq i}, GID, v) \to SK_{i,GID,v}$.

5.4   Proposal

When the user wants to add a transaction to the block, it needs to run the Proposal algorithm. In this stage, the message that the user will publish is encrypted with a series of attributes and then released to the network. The primary node collects related transactions from the network, integrates them into specific types of blocks, and publishes messages to the blockchain through PBFT consensus mechanism [21]. At the Encrypt stage, first, construct a ciphertext policy vector x, which length is $l + 1$. Above, we defined A as the set of all attributes in the system. Define S as the set of attributes with ciphertext policy. So, the first l elements of vector x is defined as: if $i \in S$, $x_i = r_i$, otherwise $x_i = 0$, where r_i is randomly choose in $\mathbb{Z}_p$. x_{l+1}, the last element of vector x, is define as $-\sum_{i=i}^{l} x_i(modp)$. Then choose a random vector s, let M be the plaintext of the message and $\alpha = \sum_{i=1}^{n} \alpha_i$, the ciphertext CT is divided into three parts: $C_0 = g_1^{As}, C_1 = g_1^{(x_iU^T+W_i^T)As}$ and $C' = M \cdot \prod_{i=1}^{n} \widehat{e}(g_1, g_2)^{\alpha_i^T As} = M \cdot \widehat{e}(g_1, g_2)^{\alpha_i^T A}$ that is $CT = (C_0, \{C_i\}_{i=1}^{n}, C')$. So, the Encrypt stage can be shown as: $Encrypt(MK, PK_i, x, M) \to CT$. Before publishing the ciphertext of message, the user needs to add their own signature to the message, and then publish the *ProposalRecord*. At the Proposal phase, in addition, backup nodes that can publish transactions, primary nodes need to collect transactions in the network and add them to the block. In our system, the PBFT consensus mechanism is used to achieve this step. There are many different types of transactions in the system, just as blocks have their own type. Primary nodes need to store transactions in corresponding blocks by consensus mechanism.

5.5 Verification

When users want to access a transaction on the blockchain, they first need to verify the digital signature of the transaction to ensure message integrity and authenticate the identity of the transaction creator. In our system, the ECDSA algorithm [22] is used as a digital signature algorithm. ECDSA became the ANSI standard in 1999 and became the IEEE and NIST standard in 2000. In this stage, the user first visits the block in which the transaction is located and verifies the block with the block generator's verification key. If the validation fails, the block is considered invalid. Otherwise, further, verify the legality of the transaction using ECDSA. The transaction is legal if and only if $Ver(vk, Block, ProposalRecord, \sigma_{Block}, \sigma_{proposalRecord}) = 1$, otherwise, verification failed. It's also worth mentioning that all users can verify the validity of each transaction, but only with specific attributes can the transaction data be decrypted.

5.6 Access

At the Access phase, the user can decrypt the encrypted message with the correct attribute set. If the user's attribute-based key is satisfied with the cipher policy of the ciphertext CT, it can access the message successfully. Otherwise, he cannot access the data on the blockchain. This algorithm takes the ciphertext $CT = (C_0, \{C_i\}_{i=1}^{n}, C')$, the secret key set $\{K_i := sk_{i,GID,v}\}_{i=1}^{n}$ based on the attributes and the attribute vector v as input. Then calculate the plaintext in this way: $M = \frac{C'}{\widehat{e}(C_0, \prod_{i=1}^{n} K_i) \cdot \widehat{e}(\prod_{i=1}^{n} C_i^{v_i}, H(GID,v))}$. In the above, we construct vector x and vector v as follows: if $i \in S$, $x_i = r_i$, otherwise $x_i = 0$, $x_{l+1} = -\sum_{i=1}^{l} x_i(modp)$, and if $i \in R$, $v_i = 1$, otherwise $v_i = 0$, $v_{l+1} = 1$. Therefore, if users want to decrypt data with attributes that are encrypted, then $<x, v> = 0$. So that plaintext can be restored. This process can be expressed as $Decrypt(\{sk_{i,GID,v}\}_{i=1}^{n}, CT, v) \to M$.

6 Security Analysis

In this section, we will analyze the security of the electricity trading blockchain from three aspects: anonymity, fine-grained access control, collusion attack, and non-repudiation.

Anonymity: In the blockchain, each person has a virtual identity on the blockchain that is independent of the real identity. Anonymity means that the identity of each person cannot be known. In this paper, the identity of each user is identified by attributes, that is, the user has a series of private keys based on their attributes. Only the authority agencies know the user's true identity and publish their attribute certificate to the user after verifying their identity. After that, the user's behavior in the system only needs to be based on their attributes. For other system users, they have no way of knowing the true identity of the user who posted the transaction. Therefore, the system has further improved anonymity in the blockchain.

Fine-Grained Access Control: In this paper, the attribute-based cryptosystem is used to enable automatic fine-grained access control. When publishing a transaction to a blockchain, it is necessary to encrypt the transaction information by using a series of attributes, and the user can obtain the corresponding private key only when it accesses the encrypted data in the blockchain only if it has a specific attribute set. Therefore, ABE has the good nature of fine-grained access control and user privacy protection required for blockchain platform data sharing.

Collusion Attack: In our proposed scheme, attribute-based encryption is decentralized, so user attributes can be issued by n different authority agencies. For collusion attacks by authority agencies, our scheme can resist attacks jointly launched by up to $n-1$ authority agencies. If the corrupt authority agencies are greater than or equal to n, the user's attribute key can be forged. On the other hand, users can not initiate collusion attacks. In this scheme, each user has his own global identity GID. Assuming that a user's global identity is GID_1, and he wants to forge the attribute key based on attribute set S that he does not own. Another user GID_2 has the attribute S, so they want to unite to forge keys. When decrypt the data in the transaction, the user GID_1 need to calculate $\hat{e}(\prod_{i=1}^{n} C_i^{v_i}, H(GID_1, v))$ with his attribute key, and the user GID_2 need to calculate $\hat{e}(\prod_{i=1}^{n} C_i^{v_i}, H(GID_2, v))$ that associated with attribute set S. Therefore, different GIDs make it impossible for them to forge a complete combination of attribute keys, thus preventing them from completing collusion attacks on the system.

Non-repudiation: The blockchain technology has the characteristics that data cannot tamper and traceable. Each transaction in the blockchain is ciphered in series with two adjacent blocks, so any transaction in the blockchain can be traced back. In our proposed scheme, blockchain technology is used to store data on electricity trading. Therefore, each transaction in the electricity trading blockchain can no longer be tampered with once it is confirmed. This guarantees the security of the electricity trading record.

7   Evaluation

We implement the prototype described in this paper in C++ on a client machine with Intel i7-4600U 2.70 GHz CPU, and 4 GB RAM. We choose secp256k1 (Standards for Efficient Cryptography Group (SECG) curve over a 256-bit prime field) as ECDSA algorithm. Figure 2 shows the computation overhead of proposal stage and access stage. The proposal stage mainly contains encryption step and signing step. The access stage is actually a decryption process. In the figure, let n be the number of the attributes required in the process of proposal and access. We vary n from 1 to 10. We can see that it takes about 31.5 ms to generate a transaction with only one attribute. When the number of attributes is increased to 10, the time to generate a transaction is increased to about 74.3 ms. In the access stage, the time cost of access is about 105 ms when there is only one attribute, and when the number of attributes is increased to 10, it takes about 602 ms to access a transaction. The time costs of proposal and access a block depend on the number of transactions contained in a block. From the preceding experiment results, we can see that our scheme has certain advantages and availability in efficiency, and its performance can support its application in the field of electricity trading.

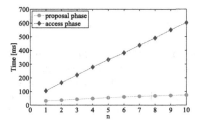

Fig. 2. Computation overhead of proposal and access.

8   Conclusion

We have proposed a privacy-preserving electricity trading blockchain to record every transaction in the system. In this scenario, we have made the following main contributions: First, we apply blockchain technology to the power sector to ensure that every transaction is non-tampered, unforgeable and verifiable. Second, we use a decentralized policy-hiding attribute-based encryption scheme. ABE provides fine-grained access control and protects user privacy, while decentralized policy-hiding attribute-based encryption makes user attributes can be distributed by multiple different authority agencies without the need for a central authority. Finally, we conducted a security analysis of our proposed solution, and analyzed that our system can be well applied to power trading scenarios.

References

1. Nakamoto, S.: Bitcoin: a peer-to-peer electronic cash system. www.bitcoin.org. Accessed 20 Mar 2019
2. Meiklejohn, S., et al.: A fistful of bitcoins: characterizing payments among men with no names. In: Proceedings of the 2013 Conference on Internet Measurement Conference (IMC 2013), pp. 127–140 (2013)
3. Neisse, R., Steri, G., Nai-Fovino, I.: A blockchain-based approach for data accountability and provenance tracking. In: International Conference on Availability, Reliability and Security, p. 14. ACM (2017)
4. Christidis, K., Devetsikiotis, M.: Blockchains and smart contracts for the internet of things. IEEE Access **2016**(4), 2292–2303 (2016)
5. Zhao, H., Li, X., Zhan, L., Zhongcheng, W.: Data integrity protection method for microorganism sampling robots based on blockchain technology. J. Huazhong Univ. Sci. Technol. (Nat. Sci. Ed.) **43**(s1), 216–219 (2015)
6. Jordi, C., Jordi, P.: Distributed immutabilization of secure logs. In: International Workshop on Security and Trust Management, pp. 122–137 (2016)
7. Zhang, J., Xue, N., Huang, X.: A secure system for pervasive social network-based healthcare. IEEE Access **4**(99), 9239–9250 (2016)
8. Siddiqi, M., All, S.T., Sivaraman, V.: Secure lightweight context-driven data logging for bodyworn sensing devices. In: International Symposium on Digital Forensic and Security, pp. 1–6 (2017)
9. Kosba, A., Miller, A., Shi, E., Wen, Z., Papamanthou, C.: Hawk: the blockchain model of cryptography and privacy-preserving smart contracts. In: IEEE Security and Privacy, pp. 839–858 (2016)
10. Greenspan, G.: MultiChain Private Blockchain-White Paper. http://www.multichain.com/white-paper/. Accessed 20 Mar 2019
11. ElementsProject/Elements: Feature Experiments to Advance the Art of Bitcoin. https://github.com/ElementsProject/elements. Accessed 15 Mar 2019
12. Maxwell, G.: Confidential Transactions. https://www.elementsproject.org/elements/confidential-transactions/. Accessed 20 Mar 2019
13. Lazarovich, A.: Invisible Ink: blockchain for data privacy, Massachusetts Institute of Technology (2015)
14. Zyskind, G., Nathan, O., 'Sandy' Pentland, A.: Enigma: decentralized computation platform with guaranteed privacy. Comput. Sci. (2015)
15. Maymounkov, P.: Mazières, D.: Kademlia: a peer-to-peer information system based on the XOR metric. In: The First International Workshop on Peer-to-Peer Systems, pp. 53–65 (2002)
16. Bonneau, J., et al.: SoK: research perspectives and challenges for bitcoin and cryptocurrencies. In: IEEE Symposium on Security and Privacy, pp. 104–121 (2015)
17. Sahai, A., Waters, B.: Fuzzy identity-based encryption. In: Cramer, R. (ed.) EUROCRYPT 2005. LNCS, vol. 3494, pp. 457–473. Springer, Heidelberg (2005). https://doi.org/10.1007/11426639_27
18. Goyal, V., Pandey, O., Sahai, A., Waters, B.: Attribute-based encryption for fine-grained access control of encrypted data. In: Proceedings of the 13th ACM Conference on Computer and Communications Security (CCS 1006), pp. 89–98 (2006)

19. Bethencourt, J., Sahai, A., Waters, B.: Ciphertext-policy attribute-based encryption. In: Proceedings of the 2007 IEEE Symposium on Security and Privacy (SP 2007), pp. 321–334 (2007)
20. Michalevsky, Y., Joye, M.: Decentralized policy-hiding ABE with receiver privacy. In: Lopez, J., Zhou, J., Soriano, M. (eds.) ESORICS 2018. LNCS, vol. 11099, pp. 548–567. Springer, Cham (2018). https://doi.org/10.1007/978-3-319-98989-1_27
21. Castro, M., Liskov, B.: Practical Byzantine fault tolerance. In: USENIX Technical Program - OSDI 1999 (1999)
22. Johnson, D., Menezes, A., Vanstone, S.: The elliptic curve digital signature algorithm (ECDSA). Int. J. Inf. Secur. 1(1), 36–63 (2001)

A Novel Facial Expression Recognition Scheme Based on Deep Neural Networks

Zhuohua Liu[1], Hui Suo[1], and Bin Yang[2(✉)]

[1] School of Computer and Design, Guangdong Jidian Polytechnic,
Guangzhou, China
[2] School of Internet of Things, Jiangnan University, Wuxi, China
Yangbin@jiangnan.edu.cn

Abstract. Automated emotion recognition in the wild from facial images remains a challenging problem. Although recent advances in Deep Learning have supposed a significant breakthrough in this topic, strong changes in pose, orientation and point of view severely harm current approaches. With the transition of facial expression recognition (FER) from laboratory-controlled to challenging in-the-wild conditions and the recent success of deep learning techniques in various fields, deep neural networks have increasingly been leveraged to learn discriminative representations for automatic FER. In this paper, we propose a Low-rank Multimodal Fusion (LMF) method, which performs multimodal fusion using low-rank tensors to improve efficiency. Experimental results performed on emotion datasets demonstrate that our proposed method outperforms state-of-the-art.

Keywords: Facial expression recognition · Deep neural networks · Low-rank Multimodal Fusion

1 Introduction

Facial expression is one of the most powerful, natural and universal signals for human beings to convey their emotional states and intentions. Comparing to feature extraction based on expert's knowledge, deep learning is considered a more effected way to discover the discriminant representations inherent in human faces by incorporating the feature extraction into the task learning process. Deep learning can be used by non-experts for their researches and/or applications, especially in FER field.

FER systems can be roughly grouped into two categories: static image and dynamic sequence [1]. In static-based methods, the facial features [2] are generated with only spatial information from the current single image. On the other hand, dynamic-based methods consider the temporal relation among contiguous frames in the input facial expression sequence [3]. Multimodal research has shown great progress in a variety of tasks as an emerging research field of artificial intelligence. However, multimodal fusion is still an important problem yet to be handled in this domain [4]. The goal of fusion is to combine multiple modalities to leverage the complementary of heterogeneous data and provide more robust predictions. Thus, an important challenge has been on scaling up fusion to multiple modalities while maintaining reasonable model

© Springer Nature Switzerland AG 2019
X. Sun et al. (Eds.): ICAIS 2019, LNCS 11635, pp. 612–622, 2019.
https://doi.org/10.1007/978-3-030-24268-8_56

complexity. Compared with the current state-of-the-art of FER techniques, the contribution of our work can be summarized as follows:

- A method, which leveraging low-rank weight tensors to make multimodal fusion efficient without compromising on performance, is proposed.
- The proposed scheme is computationally efficient and has fewer parameters in comparison to previous tensor-based methods.
- The proposed model outperformed state-of-the-art models in performance on several public datasets.
- A novel wild-wise database is generated to simultaneously train a multi-task, multi-label and multi-domain model.

The rest of the paper is organized as follows. Section 2 presents the review of FER approaches. The proposed method is presented in Sect. 3. Section 4 presents the experimental results and discussions. Finally, the concluding remarks are given in Sect. 5.

2 Related Works

Although, various approaches represent important results for FER, especially considering that the problems they tackle were previously (almost) unexplored. A large set of tools is now available. Among them, methods based on artificial neural networks were proven to be promising for exposing some challenge exemplars. CNN [5] has been extensively used in diverse computer vision applications, including FER.

Facial expression recognition is a multidisciplinary research field, studied in machine learning, computer vision, cognitive science, psychology, neuroscience and applied health sciences. The number of computer vision researchers working in the field of facial expression analysis has increased since the early 90s, and a large amount of published works in the topic exist. Depending on the features used for the recognition task, we can distinguish two prevailing methodologies: geometric based approaches and appearance-based approaches. In the first case, algorithms focus on localizing and tracking specific fiducial facial landmarks, in order to train a classifier based on distances and relative positions of these landmarks.

Many existing networks for FER focus on a single task and learn features that are sensitive to expressions without considering interactions among other latent factors. In the real-world, FER is intertwined with various factors, such as head pose, illumination, and subject identity (facial morphology) [6]. Early fusion is a technique that uses feature concatenation as the method of fusion of different views.

Tao et al. [7] propose a novel attitude restoration method based on multi-layer deep neural network non-linear mapping is. It is based on multi-modal fusion feature extraction and anti-propagation in-depth learning. In multimode fusion, they construct a hyper-graph Laplacian with low rank representation. A unified feature description is obtained by standard eigenvalue decomposition of hypergraph Laplacian matrix. In the in-depth learning of anti-propagation, they learned the non-linear mapping from two-dimensional image to three-dimensional attitude under fine-tuning of parameters. The experimental results of three groups of data show that the recovery error of this method is reduced by 20%–25%, which proves the effectiveness of this method. Several components/models that are independently designed and optimized, leading to sub-optimal performances.

To handle such problem, Wang et al. [8] propose a new reasoning embedded multi-task learning framework for predicting human posture from depth images. Their framework is implemented with the deep structure of neural networks. They handle firstly generating the heat (confidence) maps of body parts via a fully convolutional network. Secondly, they seek the optimal configuration of body parts based on the detected body part proposals via an inference built-in MatchNet, which measures the appearance and geometric kinematic compatibility of body parts and embodies the dynamic programming inference as an extra network layer. Features come from different sub-network were simultaneously trained by using multiple loss functions. The weakness of their approach was that they only use a single source of data. All images for training must be labeled with all the tasks involved. This may be a limitation in real-word applications, such as emotion recognition.

Various subspace clustering methods based on multi-view sparse and low-order representation are also proposed. In particular, a multi-view subspace clustering method called low-order tensor constrained multi-view subspace clustering (LT-MSC) was recently proposed in [9]. In the LT-MSC method, all subspace representations are integrated into a low-order tensor, which captures high-order correlation based on multi-view data.

Abavisani and Patel [10] propose multimodal extensions of the recently introduced sparse subspace clustering (SSC) and low-rank representation (LRR) based subspace clustering algorithms for clustering data lying in a union of subspaces. Given multi-modal data, their method simultaneously clusters data in the individual modalities according to their subspaces. They further exploit the self-expressiveness property of each sample in its respective modality and enforce the common representation across the modalities. Their model is modified to be robustness to several types of noise. Moreover, their proposed algorithms are evaluated to process nonlinearity-data.

Inspired by the promoting works based on multimode fusion technique, a multi-mode architecture of neural network was proposed in this paper. By using such network, knowledge could be transferred from other relevant tasks. In the meanwhile, the disturb factor would be disentangled.

3   Multimodal Sparse and Low-Rank Subspace Clustering

3.1   Sparse Subspace Clustering

In this section, we firstly give a brief background on Sparse Subspace Clustering (SSC) schemes [11]. SSC demonstrates that the noiseless data in a union of subspaces are self-expressive. Every data point can be represented as a sparse linear combination of other data points.

Let $Y = [y_1, \cdots, y_n] \in R^{D \times N}$ be a collection of N signals $\{y_i \in R^D\}_{i=1}^N$ drawn from a union of n linear subspaces $S_1 \cup S_2 \cup \cdots \cup S_n$ of dimensions $\{d_l\}_{l=1}^n$ in R^D. Let $Y_l \in R^{D \times N}$ be a sub-matrix of Y of rank d_l with $N_l > d_l$ points that lie in S_l with $N_1 + N_2 + \cdots + N_n = N$. Given Y, the task of subspace clustering is to cluster the signals according to their subspaces.

The goad of SSC algorithm is to find a sparse matrix $C \in R^{N \times N}$ by solving the following optimization problem:

$$\min \|C\| \tag{1}$$

where $\|C\| = \sum_{i,j} |C_{i,j}|$ is the l_1-norm of C. In the case when the data is contaminated by noise and outliers, one can model the data as:

$$Y = YC + N + E \tag{2}$$

where N is arbitrary noise and E is a sparse matrix containing outliers. In this case, the following problem can be solved to estimate the sparse coefficient matrix C.

$$\min_{C,E} \frac{\delta}{2} \| Y - YC - E \|_F^2 + \|C\| + \delta_e \|E\| \tag{3}$$

where δ and δ_e are positive regulation parameters.

3.2 Multimodal Sparse and Low-Rank Representation-Based Subspace Clustering

The traditional subspace clustering methods are specifically designed for unimodal data. These methods cannot be easily extended while the problem has changed to heterogeneous data. Therefore, a multimodal extension of the sparse and low-rank subspace clustering algorithm [11] is selected in our proposed scheme. Given N paired data samples $\{(y_i^1, y_i^2, \ldots, y_i^m)\}_{i=1}^N$ from m different modalities, define the corresponding data matrices as:

$$\{Y^i = [y_1^i, y_2^i, \ldots, y_N^i] \in \mathbb{R}^{D \times N}\}_{i=1}^m \tag{4}$$

The m paired set of sample points are assumed drawn from a union of n linear subspaces in $\{\mathbb{R}^D\}_{i=1}^m$, respectively. In the case of data contaminated by noise and outliers, the data can be written as:

$$\{Y^i = Y^i C^i + N^i + E^i\}_{i=1}^m \tag{5}$$

Where $\{C^i\}_{i=1}^m$, $\{N^i\}_{i=1}^m$ and $\{E^i\}_{i=1}^m$ are the corresponding sparse coefficient matrix, noise and error terms, respectively.

The subspace representations of different modes are coerced to be the same. In some previous methods, the subspace representations of different modes are different, but they are combined in some way by enforcing some kind of regularization on the representations. The correlation and coupling between different modes are able to be utilized by extracting common sparse and/or low-order representations of different modal data. The optimization problem can be defined as:

$$\min_{C,E} \vartheta(C, E) + \frac{\delta}{2} \sum_{i=1}^{2} \left\| Y^i C^i - N^i - E^i \right\|_F^2 \tag{6}$$

When $\vartheta(C, E) = \|C\| + \delta_e \|E\|$, multimodal SSC (MSSC) algorithm can be obtained. The optimization problem can be redefined as:

$$\min_{C,E} \|C\| + \delta_e \|E\| + \frac{\delta}{2} \sum_{i=1}^{2} \left\| Y^i C^i + N^i + E^i \right\|_F^2 \tag{7}$$

To enhance the results of optimization, [11] slightly modify the formulation into:

$$\min_{C,E} \frac{\delta}{2} \sum_{i=1}^{m} \left\| Y^i - Y^i A - E^i \right\|_F^2 + \|A\| + \delta_r \|C\| + \delta_e \|E\| \tag{8}$$

Where $A = C\text{-}diag(C)$, E is a compact representation for $\{E^i\}_{i=1}^{m}$. When C is estimated, spectral clustering methods can be applied on the affinity matrix $W = |C| + |C|^T$ to obtain the simultaneous segmentation of the data $\{Y^i\}_{i=1}^{m}$.

4   Architecture of Deep Neural Network

Because computing power is still limited, especially in wearable devices, multipurpose is more appropriate in some cases. The proposed work requires a more convenient way of accommodation in the real world. Many existing fer networks only focus on one task and learn expression-sensitive features without considering the interaction between other potential factors. In the real world, different factors can distract the attention of FER tasks, such as lighting, head posture, etc. On this basis, we use multi-task learning technology to transfer knowledge from other related tasks.

As shown in Fig. 2, the proposed facial expression recognition architecture includes a pair of identical CNN components. Each CNN consists of six convolution layers. After the final convolution layer, a fully connected (fc) layers consisting of 1024 neurons were used which is shown in Fig. 1. The maximum pool layer is used to reduce the size of feature mapping after the convolution layer. Let L represent the index of the largest pool layer. The output of the layer is a set of square mappings of wl size. We get P_l from P_{l-1}. The square mapping size WL is obtained by $wl = wl - 1/k$, where k is the maximum square pool core size. As an extension of the activation function of the correction linear unit (ReLU) [12], the series correction linear unit (CReLU) proposed to reduce the number of calculations by half without losing precision [13].

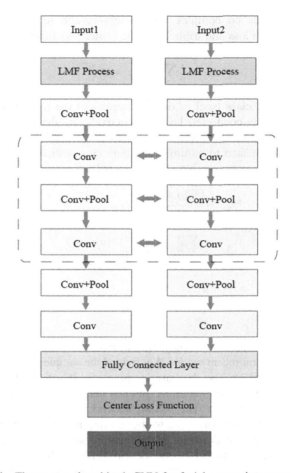

Fig. 1. The proposed multitask CNN for facial expression recognition.

One of the main difficulties with multi-task approaches using different databases is the fact that not all the samples are labeled for all the tasks [6]. Different loss functions for each task and train alternatively for the different domains were developed to handle such problem. Softmax loss technique is usually used in convolutional CNN to force the features of different classes staying apart. Features form clusters corresponding to different expressions in the feature space. But the features in different cluster may scattered due to high intra-class variations. And the clusters often overlap because of high inter-class similarities. To deal with these problems, center loss [14] is developed to reduces the intra-class variations. It simultaneously estimates the center of each class features and penalizes the distances between the features belonged to different class centers. Center loss algorithm can gather together features to their corresponding class centers. The gradient and update equation of center loss function are easy to derive and the resulting CNN model is trainable. Center loss enjoys the same requirement as the softmax loss and needs no complex sample mining and recombination, which is inevitable in contrastive loss and triple loss. The center loss function L_C is defined as:

$$L_C = \frac{1}{2}\sum_{i=1}^{k}\left\|x_i - c_{y_i}\right\|^2 \tag{9}$$

where y_i and x_i are the class label of the ith sample and the feature of the ith sample generated from the fully-connected layer, respectively. c_{y_i} denotes the center of the cluster in which all samples are labelled as y_i, and k is the number of the samples. Joint supervision loss is calculated to minimize the intra-class variations while keeping the features of different classes separable. The backward computation is:

$$\frac{\partial L_C}{\partial x_i} = x_i - c_{y_i} \tag{10}$$

$$\Delta c_j = \frac{\sum_{i=1}^{m}\delta(y_i = j)\cdot(c_j - x_i)}{1 + \sum_{i=1}^{m}\delta(y_i = j)} \tag{11}$$

5   Experiment

For deep feature learning, we employ the TensorFlow implementation, which is commonly used in several recent works. We divided the samples data into training data (70%) and test data (30%). The database learning rate is set to 0.02, which will be divided by 10 after every 10,00 iterations. In each iteration, 256 samples are used for stochastic gradient optimization. The second network was pre-trained on the SFEW dataset. The training strategy was same to the training in first network. We manually labelled subject for the SFEW database. In the fine-tune stage, we exchanged the tuning database, that is, SFEW for the first network and MTE for the second one. The base learning rate is changed to 0.01. The validation accuracy is converged after 200 epoch's fine-tuning. All the experiments in this work were developed on NVIDIA GeForce GTX Titan GPU. We used dropout technique to each fully-connect layer with a probability of 0.65. Accuracy measures the number correctly classified examples; it is defined as follows:

$$accuracy_i = \frac{TP_i + TN_i}{N} \tag{12}$$

where i species the class, i.e., the i-th emotion category, TP_i (true positives) are correctly identified test instances of class i, TN_i (true negatives) are test images correctly labeled as not belonging to class i, and N is the total number of test images.

5.1   Generation of the Emotion Database

For developing a FER approach, it is important to have enough label images, including as many popular and environmental changes as possible. We generated an emotion experimental database to enrich the training images of tags. This database consists of two main data sets, facial expression data and facial expression data in wild scenes. The former includes FERD 2013 [15] data set and experimental image acquisition. Fer2013 is a large, unconstrained database automatically collected by the Google Image Search API. After rejecting frames with error markers and adjusting the clipping area, all images are registered and adjusted to 48 * 48 pixels. FERD 2013 contains 28709 training images, 3589 validation images and 3589 test images with seven expression tags.

Multimodality is an important feature to obtain accurate results. On the other hand, different modalities are difficult to fuse in emotional recognition. FER systems are usually either rule-based or widely trained through facial emotional data. In either case, such HCI systems should be able to adapt knowledge to specific users or interaction contexts. At one point, we recruited 40 subjects of Human's face age from 20 to 50 through online advertising. Each participant was asked to provide seven facial expressions (happiness, sadness, surprise, anger, aversion, fear and neutrality). We took ten pictures of each emotion of different subjects, and finally got five pictures approved by three experienced psychologists. Finally, we obtained a total of 1400 images. A sample of the data set is shown in Fig. 2.

Fig. 2. Sample images in SFEW

Face alignment is important in many facial recognition applications. In this work, the face alignment strategy proposed in [16] is selected to robustly align human face 'in-the-wild'. Finally, each aligned facial image on SFEW was cropped into 48 × 48 pixels and was transformed to grayscale.

5.2 Experimental Results

The confusion matrix of the proposed method evaluated on the FER2013 database is shown in Table 1.

Table 1. Confusion matrix (in percentage) of the proposed method evaluated on the FER2013 database. The ground truth and the predicted labels are given by the first column and the first row, respectively.

	Happy	Sadness	Surprise	Anger	Disgust	Fear	Neutral
Happy	**80.1**	2.7	5.7	2	3.7	5.7	2.1
Sadness	0	**81.7**	5.2	5.8	3.7	5.7	2
Surprise	5.2	0	**88.4**	2	3.2	19.8	0
Anger	1.4	1.7	3	**74.5**	8.6	5.5	2.2
Disgust	5.7	8.7	0	5.7	**70.4**	3	5.8
Fear	4.5	7.7	21.5	5.5	2.4	**76.7**	3.5
Neutral	3.3	5.7	0	0	8.9	5.7	**80.8**

A CNN consists of three types of heterogeneous layers: convolutional layers, pooling layers, and fully connected layers. The convolutional layer has a set of learnable filters to convolve through the whole input image and produce various specific types of activation feature maps. Therefore, we only compare our work to CNN based FER methods. Four methods [14, 17–19] were implemented and applied to the same database. The obtained results are summarized in Table 2. The experimental results show that our scheme achieves better reconfiguration performance than other schemes.

Table 2. Performance comparison of different methods.

Method	Characteristic	Accuracy %
Wen et al. [14]	A new supervision signal for face recognition task is proposed	68.77
Cai et al. [18]	The IL is designed to reduce the intra-class variations while enlarging the inter-class differences simultaneously	71.11
Zhang et al. [17]	A bridging layer is used to leverage the inherent correspondences among of datasets	70.14
Yang et al. [19]	A semantic domain/task descriptor is developed to unify various existing multi-task/multi-domain algorithms within a single matrix factorisation framework	73.30
Proposed method	Low-rank multimodal fusion method is proposed to increase the performance	76.72

6   Conclusion

Comparing to feature extraction based on expert's knowledge, deep learning is considered a more effected way to discover the discriminant representations inherent in human faces by incorporating the feature extraction into the task learning process. In this paper, a novel facial expression recognition method is proposed. Multimodal sparse and low-rank subspace clustering is developed and used in the facial feature clustering process. Extensive experiments show that the proposed method is able to capture both global and local information of faces and performs significantly better than many competitive algorithms for each of these two tasks. In future, we will evaluate the performance of our method on other applications such as simultaneous human detection and human pose estimation, object recognition and gender estimation.

Acknowledgments. This paper is one of the results of the 2016 Guangdong Provincial Higher Vocational Education Leading Talent Project (Hui Suo); and partly supported by the National Natural Science Foundation of China (NO. 51505191), the Humanities and Social Sciences projects of the Ministry of Education (NO. 18YJC760112) and the Chinese Postdoctoral Science Foundation (NO. 2018M632229).

References

1. Li, S., Deng, W.: Deep facial expression recognition: a survey (2018)
2. Mollahosseini, A., Chan, D., Mahoor, M.H.: Going deeper in facial expression recognition using deep neural networks. In: Applications of Computer Vision, pp. 1–10 (2016)
3. Jung, H., Lee, S., Yim, J., Park, S., Kim, J.: Joint fine-tuning in deep neural networks for facial expression recognition. In: IEEE International Conference on Computer Vision, pp. 2983–2991 (2015)
4. Zhang, Y., Wang, Q., Li, Y., Wu, X.: Sentiment classification based on piecewise pooling convolutional neural network. Comput. Mater. Continua **56**, 285–297 (2018)
5. Cui, Q., Mcintosh, S., Sun, H.: Identifying materials of photographic images and photorealistic computer generated graphics based on deep CNNs. Comput. Mater. Continua **55**, 229–241 (2018)
6. Pons, G., Masip, D.: Multi-task, multi-label and multi-domain learning with residual convolutional networks for emotion recognition (2018)
7. Tao, D., Hong, C., Yu, J., Wan, J., Wang, M.: Multimodal deep autoencoder for human pose recovery. IEEE Trans. Image Process. **24**, 5659–5670 (2015). A Publication of the IEEE Signal Processing Society
8. Wang, K., Zhai, S., Hui, C., Liang, X., Liang, L.: Human pose estimation from depth images via inference embedded multi-task learning (2016)
9. Zhang, C., Fu, H., Si, L., Liu, G., Cao, X.: Low-rank tensor constrained multiview subspace clustering. In: IEEE International Conference on Computer Vision (2015)
10. Abavisani, M., Patel, V.M.: Multimodal sparse and low-rank subspace clustering. Inf. Fusion **39**, 168–177 (2018)
11. Ehsan, E.: Sparse subspace clustering: algorithm, theory, and applications. IEEE Trans. Pattern Anal. Mach. Intell. **35**(11), 2765–2781 (2013)
12. Nair, V., Hinton, G.E.: Rectified linear units improve restricted Boltzmann machines. In: International Conference on Machine Learning, pp. 807–814 (2010)
13. Shang, W., Sohn, K., Almeida, D., Lee, H.: Understanding and improving convolutional neural networks via concatenated rectified linear units, pp. 2217–2225 (2016)
14. Wen, Y., Zhang, K., Li, Z., Qiao, Yu.: A discriminative feature learning approach for deep face recognition. In: Leibe, B., Matas, J., Sebe, N., Welling, M. (eds.) ECCV 2016. LNCS, vol. 9911, pp. 499–515. Springer, Cham (2016). https://doi.org/10.1007/978-3-319-46478-7_31

15. Goodfellow, I., Erhan, D., Luc, C.P., Courville, A., Mirza, M., Hamner, B., et al.: Challenges in representation learning: a report on three machine learning contests. Neural Netw. **64**, 59–63 (2015)
16. Asthana, A., Zafeiriou, S., Cheng, S., Pantic, M.: Incremental face alignment in the wild. In: Computer Vision and Pattern Recognition, pp. 1859–1866 (2014)
17. Zhang, Z., Luo, P., Loy, C.C., Tang, X.: Learning social relation traits from face images (2015)
18. Cai, J., Meng, Z., Khan, A.S., Li, Z., Tong, Y.: Island loss for learning discriminative features in facial expression recognition (2017)
19. Yang, Y., Hospedales, T.M.: Unifying multi-domain multitask learning: tensor and neural network perspectives. In: Csurka, G. (ed.) Domain Adaptation in Computer Vision Applications. ACVPR, pp. 291–309. Springer, Cham (2017). https://doi.org/10.1007/978-3-319-58347-1_16

Active Defense System of Industrial Control System Based on Dynamic Behavior Analysis

Wenjin Yu$^{(\boxtimes)}$, Yixiang Jiang, and Yizhen Lin

China Tobacco Zhejiang Industrial CO., LTD., Ningbo, China
{yuwj,linyizhen}@zjtobacco.com,
jiangyxlunwen@sina.com

Abstract. The Internet and the traditional network continue to converge. With the continuous occurrence of security incidents for industrial control systems such as the "Stuxnet" and the Ukraine power grid incident, the security of industrial control systems has attracted more and more attention from the state and enterprises. In order to cope with the continuous attacks, an active defense system for industrial control systems based on dynamic behavior analysis is proposed in this paper. By analyzing the traffic of the captured intruder and the attack behavior of the intruder, the system can make corresponding counter-measures when the attack occurs. The system realizes the expected goal of the industrial control system to actively defend against the intrusion behavior.

Keywords: Industrial safety · Active defense · Dynamic behavior analysis

1 The Introduction

1.1 The Research Background

With the continuous development of science and technology, the integration of industrial network and IT network has accelerated the development of industrial system greatly. However, the security problem in the traditional network is introduced into the industrial control system at the same time [1]. Industrial control systems are usually used in the infrastructure related to national security, such as water, electricity, oil and other industries. Once these industries are invaded, the loss will be huge. For example, Iran's "Stuxnet" virus attack, most centrifuge failures at nuclear power plants, Ukraine electrical system invasion events, and so on [2].

Due to the requirement of real-time and availability of communication, there are usually some defects at the beginning of design in industrial control system, such as the lack of authentication mechanism in the design of communication protocol and the untimely update of upper computer software. Compared with the traditional network, the industrial control system network has more attack surfaces [3]. With the continuous development of science and technology, the intrusion methods of attackers are developing. It is difficult for traditional defense methods to completely intercept the endless attacks. So researchers are shifting from traditional passive defense to active defense based on dynamic behavior. Honeypot is a typical active defense technology. Honeypot can lure attackers and obtain their purpose by analyzing their behaviors, so

© Springer Nature Switzerland AG 2019
X. Sun et al. (Eds.): ICAIS 2019, LNCS 11635, pp. 623–636, 2019.
https://doi.org/10.1007/978-3-030-24268-8_57

as to reinforce the industrial control system and achieve the purpose of active defense. In order to explore effective active defense technology, an active defense system based on dynamic behavior analysis is designed in this paper. Through the analysis of network attack traffic in the system, the attacker's purpose and behavior are obtained, so that better countermeasures can be made in a targeted manner.

1.2   Status Quo at Home and Abroad

The research on industrial control system security in Europe and America started early and has been in a leading position. A number of state-level industrial control security laboratories have been established. With the outbreak of "stuxnet" virus in 2010, various countries began to pay attention to industrial control system security, and unified industrial security issues with national infrastructure security [4].

There is a certain gap between China and developed countries in the field of industrial control. In recent years, China has gradually increased the research on industrial control system security, such as the National Cyberspace Space Security Strategy issued in 2016, which proposes that the core of industrial control system security is information security. There are also many well-known industrial control security manufacturers in China, such as: qiming stars (Venustech), green alliance (NSFOCUS). These manufacturers also greatly accelerate the domestic research on industrial control control security issues.

2   Overview of Industrial Control Systems

This chapter mainly analyzes the security requirements of security awareness of workers, industrial control components, vulnerability of industrial control network, general steps of industrial control attack and industrial control system. Analysis of these contents can help to build a more targeted industrial control system defense system.

2.1   Vulnerability of Industrial Control System

Industrial control system is different with the traditional IT network in communication protocol and the operating system, such as industrial control network operating systems generally use special embedded operating system, the communication protocol is also a special communication protocol. Because the industrial control system can't shut down in production, it requires the system to run stably for a long time. These are all important factors for the safety risk of industrial control system [5, 6]. Its vulnerability is mainly reflected in the following aspects:

(1)   Weak security awareness

Due to the lack of corresponding security training, the security awareness of practitioners is insufficient, and the corresponding security norms can't be followed in actual operation, which results in the exposure of the industrial control system in the network, making it face greater security threats. For example, workers may insert virus-infected USB flash drive into the industrial control system, causing the system to be attacked. These are caused by the weak security awareness of the staff.

(2) Vulnerabilities in industrial control components

The hardware, software and operating system of industrial control system are designed without strict security consideration. Due to its stability requirements, the industrial control system equipment can't be shut down and updated during running, which makes the system vulnerability can't be repaired for a long time and makes it easier for attackers to invade the system.

(3) Vulnerability of industrial control network

Industrial control system requires high real-time communication, therefore, in the design of the communication protocol of the industrial control system, the security of the communication, such as the security authentication mechanism, is not considered. These protocol vulnerabilities bring great security risks to industrial control system. In addition, at the beginning of the design, the unclear network boundary between the industrial control system and the enterprise network also brings unstable factors to the system security.

2.2   General Steps of an Attack on an Industrial Control System

Generally speaking, the attack steps for industrial control system can be divided into four steps: information collection, detection and discovery, intrusion and penetration, and attack:

(1) Information collection

The attacker collects the basic information of the target system through various means, including the protocol, equipment, operating system, and so on, and then finds the vulnerability or backdoor for the equipment used by the system.

(2) Exploration and discovery

The attacker uses the communication protocol and specific port used by the target system to obtain the specific location of the target system. And the attacker can detect the system more deeply through the industrial communication protocol used by the system. For example, if you want to obtain the equipment information of Modbus protocol PLC, you can send function code no. 43 to the system.

(3) Intrusion and infiltration

In order to obtain the control authority of the target system, it needs to invade and infiltrate the system. For example, an attacker can take advantage of the vulnerability of the operating system to obtain the HMI authority of the system. Based on this, it can also use the system as a springboard to invade and infiltrate other devices in the system.

(4) Implement an attack

After the attacker gets the control authority of the system, the target system can be operated purposefully by the attacker. For example, start and stop the corresponding equipment, turn off the alarm function.

2.3 Industrial Control System Safety Requirements

The original industrial control system was designed to run on the private network without considering access to the public network. With the development of information technology, the integration of industrial control system network and Ethernet makes it face greater intrusion risk [7]. The primary goal of traditional information systems is confidentiality, while industrial control systems focus more on stability and availability.

(1) Availability

Industrial control system is a system with special requirements for communication time. Only when strict communication time requirements are met can normal execution of operation instructions be guaranteed [7]. Communication delay will affect the normal running of the system, and serious conditions lead to system downtime. Therefore, availability is one of the most important security requirement of industrial control system. Therefore, the impact on system availability is considered in both the design and deployment of security mechanisms.

(2) Integrity

Ensuring the integrity of communication is also a very important requirement of industrial control system. In order to meet real-time requirements, the communication protocol of the industrial control system does not provide a window mechanism for retransmission of corrupted datagram, but realizes data integrity detection mechanism such as cyclic redundancy inspection to detect corrupted datagram. A single transport layer integrity check can only detect errors and cannot provide other security mechanisms, so it cannot meet the integrity requirements of industrial control system communication.

(3) Confidentiality

Different from traditional information systems, confidentiality is not the most important security requirement in industrial control systems [8]. Due to the limited computing resources in the system, any encryption and decryption operation will take up computing resources, increase the system overhead and cause a certain delay, which may make the industrial control system fail to meet the real-time requirements of communication and affect the normal running of the system. Therefore, the communication protocol of general industrial control system does not encrypt the data packets transmitted in the network.

3   Active Defense System Framework Design

This chapter makes a detailed comparison of mainstream information security technology. According to the content analyzed in the previous chapter, the design framework of the active defense system is proposed.

3.1   Mainstream Information Security Technology Comparison

At present, the commonly used security technologies include intrusion detection, honeypot, and so on. Often different security technologies will correspond to different security needs. Common security capabilities include intrusion detection, entrapment, and response capabilities. The comparison table of common security devices by capability is as follows:

Table 1. Comparison table of common safety devices by capacity.

	Ability to find		Ability to trap	Responsiveness
	Known intrusion	Unknown intrusion		
Intrusion detection	Strong	Null	Null	Null
Firewall	Null	Null	Null	Strong
Honeypot	Little	Little	Strong	Little
Antivirus	Strong	Mull	Null	Null
Security audit	Strong	Strong	Null	Null
Switches	Null	Null	Null	Null

According to Table 1, it can be found that intrusion detection has a strong ability to detect attack behaviors. It matches the target network data collected with its own attack characteristic database to detect abnormal behaviors in the network. Honeypot system is to attract attackers by exposing known vulnerabilities and imitating the real system. By analyzing the attacker's attack behavior and the captured data, the protection scheme of industrial control system is designed or strengthened according to the analysis results. The active defense system in this paper is based on the characteristics of intrusion detection and honeypot system.

3.2   Active Defense System Framework Design

Based on the analysis of the characteristics of existing security technology, an active defense system is proposed in this chapter which consists of industrial honeypot systems and industrial intrusion detection systems. The active defense system in this paper is composed of firewall, intrusion detection system and honeypot system. This system attracts the attack of hackers through the open port 502 in Modbus protocol, and analyzes the attack data through the intrusion detection system, the attack data will be introduced into the industrial honeypot system. The attacker's attack behavior is recorded in the honeypot system and the attack data is processed for subsequent research. Figure 1 is the active defense system framework.

At present, the mainstream intrusion detection methods generally use empirical model or neural network model. However these methods are not mature and the matching database can't be updated in a timely manner for the real-time characteristics of industrial control system. As a result, unknown attacks cannot be detected in time and the false alarm rate tends to be high. Intrusion detection does not have the ability to trap attacks, and honeypot does not have the ability to detect consistent attacks. The combination of the two can make up for each other's shortcomings, and form a complete active defense system. However, the intrusion detection delay in the traditional network is high, which will lead to the high delay of the system and can't meet the real-time communication requirements of the system. In order to improve the detection accuracy and reduce the amount of data analysis, the system uses pre-configured rules to filter the data packets of the target network. Then the data package accessing the industrial control system is imported into the honeypot system, and all other data are discarded. A honeypot system is designed which can satisfy the characteristics of industrial control system in this paper. In order to attract attackers to deploy honeypot system, it can be disguised as a specific industrial system during actual deployment.

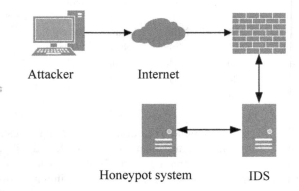

Attacker   Internet

Honeypot system   IDS

Fig. 1. Active defense architecture framework.

4   Industrial Intrusion Detection System

This chapter briefly introduces Snort system. An intrusion detection system suitable for industrial control system is designed in this chapter and each module and workflow of the system are introduced in detail.

4.1   Introduction of Snort

Snort is a powerful intrusion detection system. Snort can support a mainstream operating system, and Snort can recognize a lot of attacks based on its matching rules. If the attack is successfully matched with its own feature library, the attack can be considered to have occurred. Because of lightweight nature, Snort doesn't affect the normal network when it detects. The data generated by the attack behavior in the database is saved in the database and displayed through the web interface.

4.2   Industrial Intrusion Detection System Framework Design

Combined with the characteristics of Snort and industrial control system, framework of industrial intrusion detection system is designed in this chapter, which is shown in Fig. 2.

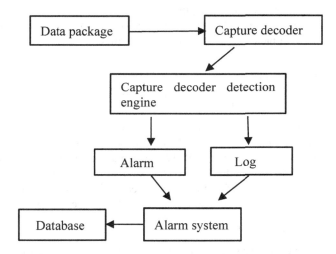

Fig. 2. Industrial intrusion detection system framework.

(1) Capture decoder

The packet catcher module is implemented by Libpcap, which is mainly used to collect traffic data on the target network. Users can select dedicated functions from the function library and configure the packet filter to achieve the specific function [8]. The Snort network intrusion detection system can detect attacks in multiple types of interface packets. Users can use Libpcap to obtain packets of the target network through a simple configuration. Packets can be filtered by specifying a set of rules such as destination port, IP address, and so on.

Packet decoding, also known as protocol parsing, mainly matches captured packets according to protocol format. The main process of packet decoding is to first obtain the field information of the current data header. According to this packet header information, the parsing function is called, and the results of protocol parsing will be stored in the corresponding data. These parsing results will provide data support for future work.

Data preprocessing before packet analysis can improve the efficiency of analysis. Users can specify the type and associated parameters of processing in the configuration file as needed, which allows users to easily extend the preprocessor.

(2) Detection of engine module

The main metrics to measure the performance of an intrusion detection system include detection efficiency and detection accuracy. The feature and rule selection of detection attack have great influence on the accuracy of detection engine. The architecture of the detection engine determines the efficiency of the detection system. Detection engine is usually deployed after pre-processing, and the detection engine performs in-depth detection of the pre-processed information according to the rules configured in advance.

(3) Alarm/log

Snort provides users with two output modes, alarm and log. The log is used to record the attack information. Detection results of alarm processing can also be selected, including complete mode and quick alarm mode.

4.3   The Working Process

(1) Main function processing flow

Initializing the main function is the main part of this processing flow. During the processing, the main function can parse the command line and effectively process the corresponding rules at the same time [10]. The initialization process is generally a valid configuration of the directory. In this process, the command line parsing function needs to be called, and the corresponding functions can be realized by calling different functions. For example, use the OpenPcap function to intercept and detect the specified data.

(2) Rule base parsing process

According to the characteristics of each attack, the intrusion detection system stores the rules as a linked list on the basis of the rule tree and five kinds of rules during initialization. The horizontal position of the rule in the two-dimensional linked list depends on the rule header, while the vertical position of the rule is determined by the rule options. The rule parsing process is shown in Fig. 3.

(3) Packet processing process

The ProcessPackek function decodes each packet. Only in intrusion detection mode can the system obtain data packets with preprocessed linked list. Detect function detects the data packets after preprocessing, and If the data packets can't pass the matching rule, the corresponding output function is called to process in a specific way, such as alarm, log, discard. If the packet passes all matching rules, the above process is repeated for the next packet.

5   Industrial Honeypot Technology

This chapter briefly introduces the honeypot system, introduces the overall design of honeypot system in detail, and makes a simple introduction to the implementation of honeypot.

5.1   Overview of Industrial Honeypot System

The honeypot system designed in this paper can make it more convenient for users to detect security events in the network, and can also analyze the captured data, attack purpose, attack characteristics to obtain the identity and location information of the attacker.

In this paper, B/S structure is adopted to realize our industrial honeypot system. The server is mainly used to capture attack data in the network and perform corresponding processing. The browser side mainly displays the data captured by the server and processing results to the user graphically. The honeypot system is expected to achieve the following objectives [11].

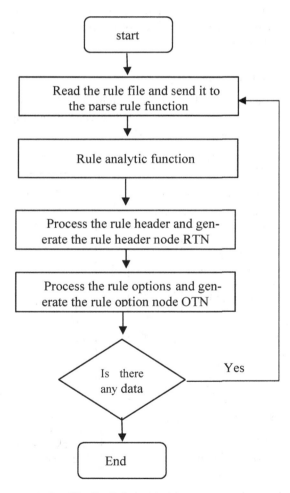

Fig. 3. Rule resolution process.

(1) Capture all attack data in the system

In order to better predict the threat to the industrial control system in the network, the system needs to be connected to the honeypot and capture all attack data.

(2) Convenient management

Since the data in the honeypot is huge and without the function of status monitoring, the management error rate will be very high if it is manually monitored. Therefore, in order to facilitate the administrator of honeypot management, it is necessary to realize the management function and status monitoring function of the honeypot in the system.

(3) Security event monitoring and analysis

In order to make it convenient for administrators to acquire attack information, it is required that the system can detect the attack of information security in real time and analyze the attack data in detail.

5.2   Honeypot System Overall Design

Industrial honeypot system is divided into front-end visual interface, industrial honeypot system server, attack detection and data acquisition. Figure 4 shows the structure diagram of industrial honeypot system:

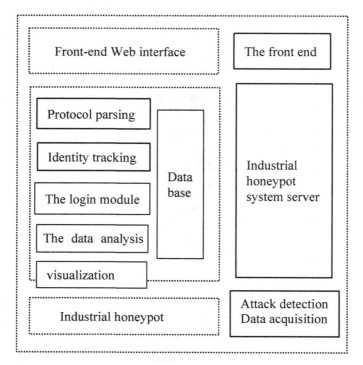

Fig. 4. Industrial honeypot system architecture diagram.

(1) Data visualization

The main function of the front-end interface is to receive the data analysis results of the industrial system server and present the results to the user graphically after classifying and summarizing.

(2) Industrial honeypot system server

Industrial honeypot system consists of several submodules, including user login module, honeypot management module, protocol parsing module, data analysis and visualization module. These modules analyze and process the data and push the results to the front-end Web for visualization.

(3) Attack detection and data acquisition

The attack detection and data acquisition part is implemented by the industrial honeypot, which is used to detect the target network all day and detect external attacks in time.

5.3   Industrial Honeypot Realization

The industrial honeypot in this paper is realized by improving Conpot, and the improved honeypot can simulate Modbus protocol. We can deploy honeypot in the network that needs to be monitored, so that attacks can be detected and attack data can be obtained [12].

Design Ideas. The main function of honeypot in this paper is to monitor attack data in real time and send attack data to the industrial honeypot server [13]. In this way, it can prevent the attacker from invading the honeypot and changing the information such as honeypot log, and make it convenient for system to process data by concentrate the data. The honeypot of this paper mainly includes two parts in function: attack monitoring and recording part, data remote push part. Figure 5. shows the industrial honeypot function module diagram:

The attack monitoring and recording part is mainly responsible for monitoring the commonly used ports of industrial control protocol. After the attack data are captured, the attack data will be stored locally and pushed to the web front end in real time. The data remote push part can use the configuration file to configure the push function of honeypot.

The Working Process. The honeypot system designed in this paper will listen to the commonly used ports of industrial control protocol in a loop. When a data flow is detected on a certain port, the main program of honeypot system will create sub-threads and call relevant programs to capture the attack data under the port, and the main program will continue to listen to the port in a loop.

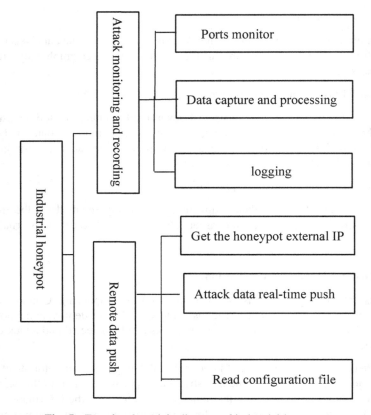

Fig. 5. Functional module diagram of industrial honeypot.

In actual deployment, he honeypot can be disguised as an actual industrial control system. For example, electric Power Monitoring System, weak password, SQL injection vulnerability and other attack data can be set to attract attackers in the system login interface [14]. The attacker can also modify the corresponding parameters, so that the system can make corresponding protection according to the attack intention of the attacker [15].

6 Summary and Prospect

6.1 Summary

After the "Stuxnet" incident, industrial control security has been widely concerned, and has achieved certain achievements at home and abroad. It mainly analyzes the attack characteristics of industrial control system and the general steps of attack in this paper. On this basis, an active defense system of industrial control system based on honeypot system and intrusion detection is proposed in this paper. The system makes full use of the advantages of the honeypot system and the intrusion detection system. It uses the intrusion detection technology to import the data of the industrial control system into the honeypot system, and the rest data traffic is discarded. Finally, the honeypot system analyzes the attacker's attack data and obtains the attack method. According to the characteristics of the attacker, the corresponding protective measures are formulated. The specific work is summarized as follows:

(1) The active defense system of industrial control system based on dynamic behavior analysis designed in this paper combines the advantages of honeypot system and intrusion detection system.
(2) An industrial honeypot system supporting a variety of protocols is designed, which can capture attacking data of various industrial control protocols and push them remotely.
(3) In this paper, intrusion detection technology is applied to industrial control honeypot, and attacking data targeted at industrial control system are drained to honeypot system to realize data analysis.

6.2   Prospect

The active defense system designed in this paper still has the following problems to be improved in the later stage:

(1) The honeypot system designed in this paper needs to be further improved in terms of interaction. The honeypot isn't high attractive to attackers, resulting in less attack data captured. In the later stage, it is necessary to further study how to improve the interaction degree of honeypot system, so as to attract attackers and capture more attack data.
(2) The attack data analysis function of this system for various industrial control protocols is not perfect enough. Currently, this system only supports the analysis of attack data of Modbus protocol, and further studies are needed to analyze more types of attack data.
(3) Although the system can trace the identity of an attacker, the main method is manual analysis. In the next step, clustering and deep learning algorithm can be considered to be applied to the system to classify the attacking IP and its behavior characteristics, so as to improve the traceability efficiency.

References

1. Xia, C., Liu, T., Wang, H., et al.: Current situation and development trend of information security in industrial control systems. Inf. Secur. Technol. 4(2), 13–18 (2013)
2. Fan, K., Gao, L., Yao, X., et al.: Information security guidelines for industrial control systems, pp. 102–110. Science Press, Beijing (2016)
3. Tang, W.: Information security of industrial automation control system based on defense concept in depth. China Instrum. (S1), 112–118 (2013)
4. Cheng, J., Xu, R., Tang, X., et al.: An abnormal network flow feature sequence prediction approach for DDoS attacks detection in big data environment. CMC: Comput. Mater. Continua 55(1), 095–119 (2018)

5. lv, S., Sun, L., Shi, Z., et al.: Discussion on safety supervision and protection of industrial control system in key infrastructure. Sci. Technol. Confid. (9), 12–17 (2016)
6. Creery, A.A., Byres, E.: Industrial cybersecurity for a power system and SCADA networks-Be secure. Ind. Appl. Mag. IEEE **13**(4), 49–55 (2007)
7. Wade, S.M.: SCADA honeynets: the attractiveness of honeypots as critical infrastructure security tools for the detection and analysis of the advanced threats (2011)
8. Krutz, R.L.: Securing SCADA Systems. Wiley, Hoboken (2005)
9. Jack, K., Cleo, Wu, P., et al.: Practical solutions for Snort intrusion detection. China Machine Press (2005)
10. Yin, L.: Research and development of intrusion detection technology. In: Electrical & Electronics Engineering, pp. 389–391. IEEE (2012)
11. Wang, Y., Ai, Z., Zhang, X.: Research and implementation of tracing technology based on honey label and honeypot. Inf. Technol. (03), 108–112 (2018)
12. Hu, H.: Design and implementation of industrial control intrusion acquisition system based on honeypot technology. Zhengzhou University (2017)
13. Bao, J., Ji, C.P., Gao, M.: Research on network security of defense based on Honeypot. In: International Conference on Computer Application and System Modeling, pp. V10-299–V10-302. IEEE (2010)
14. Qiao, P., Yue, Y.: Application of honeypot technology in network security. J. Harbin Univ. Sci. Technol. (03), 37–41 (2009)
15. Cheang, C.F., Wang, Y., Cai, Z., Xu, G.: Multi-VMs intrusion detection for cloud security using Dempster-shafer theory. CMC: Comput. Mater. Continua **57**(2), 297–306 (2018)

Research on Active Defense Technology of Smart Grid Control Terminal Based on Dynamic Trust

Xiao Liang[1(✉)], Yunpeng Li[2], Baohua Zhao[1], Zhihao Wang[1], and Ningyu An[1]

[1] Computing and Application Technology Department, Global Energy Interconnection Research Institute Co. Ltd., Beijing, China
liangxiao_geiri@126.com, {zhaobaohua, wangzhihao, anningyu}@geiri.sgcc.com.cn
[2] Nantong Power Supply Company, State Grid Jiangsu Electric Power Co. Ltd., Nanjing, Jiangsu, China
ntliyp@js.sgcc.com.cn

Abstract. With the construction of smart grid and smart energy city, a large number of smart terminals will be deployed in non-traditional areas by power grid enterprises. On the one hand, these intelligent terminals will realize flexible interaction with the power grid. On the other hand, they are also vulnerable to external attacks. Therefore, the industrial control security risk of intelligent terminals has become the focus of attention of society and enterprises. After explaining the industrial control risks faced by smart terminals, the protection scheme of smart grid control terminals based on dynamic trust is introduced in detail in this paper, and multiple protection of control terminals in complex network environment is realized.

Keywords: Dynamic trust · Intelligent terminal · Security protection

1 Introduction

With the development of Internet technology, large-scale distributed computing environments are gradually being applied to the smart grid field. Application patterns in such computing environments typically appear as dynamic collaborative systems consisting of multiple heterogeneous systems or software services. The form of the system is shifting from a closed, familiar-user-oriented, and relatively static model to an open, public-user-oriented, dynamic collaboration model. Traditional security technologies such as cryptography, digital certificates, and access control can solve trust issues such as entity authentication and authorization in the system. But in such large-scale distributed computing environments, there is no centralized management authority to rely on, the information of a subject can't be obtained completely, or the subject is not recognized at all, which makes it difficult to use these traditional security technologies to solve security problems in large-scale distributed environments [1]. At the same time, the behaviors of these subjects are also very uncertain, and even the

X. Sun et al. (Eds.): ICAIS 2019, LNCS 11635, pp. 637–648, 2019.
https://doi.org/10.1007/978-3-030-24268-8_58

distributed computing environment itself is constantly changing dynamically. Traditional security technologies are mainly aimed at subjects in static environments. Their behaviors are generally predictable. The dynamics of subjects and environments also seriously weaken the effectiveness of these traditional security technologies [2]. Therefore, dynamic trust management technology provides a new idea for solving the security problem of new application forms in large-scale distributed computing environments.

The information communication of smart grid has the characteristics of high integration and friendly interactivity, by using complex control and algorithm, efficient decision capability, security, reliability, economic are achieved in smart grid. The excellent performance of smart grid has also attracted the attention and recognition of governments all over the world. Since the 21st century, western countries, represented by Europe and the United States, have already prepared to take smart grid as the future direction of power grid development. China will build a smart grid system by 2020. Therefore, it is urgent to solve the security protection problem of smart grid industry.

In June 2010, Stuxnet virus was first detected. It is transferred between separate networks primarily via USB media. Firstly, Siemens monitoring and data acquisition system is regarded as the target of attack, and the directed attack on infrastructure (energy) facilities is realized. In 2015, a large-scale blackout occurred in Ukraine and the SCADA system was seriously damaged. After investigation, the reason is that there was a variant of BlackEnergy inside the system. Disseminated by of power secondary system, BlackEnergy Lite can cause significant damage to the system. The incident was considered the first major blackout event caused by network attack [3, 4]. In order to prevent these phenomenon from occurring again, after analyzing the industrial control security risk of smart grid, the security protection scheme of smart grid control terminal based on dynamic trust is put forward.

2   Security Risk Analysis of Smart Grid Control Terminals

2.1   Lack of Security Standards for Smart Grid

With the development of modern science and technology, the scale of smart grid is expanding constantly, and the terminals in different places are also tend to be distributed on a large scale. In order to reflect the Internet's thinking mode, the power system structure will become increasingly complex in the smart grid, and the security and reliability of power systems will face enormous challenges. At the same time, the connection of large-scale terminals will lead to an increase in the number of different interfaces, and the data interaction between different systems will also increase geometrically. This growth is unpredictable, and traditional network protection solutions can't solve such problems. Within the power system, the traditional security zone division method is difficult to meet the security protection requirements of the future power system structure [5]. However the risks existed in this new form of grid environment can be solved by the dynamic trust protection scheme.

2.2   Information Security Risk Introduced by Power Intelligent Terminal

While deepening the construction of smart grids, a large number of intelligent programmable devices will be connected to the grid. Through real-time monitoring of the grid operation, fault location and fault handling can be effectively performed to improve the stability, thereby improving the stability and reliability of the grid system. These smart devices can also support remote control such as remote connection, disconnect, configuration, upgrade, and so on. Although these technologies bring convenience, a large number of security vulnerabilities are inevitably accompanied. When a smart device is hacked, the hacker can completely control the smart device, destroy some of its functions, and even control the local power system through the smart device, resulting in more serious consequences. Therefore, the distributed deployment of smart devices imposes more strict requirements on the overall protection of information security [6, 7].

2.3   Complicated Power Grid Environment and Intelligent Attack Means

With the in-depth advancement of the smart grid, the probability of hackers conducting network attacks will increase dramatically. So intelligent terminal equipment puts higher demands on the network access environment and network performance. Wireless technologies such as WiFi and 4G/3G/2G bring network access convenience to the production, management and operation of smart grids. At the same time, due to the wide coverage of wireless signals, the secure transmission based on wireless networks needs to be strengthened, and wired network security requirements will be higher. At present, power companies transmit important data through wireless virtual private networks (through wireless public networks such as China Mobile, Telecommunications, China Unicom, etc.), and under certain conditions, which may also pose a potential threat to smart grid security. It is expected that future network attacks will be large-scale, organized, and the means of attack will be flexible, which will certainly bring new challenges to grid security.

2.4   Security Threats on User Side

With the continuous deepening of the integration process of "two transformations", two-way interaction between users and the power grid has been realized. Relying on the AMI (Advanced Metering Infrastructure) system, the intelligent terminals and devices of the client (such as smart appliances, plug-in electric vehicles, and so on) will be directly connected to the power system. These connection methods inevitably bring unknown security risks to users: the information between the user and the power company is transmitted over the public network. As we all know, transmission through the public network will inevitably bring information security risks. These devices are completely exposed to the public network, and the probability of being illegally invaded is greatly increased. In addition, smart grid information security issues involve other factors, such as the malicious damage caused by dissatisfied employees, industrial espionage and terrorist attacks, and unintentional damage to the information infrastructure caused by user errors, equipment failures and natural disasters. The natural complexity and vulnerability of smart grids make it easy for malicious attackers to sneak into, control power production systems, and undermine power load conditions, which can cause grid collapse in extreme cases.

2.5   Many Vulnerabilities in Industrial Control Systems

With the development of smart grids, SCADA (Supervisory Control And Data Acquisition) systems are used for power dispatching and support, and there are many loopholes in the integration of Internet of Things and industrial control systems. The type of vulnerability of industrial control systems is shown in Fig. 1.

The workstation operating system is vulnerable. Since the industrial control system is almost never upgraded after the completion of the operating system, many vulnerabilities have accumulated.

(1) Application software vulnerabilities. Industrial control software generally conflicts with anti-virus software. The industrial control network basically does not have anti-virus software installed. The virus can exist in the industrial control network. The application software vulnerabilities are usually easier to identify. Once the system is exposed to the public place IC network, the consequences could be disastrous.

(2) Network protocol vulnerabilities. Industrial control networks are mostly based on common protocols, such as TCP/IP protocol and OPC (Object Linking and Embedding (OLE) for Process Control) protocol. Currently, key protocol switching devices such as OPC servers rely on foreign imports. In order to meet the needs of engineering services, manufacturers usually retain the back door. Once an information war breaks out, the initiative must be in the hands of equipment manufacturers.

(3) Security management loopholes. In the engineering construction, usually different people contact and operate industrial control equipment, using different peripheral devices, such as U disk, laptop connection, and so on. It's possible for this to give the virus a chance to invade.

(4) Vulnerability of virus protection equipment. Currently, the security level of virus protection equipment on the market is uneven. These equipments are not only protection equipment but also attacking sources.

(5) The network port is vulnerable. When the industrial control device is in operation, various control network ports do not necessarily use special components for operation. It is likely that an inappropriate person can insert any peripheral device without special training, which brings potential risk of attack.

(6) Operational behavioral vulnerability. Since some young operators often do not have professional on-site training to illegally connect workstations to the public network during night shifts, providing opportunities for external attacks.

In summary, the new distributed computing smart grid environment will face many new challenges, how to effectively manage in a large-scale distributed computing environment, how to share resources and work collaboratively across autonomous domains, how to effectively aggregate and manage heterogeneous and huge network resources. When faced with a large number of uncontrollable and service resources lack of trust, how to ensure reliable trust relationships between shared and collaborative resources to adapt to such computing environments and the demand for application model development has become a key issue in the current smart grid industry.

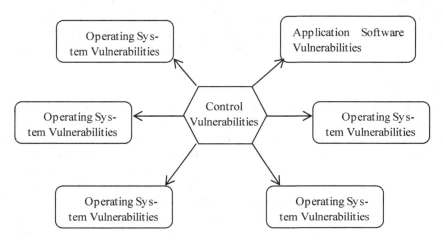

Fig. 1. Active defense architecture framework.

3   Active Defense Technology of Smart Grid Control Terminals Based on Dynamic Trust

According to the risk analysis in the previous part, the smart terminal devices oriented to users will face more risks, including the risks of intelligent interactive terminals, power robots, programmable devices, smart meters, smart appliances, plug-in electric vehicles. The power information collection system is a typical application of smart devices. A comprehensive, three-dimensional smart grid control terminal security protection scheme is proposed combining the concept of dynamic trust with the original power information collection technology.

3.1   Dynamic Trust Technology in Distributed Network Environment

The dynamic nature of large-scale distributed computing environment brings challenges far beyond the traditional network application environment to trust management in this environment. The quantity scale of the participating entities, the dynamic nature of the entities themselves, and the lack of central control mechanism make traditional trust management mechanism unsuitable in this environment. In order to explore dynamic trust models for large-scale distributed computing environments, the paper will first study the characteristics of large-scale distributed computing environments.

(1) Heterogeneity

Heterogeneity refers that there are great differences in the attributes of various resources in such computing environments. For example, computing resource platforms vary greatly due to the difference of hardware vendors; data resources are stored in different ways and data storage devices are also quite different; there are also great differences in the operating systems used by users, in addition, there are various communication devices and different communication protocols running in the network. Which increase the difficulty of the unified management and utilization of resources in such environments.

(2) Discreteness

Discreteness refers that there is usually no centralized management control mechanism in such computing environments. In a large-scale distributed computing environment, entities can join the computing environment anonymously at anytime from anywhere, realize resource access or data processing. This makes the traditional centralized system management mechanism difficult to adapt. In the traditional centralized management mechanism, it uses a specific security architecture to partition entities to achieve the management of participating entities, that is, adding a hierarchical management control server to complete identity authentication and authorization. However, in a large-scale distributed computing environment, even if the above-mentioned traditional security management mechanism has been applied, only a plurality of security domains that are not related to each other are formed. There are still many difficulties in current research on how to resolve the differences between these security domains to achieve effective resource access and utilization between different security domains. The current common solution is to establish a unified management environment and map multiple security domains to it. This kind of scheme has a good effect in the case of a small network and a small number of participating entities. However, for a larger-scale smart grid environment, the number of entities tends to be massive, and such schemes will become ineffective. At the same time, discreteness also makes centralized resource authorization, entity management, and trust management difficult in such computing environments. At present, how to implement trust management in discrete distributed computing environment is a key issue in research, and further research is needed in research fields such as cross-domain access, trust delegation and trust negotiation.

(3) Autonomy

Autonomy refers to the characteristics of autonomy and autonomy of participating entities and resources in such computing environments. Such application models are generally based on the principle of "voluntary participation, independent collaboration". Simply put, resources are subordinate to different organizations and individuals. Resource providers can choose to provide services or refuse services according to their own wishes when facing requests from resource requesters. The participating entities have autonomy in the whole process of participating in the system. The entity can choose to join or withdraw from the system at any time, and the independent choices communicate with other entities or services. The system can't manage and control these behaviors. Autonomy makes the behavior of an entity only depending on its own interests-driven or behavioral strategies, and it is impossible to perform centralized control at the system level. Therefore, compared with the traditional computing environment, such large-scale distributed computing environments usually show greater uncertainty and dynamic characteristics in running characteristics and running trajectories [7]. How to manage the behavior of an entity in such a computing environment and achieve the overall goal of the system through the autonomous behavior of the entity is a huge challenge.

(4) Dynamism

Dynamicity refers to the dynamic characteristics that the behavior of entities, the relationship between entities, and even the architecture of the network itself are constantly changing in such computing environments. Large-scale distributed computing environments are open systems, and the entities participated in are always dynamically joining and exiting, and the behavior of entities is always unpredictable. This causes the system architecture, resource characteristics, and participating entities in such computing environments to always be in dynamic evolution. Dynamics leads to a system's collaborative environment and trust relationships that need to change as the system changes, and the need for effective trust management implementation is greatly enhanced.

(5) Collaboration

Collaboration is the process of interaction between multiple entities to accomplish a common task. All of the above features make it difficult for entities to collaborate in large-scale distributed computing environment. However, the application patterns in this environment are usually implemented for a certain overall goal. For example: file sharing, grid computing for large-scale computing tasks, and more. These overall goals are precisely the need for extensive collaboration between autonomous entities or autonomous domains. Therefore, the application system in a large-scale distributed computing environment must be able to establish trust relationships for different entities and domains. It must be able to implement unified management according to the different requirements of different domains, and must be fostered synergies among a large number of unfamiliar and autonomous entities.

Aiming at the above characteristics, the concept of dynamic trust is introduced in this paper. In order to better understand this concept, let's first briefly understand the Markov process. Markov property is that the conditional distribution of the future state has nothing to do with the previous state under the premise that the current state of the system is known, it is also known as no aftereffect. Stochastic processes with Markovian properties are called Markov processes. In the context of the continuous development of smart grids, for the characteristics of heterogeneity, discretization, dynamics, etc., the change of trust relationship between terminals is only related to the current state, and has nothing to do with the past state, so it conforms to the Markov property. This type of trust is called dynamic trust [8–10].

3.2   Overall Architecture of Security Protection Based on Dynamic Trust

The security protection model of the smart grid information management system is shown in Fig. 2. Security protection is independently designed in the information intranet according to the three-level protection principle.

Desktop Terminal	Secondary system domain	Security Control System of Departments
First level system	Second level system	Third level system
Security Protection Measures		

Fig. 2. Security protection schematic diagram.

Provides reliable data source authentication, anti-replay, data encryption, data integrity verification and other reliable security protection for the system for different systems between different master systems through remote security encryption channels, identity authentication, network perimeter security protection, and isolation devices. The comprehensive network security protection effectively responds to various threats that may exist in the network, thereby effectively ensuring the security of related data.

The general principles of dynamic trust security protection system are: to isolate the information network by logical strong isolation device; to ensure the security and integrity of remote data transmission by network encryption system; to strictly verify the identity of terminal and user to ensure the uniqueness and authenticity of user identity. The information system is divided into a boundary layer, a network environment layer, a host system layer, and an application system layer, and security protection design is implemented to implement progressive and deep defense.

3.3   Security Protection Scheme of Intelligent Terminal

The main ideas of intelligent terminal security protection are as follows:

(1) The antivirus server is deployed on the PC and server by deploying the antivirus center server inside the main station system to effectively prevent illegal code, potential virus threats and attacks.

(2) Two sets of firewalls are deployed at the boundary of the primary system to implement security isolation and security policy protection at the boundary.

(3) The IDS (Intrusion Detection System) embedded in the self-trust evaluation model is directly connected to the core switch of the primary station system, and the suspicious traffic existing in the network is discovered in a timely manner by means of bypass.

(4) The vulnerability scanning system is deployed on the core switch to periodically scan for possible loopholes in the device terminals and servers, and patch them in time.

3.3.1 Embedded Self-confidence Assessment Model

The model is mainly based on the "emergence" learning model in evolutionary computation, introduces machine learning into trust management, and proposes a dynamic evaluation system for multi-attribute trust relationships. The system can integrate multiple pairs of trust attributes, and can independently learn and autonomously improve the execution ability of the model's evaluation tasks in the process of continuously performing dynamic evaluation tasks, thus adapting to the above dynamic and fuzziness. By adding this model to nodes in a complex network environment, these nodes can be made to autonomously establish and manage trust relationships between them. When user selects a data source for transmission, the node can use this model to select the appropriate data source.

The model is implemented by a classifier system, which applies genetic learning to rules in a production system. The structure of the classifier system is shown in Fig. 3.

The various trust evaluation information from the feedback system is encoded into a finite-length internal message by a detector of the classifier system and then sent to an internal message list; the triggered classifier in the message table sends internal messages to the message table, which perform corresponding operations on external entities through effectors.

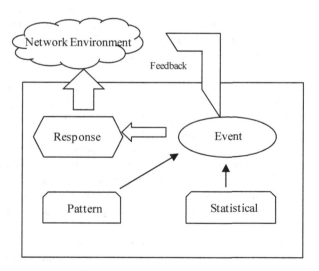

Fig. 3. System structure of multi-trust evaluation model

3.3.2   Working Mode of Self-confidence Model

The working process of the adaptive dynamic trust evaluation model proposed in this paper is as follows: Assume that when the entity q needs to perform operational authorization, the entity q first detects whether there is an entity in the neighbor that provides the authorization service. If there is an entity p that meets the requirements, q evaluates p according to its own trust evaluation model and makes a decision whether to make a request. Then it optimizes its own evaluation system according to the results of decision-making.

In the above problems solving process, a message is first sent from the environment to the classifier system, such as: the reputation of an entity. This message is first preprocessed into an internal message and placed in the internal message list. By bidding, the "strongest classifier rule" will be selected, this bidding should be a function of the fitness of the rules accumulated in the classifier and the matching quality of the input message and the mode condition. This motivated rule will send a message to the effector in its own actions and act on the external environment.

The learning evolution process of the classifier system itself is divided into two phases. The first stage is to adjust the fitness of the rules of the classifier through the reward system. The winner gives the reward and the loser gives the punishment. If the output of the system is the result of a series of rules, then the fitness of this series of rules needs to be allocated. For example, the first three rules make the behavior of not trusting the target entity and finding the next target. The fourth rule makes the act of trusting the target entity and initiating the request. Eventually the target entity allowed the service request and provided the correct service. The first three rules all contribute to the formation of the final rule, and all four rules need to be rewarded. Chained scoring in the model will assign adaptive values to these rule chains.

The second stage of learning is to use the genetic operator to change the rules themselves so that successful rules can be preserved, and successful rules can be combined into new classifier rules, while unsuccessful rules will disappear. That is, the rule set evolution process during the execution of the classifier. The classifier performs the first phase of learning in the history window h. When it reaches the h times operation of the history window, the classifier will evolve according to the fitness values accumulated by the rules in this period to form the Next Generation Rule Set. Evolution is accomplished by selection, crossover and mutation of genetic operators. The selection of the history window h must be set by experience. When this value is set large, the system can perform correct and effective evolution, but it takes a long time. Within this window, the system will maintain the original rule set and cannot make the expected changes. If the history window h is set too small, it will cause the rules to not fully play the cumulative fitness value during the period, making the evolutionary results less effective.

The model in this paper is not use evolutionary computation to find the optimal solution to a problem. But it is expected that through the continuous execution of the model, the entity can adaptively generate a new rule set to change its own strategy according to the changes of the network environment. Therefore, the model does not set a termination condition, but when there are resistance changes in successive generations of rule sets, the rule set will be rolled back to the previous generations.

3.3.3 Border Protection

Border Security involves how to effectively detect and control the flow of data into and out of the boundary. The boundaries of the smart grid can be divided into five categories: third-party boundaries of the information extranet, third-party boundaries of the information intranet, third-party boundaries of the information internal and external networks, information intranet vertical subordinate unit boundary and horizontal interdomain boundary. The boundaries can be divided into four categories: the third-party boundary of the information intranet, the boundary of the information internal and external network, the vertical subordinate unit boundary of the information intranet, and the horizontal inter-domain boundary.

3.3.4 Network Environment Security Protection

The security protection of network environment is oriented to the overall supporting network of smart grid, as well as the network environment facilities that provide the network support platform for each security domain. The network environment specifically includes routing devices, switching devices, and security devices and network service infrastructure introduced by the security system. The key network and security devices implement autonomous and controllable replacement, and the link communication of the network realizes the encryption processing of data.

3.3.5 Host System Security Protection

The host system security protection includes security protection for the server and the desktop terminal, the server includes a business application server, a network server, a web server, files and communications, and the like; the desktop terminal includes the desktop computers and the notebook computers as end user workstation.

The protection of the host system mainly includes timely repairing operating system patches, installing anti-virus software, updating virus database, turning off unnecessary services, setting password policies, locking policies, and opening system log audits and so on.

For the host computer, operator station, engineer station and other hosts in the industrial control network. Due to compatibility problems with anti-virus software, key file protection programs can be deployed on these systems to implement whitelist anti-virus mode, protect key files. Once you find a program that modifies key files, it will start protection.

3.3.6 Application Security Protection

Application security protection includes protection for the primary station application system, user interface security protection, security protection between data interfaces between systems, and security protection of data interfaces within the system. The goal of application security protection is to ensure the security of the application itself and the security of the data transmitted when interacting with other systems by taking security measures such as identity authentication and access control. Audit measures are taken to detect an intrusion attempt before a security incident or to conduct an audit trail after a security incident occurs.

4 Conclusion

The development of smart grids has a wide range of significance. We need to increase our attention and realize the rapid and good development of all aspects of smart grid. Since the research and construction of smart grids, especially smart terminals, are in their infancy, there are many weak links in smart terminals. Physical facilities and network communication systems are still in the integration stage. Because smart terminals are deployed in traditional management areas of non-grid enterprises, they are often the first choice for malicious users to attack. Therefore, special attention should be paid to the trust management and security protection of smart terminals.

Acknowledgment. This work is supported by the Science and Technology Project of SGCC (No. 17-JS-199) and the National Natural Science Foundation of China (No. 61833008).

References

1. Zhang, W.L., Liu, Z., Wang, M., et al.: Research progress and development trend of smart grid. Power Grid Technol. (13), 1–11 (2009)
2. Mawei. Smart grid system was initially built in 2020. Sci. Technol. China (7), 32–35 (2015)
3. Shao, X., Zhang, N.: Computer application in network information processing and security. Inf. Comput. (Theoret. Version), 2019 (01), 232–233 (2016). Xinhua Smart grid system [EB/OL] was initially built in 2020
4. Cao, J., Wan, Y., Tu, G., et al.: Research on the architecture of smart grid information system. J. Comput. Sci. (1), 143–167 (2013)
5. Tang, Y., Wang, Q., Ni, M., et al.: Network attack analysis in power information physical fusion system. Power Syst. Autom. (6), 4 (2016)
6. Chen, S., Song, S., Li, L., et al.: Overview of smart grid technology. Power Grid Technol. **33** (8), 1–7 (2009)
7. Meng, R., Rice, S.G., Wang, J., Sun, X.: A fusion steganographic algorithm based on faster R-CNN. CMC: Comput. Mater. Continua **55**(1), 001–016 (2018). North China Electric Power University (Beijing), (2018)
8. Cui, J., Zhang, Y., Cai, Z., Liu, A., Li, Y.: Securing display path for security-sensitive applications on mobile devices. CMC: Comput. Mater. Continua **55**(1), 017–035 (2018)
9. Huang, C., Wang, Z.: Research on dynamic trust relationship modeling and management technology. Ph.D. thesis. Changsha University of Defense Science and Technology (2005)
10. Zhang, G., Zhang, Y.: Network trust management review. Comput. Sci. **37**(9), 6–12 (2010)

Author Index

Printed in the United States
By Bookmasters